Religion, Education and the Law: A Comparative Approach

Published by
Tottel Publishing Ltd
Maxwelton House
41–43 Boltro Road
Haywards Heath
West Sussex
RH16 1BJ

Tottel Publishing Ltd
Fitzwilliam Business Centre
26 Upper Pembroke Street
Dublin 2

ISBN 978 1 84766 064 0

British Library Cataloguing-in-Publication Data
A catalogue record for this book is available from the British Library

Typeset by Marie Armah-Kwantreng, Dublin, Ireland
Printed and bound in Great Britain by
Athenæum Press Limited, Gateshead, Tyne & Wear

Religion, Education and the Law: A Comparative Approach

Dr Dympna Glendenning
BA, M Ed, PhD,
Barrister-at-Law

Tottel publishing

In memory of my late sister Una Moore (nee King)

PREFACE

This book considers the basic church-state (ecclesiastical law) arrangements made by six countries to accommodate religion in public life and to provide for religious freedom and freedom of education in publicly-funded schools in a comparative context. The countries chosen for consideration are England, Germany, Spain, Ireland and the United States of America (US) because, while sharing many common features, they illustrate a number of distinctive approaches to the place of religion in public life and in public education. In each of these countries the author seeks to abstract the main constitutional, statutory or other arrangements which uphold freedom of religion and freedom of education particularly as it relates to education in first and second level schools. In the five European countries chosen, some of the main historical developments which shaped the character, substance and direction of religious education in each country will be included, with an awareness that the author is neither a historian, a sociologist or a theologian. Rather, the author approaches the topic in this book from a legal perspective and strives, in so far as that is possible, to view the subject matter from that viewpoint. Since all five European countries chosen, are members of the European Union (EU), they are considered, not just from the viewpoint of national law, but in the broader context of Community law and international human rights law. It is the author's opinion that this book would be incomplete without some discussion of the unique relationship between church and state in the US and this is included in the penultimate chapter.

Following an Introduction, and prior to looking at the European countries chosen, some relevant aspects of the evolution of the history of church-state relations in Europe, are considered in **chapter 2**. This is considered necessary in so far as historical experiences appear to have influenced, not only the character and direction of religion and its relations with education and law, but also the degree of separation of church and state which emerged in the member states. **Chapter 3** contains an outline of the legal framework of EU law which supports, *inter alia,* freedom of religion and freedom of education in the member states. In **chapter 4** international human rights are considered in so far as they pertain to freedom of religion and freedom of education. **Chapter 5** looks at church-state separation in England, at the concept of establishment of religion there and at the provision made for religious freedom and freedom of education in the state education system. The subject-matter of **chapter 6** is relevant features of Germany's ecclesiastical law and the accommodation made for religion and specifically for religious education and religious instruction in the public schools. In

chapter 7 the evolution of the separation of church and state in France is considered and its influence on the place of religion in its public and private schools there. Spain's metamorphosis from a highly conservative Catholic country to one of the most liberal countries in Europe is the topic in **chapter 8**. This chapter also considers ecclesiastical law in Spain, recent education reforms and Spain's current provision for religious education/instruction in the public schools. **Chapter 9** looks at Ireland, at a time when its church-state relations are in transition, and at the provision made for freedom of religion and education in its publicly-funded education system. By way of contrast the following **chapter 10** examines the Separation of church and state principle in the US, in so far as it illuminates the place of religion, if any, in its public schools. Each chapter draws on history but only in so far as it relates to the subject matter in hand. The final **chapter 11** draws together certain common values and approaches found to exist in earlier chapters and draws conclusions. This book considers the relevant aspects of the law as it applies on 1 September 2008.

Like most other books, the writing of this book proved to be more complex and demanding than at first anticipated. Indeed, it could not have been written without the support and advices of a number of people including experts in the relevant subject matter from England, Germany, Spain, Ireland and the US. Not only does this book build on the knowledge of others, as the footnotes illustrate, but it rests on the support and advices of family, friends and colleagues during the four year period of its gestation. I am especially indebted to Mr Murray Smith BL who read the final draft and for his erudite insights along the way and to Professor Wylie of Cardiff University who read an early draft of the book.

I also wish to acknowledge the kind assistance and valued suggestions of those who read and advised on individual chapters including my colleague Mr James O' Reilly SC who read and advised on **chapter 3** (EU law); Professor Gerry Whyte of Trinity Law School, Dublin and Professor Áine Hyland, formerly of University College, Cork, and Mr Oliver Mahon BL all of whom read and assisted me with **chapter 9** (Ireland); Professor Charles J Russo, University of Dayton, Ohio who read and advised on **chapter 10** (US); Dr Paul Meredith, University of Southampton, who read and made much valued suggestions relating to **chapter 5** (England); Prof Barbel Dörbeck-Jung, University of Utwente, the Netherlands, for her valued assistance with **chapter 6** (Germany); Dr Arnaud Crass of University College, Dublin who read and assisted me with **chapter 7** (France); Ms Rosario Hernandez of University College, Dublin and who read and assisted with **chapter 8** (Spain) and my colleague Mr Edmund Sweetman BL who read an early draft of the same chapter. Finally my thanks goes to brother Desmond King for his many insights during the drafting period. Any mistakes in this book are entirely my own and I would appreciate if these were brought to my attention.

This book is not intended as a manual which might substitute for legal advice. Where such advice is needed, it should be sought from independent professional sources. Rather, this book is written in the hope that it will generate public discussion on the interplay between freedom of religion with education and with the law, both nationally and internationally as the EU moves towards greater unity, integration and harmonisation.

Finally I would like to express my gratitude to the professionals at Tottel Publishing who produced this book and for their assistance and patient support during its preparation. I am particularly grateful to Ms Amy Hayes, Managing Editor, and to Ms Sandra Mulvey, Editor, Ms Jennifer Lynch, Marketing Manager and Ms Marie Armah-Kwantreng, Typesetter.

ABBREVIATIONS

Art = Article

CPSMA = Catholic Primary Schools Management Association

CRC = UN Convention on the Rights of the Child 1989

CKREE = Christian Knowledge and Religious and Ethical Education

ECHR = European Convention on Human Rights 1950

DIK = Deutsche Islam Konferenz

DCSF = Department for Children, Schools and Families

ECJ = European Court of Justice

ECtHR = European Court of Human Rights

EU = European Union

FRA = European Union Agency for Fundamental Rights

GDR = German Democratic Republic

HSE = Health Service Executive

IBHR = UN International Bill of Human Rights 1966

ICCPR = UN International Covenant of Civil and Political Rights 1966

ICESR = UN International Covenant on Economic and Social Rights

ICESCR = UN International Covenant on Economic, Social and Cultural Rights

JMB = Joint Managerial body for Secondary Schools

LEA = Local Education Authoritie

para, paras = paragraph, paragraphs

reg = Regulation

RI = religious instruction

UNDHR = UN Universal Declaration on Human Rights 1948

UNDHR = UN Universal Declaration on Human Rights 1981

UNCDE = UN Convention against Discrimination in Education 1962

s, ss = section, sections

SACRE = Standing Advisory Council for Religious Education

SSFA = School Standards and Framework Act 1998

TEU = Treaty on European Union

USA = United States of America

VEC = Vocational Education Committee

CONTENTS

TABLE OF CASES

Abingdon School District v Schempp (1963)
374 US 203 .... 1.052, 10.005, 10.043, 10.044, 10.047, 10.050, 10.068
AG for the State of Victoria; Ex rel Black v The Commonwealth
(1981)146 CLR 559, 595–7 .... 1.054
AG v Pearson 3 Merivale, 353 .... 10.062
Aguilar v Felton (1985) 473 US 402 .... 10.020
Ahmad v United Kingdom (1981) 4 EHRR 126 .... 4.023, 4.028
Ali v Headteacher and Governors of Lord Grey School
[2006] UKHL 14; [2006] 2 WLR 690 .... 4.047, 5.038
American Civil Liberties Union v McCreary County, Kentucky
(2003) 354 F 3d 438 [184 Educ L Rep. 67] (6th Cir) 10.052
Anderson v Mexico Academy and Cent School (2003)
56 Fed Appx 549 (2d Cir) 10.054
Angelini v Sweden (1988) 10 EHRR 123 .... 4.056, 4.068
Aquillard (1987) 482 US 578 .... 10.041
Aronow v United States (1970) 432 F 2d 242 (9th Cir) 10.006
Arrowsmith v UK (1978) 19 DR 5 .... 1.050
Article 26 of the Constitution and in the Matter of the Reference to the Court of the Regulation of Information (Services outside the State for Termination of Pregnancies) Bill 1995, Re
[1995] 2 ILRM 81 .... 2.009, 9.010
Article 26 and the School Attendance Bill 1942, Re
[1943] IR 334 .... 4.061, 9.091
Article 26 and the Employment Equality Bill 1996, Re
[1997] 2 IR 321 .... 9.036
Article 26 of the Constitution and the Criminal Law (Jurisdiction)
Bill 1975, Re [1997] IR 129 .... 9.011

Baghwan Case 196/87 [1988] ECR, p 6159 .... 3.011
Baker v Adams County/Ohio Valley School (2004) 86 Fed App 104
[184 Educ L Rep 745] 6th Cir 10.052
Barralet and Others v Attorney General [1980]
3 All ER 918 .... 1.047, 5.004, 5.011
Baumgartner v First Church of Christ, Scientist (1986) 490 NE 2d 1319
(111 App) 10.063
Belgian Linguistic Cases (1967) 1 EHRR 241;
(1979) 1 EHRR 252 .... 4.043, 4.045, 4.046, 4.047, 4.049
Bishop of Exeter v Marshall (1868) LR 3 HL 17 .... 5.011
Board of Education of Central School District No 1 v Allen (1923)
392 US 236, 88 S Ct 10.029, 10.070, 10.071

Boy Scouts of America v Dale (2000) 530 US 640, 160 NJ 562, 734A 2d 1196 .... 3.012, 10.055, 10.075
Boyd v Harding Academy of Memphis CA 6, No. 95–5945, 7/9/96) 10.073
Braunfeld v Brown (1961) 366 US 599 .... 10.068
Bruker v Markovitz [2007] SCC 54 .... 5.040
Bryan v Watchtower Bible and Tract Society (1999) 738 A 2d 839, 848 (Me) 10.063
Buscarini & Others v San Marino (24645/94) [1999] ECHR 7 (18 February 1999) 1.050, 4.035

Caldwell v Stuart (1985) 1 WWR 620 .... 9.076, 10.073
Campaign to Separate Church and State v Minister for Education [1996] 2 ILRM 241; [1998] 2 ILRM 81; 3 IR 321 .... 6.003, 6.034, 7.034, 9.036, 9.037, 9.039, 9.066, 9.067, 9.078, 9.096, 10.044
Campbell and Cosans v UK (1982) 4 EHRR 165 .... 2.014, 4.044, 4.045, 4.046, 4.060, 4.070
Cantwell v Connecticut (1940) 310 US 296 .... 10.019, 10.023, 10.024, 10.028
CH ex rel ZH v Oliva (2000) (CH) 226 F 3d 198 (3d Cir) 10.005
Cha'are Shalom Ve Tsedek v France (2000) 9 BHRC 27 .... 4.026
Cheema v Thompson (1995) 67 F 3d 883 [104 Educ L Rep 57] (9th Cir) 10.038
Chalifoux v New Caney Independent School District, 976 S Supp 659 .... 1.037
Choudbury v Governors of Bishop Challoner Roman Catholic Comprehensive School [1992] 3 All Eng 277 .... 3.024, 5.016, 5.025
Christian Education South Africa v Minister for Education [2001] 1 LRC 441 .... 5.038
Church of Scientology Moscow v Russia Application No 18147/02, judgment of 5 April 2007 .... 1.046, 4.012, 4.021, 4.027, 4.040, 5.004, 8.024
Church of the New Faith v Commissioners for Pay-Roll Tax [1983] 1 VR 97 .... 1.049
Christian Education South Africa v Minister of Education CCT 13/98 ZACC 16; 1999 (2) SA 83; 1998 (12) BCLR 1449, 14 October 1998 .... 4.027
Ciftci v Turkey Application No 71860/01, Decision of 17 June 2004 .... 4.067
CJ, JJ and EJ v Poland (1996) 84-A Eur Comm'n HR Dec & Rep 46 .... 4.068
Cline v Catholic Diocese of Toledo (2000) 206 F 3d 651 (6th Cir) 10.073
Cochran v Louisiana State Board of Education (1930) 281 US 370 .... 10.069
Commissioners of Special Income Tax v Pemsel [1891] AC 531 .... 5.010, 5.014
Commonwealth v Herr 78 A 68 (Pa 1910) 10.039
Constitution in Everson v Board of Education 330 US 63 .... 10.008

Conway v Independent Newspapers (Ireland) Limited [2000] 1 IRLM 426 ..... 3.023
Conway v INTO [1991] 2 IR 305 ..... 9.030
Cooper v Eugene School District No 4J 723 P 2d 298 [34 Ed L Rep 614] 10.039
Copsey v WWB Devon Clays Ltd 2005 EWCA Civ 932,
[2005] 1 CR 1789 ..... 4.028
Corporation of Canadian Civil Liberties Association v Ontario
(1990), 71 OR (2d) 341 (CA) 4.066
Craigdallie v Aikman (1813) 2 Bligh, 529; 1 Dow 1 ..... 10.062
Crowley v Ireland [1980] IR 102 ..... 9.030, 9.091
Curran v Catholic University of America (1989) No 1562–87
(Sup Ct DC, February 28) 10.074
Cyprus v Turkey (2002) 35 EHRR 30 ..... 4.047, 4.069

Dahlab v Switzerland Case 44774/98, 29 June 2004 ..... 2.016, 4.035, 9.048
Darby v Sweden (1991) 13 EHRR 774 ..... 1.013
Darling v Minister of Education, Jones v Minister of Education
(1962) Times, 7 April 5.024
Delahunty v South Eastern Health Board, St Joseph's Industrial School,
Kilkenny and the Minister for Education & Science [2003] 4 IR 361 ..... 9.088
Delahunty v South Eastern Health Board and St Joseph's Industrial School,
Kilkenny [2000] 4 IR 361 ..... 9.030
DO'C v AM McD, The Minister for Education and Science, Ireland
and the Attorney General [2006] IEHC 299 ..... 9.088
DPP v Best [1998] 2 ILRM 549 ..... 1.024

Education South Africa v Minister for Education 2000 (4) SA 757 (CC);
2000 (10) BCLR 1051 (CC) 1.042
Edward v Aguillard (1987) 482 US 578. ..... 10.027, 10.032, 10.033
Eklund v Byron Union School District (2006) 153 Fed Appx 648
(9th Cir 2005) cert denied, 127 S Ct 6 ..... 10.005
Employment Division, Department of Human Resources of Oregon
v Smith 494 US 872 (1990) 5.031
Employment Equality Bill 1996 [1997] 2 IR 321 ..... 9.037, 9.043, 9.068
Engel v Vitale (1962) 370 US 421 ..... 10.001, 10.002, 10.003, 10.010,
10.042, 10.043, 10.047
Epperson v Arkansas (1968) 393 US 97 ..... 10.029, 10.031
Equal Employment Opportunity Commission (EEOC)
v Catholic University of America (1996)
83 F 3d 455 (DC Cir) 10.074
Erin v Turkey, Application No 60856/00 (7 February 2006, unreported) 4.047
Everson v Board of Education (1947) 330 US 1 ..... 1.054, 10.001, 10.002,

10.003, 10.007, 10.010, 10.011, 10.013, 10.019, 10.027–10.029, 10.031, 10.065, 10.066, 10.068, 10.070

Fleming v Jefferson County School District (2002) (DC No 99-D 1932) dec on 27 June 2002, 10th Circuit Court of Appeal 10.053
Flynn v Power [1985] IR 648; [1985] ILRM 336 ....9.074, 9.076, 10.073
Fox v Higgins (1912) 46 ILTR 222 ....9.030, 9.075, 9.088
Freedom and Democracy Party (OZDEP) v Turkey (Application No 23885/94), 8 December 1999 ....4.031, 4.032, 4.034
Freiler v Tangipahoa Parish Board of Education (2005) 185 F 3d 337 [137 Educ Law Rep 581] (4th Cir) 10.034

Ganzy v Allen Christian School (1998) 995 F Supp; 340 (EDNY) 10.073
Germain v Pullman Baptist Church (1999) 980 P 2d 809 (Wash App) 10.063
Gernetzke v Kenosha Unified School District No 1 (2001) 274 F 3d 464 [160 Ed Law Reports 25] (7th Circuit); 525 US 1017 (2002) 10.054
Gorzelik v Poland [GC], No 44158/98, paras 94–95 ....4.042
Governing Body of the London Oratory School; Adams, Goodliffe and Lindsay v The Schools' Adjudicator [2003] EWHC; [2005] ELR 162 .... 5.028, 5.029
Grand Rapids v Ball (1985) 473 US 373 ....10.040
Gundiz v Turkey Reports of Judgments and Decisions, 2003–XI, p 229 ....3.027

Hall v Baptist Memorial Health Care Corporation (1998) 27 F Supp 1029 (WD) 10.075
Handyside v the United Kingdom, judgment of 7 December 1976, Series A, No 24, p 23, para 49 ....4.032
Handyside v UK (1976) 1 EHRR 737 .... 3.023, 3.028
Hansen v Ann Arbor Public Schools (2003) 293 F Supp 2d 780 (ED Mich) 10.005
Harmon v Dreher 2 Speers Equity Reports 87, 120 (SCCt. Appeal), 1843 ....10.061
Hartikainen v Finland (Comm No 40/1078) UN Doc A/34/40, Decision of 9 April 1981 ....4.065, 4.068, 9.048, 9.056, 9.060
Hasam and Chaush v Bulgaria [GC], Application No 30985/96, para 62, ECHR 2000–XI 4.041, 9.047
Hasan and Eylem Zengin v Turkey [2008] ECHR, Application No 1448/04, Part IV...4.001, 4.002, 9.047
Hazlewood School District v Kuhlmeier (1988) 484 US 271 .... 10.009, 10.053

HE v A Hospital NHS Trust [2003] EWHC 1017 (fam); In re T (Adult: Refusal of Treatment) Court of Appeal, 1992, July 22, 23, 24 and 30 .... 1.049
Hiles v Episcopal Diocese of Massachusetts (2002) 773 NE 2d 929, 935 (Mass) 10.063
Hines v Caston School Corp. 651 N E 2d 330 .... 10.037
Hoffman v Austria (1993) 17 EHRR 293. .... 1.049
Holden v Board of Education (1966) 216 A 2d 387 (NJ) 10.016
Hurley v INTO [1991] 2 IR 328 .... 9.030
Hynes v Mayor and Council of Oradell (1976) 425 US 610 .... 10.023

Independent Russian Region of the Society of Jesus v Russia Decision No 46-O of the 13 April 2000 .... 4.040

James v UK 8 EHRR 123 .... 4.045
Jamieson v Texas (1943) 318 US 413 .... 10.023
Jersild v Denmark, judgment of 13 September 1994, Series A, No 298, p 26, para 37 .... 4.032
Leirvag v Norway Communication No 1155/2003 CCPR........ 1.027, 7.036
Jimenez and Jimenez Merino v Spain Application No 51188/99 EHRR 1.034, 4.070, 6.026, 6.034, 7.036, 8.032, 8.035, 8.036, 9.056, 11.014
Johnson v Town of Deerfield (1939) 25 Fed Supp 918 (D Mass), affirmed, 306 US 621, 59 S Ct 791 .... 10.016
Jones v Clear Creek Independent School (1992) 977 F 2d 963 (5th Circuit). (Clear Creek 11) 10.048
Jordebo v Sweden ECHR, Application No 11533/85 decision of 6 March 1987 .... 4.045

K v Sweden, Application no 13800/88, Commission Decision of 1 July 1991, Decisions and Reports 71 .... 8.036
Kalac v Turkey (1997) 27 EHRR 552 .... 4.022, 4.024, 4.028, 4.032, 4.036
Karaduman v Turkey (1993) 74 DR 93 .... 4.023
Karen B v Treen (1981) 653 F 2d 897, 901 (5th Circuit) affirmed 455 US 913 (1982) 10.041
Karnell and Hardt v Sweden (No 4733/71), (1971) 14 Yearbook 676 .... 4.055
Kedroff v St. Nicholas Cathedral 344 US at 116 .... 10.063
Kiesinger v Mexico Academy & Central School (2003) 56 Fed Appx 549 [173 Educ L Rep 709] (2nd Cir) 10.054

Kitzmiller v Dover Area School District (2005) 400 F Supp 2d 707
[205 Educ L Rep 250] (MD Pa) 10.030, 10.035
Kjelsden, Busk Madsen and Pedersen v Denmark (1976)
1 EHRR 711 .... 4.046, 4.048, 4.049, 4.051, 4.056,
4.065, 4.068, 6.010, 8.035, 9.041, 9.047,
9.054, 9.060, 10.031
Kokkinakis v Greece (1994) 17 EHRR 397 ...... 3.027, 4.012, 4.027, 4.028, 4.035,
8.037, 9.048, 10.024
KwaZulu-Natal v Pillay [2007] ZACC 21 .... 1.039

Law v Canada [1999] 1 SCR 497 .... 5.040
Lawrence v Texas (2003) 539 US 558, 602–3 .... 10.027
Lee v Butler County Board of Education (2002)
183 F Supp 2 d 1359. 869] 10.021
Lee v Wiseman (1992) 505 US 577 .... 10.021, 10.046
Leirvag v Norway Communication No 1155/2003 .... 4.015, 5.032
Lemon v Kurtzman (1971)
403 US 602 .... 10.005, 10.013, 10.014, 10.032, 10.068, 10.071
Lemon v Kurtzman (1973) 411 US 192 .... 10.013
Lingens v Austria (1986) 8 EHRR 407 .... 3.023
LO'K v LH, the Minister for Education and Science
and the Attorney General [2006] IECH 13 .... 9.088, 9.089
Locke v Davey 540 US 712 .... 1.008, 1.021, 1.034
Lovell v City of Griffin (1938) 303 US 414 .... 10.023
Ludin BverG, 2BvR 1436/02 .... 3.021
Lynch v Donnelly (1971) 403 US 602 .... 10.006, 10.013, 10.020
Lynch v Donnelly (1984) 465 US 668 .... 10.004, 10.005, 10.006, 10.017,
10.020, 10.047

Mandla v Dowell Lee (1983) 2 AC 548 .... 3.014, 3.015
Manoussakis v Greece (1996) 23 EHRR 387 .... 3.028, 4.025
Marsh v Chambers (1983) 463 US 783 .... 10.006, 10.021
Martin v City of Struthers (1943) 319 US 141 .... 10.023
Maunsell v Minister for Education [1940] IR 213 (HC) 9.030, 9.068
May, Minors, Re [1959] IR 334; 92 ILTR 1 .... 9.033
McCollum v Board of Education (1948)
333 US 203 .... 1.052, 4.055, 10.005, 10.012, 10.040
McEneaney v Minister for Education [1941] IR 430 (SC) 9.030
McGee v Attorney General [1974] IR 284 .... 2.009, 9.010
McGrath and O'Ruairc v Trustees of Maynooth College
[1979] ILRM 166 .... 6.034, 9.001, 9.036, 9.066, 9.067

McLean v Arkansas Board of Education (1982)
529 F Supp 1255 (ED Ark) 10.011, 10.030, 10.032
MDP v SMB (6 November 1988, unreported), HC 6.034
Meek v Pittenger (1975) 421 US 349 .... 10.029, 10.071
Metropolitan Church of Bessarabia v Moldova
(2002) 35 EHRR 13 .... 1.017, 4.012, 4.017, 4.028, 4.035, 4.041, 4.042, 8.037, 9.006, 9.047, 9.052
Minersville v Gobitis 310 US 586 .... 10.016
Minker v Baltimore v Conf of United Methodist Church
(1990) 894 F 2d 1354, 1355 .... 10.063
Molloy v Minister for Education [1975] IR 88 .... 9.031, 9.034
Mormon Church v United States 98 US 136 US 1 (1890) 1.049
Morse v Fredrick US Supreme Court, 25 June 2007 .... 1.038
Moscow Branch of the Church of Scientology v Russia,
Application No 18147/02, judgment of 6 April 2007 .... 4.068
Moscow Branch of the Salvation Army v Russia
Application No 72881/01, ECHR 2006, Decision No 7-O of
7 February 2002 .... 4.040, 4.042
Mulloy v Minister for Education [1975] IR 88 .... 9.033, 9.034, 9.052
Multani v Commission Scolaire Marguerite-Bourgeoys
[2006] 1 SCR 256 .... 5.040, 10.036
Murdock v Pennsylvania (1943) 319 US 105 .... 10.023
Murphy v IRTC [1999] 1 IR 12 .... 9.043
Myers v Loudoun County Public Schools (2005)
418 F 3d 395 (4th Cir) 10.018

Nelly v Grace Community Church of the Valley (1988)
763 P 2d 948 (Cal) 10.063
New York State Club Assn, Inc, v City of New York (1988)
487 US 1 .... 10.057
Newdow v US Congress (2003) 292 F 3d 597 (9th Cir 2002);
203 WL 554742 (9th Cir) 10.007, 10.017, 10.018

O (a Minor)(Blood Transfusion) [1993] 2 FLR 757 .... 1.049
O' Keefe v Minister for Education and Science [2006] IEHC 13 .... 9.030
O'Callaghan v McDonnell, The Minister for Education and Science
[2006] IEHC 299 .... 9.030
O'Callaghan v Meath VEC, (20 November 1990, unreported) HC 9.062, 9.065
O'Callaghan v O'Sullivan [1925] 1 IR 90 .... 5.012, 9.094, 9.095
O'Connor v Hendrick (1906) 77 NE 612 (NY 10.039
O'Hair v Blumenthal (1979) 442 US 930, 99 S Ct 2862,
61 L Ed 2d 298 .... 10.006

O'Hair v Murray (1979) 588 F 2d 1144 (5th Cir) 10.006
O'Keefe v Cardinal Cullen 2 QB 1873 CL 7 319
and 1873–1874 IR,
Common Law, Vol VII, p 319 .... 5.008, 5.011, 5.012, 9.094, 10.062
O'Shiel v Minister for Education [1992] 2 IR 321 .... 1.024
Olson v Luther Memorial Church (1996) WL 70102 (Minn) 10.063

P v B (26 February 1999, unreported), SC 6.034
Paridul Comunistilor (Nepeceristi) and Ungureanu v Romania
No 46626/99, para 49, ECHR 2005–1 .... 4.042
Peloza v Capistrano School District 917 F 2d 1004 .... 10.033
Percy v Church of Scotland Board of National Mission, 199 SLT 1228
(Employment Appeal Tribunal) 5.009
Petruska v Gannon Univ (2005) US Ct of Appeal for Third Circuit,
83 F 3d 455 (DC) 10.063
Pierce v Society of Sisters (1925) 268 US 510 .... 2.008, 10.064
Prais v Council C–130/75 [1976] ECR 1589 .....2.016, 3.005, 3.007, 3.031, 11.007
Prosecutor General v Ake Green, Judgment of Supreme Court of Sweden,
Issued 29 November 2005, p 4 .... 3.026, 3.028
Pyle v South Hadley School Committee 55F.3d 20,
West's Education Law Reporter, 100, 579–581, 27 July 1995 .... 1.038

Quinn's Supermarket v Attorney General
[1972] IR 1 .... 9.001, 9.033, 9.034, 9.043, 9.067

R (Amicus) v Secretary of State for Trade and Industry
[2004] IRLR, pp 436–7 .... 5.031
R (Begum) v Denbigh High School [2004] EWHC Admin 1389,
[2004] ELR 374 (QBD), [2005] EWCA, Civ 199,
[2005] ELR 198 (CA), [2006] UKHL 15,
[2006] 2 WLR 719, [2006] 2 All ER 487 ....4.022, 5.036, 5.037
R (K) v London Borough of Newham [2002] ELR 390 .... 5.026, 5.027
R (O) v St James RC Primary School Appeal Panel [2001] ELR 469 .... 5.027
R (Williamson) v Secretary of State for Education and Employment
[2005] UKHL 15; [2005] ELR 291; [2005] 2 AC 246 ....1.047, 1.050, 4.027,
4.028, 5.031, 5.038
R v Bedfordshire ex parte WE, (8 November 1996, unreported) 5.026
R v Big M Drug Mart [1985] 1 SCR 295 .... 5.039, 5.040
R v Bow Street Magistrates Court (1991) 91 Crim Appeal r 393 .... 3.024
R v East Sussex County Council ex parte D [1991]
COD 374, 15 March 1991 .... 5.026
R v Essex CC ex parte C [1994] ELR 54 at 63 G and 65G 5.026

R v Governors of Bishop Challoner Roman Catholic Comprehensive Girls School ex parte Choudhury [1992] 3 All ER 277 .... 5.028
R v Governors of La Sainte Union Convent School [1996] ELR 98 .... 5.028
R v Greenich London Borough Council ex parte Governors of John Bull Primary School (1990) 154 LGR 678 CA 5.027
R v Headteacher and Governors of Denbigh High School [2006] UKHL 15 .... 4.022, 4.028
R v Registrar General ex parte Segerdal [1970] 2 QB 697; [1970] 3 All ER 886 .... 1.046, 1.048, 5.004, 5.011
R v Secretary of State for Education ex parte Williamson [2005] UKHL 15; [2005] ELR 291, HL 1.049, 2.006
Raihon Hudoyberganova v Uzbekistan Communication No 931/2000, UN Doc CCPR/C/82/D/931/2000 (2004), par 62 .... 4.025
Refah Partisi v Turkey [2003] ECHR 87 .... 1.006, 4.028, 4.029, 4.031, 4.032, 4.033, 4.034, 4.037, 4.041, 9.059, 11.005
Refah Partisi (The Welfare Party) v Turkey [2003] EHRR 1 ..... 1.008, 4.041, 4.068
Religious Society of Jehovah's Witnesses in Yaroslav and Christian Glorification Church v Russia Decision No 16-P of 23 November 1999 .... 4.040
Reynolds v United States (1878) 98 US 145, 164 .... 1.049, 10.029
Roberts v US Jaycees (1984) 468 US 609, 622 .... 10.056, 10.057

Sahin v Turkey (1996) 84 (Application 44774/98), (10 November 2005, unreported), Grand Chamber 4.045, 4.046
Sahin v Turkey (2005) 41 EHRR 8 .... 2.016, 4.022, 4.028, 4.045, 4.046, 7.024, 11.004
Sahin v Turkey Application 44774/98, judgment of 29 June 2004 .... 4.018
San Antonio Independent School District v Rodriguez 10.007
Santa Fe Independent School District v Doe (2000) 530 US 290 .... 10.014
Schneider v State (Township of Irvington) (1939) 308 US 147 .... 10.023
Scopes v State (1924) 289 SW 363 (Tenn) 10.030
Seidman v Paradise Valley Unified School District No 69 (2004) 327 F Supp 2d 1089 [191 Educ L rep. 175] (d Ariz) 10.054
Selman v Cobb County School District (2005) 390 FSupp 2d 1286 [203 Educ L Rep 637] (n D Ga) 10.034
Selman v Cobb County School District (2006) 449 F 3d 1320 [210 Educ L Rep 52] (11th Cir) 10.034
Sheehan v INTO [1997] 2 IR 327 .... 9.030
Sherbert v Verner (1963) 374 US 398 .... 10.013
Shofman v Russia No 74826/01, 24 Nov 2005, para 53 .... 4.042
Sidiropoulos v Greece Judgment of 10 July 1998, Reports of Judgments and Decisions 1998–IV 4.041, 4.042

Skoros v City of N York (2007) 437 F3d (2d Cir 2006) cert denied,
127 S Ct 1245 .... 10.005
Socialist Party v Turkey 20/1997/804/1007, 25 May 1998 .... 4.031, 4.032, 4.034
Soering v UK, judgment of 7 July 1989, Series A, No 161 .... 4.032
Stankov and the United Macedonian Organisation Ilinden v Bulgaria
Nos 2922/95 and 29225/95, para 84, ECHR 2001–IX 4.042
Stedman v United Kingdom (1997) 23 EHRR 168 .... 4.023
Stone v Graham (1980) 449 US 39 .... 10.050
Sulak v Turkey (1996) 84–A-DR 98 .... 4.046
Suleiman v Juffali 1 FLR 479 at 490 (2002) 5.013
Sunday Times v UK Series A, No 30, judg of 26 April 1979 .... 3.028
Syndicat Northcrest v Amselem [2004] 2 SCR 551 .... 5.031, 5.040

Tilston, Infant, Re [1951] IR 1 .... 9.031, 9.033
Timishev v Russia (Application Nos 55762/00 and 55974/00),
(13 December 2005, unreported) 4.046
Tinker v Des Moines Independent Community School (1969)
484 US 271 .... 10.009, 10.037, 10.053
TM v JH, JM and the Minister for Education [2006] IECH 26 .... 9.030, 9.088
Towne v Eisner 245 US 418, 425 (1918) 1.044

Unification Church v Spain, judgment of 15 February 2001 .... 8.003, 8.004
United Communist Party of Turkey v Turkey
Judgment of 30 January 1988, 133/1996/752//951
Reports of Judgments and Decisions 1998–1 .... 4.008, 4.030, 4.031, 4.032,
4.033, 4.034, 4.041, 4.042, 4.068
United States v Seeger 380 US 163 (1965) 1.050

Valsamis v Greece [1998] ELR 430 .... 1.050, 4.053, 5.026
van Rosmaalen v Bestuir van de Betrijfsvereinigingen Case 300/84
[1986] ECR 3.011
Verein v Gemeinsam Lernen v Austria N 23419/94,
Decision 6 September 1995, 82 DR 41 .... 4.064
Vigars v Vally Christian Centre of Dublin (1992) Cal 805 F Supp,
802 (ND Cal) 10.073

Walker v Hussain [1996] ICR 291 .... 3.014, 3.016
Wallace v Jafree (1985) 472 US 38 .... 10.045
Wang v Minister for Immigration and Multicultural Affairs
[2002] FCA 5 .... 1.047, 1.050
Washegesic v Bloomingdale Public Schools (1994)
33 F 3d 679 (6th Cir) 10.054

Watchtower and Bible Tract Society of New York v Village of Stratton (2002) 536 US 150 .... 10.023, 10.026
Watson v Jones 80 US (13 Wall) 677, 679, 730 (1871) (Court of Appeals of South Carolina) 10.010, 10.059, 10.061, 10.063, 11.017
Watt v Kesteven CC [1955] 1 QB 408, 1 All ER 473, CA 5.024
Webster v New Lennox School District (1990) 122, 917 F 2d 1004 (7th Cir) 10.033
Wells v City of Denver (2001) 257 F 3d 1132, 1144 (10th Cir) 10.009, 10.053
West Virginia State Board of Education v Barnette (1943) 319 US 624 .... 10.007, 10.016
Williams v Episcopal Diocese of Massachusetts (2002) 766 NE 2d 820, 825 (Mass) 10.063
Willoughby v Stever 504 F 2d 1975 .... 10.032
Wood v Ealing BDC [1967] Ch 364, [1966] 3 All ER 514 .... 5.024

X v Denmark (1976) 5 DR 157 .... 4.024
X v UK No 7782/77, Decision of 2 May 1978, 14 DR 179 .... 4.062, 4.063
X v UK, No 7992/77, Commission Decision of 12 July 1978, DR 14 .... 4.036, 4.058
X v UK, No 8160/78, Commission Decision of 12 1981, Decision and Reports, (DR) 22 .... 4.036
X v United Kingdom Application No 7291/75, admissibility decision of 4 October 1977 .... 5.031
X v United Kingdom, No 8160/78, Commission Decision, 12 March, 1981, Decisions and Reports, (DR) 22 .... 4.058
Xengin v Turkey Application No 1448/04 (2008), judg del 9 Jan 2008 .... 6.034

Yanaisk v Turkey (1993) 74 DR 98 .... 4.032, 4.046
Young, James and Webster v UK (1982) 4 EHRR 38 .... 11.004

Zengin v Turkey Application 1448/04 EHRR, judg del 9 Jan 2008 .... 3.046, 7.036
Zorach v Clauson (1952) 343 US 306 .... 10.005, 10.006, 10.017, 10.040

TABLE OF STATUTES

Catholic Relief Act 1829 .... 5.004
Censorship of Public Acts
1929–1967 .... 6.004
Censorship of Publications
Act 1929 .... 9.075
Child Care Act
1991 ....9.087, 9.092
Pt VII 9.078
Child Trafficking and Pornography
Act 1998 .... 9.087
Children Act 1908 .... 9.092
Children Act 2000 .... 9.087
Children Act 2001 .... 9.092
Commission to Inquire into Child
Abuse Act 2000 ....9.085, 9.086
Criminal Justice Act 2006
s 176 (2) 9.087
Criminal Justice and Immigration
Act 2008 .... 3.024, 5.005

Education (Miscellaneous Provisions)
Act 2007 .... 9.016
Education (Welfare) Act
2000 .... 9.016
Education Act 1944 .... 5.017, 9.012
Education Act 1964 .... 5.019
Education Act 1967 .... 5.019
Education Act 1968 .... 5.019
Education Act 1981 .... 5.019
Education Act 1996 .... 5.019
Education Act
1998 .... 1.025, 1.026, 4.061, 6.025, 9.010, 9.011, 9.012, 9.016, 9.031, 9.044, 9.046, 9.049, 9.051, 9.052, 9.054, 9.055, 9.058, 9.063, 9.068, 9.080
s 7 .... 1.026
(4)(a)(iv) ... 9.051, 9.063
8 .... 9.032
9 (d) 9.056
10, 12 .... 9.003
14 .... 9.032
15 .... 9.032
(2) (d) 9.077
16 .... 9.032
17 .... 9.032
30 .... 6.033, 9.044, 9.056, 9.058, 9.059, 9.060
(1) 9.056, 9.057
(2) (d) 9.057
(e) 9.026, 9.049, 9.057
(4) 9.057
37 ....9.068, 9.071
(1) 9.071, 9.076
Pt II 9.032
Education Act 2002 .... 5.019
s 100 .... 11.001
101 .... 11.001
Education Act 2005 .... 5.033
Education for Persons with Special
Needs Act 2004 .... 9.016
Education Reform Act
1988 .... 5.017
Elementary Education
Act 1876.............................. 9.092
Employment Equality Acts
1998–2004 .... 9.070
Equal Status Act 2000
s 7 .... 9.078
(3) (c) 9.013, 9.021, 9.077, 9.078, 9.079, 9.080
Equal Status Act 2004
s 6 .... 9.021, 9.077, 9.080
Equality Act 2004 .... 9.070

Equality Act 2006 .... 5.007
Equality Acts 1998–2004 .... 9.076

Fifth Amendment of the Constitution
Act 1972 .... 9.033

Government of Ireland Act 1920
s 5 .... 9.026

Industrial Schools Act 1868 ..... 9.085
Intermediate Education (Ireland)
Act 1878
s 7 .... 9.026
Irish Church Act 1869
s 20 .... 9.094

Non-Fatal Offences against
the Person Act 1997 .... 9.085

Prohibition of Incitement
to Hatred Act 1989 .... 3.023
Protection of Persons Reporting
Child Abuse
Act 1998 ....9.016, 9.087
s 10 .... 9.016

Residential Institutions Redress Act
2002 .... 9.086
Roman Catholic Relief
Act 1829 .... 5.004
Sex Offenders Act 2001 .... 9.087
Shops (Hours of Trading) Act 1938
s 25 .... 9.033
Statute of Limitations (Amendment)
Act 2000 .... 9.087

Unfair Dismissals Act 1977 ..... 9.076
s 6 (2) (f) 9.076
Vocational Education
Act 1930 .... 9.062
Vocational Education Act
Acts 1930–1970 ...... 9.035, 9.064
Vocational Education Acts
1930–2001 .... 9.019
Vocational Education (Amendment)
Act 1970
s 1 ....9.064
Vocational Education Act
Acts 1930–2001 ..... 9.012, 9.018,
9.019, 9.021,
9.062, 9.066,
9.076

Canada

Charter of Rights and
Freedoms 1982 ....4.066, 5.039
Human Rights Act 1978 ....5.039

Denmark

Executive Order of 1972
s 1 (3) 4.052
State Schools Act 1970 ......4.048

Finland

Comprehensive School Statute 1970
para 16(3) 9.060
School System Act
1968 ....9.060, 9.061
s 6 ....9.060

France

About-Picard Law
of 2001 .... 7.005, 7.022, 7.023
Act of 15 March 1882 ....1.032
Astier law of 25 July 1919 ....7.033
Civil Code of 1804 .... 7.001, 7.040
Debré Law, No 59–1557 of 31
December 1959 .... 7.033, 7.038
Falloux law of
15 March 1850 ....7.033
Ferry Laws 1880 ....11.014
Ferry's laws of 1881–2 ....7.027
Ferry Law of 1882 ....7.035

Ferry Laws 1882–1886 .... 7.016
French Civil Code of 1804
Art 180 .... 7.040
Goblet law
of 30 October 1886 .... 7.033
Law of 28 March 1882 .. 7.006, 7.030
Law of 30 October 1886 .... 7.006
Law of 1901 .... 7.032
Law of 1905 .... 7.006, 7.009, 7.017, 7.019, 7.020, 7.023, 7.028, 7.030, 7.032, 7.041, 7.044, 9.035
Art 1 .... 7.017
2 .... 7.018
30 .... 7.016
Law of 1907 .... 7.032
Law of 2001 .... 7.041
Law of 2004 .... 3.029, 7.024, 7.025, 7.026, 7.041
Napolonic Concordat
of 1808 .... 7.028
Ordinance No 2000–549 of 15 June
2000, Art 7 .... 7.016

Germany

Federal Statute of
23 September 1990 .... 1.005, 6.001, 6.004
Fiscal Code
s 51–68 .... 6.016
Grundgesetz
(Basic Law) 1.005, 11.011
Art 3 .... 6.013
(1) 6.018
(3) 6.013, 6.018
4 .... 6.004, 6.005, 6.013, 6.033
(1) 6.008, 6.018, 6.026
5 .... 6.004
7 (1) 6.010, 6.021, 6.022, 6.024, 6.026, 6.034
(2) 6.023
(3) 6.007, 6.022, 6.023, 6.024, 6.027, 6.033, 6.034
(4) 6.004
33 .... 6.008, 6.009, 6.011, 6.012, 6.018
137 (1) 6.004
138 .... 6.004
140 ...... 6.001, 6.007, 6.008, 6.014, 6.015, 6.017, 6.023, 6.029
141 .... 6.023
Religious Education
of Children Act 1921 .... 6.010
Religious Peace
of Augsburg 1555 .... 6.001
Treaty of Westphalia
1648 .... 2.004, 2.005
Unification Treaty
31 August 1990 ...... 1.005, 6.001, 6.004, 6.017
Vocational Education Acts
1930–2001 .... 6.010

Italy

Edict of Milan
(313 CE) 2.002, 2.006
Family Law (Divorce)
Act 1996 .... 1.043

Norway

Non-Conformist Act 1845 .... 4.015

Russia

Federal Law on the Freedom of
Conscience and Religious
Associations 1997 .... 4.039

Religions Act 1997 ....4.040, 4.041

San Marino

Elections Act 1.050

South Africa

Equality Act 2000 .... 1.042

Promotion of Equality
and Prevention of Unfair
Discrimination
Act 2000.................... 1.039, 1.041

Spain

Act of Religious Freedom
1980 ....8.023, 8.024, 8.038
Art 7 (1) 8.023

Criminal Code
Art 510 ....3.025
522–526 .... 3.025
Ch XXI 3.025

Education and Educational
Reform Financing
Act 1970............................... 8.012

Institutional Act 8/1985
s 4 .... 8.033

Institutional Law 1/1999
Preamble 8.017

Law of University Reform
1983 .... 8.025

Organic Act on Freedom
of Religion 1980 .... 8.004

Organic Law on the Right to
Education 1985 ....8.025, 8.026

Organic Law on the General
Organisation of the
Educational System
1990 ....8.025, 8.027

Sweden

Criminal Code
Ch 16 ....3.026, 3.027

Decree on Schools 1971 .... 4.054

School Act 1962 ....4.054

School Law 1985
Ch 3 s 12 ....4.057

Turkey

Criminal Code
Art 163 ....4.032

Law No 2820
s 78 ....4.032
90.1 ....4.032
101 ....4.032
103 ....4.032
107.1 ....4.032

United Kingdom

Accession Declaration
Act 1910 .... 5.008, 5.013

Act of Settlement
1701 ....5.008, 5.013, 5.042

Act of Succession 1534 ....5.008

Act of Supremacy 1534 ....5.008

Act of Supremacy 1559 ....5.008

Act of Toleration 1688 ....5.004

An Act for Explaining
and Emending an Act
entitled An Act
to Prevent the Further Growth
of Popery 1709 ....9.024

An Act for the English Order,
Habite and Language
1537....................................9.024

An Act for the Uniformity
of Public Prayers and
Administration
of Sacraments 1665 ....9.024

An Act to Prevent
the Further Growth
of Popery 1703 ....9.024

An Act to Restrain Foreign
Education 1695.....................9.024

United Kingdom (contd)
Balfour Act 5.018
Bill of Rights
Act 1688 .... 5.008, 5.013
Butler Act 5.019
Catholic Relief Act 1793 .... 5.004
Catholic Relief Act 1828 .... 5.004
Catholic Relief Act 1829 .... 5.004
Catholic Reliefs Act 1778 .... 5.004
Church of England Assembly
(Powers) Act 1919 .... 5.009
Coronation Oath
Act 1688 .... 5.008, 5.013
Corporation Act 1661 .... 5.004
Education (Grants and Awards)
Act 1984 .... 5.019
Education (Miscellaneous
Provisions) Act 1948 .... 5.019
Education (Miscellaneous
Provisions) Act 1953 .... 5.019
Education (Objections
to Admission Arrangements)
Regulations 1999
(SI 1999/125) 5.029
reg 7 .... 5.029
Education (School Leaving Dates)
1976 .... 5.019
Education (Schools)
Act 1992 .... 5.019, 5.021
Education (Work Experience)
Act 1973 .... 5.019
Education Act (NI) 1923 .... 9.022
Education Act 1880 .... 5.018
Education Act 1902 .... 5.018
Education Act 1918 .... 5.018
Education Act
1944 .... 5.015, 5.019, 5.024,
5.032, 5.044
s 25 .... 5.019
55 .... 5.026
76 .... 5.023
Sch 5 .... 5.019, 5.034
Education Act 1946 .... 5.019
Education Act 1959 .... 5.019
Education Act 1962 .... 5.019
Education (No 2) Act 1968 ...... 5.019
Education Act 1973 .... 5.019
Education Act 1975 .... 5.019
Education Act 1976 .... 5.019
Education Act 1979 .... 5.019
Education Act 1980 .... 5.019
Education Act 1981 .... 5.019
Education Act 1993 .... 5.019, 5.034
Sch 9 .... 5.026
Education Act
1996 .... 5.019, 5.024,
5.032, 5.033,
5.034
s 9 .... 5.023
375 .... 5.021, 5.033, 5.034
376 .... 5.033
381 .... 5.021
386 .... 5.032
387 .... 5.032
389 .... 5.032
397 .... 5.033
398 .... 5.033
509 .... 5.026
548 .... 5.031
579 .... 5.033
Sch
27 .... 5.023
31 .... 5.034
31 .... 5.019
Ch 111 .... 5.034
Pt 1 .... 5.019
Education Act 1998 .... 11.011
Education Act 2002
s 80 .... 5.019
159 .... 1.052
Pt 10 .... 5.022

TABLE OF EUROPEAN LEGISLATION

TABLE OF CONSTITUTIONS

TABLE OF CONVENTIONS, COVENANTS AND DECLARATIONS

BIBLIOGRAPHY

Gilby (trans), Thomas Aquinas, *Summa Theologiae* (McGraw Hill, 1964)

Adams and Emmerich, *A Nation Dedicated to Religious Liberty* (University of Pennsylvania Press, 1990)

Ahdar and Leigh, *Religious Freedom the Liberal State* (Oxford University Press, 2005)

Akenson, *The Irish Education Experiment* (Routledge, 1970)

Akenson, *A Mirror to Kathleen's Face: Education in Independent Ireland 1922–60* (McGill-Queens, 1975)

Lipscomb and Bergh (eds), 16 *Writings of Thomas Jefferson* 281 (Thomas Jefferson Memorial Association of the United States, 1903)

Auchmuty, *Irish Education: a Historical Study* (Hoggis Figgis, 1937)

Aversarius, *Religious Education in Public Schools*

Babbs, Martin and Hazelwindt (eds), *Focus on Social Inequalities* (TSO, 2004)

Barbier, *La laïcité (The secular principle),* (L'Harmattan, 1995)

Bates, *Religious Liberty: An Inquiry* (Harper, 1945)

Bettison (ed*), Documents of the Christian Church* (3rd edn, Oxford University Press, 1999)

Bhargava (ed), *Secularism and its Critics* (Oxford University Press, 1999)

Burke, *The Works of the Right Honourable Edmund Burke* (Rivington, 1815)

Bonney, *The Thirty Years War 1618–1648* (Osprey Publications, 2002)

Borkenau, *The Spanish Cockpit* (Osprey Publishing, 2002)

Bolt, *A Man For All Seasons* (Vintage, 1990)

Borowick and Babiski (eds), *New Religious Phenomena in Central and Eastern Europe* (Nomos, 1997)

Boston, *Why the Religious Right is Wrong about Separation of Church and State* (Prometheus, 1993)

Brenan, *The Spanish Labyrinth: an Account of the Social and Political Background of the Spanish Civil War* (Cambridge University Press, 1960)

Brown and Bell, with assistance from Galabert, *French Administrative Law* (5th edn, Clarendon Press, 1998)

Bunson, Edict of Milan, *Encyclopedia of the Roman Empire* (New York, 1994)

Buckley, Skehill and O'Sullivan, *Child Protection in Ireland: A Case Study* (Oak Tree Press, 1997)

Burke, *Reflections on the Revolution in France, 1790* (Harvard Classics, Collier & Son 1909–1914)

Burke, *The Works of the Right Honourable Edmund Burke* (Rivington, 1815)

Butler, *Historical Memoirs of English, Scottish, and Irish Catholics* (John Murray, 1819–22)

Butler, *The Life of Hugo Grotius* (John Murray, 1826)

Butler, *The Coronation Oath* (Bibliotheca Heraldica, 1801)

Butler, *The French Church* (1817)

Carr and Fusi, *Spain: Dictatorship to Democracy* (George Allen and Unwin, 1979)
Carr, *Spain 1808–1975: A History* (Oxford University Press, 1982)
Cassells English Dictionary (Cassells, 1971)
Chadwick, *Shifting Alliances: Church and State in English Education* (Geoffrey Chapman Publishers, 1997)
Clarke, *Church and State: Essays in Political Philosophy* (Cork University Press, 1984)
Cole, *Education, Equality and Human RIghts: Issues of Gender,'Race', Sexuality, Disability and Social Class* (Routledge Falmer, 2006)
Connolly (ed), *The Oxford Companion to Irish History* (Oxford University Press, 1999)
Cook, *The Laws of Moses and the Code of Hammurabi* (Adam and Charles Black, 1903)
Coolahan, *Irish Education: History and Structure* (Institute of Public Administration, 1981)
Coolahan (ed), *Report on the National Education Convention. Ireland: The National Education Convention Secretariat* (Government Publications, 1994)
Cooney, *John Charles McQuaid: Ruler of Catholic Ireland* (O'Brien Press, 1999)
Costello and Barry (eds), *The New Equality Directives* (Irish Centre for European Law, 2003)
Coulton, *The Inquisition* (Ernest Benn, 1929)
Cox, *The English Churches in a Secular Society: Lambeth, 1870–1930* (Oxford University Press, 1982)
Cruise O' Brien, *Ancestral Voices, Religion and Nationalism in Ireland* (University of Chicago Press, 1995)

Darwin, *On the Origin of Species by Means of Natural Selection* (John Murray, 1859)
Davison Hunter, *Culture Wars: the struggle to define America* (Basic Books, 1991)
Dawkins, *The God Delusion* (Bantam Press, 2006)
Dawood (trans), *The Koran* (Penguin Classics, 1990)
de Groof (ed), *Subsidiaritty and Education: Aspects of Comparative Educational Law* (Acco, 1994)
Debray (ed) *Contretemps: Eloges des idéaux perdus* (Gallimard, 2004)
Dershowitz, *America Declares Independence* (Wiley & Sons, 2003)
Doerr and Menendez, *Religious Liberty and State Constitutions* (Prmoetheus Books, 1993)
Dunford and Sharp, *The Education System in England and Wales* (Longman, 1990)
Durand-Prinborgne, *La Laïcité* (Dalloz, 1996)

Encyclopedia Brittanica (11th edn)

Esdaile, *Spain in the Liberal Age: From Constitution to Civil War, 1808–1939* (Blackwell, 2000)
Evans, *Freedom of Religion Under the European Convention on Human Rights* (Oxford University Press, 2001)

Feldman, *Divided by God* (Farrar, Straus and Giroux, 2005)
Ferguson and Kenny (eds), *On Behalf of the Child* (A & A Farmar, 1995)
Ferrari, Cole-Durham and Sewell (eds), *Law and Religion in Post-Communist Europe* (Peeters, 2003)
Figgis, *From Gerson to Grotius*, 1414–1625 (Batoche Books, 1999)
Fink, *De Concordatis* (Louvain, 1879)
Flannery, *The Anguish of the Jews* (Paulist Press, 1985)
Flannery, *The Death of Religious Life* (Columba Press, 1997)
Foley (ed), *Jeffersonian Cyclopedia* (Funk & Wagnells, 1900)
Fuller, *Irish Catholicism since 1950: The Undoing of a Culture* (Gill and MacMillan, 2004)

Galerius, *Edict of Toleration*
Gallup and Jones, *The Next American Spirituality: Finding God in the Twentieth Century* (Chariot Victor Pubs, 2000)
Gallup and Jones, *The Saints Among Us* (Morehouse Pubs, 1993)
Gallup and Lindsay, *The Gallup Guide: Reality Check for 21st Century Churches* (Gallup, 2002)
Gallup and Lindsay, *Surveying the Religious Landscape* (Morehouse Pub Co, 1999)
George Orwell, *Animal Farm* (Harcourt, Brace, 1946)
Gidron (ed) *Government and the Third Sector: Emerging Relationships in Welfare States* (Jossey-Bass Publications, 1992)
Glenn, *The Ambiguous Embrace: Government and Faith-based Schools and Social Agencies* (Princeton University Press, 2001)
Glenn and de Groof, *Finding the Right Balance, Freedom, Autonomy and Accountability in Education* (Lemma, 2002)
Glenn and de Groof, *Balancing freedom, autonomy and accountability in Education* (Wolf Legal Publishers, 2005)
Glendenning and Binchy (eds*), Litigation against Schools: Implications for School Management* (First Law, 2006)
Glendenning, *Education and the Law* (Tottel Publishing, 1999)
Gonzalo Ojea Puente, *La formación del cristianismo como fenómeno ideológico (España Editores, SA*, 1993)
Gordon and Stack (eds) *Citizenship Beyond the State* (Routledge, Taylor and Francis, 2007), vol 11, issue 2
Graham and Labanyi (eds), *Spanish Cultural Studies: An Introduction: The Struggle for Modernity* (Oxford University Press, 1995)
Gray *Black Mass: Apocalyptic Religion and the Death of Utopia* (Allen Lane, 2007).

Gregor (trans), Kant, *The Metaphysics of Morals* (Cambridge University Press 1991)
Green, *Education and State Formation* (Macmillan, 1991)
Griffiths, *The Marriage of East and West* (Wm Collins & Son, 1982)
Grotius, *On the Truth of the Christian Religion* (Paris, 1627)

Halsbury's Laws of England (Lexis Nexis/Butterworths, 2006), vol 15
Hand and McBride, *Droits sans Frontieres: Essays in Honour of L Neville Brown* (Holdsworth Club, 1991)
Harper, *The Code of Hammurabi, King, of Babylon* (Lawbook Exchange Ltd, 1991)
Harris, *Education and Diversity* (Hart Publishing, 2007)
Hatfield (ed), *Judicial Review: a Thematic Approach* (Gill and Macmillan, 1995)
Hauben (ed), *The Spanish Inquisition* (John Wiley, 1969)
Healey, *The French Achievement: Private School Aid-a Lesson for America* (Paulist Press, 1974)
Heffernan (ed), *Human Rights, a European Perspective*, (Round Hall Press, 1994)
Heimbrock, Scheilke, Schreiner (eds), *Towards Religious Competence. Diversity as a Challenge in Europe* (LIT Verlag, 2001)
Herold (ed), *Napoleon 1, Emperor of the French, The Mind of Napoleon: A Selection from his Written and Spoken Words* (Columbia University Press, 1955)
Hexham, *Concise Dictionary of Religion* (Regent College Publications, 1998)
Hitchens, *God is Not Great* (Hachette Book Group, 2007)
Hogan and Whyte, *J M Kelly: The Irish Constitution* (4th edn,Tottel Publishing, 2003)
Hollifield and Ross, *Searching for the New France* (Routledge, 1991)
Honore, *Law in the Crisis of Empire 379–455* (Oxford University Press, 1998)
Horton and Mendus (eds), *John Locke, A Letter Concerning Toleration, in Focus* (Routledge, 1991)
Hyland and Milne (eds) *Irish Educational Documents* (Church of Ireland College of Education, 1987)
Hylson-Smith, *The Churches in England from Elizabeth I to Elizabeth II* (Canterbury Press, 1996–1998)

Inglis, *Global Ireland: Same Difference* (Routledge, 2007)
Irujo, *El Tribunal Constitucional y la proteccion de la libertades publicas en al ambitio privado, en El Tribunal Constitucional* (IEF, 1981)
Israel (ed), *Major Peace Treaties of Modern History: 1648–1967* (McGraw-Hill Book Company, 1970)

Jacobi, *Collected Works*, The Theory of Psychoanalysis (1913) Vol 4
Jacobi (ed), *Psychological Reflections: An Anthology of the Writings of C G. Jung* (Routledge and Kegan Paul, 1953)
James, *The Varieties of Religious Experience: a Subject on Human Nature* (Modern Library, 1994)

Jarman, *Landmarks in the History of Education* (John Murray, 1963)
Jenkins, *The Next Christendom: the Coming of Global Christianity* (Oxford University Press, 2003)
Jeuffroy, Tricard and Durand, *Liberté religieuse et regimes des cultes en droit francais 1031–1034* (Editions du Cerf, 1996)
Jewish Enclyclopedia (Funk and Wagnalls, 1901–1906)
Johns, *Babylonian and Assyrian Laws, Contracts and Letters* (Adamant Media Corporation, 2000)
Josephus, *The Works of Josephus* (Loeb Classical Library, Heinman, 1926)

Kagan, Ozment and Turner, *The Western Heritage* (7th edn, Prentice Hall, 2001)
Kahn-Freund, Rudden, Levy, *A Source Book on French Law* (3rd edn, Clarendon Press, 1991)
Kamen, *The Rise of Toleration* (Weidenfeld and Nicholson, 1967)
Kamen, *The Spanish Inquisition and Society in Spain in the Sixteenth and Seventeenth Centuries* (Indiana University Press, 1985)
Kelly, *Fundamental Rights in the Irish Law and Constitution* (2nd edn, Oceana Publications, 1968)
Kennedy, *Just Law* (Vintage, 2004)
Kommers, *The Constitutional Jurisprudence of the Federal Republic of Germany* (2nd edn, Duke University Press, 1997)

Lactantius, *Edict of Milan*
Lane (ed), *Religion, Education and the Constitution* (St Columba's Press, 1992)
Langdon-Davies, *The Spanish Inquisition* (Longman, 1969)
Larson, *Summer of the Gods* (Basic Books, 1997)
Lea, *A History of the Inquisition in the Middle Ages* (1988, Harbor Press, 1955)
Lee (trans), *Plato and the Republic* (Penguin Classics, 1974)
Bray (trans), *Montaillou: The Promised Land of Error* (Vintage Books, 1979)
Lewis, Hooper (ed), *God in the Dock: Essays on Theology and Ethics* (William B Eerdmans Publishing Co, 1971)
Lewis, Sharland and Moffat, *Education and the Courts* (2nd edn, Jordans, 2003)
Liell (ed), *The Law of Education* (9th edn, Butterworths, 1984)
Littleton and Maher (eds), *Contemporary Catholicism: a Critical Appraisal* (Columba Press, 2008)
Lloyd, *The Church of England, 1900–1965* (SCM Press, 1966)
Lodge and Lynch (eds) *Diversity at School* (Equality Authority, 2004)
Lundy, *Education Law: Policy and Practice in Northern Ireland* (SLS, 2000)

McArdle (ed) *Cambridge Lectures 1991* (Comansville Editions Yvon Blais, 1993)
Macbeth, *Studies: The Child Between* (Office for Official Publications, 1984)
Machiavelli, *The Prince* (first published in 1531) (Penguin Books, 2004)
Mackey and McDonagh (eds), *Religion and Politics in Ireland at the Turn of the Millennium* (Columba Press, 2003)

Mansfeld and Wintrop (trans and ed), de Toqueville, *Democracy in America* (University of Chicago Press, 2000 (hardcover), 2002 (paperback))
Marcus, *Saeculum: History and Society in the Theology of St Augustine* (2nd edn, Cambridge University Press, 1989)
Margolis and Marx, *A History of the Jewish People* (Atheneum, 1927)
Marx, *Contribution to Critique of Hegel's Philosophy of Right* (Cambridge University Press, 1970)
Matthews, *Laying Down the Law: A Study of the Theodosian Code* (Yale University Press, 2000)
Mayfield, *The Church of England* (2d edn, 1963)
McBeth, *A Sourcebook for Baptist Heritage* (B&H Publishing Group, January 1990)
McCarthy, *The Distasteful Challenge* (Institute of Public Administration, 1968)
McGahern, *Memoir* (Faber and Faber, 2005)
McGrath, *The Dawkins Delusion* (Society for the Promotion of Christian Knowledge, 2007)
McMahon and Binchy, *Law of Torts* (3rd edn, Tottel Publishing, 2000)
McManus, *Education and the Courts* (2nd edn, Jordans, 2004)
Merino-Blanco, *Spanish Law and Legal System* (2nd edn, Sweet and Maxwell, 2006)
Mitchell, *Betrayal of the Innocents: Desire, Power and the Catholic Church in Spain* (University of Pennsylvania Press, 1998)
Mitchell, *Passional Culture: Emotion, Religion and Society in Southern Spain and Violence* (University of Pennsylvania Press, 1990)
Mitchell, *Piety in Spanish Folklore* (University of Pennsylvania Press, 1988)
Monter, *Frontiers of Heresy: The Spanish Inquisition from the Basque Lands to Sicily* (Cambridge University Press, 2003)
Murdoch's Dictionary of Irish Law, (5th edn, Tottel Publishing, 2008).
Murray, *The Soul of Europe and other Selected Writings* (Veritas, 2002)

Nagy (ed), Boros-Kazai (trans), *Democracy, Revolution, Self Determination* (Columbia University Press, 1991)
Neuhaus, *The Naked Public Square: Religion and Democracy in America* (WB Eerdmans Publishing Co, 1983)
NCB Stockbrokers, *2020 Vision: Ireland's Demographic Dividend* (2006)
Norman, *Ethos and Education in Ireland* (Peter Lang Publishing, 2003)

O'Brien, *The Inquisition* (Macmillan Publishing, 1973)
O'Buachalla, *Educational Policy in Twentieth Century Ireland* (Merlin Publishing, 1988)
O'Connell, *A History of the INTO* (Irish National Teachers' Organisation, 1968)
O'Dair and Lennon, *Law and Religion* (OUP, 2001)
O'Donoghue, *The Catholic Church and the Secondary School Curriculum in Ireland 1922–62* (1999)

Paine, *The Rights of Man*, (Penguin Classics, 1984)
Peters, *Inquisition* (California University Press, 1989)
Peterson (ed) *Thomas Jefferson: Writings* 1186–1187 (Library of America, 1984)
Pierson, *The History of Spain* (Greenwood, 1999)
Plato, Pangle (trans), *The Laws of Plato* (Basic Books, 1980)
Plato, Grube (trans), *The Republic* (Hackett Publishing Company, 1992)

Radau, *Early Babylonian History* (Wipf & Stock Publishers, 2005)
Reich (ed), *Select Documents Illustrating Medieval and Modern History* (PS King, 1905)
Robbers (ed), *State and Church in the European Union* (Nomos, 2005)
Robinson, *Readings in European History* (Ginn, 1906)
Roth, *The Spanish Inquisition* (Columbia University Press, 1987)
Rousseau, *The Social Contract* (Penguin Books, 2004)
Rousseau, *The Social Contract or the Principles of Political Right* (New American Library, 1974)
Russo, *Reutter's The Law of Public Education* (6th edn, Foundation Press, 2006)

Schwarze (ed), *Administrative Law under European Influence* (Sweet &. Maxwell, 1996)
Seneca, *On the Shortness of Life* (Penguin Classics, Penguin, 1997)
Shaw, *The Doctor's Dilemma* (1906)
Shatter's Family Law (4th edn, Tottel Publishing, 1997)
Shorter Oxford English Dictionary
Skinner, *The Foundations of Modern Political Thought* (Cambridge University Press, 1978)
Szabo, *Cultural Rights* (Sijthoff, 1974)

Tamanaha, *Law as a Means to an End: Threat to the Rule of Law* (Cambridge, 2006)
Tamanaha, *Law as a Means to an End: Threat to the Rule of Law* (Cambridge University Press, 2006)
Tamanaha, *On the Rule of Law: History, Politics, Theory* (Cambridge, 2004)
Taus-Bolstad, *Spain in Pictures* (Visual Geography), (Lerner Publishing Group, 2004)
Taylor, *A Secular Age* (Harvard University Press, 2007)
Teaching Religion in the Primary School: Issues and Challenges (Irish National Teachers Organisation, 2003)
Teigten, *Collected Edition of the Travaux Preparatoires of the European Convention on Human Rights* (Council Of Europe, 1985)
The Educational Structures in the Member States of the European Community (Office for Official Publications of EC, Luxembourg, 1989)
Titley, *Church-State and the Control of Schooling in Ireland* (McGill-Queens, 1983)

Tooley (trans), Bodkin, *Six Books of the Commonwealth* (original 1576, Basil Blackwell, I955)
Treacy and Whyte (eds), *Religion, Morality and Public Policy* (Dominican Publications, 1995)

Vatican's Statistical Yearbook
Vincent, Scanlan (trans), *Judaism*, (Sands & Co, 1934)

Wakefield, *Heresy, Crusade, and Inquisition in Southern France, 1100–1250* (University of California Press, 1974)
Watson, *The Church of England* (Kessinger Publishing, 2004)
Weinberg, *Dreams of a Final Theory: The Scientific Search for the Ultimate Laws of Nature* (Vintage, 1993)
Whyte, *Church and State in Modern Ireland, 1923–70,* (Gill & Macmillan, 1971)
Winton (ed), *Documents from Old Testament Times* (Harper and Row, 1958)
Witte and van der Vyver (eds), *Religious Human Rights in Global Perspective: Religious Perspectives* (Martinus Nijhoff Publishers, 1996)
Wolf, *Toward Consensus: Catholic-Protestant Interpretations of Church and State* (Doubleday: Anchor Books, 1968)
Wokler, *Rousseau* (Altýn Kitaplar Yayýnevi, 2003)
Words and Phrases Legally Defined (Lexis Nexis/Butterworths, 1998)

Chapter 1

INTRODUCTION

Man was born free, and he is everywhere in chains. Those who think themselves the masters of others are indeed greater slaves than they.[1]

[1.001] Despite the tensions that have existed between them over the centuries, it has been argued that religion, education and the law are the pillars of civilization.[2] Some fear that the pillar of religion is gradually being removed from the dialogue with education and the law thus weakening the structural edifice of modern civilization, so to speak. On the other hand, countries such as France, Turkey and the United States of America (US) have determined that religion has no place in public education and have embodied the principle of secularism in their laws and constitutions. However, just as sociologists of religion and others were predicting a worldwide decline in the practice of religion, religion seemed to revive itself towards the end of the last century[3] with Pentecostalism and Islam being the most dynamic religious movements.[4] Undoubtedly, the place of religion in society has altered profoundly during the twentieth century and a number of so-called 'new religions' have emerged as people strive to make sense of their lives and their spiritual beliefs in an increasingly secular age.[5] With the growth in the more conservative forms of religion, the pressing need for mutual understanding among religions has been recognised together with the need for carefully-devised legal protections for religious freedom and freedom of education. Moreover, the emergence of multi-faceted problems, many of them social and religious, has led to calls for a more open, tolerant approach to religion generally speaking. Regrettably, media coverage following the tragic events of 9/11 tended to label all conservative religious adherents as 'fundamentalists' leading to societal pressure on sincere

---

1. Rousseau, *The Social Contract* (Penguin Books, 2004) p 2.
2. Lane (ed), *Religion, Education and the Constitution* (St Columba's Press, 1992) p 4.
3. Ahdar and Leigh, *Religious Freedom the Liberal State* (Oxford University Press, 2005) p 1: Berger, 'Secularism in Retreat', *The National Interest*, Winter 1996/7, 3.3.
4. Berger, 'Religions and Globalisation' (2003) 36 *European Judaism*, 4, 7.
5. Taylor, *A Secular Age* (Harvard University Press, 2007).

religious adherents to conform to the norms and values of the liberal and secular state.[6] While it is estimated that Christianity[7] remains the world's largest broad religious category,[8] comprising approximately 33 per cent of the world's total population, research indicates that Muslims now outnumber Catholics for the first time[9] which raises new questions as to the law on religion throughout Europe.[10]

[1.002] In Europe, where many countries share the main hallmarks of Christianity, differing approaches to the ideological and philosophical basis of political authority are apparent which are manifested in the provision made for religion in each country and for the teaching of any religion, if any, in publicly-funded schools. In France, where public education is a key agency for unity and social cohesion, there is, generally speaking, no place for religion in the public schools,[11] although there is public funding for its mainly Catholic private schools, albeit on strict conditions.[12] By contrast, religion is part of the state system of education in Germany, England, Ireland and Spain. Alternatively, there may be a long-established tradition of the provision of education mainly by others (eg the churches and religious orders), provided state imposed standards are met, as is the case in Ireland.

[1.003] Although the churches were the early providers of education in most Western democracies, the state has been intimately involved with the educational systems at least from the mid-nineteenth century onwards and earlier in some instances.[13] As with other services, the assumption of

6. Ahdar and Leigh, *Religious Freedom in the Liberal State* p 2.
7. The doctrines and precepts taught by Christ, faith in Christ and his teaching; Christian character and conduct; the state of being a Christian. *Cassell's English Dictionary* p 199.
8. Jenkins, *The Next Christendom: the Coming of Global Christianity* (Oxford University Press, 2003) p 5.
9. Kington, 'Vatican says Muslims outnumber Catholics', (2006) *Irish Times*, citing Vittorio Formenti (ed) Vatican's Statistical Yearbook.
10. Robbers (ed), *State and Church in the European Union* (Nomos, 2005) pp 577–589, 578.
11. See, however, the position of the religious public schools in Alsace-Moselle discussed in **para [7.031]**.
12. See further **para [7.032]**.
13. Glenn and de Groof, *Balancing freedom, autonomy and accountability in Education* (Wolf Legal Publishers, 2005) chapter 10.

responsibility by the state, with its greater capacity to raise resources, gradually moved to the fore frequently co-opting many schools that had emerged without state assistance.[14] These non-state schools were over time required to align their programmes of education and standards with those of state schools and increasingly they were regulated in common with state schools. Thus, many non-state schools came to be perceived as providing the public service of education, and they became, at least to some degree, 'organs of the state'.

[1.004] In the European Union (EU hereafter), these regulated schools became subject to relevant Community law and to the requirements of international human rights law in certain spheres. In recent years the appropriate place of religion in public life has been propelled into the forefront of global debate and the potential of religion to influence political life is being scrutinised in an unprecedented manner as the EU enlarges.[15] Generally, in denominational systems of education, the school is perceived not just as the primary environment for the socialisation of children but as the cradle of religious belief in that the more intensively religion has stamped its character on the child in the early days at school, the more likely he is to pass his value system on to the next generation.[16] As many countries strive to find an acceptable balance between freedom of religion for the individual and a religiously neutral education for children, the place of religious symbols in public schools and the so-called 'headscarf' cases have entered the courtrooms and many of these cases are discussed later in this book.[17] Some flavour of a country's approach to religion, or its absence, may be gleaned from the Preamble to its constitution.

Deities in Constitutional Preambles

[1.005] Certain countries invoke the blessings of a deity in their preambles while others go further and enshrine principles relating to religion in the

---

14. Glenn and de Groof, *Balancing freedom, autonomy and accountability in Education* (Wolf Legal Publishers, 2005) p 268.

15. For example see *Judgments of the Federal Constitutional Court in Germany*, BVerfGE 89, 155 in which the Court upheld the constitutionality of Germany's participation in the EU. However, this judgment also set down serious reservations which became the basis of widespread debate on this issue.

16. Jacobi (ed), *Psychological Reflections: An Anthology of the Writings of C G Jung* (Routledge and Kegan Paul, 1953), p 83.

17. See **paras [3.021]**, **[4.023]** and **[6.011]**.

body of their constitutions. What is meant by God or a deity may vary, quite considerably, from country to country and in accordance with various beliefs, tenets and eras. For example, the Swiss Constitution (1998) was adopted by the people 'in the name of Almighty God' while Greece's Constitution (1975), which omits a preamble, is enacted in 'the name of the Holy and Consubstantial and Indivisible Trinity.' The amended Preamble of the Basic Law for the Federal Republic of Germany (1990) opens with the words 'Conscious of their responsibility before God and Men, Animated by the resolve to serve world peace as an equal partner in a united Europe, the German people have adopted, by virtue of their constituent power, this Basic Law.'[18] Ireland's preamble to its Constitution (1937), which has been described as 'probably unique among modern written constitutions',[19] invokes 'the Name of the Most Holy Trinity, from whom is all authority and to Whom as our final end, all actions of men and states must be referred' and it acknowledges 'all our obligations to our Divine Lord, Jesus Christ, Who sustained our fathers through centuries of trial and it concludes with the phrase 'Dochum Glóire Dé agus Onóra na hÉireann' ('For the Glory of God and the honour of Ireland'). The Australian Constitution simply calls down 'the blessing of Almighty God' while the preamble to the South African Constitution declares 'May God protect our people' in four languages. By contrast, the Constitution of India describes the state as 'a sovereign, socialist, secular, Democratic Republic.'

[1.006] In an integrating Europe, it is clear that certain common legal principles and shared democratic values have emerged from its Christian heritage, rooted in the Middle East, and from the constitutional traditions in the various member states, and that these constitute the general principles of the EU's law, together with rights guaranteed in the European Convention on Human Rights and Fundamental Freedoms (ECHR). At the same time, Europe must meet the challenge of equitably accommodating its growing Islamic population, whose beliefs and values may, on occasion, sit uneasily with the upholding principles of a democratic society.[20] Ironically, as Europe secularises, it is now striving to meet the rights of religious minorities, and those growing numbers who profess no religion, who are seeking accommodation in public life and in publicly-funded education, thus

18. Germany's Basic Law (*Grundgesetz*), see Unification Treaty, 31 August 1990 and Federal Statute of 23 September 1990, *Federal Law Gazette* 11 p 885.

19. *Revista Xaveridna*, Bogota, Columbia, December 1937 in a newspaper article written at the request of the editor.

20. *Refah Partisi (The Welfare Party) v Turkey* [2003] EHRR 1.

ensuring that religion will continue to be one of the most significant social and political issues of this century.

[1.007] Many individuals are understandably fearful of religion because of the wars and persecutions fought in its name through the centuries and in view of the fact that the Crusades, the Inquisition and the Holocaust comprise part of the collective memory of Europe.[21] Perhaps, as the United Nations Declaration on Human Rights 1948 (UNDHR) indicates, it was disregard and contempt for human rights which 'resulted in barbarous acts which have outraged the conscience of mankind'[22] rather than religion *per se* which brought war and great suffering to mankind. Whatever the reason, legal protection for the right to freedom of religion was dilatory in arriving on the world stage, so to speak. However, such protection is now to be found in various international human rights instruments dealing with freedom of thought, conscience and religion and related rights.[23]

FREEDOM OF RELIGION

[1.008] Freedom of religion is a fundamental right and it is, according to the European Court of Human Rights (ECtHR hereafter) 'one of the foundations of a democratic society.'[24] Yet, religion is clearly under pressure in the West, as Ahdar and Leigh observe, and they suggest a number of reasons for this.[25] Firstly, they note a greater number and diversity of

---

21. Drinan, 'Can God and Caesar Coexist? Balancing Religious Freedom and International Law' *The British Yearbook of International Law* (2004) pp 89 and 15.

22. Preamble to United Nations Declaration on Human Rights (1948) proclaimed by the General Assembly, Resolution 217(A)(111) of 10 December 1948.

23. International treaties which contain provisions relating to religion are the European Convention on Human Rights 1950 and Article 2 of Protocol I; The United Nations Declaration on the Elimination of all Forms of Intolerance and of Discrimination Based on Religion or Belief 1981: UN Convention on the Rights of the Child 1989, Art 14; Art 18 of the UN Declaration on Human Rights (1981) (UNDHR); while germane provisions dealing with education include: Art 26 of the UNDHR; Art 2 of Protocol 1 of the ECHR; Art 13(3) of the UN International Covenant on Economic, Social and Cultural Rights 1966 (ICESCR) and Art 18 of the UN International Covenant on Civil and Political Rights (ICCPR).

24. *Refah Partisi (The Welfare Party) v Turkey* [2003] EHRR 1.

25. Ahdar and Leigh, *Religious Freedom in the Liberal State* p 5: see also Lewis, Hooper (ed), *God in the Dock: Essays on Theology and Ethics* (William B Eerdmans Publishing Co, 1971) chapter 12.

religions (and 'spiritualities') in modern liberal democracies than in past centuries together with easy international travel and greater religious pluralism accelerated by immigration. Secondly, they observe the rapid growth of Islam in the west[26] and they believe that Islam will not so readily acquiesce to the privatisation of belief that Christians have accepted.[27] Thirdly, they refer to the expansion of the state and its penetration into most spheres of social interaction. Fourthly, they argue that classical liberalism, which was not opposed to religion, has mutated to a secularised comprehensive form of liberalism that promotes, what Justice Scalia, of the US Supreme Court described in *Locke v Davey*[28] as 'a tepid, civic version of the faith.' Although it has ancient antecedents, it is only in the last century that religious freedom has been recognised globally as a legal right although it is probably more difficult to enforce than the more established rights such as freedom of expression and freedom of association. The proclamation of the right to freedom of religion or belief in the 1950s as a universal human right[29] to be guaranteed by contracting states as a matter of law, was undoubtedly a singular step forward in human history.

Religion in Public Life

[1.009] In the past, Edmund Burke had few doubts as to the place of religion in society since he declared: 'we know and, what is better, we feel inwardly, that religion is the basis of civil society and the source of all good and all comfort'.[30] Others contend that religion has no place in public life or public education, that the law should reflect a clear separation of church and state and that it should provide a secular and rational pillar to support public policy.[31] In recent decades there is a tendency to demonise religion as one of the root causes of the world's greatest evils as the growth in the sales of

---

26. Ahdar and Leigh, *Religious Freedom in the Liberal State*, citing Ferrari 'Individual Religious Freedom and National Security in Europe after September 11', *BYUL Rev* 357.

27. Ahdar and Leigh, *Religious Freedom in the Liberal State* p 5.

28. *Locke v Davey* 540 US 712.

29. ECHR, Art 9.

30. See *The Works of the Right Honourable Edmund Burke* (Rivington, 1815) Vol 5, p 173.

31. Marx, *Contribution to Critique of Hegel's Philosophy of Right* (Cambridge University Press, 1970), Darwin, *On the Origin of Species by Means of Natural Selection* and *On Natural Selection*) and Dawkins, *The God Delusion*.

literature of what has been termed 'proselytising atheism' indicates,[32] but that debate has not been entirely one-way.[33] While atheism need not necessarily be missionary in its outlook, 'zealous atheism', it has been argued, renews some of the worst features of both Christianity and Islam in that it constitutes a project of universal conversion which is right for everybody,[34] thereby downgrading the right to religious freedom, which is recognised as one of the most significant of all human rights.[35]

Tensions Relating to Religion in Europe

[1.010] Although the practice of religion continues to decline in Europe, religion itself remains an important element of social life and it has become in recent years a significant element on the political agenda which the civil ecclesiastical law (the law relating to church and state) of the EU recognises.[36] There are few spheres of law in which historic experience, emotional ties, tradition and basic convictions have as direct an influence as in civil ecclesiastical law generally speaking.[37] Internal tensions may arise between the established citizens in the member states, or between those citizens and the new immigrants, the former perceiving risks to their traditional values, culture and faith while the latter may feel misunderstood, alienated or even threatened in their new situation.

[1.011] Tensions may also arise within the member states from the conflicting perspectives of some religions and the secular values embodied in EU law and in human rights law. These latter conflicting perspectives

32. Gray, 'The atheist delusion' (2008) *Irish Times,* 20 March, referring to Dawkins, *The God Delusion,* see also Hitchens, *God is Not Great* (Hachette Book Group, 2007) and *Black Mass: Apocalyptic Religion and the Death of Utopia* (Allen Lane, 2007).

33. Taylor, *A Secular Age*, McGrath, *The Dawkins Delusion* (Society for the Promotion of Christian Knowledge, 2007), *Darwin's Angel: An Angelic Riposte to The God Delusion.*

34. Gray, *Black Mass: Apocalyptic Religion and the Death of Utopia.*

35. In *R v Secretary of State for Employment ex parte Williamson* [2005] UKHL 15: Art 9 of the European Convention on Human Rights but other rights may also be involved depending on the context eg Arts 13, 14 and Art 2 of Protocol 1.

36. Robbers (ed), *State and Church in the European Union* (Nomos, 2005) p 577: Perry, 'Religion, Politics and Human Rights' in Treacy and Whyte (eds), *Religion, Morality and Public Policy* (Dominican Publications, 1995) pp 16, 19.

37. Robbers (ed), *State and Church in the European Union*, p 577.

become apparent most frequently in value-laden issues relating, for example, to the fostering and adoption of children; same-sex marriage; abortion; euthanasia; stem-cell research; the right to manifest religion in public life; and the teaching of religious education in schools. Such tensions run deeper than mere uneasiness, however, since they derive from different ideological conceptions of moral authority in spheres of mutual concern to church and state. That inherent conflicts have long existed in these intersecting areas of life is clear from the probing questions of the Pharisees to Jesus, as to the legality of paying taxes to the Roman secular government and from Jesus' reply: 'Render unto Caesar the things that are Caesar's, and unto God the things that are God's.'[38] However, it may require the wisdom of Solomon and the patience of Job to determine precisely what is Caesar's due and what is rightfully God's, when religion and education intersect with law in harmonising Europe. Approaches to such problems, globally, are many and varied depending on each individual country's historical experience and ideological struggles and they may range from theocracy, through accommodation of religion in public life, to various degrees of secularism described as 'passive', or as 'assertive', or 'militant' as in France and Turkey.[39]

[1.012] One of the most intractable challenges facing an increasingly diverse Western Europe is that of striking an appropriate balance in society between respecting individual and group rights to religious and cultural freedom while fostering social cohesion at a time of perceived social tensions.[40] Although church-state relations may evolve from distinctions relating to norms and values that are essentially philosophical and ideological/religious in character, legislation, the media, judicial decisions, politics, public education and human rights all have an immense influence on civil ecclesiastical law. Because the relationship between church and state in each country ebbs and flows in response to public demands, political exigencies, judicial decisions, legislative and other structural changes, it is in a state of constant flux, being rendered 'new' by each successive generation which adds fresh insights and new perspectives to the legacy of the past.

38. Mark 12: 17 (King James), Matthew 22:21 and Luke 20:25.

39. For an interesting article on these approaches see Kuru, 'Passive and Assertive Secularism: Historical Conditions, Ideological Struggles and state Policies toward Religion', *World Politics,* Vol 59, no 4, July 2007, 568–594.

40. Harris, *Education and Diversity* (Hart Publishing, 2007) p 361 and generally **chapter 2**.

Church-State Relations in Europe

[1.013] In most European countries, generally speaking, one predominant church of the majority still retains close relationships with the state, with the exception of Germany where two main religions are recognised. In Northern Europe these countries tend to be Protestant, with the exception of Ireland, while in the South they are generally Catholic. There is a global tendency to abolish the established churches, although, as the ECtHR held in *Darby v Sweden*,[41] establishment *per se* does not violate Art 9 of the ECHR. Nonetheless, Sweden abolished her established church in 2002. The General Synod of the Lutheran Church of Norway has announced that it will relinquish its traditional ties with the Norwegian State shortly. This latter decision was taken following a government commission's recommendation that the privileged civic church-state relationship should be abolished. In the UK, however, the established Church of England still exists and is considered in **chapter 5** below. Although the relevance of the Established churches has greatly declined in latter years, traditional church-state structures generally remain in place in the countries which have abolished the legal status of establishment.

[1.014] In addition, external forces emanating from globalisation, harmonisation and from the influence of international human rights law are influencing the laws of the member states, a process which Heinig succinctly describes when he states: 'The processes of Europeanization, internationalisation and globalisation thoroughly penetrate the law.'[42] The removal of national boundaries in Europe as a consequence of the enlarging EU and the emergence of new technologies have facilitated mass migration, immigration and globalisation.[43] However, it is the scale of modern migration, the rapidity with which it is occurring and the perceived threat to global peace and to Western economies and their security and way of life,

---

41. *Darby v Sweden* (1991) 13 EHRR 774 at 45.

42. Heinig, 'Law on Churches and Religion in the European Legal Area-Through German Glasses,' 8 *German Law Journal*, No 6 (1 June 2007).

43. Seneca (4 BC–65 AD) reminds us it is part of the human condition to be forever on the move: 'Different reasons roused different peoples to leave their homes; but this at least is clear, nothing has stayed where it was born. The human race is always on the move: in so large a world there is every day some change-new cities are founded and new names of nations are born as former ones disappear or are absorbed into a stronger one .... What does it matter what ground I stand on?' On the shortness of Life (De Brevitate Vitae).

which makes the modern phenomenon unprecedented and Western man anxious.

[1.015] With regard to state-church relations in the EU, Robbers[44] has identified three basic types of civil ecclesiastical law systems. In the first of these categories, he finds a state church or predominant religion with 'close links between state power and the existence of the church.' eg England, Greece, Malta and Finland. In the second category Robbers places those systems established on the principle of a strict separation of church and state eg France, with the exception of the three eastern départments, and also the Netherlands.[45] While Robbers states that there is to a great extent a legal separation in Ireland also, he astutely suspects that the religious influence on the state in predominantly Catholic Ireland is probably stronger and more direct than the constitutional provisions suggest.[46] This is particularly so with regard to education, which is an exception to the general principle of church and state separation in Ireland,[47] as is clear from **chapter 9** below. In the third category, Robbers identifies the basic church-state separation principle in operation in certain countries, while, simultaneously a multitude of common tasks are recognised in a co-operative fashion eg Belgium, Poland, Spain, Italy, Hungary, Austria, Portugal and the Baltic States.[48] But, as Robbers is the first to acknowledge, this categorisation according to legal and theoretical considerations is immediately overlaid and rendered questionable by social conditions which suggest different groupings and some covenantal agreements.[49]

[1.016] While the law may be employed in one country to establish the pre-eminence of one particular religion or more, it may facilitate and foster a co-operative approach to all religions and none, or it may be employed to sequester religion and press it into the private sphere, in so far as this is possible. Thus, the provision made for religion in publicly-funded schools in Europe, if any, will be strongly influenced by the church-state relationship in each country and by the degree of separation between them. This

44. Robbers (ed), *State and Church in the European Union* p 578.

45. Robbers (ed), *State and Church in the European Union.*

46. Robbers (ed), *State and Church in the European Union* pp 578–9.

47. See Casey, 'State and Church in Ireland' in Robbers (ed), *State and Church in the European Union* pp 187–208 at 191.

48. Robbers (ed), *State and Church in the European Union* pp 578–579.

49. Robbers (ed), *State and Church in the European Union* p 579.

relationship, in turn, will be deeply influenced by historical and other experiences, being indelibly marked in some instances by seismic events, such as revolution or reformation.

Models of Religion

[1.017] Ahdar and Leigh[50] consider that religion, in the global sense, generally falls into one of the following categories: theocracy,[51] erastianism,[52] separationism (the secular state), establishment (a state religion), pluralist models, neutrality models and competitive market models.[53] At one end of the spectrum lie those countries which strive to retain their homogeneity by restricting individual freedom of expression, by imposing the religious values of the majority on all, or by protecting religion or ideology, in one form or another, in their constitutions. The ECtHR has clarified, in a number of cases, that theocracy is incompatible with democracy and that is one of the main upholding principles of the ECHR.[54]

[1.018] There are also those countries, which may be moving towards democracy and such countries may have somewhat conflicting principles enshrined in their constitutions. In the Constitution of the Republic of Iraq 2005,[55] for example, not only is Islam the first religion, it is recognised in

50. Rousseau, *The Social Contract* (Penguin Books, 2004).

51. 'Government by the immediate direction of God or through a sacerdotal class; a state so governed.' This definition is taken from *Cassells English Dictionary* (Cassells, 1971) p 1168.

52. 'One holding the opinions on ecclesiastical matters attributed to Erastus, a German physician (1524–1583); one holding that the state has supreme authority over the church.' *Cassell's English Dictionary*, p 386. See further Ahdar and Leigh, *Religious Freedom in the Liberal State* p 71 *et seq*.

53. Ahdar and Leigh, *Religious Freedom in the Liberal State* p 70 *et seq*.

54. *Metropolitan Church of Bessarabia v Moldova* (2002) 35 EHRR 13.

55. The Preamble of Iraq's Constitution reads as follows: 'In the name of God, the most merciful, the most compassionate. 'We have honoured the sons of Adam. We are the people of the land between two rivers, the homeland of the apostles and prophets, abode of the virtuous imams, pioneers of civilization, crafters of writers and cradles of numeration. Upon our land the first law passed by man was passed, the most ancient just pact for homelands policy was inscribed, and upon our soil, companions of the Prophet and saints prayed, philosophers and scientists theorised and writers and poets excelled.' http://www.geocities.com/haniqassim/Iraq_Constitution_English.pdf, accessed on 1 October 2008.

Art 2 of the Constitution as 'a fundamental source of legislation.' Article 2A provides: 'No law that contradicts the established provisions of Islam may be established', a provision which sits uneasily with Art 2B which provides: 'No law that contradicts the principles of democracy may be established.'[56] When conflict arises between Islam and the principles of democracy in Iran, it is conceivable that the Federal Supreme Court may decide to balance these rights in favour of the Islamic religion since the Constitution makes provision for the appointment to that Court of Experts in the Islamic jurisprudence who may not have any training/education in civil law or relevant subjects.[57]

[1.019] Afghanistan's new Constitution also enshrines the *sharia* and secular law but it is as yet unclear how these laws will co-exist in practice.[58] It appears that to renounce one's religion, if one is of the Muslim faith, is still a crime under the traditional *sharia* and is punishable by execution and this sits uneasily with the guarantee in Art 7, Ch 1 of the Constitution to abide by the UN international law treaties. Abdul Rahman, who converted to Christianity in 1990 was, following the fall of the Taliban, prosecuted for the crime of conversion from Islam by the new Afghan government. It has been reported that the trial judge declared: 'We will ask him if he has changed his mind. If so we will forgive him.' Fortunately for Rahman he did change his mind, at least until he arrived in Italy, where he was granted asylum, having been permitted to emigrate there.[59]

[1.020] At the other end of the spectrum lie the countries which have adopted the strict separation of church and state as the Republic of France, Turkey

---

56. http://www.geocities.com/haniqassim/Iraq_Constitution_English.pdf, accessed on 1 October 2008.

57. See further United States Commission on International Religious Freedom, 6 October 2005, Analysis of Proposed Iraqui Constitution: Ambiguities in Text Threaten Human Rights Protection, available online at http://www.uscirf.gov/index.php?option=com_content&task=view&id=1389&It, accessed on 1 October 2008.

58. See http://afghansite.com/afghanistan/afghanConstitution.asp, accessed on 1 October 2008 and in particular Art 3, Ch 3 and Art 7, Ch 1,: see further Elliott, 'In Kabul, a Test for Shariah' (2006) *New York Times,* 26 March, para 4 at 43.

59. 'Afghan on Trial for Christianity', BBC News, 20 March 2006: http://news.bbc.co.uk/2/hi/south_asia/4823874.stm, accessed on 1 October 2008: Fisher and Povoledo, 'Italy grants asylum to Afghan Christian Convert' (2006) *New York Times*, 30 March.

and the US although significant distinctions are apparent between these approaches. In particular, France's influence on European affairs generally and in human rights law in particular, continues to be quite profound, as may be seen in **chapter 7** below. At the heart of these matters lie some fundamental ideological distinctions which arise from the age-old debate between the supporters of 'the natural law' and the adherents of the more secular form of 'the natural rights philosophy', a debate which has exercised the minds of some of the world's finest minds through the ages, which is discussed in the European context later in this book.[60]

Religious Trends in the USA

[1.021] As Europe adopts a more secular character, demands are being increasingly expressed in the US for greater governmental religious expression.[61] George Gallup Junior, who has conducted many surveys on American life, believes that it is impossible to understand America without acknowledging the influence and impact of religion.'[62] Despite the glaring lack of relevant knowledge regarding the doctrine, traditions and the Bible at the basis of their professed religion, Gallup identified a current of individualistic deep spiritual questing which arises, he believes, partly from disenchantment with the perceived failure of twentieth century materialism.[63] Perhaps the popular approach of US culture towards religion was best summarised by Justice Scalia in *Locke v Davey* when he stated: 'One need not delve too far into modern, popular culture to perceive a trendy distain for deep religious conviction.'[64] Many Europeans would argue

60. See **para [3.008]** *et seq.*

61. Fischer and Wallace, 'God and Caesar in the Twenty-First Century: What Recent Cases say about church-state Relations in England and the United States, *Florida Journal of International Law*, vol 18.

62. Gallup and Lindsay, *Surveying the Religious Landscape* based on a number of statistical surveys: see also Gallup and Jones, *The Next American Spirituality: Finding God in the Twentieth Century* (Chariot Victor Pubs, 2000); Gallup and Jones, *The Saints Among Us* (Morehouse Publishers, 1993) and Gallup and Lindsay, *The Gallup Guide: Reality Check for 21st Century Churches* (Gallup, 2002).

63. Gallup and Lindsay, *Surveying the Religious Landscape* based on a number of statistical surveys: see also Gallup and Jones, *The Next American Spirituality: Finding God in the Twentieth Century*: Gallup and Jones, *The Saints Among Us* and Gallup and Lindsay, *The Gallup Guide: Reality Check for 21st Century Churches*.

64. *Locke v Davey* 540 US 712, 733.

that this 'trendy distain for deep religious conviction' is also a feature of modern popular culture in Europe, where religion among the youth continues to decline.[65] Nonetheless, in most European countries there is a close link between religion and education and the role of the churches in education, generally speaking, continues to be significant.

THE RIGHT TO EDUCATION

[1.022] There is now a well-established consensus in Europe that the right to education is a fundamental human right and its delivery constitutes one of the most significant central functions the modern state discharges on behalf of the citizen. In contemporary Europe, education is generally viewed as a national obligation falling on the state and the right to education is perceived as one of the social rights the state undertakes to vindicate on the citizen's behalf.[66] In order to achieve its social and economic objectives for society, the modern state increasingly controls and regulates education in the interests of the common good. But, as Neuhaus reminds us, 'The state is not the source but the servant of the law'[67] and the state itself may be constrained in its action by individuals or groups having certain legal or fundamental rights and/or international human rights. In tandem with the globalisation of education, international human rights are becoming increasingly more relevant to the interface of education with religion particularly in publicly funded schools and this fact is reflected in the growing number of decisions of the ECtHR in this sphere, some of which relate to dress codes for students and teachers in public schools.

[1.023] It is not a simple matter to ascertain what the appropriate, democratic role of the state is in a sphere of life which is value-laden such as education. Is it appropriate for the state, for example, to seek to form its own citizens in public schools through the teaching of compulsory citizenship, ethics, religious education, moral education, or human rights programmes, which may conflict with parental wishes? If the state has that right, under national

---

65. Robbers (ed), *State and Church in the European Union.*

66. *The Educational Structures in the Member States of the European Community,* 1989, Luxembourg, Office for Official Publications of EC, p 101: Macbeth, 'The Child Between' *Studies* (1984) Office for Official Publications, Luxembourg, p 11: http://openlibrary.org/b/OL2615545M, accessed on 1 October 2008.

67. Neuhaus, *The Naked Public Square: Religion and Democracy in America* (WB Eerdmans Pubs Co, 1983) p 259.

and international law, how are those parents who have differing religious and philosophical convictions to be accommodated by the state? Such issues have led to controversy between individual parents and the state in many countries culminating in litigation, *inter alia,* under national law in Germany and under national and international law in the case of Spain. Since the state is the servant and not the source of the law should it have total control of the entire curriculum, including religious instruction/education as in Germany, or should constitutional constraints be imposed on the state's role in this regard, as in Ireland? In the light of the abuses that have arisen in totalitarian states, these are matters which need profound analysis and thoughtful reflection as the EU harmonises and coheres.

Freedom of Education

[1.024] Freedom of education is generally guaranteed in national constitutions and in international law and it has two distinct elements. The first of these is a collective entitlement, the freedom of bodies and groups of persons, within specific legal limits, to set up and administer schools that are independent of the state grounded in a particular religious denomination, philosophy or pedagogy. Secondly, there is the individual freedom of parents, again within express legal limits, to choose the school that they wish their children to attend. Thus, while the state may establish public schools as an option for parental choice, the freedom to establish state-funded or state-subsidised independent schools or private schools exists together with certain rights to appoint staff in accordance with the requirements of the school and its characteristic spirit, ethos or philosophy of the school, provided such staff meet the educational standards of the state.[68] Such options are generally open to parents who do not wish to avail of the full state sector schools which exist in most Western democracies to various degrees. In some countries, the option also exists to educate in the home subject provided the standards imposed by the state are discharged by parents.[69] More recently, the right to education is also recognised in the EU Charter of Fundamental Freedoms together with the right to vocational and

68. See further Glenn and de Groof, *Finding the Right Balance, Freedom, Autonomy and Accountability in Education* (Lemma, 2002). In the Irish context see *O'Shiel v Minister for Education* [1992] 2 IR 321.

69. For example in England and in Ireland: in the Irish context see further *DPP v Best* [1998] 2 ILRM 549.

continuing training.[70] Furthermore, the freedom to found educational establishments is also recognised, with due respect for democratic principles and the right of parents to ensure the education and teaching of their children in conformity with their religious, philosophical and pedagogical convictions, shall be respected, in accordance with the national laws governing the exercise of such freedom and right.[71]

Funding of Public Education

[1.025] When comparing and contrasting different systems, difficulties arise from the fact that different countries draw the boundaries of 'public education' in a variety of ways, as Glenn and de Groof observe:

> Most Catholic schools in England or Ontario are part of the 'public' system, while in the Netherlands or Belgium, while receiving the same full funding from the state, they would be regarded as 'private.' And what about 'charter schools' in the United States, privately – initiated, privately-operated, yet considered public and subject to the legal requirements for public schools? On the other hand, schools which respond to the demand of parents for education with a religious character are definitely private and not eligible for 'charter' status; in effect, state charter school legislation promises that educators and parents can work together to create any sort of school they want, so long as it is not religious![72]

And, given the absence of a full public education sector, how does one categorise Ireland's privately-owned, denominational primary schools in which the churches employ the teachers, but the state remunerates, supervises and regulates them? Since the teachers are public servants, one must conclude they deliver a public service, that of education, to students. But the matter does not end there, since the teachers in this instance are required to promote the ethos of the school, and to teach religious instruction, for which provision is made in the Education Act 1998. The dual character of the denominational teachers' role and function in Ireland is discussed later in **chapter 9**.

70. Art 14.1, C 364/11.

71. Art 14.3, C 364/11.

72. Glenn and de Groof, *Finding the Right Balance, Freedom, Autonomy and Accountability in Education* at 271.

Public Funding of Private Education

[1.026] The degree to which private schools should be publicly-funded, and the balance to be achieved between the provision made for private schools and other school types is controversial in many member states, and this too may vary considerably under national laws and constitutions. Fears have been expressed in England,[73] Ireland[74] and Spain[75] that fee-paying schools are creating a two-tiered education system. Possibly in response to these concerns, the Department of Education and Science in Ireland has recently announced that it will not fund any new fee-paying schools.[76] But such a decision could impose constraints on the constitutional entitlement of parents to establish private schools,[77] although this parental right is not an absolute right[78] since it must be weighed against the rights of others to a fair share of national resources. Nonetheless, since private schools facilitate freedom of religion and freedom of education, the need to establish them in a democratic society is axiomatic and it is for the state to decide to what degree they will be publicly-funded. To close off all funding for new private schools would seem arbitrary, however, and this measure is likely to invite a legal challenge.

[1.027] As will be seen later, many parents in Europe are finding that certain state-promoted secular programmes of religious education and ethics in publicly-funded schools are incompatible with their religious and philosophical convictions, and they are being obliged to seek private education for their children in accordance with their convictions.[79] If

---

73. See **para [5.031]** *et seq*.

74. See **para [9.016]**.

75. See **para [8.025]** *et seq*.

76. McGreevy, 'Education Department will not fund any new fee-paying schools' (2007) *Irish Times*, 9 October.

77. See Art 42.1 in which the Family is the natural educator of the child; Art 42.2 in which parents are free to provide this education, *inter alia,* in private schools; Art 42.3 under which the state shall not oblige parents in violation of their conscience and lawful preference to send their children to schools established by the state, or to any particular type of school designated by the state.

78. Education provision must now be made pursuant to the Education Act 1998 and in carrying out his/her functions under s 7(4)(a)(i) the Minister is required to have regard to the resources available ('shall have regard ...').

79. *Jimenez and Jimenez Merino v Spain* Application no 51188/99, ECHR Reports of Judgments and Decisions 2000–VI: *Leirvag v Norway Communication* no 1155/2003, 23 Nov 2004, CCPR/C/82/D/1155/2003, decision of the UN Human Rights Committee.

publicly-funded schools fail to accommodate the convictions of these parents within the public school sector, there may be a heavier onus on states in the future to support private schools. While international law permits non-state schools to exist, it does not place an obligation on states to create favourable conditions for their existence.[80]

[1.028] States may, however, impose stricter obligations in this regard under their national laws. For example, in a decision of 8 April 1987 the German Federal Constitutional Court held that the Länder are required to support the system of private schools, which is considered equal to the public system, on parallel lines with the public school system, and to safeguard its existence. This decision has implications not solely for the law relating to private schools in Germany but for the concept of fundamental rights generally in that it seeks to harmonise the fundamental right of parents to the choice of private or state schools with the realities of contemporary life. From the perspective of freedom of education and freedom religion, this is a landmark decision for German parents. However, as Frank-Rudiger Jach points out, the reality is that parents who establish a private school in Germany have to make sacrifices during the qualifying period and they must source permanent additional resources through donations, loans and contributions.[81]

[1.029] As secularism increases in the West, religion and its place in public life and public education is coming under unprecedented scrutiny while the spectre of religious extremism continues to threaten world peace and security.[82] Some of the inherent ideological conflicts are illustrated in those cases relating to the wearing of the Islamic headscarf in public places which have come before the courts of the member states or before the ECtHR, specifically with regard to public education, which are discussed later. Within the member states, the outcome of these cases is reflective of the

---

80. van Bueren, 'Education: Whose Right is it Anyway?' in Heffernan (ed), *Human Rights: a European Perspective* p 339 at 347.

81. Jach, (Special Agreement Schools), *Le scuole private sono*, 1998/1999 USR/DIE, 81–7, cited in Glenn and de Groof, *Finding the Right Balance: Freedom, Autonomy and Accountability in Education.*

82. Taylor, *A Secular Age* (Harvard University Press, 2007); Glenn, *The Ambiguous Embrace: Government and Faith-based Schools and Social Agencies* (Princeton University Press, 2001): Green, *Education and State Formation* (Macmillan, 1991); Lundy, *Education Law: Policy and Practice in Northern Ireland* (SLS, 2000); Chadwick, *Shifting Alliances: Church and State in English Education* (Geoffrey Chapman Publishers, 1997).

established relationship between church and state and the character and degree of separation that exist between them[83] but this relationship must now take cognisance of germane international law constraints and relevant EU law. As Europe unifies and integrates, it places its trust for the future in democracy, education, human rights and the rule of law,[84] but it also recognises certain human rights, such as freedom of thought, conscience and religion and freedom of education, to which I return later.

THE RULE OF LAW

[1.030] The towering significance of the rule of law has long been universally recognised. As Blackstone puts it 'The law is the embodiment of the moral sentiment of the people.'[85] Moreover, the rule of law is a political ideal which has achieved global endorsement.[86] Law is at the core of human relationships, controlling our conduct, regulating our economies and safeguarding our security and, unless we are to revert to the law of the jungle, law is the supreme and rational regulator in a rapidly changing world.[87] As Machiavelli remarked in *The Prince* (1531):

> ... there are two ways of fighting: by law or by force. The first way is natural to men, and the second to beasts .... And nothing brings a man greater honour than the new laws and new institutions he establishes. When these are soundly based and bear the mark of greatness, they make him revered and admired.[88]

However, the law can be unduly prescriptive and a democratic society seeks to achieve an appropriate equilibrium between the competing interests in the interest of the common good. Good law, therefore, is essentially about

---

83. See further Gallala, 'The Islamic Headscarf: An Example of Surmountable Conflict between *Shari'a* and the Fundamental Principles of Europe' (2006) *European Law Journal,* Vol 12, no 5, September, pp 593–612.

84. On the rule of law in economics see 'Briefing Economics and the rule of law,' Order in the Jungle (2008) *The Economist*, 15 March, pp 83–5.

85. Blackstone (1723–1780), *Commentaries on the Laws of England* available at http://onlinebooks.library.upenn.edu/webbin/book/look/lookupname?key=Blackstone, accessed on 1 October 2008.

86. Tamanaha, *Law as a Means to an End: Threat to the Rule of Law* (Cambridge University Press, 2006); Tamanaha, *On the Rule of Law: History, Politics, Theory* (Cambridge, 2004).

87. Kennedy, *Just Law* (Vintage, 2004) p 9.

88. Machiavelli, *The Prince* (first published in 1531) (Penguin Books, 2004) pp 74, 111.

achieving an equitable balance between competing interests grounded in legal principles. Certain fundamental freedoms including, *inter alia*, freedom to profess and practice religion; freedom to hold and manifest religious beliefs; freedom to associate with others in giving expression to religious faith; and guarantees of equality and non-discrimination between the religions; are widely acknowledged as key indicators of a democratic society which show commitment to the rule of law. As Helena Kennedy QC observes:

> The rule of law is one of the tools we use in our stumbling progress towards civilising the human condition: a structure of law with proper methods and independent judges, before whom even a government must be answerable. It is the only restraint upon the tendency of powers to debase its holders .... It is precisely when there is high political fever that the controlling power of the judiciary and lawycrs bccomes so important. The judges have to curb governmental excess; they are the guardians of the rule of law, and it is crucial that they do not allow themselves to be co-opted by the Executive.[89]

In the Lisbon Treaty, the Union accedes to the ECHR which constitutes general principles of the Union's law. At the time of writing (October 2008), there is considerable uncertainty surrounding the Lisbon Treaty, due mainly to Ireland's rejection of the Treaty in referendum.

EDUCATION AND INTEGRATION

[1.031] Education, with its immense potential to reconcile divisions, to harmonise differences and to foster harmony and social cohesion, lies at the heart of Europe's integration. Education for the masses has long been recognised as a powerful instrument for modern nation building and for transmitting national identities and ideologies from one generation to the next. For example, the unique potential of public education for promoting social cohesion had already been identified, *inter alia*, in Greece by Plato, in France by Napoleon Bonaparte, Alexis de Tocqueville,[90] and others[91] and by the founding fathers in the US.[92] Both the European

89. Kennedy, *Just Law* (Vintage, 2004) p 15.

90. Education is, de Toqueville states, 'the only guarantee we have against the aberrations of the masses.' *see* 'Essay on American Government and Religion'.

91. By Rousseau and others.

92. **Para [10.012]** *et seq*.

Commission[93] and the Council of Europe[94] have identified the beginnings of a 'new' approach to civic education in Europe together with a widening consensus that the stability and welfare of democracies and the advancement of human rights do not solely depend on good governance by the state but, more significantly on the quality of individual citizens.

[1.032] This approach to democratic citizenship, which has emerged in many member states, is reflected in the curricula of publicly-funded schools during the past decade. In other words, citizenship has become more than a legal status, it is now a pivotal subject promoted in European schools as well as in the wider society. There is nothing 'new' is this approach since France's Jules Ferry[95] employed the same philosophy when building up secularity and social cohesion in nineteenth century France. When striving to establish a secular state in France, Ferry introduced mandatory, free, secular education at elementary level pursuant to the Act of 15 March 1882 and he brought forward citizenship programmes and ethics to take the place of religious programmes. A somewhat similar process is occurring at a macro level in Europe. As the EU unifies and harmonises education across Europe is becoming more secular, reflecting the growing secularity of the wider society.

[1.033] When it comes to the establishment of national, intra-national or trans-national structures, education has also been identified as central in promoting a foundation of common values and norms. Perhaps the EU was

---

93. European Commission, Accomplishing Europe through education and training, Office for Official Publications of the European Communities, Luxembourg, 1997: European Commission, Education across Europe, Statistics and Indicators 1999, Office for Official Publications of the European Communities, Luxembourg, 2000: European Commission, Evaluating quality in school education, A European pilot project, Office for Official Publications of the European Communities, Luxembourg, 1999: European Commission/Eurydice/ Eurostat, Key data on education in Europe 1999–2000, Office for Official Publications of the European Communities, Luxembourg, 2000.

94. Council of Europe, Recommendation 59 (1999) on 'Europe 2000-Youth Participation, The Role of Young Persons as Citizens, June 1999 and further Claire Wallace. George Datler and Reingard Spannring, *Young People and European Citizenship,* Institute for Advance Studies, Vienna, February 2005.

95. Who was Minister for Public Instruction and Fine Arts from 1882–1883 and was twice Prime Minister of France (1880–1881) and (1883–1885). Ferry is credited with the secularisation of French education and the colonial expansion of France.

dilatory is recognising the significance of education in its plans for unification and integration and its powers in this sphere emerged gradually from an extremely limited jurisdictional base.[96] With the passage of time, education's key potential was, however, recognised as Jean Monet's celebrated statement indicates, 'If I were to do it all again, I would start with education.'[97] In retrospect, Monet's ambition could scarcely have been realised at the earlier stages of integration because of inherent sensitivities and tensions in this particular area of life.

[1.034] In addition to citizenship programmes, most modern European publicly-funded schools provide some form of comparative, religious, philosophical, ethical or moral programmes, with a view to reinforcing common values through education by providing a universal framework for good behaviour and responsible sexual conduct. Such programmes are generally included in curricular programmes devised under national legislation.[98] These programmes of citizenship and comparative religious education are discussed later in **[4.010]**. However, concerns are being expressed by some individuals and religious groups that, in these programmes, their cultural and/or religious values are being downgraded or replaced by the secular values of the state, a change which has resulted mainly from the modern state's advance into many social spheres of life including education. As the EU moves to closer unity, is there a danger that the right to instil values, formerly vested in parents or in the churches on their behalf, will be replaced by civic values validated by secular international human rights laws leading to 'a tepic civic version of the faith'?[99]

In Spain, one such programme, (Programme for Citizenship and Human Rights), was unsuccessfully challenged by Spanish parents in *Jimenez and Jimenez Merino v Spain*.[100] In that case, the ECtHR unanimously held that, not only may the Spanish State lawfully determine a programme of morals in which sensitive issues of morality and spirituality intersect in its public

96. See further Glendenning, *Education and the Law* (Tottel Publishing, 1999) 208.

97. Cited in European Parliament, Session Documents 1988/89, Document A 2–0285/88, Series A, Explanatory Statement, p 11.

98. For example see Fussel, Germany, 'Ethics or Religious Instruction'?, *European Journal for Education Law and Policy,* Vol 3, no 1 1999, pp 59–60.

99. *Dictum* of Scalia J in *Locke v Davey* 540 US 712.

100. *Jimenez and Jimenez Merino v Spain* Application No 51188/99, Reports of Judgments and Decisions 2000–VI.

schools, but it may make such programmes mandatory on students even when their parents do not accept the norms and values inherent in these programmes. This disquieting decision, which does not appear to adequately accommodate the right to freedom of religion for parents, is discussed further in **chapter 8** below.

State Funding of Religious Education in Publicly Funded Schools

[1.035] The state's role in the funding or sponsoring of religious education in publicly-funded schools can be a controversial issue given the diversity of human beliefs and non-beliefs. Even in European countries, a variety of approaches is apparent. Those who favour some form of religious education in publicly-funded schools contend that it is beneficial for students in that it socialises them, fosters self-discipline and establishes sound values. Others argue that the provision of religious education in such schools constitutes state sponsorship of religious beliefs which serves to isolate those students who do not share in the beliefs taught or unduly presses such students into conformity with the norm. Much will, of course, depend on the ecclesiastical law relationship (the church-state relationship) which exists in the individual country and on the provision made by the state to accommodate parental wishes in this regard.

[1.036] In most Western European countries, private education is an option for those who can afford it, and parents are free to avail of a private denominational education for their children. What is the most appropriate option for those students who are not so advantaged? With regard to public education, the courts in many countries have been called upon to reconcile two important legal principles, religious freedom for all[101] and the right of students to have a religiously-neutral education. The intersection of these two sets of rights is possibly most manifest in cases dealing with appropriate dress codes for teachers and students in public schools.[102]

---

101. See Schachter, 'Public school teachers and religiously distinctive dress: A diversity-centered approach', *Journal of Law and Education* 22 (1), 61–69, Winter 1993.

102. Burstall, 'A comeback for strict dress codes' (schools in Great Britain) (1994) *Times Educational Supplement,* 20 May.

DRESS CODES IN PUBLIC SCHOOLS

[1.037] In public education, dress codes for students are frequently perceived as being related to issues such as the maintenance of order, discipline and national identity in schools and, generally speaking, common sense prevails. When the concept of religious freedom for the individual conflicts with the right of others to a religiously neutral space in public education, such matters may result in litigation[103] or they may even be regulated by legislation, as in France, a matter considered in **[7.017]** below. Prohibitions on dress codes are imposed with greater stringency in countries which support the secular principle, eg Turkey or France. Accordingly, the vigour with which dress codes are enforced may vary considerably in schools from country to country, depending on the church-state relationship, the relevant law and the context. For example, when students wore rosaries as necklaces in a US public school, a federal trial court in Texas ruled that educators who prohibited them violated the students' pure speech right under the First Amendment of the US Constitution.[104] On the other hand, rosaries worn by students in a French school would most likely be classified as 'conspicuous religious symbols', thus violating the 2004 law banning such symbols.[105]

[1.038] We may conclude, therefore, that the vigour with which dress codes are enforced may vary considerably, not only from country to country, depending on the church-state relationship and the general law, but they may also vary within countries,[106] including those countries which promote the secular principle. In some states in the US students have challenged the enforcement of student dress codes by public school authorities and they have sought relief against its enforcement arguing their entitlement to freedom of expression,[107] an issue which is considered later in **chapter 10**.

---

103. In what the Americans refer to as 'the garb law'. See 'The Constitutionality of "garb laws" in the context of the public high school', *Journal of Law and Education,* 23 (4), 549–569, Fall, 1994 and further Russo, *Reutter's The Law of Public Education* (6th edn, Foundation Press, 2006) pp 65–66, which deals with religious garb for students and teachers including the wearing of nun's habits when teaching.

104. *Chalifoux v New Caney Independent School District*, 976 S Supp 659.

105. See further **chapter 5**.

106. For example, the German *Länder.*

106 *Pyle v South Hadley School Committee* 55F.3d 20, West's Education Law Reporter, 100, 579–581, 27 July 1995. This case, in which the students challenged the dress code of the school authorities and sought an injunction against its enforcement, was heard in the US Court of Appeals, First Circuit. (contd .../)

[1.039] At a time when world-wide controversy surrounds the wearing of culturally or religiously significant clothing in public schools, such as the hijab and the turban, perhaps there is something to be learned from the Constitutional Court of South Africa's recent judgment in *MEC for Education: KwaZulu-Natal v Pillay & Others (Pillay* hereafter).[108] This case is significance, not alone for the scope and the depth of its jurisprudential analysis, but for its many insights. It is, however, a case in which context is pivotal, set as it is against the background of the former apartheid system and it constitutes an exacting test for the vitality of the non-discrimination guarantees in Art 9[109] of the South African Constitution[110] and for the statutory guarantees, which give effect to them, the Promotion of Equality and Prevention of Unfair Discrimination Act 2000 (the Equality Act). In other words, freedom of expression, culture and religion are protected in the Constitution and in legislation in South Africa and the concept of 'reasonable accommodation' in the Equality Act is an important one, as it is also in Canada. At the centre of this searching and erudite analysis of cultural and religious expression was a tiny gold nose stud worn by a High School student, Sunali Pillay (Sunali), a Tamil *learner*[111] from Southern India whose faith had previously been subjected to serious discrimination in South Africa.

[1.040] Prior to her admission to the school, Sunali's mother had signed the School Code (the Code) and undertaken to comply with it. The Code permitted one small round gold stud in each ear but otherwise forbad the wearing of jewellery. On reaching physical maturity, Sunali had her nose

---

107. (contd) See further Ray, 'A Nation of Robots? The constitutionality of public school uniform codes, *The John Marshall Law Review*, 28 645, Spring 1995: see *Morse v Fredrick*, US Supreme Court, 25 June 2007 commonly referred to as the 'Bong Hits 4 Jesus' case. This latter case was concerned centrally with student freedom of expression in public schools, student discipline, and the promotion of drugs in school-related activities.

108. *MEC for Education: KwaZulu-Natal v Pillay* [2007] ZACC 21, case decided on 5 October 2007, Case CCT 51/06. I am grateful to Professor Jan de Groof for drawing my attention to this significant case.

109. Which prohibits discrimination, *inter alia,* in Art 9(3) on the grounds of race, gender, sex, pregnancy, marital status, ethnic or social origin, colour, sexual orientation, age, disability, religion, conscience, belief, culture and language and birth. Other provisions in Art 9 may also be relevant.

110. The Constitution of the Republic of South Africa, 1996, as adopted on 8 May 1996 and amended on 11 October 1996 by the Constitutional Assembly.

111. The term used in South Africa for a student or a pupil.

pierced, while being prayed over, as part of a 4,000–5,000 year-old tradition and had a small gold stud inserted in her left nostril. This ceremony, which honoured her coming of age, also indicated to the community that she was ready for marriage. When Sunali returned to school after the holidays, the school authorities prohibited the wearing of the nose stud since it did not comply with the school Code. For her consistent refusal to comply with the Code, Sunali was threatened with disciplinary proceedings. In the interim, however, her mother appealed to the Equality Court which dismissed the claim but the Equality Appeal Court reversed and upheld the claim. On appeal, the High Court declared the school's decision as unfair discrimination and 'null and void.'

[1.041] When the Minister for Education and the school authorities appealed the matter to the Constitutional Court, it affirmed the High Court's finding of unfair discrimination and also found that the Code too was discriminatory because it lacked a clear exemption procedure for cultural and religious practices. Although the issue *per se* was moot, because Sunali had left school, Chief Justice Langa, who wrote the majority decision, considered that it was in the interests of justice for the court to consider the matter because of the impact the decision would have on schools nationwide. He stated that the prohibition on the wearing of jewellery in this instance had the potential for indirect discrimination because it permitted certain groups of students to express their religious and cultural identity freely, by wearing earrings, while denying that right to others. Presumably, the court was referring to the permission given in the Code to the occidental custom of wearing earrings, which was denied to the oriental custom of wearing nose-rings. Evidence before the court indicated that the custom of wearing a nose stud was a voluntary religious practice[112] and an element of Sunali's South Indian Tamil culture, which was inextricably intertwined with the Hindu religion. The court emphasised the necessity of protecting religious practices even when these were voluntary practices. It stated that 'religion is ordinarily concerned with personal faith and belief, while culture generally relates to traditions and beliefs developed by a community.' Nonetheless, it acknowledged that there was a good deal of overlap between religious practices and culture:

> religious practices are frequently informed not only by faith but also by custom, while cultural beliefs do not develop in a vacuum and may be based

[112] Both obligatory and voluntary practices qualified for protection under the Promotion of Equality and Prevention of Unfair Discrimination Act 4 of 2000.

> on the community's underlying religious or spiritual beliefs. Therefore, while it is possible for a belief or practice to be purely religious or purely cultural, it is equally possible for it to be both religious and cultural.[113]

Applying these principles, the court determined that the school had interfered with the student's religion and culture and since that burden was not placed on others, its interference with this right constituted discrimination against Sunali. A subjective test was applied by the court.[114] No evidence was submitted that granting this specific exemption would imperil uniformity or school discipline. The court concluded, therefore, that the school's discrimination was unfair because it failed to implement an exemption procedure and it made an order declaring that the school's refusal to grant an exemption unfairly discriminated against Sunali. It was not sufficient, the court stated, to state that Sunali could enrol in another school, since the Constitution requires the community to affirm and reasonably accommodate difference, not merely to tolerate difference, as a last resort. Furthermore, the court ordered that the school in consultation with learners, parents and staff, amend the Code and provide for a procedure to reasonably accommodate religion and cultural practices. The court also granted a declarator that Sunali has been discriminated against unfairly by the school.

[1.042] Langa CJ stated that it was always desirable, and may sometimes be vital, to hear from the person whose religion or culture is at issue and that this is particularly so when that person is a child. He cited with approval an earlier case from the Constitutional Court, *Christian Education South Africa v Minister for Education*,[115] which concerned children and he considered that their 'actual experiences and opinions would not necessarily have been decisive, but they would have enriched the dialogue, and the factual and experiential foundations for the balancing exercise in this difficult matter would have been more secure.' Indeed, Langa CJ concluded that the need for the child's voice to be heard was perhaps even more acute when it concerns children of Sunali's age who should be increasingly taking responsibility for their own actions and beliefs. It appears from this case that some of the

113. O'Regan J dissented in part from one of the Orders made (the Order granting the declarator to Sunali). Her judgment, however, is exceptional is its analysis of many of the features of public schools in South Africa and is worthy of attention.

114. O'Regan J disagreed with this subjective test for reasons outlined in her judgment.

115. *Education South Africa v Minister for Education* 2000 (4) SA 757 (CC); 2000 (10) BCLR 1051 (CC).

public schools may still harbour residual bias from the apartheid era, which tends to favour white Western values and religion over less established religions and cultures, thereby leading to unfair discrimination. However, the court's application of reasonable accommodation principles for religious and cultural minorities through the aegis of the Equality Act 2000, which gives effect to the constitutional guarantees of non-discrimination, gives cause for hope. When applying EU Directives on Equality and non-discrimination to the member states, perhaps there are lessons to be learned, *inter alia,* from the *Pillay* case which illustrates the flexibility which the application of reasonable accommodation principles afford when dealing with equality and non-discrimination in religious and cultural issues in the public sphere.

Secularism

[1.043] As the EU coheres and integrates, the values of a secular society embodied in international human rights law are being increasingly reflected in public life,[116] while freedom to manifest religious belief in public life is being curtailed. Even in traditionally Catholic countries, where religion has become the subject of political scrutiny and legislative intervention, the secular principle is advancing despite the opposition of church leaders in Europe. Italy enacted legislation permitting abortions in 1978 while Ireland recognised divorce in 1995 following a referendum.[117] In 2004 France prohibited by legislation 'conspicuous religious symbols' in its public schools[118] while Spain has recently passed the most liberal laws in Europe legalising marriage between same sex couples and introducing radical reform of education.[119]

KEY TERMS

[1.044] As Oliver Wendell Holmes Jr (1841–1935) observed in *Towne v Eisner,*[120] the meaning of a word may vary in accordance with context and time since, 'a word is not a crystal, transparent and unchanged, it is the skin

116. Defeis, 'Religious Liberty and Protections in Europe', *Journal of Catholic Legal Studies* Vol 45:73: Ahdar and Leigh, *Religious Freedom the Liberal State.*

117. The Family Law (Divorce) Act 1996.

118. French legislation enacted on 15 March 2004.

119. This legislation was enacted by the Spanish Parliament (*Cortez*) on the 13 June 2005 and came into force on the 3 July 2005, see **para [8.001]** below.

120. *Towne v Eisner* 245 US 418, 425 (1918), *per* Holmes J.

of a living thought and may vary greatly in colour and context according to the circumstances and time in which it is used.' Despite this caveat, an attempt will now be made to define, as far as possible, some of the terms used in this book, bearing in mind that words and terms may carry different shades of meaning within the countries discussed and, accordingly, from chapter to chapter of this book. For example, for some the meaning of the word 'God' is a personal God (the Christian God); to others such a concept may be alien and even naïve. As Weinberg states in his *Dreams of a Final Theory*, 'Some people have views of God that are so broad and flexible that it is inevitable that they will find God wherever they look for him. One hears it said that 'God is the ultimate' or 'God is our better nature'. Of course like any other word the word 'God' can be given any meaning we like.'[121] Thus, the personal God referred to in the Preamble to the Polish Constitution 1997[122] or in the Constitution of Ireland 1937 may be distinguished from the God of the Enlightenment writers[123] or perhaps the God of the American Declaration of Independence.[124] Although Rousseau acknowledges that all justice comes from God, who alone is its source, he also recognises a universal justice deriving from reason alone, and he considers that the laws of natural justice, lacking any natural sanction, are unavailing among men. Consequently, he argues, there must be covenants and positive laws to unite rights with duties and to direct justice to its object.[125]

---

121. Weinberg, *Dreams of a Final Theory: The Scientific Search for the Ultimate Laws of Nature* (Vintage, 1993). Weinberg is theoretical physicist and winner of Nobel Prize for physics. See also interview with Weinberg at www.pbs.org/faithandreason/transcript/wein-body.html, accessed on 1 October 2008.

122. Adopted on 2 April 1997.

123. See further **para [2.008]**.

124. See further Dershowitz, *America Declares Independence (*John Wiley & Sons, Inc 2003) and in particular chapter 1, 'Who is the God of the Declaration?', p 9.

125. Rousseau, *The Social Contract* p 40. 'All justice comes from God, who alone is its source; and if only we knew how to receive it from that exalted fountain, we should need neither governments nor laws. There is undoubtedly a universal justice which springs from reason alone, but if that justice is to be acknowledged as such it must be reciprocal. Humanly speaking, the laws of natural justice, lacking any natural sanction, are unavailing among men .... So there must be covenants and positive laws to unite rights with duties and to direct justice to its object.'

[1.045] Many attempts have been made over the years by philosophers,[126] political theorists,[127] theologians and others to define religion,[128] with varying degrees of success.[129] Perhaps de Toqueville best distilled the essence of religion when he stated: 'Religion is, therefore, only a particular form of hope, and it is as natural to the human heart as hope itself.'[130]

[1.046] The US Civil Rights Act of 1964 states 'To be a *bona fide* religious belief entitled to protection under either the First Amendment or Title VII, a belief must be sincerely held, and within the believer's own scheme of things religious.'[131] However, the very fact that there are so many and such diverse definitions of 'religion' is sufficient to show that this term cannot stand for any single principle or essence and that it has altered over the centuries[132] and is now a collective name which is impossible to describe precisely.[133] Yet

126. See MJB Allen, *Ficino Marsilio: His Theology, His Philosophy, His Legacy*; Aquinas, *Summa Theologiae*; Kant, *The Metaphysics of Morals*; Locke, *A Letter Concerning Toleratio*n (1689).

127. Grotius, *On the Truth of the Christian Religion*; Bodkin, *Six Books of the Commonwealth.*

128. See Hexham, *Concise Dictionary of Religion* (Regent College Publications, 1998). The twelve classical world religions have been identified by one source as Baha'i, Buddism, Christianity, Confucianism, Hinduism, Islam, Jainism, Judaism, Shinto, Sikhism, Taoism and Zoroastrinism; see 'World Major Religions,' *New York Public Library Students Desk Reference* (Prentice, 1993), 271.

129. See www.adherents.com/Religious_By_Adherents.html, accessed on 1 October 2008. A major source, *inter alia,* for these estimates is Barrett's religious statistics organisation whose figures are published by the Encyclopaedia Brittanica (incl. annual update and Yearbooks) and also the World Christian Encyclopaedia (2001).

130. de Toqueville, *Democracy in America.*

131. USCA Const. Amend 1: Civil Rights Act 1964 701 *et seq*, 717 as amended 42 USCA 2000–16.

132. See Hylson-Smith, *The Churches in England from Elizabeth I to Elizabeth II* (Canterbury Press, 1996–1998), chapter 4, in which the author cites Elizabeth I's Chief Minister, Sir Wm Cecil: '[t]he state could never be in safety, where there was toleration of two religions. For there is no enmity so great as that of religion, and they that differ in the service of God, can never agree in the service of their country.'

133. See James, *The Varieties of Religious Experience: a Subject on Human Nature* (Modern Library, 1994) p 46.

some broad definition or description of religion is necessary since only beliefs, convictions and practices grounded in religion, as opposed to those that are secular, social or conscientiously held, are protected by the guarantee of freedom of religion in international human rights law. Moreover, many legal systems in Europe confer special status and entitlements on religious bodies and churches,[134] so the question of what constitutes a 'religion' is significant also in that sense since it may confer access to public funding, status, and tax concessions.[135] Indeed, protracted legal battles have been fought in many countries for the privilege of registration as a church. In particular, the Church of Scientology[136] and the Jehovah's Witnesses have fought tenaciously for this right and a number of these cases are discussed later in this book.[137]

[1.047] In the House of Lords case *R (Williamson) v Secretary of State for Education and Employment*[138] Lord Walker of Gestingthorpe, commenting on the inherent difficulties traditionally encountered in earlier precedents in defining religion, stated that it was certainly not necessary and probably not useful for the court to reach a precise definition of religion in that case.[139] However, as Ferrari observes,[140] the absence of a precise legal definition of 'religion' does not exclude the existence of a paradigm of religion which broadly offers some guidelines to court and administrative

134. Such as Spain (the Roman Catholic Church) and Germany. See further **chapters 6** and **8**.

135. In *R (Senergal) v Registrar General* [1970] AC 3 All Eng 886 at 887, Lord Denning MR referred to the considerable privileges which a 'place of meeting for religious worship' acquires under The Places of Worship Act 1855 in the following terms: 'They will have taken one step towards getting a license to celebrate marriages there; they will be outside the jurisdiction of the Charity Commissioners; and the building itself may become exempt from paying rates. All of this depends on whether it is properly a "place of meeting for religious worship"'. For the ECtHR's recent decision recognising Scientology as a religious association see further *Church of Scientology v Russia* No 18147/02, judgment of 5 April 2007.

136. *Church of Scientology v Russia* No 18147/02, judgment of 5 April 2007.

137. **Paras [4.041]**, **[8.024]**, **[9.018]**, **[9.033]** and **[10.016]**.

138. *R (Williamson) v Secretary of State for Education and Employment* [2005] UKHL 15.

139. See further his reasons given at para 55 of the judgment.

139 Ferrari, 'New Religious Movements in Western Europe', *Religscope,* Research and Analyses, No 9, October 2006, p 4; (contd .../)

bodies called upon to deal with religion. The Oxford English Dictionary gives as one of its definitions of religion, 'a particular system of faith and worship ... recognition on the part of man of some higher, unseen power as having control of his destiny and as being entitled to obedience, reverence and worship.' Religion tends to involve belief in a divine, superhuman, transcendent or controlling power.[141] Some religious rites may be privately practised by individual believers but the major world religions also require or encourage their adherents to attend services, mass or holy communion regularly, while followers of Islam are expected to attend prayers, particularly on Fridays.[142] The form and content of communal rites is frequently a matter of considerable importance for adherents of a particular religion, as is their system of governance and many wars have been waged and many people martyred because of disagreements over such matters.[143] Perhaps one of the most pragmatic definitions of that chameleon word 'religion' was delivered by Dillon J in *Barralet and Others v Attorney General*[144] when the Chancery Court was called upon to decide whether the objects of the South Place Ethical Society (a humanist association) were for the advancement of religion or otherwise charitable, or not charitable. Having considered the objects of the Society together with the study and dissemination of ethical principles and the cultivation of a rational religious sentiment,[145] Dillon J stated:

> Religion, as I see it, is concerned with man's relations with God, and ethics are concerned with man's relations with man. The two are not the same, and are not made the same by sincere inquiry into the question, what is God. If reason leads people not to accept Christianity or any known religion, but they do

140. (contd) see http://religion.info/pdf/2006_10_ferrari_nrm.pdf, accessed on 1 October 2008; Ferrari, 'The European Pattern of Church and State Relations', *Comparative Law*, vol 20, Nihon University, Tokyo, 1–24; Ferrari 'Individual Religious Freedom and National Security in Europe after September 11', *Brigham Young University Law Review*, Vol 2004, no 2, 357–383; Ferrari, Cole-Durham and Sewell (eds), *Law and Religion in Post-Communist Europe* (Peeters, 2003).

141. *Words and Phrases Legally Defined* (Lexis Nexis/Butterworths, 1998) p 737.

142. *Shorter Oxford English Dictionary*, p 737, cited in *Words and Phrases Legally Defined* (Lexis Nexis/Butterworths, 1998) p 737.

143. *Wang v Minister for Immigration and Multicultural Affairs* [2002] FCA 52 at 35, *per* Nicholson J.

144. *Barralet and Others v Attorney General* [1980] 3 All ER 918.

145. Stated in Rule 2 of the Rules of the Society.

> believe in the excellence of qualities such as truth, beauty and love, or believe in the Platonic concept of the ideal, their beliefs may be to them the equivalent of a religion, but viewed objectively they are not religion.[146]

Dillon J considered that the two essential attributes of religion are faith and worship; faith in a god and worship of that god.

[1.048] In *R (Segerdal) v Registrar-General*[147] the matter before the court was whether a Chapel of Scientology was 'a place of meeting for religious worship' for the purposes of ss 2 and 3 of the Places of Worship Act 1855 (the 1855 Act). Buckley LJ's interpretation of 'worship' in the context of that case was as follows: 'Worship, I take to be something which must have, at least, some of the following characteristics: submission to the object worshipped, veneration of that object, praise, thanksgiving, prayer or intercession.'[148] However, he went on to state that he could find nothing in the Scientology wedding ceremony to distinguish it from a purely civil, non-religious ceremony conducted in a registry office, and that it contained none of the elements which he considered to constitute necessary elements of worship. It was not necessary to find every element in every act that could properly be described as worship, he continued, but when you find an act which contains none of these elements it cannot answer to the description of an act of worship.[149] Accordingly, the Appeal Court decided that, while the objects of the Scientology association were charitable, they were not for the advancement of religion for the purposes of the construction of the 1855 Act. In *Church of Scientology of Moscow v Russia*[150] the ECtHR recognised the Church of Scientology as a religious organisation and this decision has significient implications for all the contracting states and it is discussed below in **chapter 4**.

---

146. *Barralet and Others v Attorney General* [1980] 3 ALL ER 918.

147. *R v Registrar General ex parte Segerdal* [1970] 2 QB 697; [1970] 3 All ER 886 at 892.

148. *R v Registrar General ex parte Segerdal* [1970] 2 QB 697; [1970] 3 All ER 886.

149. *R v Registrar General ex parte Segerdal* [1970] 2 QB 697; [1970] 3 All ER 886.

150. Decision of ECtHR, Application No 18147/02, judgment delivered on 5 April 2007.

[1.049] Christianity has been recognised as a religion,[151] but those who are Christian belong to many churches and different denominations and they may have some conflicting beliefs. For example, some Christians believe that polygamy was not just permitted by the Bible but, rather, enjoined by it,[152] whilst other Christians believe that medical treatment involving blood transfusions is prohibited by the Bible and is sinful even in circumstances where it is the sole avenue for saving life.[153] Many courts have dealt with this issue involving complex decisions seeking to balance the best interests of children and adults against respect for religious and philosophical convictions.[154] Recently, the Irish High Court granted an order to a hospital to give a blood transfusion to the child of a Jehovah Witness mother who had refused the transfusion on the grounds of her religious convictions.[155] The case was decided in the best interest of the child who was not old enough to make an informed decision on such issues. Such matters become more complex when a competent adult refuses to give informed consent to the transfusion since they are entitled to have their religious and philosophical convictions respected by the state under Art 2 of Protocol 1 of the ECHR[156] and in that regard the

151. *R v Secretary of State for Education ex parte Williamson* [2005] UKHL 15; [2005] ELR 291, HL.

152. See *Mormon Church v United States* 98 US 136 US 1 (1890); *Reynolds v United States* 98 US 145 (1879).

153. See *O (a Minor)(Blood Transfusion)* [1993] 2 FLR 757. There are a number of scriptural references which allegedly support this belief. It is stated in Leviticus at 17:10: 'And any man from the house of Israel, or from the aliens who sojourn among them, who eats any blood, I will set my face against that person who eats blood, and will cut him off from among his people.' See also Genesis: 4, Acts 15:29 and Acts 21: 25.

154. For example, in the English context, see *HE v A Hospital NHS Trust* [2003] EWHC 1017 (fam); *In re T (Adult: Refusal of Treatment)* Court of Appeal, 1992, July 22, 23, 24 and 30 also at [1992] 3 WLR.

155. www.IrishExaminer.com, 'Breaking news', accessed 5 January 2008, and Lawlor, 'Lifeblood: the Right of the Child' (2004) *The University Observer Online*, vol xi, Issue 2, 27 September.

155 On this point, see Murphy, 'The Right to die for Jehovah' *BBC News*, 5 November 2007. In this case a young Jehovah's Witness, who had signed a form refusing blood transfusions, died having giving birth to twins. Doctors respected her decision made on religious and/or philosophical grounds and did not intervene; other countries may take a more pro-life approach. (contd .../)

ECtHR decision in *Hoffman v Austria*[157] is instructive. Others Christians believe that corporal punishment of children is not just simply permitted by the Bible but that it is encouraged by it.[158] Apart from the difficulties surrounding a legal definition of religion, the categories are not closed and the emergence of the so-called 'new religions' from the 1970s onwards has raised questions for society as to whether these can be classified as religions in the true sense and whether they constitute a danger to the individual and to the common good of society in certain extreme circumstances. The test of religion, it has been held, should not be confined to theistic religion, since there are some religions which do not profess a God and some of the Australian cases illuminate this issue. In *Church of the New Faith v Commissioners for Pay-Roll Tax*[159] the Supreme Court of Victoria stated:

> If by God is meant the Supreme Being, Creator and Ruler of universe, with the usual Western connotations of an Ultimate Deity who is personal and with whom man can or should have a relationship, it must be noted there are religious traditions without a God. In classical Hindu thought there are many gods but beyond all the gods there is one Ultimate Reality (Brahman) beyond description or comprehension, who is not the creator, who is utterly transcendent to creation, and to whom no worship is directed. The word is neuter, so that 'who' is an inappropriate pronoun; cf. Benjamin Walker, *The Hindu World; An Encyclopedia of Hinduism* (1968), pp 393–395, Margaret and James Stutley, *A Dictionary of Hinduism* (1977), pp 49–51.

[1.050] In the High Court of Australia in the same case, Wilson and Deane JJ pointed out that the trend of authority is towards a 'newer more expansive reading' of religion, as is the case also in the jurisprudence of the US,[160] which is not surprising in an age of increasingly multicultural societies and

---

156. (contd) See also the decision of the Irish High Court in the *Ms K case* in which the High Court ordered a young Jehovah Witness mother to have a transfusion which she had refused, on the grounds that the right of the newborn child to have a family life overruled the right of the mother to refuse treatment. See further McDonald and Managh, 'Jehovah Witness forced to have life-saving transfusion' (2006) *The Irish Independent*, 23 September and (2006) *Irish Times*, 22 September.

157. *Hoffman v Austria* (1993) 17 EHRR 293.

158. *R v Secretary of State for Education ex parte Williamson* [2005] UKHL 15; [2005] ELR 291, HL.

159. *Church of the New Faith v Commissioners for Pay-Roll Tax* [1983] 1 VR 97, reversed.

160. Citing Wilson and Deane JJ.

growing respect for human rights. Art 9 of the ECHR protects not just the *forum internum* of religious belief, but freedom of 'thought, conscience and religion' which covers a wider field than even the most expansive notion of religion. For example it has been held that pacifism,[161] vegetarianism and total abstinence from alcohol, are uncontroversial examples of beliefs that would fall within the ambit of Art 9.[162] In *Buscarini & Others v San Marino*[163] the ECtHR held that the protection available under Art 9 of the ECHR also implies the freedom to hold or not to hold religious beliefs and the freedom to practice or not to practice any religion. The applicants, who had been elected to the parliament of San Marino, took their oath of office in written form, having omitted the reference to the Gospels that was required by the Elections Act. However, the parliament of San Marino ordered them to retake the oath on the Gospels on pain of forfeiting their seats in parliament. Although the applicants complied with the order, they complained to the ECtHR that their right to freedom of religion and conscience as guaranteed by Art 9 of the ECHR had been violated by the parliament. A Grand Chamber of 17 judges of the court unanimously agreed that a violation of Art 9 had occurred since requiring the applicants to take the oath on the Gospels had been tantamount to requiring two elected representatives of the people to swear allegiance to a particular religion, a requirement that was not compatible with Art 9. It would be contradictory to make the exercise of a mandate intended to represent different views of society within parliament subject to a prior declaration of commitment to a particular set of beliefs, the court stated. The limitation complained of, therefore, could not be regarded as 'necessary in a democratic society'.[164] In

161. See *Valsamis v Greece* [1998] ELR 430 and *Arrowsmith v UK*, App No 7050/75 (1978) 19 DR 5.

162. *R (Williamson) v Secretary of State for Education* [2005] UKHL, *per* Lord Walker of Gestingthorpe, who also pointed out at para 55 that pacifism and other comparable religious beliefs can be based either on religious convictions but also on ethical considerations which are not religious but humanist. This was the type of problem which faced the US Supreme Court in *United States v Seeger* 380 US 163 (1965), in which the germane statute recognised conscientious objection to military service only if it arose from 'religious training and belief', which was defined as requiring belief in a Supreme Being and excluding 'essentially political, sociological, or philosophical views or a merely personal moral code.'

163. *Buscarini & Others v San Marino* (24645/94) [1999] ECHR 7.

164. At the time of the hearing San Marino had enacted Law No 115/1993 changing the law in this regard.

this book the author will be concerned mainly with the meaning of 'religion' in the context of the ECtHR, which was considered by the full court in *Wang v Minister for Immigration and Cultural Affairs*:[165]

> Accordingly, it is appropriate to consider Art 18 of the Universal Declaration and the objects of the Convention in interpreting Art 1 A (2). When regard is had to those matters it is clear that there are two elements to the concept of religion for the purposes of article 1A(2): the first is as a manifestation or practice of personal faith or doctrine, and the second is the manifestation or practice of that faith or doctrine in a like-minded community. I would add that that interpretation is consistent with the commonly understood meaning of religion as including its practice in or with a like-minded community.

[1.051] The meaning of the term 'religious education' may vary considerably from country to country. It may be akin to:

(a) ethics or philosophy, as in Germany;

(b) comparative religions and programmes of good behaviour, responsible sexual conduct and citizenship, as in the UK;

(c) the predominantly orthodox 'religious education' in Greece;

(d) the new world programme of 'religious education' in Norway, which includes humanism; or

(e) the comparative secular programme of 'religious education', which is part of the state examinations syllabus in Ireland.

On the other hand, the term 'religious instruction' or 'religious worship' will mean religious instruction and religious worship in one religious denomination, although this definition may vary from country to country. The phrase 'denominational education' refers to a class or type of education pertaining to a particular denomination or to a system of education grounded in the principles of a religious denomination, which may be referred to as sectarian.[166]

[1.052] In this book 'public education' generally means the service of education provided to the public by the state in state schools or in schools where such service is largely state-funded or state maintained. In England,

165. *Wang v Minister for Immigration and Cultural Affairs* (2000) FCA 1599 at para 81 *per* Merkel J

166. See *Cassell's English Dictionary*, p 299.

however, the term 'public schools' refers to a system of regulated[167] private schools which are fee paying and are owned and operated by private bodies. In the US, the term 'public schools' applies to elementary and secondary schools which are designed to serve as vital institutions for the preservation of national cohesion and perhaps the most powerful agency for promoting cohesion among a heterogeneous democratic people.[168] It is not surprising, therefore, that the constitutional prohibitions meet their severest test in the US when they are sought to be applied in the public school classroom.[169]

[1.053] Any reference to 'ecclesiastical law' will mean the law relating to church and state relations, which varies from country to country depending, *inter alia,* on historical, cultural and religious identities. The term 'canon law' will mean church law as promulgated by Popes and Councils of the church, in the case of the Catholic Church, or by the governing bodies and structures of the other main churches.

[1.054] The term 'establishment' is not a legal term but a contextually defined word that may have different meanings.[170] As Bates points out, the establishment of a religion can be achieved in a number of ways:

> The church and state can be one; the church may control the state; or the state may control the church; or the relationship may take one of several possible forms of a working arrangement between the two bodies.[171]

When interpreting Art 116 of the Australian Constitution, Gibbs J pointed to different ways in which a religion could be 'established' by law. Firstly, he noted, the broadest of these is simply to protect by law. The more common contemporary meaning is the conferring on a religion or a religious body of the position of a state religion or a state church. Secondly, when employed in relation to the establishment principle, the word means to support a church in the observance of its ordinance and principle and this meaning can extend

167. Education Act 2002, s 159(1) and see generally McManus, *Education and the Courts* (2nd edn, Jordans, 2004), chapter 9.

168. *McCollum v Board of Education* 333 US 203, 216–217 (1948) and *Abingdon School District v Schempp* 374 US 203 *per* Brennan J.

169. *Abingdon School District v Schempp*, 374 US 203, (1963) US.

170. See Munro, 'Does Scotland have an Established Church?' (1997) 4 *Ecclesiastical Law Journal*, Issue 20, 639–45.

171. Bates, *Religious Liberty: An Inquiry*, pp 9–14, 239–252 cited with approval by Black J delivering judgment of the US Supreme Court in *Everson v Board of Education* 340 US 1 at 18.

to churches which are unconnected to the state and are supported solely by voluntary contributions. A third possible meaning of the word 'establish' is to set up a new church or religion.[172] Although the US repudiated the concept of establishment of religion in the First Amendment to their Constitution,[173] the task of separating the secular from the religious, particularly in education, is one of magnitude, complexity and considerable sensitivity. A number of European countries have established systems which institutionalised a state church or predominant religion that retained close ties with state powers – for example, England, Denmark, Finland,[174] Greece and Malta. However, there is now a definite tendency in Europe towards the disestablishment of the established churches.[175]

[1.055] The term 'Europe' throughout this book will refer to the European Union and its member states rather than to any geographical area unless otherwise indicated. Finally, the term 'Ireland' will not include Northern Ireland since this sphere has already been comprehensively covered by other authors in recent times.[176]

---

172. *AG for the State of Victoria; Ex rel Black v The Commonwealth* (1981)146 CLR 559, 595–7; and further McConnell, 'Establishment and Disestablishment at the Founding, Pt 1, Establishment of Religion' (2003) 44 *Wm & Mary Law Rev* 2105, 2131; Ogilvie, 'What is a Church Established?' (1990) 28 *Osgoode Hall LJ* 179, 196.

173. Although nine of the thirteen states which formed the Union had established churches.

174. See further Kaariainen, *Churches and Religion,* 16 November 2007, available at http://virtual.finland.fi/finfo/english/uskoeng.html, accessed on 1 October 2008.

175. Robbers (ed), *State and Church in the European Union* (Nomos, 2005) p 579.

176. Gallagher and Lundy, 'Religion, education and the law in Northern Ireland', Martinez Lopez-Muniz, de Groof and Lauwers (eds), *Religious Education in Public Schools: Study of Comparative Law: Yearbook of European Association for Education Law and Policy,* Vol VI, (Springer, 2006) pp 171–195: Lundy, *Education Law: Policy and Practice in Northern Ireland* (SLS Legal Publishers, 2000): Richardson, 'Religious Education in Northern Ireland: Towards Mutual Respect?', Paper for Teaching for Tolerance, Respect and Recognition in Relation with Religion or Belief, Oslo, 2–5 September 2004, available online at http://folk.uio.no/leirvik/OsloCoalition/Richardson0904.htm.

Chapter 2

CHURCH-STATE RELATIONS: HISTORICAL EVOLUTION

ANCIENT RIGHTS REFORMULATED

[2.001] Since time immemorial, there have been certain rights and freedoms which have not been subject to temporal rule or secular law – such as freedom of thought, conscience and religion, freedom to manifest religion and freedom of association and expression – provided that their free exercise did not impact adversely on the common good. It is commonly thought that it was in Iraq, generally considered 'the cradle of civilisation', that the concept of a constitutional code was first formally promulgated by Hammurabi, King of Babelonia (1792–1750 BC) as a uniform system of law.[1] The Code of Hammurabi is acknowledged in legal literature as one of the most ancient surviving legal codes. By carving certain fundamental laws into pillars of basalt eight feet high, the ancient Babelonians sought to underscore the immutability of the various Codes of Law[2] that bound all persons, from slave to monarch.[3] Significantly, the Code recognised the existence of a well-established legal system, which had faith in the perceived ruling gods, and it acknowledged the principle that some laws are so fundamental and immutable, that they are above positive or man-made law, being so sacrosanct that even a sovereign may not interfere with them.[4]

---

1. It seems that the Hammurabi Code is just one of a series of laws which regulated the organisation of society in the Ancient Near East and some of these contain somewhat similar Codes; for example, the Hittite Code (c 1300 BC), the Ur–III dynasty (c 2050 BC) and the Mosaic Law (according to the Torah redactor theory 400–300 BC) circa 1200 BC. See further Winton (ed), *Documents from Old Testament Times* (Harper and Row, 1958).
2. Winton, from Code 1–282 with numbers 13 missing and also nos 66–99. This unique stone was found in 1901 in a city of the Persian mountains.
3. See further Radau, *Early Babylonian History* (Wipf & Stock Publishers, 2005); Johns, *Babylonian and Assyrian Laws, Contracts and Letters* (Adamant Media Corporation, 2000); Harper, *The Code of Hammurabi, King, of Babylon* (Lawbook Exchange Ltd, 1991); Cook, *The Laws of Moses and the Code of Hammurabi* (Adam and Charles Black, 1903).
4. Cook, *The Laws of Moses and the Code of Hammurabi* (Adam and Charles Black, 1903).

Remarkably, religious faith had been identified by the ancient Babelonians as one of the fundamental rights which lay beyond the remit of the temporal sovereign, since it remained with the individual. Arguably, individual human rights were further endorsed by many ancient, respected sources, including the Old Testament (1200–300 BC), Confucius (551–479 BC), the New Testament (AD 40–100), the Koran (AD 644–656), the Magna Carta Libertatum (AD 1215) and the Aztec Code of Nezahualcoyotl (AD 1400).[5]

[2.002] In the early centuries AD, as cross-border migration increased and religions mingled and diversified, social cohesion and integration posed pressing problems for the Roman Empire, particularly amongst the Jews and early Christians. Some form of church-state compromise was indicated, although the formalisation of concepts of toleration and justice for all religions were slow to emerge. Even within the Christian church the recognition of religious liberty was a tardy and tortuous process.[6] Gradually, these concepts began to be embodied, albeit briefly, in the decrees and edicts of certain emperors. Following the persecutions of the early Christians by Diocletian,[7] Galerius enshrined the concepts of justice and toleration for all religions in the Edict of Toleration (311 CE),[8] but these norms were inconsistently applied throughout the Empire, it appears. As a result of political and military victories, the Emperor Constantine 1 was able to reach an agreement with Licinius[9] that led to the Edict of Milan (313 CE),

5. Cook, *The Laws of Moses and the Code of Hammurabi.*
6. Ahdar and Leigh, *Religious Freedom in the Liberal State,* p 22 and generally chapter 1.
7. These persecutions were documented by Lactantius (ca 245–325 CE) in Latin and by Eusebius (ca 260–340 CE) in Greek. Both the *Edict of Toleration* and the *Edict of Milan* are to be found in Lactantius's *On the Deaths of the Persecutors.*
8. See *Edict of Toleration* by Galerius, 311 AD, from Lactantius, *De Mort Pers,* Chs 34, 35. Opera, ed OF Fritzche 11, p 273 (Bibl Patt Ecc Lat XI, Leipsig 1844, translated by Department of History, University of Philadelphia Press, [1897–1907] vol 4;1, pp 28–30, accessible at www.fordham.edu/halsal/source/edict-milan.html accessed on 16 November 2007. This service is part of the Internet Medieval Sourcebook. See also Fairley (ed), *Translations and Reprints from the Original Sources of European History.* See later Edict of Toleration issued by Joseph 11, Emperor of Austria in 1781 and extended in 1782, which conferred religious and political rights to all minority religions except the Jews.
9. Emperor in the East. See Ahdar and Leigh, *Religious Freedom in the Liberal State,* p 13.

confirming the earlier Edict of Toleration, which conferred on all Christians and other religions the right to follow freely the religion of their choice and the free opportunity to worship as they pleased.[10] In addition to the many problems presented by the early Christians, the various widely-dispersed branches of the Jewish Diaspora constituted a serious threat to the Roman Empire. In order to bring the Diaspora under its control, Rome divested the Jews of their pivotal judicial function while permitting them the freedom to practice their religion. However, Rome set limits to the boundaries of religious freedom since it continued to monitor Jewish propaganda, of which it was suspicious. Rome also banned the proselytising of Christian freed men and slaves and forbad Jews to have non-Jewish slaves or to marry Christian women.[11] Such matters, which did not pertain to the purely religious domain, remained subject to Roman law.

[2.003] It is notable that the early Christian church identified toleration as a virtue, supported toleration of all religions and defended the Edict of Milan as being '*testes veritatis*', the living proof of Christianity in action.[12] These early guarantees of religious freedoms were short-lived, however. With the reign of Theodosius 1 (AD 378–395), Christianity became the official religion of the Empire and all other religions were declared illegal.[13] The

---

10. *Edict of Milan* 313 AD from Lactantius, *De Mort Pers* Ch 48, accessible at www.fordham.edu/halsal/source/edict-milan.html assessed on 16 November 2007, this service is part of the Internet Medieval Sourcebook, Matthew Bunson, Edict of Milan, *Encyclopedia of the Roman Empire,* New York, 1994.

11. See further Vincent, *Judaism* (Sands & Co, London, 1934), Trans by Scanlan, pp 32–35.

12. Vincent, *Judaism* p 32 referring to the Edict of Milan 313. Significantly Locke also identified toleration as the chief characteristic of the true church, *A Letter concerning* Toleration (1689) reproduced in Horton and Mendus (eds), *John Locke, A Letter Concerning Toleration, in Focus* (Routledge, 1991), 14: James Madison warned that if freedom of religion be abused, it is an offence against God, not against man, Memorial *and Remonstrance against Religious Assessments* (1785): reproduced in Adams and Emmerich, *A Nation Dedicated to Religious Liberty,* 104.

13. *The Theodosian Code* XV1.1.2 was the legal Code of the Roman Empire promulgated in 438 by Theodosius 11 in the East and accepted by Valentinian 111 of the West. See further Bettison (ed), *Documents of the Christian Church,* p 31 *et seq*; also Vincent, Scanlan (trans), *Judaism* (Sands & Co, 1934); Honore, *Law in the Crisis of Empire 379–455* and Matthews, *Laying Down the Law: A Study of the Theodosian Code* (Yale University Press, 2000).

principles of religious freedom advanced by Tertullian at the turn of the second century AD were regrettably abandoned and many centuries of intolerance followed, practised by later Christian sovereigns and emperors.[14]

[2.004] From the suppression of the non-Christian religions in AD 378 until the Enlightenment of the eighteenth century, freedom of religion and worship in the formal sense did not exist in many parts of Europe. By the medieval period, the Roman Catholic Church had become the sovereign common authority and in the late medieval period that Church was the predominant influence in Western Europe.[15] During this period, Judaism was repressed[16] and the notorious crusades took place.[17] Following the Reformation, bitter 'Wars of Religion' took place between warring factions of Catholics and Protestants in Europe, although power-struggles between ecclesiastical and secular rulers pre-date the Reformation. This was particularly the case in England, Germany and Scandinavia where church-state concordats had not been agreed.[18] Writers generally trace the existence of the modern secular state, based on the recognition of the existence of a plurality of sovereign 'powers', and the origin of international human rights law and international relations to the Treaty of Westphalia (1648),[19] which

14. Ahdar and Leigh, *Religious Freedom in the Religious State*, p 14 citing Kamen, *The Rise of Toleration* (Weidenfeld and Nicholson, 1967) and Marcus, *Saeculum: History and Society in the Theology of St Augustine* (2nd edn, Cambridge University Press, 1989) and Tierney, 'Religious Rights: An Historical Perspective', in Witte and van der Vyver (eds), *Religious Human Rights in Global Perspective: Religious Perspectives* (Martinus Nijhoff Publishers, 1996), 20.

15. Figgis, *From Gerson to Grotius*, 1414–1625 (Batoche Books, 1999) p 5.

16. See Flannery, *The Anguish of the Jews* (Paulist Press, 1985).

17. Defeis, 'Religious Liberty and Protections in Europe', *Journal of Catholic Legal Studies* Vol 45:77.

18. Skinner, *The Foundations of Modern Political Thought* (Cambridge University Press, 1978), vol 11, pp 59–60.

19. See Peace Treaty between the Holy Roman Emperor and the king of France and their Respective Allies, 24 October 1648, reprinted in Israel (ed), *Major Peace Treaties of Modern History: 1648–1967*, at 7. The Treaty of Westphalia brought to an end the 30 Years War which had its origin in religious strife between Catholic and Protestant states within the Empire and it indicates the emergence of the modern secular state system grounded in the existence of a plurality of sovereign 'powers'.

brought to an end the Thirty Years War that had its origin in religious strife between Catholic and Protestant states within the Empire.[20]

[2.005] The Treaty of Westphalia laid down guarantees of religious freedom for religious minorities (human rights), which had their genesis in the earlier theories of Aristotle, Plato and the ancient Greeks. These guarantees were later reconstructed and re-interpreted by Thomas Aquinas and the Scholastics in the twelfth and thirteenth centuries[21] and, much more radically so, by Rousseau and the Enlightenment writers during the eighteenth century, which in turn influenced, *inter alia*, the French Revolution of 1789 (the Revolution).

THE CONCEPT OF TOLERANCE RE-EMERGES

[2.006] Many writers, including John Locke[22] and James Madison[23] have identified religious toleration as the hallmark of the 'true church'. As has been seen, with some notable exceptions,[24] following the Edict of Milan, the early Christian Church paid little heed to this principle, with the result that suppression and religious persecution became common down through the centuries.[25] In contemporary times, however, Christians have come to re-

20. Drinan, 'Can God and Caesar Coexist? Balancing Religious Freedom and International Law' *The British Yearbook of International Law* (2004) 86–95; and further Borgen, 'Triptych: Sectarian Disputes, International Law, and Transitional Tribunals in Drinan's Can God and Caesar Coexist?' *St. John's Law Review,* vol 45, No 11, p 11–58; also Defeis, 'Religious Liberty and Protections in Europe', *St John's Law Review,* vol 45, No 1.

21. Aquinas, *Summa Theologiae* (Blackfriars, 1963–1975).

22. See 'A Letter Concerning Toleration' (1689), reproduced in Horton and Mendus (eds), John Locke, A Letter Concerning Toleration, in Focus (Routledge, 1991).

23. Memorial and Remonstrance against Religious Assessments (1785), reproduced in Adams and Emmerich, *A Nation Dedicated to Religious Liberty* (Pennsylvania Press, 1990).

24. See further Johnson, 'Religious Rights and Christian Texts' in Witte and van der Vyver (eds), *Religious Human Rights in Global Perspective: Religious Perspectives* (Martinus Nijhoff Publishers, 1996), 65, 68.

25 See *dictum* of Lord Walker of Gestingthorpe in *R v Secretary of State for Education and Employment, ex p Williamson* [2005] UKHL, 15, [56]; Ahdar and Leigh, *Religious Freedom in the Liberal State,* p 15 *et seq*; Curran, 'Religious Freedom and Human Rights in the World and in the Church; a Christian Perspective' in Swindler (ed), *Religious Liberty and Human Rights,* 143, 145; (contd .../)

embrace tolerance and religious freedom.[26] In Vatican II, one finds the Catholic Church's official approach to tolerance in the Declaration on the Relationship of the Church to Non-Christian Religions (*Nostra Aetate*).[27] This Declaration, which was signed in 1965, states that all men comprise a single community, having a single origin and a final goal: God.[28] It stresses inter-church common ground and points out that the Catholic Church rejects nothing which is true and holy in these religions (ie Hinduism, Buddism, Islam and Judaism). The Declaration makes it clear that it looks with esteem on the Moslems[29] and cannot forget that it received the revelation of the Old Testament from the Jews.[30] Furthermore, Vatican II points to the fundamental significance of a free, personal response to faith in *Dignitatis Humanae*:

> It is one of the major tenets of Catholic doctrine that man's response to God in faith must be free .... The act of faith is of its very nature a free act .... It is therefore completely in accord with the nature of faith that in matters religious every manner of coercion on the part of men should be excluded.[31]

When freedom of religion, as a human right is mentioned, however, many point to the Enlightenment writers and the emergence of the modern state.

The Emergence of the Modern State

[2.007] The events that culminated in the French Revolution eventually led to the proclamation of the Declaration of the Rights of Man and the Citizen (the Declaration),[32] which was deeply influenced by the liberal principles

25. (contd) Wolf, *Toward Consensus: Catholic-Protestant Interpretations of Church and State* (Doubleday: Anchor Books, 1968) pp 102–3.
26. See Hudson, 'The Theological Basis for Religious Freedom' (1961) 3 *Journal of Church and State*, 130, 134.
27. For the official English translation, see Abbott, *The Documents of Vatican II*, 660–8. 689–690, *Dignitatis Humanae,* section 10.
28. Abbott, *The Documents of Vatican II*, para 1.
29. Abbott, *The Documents of Vatican II*, para 3.
30. Abbott, *The Documents of Vatican II*, para 4.
31. Abbott, *The Documents of Vatican II*, 689–690, Dignitatis Humanae, section 10.
32. See **Appendix 2** of this book.

enshrined in the American Declaration of Independence (1776).[33] In this manner, the seeds of a new civil structure had been sown and the combined effect of the social upheavals of the sixteenth and seventeenth centuries culminated in the replacement of ecclesiastical dominance with the civil authorities through the setting up of the modern state in most European countries.[34] The events in France led to a seismic shift in the perception of individual rights and religious freedom, which the separation of church and state was perceived as an essential element of the newly established democracy with its upholding tenets of liberty, equality and fraternity. As a consequence of the writings of the French[35] and English[36] humanists, the modern concept of the state emerged as a sovereign political body within a specific jurisdiction having a distinctive existence from governor and governed.[37] With the emergence of the modern state, a framework of ecclesiastical law evolved over the centuries in each country to accommodate the fundamental rights of the individual and the rights of the various churches and communities that represent them in germane spheres. Such rights were eventually enshrined in modern constitutional codes and statutes and international treaties, which included concordats with the Holy See in certain countries. Each country's ecclesiastical law framework is shaped by its historical and cultural experience but, even in Europe differing ideological perspectives may arise on fundamental issues.

Differing Philosophical Approaches in Europe

[2.008] There are fundamental differences between medieval and modern concepts of natural law, the origin of political authority and the juridical basis for society in Europe. The medieval concept asserts that God is the fount of political power and is frequently referred to as 'the natural law

---

33. Declaration of Independence, 4 July 1776. See further White, 'The Influence of American Ideas upon the French Revolution' American Historical Association, available at www.historians.org/info/AHA_History/adwhite2.htm, accessed on 1 October 2008. See **Appendix 1A**.

34. Figgis, *Political Thought From Gerson to Grotius: 1414–1625* identifies Martin Luther, Henry VIII of England and Philip II of Spain as the main architects of this transformation.

35. Chiefly Voltaire, Montesquieu and Rousseau.

36. For example, John Locke and Hobbes.

37. Figgis, *Political Thought From Gerson to Grotius, 1414–1625* pp 5–6.

philosophy', which has many forms. The modern concept views man and his rationality as the source of political authority. In the latter, generally termed 'the natural rights philosophy', natural law is perceived as remaining valid even if God does not exist. Arguably the most significant period in the development of this ancient philosophy[38] was that of the Enlightenment,[39] Jean-Jacques Rousseau (1749–1762) being particularly important. Rousseau's concept of self-determination and reason and 'the natural rights philosophy' generally have become so universally accepted that, arguably, they now underpin the whole edifice of international law norms and values supporting human rights globally. Those who promote the natural rights philosophy consider that democratic rights and all civil authority are vested in man, who is a free and rational being; that such rights derive essentially from the will of the people or the multitude, and that God, or any superior being, may or may not be in the picture, so to speak. They tend to view the neutral space of public life and public education as the most successful guarantor of personal and religious freedom and they may be assertive of this to varying degrees, as it clear from the contrast between France and the US, for example. The supporters of the natural rights philosophy point to human rights law and to the secular state established by the American Constitution as the ideal model, claiming that it has created a neutral space between various religions within which religious freedom is protected, including that of the Catholic minority.[40] They contend that positive law derives solely from the democratic rights vested in man by his nature and that the Christian God (or personal God) is not the source of such rights. Given these fundamental distinctions at the base of political authority, it

38. The history of the European Enlightenment goes back at least to Aristotle and was reconstructed by Thomas Aquinas in the thirteenth century and once again by the 'humanists' of the fourteenth and fifteenth centuries. See further Hooker's *History of the European Enlightenment*, Internet Resources at http://www.resourcehelp.com/his_europe.htm, accessed on 1 October 2008.

39. Voltaire, Diderot, Montesquieu and Rousseau in France; Locke, Wollstonecraft and Hobbes in England.

40. See O'Toole, 'Space for Religious Freedom' (2004) *Irish Times*, 21 January, p 16. For a fascinating discussion on related matters, see Russo, 'The Ten Commandments in American Public Schools: An Enduring Controversy', (2003) *Education Law Journal*, p 90. Russo points out that, as with most legal issues in US education, such a discussion is not applicable to non-public schools, whether they are religiously affiliated or not, since most matters in non-public schools are subject to contract law and not constitutional principles. See *Pierce v Society of Sisters* (1925) 268 US.

comes as no surprise that ideological tensions surrounded certain aspects of the failed Constitutional Treaty for Europe, and the proposed Lisbon Treaty.

THE THEISTIC NATURAL LAW

[2.009] Those who support the natural law paradigm, in whatever form it takes, assert that fundamental rights derive from a divine power, that is superior and antecedent to positive law and that such rights are fundamental and, accordingly, immune from change by the parliamentary process. For example, the controversial decision of the Irish Supreme Court in 1995, *Re Article 26 of the Constitution and in the Matter of the Reference to the Court of the Regulation of Information (Services outside the State for Termination of Pregnancies) Bill 1995*,[41] indicated a seismic shift away from the natural law based fundamental principle of protection for the unborn, embodied in the Constitution of Ireland 1937, in the direction of positive law. By adjusting Irish jurisprudence away from the theistic natural law, the Supreme Court broke with tradition and permitted Ireland to align itself with the upholding 'natural rights philosophy' of much of Western Europe, which in turn upholds international human rights law. Professor Binchy describes this precedent as one of the most significant legal decisions since the foundation of the state[42] and one which, he considers, destabilised the whole scaffolding of human rights protection in the Constitution. The significance of this decision, he argues, lies not in the development of any new constitutional principle but in its implicit denial of the very concept of a fundamental principle of law.[43] As will be seen in **chapter 9**, however, educational practice and policies in Ireland are still in the process of alignment with certain aspects of constitutional jurisprudence[44] and human rights law as

41. *Re Article 26 of the Constitution and in the Matter of the Reference to the Court of the Regulation of Information (Services outside the State for Termination of Pregnancies) Bill 1995* [1995] 2 ILRM 81.

42. Binchy, 'Abortion ruling one of the most significant legal decisions since the foundation of State' (1995) *Irish Times*, 15 May.

43. Whyte, 'Natural Law and the Constitution' (1996) ILTR 14 ILT (ns) 8 and Twomey, 'The Death of the Natural Law' (1995) ILT (ns) 270.

44. As may be seen, some Irish cases indicate a clear shift in direction towards more liberal values, eg *McGee v Attorney General* [1974] IR 284; *Re Art 26 of the Constitution and in the Matter of the Reference to the Court of the Regulation of Information (Services outside the State for Termination of Pregnancies) Bill 1995* [1995] 2 ILRM 81 and also the recognition by the state of divorce and of same-sex unions.

educational reforms, *inter alia,* continue to evolve in the direction of the western European norm.

Potential Spheres of Conflict

[2.010] When certain laws applicable throughout the enlarged EU are being harmonised, some conflicting values may arise with regard to the more conservative states, particularly when those laws touch on sensitive issues such as education, adoption, abortion or marriage laws. Such member states may have certain religious affiliations and/or practices that do not fully accord with the Union's more liberal aims and objectives and they may legislate in accordance with their religious principles, which may be embodied in constitutional or legislative measures. For example, Poland has recently enacted legislation so as to ensure religious freedoms for its largely Catholic population since the members of the Polish Parliament have voted to prohibit trading on Catholic feast days following complaints that large foreign supermarkets demand excessive working hours and ignore employees' religious needs. Under this legislation, trading is to be banned on 12 days annually to allow families to fulfil a key family role in the home on important religious occasions.[45] It will be recalled that the EU's Green Paper (2004),[46] which aimed to create a common judicial area in the field of family law so as to facilitate its citizens seeking divorce in cross-border cases was opposed by predominantly Catholic Ireland,[47] which has more conservative divorce laws than the European norm.[48] Ireland objected to this

45. Luxmoore, 'Poland stops supermarkets from trading on feast days' (2007) *The Universe*, 15 July. Under the legislation, trading is to be banned on twelve days annually, including Easter, Pentecost, Corpus Christi, Assumption day, All Saint's Day and Poland's National Constitution and Independence days. See further, Kraynak, *Christian Faith and Modern Democracy: God and Politics in the Fallen World* (University of Notre Dame Press, 2001).

46. 'Public Consultation on the Law applicable to International Divorces', 14 March 2004.

47. Approximately 63 per cent voted in the referendum in 1986 against divorce legislation. In a second referendum to amend the Constitution in 1995, the mandate to amend was carried forward by a slim 50.3 per cent margin.

48. The Family Law (Divorce) Act 1996, s 5 requires, *inter alia,* that '(a) at the date of the institution of proceedings, the spouses have lived apart from one another for a period of, or periods amounting to, at least four years during the previous five years.' See further *Shatter's Family Law* (4th edn, Tottel Publishing, 1997) chapter 9.

proposed harmonisation on the grounds that this would conflict with its statutory and constitutional provisions relating to divorce.

[2.011] In Ireland, some fear that their national policies and practices will be unduly influenced by what they perceive as the EU's 'supra-national powers' and human rights secular ideology and that this will ultimately pose a threat to the ideological basis on which their church-state system has been established. Concerns have been expressed that EU structures and perspectives, dominated by legal positivism and individualism, could undermine, in particular, the culture of member states where the Catholic Church's viewpoint enjoys a stronger adherence than within the Union generally and that pluralism, as it applies in the EU, may be a cloak for 'an aggressive secularism', which may harden into an ideology that may exclude religious perspectives from public life.[49] Essentially, they fear that religion is being replaced by 'a new religion' of human rights norms and principles, or a new morality, which is striving to erect a metaphorical 'wall of separation between church and state.'[50] Since religion is not just 'a purely private matter', they argue, there should not be a false division between politics and religion.[51] In his book, *The Soul of Europe*, Bishop Donal Murray succinctly summarises these fears:

> It is no accident that modern democracies and the European Union itself, seem to be marked by a profound disillusionment with the political process. This is at least partly because the whole concept risks seeming to tell people 'Do not enter here with your whole self. Your religious views must be kept to yourself; they are a private matter. Your moral views must not intrude into political life, they are divisive .... But there is a danger that we may find ourselves with no heritage to be proud of and no foundation on which to stand .... The

49. Editorial (2004) *Irish Independent*, 3 December.

50. A reference to the well-known phrase taken from Thomas Jefferson's letter to the Danbury Baptist's Association, of 1 January 1802; Andrew (ed), *16 Writings of Thomas Jefferson 281*.

51. McGarry, 'EU may threaten Catholic vision' (2005) *Irish Times*, 27 September. Pope Benedict has also challenged today's ideas in education: see pastoral letter of the Catholic bishop of Limerick, Dr Donal Murray, 'To live as God's people: Reflections on the Visit of Pope John Paul to Limerick' in which he states 'We are not faced with State atheism but with the false and destructive notion that religion is a purely private matter.' See further, Archbishop Martin of Dublin, 'Michael Littleton Lecture', 2 November 2004; 'Prelate warns secularism must not smother religion' (2004) *Irish Independent*, 3 November.

> underlying fear in contemporary society is the fear of meaninglessness .... We are afraid of chaos.[52]

[2.012] Catholics point to the manner in which Rocco Buttiglione, the Italian nominee to the European Commission, was prevented from taking up his first position in the Commission[53] because of his orthodox Catholic views. Buttiglione's critics implied that his religious beliefs would affect his ability to properly carry out the position for which he was nominated. More recently, a German Minister for Culture and Education, Karin Wolff, came under pressure for suggesting that the biblical story of creation should be discussed in school science classes, since it calls into question the separation of church and state in German public schools. Ms Wolff, a theologian and former religion teacher, it is reported, sees no contradiction between biological evolution and the biblical explanation for the origin of the world but she has been subjected to serious criticism and described as a 'Christian fundamentalist' by other politicians.[54] Of particular interest in this regard is the refusal of the English government to grant exemptions for Catholic adoption agencies from the 2003 Regulations which implement the EU Equality Directives, which are discussed later in **chapter 3**, a decision which has much wider ramifications, particularly in education.[55]

POST-1989: A NEW ERA FOR RELIGION

[2.013] Many commentators draw attention to the fall of the Berlin Wall, which commenced in November 1989, as the start of a new era for religion in Europe. Religions whose presence in communist countries had been restricted or prohibited moved rapidly into new territory that was free from strict societal control and restrictive travel regulations.[56] Moreover, many so-called 'New Age' religions were quick to see the potential for new members in this unprecedented occurrence. Faced with new challenges, some well-

---

52. Murray, *The Soul of Europe and other Selected Writings* (Veritas, 2002) pp 96–98.

53. By a majority of Members of the European Parliament.

54. Scally, 'German Minister caught in creationism row' (2007) *Irish Times,* 21 July, p 11 citing the Social Democrat and Green Party.

55. Siggs, 'Catholics urged to lobby MPs over adoption ruling: Cardinal expresses fears of "a new kind of morality"' (2007) *The Universe*, 4 February.

56 Kent, 'The French and German Versus American Debate Over "New Religions", Scientology and Human Rights', in *Marburg Journal of Education*, Vol 6, No 1 (January 2001). (contd .../)

established religions found it necessary to redefine themselves following the loss of political power by communism. But it is where East and West meet that the most fundamental distinctions become apparent which is clear from Turkey's attempts to obtain membership of the EU.[57]

The Significance of Education

[2.014] For Plato, the key to creating and maintaining his ideal Republic was education.[58] The individual was best served, he considered, when he was subordinated to a just society in which education was the responsibility of the state. Education, which ought to be universal, he opined, should effectively mould children to discharge their future role in a just society. Despite his autocratic methodology and undoubted meritocracy, Plato's views set down the foundation from which much of the later democratic philosophy of education would emerge, although many would disagree with his views on education and vehemently resist any such state-imposed ideology (statism). In particular, the Catholic Church perceives education as a right and duty of parents and the family. Statism, on the other hand, regards education as a right and duty of the state, or the government for the time being. From the Catholic Church's point of view the individual is immortal, while the state is merely transitory and its concept of education corresponds to a materialistic view of humanity which ends with death.[59] Contemporary Europe, on the other hand, views education as an obligation to be discharged nationally by the member states as a social right and as an increasingly significant human right guaranteed in international law[60] (although the

56. (contd) Maxwell, 'New Kingdoms for the Cults', in (1992) *Christianity Today,* 13 January, pp 37–40. Morvant, 'Sects Prompt Protests in Eastern Europe' in Hungarian American List, Open Media Analytical Brief, 2 July 1996, Richardson, 'New Religions and Religious Freedom in Eastern and central Europe: a Sociological Analysis' in Borowick and Babiski (eds), *New Religious Phenomena in Central and Eastern Europe* (Nomos, 1997) pp 257–282.

57. See Griffiths, *The Marriage of East and West.*

58. Plato, Grube (trans), *The Republic* (Hackett Publishing Company, 1992), Books 1–5 trans by Grube and revised by Reeve (Loeb Classical Library, Harvard University Press, 1992)

59. McNeill, 'Guidelines for an Irish Education Policy' (1979) *Irish Jurist* (ns) 378 at 380 with an Introduction by Professor Osborough at 378.

60. *The Educational Structures in the Member States of the European Community,* p 101. Macbeth, *Studies: The Child Between* (Office for Official Publications, 1984) p 11.

vindication of this may in practice prove problematic). From the human rights perspective, second only to the family, the most ancient of all societies, education is the vehicle by which values and attitudes are transferred from one generation to the next. The ECtHR distinguished between education and teaching in *Campell and Cosans v UK* when it stated:

> The Court would point out that the education of children is the whole process whereby, in any society, adults endeavour to transmit their beliefs, culture and other values to the young whereas teaching or instruction refers in particular to the transmission of knowledge and to intellectual development.[61]

[2.015] It is in school where children learn to construct their own identities as believers or non-believers and to face the diverse beliefs of the school community, which is a microcosm of the wider world. Without the regulation provided by the law, however, the relationship between education and religion in the wider society could become unbalanced or partisan or, in exceptional instances, a vehicle to promote corruption, violence, extremism or radicalism. But to what degree should the law regulate the interface of religion and education? Or should religion, as some argue, be relegated by law to the private sphere, thereby creating a sacrosanct space from which all religion and religious beliefs would be omitted?[62]

CONCLUSION

[2.016] Churches in Europe and in the US were the dominant providers of education until the late eighteenth century and in some countries for a hundred years later or more.[63] With the growth of democracy, the main powers in public education gradually moved from the churches to the state, a transformation which was reflected in national constitutions and was embodied in legislation in many countries. During the nineteenth century, a common feature in Europe and the US was the state's growing responsibility for education, despite distinctions in the social, economic, political and

61. See the ECtHR definition of 'education' in *Campbell and Cosans v UK* (1982) 4 EHRR 165.

62. See Neuhaus, *The Naked Public Square: Religion and Democracy in America* (WB Eerdmans Pubs Co, 1983).

63. Glenn and de Groof, Balancing *freedom, autonomy and accountability in Education*, at 28. See in particular **chapter 9** below, which shows that the significant influence of the churches in education has continued in Ireland much later than in other EU countries generally.

ideological forces that underpinned this development.[64] Each country created the national framework and public policies within which religious needs were met in accordance with its law and constitution. However, in time, issues relating to religion transcended national boundaries and domestic legal systems and became part of international human rights law jurisprudence[65] and, to some degree, EU law. The European Commission, for example, has dealt with religious issues in the equality and anti-discrimination law context,[66] while the ECtHR has also ruled on a large corpus of cases relating to religion[67] and the right to participate in religious teaching as protected by Art 9 of the ECHR. Furthermore, the Draft/EU Reform Treaty makes provision of general application for the status of the churches and non-confessional organisations. It is a fact that the education systems of many countries, democratic and otherwise, have maintained close ties with religion. As Beverly McLachlin (Chief Justice of Canada), stated when speaking to a World Conference on Religion and Education in the Netherlands in 2004, it is difficult to exclude religion from public life,[68] since it is a cultural form which expresses itself in the public sphere:

> By their very nature, the many shades of religious beliefs that we find in our midst are bound to find expression in the public sphere. Religion is a cultural form that imbues all facts of the adherent's life. It touches not only upon beliefs about transcendent aspects of the universe, but affects all aspects of the way people move within the social and political world. There are no limits to the claims made by religion upon the self. Religion claims the believer's entire being, and makes demands that exceed her internal conscience. Believers must respond to these demands in their lives, and in their interaction with others in the world.[69]

---

64. Glenn and de Groof, *Finding the Right Balance, Freedom, Autonomy and Accountability in Education* and also see Harris, *Education and Diversity*, p 90.
65. See **chapter 4**.
66. Council Directive 200/78/EC, 27 November 2000 setting up a general framework for equal treatment in employment and occupation, Official Journal L 303, 2–12–2000, 16.
67. *Prais v Council* C–130/75 [1976] ECR 1589 and in particular 1598–1599. *Sahin v Turkey* (2005) 41 EHRR 8. *Dahlab v Switzerland* Case 44774/98, 29 June 2004.
68. Organised by the European Association for Education Law and Policy. See further the Journals of the European Association for Education Law and Policy, Kluwer Law International.
69. See further, McLachlinn, 'Who owns our Kids? Education, Health and Religion in a Multi-cultural Society', McArdle (ed) *Cambridge Lectures 1991* (Comansville Editions Yvon Blais, 1993) p 147.

Many European countries would agree with McLachlin CJ that it is well nigh impossible to exclude religion from public life and this is particularly difficult in the case of public education, as the experience in the US over the past eight decades has shown – a matter which is discussed in **chapter 10** below.

Chapter 3

RELIGION, EDUCATION AND LAW IN THE EUROPEAN UNION

The law is not a 'light' for you or any man to see by; law is not an instrument of any kind. The law is a causeway upon which so long as he keeps to it a citizen may walk safely.[1]

INTRODUCTION

[3.001] The failure of the Draft European Constitution to be adopted by the member states and the current difficulties surrounding the Lisbon Treaty)[2] lead some to consider that ideological issues may be at the heart of the matter. However, the post-Referendum Eurobarometer survey indicates otherwise.[3] The Irish electorate's rejection of Lisbon Treaty has given rise to considerable public debate on the impact of EU membership on Irish identity and values.[4] Referring to the Referendum on the Lisbon Treaty, Ireland's Catholic Cardinal, Sean Brady, suggested recently that Ireland's rejection of the complex Lisbon Treaty could be attributed in part to a growing unease concerning the direction the EU is now taking.[5] In a wide-

1. Bolt, *A Man For All Seasons* (Vintage, 1990).
2. 2007/C 306/01, Treaty of Lisbon amending the Treaty on European Union and the Treaty establishing the European Community signed at Lisbon, 13 December 2007, to be renamed the treaty on the Functioning of the European Union.
3. Conducted by Gallup on 13–15 June 2008 at the request of the European Commission, 18/VI/2008, available online at http://ec.eupora.eu, accessed on 1 October 2008.
4. See (2008) *Irish Times* Letters to the Editor, 30 August, p 15 and in particular that of Dr John Brennan, Lecturer in European Politics and Society, National University of Ireland, Maynooth, Co Kildare.
5. The Cardinal was speaking at the Humbert School in Killala, Co Mayo. This lecture is available online at http://www.irishtimes.com/newspaper/frontpage/2008/0825/1219616651409.html, accessed on 1 October 2008 and extracts are covered in the print edition of 25 August, 2008, McGarry, 'Cardinal criticises EU attitude to Christian way of life', p 1.

ranging address, the Cardinal referred to 'a fairly widespread culture in European affairs which relegates manifestations of religious convictions to the private and subjective sphere.' Essentially, the Cardinal's plea appears to be for reasonable accommodation of the churches and religion within EU structures; a plea for religious freedom as reflected by the application of the principle of pluralism rather than the principle of secularism. As the EU puts in place its 'common causeway of law', so to speak, on which the member states can walk safely, is there a danger that some well-founded individual religious freedoms could be submerged by the consensus emerging from the more powerful secular states and from the demands of equality and non-discrimination?

[3.002] The post-Referendum Flash Eurobarometer survey suggests that over half the people who did not vote in the referendum said this was due to a lack of understanding of the relevant issues.[6] Nonetheless, it is remarkable that the same survey found that support for Irish membership of the Union was 98 per cent among those who voted 'yes' and 80 per cent among those who voted 'no'.[7] Just two per cent of respondents gave as their chief reason for voting against the Treaty the possibility that it would allow the introduction of European legislation in Ireland permitting same-sex marriage, abortion and euthanasia. It is worth recalling that the Lisbon Treaty was negotiated and signed by all 27 member states, who were directly elected by their people in the national contexts, and that they all were actively involved in the Convention on the future of Europe which contributed to the Draft EU Constitution in 2004. There was a lively public debate at that time on whether the Draft EU Constitution should include a reference to God and the Europe's Christian heritage. Perhaps it should come as no surprise that the EU with its 27 member states should encounter problems relating to religion as it harmonises, for this is traditionally one of the most difficult spheres in which to build a consensus as was also apparent during the drafting of the US Constitution, which is discussed later in **chapter 10**.

[3.003] What is not yet clear is the approach the EU will adopt in the future: will it leave sufficient autonomy to the churches, for example, to maintain

6. Eurobarometer Survey, p 2.

7. Eurobarometer Survey, p 2, policy issues of concern for those who voted 'No' were (a) the maintenance of Irish foreign policy neutrality; (b) the continuation of corporate tax status; and (c) the preservation of the EU's existing institutional structures which would ensure a strong voice for Ireland.

their interests in the social spheres, such as health and education, or will it follow the principle of secularism, as best exemplified by France? This chapter outlines the general legal framework of EU law in so far as it gives support to freedom of religion and freedom of education principles. It looks at the EU's equality and non-discrimination Directives, germane case law, and the Charter of Fundamental Rights (the Charter). Although the Charter was signed and proclaimed by the Presidents of the European Parliament, the Council and the Commission at the European Council meeting in Nice on 7 December 2000,[8] it does not currently have full legal effect in the member states.[9]

Religious Identity of the Union

[3.004] In the past decade the religious identity of the EU has been controversial both nationally and internationally. Recent developments, however, show a striking consciousness of the religious element in the life of the Union[10] as it strives to achieve greater unity, cohesion and solidarity in the future. In the early decades of the Community's existence, there was a general awareness of the inherent sensitivities in matters relating to religion and so primary Community law eschewed this sphere of law. The Draft Treaty establishing a Constitution for Europe[11] refers to fundamental rights germane to religion in the common constitutional traditions of the member states; in the Charter, and in the European Convention on Human Rights (ECHR). Art 1.51 of the Draft Treaty provides for the legal position of the churches:

1. The Union respects and does not prejudice the status under national law of the churches and religious associations or communities in the member states.

---

8. 2000 OJ (C364), 1 (7 December 2000): A copy of the Charter is available at the European Parliament website at http://.europarl.europa.eu/charter/default_en.htm, accessed on 1 October 2008: see also Europe Alive at www.robert-schuman.org/breve.php?num+4515&typ=art, accessed on 1 October 2008.

9. Until the treaty of Lisbon is adopted by all 27 member states.

10. Robbers, 'State and Church in the European Union' in Robbers (ed), *State and Church in the European Union* (Nomos, 2005) p 580–581.

11. Treaty establishing a Constitution for Europe, Official Journal, C 310 of 16 December 2004 adopted by consensus by the European Convention on 13 June and 10 July 2003, Arts 1–7.

2. The Union equally respects the status of philosophical and non-confessional organisations.
3. Recognising their identity and their specific contribution, the Union shall maintain an open, transparent and regular dialogue with these churches and organisations.[12]

Even though the above provisions (1–3 of Art 1.51) failed to achieve a constitutional status, because the EU Constitution was not adopted, they are nonetheless binding constitutional law because their original status still stands as Declaration No 11 of the Final Act in the Amsterdam Treaty. Accordingly, the churches are recognised in EU law as entities of Community law, and the competences of the member states are currently respected in regard to the churches and not prejudiced. Furthermore, the contribution of the churches is recognised and provision is also made for dialogue which is 'open, transparent and regular'. As the EU evolves, this will most likely become an established feature of the general framework, which will introduce greater flexibility into relations with the churches.

[3.005] When the ECJ ruled in *Prais v Council*[13] that freedom of religion was a fundamental principle of European law, the foundation stone was laid, so to speak, for the religious identity of the Union. This case arose out of circumstances in which the Jewish applicant for a position as a translator with the EC Council was required to sit a test on a Jewish festival (Shavuot or Pentecost), during which it is not permitted to travel or to write. Vivien Prais notified the Council of her conscientious difficulties after the date for the test had been fixed, and the other candidates had already been convoked. The Council, however, refused to change the test date and Ms Prais then sued them. The plaintiff alleged that, because the defendant refused her request, by reason of her religious convictions, she was prevented from taking part in the competition, although staff regulations (Art 27) expressly provided that officials were to be selected without reference to race, creed or sex. Furthermore, the plaintiff claimed that religious discrimination was prohibited by Community law, as being contrary to the fundamental rights of the individual, respect for which the court was bound to ensure. In addition, the plaintiff relied on Art 9.2 of the ECHR being the right to manifest one's religion or beliefs, subject only to such limitations as are prescribed by law and are necessary in a democratic society in the interests of public safety, for the protection of public order, health or morals, or for the protections of the

12. Official Journal, C 340, 10/11/1997, p 133.

13. *Prais v Council* C–130/75 [1976] ECR 1589.

rights and freedoms of others. The plaintiff contended that since the ECHR had been ratified by all the member states, the rights enshrined in it were to be regarded as included in the fundamental rights to be protected by Community law. Accordingly, she claimed that Art 27 of the staff regulations was to be interpreted so as to require the Council to arrange the date of tests for the positions to enter its service which would enable every candidate to participate in the tests, whatever his or her religious circumstances, or in the alternative, that the right of freedom of religion guaranteed by the Convention requires this.

[3.006] The ECJ considered that it is of great importance that the date of the written tests should be the same for all candidates but the interests of participants not to have a date fixed for the test which is unsuitable for them must be balanced against this necessity. If a candidate fails to inform an appointing authority in good time of his or her difficulties, the appointing authority would be justified in refusing to afford an alternative date, particularly if there are other candidates who have been convoked for the test. It is desirable, the court continued, that an appointing authority informs itself generally of dates which might be unsuitable for religious reasons, and seeks to avoid fixing such dates for tests. However, neither staff regulations nor the said fundamental rights can be considered to impose on the appointing authority a duty to avoid a conflict with a religious requirement of which the authority has not been informed. In the instant case, in so far as the defendant, if informed of the difficulty in good time, would have been obliged to take reasonable steps to avoid fixing for a test a date which would make it impossible for a person of a particular religious persuasion to undergo the test, it can be said that the defendant was not informed of the unsuitability of certain days until the date for the test had in fact been fixed. Accordingly, the defendant was in its discretion entitled to refuse to fix a different date when the other candidates had been convoked. This carefully balanced decision is of pivotal importance as it demonstrates the extent to which the court was prepared to go in order to protect the freedom of religion principle. The court ruled that the Community and its institutions cannot interfere with the rights of an individual to practice his or her religion to the degree that it constitutes religious discrimination. This was one of the earliest cases to make reference to the ECHR and it was the first case in which religion entered into the ECJ's jurisprudence.

LEGAL STRUCTURES OF THE EU

[3.007] Common legal principles, deriving from Community Law, increasingly bind the member states. Respect for human rights and fundamental freedoms are values shared by all member states as Art 6.2 EC indicates:

> The Union shall respect fundamental rights, as guaranteed by the European Convention for the Protection of Human Rights and Fundamental Freedoms signed in Rome on 4 November 1950 and as they result from the constitutional traditions common to the member states, as general principles of community law.

The right to self-determination of the churches finds its genesis in the freedom of religious principle which was first recognised by the European Court of Justice (ECJ) in *Prais v Council*, as discussed above.[14] Article 6.2 EU respects the fundamental rights as guaranteed by the ECHR and arising from the common constitutional traditions of the member states as general principles of Community law. Article 9 of the ECHR protects freedom of thought, conscience and religion both as an individual right and as a right of communities. Both the churches and religious communities have a right of complaint before the ECHR if they have a claim to being damaged in their rights pursuant to Art 9 of the Convention.[15]

[3.008] The principle of subsidiarity[16] acts as a constraint on Community action in the law on religion in the member states. In particular Art 5 restrains such action, by providing that, in all areas which do not fall within its exclusive competence, the Community shall take action in accordance with the principle of subsidiarity only if and so far as the objects of the proposed action cannot adequately be achieved by the member states, or because of their scale or effects can be achieved better at Community level.[17] Accordingly, if the objects of the proposed action can adequately be achieved at the level of the member states, then the states ought to be given the right and the opportunity to achieve those objects.

---

14. *Prais v Council* C–130/75 [1976] ECR 1589.
15. Robbers (ed), *State and Church in the European Union* (Nomos, 2005) p 583.
16. See further Glendenning, *Education and the Law*, [1.13], [2.48], [2.86], [3.22], [3.41], [3.64], [3.126], [4.50], [4.71], [6.10], [6.24].
17. Art A 3B of the EC Treaty and Art B of the TEU, and the Official Journal of the EC, C 325/42, 24 December 2002.

[3.009] In Art 6.2 EU Constitutional traditions common to the member states, are recognised as general principles of Community law[18] and this establishes a basis in Community law for the development of the law relating to religion in the member states. In all European countries, the freedom of religion principle is recognised and the churches have institutional autonomy within the rule of law and they play an important role, *inter alia,* in private education and in publicly-funded education, with the exception of France, where the secular principle prevails in the public schools generally speaking.[19]

[3.010] Article 6.3 EU provides that the Union shall respect the national identity of the member states. In Art 151 EC,[20] the common cultural heritage of Europe is recognised. Indeed, the Community itself contributes to the evolution of the cultures of the member states, while protecting their national and regional diversity. Cultural competences indicate the categories of culture envisaged in Art 151, which includes research and education and general and professional education. Nonetheless, the concept of culture enshrined in Art 151 appears somewhat shallow. Community competences for professional and general education may also arise from Art 149 EC. As Robbers points out, in this manner all church educational institutions, for example, private schools, theological faculties and church academies together with religious education classes, derive support from Community law.[21] In accordance with Art 307 EC the rights and obligations arising out of those treaties, made between one or more states and one or more third countries, prior to the coming into force of the EC Treaty on 1 January 1958, are not affected by the provisions of the EC Treaty, or in the case of acceding states, before the date of their accession. It would appear, therefore, that the concordats made in a number of countries with the Holy See are protected by Art 307 EC. Robbers makes the point that, pursuant to Art 300 EC read together with Arts 282 EC and 308 EC and the general principle of equality, the Union can conclude treaties with other states:

> The clearer the implications of Community law for the position of the religious communities become, the more it becomes reasonable to take this possibility of contractual regulation into consideration.[22]

---

18. OJ C 325/5.

19. For the position in state schools in Alsace-Moselle and in the private schools in France, see **para [7.031]** below.

20. Renumbered following the Treaty of Amsterdam.

21. Robbers (ed), *State and Church in the European Union* (Nomos, 2005) p 584–5.

22. Robbers, *State and Church in the European Union* p 585.

Such provisions have considerable potential for the development of contractual arrangements between the states in the future.

[3.011] When it comes to the interface of the various churches with EU law in the employment sphere, complex issues may arise as is well illustrated by the *Baghwan* case.[23] In this decision, the ECJ held that Art 2 EC must be interpreted as meaning that activities performed by a member of a community based on religion or other philosophy, as part of the activities of the community, constitute economic activities within the EU.[24] Thus, paid labour and services delivered in the setting of economic activity of the religious community can be considered as part of the economic life within the framework of EU law. In *van Rosmaalen v Bestuir van de Betrijfsvereinigingen*[25] the ECJ defined self-employment as genuine and effective economic activity when performed outside a relationship of subordination. As a result, a missionary priest in Zaire, who had for many years been maintained by the members of his missionary community rather than by his religious order, was held by the court to be self-employed under Community law, and accordingly he was entitled to receive a pension in line with the laws of the member state.

Specific Protection of Religious Autonomy

[3.012] Apart from places of worship, such as churches and mosques, collective religious liberties may be given expression in a number of social contexts such as schools, hospitals or adoption agencies. Many of these institutions employ large numbers of staff and they are frequently state-funded. In particular, Germany and Ireland[26] have traditionally conferred considerable autonomy on the churches[27] in social spheres. A pivotal issue is whether and/or to what extent such bodies are entitled to select for employment solely those persons who share in their religious faith and

23. Case 196/87 [1988] ECR, p 6159.

24. However, when the person leaves the member state and goes to another member state, Arts 59 EC and 60 EC do not apply.

25. *van Rosmaalen v Bestuir van de Betrijfsvereinigingen* [1986] ECR, p 3097.

26. See further **para [9.010]** below.

27. In Germany this autonomy has been conferred on the Protestant and Catholic Churches because of this special legal status as public corporations, see further **para [6.015]**.

convictions. An analogous issue is whether, and/or to what extent the religious employer may determine that the conduct, private life and example of their employee must reflect the religious employer's ethos or characteristic spirit. In practical terms, such issues are normally dealt with through the implementation of legal protections or exemptions from the binding obligations under the law.[28] There is a clear conflict here between the rights of the religious employer to associate with others of like faith and to promote its ethos, and the rights of the individual to equality and not to be subjected to discrimination.[29] In the US, it has been held by the Supreme Court in *Boy Scouts of America v Dale* that freedom to associate with others of like mind includes within its compass the right to exclude others who do not share in the beliefs at issue.[30] As Ahdar and Leigh point out, a variety of limiting strategies may be employed to protect collective religious liberty for religious bodies in the liberal state in the face of claims taken by employees, or office-holders under anti-discrimination legislation, but the underlying issue is 'the extent to which any exceptions or exemptions are framed and applied by the courts to allow space for religious pluralism.'[31] The coming into effect of the employment equality Directives marked a huge step forward in the social policy sphere for Community law in the member states, but these measures have not been unattended by controversy.

(i) Protecting Religion through Anti-Discrimination Legislation

[3.013] The Treaty of Amsterdam was approved unanimously by the member states in 1997. Article 13 of that Treaty granted the Community additional powers to combat discrimination which gave rise to two new Directives which aimed to implement the non-discrimination principles across the EU. These Directives, with their innovative approach, raise the status of the

28. Ahdar and Leigh, *Religious Freedom the Liberal State* p 308. See generally and **chapter 10** on Employment which contains a very useful analysis of this complex area of law.

29. Whyte, 'Protecting Religious Ethos in Employment Law: a Clash of Cultures', 27 DULJ 2005.

30. *Boy Scouts of America v Dale* 530 US 640 (2000). However, this case arises out of an entirely distinctive model of church-state separation to that pertaining in any EU member state.

31. **[10.038]** *et seq.*

principle of equality to a new level in EU law[32] and they are relevant to both religious freedom and freedom of education in the member states.

(a) Council Directive 2000/43/EC (the Race Directive) implements the provision of equal treatment irrespective of racial and social origin in relation to, *inter alia,* education; and the churches

(b) Council Directive 2000/78/EC (The Framework Directive) establishes a general framework for equal treatment in employment and occupation in relation to, *inter alia*, the churches and in education and training.

A. The Race Directive

[3.014] The Race Directive has a much wider scope than the Framework Directive and it bears some relevance to the issue of religion and education. As well as prohibiting direct and indirect racial and ethnic discrimination in employment and occupation, it also applies to the provision of goods and services[33] by private and public sectors, which includes education.[34] In view of the fact that the ECJ has few precedents relating to religious or racial discrimination, the court may well draw upon the established case law of other member states as an aide to the interpretation of the non-discrimination Directives. Riley is of the view that considerable weight will be attached to British case law, and particularly the decisions of the House of

---

32. See further Thusing, 'Following the US example: European employment discrimination law and the impact of Council Directive 2000/43/EC and Directive 2000/78/EC', *International Journal of Comparative Labour Law and Industrial Relations*, vol 19, pp 187–218 and O'Hare, 'Enhancing European Equality Rights: a New Regional Framework', *Maastricht Journal of European and Comparative Law*, vol 8, p 144.

33. Arguably, if education is publicly-funded, then it is a public service, even if delivered in a privately-owned school.

34. Although this point is uncertain since the Community general competence to legislate in this sphere is open to doubt. Article 149(4) expressly excludes harmonisation in the area of education. There is, however, an alternative view that Art 13 confers on the Community express jurisdiction in regard to discrimination issues, and to this extent acts a *lex specialis.* See Riley, 'Headscarves, skull caps and crosses: Is the proposed French ban safe from European legal challenge?' available to download at http://www.muslim-lawyers.net/news/index.php3?aktion=show&number=248, accessed on 1 October 2008.

Lords, since the UK has the most developed case law of all member states,[35] although racial discrimination cases are surprisingly rare.[36] However, the phrase 'race or ethnic origin' can be expanded through judicial activism so to protect religious groups who share the same racial or ethnic origins.[37] It should be said that England's approach in bringing ethnic origins (specifically Jews, Sikhs and Muslims) within the scope of indirect discrimination under the Race Relations Act 1976 is a fine example of judicial creativity which is exemplified in the following cases.[38]

[3.015] The main significance of the judgment in *Mandla v Dowell Lee*[39] was the court's finding that the protection provided by the Race Relations Act 1976 could be extended to embrace certain religious categories defined by ethnic origins and that Sikhs and Jews fall within that definition. In this case the school was held to have indirectly discriminated against a Sikh pupil who attended his private school while wearing his turban, which was contrary to the school rules. When considering the term 'ethnic origin', the court took into account, among other factors, whether the group had a common religion different from neighbouring groups or from the local community, and the fact of being a minority, or of being an oppressed or a dominant group within a wider community. However, the case also points up how indirect discrimination can arise when school rules are enforced without due regard to the cultural norms and values of minorities in schools, a lesson that has also been learned in Canada, in relation to the wearing of the kirpan by a Sikh student in a Canadian school.[40]

[3.016] In another English case, *Walker v Hussain,*[41] the court found that 17 Muslims had suffered indirect racial discrimination as their case fell within s 57(3) of the Race Relations Act 1976. The workers had taken a day off for Eid which the court compared to Christmas day among Christians. When

---

35. Riley, 'Headscarves, skull caps and crosses: Is the proposed French ban safe from European legal challenge?' available to download at http://www.muslim-lawyers.net/news/index.php3?aktion=show&number=248 p 2, accessed on 1 October 2008.

36. Harris, *Education, Law and Diversity* p 154.

37. Harris, *Education, Law and Diversity* p 154.

38. *Mandla v Dowell Lee* (1983) 2 AC 548: *Walker v Hussain* [1996] ICR 291.

39. *Mandla v Dowell Lee* (1983) 2 AC 548.

40. See **para [10.038]**.

41. *Walker v Hussain* [1996] ICR 291.

they returned to work they were disciplined and given a final warning. The Employment Appeals Tribunal found that they did not fall within the ambit of the Race Relations Act 1976 but the court reversed that finding. This creative approach to the expansion of anti-discrimination legislation to include distinct ethnic origins has substantially expanded the scope and protection of the Race Relations Act 1976.

B. The Framework Directive

[3.017] By contrast with the Race Directive, the Framework Directive has a narrow scope, applying only to employment and occupation and vocational courses. The Framework Directive implements the principle of equal treatment in employment and occupation irrespective of religion and belief, disability, age or sexual orientation in employment, training and membership and involvement in organisations of workers and employers. The Directive extends to conditions for access to employment, working conditions, remuneration and dismissals. Since it includes vocational training, it extends to vocational courses given in schools and colleges. It prohibits direct and indirect discrimination on the specified grounds. With regard to the religion and belief ground, the Framework Directive allows for limited exceptions to the principle of equal treatment, for example, where the ethos of a religious organisation needs to be preserved. Para 23 of the Directive provides:

> In very limited circumstances, a difference of treatment may be justified where a characteristic relating to religion or belief, disability, age or sexual orientation constitutes a genuine and determining occupational requirement, when the objective is legitimate and the requirement is proportionate. Such circumstances should be included in the information provided by the member states to the Commission

Thus, 'in very limited circumstances', a difference of treatment may be justified, where a characteristic relating to religion or belief constitutes a genuine and determining, proportionate, occupational requirement. Such limited circumstances include particular circumstances in which philosophical or ideological characteristics may justify a difference in treatment. Notwithstanding the prohibition as set out in the Framework Directive, member states may provide:

> that a difference of treatment which is based on a characteristic related to any of the grounds referred to in art. 1 shall not constitute discrimination where, by reason of the nature of the particular occupational activities concerned or of the context in which they are carried out, such a characteristic constitutes a

genuine and determining occupational requirement, provided that the objective is legitimate and the requirement is proportionate.

[3.018] A potential sphere of exception is envisaged by Art 4(2) and (3) of the Framework Directive which is germane to the churches and religious schools, the text of which provides:

> 4.2 Member states may maintain national legislation in force at the date of adoption of this Directive or provide for future legislation incorporating national practices existing at the date of adoption of this Directive pursuant to which, in the case of occupational activities within churches or other public or private organisations the ethos of which is based on religion or belief, a difference of treatment based on a person's religion or belief shall not constitute discrimination where, by reason of the nature of these activities or of the context in which they are carried out, a person's religion or belief constitute a genuine, legitimate and justified occupational requirement, having regard to the organisation's ethos. This difference of treatment shall be implemented taking account of member states' constitutional provisions and principles, as well as the general principles of Community law, and should not justify discrimination on another ground.
>
> 4.3 Provided that its provisions are otherwise complied with, this Directive shall thus not prejudice the right of the churches or other public or private organisations, the ethos of which is based on religion or belief, acting in conformity with national constitutions and laws, to require individuals working for them to act in good faith and with loyalty to the organisation's ethos.

Article 4(2) and (3) expressly leave open the possibility in occupational activities within churches and other public or private organisations, which have an ethos based on religion or belief, (eg schools), for treatment based on the religious identity and ethos of the organisation, when recruiting personnel for such organisations. But this exemption is not open-ended: it only operates when the potential employee's religion or belief constitutes 'a genuine, legitimate and justified occupational requirement, having regard to the organisation's ethos.'

Applying the Framework Directive: the Religion Ground

[3.019] Since only existing arrangements or practices fall within the Directive's ambit, the point of departure concerning the application of Art 4(2) is whether, at the date of the adoption of the Framework Directive, a national practice or legislation already existed in the member state which accorded with its national laws and constitution. Because the 'justified occupational requirement' is not restricted to express characteristics of a function to be exercised, it extends to the wider context. Thus, wider contextual factors might include:

(i) the relevance of the religion in question;

(ii) its values, norms or ethos as expressed in the institution's foundational documents;

(iii) the vigour with which that ethos is asserted and promoted in practice in the institution; and

(iv) the general context in which the ethos or characteristic spirit is exercised in practice.

When discussing the impact of the Framework Directive in Germany, where the traditional autonomy of the Protestant and Catholic ChurchCatholic Churches from state regulation is a significant feature of the German law, Joussen[42] and Reichold[43] hold that the Directive contains sufficient flexibility to protect church autonomy. Referring to the obligation on employees 'to act in good faith and with loyalty to the organisation's ethos,' both authors interpret the Directive as meaning that churches can still require their main employees to be members of the relevant church. Furthermore, they consider that the 'good faith' requirement in Art 4(2) gives reassurance to the churches that they can impose heightened loyalty duties on their employees.

[3.020] Reichold contends that the exemptions should be interpreted broadly and that this would permit the loyalty requirement to be extended to other employees such as cooks, cleaners, or nurses employed by religious

---

42. Joussen, '*Die Folgen de Europaischen Diskriminierungsverbote für das kirchliche Arbeitsrecht*' [Consequences of the European prohibitions of discrimination for church specific employment law] (2003) *Reic der Arbeit, pp* 32–39, cited in English in *Critical Review of Academic Literature relating to the EU Directives to Combat Discrimination*, Employment and Social Affairs, EU Commission, July 2004, p 17. Available online at http://www. eu.europe.eu, accessed on 1 October 2008.

43. Reichold, 'Europarecht und das kirchliche Arbeitsrecht', [European law and church specific employment law] (2001) *Neue Zeitschrift für Arbeitsrecht pp* 1054–1060 cited in English in *Critical Review of Academic Literature relating to the EU Directives to Combat Discrimination*, Employment and Social Affairs, EU Commission, July 2004, p 17. Available online at http://www. eu.europe.eu, accessed on 1 October 2008.

organisations. Furthermore, he concludes that dismissal on the grounds of overt homosexuality could be justified under the Directive.[44] By contrast, Joussen[45] is of the view that the Directive would not permit dismissal on the sole ground of sexual orientation[46] which is likely to be the correct conclusion. Clearly, the discrimination on the ground of religion will only be upheld provided it does not constitute discrimination on any other ground. Kimber argues that a broad interpretation of this 'good faith' obligation could result in violations of an individual's right to private life. Yet, she also observes that a narrow reading of Art 4(2) could breach the freedom of religion principle in regard to the churches.[47] It will be for the ECJ to balance and reconcile these competing interests and when doing so, it is likely to be influenced by similar cases from the jurisprudence of the member states.

[3.021] One case of considerable significance is that of *Fereshta Ludin*[48] in which the German Constitutional Court weighed two significant constitutional principles: the freedom of religion principle and principle of neutrality in public institutions. The court had already ruled on laws relating to religious freedom, when it upheld the right of a Turkish woman in her position as a sales assistant in a big department store to wear the Islamic headscarf at work. But in *Ludin*, the court distinguished the *locus* in which the headscarf had been worn and the fact that Ms Ludin was a civil servant working in the context of a public school. In a 3:2 decision, the court stated that a business did not bear the burden of religious neutrality required in schools or other state institutions. The court's decision that Ms Ludin could

44. Reichold, 'Europarecht und das kirchliche Arbeitsrecht', [European law and church specific employment law] (2001) *Neue Zeitschrift für Arbeitsrecht* pp 1054–1060.

45. Joussen, 'Die Folgen de Europaischen Diskriminierungsverbote *für* das kirchliche Arbeitsrecht' [Consequences of the European prohibitions of discrimination for church specific employment law] (2003) *Reic der Arbeit, pp* 32–39, cited in English in *Critical Review of Academic Literature relating to the EU Directives to Combat Discrimination*, Employment and Social Affairs, EU Commission, July 2004, p 17. Available online at http://www. eu.europe.eu, accessed on 1 October 2008.

46. See the position arising under *Boy Scouts of America* case in **para [10.055]**.

47. Kimber, 'Recent Developments in EC Equality Law', in Lucey and Keville, *Irish Perspectives on EC Law* (Round Hall Press, 2003) pp 291–317.

48. BverG, 2BvR 1436/02.

wear her headscarf because the state of Baden-Wuerttemberg, which refused to employ her as a teacher in 1998, had no legislation providing for this issue. In addition, the court pointed out the pivotal distinction between religious symbols placed on public property by order of the state, and the state's toleration of the personal decision of a person to wear a religious symbol herself.[49] This case in discussed further at **[6.014]**. At this juncture, it is sufficient to observe that the principle of freedom of religion and the principle of secularity and state neutrality were well ventilated, so to speak, by the German court in the *Ludin* case and that the ECJ is likely to draw on this landmark decision when considering germane cases in the future.

Because of the wide sweep of the EC equality and non-discrimination legislation, their effect is now being experienced across the member states as national laws align their laws with the Directives. In England, specifically with regard to the adoption and fostering of children, the religious communities (Christian, Jewish and Muslim) have collectively objected to the Equality Regulations 2003[50] which they claim are forcing them to abandon long-established practices.[51] More recently, the Catholic Church in Ireland has expressed concerns that the long-established ethos of its nationwide network of Catholic schools may be at risk of being curtailed by the impact of the employment equality Directives.[52] Germany has been under pressure from the Commission to align its marriage laws with the Directives by introducing same-sex marriage while Spain has experienced difficulties regarding its competition laws which favour, in some respects, the Catholic Church.

[3.022] While the academic literature acknowledges that the Directives contribute substantially to equality and non-discrimination in the member states, it also focuses on the tensions that can arise with other human rights, including the right to privacy, freedom of religion, or freedom of association.[53] Dollat points to the need for a dialogue between the ECJ and

49. BverG, 2BvR 1436/02, see further, Mattias Mahlmann, 'Religious Tolerance, Pluralist Society and the Neutrality of the State: The Federal Constitutional Court's Decision in the Headscarf case', *German Law Journal,* Vol 4, No 11.

50. Employment Equality (Religion or Belief) Regulations 2003 (SI 1660/03) UK.

51. See **chapter 5**.

52. http://www.irishtimes.com/newspaper/ireland/2008/0405/1207332821483.html, accessed on 1 October 2008.

53. *Critical Review of Academic Literature relating to the EU Directives to Combat Discrimination*, Employment and Social Affairs, EU Commission, July 2004.

the ECtHR so as to avoid conflicts emerging in the interpretation of the right to non-discrimination.[54] As will be seen in **chapter 4** below, some ambiguity is apparent in human rights jurisprudence arising out of the fact that the ECtHR has declared that the plurality principle and the principle of secularism are both upholding principles of a democratic society. As is argued in the following chapter, there is an inherent contradiction in upholding both principles which needs to be reconciled by the ECtHR. Undoubtedly, a clear recognition of the human rights dimension to non-discrimination law of the EU will be an important requirement for the future harmonious development of the law in this sphere. A number of authors have argued that the 'reasonable accommodation' principle included in the Framework Directive for people with disabilities could have been usefully applied to other grounds, including the religion ground.[55] In the opinion of the author, this could have facilitated a greater flexibility regarding the application of the Directive, when dealing with religiously-sensitive issues and the churches, particularly in countries whose ecclesiastical law maintains closer church-state relations in education and in health than the European norm. One issue of considerable public debate, arising from the controversy surrounding the publication of caricatures of the Prophet Muhammad in 2006, was the right to offend within the law and the parameters of that right.

Respecting Religion

A Offending within the Law

[3.023] While tolerance and respect for the feelings and beliefs of others is most desirable in any civilised society, the right to give offence within the parameters of the law is also a right protected by Western democracies in their laws and constitutions and by the ECHR.[56] Must those of the Islamic

54. Dollat, '*Vers la reconnaissance generalisé du principe de l'égalité de traitement entre les personnes dans l'Union Europeénne*,' *Journal de Tribunaux,* No 87, pp 57–65.

55. *Critical Review of Academic Literature relating to the EU Directives to Combat Discrimination*, Employment and Social Affairs, EU Commission, July 2004 p 6 citing Thusing, and Bell and Waddington, 'Reflecting on Inequalities in European Equality Law,' *European Law Review*, 2003, vol 8, p 144.

56. See Art 10 of the ECHR, also *Handyside v UK* (1976) 1 EHRR 737: and in re significance of political speech, *Lingens v Austria* (1986) 8 EHRR 407.

faith and others, who have chosen to live in the EU, accept the established norms and values of the host country in public life, or should western democracies, in the interest of world peace and tolerance, set stricter legal limits to freedom of speech and press freedoms when it intends to incite hatred or racism or to ridicule religion?[57] In England, there was a decision concerning Salman Rushdie's book *The Satanic Verses*, where a magistrate refused to grant a summons against Rushdie and his publisher for alleged blasphemous and seditious libel. The Chief Magistrate found that Rushdie's book was neither blasphemous nor a seditious libel.

[3.024] When judicial review of this decision was sought in *R v Bow Street Magistrates Court, Ex parte Choudhury*, it was rejected by the Queen's Bench Divisional Court, which held that the common law offence of blasphemous libel only extended to Christianity.[58] In its single judgment, delivered by Watkins LJ, the court stated: 'the mere fact that the law is anomalous or unjust does not in our view justify the court in changing it ...'. Accordingly, the court affirmed that the law as it then stood did not extend to religions other than Christianity.[59] In the context of England's celebrated tolerance of religious diversity, this remarkably restrictive decision failed to expand the protection of the common law to any category of religion other than Christianity or to align, update the law with the ethnic, cultural and religiously diverse society of 1990s England. This anachronistic decision lacked the dynamic which enables creative judicial interpretation to reconcile and harmonise the law with modern conditions and exigencies. Moreover, it failed to take account of well-founded international human rights and religious freedoms, and particularly Art 9 of the ECHR, which are considered in **chapter 4** below. The *Choudhury* decision promoted

57. In England see Racial and Religious Hatred Act 2006 which makes provision for the prosecution of offences involving stirring up hatred against persons on racial or religious grounds, which amends the Public Order Act 1986. In Ireland see Prohibition of Incitement to Hatred Act 1989; Art 40.6.1°(i) of the Constitution of Ireland; *Conway v Independent Newspapers (Ireland) Limited* [2000] 1 IRLM 426 and Law Reform Commission's Report on the Crime of Libel (LRC 41–1991)**:** see Joint Committee on the Constitution, First Report, Art 40.6.1°(i), Freedom of Expression, July 2008, with regard to the position in Spain, see Iban, 'State and Church in Spain in Robbers (ed), *State and Church in the European Union* (Nomos, 2005) 139 at p 154.

58. *R v Bow Street Magistrates Court* (1991) 91 Crim Appeal r 393; also *Times Law Reports*, 10 April, 1990.

59. *R v Bow Street Magistrates Court* (1991) 91 Crim Appeal r 393.

considerable controversy in its wake, and led to further discord between the Muslim and non-Muslim community in England and further afield.[60] One may conclude, therefore, that the *Choudhury* decision was indeed a lost opportunity[61] to extend the protection the law afforded to others to all religions and none. Some five years after the *R v Bow* decision, the Incitement to Hatred Act 2006 was enacted, most of which came into force on 1 October 2007 and the Criminal Justice and Immigration Act 2008 abolished the common law offences of blasphemy and blasphemous libel and introduced a new criminal offence of incitement to hatred on the grounds of sexual orientation. Spain and Sweden also deal with such issues under the Criminal Code.

B Remedies Under The Criminal Law

[3.025] Chapter XXI of the Spanish Criminal Code (Crimes against the Constitution) contains one section which is headed 'Crimes against the freedom of conscience, religious sentiments and respect for the deceased' (Arts 522–526). These Articles classify the following as crimes: the public ridicule of religious sentiments, the violation of tombs, offending religious sentiments in places of worship, impeding religious acts, disturbing religious acts of 'registered religious communities' and forcing the practice of religious acts.[62] Furthermore, the fact that discriminatory treatment might arise from religious motives is considered by the criminal legislator to constitute aggravation.[63] Articles 510.1 and 510.2 of the Spanish Criminal Code prohibit as a crime incitement to discrimination, hatred and violence on racist, anti-Semetic, ethnic or racial grounds as well as, *inter alia*, on grounds relating to ideology, religion and beliefs.[64]

---

60. See Tregilgas-Davey, '*Ex parte Choudbury* – An Opportunity Missed', *The Modern Law Review,* Vol 54, No 2, pp 294–299.

61. See Tregilgas-Davey, '*Ex parte Choudbury* – An Opportunity Missed', *The Modern Law Review,* Vol 54, No 2, pp 294–299

62. Iban, 'State and Church in Spain', Robbers (ed), *State and Church in the European Union* (Nomos, 2005) pp 139–155, 154. It should be noted, however, that this book was published in 2005 and that legislation is always 'on the move' and may have been altered or amended since then.

63. Iban, 'State and Church in Spain', Robbers (ed), *State and Church in the European Union* (Nomos, 2005) pp 139–155, 154.

64. See further http://www.legislationonline.org.

[3.026] Chapter 16 of the Swedish Criminal Code provides that a person becomes guilty of agitation against a group by making a statement or otherwise spreads a message that threatens or expresses contempt for an ethnic group or any other group of people with reference to their race, skin colour, nationality or ethnic origin, religious belief or sexual orientation. This Act was amended on 1 January 2003 to criminalise incitement against homosexuals as a group.[65] The 2003 amendment was intended to satisfy the requirements regarding the restrictions of freedom of speech, based on Swedish constitutional protection of this right, as well as the requirements of the ECHR.[66]

[3.027] In July 2003 Pastor Ake Green preached a sermon[67] to approximately 50 people in a Swedish church concerning homosexuality stating, *inter alia*, that: 'The Bible discusses and teaches us about these abnormalities. And sexual abnormalities are a serious cancerous growth on the body of a society.' Pastor Green was prosecuted under chapter 16 of the Criminal Code as amended and given a sentence of one month in prison which was suspended. When the matter reached the Supreme Court on appeal from the Court of Criminal Appeal, the court reviewed the said domestic legislation which fits within the limits set forth in the ECHR and concluded that the question was, whether applying these provisions in the instant case would violate Sweden's commitments under the Convention. Accordingly, the court considered the germane case law of the ECHR and in particular the scope and application of Art 9 and the cases of *Kokkinakis v Greece*[68] and *Gundiz v Turkey*[69] and it concluded that the determining factor was whether the restriction of Ake Green's freedom to preach was necessary in a democratic society.

65. The *Travaux Preparatoires* of the ECHR pointed out that homosexuals are a vulnerable societal group and are frequently victims of crime as a result of their sexual orientation and that Nazis and other groups targeted them and interlinked them with racist and anti-Semitic campaigns, see *Prosecutor General v Ake Green*, Judgment of Supreme Court of Sweden, Issued 29 November 2005, p 4. http://www.domstol.se/Domstolar/hogstadomstolen/Avgoranden/2005/Dom_pa_engelska_B_1050-05.pdf, accessed on 1 October 2008. The court was citing from the Swedish Government's Bill 2001/02: 59, p 32 *et seq*.

66. Freedoms (Government) Bill 2001/02: 59, 34 *et seq*.

67. The sermon was entitled 'Is homosexuality congenital or the powers of evil meddling with the people?'

68. *Kokkinakis v Greece* (1994) 17 EHRR 397.

69. *Gundiz v Turkey* Reports of Judgments and Decisions, 2003–XI, p 229.

[3.028] It was necessary, the court considered, to assess whether the restriction was proportionate to the protected interest and it noted the 'certain flexibility' or margin of appreciation accorded the signatory state in such instances.[70] The court reviewed the case law of the ECHR in regard to Art 10 (freedom of expression), and in particular *Handyside v UK*.[71] The court noted that when the ECHR determines whether the restriction imposed meets 'a pressing social need', it goes on to determine whether it is 'proportionate to the legitimate purpose to be achieved', and whether the reasons asserted by the national authorities are 'relevant and sufficient'.[72] While the court concluded that Pastor Green's sermon must be viewed as 'extreme', nonetheless, he made his statements in a sermon to his congregation regarding a theme found in the Bible.[73] Moreover, the legitimacy of Green's beliefs, on which he based his sermon, would not be considered by the ECHR.[74] Under these circumstances, the court concluded that it was most likely that the ECtHR, in a determination of the restriction of Pastor Green's right to preach his Biblically-based sermon, would find that this restriction was not proportionate, and that it would, therefore, be a violation of the Convention. In the light of the above the court decided to dismiss the indictment of Ake Green. Possibly the most significant aspect of this judgment is that the Swedish Supreme Court saw the Swedish Constitution as posing no threat to Green's prosecution, but that it, nonetheless, proceeded to judge the issue almost entirely on its perception of how Green would be judged before the ECtHR. If other countries adopt a similar approach in the future, then it is easy to see how the decisions of the ECtHR will influence the jurisprudence in the member states, a matter which is discussed further in **chapter 4** below.

The ECJ and the Principle of Secularism

[3.029] Because of the lack of precedents in this sphere, it is unclear how the ECJ will approach the principle of secularism when deciding cases which come before it. Undoubtedly, the court will put the secular principle under

70. *Prosecutor General v Ake Green*, p 12.

71. *Handyside v UK* 1979 1 EHRR 737.

72. *Sunday Times v UK* Series A, No 30, judgment of 26 April 1979, p 62.

73. *Prosecutor General v Ake Green*, http://www.domstol.se/Domstolar/hogstadomstolen/Avgoranden/2005/Dom_pa_engelska_B_1050-05.pdf, accessed on 1 October 2008.

74. *Manoussakis v Greece* (1996) 23 EHRR 387.

intense scrutiny and severe assessment. Clearly, the ECHR protects religious freedom to a much lesser extent than Community law, since it permits 'a margin of appreciation' for the member states, when considering what state interferences are justifiable under the Convention. Again, by contrast with the ECHR, EU law demands strict objective justification of interference with established rights such as religious freedom. While a direct challenge under the Framework Directive could be mounted to the legislative ban on 'conspicuous religious symbols' in the Law of 2004, the ambit of that Directive would restrict any such challenge to schools and colleges providing vocational courses or vocational training.

[3.030] On the other hand, some potent grounds exist for contending that 'race or ethnic origin' can be applied by the court to protect religious groups who share the same or similar ethnic origins. For example, the secular principle is not universally applied in France, so to some degree France has breached its own secularist principle.[75] Traditionally, France has exempted the Alsace-Moselle region from the requirement to implement the secularist principle in its state-funded public schools, for historical reasons discussed in **chapter 7**. In this region, the state funds public religious schools directly. If the Alsace-Moselle public schools are accorded this right, it can be argued that all other public school students throughout France, who are being adversely affected by the legislative ban on conspicuous religious symbols, are being discriminated against. Moreover, France has exempted the generously state-funded private school sector from the obligation to apply the secularist principle: in these predominantly Catholic schools religious instruction is taught and conspicuous religious symbols are permitted to be worn. The fact that France has made exceptions to the application of the secular principle, and permitted certain sectors to breach it, could make it more difficult for it to maintain that secularism is a legitimate aim capable of justifying the prohibition of conspicuous religious symbols in its diverse public schools.[76] However, the most potent argument against that contention arises from the fact that the partial ban in public schools, which the Law of

---

75. Riley, See Riley, 'Headscarves, skull caps and crosses: Is the proposed French ban safe from European legal challenge?' available to download at http://www.muslim-lawyers.net/news/index.php3?aktion=show&number=248, p 2, accessed on 1 October 2008.

76. Riley, See Riley, 'Headscarves, skull caps and crosses: Is the proposed French ban safe from European legal challenge?' available to download at http://www.muslim-lawyers.net/news/index.php3?aktion=show&number=248, accessed on 1 October 2008.

2004 imposes, while having the appearance of being neutral, extends to 'conspicuous religious symbols' only and that this ban mainly affects those of a certain class or religious tradition, those of the Muslim faith giving rise to indirect discrimination.

[3.031] When interpreting the secularist principle, the court is likely to take cognisance of its own jurisprudence in *Prais v Council*,[77] of the relevant case law of the ECHR, and in the International Covenant on Civil and Political Rights 1966 (ICCPR) and International Covenant on Economic, Social and Cultural Rights 1966 (ICESC), of the Charter and of the major cases in the jurisprudence of the member states. As has been seen, Community law has established that freedom of religion is a fundamental principle of the EU[78] and the ECJ requires strict, objective justification of any breaches of this established right.

The Charter of Fundamental Rights

[3.032] Considerable protection for religious freedom can be found in Art 10 of the Charter which provides:

> 1. Everyone has the right to freedom of thought, conscience and religion. This right includes freedom to change religion or belief and freedom, either alone or in community with others and in public or in private, to manifest religion or belief, in worship, teaching, practice and observance.
>
> 2. The right to conscientious objection is recognised, in accordance with the national laws governing the exercise of this right.

The Charter[79] needs to be viewed in the wider setting of the EU's well-established commitment to fundamental freedoms and human rights and its policy in the spheres of justice, freedom and security. The Treaty of Amsterdam (1997),[80] which came into operation on 1 May 1999, laid down procedures which were intended to secure the protection of these rights and freedoms.[81] Article 6 of the Charter reiterates that the EU is founded on the principles of liberty, democracy, respect for human rights and fundamental freedoms, and the rule of law, principles that are common to the member states. In Art 2 of the Charter, the Union undertakes to respect fundamental

77. *Prais v Council* C–130/75 [1976] ECR 1589.

78. *Prais v Council* C–130/75 [1976] ECR 1589.

79. A copy of the Charter is included in the **Appendix 9** of this book.

80. Which updated the Treaty of Maastricht.

81. Article 6 TEU; Art 7 TEU; Art 46 TEU and Art 49 TEU.

rights as guaranteed by the ECHR and as they result from the constitutional traditions common to the member states, as general principles of Community law. Art 6(2) provides for the accession of the EU to the ECHR. Article 6(3) concludes:

> Fundamental rights, as guaranteed by the ECHR and as they result from the constitutional traditions common to the member states shall constitute general principles of European law.

[3.033] Article 11 of the Charter guarantees freedom of expression and information while the following Article guarantees freedom of assembly and of association. In Art 14 the right to education is guaranteed together with access to vocational training:

> 1. Everyone has the right to education and to have access to vocational and continuing training.
>
> 2. This right includes the possibility to receive free compulsory education.
>
> 3. The freedom to found educational establishments with due respect for democratic principles and the right of parents to ensure the education and teaching of their children in conformity with their religious, philosophical and pedagogical convictions shall be respected, in accordance with the national laws governing the exercise of such freedom and right.

[3.034] Article 14 guarantees the right to education and the right to have access to vocational and continuing training. This right includes the possibility to receive free education. In essence the Charter sets down the fundamental rights, as its name indicates, of Europe's citizens including non-discrimination, equality, the right to life, the prohibition of torture, respect for private and family life, the right to an effective remedy and to a fair trial. In Art 22 of the Charter, the Union undertakes to respect cultural, religious and linguistic diversity. Poland has included a unilateral Declaration stating that:

> The Charter does not affect in any way the right of member states to legislate in the sphere of public morality, family law as well as the protection of human dignity and respect for human physical and moral integrity.

While the Charter has been taken into account by the ECJ and has been referred to, from time to time, in its case law as a source of inspiration or reference in much the same way as the ECHR, and has been referred to in various EU Directives, it will not have full legal effect until the Lisbon Treaty has been adopted by all 27 member states.

The European Union Agency for Fundamental Rights

[3.035] The European Union Agency for Fundamental Rights (the Agency) was established in Vienna in 2007 to provide relevant Community institutions and authorities with support and expertise when implementing Community law and taking appropriate action. The Agency will also collect germane data and foster dialogue with civil society in order to raise public awareness of fundamental rights.[82] Dialogue at all levels is central to advancing to an understanding of Community law and structures and on how they interface with the law of the member states. Some national governments have been accused of deliberately undermining the Agency by excluding major areas from its scrutiny thereby preventing it from investigating breaches of human rights perpetrated by state bodies. At a time when consolidating Europe puts its trust in human rights, democracy and the rule of law, concerns are being expressed that certain well-established religious or ideological freedoms may be at risk of being unduly curtailed, undermined, or eroded in sensitive social spheres such as adoption, divorce, abortion, euthanasia,[83] and religious education. Not surprisingly, these issues are of greater concern in the more conservatively religious countries such as Ireland and Poland, where Catholicism is the predominant religion, but it most likely also to be of concern to those of other faiths in Europe. Only open and constructive dialogue can dispel these concerns.

Significance of Churches in Europe for Social Cohesion

[3.036] Applying the principle of subsidiarity which is consistently recognised in the Treaties, Robbers is of the view that in the sphere of religious matters, a better achievement of objectives generally means that the needs of historically developed religious beliefs determined by national and regional circumstances, emotional ties and historical experience must be

---

82. The Agency replaces the European Monitoring Centre on Racism and Xenophobia. The Agency has just published its first report which indicates a rise in racist attacks in several member states of the EU. The scope of the FRA has been seriously restricted, however, by certain member states eg the UK and Ireland.

83. Hastings, 'Euthanasia is 'not a matter of human rights' (2007) *The Catholic Times,* 15 July. Only two EU countries permit medically-assisted dying. Hastings cites Liberal Democratic MEP Chris Davies, who has stated that euthanasia should not be a question of health policy but of human rights across Europe.

given space. Because of their inextricable ties with traditions, and the history and culture in the member states, he perceives the churches as pivotal in accomplishing European integration and unification:

> European unification in its very existence must depend on the churches to give the necessary anchoring in culture, in tradition and history a secure long-term future. Such culture is based on autonomy and self-determination. Community law must not monopolise the religious communities, it must not eradicate the differences between them. Anything else would promote the opposition of the churches, would endanger European unification, because internal disagreements would create fronts the destructive energy of which the otherwise mainly economic unity would not be able to counteract with anything substantial.[84]

In other words, the Union and the churches are mutually dependent in achieving the aims and objectives of a united and cohesive Europe in which freedom of religion means that there is a place in the new Europe for all religions and none on terms of equality and non-discrimination.

THE THREAT OF TERRORISM

[3.037] So-called 'Militant Islam' is now perceived as the major terrorist threat in the enlarged EU but, of course, such threats are not confined to any one quarter. An EU paper has been drafted which includes a strategy for combating radicalisation and recruitment; it aims to monitor radical imams and Internet 'hate speech' and to train teachers and police on the dangers of Islamic militancy.[85] The paper, which is based on an EU action plan established in 2005, urges governments to monitor 'travelling imams inciting to violence, talent spotters, recruiters and other leading figures and their movements within the European Union.'[86] It stresses the significance of moderate, home-grown Islam and calls on member states to support the training of imams in language and teaching skills and modern Islamic literature to 'counteract the effect of the radical message and stress the incompatibility of such a message with the main principles and values of Islam.' The paper further advises member states to encourage the Muslim

---

84. Robbers (ed), *State and Church in the European Union* (Nomos, 2005) pp 587–8.
85. Melander, 'EU calls for plan to tackle radical imams', Reuters Report (2007) *Irish Times*, 6 February.
86. Melander 'EU calls for plan to tackle radical imams', Reuters Report (2007) *Irish Times*, 6 February.

community not to rely on external imams, but rather to ensure that imams are recruited from their own communities. Member states are also encouraged to ensure that police forces reflect the communities they police and that their basic training, as well as that of teachers and social workers, includes teaching on mainstream Islam. The paper also urges governments to share information with partner countries on radical individuals 'with due regard for data protection considerations' and to monitor radical Internet sites.[87]

[3.038] This paper is not without its critics, however, who cite certain inherent difficulties involved in all of this, including issues of free speech, data protection and privacy laws. In dealing with such matters, an appropriate balance will need to be struck between basic human rights for the Muslim communities in the member states and the common good of society to protect itself from militant and unexpected terrorist attacks. While such measures may improve the security situation in Europe, this approach fails to address the deeper reasons for radicalisation, extremism and terrorism and how its causes can equitably be addressed. The European Council is devising a comprehensive migration policy on the basis of an interim report from the Commission[88] and a common policy on asylum, immigration and external border control based on solidarity between member states, which is fair towards third country nationals.[89] The EU also plans to take decisive action to preserve Europe's freedom and security, particularly in fighting terrorism and organised crime. With the growing prominence of Islam in Europe and the challenges arising from the integration process worldwide, issues of religion and ideology have moved centre stage and have become politicised.

The Lisbon Treaty

[3.039] With the failure of the Draft Constitution for Europe in 2005,[90] plans to reform and re-structure decision-making processes in the EU were delayed for two years. However, during its Presidency Germany held bilateral negotiations with all 27 member states with the hope of reviving the

87. Melander 'EU calls for plan to tackle radical imams', Reuters Report (2007) *Irish Times*, 6 February.

88. EU Presidency Conclusions, 21–22 June 2007.

89. Chapter 4, Art 111–257, para 2 of Draft Constitutional Treaty.

90. OJ 306, vol 50, 17 December 2007.

Constitution or of negotiating a new treaty which would satisfy all member states. Agreement was finally reached that Europe did not need an over-arching 'constitutional treaty' but rather a new treaty amending existing treaties and streamlining their effectiveness. The concept of a Constitutional Treaty was finally abandoned, with all its emblems, flag, hymn etc and a new treaty text was drafted which would amend, supplement and consolidate the current treaties.[91] The EU Reform Treaty (the Lisbon Treaty)[92] was signed by heads of state or governments of the 27 member states in Lisbon on 13 December 2007. The Lisbon Treaty amends the Treaty on European Union (TEU) and the Treaty Establishing the European Community and replaces the TEU so as to complete the process commenced by the Treaty of Amsterdam and the Treaty of Nice. The Lisbon Treaty was planned with a view to enhancing the pragmatic efficiency and democratic efficiency of the Union. Several Protocols and Declarations were also attached to the Treaty.

[3.040] The Preamble of the Lisbon Treaty reads as follows:

> Drawing inspiration from the cultural, religious and humanist inheritance of Europe, from which have developed the universal values of the inviolable and inalienable right of the human person, freedom, democracy, equality and the rule of law ….

[3.041] Article 2A(4) provides that the Union shall have competence in accordance with the provisions of the TEU to define and implement a common foreign and security policy, including a progressive framing of a common defence policy. Article 2B inserts specific amendments including the spheres in which the Union will have exclusive competence:

(a) in customs;

(b) in establishing competition rules necessary for the functioning of the internal market;

(c) in monetary policies for the member states where the euro is the currency;

---

91. Smyth, European Correspondent, 'EU constitution not the answer, says Dutch PM' (2007) *Irish Times*, 9 February, p 12.

92. Official Journal of the European Community, c 306, vol 50, 17 December 2007 (2007/c 306/01) to complete the process started by the Treaty of Amsterdam and the Treaty of Nice and to amend and include the Preamble.

(d) in conservation of marine biological resources under the common fisheries policy; and in

(e) common commercial policy.

Art 2C covered the areas of shared competence with the member states including, *inter alia,*[93] social policy for the aspects defined in the Treaty itself. Art 2E provides for the protection of human health, industry, culture, tourism, education, vocational training, youth and sport, civil protection and administrative co-operation. Article 5B embodied and extended the definition and implementation of all its policies and the principles of non-discrimination Article 5B of the Treaty provides:

> In defining and implementing its policies and activities, the Union shall aim to combat discrimination based on sex, racial or ethnic origin, religion or belief, disability, age or sexual orientation.' Article 2E extends the scope of EU jurisdiction, among other matters, to the protection of education and culture. Article 6(1) provides: 'The Union recognises the rights, freedoms and principles set out in the Charter of Fundamental Rights of the European Union of 7 December 2000 as adapted at Strasbourg on 12 December 2007, which shall have the same legal values as the Treaties.

[3.042] The Lisbon Treaty recognises the special position of the churches in Art 16C:

> 1. The Union respects and does not prejudice the status under national law of churches and religious associations or communities in the member states.
>
> 2. The Union equally respects the status under national law of philosophical and non-confessional organisations.
>
> 3. Recognising their identity and their specific contribution, the Union shall maintain an open, transparent and regular dialogue with these churches and organisations.

[3.043] In addition, fundamental rights, as guaranteed by the ECHR and as the result from the constitutional traditions common to the member states, shall constitute general principles of the Union's law. The Union already recognises human rights, freedoms and principles in its Charter,[94] albeit with

93. Internal market, agriculture and fisheries excluding the conservation of marine biological resources, economic. Social and territorial cohesion, trans-European networks, freedom, security and justice, common safety concerns in public health matters for the aspects defined in this Treaty, transport, consumer protection, energy, and environment.

94. Which constituted Pt 2 of the failed EU Draft Constitution.

some exceptions for Poland and the UK.[95] However, it appears that the Charter will not be given full legal effect in the member states until the Lisbon Treaty is adopted by all 27 member states.

Religious Education: Relevant Texts

[3.044] Article 18(4) of the ICCPR provides:

> The State Parties to the present Covenant undertake to have respect for the liberty of parents and, when applicable, legal guardians, to ensure the religious and moral education of their children in conformity with their own convictions.

This provision is considered in **chapter 4** (Human Rights).

Recommendations of the Parliamentary Assembly of the Council of Europe (the Assembly)

[3.045] In Recommendation 1396 (1999) on religion and democracy, adopted on 27 January 1999, the Assembly recommended that the Committee of Ministers invite the governments of the member states, among other matters,

> 13 ... (ii) to promote education about religions and, in particular, to:
>
> (a) step up the teaching about religions as sets of values towards which young people must develop a discerning approach, within the framework of education on ethics and democratic citizenship;
>
> (b) promote the teaching in schools of the comparative history of different religions, stressing their origins, the similarities in some of their values and the diversity of their customs, traditions, festivals and so on;
>
> ...
>
> (e) avoid – in the case of children – any conflict between the state-promoted education about religion and the religious faith of the families, in order to respect the free decision of the families in this very sensitive matter ....

In Recommendation 1720 (2005), adopted 4 October 2005, the Assembly recommended that the Committee of Ministers encourage the governments of member states to ensure that religious studies were taught at the primary

95. See Protocol on the Application of the Charter of Fundamental Rights of the European Union to Poland and the United Kingdom, at p 156 and also Declaration 63.

and secondary levels of state education, on the basis, *inter alia,* of the following criteria:

14.1. the aim of this education should be to make pupils discover the religions practised in their own and neighbouring countries, to make them perceive that everyone has the same right to believe that their religion is the "true faith" and that other people are not different human beings throught having a different religion or not having a religion at all;

14.2. it should include with complete impartiality, the history of the main religions, as well as the option of having no religion;

14.3. it should provide young people with educational tools that enable them to be quite secure in approaching supporters of a fanatical religious practice;

14.4. it must not overstep the borderline between the realms of culture and worship, even where a country with a state religion is concerned. It is not a matter of instilling a faith but of making young people understand why religions are sources of faith for millions;

14.5. teachers on religions need to have specific training. They should be teachers of a cultural or literary discipline. However, specialists in another discipline could be made responsible for this education;

14.6. the state authorities should look after teacher training and lay down the syllabuses which should be adapted to each countries peculiarities and to the pupils' ages. In devising these programmes, the Council of Europe will consult all partners concerned, including representatives of the religious faiths.

THE EUROPEAN COMMISSION AGAINST RACISM AND INTOLERANCE (ECRI)

[3.046] In its General Policy Recommendation No 5, 'Combating intolerance and discrimination against Muslims',[96] the ECRI has laid down its policy in this significant sphere. Having emphasised the principles of respect for equality and non-discrimination between religions, and recognising the great diversity intrinsic in the practice of Islam, it recommended that the governments of the member states 'ensure that religious instruction in schools respects cultural pluralism and make provision for teacher training to this effect.'

96. CRI, 2000, 21, 27 April 2000.

Furthermore, the ECRI, in its third report on Turkey,[97] considered, in particular, that:

> The syllabus covers all religions and is chiefly designed to give pupils an idea of all existing religions. However, several sources have described these courses as instruction in the principles of the Muslim faith rather than a course covering several religious cultures. ECRI notes that only Muslim pupils are required to follow these courses, while pupils belonging to minority religious groups can be exempted. ECRI considers the situation unclear: if this is indeed a course on the different religious cultures, there is no reason to make it compulsory for Muslim children alone. Conversely, if the course is essentially designed to teach the Muslim religion, it is a course on a specific religion and should not be compulsory, in order to preserve children's and their parents' religious freedom.

Accordingly, the ECRI urged the Turkish authorities:

> to reconsider their approach to instruction in religious culture. They should take steps either to make this instruction optional for everyone or to revise its content so as to ensure that it genuinely covers all religious cultures and is no longer perceived as instruction in the Muslim religion.

Turkey's failure to adopt and apply this recommendation subsequently led to a challenge in the ECtHR by members of the Alevi faith in *Zengin v Turkey* (2008)[98] which is considered in **chapter 4** below.

CONCLUSION

[3.047] In the EU, democracy and the rule of law build on a consensus distilled from the national communities on, *inter alia*, issues relating to the common good, shared histories, cultures, identities and human rights issues. The human rights principles which uphold these fundamental guarantees derive from the twentieth century and these latter norms may be traced to the ancient interplay between the state, religion and education,[99] which may be found in earlier bills of rights, codes and constitutions. Considerable

---

97. CRI, 2005.

98. *Zengin v Turkey* Application no 1448/04, 9 October 2007. Many of the facts in **para [4.001]**.

99. See Plato, Grube (trans), *The Republic* (Hackett Publishing Company, 1992). Plato (427 BC–347 BC) considered education to be a matter for the state alone: he also wrote on justice in the state and in the individual as well as democracy, oligarchy, tyranny, the immortality of the soul and the rewards of goodness.

common ground exists between the European countries in their approach to the unfolding of the basic freedoms in public life and in its legal framework the Union builds on the common constitutional traditions of the member states, the shared *corpus* of international human rights law and the Charter of Fundamental Rights. Increasingly international human rights organs are being called upon to establish an appropriate balance between competing interests as religion intersects with public life and public education particularly where different ideologies meet.

[3.048] Provision has been made in EU law for the recognition of the freedom of religion principle, which is a fundamental principle of EU jurisprudence, and for equality and non-discrimination in regard to religious faith and belief. However, these rights must be balanced against the competing rights and interests of individuals and other relevant parties. With regard to the manifestation of religious belief alone or in community with others, the ECJ is likely to be influenced by the germane precedents of the member states, by the case law of the ECtHR, by its own legal norms and values and by the rights embodied in the Charter when it achieves full legal effect. As the Union moves toward greater unity and solidarity, it will be necessary, it appears, for the ECJ to establish some mechanism by which to harmonise its jurisprudence with that of the ECtHR.

Despite the quite considerable provision made for freedom of religion and the recognition of the churches in EU law, the churches still fear that EU law and international human rights law will enshrine the secularism principle in its laws, rather than the principle of pluralism. The latter principle has generally been the upholding principle of church-state relations in Europe for centuries. The churches are concerned lest the application of the secularist principle evolves through cases coming before the ECJ and the ECHR and through the application of the equality and non-discrimination Directives as they penetrate the laws of the member states. If this happens to an undue degree, it will undoubtedly press the churches/religion out of the public sphere of life and into the private sphere. Indeed, the churches are already experiencing the impact of the EU Equality Directives across Europe: in state-funded adoption agencies in Britain; in ethos-related matters in the denominational school sector in Ireland; in matters relating to same-sex marriage in Germany; and in regard to certain services provided by the churches in Spain. As these Directives penetrate the laws of the member states in Europe, the churches, because of their conscientious objections and religious convictions, have little option but to move their social activities into the private sphere. Accordingly, they are increasingly of the view that, despite the many guarantees in EU law, freedom of religion, freedom of religious expression, and the freedom to manifest religion are, in practice, being curtailed.

Chapter 4

HUMAN RIGHTS: FREEDOM OF RELIGION AND EDUCATION

Democracy appears to be the only political model contemplated by the Convention and the only one compatible with it.[1]

INTRODUCTION AND GENERAL OVERVIEW

[4.001] As the ECtHR pointed out in *Zengin v Turkey* (2008),[2] religious education in Europe is now closely related to secular education and in the preponderance of the 46 Council of Europe member states, religious education is a secular subject in that it is about religion, its comparative history, evolution, beliefs etc. Approximately 43 of the 46 member states make provision for religious education classes in state schools, it appears.[3] Only France (with the exception of Alsace-Moselle), Albania and Macedonia, it appears, are exceptions to this common pattern of provision while Slovenia provides for non-confessional religious education in the final years of state education.[4]

[4.002] Religious education is a compulsory subject in 25 of the 46 member states but the obligation on students to attend these classes varies from country to country. In five member states of the Council of Europe (Norway, Sweden, Finland, Greece and Turkey), the obligation to attend such classes is absolute and all students who are adherents of the religious faith taught in these classes are required to follow them partially or fully.[5]

---

1. *United Communist Party of Turkey v Turkey* 133/1996/752/951, judgment of 30 January 1998, Reports of Judgments and Decisions.
2. *Hasan and Eylem Zengin v Turkey* [2008] ECHR, Application no 1448/04, Part IV, para 30, Comparative Law, para 30.
3. *Hasan and Eylem Zengin v Turkey* [2008] ECHR, Application no 1448/04, Part IV, para 30, Comparative Law, para 30.
4. *Hasan and Eylem Zengin v Turkey* [2008] ECHR, Application no 1448/04, Part IV, para 30, Comparative Law.
5. *Hasan and Eylem Zengin v Turkey* [2008] ECHR, Application no 1448/04, Part IV, para 31.

Of the 46 member states, ten countries (Austria, Cyprus, Denmark, Ireland, Iceland, Liechtenstein, Malta, Monaco, San Marino, and the United Kingdom) permit exemptions from religious education under certain conditions and in the preponderance of the latter member states, religious education is denominational.[6] A different approach is adopted in ten other countries (Germany, Belgium, Bosnia and Herzegovina, Lithuania, Luxembourg, the Netherlands, Serbia, Slovakia and Switzerland).[7] In the latter denominational education provision is made for denominational education in the official curriculum drawn up by the various ministries and students are required to attend unless they have chosen to opt for the substitute lesson proposed.[8] By contrast, 21 member states[9] have chosen not to compel pupils to attend classes in religious education. While religious education is generally authorised in the those 21 member states, pupils are required to attend a religious education or substitute class, but they always retain the right to opt for a secular lesson.[10]

[4.003] Despite the various provision and approaches, virtually all the member states offer at least one avenue by which pupils can opt out of religious education classes, either by the provision of an exemption or an alternative class or substitute lesson, or by providing pupils with a choice of signing up or not to a religious studies class.

[4.004] In *Zengin v Turkey* the applicants alleged that the classes in 'religious culture and ethics' in a state school in Turkey were not conducted in an objective, critical and pluralist manner, and that Turkey had failed to fulfil the criteria laid down by the ECtHR in its case law interpreting Art 2 of Protocol 1 of the ECHR.[11] The applicants, who belonged to the Alevi faith, claimed that the syllabus was taught entirely from the Sunni interpretation of the Islamic faith and tradition.

[4.005] Having examined the content of the lessons taught and the textbooks used in the religious education classes, the court noted that the texts used

---

6. *Hasan and Eylem Zengin v Turkey* [2008] ECHR, Application no 1448/04, Part IV, para 31.
7. *Hasan and Eylem Zengin v Turkey* [2008] ECHR, Application no 1448/04, Part IV, para 31, para 32.
8. *Hasan and Eylem Zengin v Turkey* [2008] ECHR, Application no 1448/04, Part IV, para 31.
9. *Hasan and Eylem Zengin v Turkey* [2008] ECHR, Application no 1448/04, Part IV, para 32.
10. *Hasan and Eylem Zengin v Turkey*, para 34.
11. *Kjelsden, Busk Madsen and Pedersen v Denmark* (1976) 1 EHRR 711.

were not limited to transmitting information on religions in general. Furthermore, these texts also appeared to provide instruction in the major principles of the Muslim faith together with a general overview of its cultural rites, such as the profession of faith, the five daily prayers, Ramadan, pilgrimage, the concepts of angels and invisible creatures, belief in the other worlds etc. In addition, pupils were required to learn several suras from the Koran by heart, to study the daily prayers and to sit a written examination for the purpose of assessment.

[4.006] The court stated that in a democratic society, only pluralism in education can enable pupils to develop a critical mind with regard to religious issues in the context of freedom of thought, conscience and religion. It referred to its numerous well-established findings that this freedom in its religious dimension is one of the most vital elements that go to make up the identity of believers and their conception of life, but it is also a precious asset for atheists, agnostics, sceptics and the unconcerned.[12] In addition, the court reiterated that in a pluralist democratic society, the state's duty of impartiality and neutrality towards various religions, faiths and beliefs is incompatible with any assessment by the state of the legitimacy of religious beliefs or the ways in which those beliefs are expressed.[13]

[4.007] The court concluded that the instruction provided in the 'religious culture and ethics' subject, therefore, did not meet the criteria of objectivity and pluralism generally, and specifically it did not respect the religious and philosophical convictions of the minor applicant's father, an adherent of the Alevi faith, on the subject of which the syllabus was silent.

[4.008] The right to religious freedom may be distinguished from other rights proclaimed in international law over the past fifty years. Rights are usually grounded in ancient concepts of human dignity which may be traced to the *Magna Carta*, or to the rights set down during the Enlightenment period, or to much earlier periods as can be seen from **chapter 2** above.[14] By contrast to other rights, the right to religious freedom was dilatory in arriving on the global scene as a legal right, but it has now been enshrined in many modern Constitutions and affirmed and reaffirmed during the past

12. *Buscarini and Ors v San Marino* (GC), no 24645/94, para 34, ECHR 1999–1.

13. *Manoussakis and Ors v Greece* (1996) 23 EHRR 387; *Hasan and Chaush v Bulgaria* (2002) 34 EHRR 55.

14. See above under 'Ancient Rights Reformulated,' **chapter 2**.

five decades in human rights covenants promulgated by the UN and by the European Convention on Human Rights (ECHR) and by the Charter of Fundamental Rights. As in the past, tolerance is perceived as pivotal in fostering an appreciation of human rights.

EDUCATING FOR TOLERANCE

[4.009] A number of human rights documents underscore the obligation on states parties to educate for tolerance, understanding and respect for the human rights of persons of other religions. For example, while stipulating that education should enable all persons to participate effectively in a free society, the International Covenant on Economic and Social Rights (ICESR) declares that education should 'promote understanding, tolerance and friendship among all nations and all racial, ethnic or religious groups' and that it should further the activities of the UN for the maintenance of peace.[15] In the UN Convention on the Rights of the Child (CRC), states are also required to direct education to the development of 'respect for the child's parents, his or her own cultural identity, language and values, for the national values of the country in which the child is living, the country from which he or she may originate, and for civilisations different to his or her own.'[16]

[4.010] Clearly, tolerance for religious, cultural and religious diversity is a central tenet of human rights which requires to be borne in mind by educators and formulators of educational policy and practice. Thus, in devising a curricular programme of religious education, human rights, civics or citizenship etc for publicly-funded schools, there is no prohibition on the inclusion of factual matters relating to culture, race, creed etc, but this needs to be balanced by the promotion of tolerance, respect and friendship for all nations including all racial, religious or ethnic groups. It would appear, therefore, that in any such programme, some factual and objective data, at least, on the main world religions should be included together with the religion that forms part of the national culture, language and values.

---

15. Article 13.1: see also UNESCO Convention 1960, Art 5.1(a): UN Convention on the Rights of the Child (CRC), 1989 Art 29 and the UN Declaration of 1981, Art 5.3.

16. CRC, Art 29(c).

The Right to Education in the ICESR and ICCPR

[4.011] The universal right to free primary education is expressly recognised in Art 13 of the ICESR, and such education is to be compulsory,[17] while the progressive introduction of free secondary education in its different forms is also recognised.[18] In the contracting states, the development of a system of schools at all levels is be actively pursued and, and 'an adequate fellowship system shall be established ...' indicating school systems at all levels. Under the ICESR, states parties further undertake to have respect for the liberty of parents and legal guardians to choose schools for their children other than public sector schools thereby respecting their convictions.[19] Thus, parents are entitled to choose private education for their children in accordance with their convictions. In Art 18(4) of the International Covenant on Civil and Political Rights (ICCPR), states parties undertake to have respect for the liberty of parents, and where appropriate legal guardians, to ensure the religious and moral education of their children in conformity with their own convictions. While this is a significant entitlement for those parents seeking to ensure a religious education for their children, it is equally an entitlement for those parents, who profess no religion[20] who may actively seek publicly-funded provision or non-denominational education for their children.

Pluralism and Democracy

[4.012] Pluralism of religious views and practice has been recognised as 'indissociable' from democracy[21] *per se*, as Parker observes:

> To the extent that pluralism of religious views and practice as a prescriptive norm is 'indissociable' from democracy itself, a government that purports to legitimately restrict manifestations of religious belief from finding full expression in society-ostensibly because such restriction is 'necessary' to

17. A copy of the ICESR appears in the **Appendix 7** of this book.
18. International Covenant on Economic, Social and Cultural Rights (ICESR) Art 13(2)(b).
19. ICESR, Art 13(3).
20. See further General Comment no 22 (1993) of the International Covenant on Civil and Political Rights (ICCPR) discussed below.
21. *Metropolitan Church of Bessarabia v Moldova* no 45701/99, para 114, ECtHR 2001–XII. In the context of freedom of association, the restriction of which necessitates justifications akin to Art 9, the ECtHR stated 'The autonomy of religious communities is in fact indispensable to pluralism in a democratic society.' See also *Kokkinakis v Greece* (1994) 17 EHRR 397, 418.

> protect that society-bears the burden of showing that a true, identifiable necessity exists to justify the restriction. Specifically, a government must identify how curbing a religious freedom in a particular instance will not violate the axiomatic principle of religious pluralism, and by extension, democracy itself. Such a view does not preclude appropriately specific justifications for curbing religious freedom, but guards against an inversion of the principle that would view robust expression of religious ideas and practice as somehow inimical to a democratic society, and thus subject to restriction simply by virtue of its religious nature.[22]

It is not easy, however, to indicate how the state should relate to the many educational enterprises and initiatives deriving from the civil society, or to parental demands in this regard.[23] Far from being abstract issues, these matters define a sphere of recurring political conflict in several countries. Different countries draw the boundaries of public education in differing ways.[24] While most Catholic schools in England or Ontario form part of the 'public' system of education, in Belgium or the Netherlands, while receiving the same full funding from the state, Catholic schools would be regarded as 'private.'[25] In certain countries, there is a full recognition of educational diversity and positive tolerance for a variety of pedagogical initiatives, as in Denmark, or to 'more uniformity and central steering, mostly when the Catholic Church is predominantly present as it is in Ireland.'[26] Durham argues that pluralism is essential to peace, that it is 'a fundamental axiom of human rights', and that peace in a pluralistic world is best maintained through building structures of mutual understanding and respect.[27] When considering religious liberty in US jurisprudence, McConnell advocates an 'animating principle of pluralism and diversity' above the maintenance of 'a scrupulous secularism' in all elements of public life touched by government,' rather than a mission to protect society from religion.[28] While

22. Parker, 'The Freedom to Manifest Religious Belief: An Analysis of the Necessity Clauses of the ICCPR and the ECHR', *17 Duke J of Comp & Int'L* 91.

23. Glenn and de Groof, *Balancing freedom, autonomy and accountability in Education* (Wolf, 2005).

24. Glenn and de Groof (2005).

25. Glenn and de Groof (2005).

26. Glenn and de Groof (2005).

27. Durham, 'Religious Pluralism as a Factor in Peace,' 2003, *Fides et Libertas*, 43(2003), 44.

28. McConnell, *Religious Freedom at a Crossroads,* 59 *U Chi L Rev* 115,116 (1992).

this latter view is cited in the US context, it reflects the established jurisprudence of the ECHR which perceives an 'indissociable' union between a democratic society and religious pluralism.[29]

Scope of the Right to Freedom of Religion

[4.013] Since the scope of the right to freedom of religion applies equally to persons with no religious convictions or faith, they too are entitled to the provision of publicly-funded secular education for their children by the state. The right to freedom of religion or belief is promulgated in Art 18 of the ICCPR[30] and it includes freedom to have or to adopt a religion, or belief of choice, and the right to manifest religion or belief in worship, observance, practice and teaching, whether individually or in community with others, whether in public or in private. The United Nations Human Rights Committee (UNHRC), in its General Comment No 22 (1993), clarified the scope or ambit of this right by declaring that it: 'protects theistic, non-theistic and atheistic beliefs, as well as the right not to profess any religion or belief.' Since Art 18 is one of the articles which is non-derogable, these rights cannot be negated by states parties even in times of public emergency.[31]

[4.014] Clearly, the scope of Art 18 extends to philosophies of life.[32] General Comment No 22 on Art 18 states that instruction in religion and ethics may, in the view of the Committee be in compliance with Art 18 if carried out in accordance with the terms of that General Comment which states:

> Article 18.4 permits public school instruction in subjects such as the general history of religions and ethics if it is given in a neutral and objective way

and public education that includes instruction in a particular religion or belief is inconsistent with article 18, paragraph 4 unless provision is made

---

29. See in particular *Kokkinasis v Greece* (1994) 17 EHRR 397, 418: *Metropolitan Church of Bessarabia v Moldova*, no 45701/99, para 114, ECtHR 2001–XII: and more recently *Church of Scientology Moscow v Russia* Application no 18147/02, judgment of 5 April 2007 which held there was also a breach of Art 11 (freedom of assembly and association).

30. The ICCPR International Human Rights Treaty based on the Universal Declaration of Human Rights (UDHR) and on part of the International Bill of Human Rights (IBHR) adopted in 1966 and came into force in 1996. United Nations. A copy of the ICCPR is contained in **Appendix 6** of this book.

31. ICCPR, Art 4.2.

32. General Comment No 22 on Art 18, adopted on 30 July 1993.

for non-discriminatory exemptions or alternatives that would accommodate the wishes of parents or guardians.

[4.015] In *Leirvag v Norway*[33] complaints were lodged with the UNHCR by a number of parents of the humanist tradition that the introduction of a new mandatory religious programme breached their freedom of religion rights under the ICCPR. By way of background, Art 2 of the Norwegian Constitution guarantees to all inhabitants of the Realm the right to free exercise of their religion, while the same Art establishes the Evangelical-Lutheran Church as the official religion of the state. Although Christianity has been taught in Norway's schools from 1739, when general mandatory education was introduced, a right of exemption existed for other religions from 1845 onwards.[34] In August 1997, the Norwegian government introduced a new compulsory religious subject into its schools called Christian Knowledge and Religious and Ethical Education (CKREE), which would replace the optional 'life stance knowledge' programme. CKREE contained only a partial exemption, which angered some minority faiths and persons with no religious faith who lodged their complaint with the UNHCR. The main issue before the Committee was whether the compulsory instruction of the CKREE subject in Norwegian schools, with only limited possibility of exemption, violated the complainants' rights to freedom of thought, conscience and religion under Art 18 of the ICCPR and more specifically the right of parents to secure the religious and moral education of their children in conformity with their own convictions, pursuant to Art 18(4). The CKREE subject combined education on religious knowledge with practising a particular religious belief eg by learning prayers and hymns by heart or requiring attendance at religious services. While parents could claim exemption from such activities by ticking a box on a form, the CKREE scheme did not, the UNHCR held, ensure that education of religious knowledge and religious practice were separated in a way which made the exemption scheme practicable.[35] In the Committee's view, the difficulties encountered by some of the claimants, and in particular the fact that some of the students had to recite religious texts in the setting of a Christmas celebration, although they were enrolled in the exemption scheme, together with the loyalty conflicts experienced by the students,

33. *Leirvag v Norway* Communication No 1155/2003.

34. Under the Non-Conformist Act 1845.

35. Compare with the Integrated Curriculum in Ireland discussed in **para [9.040]** below.

amply illustrated the difficulties encountered. The Committee held that the framework of CREE, as it was then, together with its regime of exemptions, constituted a violation of Art 18(4) of the Covenant in regard to the complainants. Thus, the state party (Norway) was under an obligation to provide the complainants with an effective and appropriate remedy that would respect their right to ensure that their children receive an education in conformity with their own convictions and to avoid similar violations in the future.

Legitimate Limits to Manifesting Religious Freedom

[4.016] The human right to have or to adopt a belief is absolute under Art 18 and states may not delimit this right. However, states may set limitations to the right to manifest a belief or faith but they must show that such limitations were 'prescribed by law' and 'necessary to protect public safety, order, health, or morals or the fundamental rights or freedoms of others.'[36] These are the sole grounds on which states parties may limit the freedom of religion or belief. The UNHRC have made it clear that, although the right to manifest religion includes the 'wearing of distinctive clothing or head coverings,'[37] states may limit this right in the interests of morality, health, public safety and public order and the fundamental rights and freedoms of others provided it is '*prescribed by law.*' Thus, while a legislative prohibition on a head covering, such as a Sikh turban, may be lawful in the interests of public safety, a legislative ban on the wearing of Muslim headscarves by teachers in public schools which permits nuns to wear their head-covering habits in the same schools, would be questionable from the perspective of human rights unless the state party could establish that the prohibition fell under the above 'the necessity principle'. Catholic Bavaria's decision to pass a law in 2004 to ban the wearing of headscarves by teachers in its public schools, but not religious habits worn by nuns and other religious symbols, has been recently upheld by the Bavarian Constitutional Court,[38] but this is now likely to be appealed to the German Constitutional Court and, if unsuccessful there, it is likely to reach the ECtHR or the ECJ.

---

36. ICCPR, Art 18.3 and ECHR, Art 9.2.

37. General Comment 22, para 4.

38. See 'Court upholds ban on Muslim teachers wearing head scarves in German state' (2007) *International Herald Tribune,* 15 January, see further http://www.iht.com/articles/ap/2007/01/15/europe/EU-GEN-Germany-Head-Scarf-Ban.php, accessed on 1 October 2008.

[4.017] When considering the phrase 'prescribed by law' in *Metropolitan Church of Bessarabia v Moldova*, the ECtHR stated that this means that an impugned measure should not only have a basis in domestic law but the law in question must be 'adequately accessible and foreseeable, that it to say, formulated with sufficient precision to enable the individual ... to regulate his conduct.'[39] Accordingly, a domestic law must afford a measure of legal protection against arbitrary interference by public authorities with the rights protected by the Convention and it must indicate with sufficient clarity the scope of any such discretion conferred on the competent authorities and the manner of its exercise.[40] Since Departmental Circulars and memoranda are not prescribed by law, and are generally not accessible and forseeable, it would most likely violate human rights, therefore, to employ such informal methods of administration to ban the 'wearing of distinctive clothing or head coverings' which manifest religion in state schools and colleges.

[4.018] The right to manifest one's religion or faith in the public sphere of life is seriously contested in certain countries with a secular political tradition, such as Turkey, France and some previously socialist countries, where this right may be perceived as endangering the secular character of the state, or as constituting a threat to the existence of a democratic society.[41] Such countries are more likely to limit the right to manifest religion in public life and particularly in public education. France, for instance, contends that its recent legislative prohibition on the wearing of 'conspicuous religious symbols'[42] by students in public schools is justified while Turkey's prohibition on the wearing of headscarves in its universities has been upheld by the ECtHR in the recent case *Sahin v Turkey*.[43] The guarantees of freedom of religion or belief and non-discrimination

39. *Metropolitan Church of Bessarabia v Moldova* (2002) 35 EHRR, 13, 333.

40. *Metropolitan Church of Bessarabia v Moldova* (2002) 35 EHRR, 13, 333.

41. *Refah Partisi (The Welfare Party) v Turkey* [2003] EHRR 1.

42. *La loi n° 2004–228 du 15 mars 2004 encadrant, en application du principe de laïcité, le port de signes ou de tenues manifestant une appartenance religieuse dans les écoles, collèges et lycées publics*: Journal Officiel, No 65, 17 March 2004, p 5190.

43 *Sahin v Turkey* Application 44774/98, judgment of 29 June 2004. See further: Evans, *Freedom of Religion Under the European Convention on Human Rights* (Oxford University Press, 2001); Beller, 'The Headscarf Affair: The Conseil d'Etat on the Role of Religion and Culture in French Society', 39 *Texas International Law Journal* 581, Summer 2004; (contd .../)

enshrined in the ICCPR and the ECHR together with the UNCRC 1989 confer recognition on the right of parents to have their children educated in accordance with their convictions. In addition some international human rights which the state is required to respect fall to be exercised in association or in community with others, for example the right to manifest religion or belief in community with like-minded others and the right to associate freely with others. Thus, in certain instances, the protection afforded by human rights extends to religious communities by extension.

THE EUROPEAN CONVENTION ON HUMAN RIGHTS AND FUNDAMENTAL FREEDOMS

[4.019] History has shown many instances where interference with freedom of thought, conscience and religion has been attempted with varying degrees of success.[44] The Council of Europe (the Council) had learned from the experience of the Second World War that these freedoms together with, *inter alia*, the right to education could be interfered with for pernicious purposes by totalitarian individuals, states and other bodies. The Council resolved to ensure that the subjugation of persons through unlawful interference with these freedoms would not recur in Europe and this resolve finally bore fruit through the regulation of certain fundamental rights in the ECHR which was adopted by the Council in 1950.[45] The ECtHR was established to hear complaints made against contracting states parties for breach of the human rights set out in the ECHR. The court adjudicates complaints taken against state parties initiated by other state parties, or by persons, including a legal person such as political party, under the jurisdiction of a state party. Contracting states undertake to abide by the final judgment of the ECtHR in

---

43. (contd) Eberle, 'Free Exercise of religion in Germany and the United States', 78 *Tulane Law Review* 1023, March 2004; Hein-On-Line, 'Religious Garb in the Public Schools: A Study in Conflicting Liberties', 22 *University of Chicago Law Review* 888, 1955; Kaminer, 'Religious Expression in the Workplace' (2004) *New York Law Journal,* 19 February, p 4; and Louis-Jacques, 'Researching the Right to Wear Garb in Public Schools in Europe: The Muslim Headscarf Issue: Religion and International Human Rights law and Policy, 2004.

44. See further Schermers, 'Freedom of Thought' in Heffernan (ed), *Human Rights, a European Perspective* (Round Hall Press, 1994) p 201–210.

45. *Travaux Preparatoires* (TV) Meeting of the Committee of Experts, Vol 111 p 262.

which they are parties and the Committee of Ministers monitor its execution.[46] In this manner, the court exercises jurisdiction over the interpretation and application of the Convention and its Protocols in the contracting states.

[4.020] Because jurisdiction is limited to interpreting and applying the Convention, the court can only decide whether the contracting state in question is in violation or not.[47] While the decisions of the court only bind the parties in the case, indicating that it is a court of limited remedy, the court's decisions, nonetheless, have application for all 46 contracting states to the Convention. Accordingly, the court operates a supranational system of review of the human rights practices of member states, rather than a judicial review process.[48] Although the court can award compensatory damages to the petitioner, it cannot compel the contracting state to amend or repeal any national law that has been violated by it.[49] The limitation of remedy indicates the subsidiary character of the ECtHR system itself and the sensitive equilibrium it must necessarily strive to achieve in practice between national sovereignty in the contracting states and supranational enforcement, as it were. In 1998 the Commission, which previously determined the admissibility of applications and sought to resolve them, was dissolved.

[4.021] Applications are now considered by a seven-judge Chamber which decides on admissibility and merits. However, a Chamber may decide to confer jurisdiction on the Grand Chamber, a 17-judge Chamber, where significant issues of interpretation are determined. Within a three-month period, following the determination of the Chamber, either party may request that the case be referred to a Grand Chamber. Final judgments of the

---

46. Art 46 of the ECHR.

47. Art 46(1) of the ECHR and see further Danchin and Forman, 'The Evolving Jurisprudence of the European Court of Human Rights and the protection of Religious Minorities' in *Protecting the Human Rights of Religious Minorities in Eastern Europe* 192, 194, Danchin and Cole (eds) 2002.

48. See further Boustead, 'The French Headscarf Law before the European Court of Human Rights', *Journal for Transnational Law and Policy,* Vol 16, no 2, Spring, 2007, Florida State University in which Ms Boustead addresses the hypothetical scenario of an expelled student taking the Headscarf Law before the ECtHR for an alleged breach of Art 9 of the ECHR.

49. Joshua Briones, 'Religious Minorities in Russia', 8 UC Davis J International & Policy 323 (2002), 325, 330 (2002).

court are binding on the respondent states who may be required to award the applicants just satisfaction. Many contracting states have incorporated the ECHR into their domestic law in one way or another and some countries have adopted it subject to their national constitutions, as in Ireland.[50] However, if the Lisbon Treaty is adopted by all the 27 member states, the Charter on Fundamental Rights will become legally binding on all member states unless exemptions have been granted. As the ECtHR has stressed in many of its decisions, not only is political democracy a fundamental feature of the European public order but the Convention was designed to promote and maintain the ideals and values of a democratic society. Moreover, the court has emphasised that democracy is the sole political model contemplated in the Convention and the only one compatible with it.[51]

Margin of Appreciation Doctrine

[4.022] When striving to determine how they are to balance and apply human rights principles in specific cases, the ECHR and the UNHCR confer certain levels of discretion on national governments as to how they comply with Convention principles such as 'the margin of appreciation' doctrine.[52] This doctrine has been described by Gordon *et al* as:

> a recognition by the [European Court] that the domestic authorities of any given member state are generally in a better position than an international court of supervisory jurisdiction to reach a decision on an individual case or to determine the extent to which a measure was 'necessary' to deal with a particular issue.[53]

Where a state's law is considered by the ECtHR to fall within the range of a number of reasonably acceptable alternatives, it is likely to uphold that law as falling within the margin of appreciation.[54] Thus, where a person has voluntarily accepted an employment role which fails to accommodate his or

50. For example Ireland, see **chapter 9** below.

51. *Church of Scientology Moscow v Russia* Application no 18147/02, judgment of 5 April 2007.

52. Parker, 'The Freedom to Manifest Religious Belief: An Analysis of the Necessity Clauses of the ICCPR and the ECHR', 17 *Duke J of Comp & Int'L* 91.

53. Gordon *et al*, *The Strasbourg Case Law: leading cases from the European Human Rights Reports* (Sweet & Maxwell, 2001) p 4.

54. *Sahin v Turkey* (2005) 41 EHRR 8 at paras 100–102: *R (on the application of Begum) v Head Teacher and Governors of Denbigh High School* [2006] 2 All ER 487 (HL) at para 64.

her religious practice or observance, or where viable alternatives exist for that person to practice or observe his religion without undue hardship or inconvenience, the Strasbourg institutions have been slow to find a breach of the right to manifest religious belief in practice or observance.[55] Clearly freedom to manifest one's religion does not mean that a person has the right to do so at any time and in any place and in any manner that accords with one's belief.[56] The application of the margin of appreciation doctrine is particularly evident where religious freedoms intersect with employment issues as the following cases show.

[4.023] In *Ahmed v United Kingdom*,[57] for example, the applicant's Art 9 claim failed because the court found that he had accepted a contract of employment, which did not contain any provision for him to absent himself from his teaching duties to attend prayers, nor had he notified his employer of his religious requirements and, moreover, he remained free to seek alternative employment which would accommodate his religious requirements. Similarly, in *Stedman v United Kingdom*[58] the applicant's claim that the obligation to work on Sundays breached her Art 9 rights failed on the grounds that she was at all times free to resign from her employment. Again in *Karaduman v Turkey*[59] the applicant was refused a graduation certificate because one of the university's requirements was a photograph of her taken without a headscarf and, for religious reasons, the applicant was unwilling to be photographed without a headscarf. The Commission held that there was no breach of her Art 9 rights under the Convention because she had chosen to pursue her higher education in a secular university in which a student submits to those university rules 'which may make the freedom of students to manifest their religion subject to restrictions as to place and manner intended to ensure harmonious coexistence between students of different beliefs.'[60]

---

55. *R v Headteacher and Governors of Denbigh High School* [2006] UKHL 15 at para 23 *per* Lord Bingham of Cornhill.
56. *R v Headteacher and Governors of Denbigh High School* [2006] UKHL 15 at para 86 citing *Kalac v Turkey* (1997) 27 EHRR 552, 558.
57. *Ahmed v United Kingdom* (1981) 4 EHRR 126, para 11.
58. *Stedman v United Kingdom* (1997) 23 EHRR 168.
59. *Karaduman v Turkey* (1993) 74 DR 93.
60. *Karaduman v Turkey* (1993) 74 DR 93.

[4.024] Once again, in *Kalac v Turkey*,[61] the applicant was unsuccessful in his Art 9 claim because, by selecting a military career, he had voluntarily accepted military discipline which implied the possibility of restrictions on certain rights and freedoms and, furthermore, he had been facilitated in fulfilling the ordinary obligations of Muslim belief. The applicant, a judge-advocate in the Turkish airforce, had been compulsorily retired because he had participated in the activities of a 'new religion' or religious sect, which was inconsistent with his obligations under military law to guarantee the secular character of the Turkish state. It was held that the applicant was free to manifest his religion in any manner he pleased but not, however, as a member of the armed forces in Turkey. Again, in *X v Denmark*[62] the ECtHR held that the applicant clergyman had accepted the discipline of his church when he voluntarily accepted his employment, and accordingly his right to leave the church guaranteed his right to freedom of religion.

[4.025] When limitations are placed by states on religious freedom, it is clear that the ECtHR will apply 'very strict scrutiny' to such cases.[63] That context may be a factor to be taken into account seems clear from the UNHCH's decision in *Raihon Hudoyberganova v Uzbekistan*.[64] In that case the Committee, having taken into account 'the specifics of the context', held that a Muslim woman, who was denied the right to wear her headscarf during classes at a state institution, had suffered a violation of her rights pursuant to Art 18 of the ICCPR. Context also appears also to have been a consideration in some of the cases relating to Turkey as a secular state.

[4.026] In *Cha'are Shalom v Tsedek v France*[65] the applicants (an association of ultra-orthodox Jews) complained that their Art 9 rights had been breached because French law did not permit them to slaughter animals in accordance with their specific opinion of what was required by Jewish religious ritual. This claim failed because it was held that the applicants could easily secure meat supplies from Belgium, which met with their requirements, and so there was no breach of their Art 9 rights. However, the court held that if the

61. *Kalac v Turkey* (1997) 27 EHRR 552.

62. *X v Denmark* (1976) 5 DR 157.

63. *Manoussakis v Greece* (1996) 23 EHRR 387, 407.

64. *Raihon Hudoyberganova v Uzbekistan Communication* No 931/2000, UN Doc CCPR/C/82/D/931/2000 (2004) par 62.

65. *Cha'are Shalom Ve Tsedek v France* (2000) 9 BHRC 27, para 81.

illegality of performing ritual slaughter made it impossible for ultra-orthodox Jews to eat meat from animals slaughtered in accordance with their religious prescriptions, then there would be interference with the freedom to manifest one's religion[66] but that was not the case in this instance. Much will depend on the character and content of the right at issue. If the right in question is fundamental to a democratic society, then the restrictions placed on its exercise must be appropriate to the aim sought to be achieved, and the means chosen must be proportionate to the 'legitimate' end. In such cases little discretion, if any, is likely to be afforded the national government.[67]

Freedom of Thought, Conscience and Religion in the Convention

[4.027] Article 9 of the ECHR provides:

> (1) Everyone has the right to freedom of thought, conscience and religion; this right includes freedom to change his religion or belief, and freedom in public or private to manifest his religion or belief.
>
> (2) Freedom to manifest one's religion or beliefs shall be subject only to such limitations as are prescribed by law and are necessary in a democratic society in the interests of public safety, for the protection of public order, health or morals or the protection of the rights and freedoms of others.[68]

The significance of the rights embodied in Art 9 has been recognised in a number of cases including *Kokkinakis v Greece*[69] in which the ECtHR held that Greece had breached Art 9 by convicting the applicant, who was a Jehovah's Witness, for proselytising. Recently the fundamental importance of Art 9 in a pluralist, multicultural society, such as England, was elucidated by Lord Nichols of Birkenhead in *R v (Williamson) v Secretary of State for*

66. *Cha'are Shalom Ve Tsedek v France* (2000) 9 BHRC 27, para 80.

67. See generally Donoho, 'Autonomy, Self-Governance and the margin of Appreciation: Developing a Jurisprudence of Diversity Within Universal Human Rights' (2001) 15 *Emory International Rev* 391,446, 451.

68. See also Art 19 (1) of the International Covenant on Civil and Political Rights (19 Dec, 1966) which states: 'Everyone shall have the right to hold opinions without interference.' Art 19 also extends to freedom of expression.

69. *Kokkinakis v Greece* (1994) 17 EHRR 397; the court awarded 4000,000 drachmas to the applicant for pecuniary damages and 2,789,500 drachmas for his costs and expenses.

Education and Employment; [70] in South Africa by its Constitutional Court in *Christian Education South Africa v Minister of Education;*[71] and by the Chamber Court of the ECtHR[72] in *Church of Scientology Moscow v Russia*.[73]

[4.028] Article 9 protects both a right to hold a belief, which is absolute, and a right to manifest belief, which is qualified.[74] However, interference with Art 9 rights is not easily established[75] and criticisms have been made concerning the timidity of the ECtHR in its resolution of disputes related to religious freedoms in Europe and concerning its appropriateness as a juridical body for this purpose, in view of the fact that secularism appears to have now become an upholding principle of the Convention in some cases. Arguably, if secularism is an upholding principle of the Convention, rather than pluralism, which is well-established,[76] then it becomes difficult for the

---

70. *R v (Williamson) v Secretary of State for Education and Employment* [2005] UKHL 15. [2005] 2 AC 246, paras 15–19.

71. *South Africa by its Constitutional Court in Christian Education South Africa v Minister of Education* CCT 13/98 ZACC 16; 1999 (2) SA 83; 1998 (12) BCLR 1449, 14 October 1998.

72. Within three months from the date a Chamber judgment is delivered, any party to the case may, in exceptional cases, request that the case be referred to the Grant Chamber (of 17 members) of the court. If that request is granted, a panel of five judges consider whether the case raises a serious issue concerning either the application or interpretation of the Convention or its protocols, or a serious issue of general significance, in which case the Grand Chamber will deliver a final judgment. Art 43 of the ECHR). The Chamber judgment becomes final (a) on the expiry of the three month period or (b) if the parties declare that they do not intend to make a request to refer to the Grand Chamber or (c) if the panel refuse the request (Art 43, para 2 of the ECHR).

73. *Church of Scientology Moscow v Russia* Application No 18147/02, judgment of 5 April 2007 which held there was also a breach of Art 11 (freedom of assembly and association).

74. At para 16 of the judgment.

75. *R v Headteacher and Governors of Denbigh High School* [2006] UKHL 15 at para 24 *per* Lord Bingham of Cornhill.

76. *Metropolitan Church of Bessarabia v Moldova*, no 45701/99, para 114, ECHR 2001–XII. In the context of freedom of association, the restriction of which necessitates justifications akin to Art 9, the ECtHR stated 'The autonomy of religious communities is in fact indispensable to pluralism in a democratic society.' See also *Kokkinakis v Greece* (1994) 17 EHRR 397, 418.

ECtHR to rule neutrally and objectively on the role and function of religion and the churches in a democratic society, since secularism is adverse to both religion and the churches. Parker contends that 'the principle of secularism' as defined primarily in the ECtHR jurisprudence is:

> ... an illegitimate justification for restrictions on religious freedom under the ICCPR and the ECHR. More specifically, the principle of secularism functioning as a principle by which religious expression may be excluded from full participation in democratic government is inimical to the ICCPR's and ECHR's vision of religious pluralism as 'indissociable' from a democratic society. Further, the European Court's application of the principle improperly equates a 'secular' government with a democratic government, and as such is in tension with prior cases in which the court had affirmed religious pluralism as axiomatic for a democratic society.

Undoubtedly, there is an inherent tension between the well-founded principle of pluralism and the principle of secularism, the latter principle being most apparent in some of the Turkish cases, particularly in *Refah Partisi v Turkey.*[77] In that case, which is discussed in some detail below, the ECtHR held that the principle of secularism was one of the indispensable conditions of democracy, which sits uneasily with pluralism, being another upholding democratic principle. In the opinion of this writer, the recognition of the secular principle in the Turkish cases, unless it is strictly limited to secular contexts (eg France and Turkey), indicates a departure for the court towards a recognition of the laic principle embodied in French jurisprudence. If the court were to adopt and apply the secularism principle throughout the EU, this could undermine the consensus in the member states which is grounded in pluralism, which generally accommodates the churches. Article 9 does not protect every act motivated or inspired by a religion or belief but is subject to the limitations set out in Art 9(2) which has generally been interpreted narrowly by the ECJ.[78] What constitutes interference with religious freedom depends on all the circumstances of the case.[79]

77. *Refah Partisi v Turkey* [2003] ECHR 87.

78. See judicial criticism of this in the Court of Appeal case *Copsey v WWB Devon Clays Ltd* 2005 EWCA Civ 932, [2005] 1 CR 1789, paras 31–39, 44–66 and in the House of Lords in *R v (Williamson) v Secretary of State for Education and Employment* [2005] UKHL 15. [2005] 2 AC 246, paras 15–19.

79. *Kalac v Turkey* (1997) 27 EHRR 552, para 27: *Sahin v Turkey* (Application No 44774/98), 11 November 2005, para 105: *Ahmad v United Kingdom* (1981) 4 EHRR 126, para 11.

Requirements of a Democratic Society

[4.029] Certain characteristics of the European public order have become identified with democracy and the rule of law: plurality; secularity; freedom of assembly; freedom of association and freedom of expression and these features have been enshrined in national constitutions and in the Convention. In latter years, the Strasbourg Court has been called upon more increasingly to adjudicate and harmonise conflicting human rights in a secular context including those cases involving the Turkish Republic. Although Turkey may be perceived as a model of Muslim secularism, it is far from a homogenous secular nation-state as recent case law in the ECJ demonstrates.[80] In practice, the Turkish State keeps a vigilant eye on religion, perceiving it as an essential social cohesive but also as a potential threat to its democratic institutions in its most extreme forms.[81]

[4.030] In *United Communist Party of Turkey and Others v Turkey*,[82] the ECtHR reiterated the primordial role played by political parties in a democratic society which enjoy the rights and freedoms embodied in Arts 10 and 11 of the ECHR. The court held that political parties were a form of association necessary to the proper functioning of a democracy and hence the protection of opinions and the freedom to express them, within the meaning of Art 10, is one of the objectives of the freedom of assembly and association enshrined in Art 11 which applies to them in their role in ensuring pluralism and the proper functioning of democracy.[83] Because the activities of political parties form part of a collective exercise of the freedom of expression, the court emphasised, they are entitled to seek the protection of Art 10 of the ECHR.[84] However, the court also noted the fact that political parties have the potential to influence the total regime in their countries by their proposals for an overall societal model which they place before the

80. *Refah Partisi and Others v Turkey* [2003] ECHR 87.

81. Birch, Growing influence of Islam alienating Alevis, Turkey's 'true second-class citizens' (2006) *Irish Times,* 20 February, p 11.

82. *United Communist Party of Turkey and Others v Turkey* Judgment of the 30 January 1988, 133/1996/752//951 Reports of Judgments and Decisions 1998–1, pp 21–22, 45.

83. *United Communist Party of Turkey and Others v Turkey* Judgment of the 30 January 1988, 133/1996/752//951 Reports of Judgments and Decisions 1998–1, pp 20–21, para 42–43.

84. *United Communist Party of Turkey v Turkey,* Judgment of 30 January 1988, Reports of Judgments and Decisions 1998–1.

electorate, and by virtue of their capacity to implement those proposals once they achieve power. For these reasons, the court concluded, political parties are to be distinguished from other organisations which intervene in the political sphere. Any measure taken against political parties, therefore, affected freedom of association and as a result, democracy in the relevant state. However, the court would, at a later date, place restrictions on the activities of political parties.

Restrictions on Political Parties

[4.031] The ECHR places limitations on the freedoms of certain political parties which, in its opinion, threaten to overturn democratic governments as the case of *Refah Partisi v Turkey* (the *Refah* case)[85] illustrates. Arguably the *Refah* case constitutes 'the litmus test', so to speak, for the concept of 'militant democracy'. Not only does this most significant case raise issues relating to the range of policies and viewpoints that a political party may lawfully espouse under Art 11 (freedom of association) of the ECHR, it is also relevant to the right of freedom of religion or belief and to the right to freedom of association and expression. At the kernel of this singular case lies the proposed plan of a political party in Turkey to establish, if it became the sole party in power, a theocratic state as an alternative to Turkey's existing secular state.[86] Refah was the fifteenth political party to have been suppressed by the Turkish authorities and three cases had been referred to Strasbourg which found that Turkey had breached Art 11 in all three cases.[87]

[4.032] The Turkish Constitution prohibits the exploitation or abuse of religion, religious feeling or things[88] as does its Criminal Code.[89] However, in order to perform its role as the neutral and impartial organiser of the exercise of religious beliefs, the state may decide to impose on its serving or future civil servants, who will be required to wield a portion of its sovereign power, the duty to refrain from taking part in the Islamic fundamentalist movement, whose goal and action plan is to bring about the pre-eminence of

---

85. *Refah Partisi v Turkey* [2003] ECHR 87.

86. *Refah Partisi v Turkey* [2003] ECHR 87 at paras 78–85.

87. *United Communist Party of Turkey v Turkey* Judgment of 30 January 1998, Reports of Judgments and Decisions 1998: *Socialist Party v Turkey* 20/1997/804/1007, 25 May 1998; *Freedom and Democracy Party (OZDEP) v Turkey* (Application No 2388594, 8 December 1999).

88. The Turkish Constitution, Art 24.4.

89. The Criminal Code of Turkey, Art 163.

religious rules.[90] The Turkish Constitutional Court dissolved the Islamic oriented *Refah Partisi* (the Welfare Party), the largest political party in Turkey, as a 'centre of activities against the principle of secularism'.[91] Basing its decision on ss 101(b) and 103(1) of Law No 2820 regulating political parties, the Constitutional Court ordered that the Welfare Party's assets be transferred to the Turkish Treasury and the court prohibited six of the party's members from sitting in Parliament and from participating in certain other political activities for five years. The main grounds cited by the Constitutional Court for dissolving the Welfare party were as follows:

(i) that it was the intention of Refah to establish a plurality of legal systems leading to discrimination based on religious beliefs;

(ii) that Refah had intended to apply sharia to the internal or external relations of the Muslim community within the context of this plurality of legal systems; and

(iii) the arguments based on the references made by Refah members to the possibility of recourse to force as a political method.[92]

The court looked at the particular context in this case. It noted that the principle of secularism is protected by the Turkish Constitution[93] on account of the country's historical experience and the specific features of Islam; that this principle was one of the indispensable conditions of democracy; and that the rules of sharia were incompatible with the democratic regime, which is a fundamental feature of the European order[94] and the only political model

---

90. See *mutatis mutandi, Yanasik v Turkey*, no 14524/89, Commission Decision of 6 January 1993, DR 74, p 14; *Kalac v Turkey* (1997) 27 EHRR 552.

91. *Yanaisk v Turkey* (1993) 74 DR 98, p 14; the decision of the Turkish Constitutional Court is discussed in detail in the above ECtHR decision. The Refah Party was founded in July 1983 and had grown in influence over the years: in the general election of 1991 it obtained 16.88 per cent of the total votes while in the general election of 1995 it had 22 per cent of the total votes and opinion polls indicated it would grow substantially.

92. Cited in the Strasbourg case of *Partisi v Turkey* at para 116.

93. See Arts 2, 4, 6, 14.1, 24.4, 68.4, 69.4. See also Law No 2820 on the regulation of political parties, ss 78, 90.1, 101, 103, 107.1 and Art 163 of the Criminal Code which set down a number of germane offences.

94. *United Communist Party of Turkey v Turkey* 133/1996/752/951, 30 January 1988: *Socialist Party v Turkey* 20/1997/804/1007, 25 May 1998; *Freedom and Democracy Party (OZDEP) v Turkey* (Application No 2388594, 8 December 1999.

contemplated by the Convention.[95] The court ruled that the principle of secularism was the foundation of freedom of conscience and equality between citizens before the law and it prevented the Turkish State from manifesting a preference for a specific religion or belief. It followed that intervention by the Turkish State to preserve the political regime had to be considered necessary in a democratic society. Where a political party pursued activities aimed at bringing the democratic order to an end and used its freedom of expression rights to issue calls to action to achieve that aim, the court concluded that the Turkish Constitution and human rights law authorised the dissolution of Refah. Two judges dissented holding that the dissolution of Refah by the Turkish State was incompatible with the Convention and its established case law and they asserted that political parties, which did not support the use of violence, should be permitted to participate in a pluralist system and that there should be room for debate about ideas thought to be disturbing or even shocking.[96] The case was finally referred to the ECJ by the Refah Partisi.

[4.033] In the ECJ, the applicants complained that their rights were violated by the Turkish government under Arts 9 (freedom of thought, conscience and religion), 11 (freedom of association and expression), 14 (prohibition of discrimination), 17 (prohibition of abuse of rights), 18 (limitations on the use of restrictions on rights) of the ECHR together with Arts 1 (protection of property) and 3 (right to free elections) of Protocol No 1. However, the court focussed largely on Art 11 and considered the range of objectives and policies which political parties in a contracting state may lawfully promote under the right to freedom of assembly and association.[97] When presenting its case to the ECtHR, the Turkish Government endorsed the opinion of the Constitutional Court and contended that a theocratic state could not be a democratic state as was manifest, *inter alia*, from Turkish history in the Ottoman period.[98] The Government also posited the view that Refah wished to abolish the principle of secularity in the Turkish Constitution and that certain actions and speeches of Refah members amounted to incitement to

---

95. *Soering v UK*, judgment of 7 July 1989, Series A, no 161, pp 35 and 88.

96. *Handyside v the United Kingdom*, judgment of 7 December 1976, Series A, no 24, p 23, para 49 and *Jersild v Denmark*, judgment of 13 September 1994, Series A, no 298, p 26, para 37.

97. *Refah Partisi (The Welfare Party) v Turkey* [2003] ECHR 87.

98. *Refah Partisi (The Welfare Party) v Turkey* [2003] ECHR 87.

popular uprising and the generalised violence characterising any 'holy war'. Moreover, the government asserted that at the material time radical Islamist groups, such as Hizbullah, were responsible for numerous acts of terrorism in Turkey and that Refah members were promoting Islamic fundamentalism in their speeches.[99]

Commenting on the relationship between democracy and the Convention, the court stated: 'Democracy is without doubt a fundamental feature of the European public order ...'. [100] This was manifest from the ECHR's Preamble which establishes a very clear connection between the ECHR and democracy and it affirms that the countries of Europe have a common heritage of political tradition, ideals, freedom and the rule of law. Within that common heritage lies the upholding values of the ECHR which was designed to promote the ideals and values of a democratic society.[101] Articles 8, 9, 10 and 11 of the ECHR require that interference with the existence of the rights enshrined in those Arts must be assessed by applying the yardstick of what is 'necessary in a democratic society' Accordingly, the court concluded that: 'Democracy thus appears to be the only political model contemplated by the Convention and, accordingly the only one compatible with it.'[102]

[4.034] By contrast with the previous cases which came before the ECtHR which were concerned with a party's policies or programme,[103] the court examined various declarations and writings made by the leaders and members of the symbolic acts and pronouncements of official party members and it concluded that, in their totality, these indicated a theocratic vision incompatible with democracy which Refah would be capable of realising through its political powers. Accordingly, a Chamber of the Court ruled that there had been no infringement of the applicant's freedom of

---

99. *Refah Partisi (The Welfare Party) v Turkey* [2003] ECHR 87.

100. *United Communist Party of Turkey v Turkey* 133/1996/752/951, 30 January 1988, Reports of Judgments and Decisions 1998–1, pp 21–22, 45.

101. *United Communist Party of Turkey v Turkey* 133/1996/752/951.

102. *United Communist Party of Turkey v Turkey* 133/1996/752/951. This decision of the ECtHR is also cited in *Refah Partisi v Turkey* [2003] ECHR 87 (13 February 2003).

103. *United Communist Party of Turkey v Turkey* 133/1996/752/951, 30 January 1988: *Socialist Party v Turkey* 20/1997/804/1007, 25 May 1998; *Freedom and Democracy Party (OZDEP) v Turkey* (Application No 23885/94, 8 December 1999.

association since the measures adopted by Turkey in suppressing it were 'prescribed by law' and necessary in a democratic society for the pursuit of legitimate aims.[104] However, three of the seven judges dissented, holding that the measures adopted by the Turkish State were disproportionate. The applicants then requested that the matter be referred to a Grand Chamber of the Court which unanimously upheld the previous judgment.[105]

The Place of Religion in a Democracy

[4.035] The place of religion in a democratic society was also considered in the *Refah* case. The ECtHR reiterates the position that, as safeguarded by Art 9, freedom of thought, conscience and religion is one of the foundations of a 'democratic society' within the meaning of the ECHR:

> It is, in its religious dimension, one of the most vital elements that go to make up the identity of believers and their conception of life, but it is also a precious asset for atheists, agnostics, sceptics and the unconcerned. The pluralism indissociable from a democratic society, which has been dearly won over the centuries, depends on it. That freedom entails, inter alia, freedom to hold or not to hold, religious beliefs and to practice or not to practice a religion.[106]

However, where several religions so-exist in a democratic society in one and the same population, the court considered that it may be necessary to place restrictions on this freedom so as to reconcile the interests of the various religious groups and ensure that everyone's beliefs is respected.[107] The court has frequently stressed the state's role as the neutral and impartial organiser of the exercise of various religions, faiths and beliefs and that this role is conducive to public order, religious harmony and tolerance in a democratic society and the case law of the ECtHR confirms this state function.[108] Nonetheless, the court also considers that the state's duty of neutrality and impartiality is incompatible with any power on the state's part to access the

104. Judgment of 31 July 2001 which contains a joint dissenting opinion at pp 35–47.

105. Judgment of Grand Chamber of 13 February 2003, *Refah Partisi (The Welfare Party) v Turkey* [2003] ECHR 87.

106. See *Kokkinakis v Greece* (1994) 17 EHRR 397, 418 and *Buscarini v San Marino* [GC], no 24645/94. para 34, ECHR 1999–1.

107. *Kokkinakis v Greece* (1994) 17 EHRR 397, p 18, para 33.

108. *Kokkinakis v Greece* (1994) 17 EHRR 397.

legitimacy of religious beliefs.[109] It has further held that in a democratic society the state may restrict the freedom to manifest a religion, for example, by wearing an Islamic headscarf in public schools, if the exercise of that freedom conflicts with the aim of protecting the rights and freedoms of others, public order and public safety.[110]

[4.036] While freedom of religion is *prima facie* a matter for the individual conscience, it also implies freedom to manifest a religion alone, in private or in community with others, and in public and within the faith circle one shares. Article 9 lists a number of forms of manifestation of religion or belief such as worship, teaching, practice and observance, but clearly it does not protect every act motivated or influenced by a religion or belief.[111] Thus, the obligation falling on a motorcyclist to wear a crash helmet, which he asserts conflicts with his religious duties, may be compatible with the freedom of religion in Art 9.[112] Likewise, the duty on a teacher to participate in normal working hours, which the teacher claims conflicts with his/her attendance at prayers, may be compatible with the religious freedom.[113] The ECtHR held that, at the time of its dissolution, the Refah Party had the potential to seize political power in Turkey, acting alone, and its monopoly of political power would have enabled it to establish the model of society it envisaged, ie a theocratic one based on *sharia* law.

[4.037] When campaigning for change in legislation or change to the constitutional or legal structures of the state, political parties enjoyed the protection of the ECHR and Art 11 so long as they discharged two conditions:

(i) the means used to these ends had to be lawful and democratic from all perspectives; and

(ii) the proposed changes had to be compatible with fundamental democratic principles.

---

109. See *Metropolitan Church of Bessarabia v Moldova*, no 45701/99, para 123, ECHR 2001–XII. The Latin phrase meaning 'the necessary changes being made', Murdoch, *A Dictionary of Irish Law* (5th edn, Tottel Publishing, 2008).

110. *Dahlab v Switzerland* Case 44774/98, 29 June 2004.

111. *Kalac v Turkey*, judgment of 1 July 1997, Reports 1997–IV, p 1209, para 27.

112. *X v UK*, App No 8160/78 (1981) 22 D&R 27 144–5.

113. *X v UK* App No 7992/77 (1978) 14 D&R 234 256, Commission Decision of 12 July 1978, DR 14, p 234.

However, political parties whose leaders incited others to do violence and/or supported political aims that were not consistent with one or more rules of democracy, or which sought the destruction of democracy and the suppression of the rights and freedoms that it recognised, could not rely on the Convention to protect them from sanctions imposed as a consequence.[114]

Restrictions on Churches by the State

[4.038] The Russian Federation is a democratic, federal law-bound state with a republican form of government.[115] Being grounded in democracy, the Constitution of the Russian Federation 1993 (Russia hereafter) recognises and guarantees the basic rights and liberties in conformity with the commonly recognised principles and norms of international law.[116] Article 28 of the Constitution provides that everyone shall be guaranteed freedom of conscience and freedom of religion, including the right to profess alone or with others any religion or to profess no religion, to freely choose, to have and share religious and other beliefs and to manifest them in practice. In addition Art 29 guarantees freedom of ideas, speech and expression, mass communication and no censorship while Art 30 guarantees the right to freedom of association.

[4.039] The Federal Law on the Freedom of Conscience and Religious Associations[117] – (The Religions Act 1997) required the founding documents of religious organisations, whose existence pre-dated the Religions Act, to conform to the new Act by amendment and to be re-registered but it imposed new requirements and a time-limit which on expiration meant certain religious organisations were liable for dissolution by a judicial decision unless they had re-registered. A number of religious organisations encountered difficulties with this new process and they initiated challenges in the Russian Constitutional Court.

[4.040] In *Religious Society of Jehovah's Witnesses in Yaroslav and Christian Glorification Church v Russia*[118] the court considered the constitutional

---

114. Judgment of Grand Chamber of 13 February 2003, *Refah Partisi (The Welfare Party) v Turkey* [2003] ECHR 87.

115. Art 1 of the Constitution of Russia 1993 which replaced the Soviet era's Constitution of 1978.

116. Constitution of Russia 1993, Art 17(1).

117. No 125-FZ of 26 September 1997.

118. *Religious Society of Jehovah's Witnesses in Yaroslav and Christian Glorification Church v Russia* Decision No 16-P of 23 November 1999.

compatibility of the requirement of the Religions Act that all religious organisations, whose existence pre-dated the Religions Act 1997, should confirm that they have existed for at least 15 years. The court held that the latter requirement would be incompatible with the principle of equality enshrined in the Russian Constitution[119] and an impermissible restriction on freedom of religion in Art 28 and the freedom of [voluntary] associations to form and to carry out their activities in Art 30. The Constitutional Court confirmed this position in *Independent Russian Region of the Society of Jesus v Russia*[120] and again in *Moscow Branch of the Salvation Army v Russia.*[121] Although the position in national law was undoubtedly well founded, the Justice Department consistently refused to re-register the Church of Scientology Moscow and this resulted in a battle of epic proportions which led to the landmark challenge in *Church of Scientology Moscow v Russia.*[122]

Refusals to Register the Church of Scientology Moscow

[4.041] The applicant made a total of 11 unsuccessful applications for re-registration under the Religions Act 1997 to the Moscow Justice Department having been registered under the old legislation for approximately three years. Having exhausted the remedies in the domestic courts, the applicant took its case to the ECtHR. The applicant complained that, under Arts 9,[123] 10[124] and 11[125] of the ECHR, it had been stripped arbitrarily of its legal-entity status resulting from the refusal to re-register it as a religious organisation under the Religion Acts 1997. Because the religious nature of the applicant had not been disputed by Russia, and the applicant had

119. Arts 13.4, 14.2, 19.1 and 19.2.

120. *Independent Russian Region of the Society of Jesus v Russia* Decision No 46-O of the 13 April 2000.

121. *Moscow Branch of the Salvation Army v Russia* Application No 72881/01, ECHR 2006, Decision no 7-O of 7 February 2002: see further Douglas Rutzen, 'Salvation in Court: the *Salvation Army v Russia*', IJNL, Vol 9, Issue 1, December 2006.

122. *Church of Scientology Moscow v Russia Application* no 18147/02, judgment of 5 April 2007 which held there was also a breach of Art 11 (freedom of assembly and association).

123. Freedom of thought, conscience and religion.

124. Freedom of expression.

125. Which prohibits discrimination on a number of grounds including religion.

received official recognition from 1994, the court found that the complaints required to be examined from the perspective of Art 11 read in the light of Art 9 of the ECHR. Referring to its settled case law, the court reiterated the fact that as enshrined in Art 9, freedom of thought, conscience and religion is one of the foundations of a democratic society within the meaning of the Convention and that in its religious dimension, it is one of the most vital elements that comprise the identity of believers and their conception of life but that it is also a precious asset for atheists, agnostics, sceptics and the unconcerned and that the pluralism indissociable from a democratic society depends on it.[126] While religious freedom is primarily a matter of individual conscience, the court continued, it also implies, among other matters, freedom to 'manifest [one's] religion' alone and in private or in community with others in public and within the circle of those whose faith one shares. Since religious communities normally exist in the form of organised structures, Art 9 must be interpreted in the light of Art 11 (the right to peaceful assembly and association) of the ECHR which protects associative rights against unjustified state interference:

> ... the right of believers to freedom of religion, which includes the right to manifest one's religion in community with others encompasses the expectation that believers will be allowed to associate freely, without arbitrary state intervention. Indeed, the autonomous existence of religious communities was indispensable for pluralism in a democratic society and is thus an issue at the very heart of the protection which Art 9 affords. The state's duty of impartiality and neutrality, as defined in the court's case law, is incompatible with any power on the state's part to access the legitimacy of religious beliefs.[127]

The court confirmed that the right to form an association is an integral part of the right granted by Art 11 and that citizens should be able to establish a legal entity so as to enable them to act collectively in a sphere of mutual interest which is one of the most significant aspects of the associative right, without which that right would be meaningless. The believers' right to freedom of religion includes the expectation that the community will be permitted to function peacefully, free from arbitrary state intervention.[128]

126. *Metropolitan Church of Bessarabia v Moldova* No 45701/99, para 114, ECHR 2001–XII.

127. Citing *Hasam and Chaush v Bulgaria* [GC], no 30985/96, para 62, ECHR 2000–XI and *Metropolitan Church of Bessarabia v Moldova* no 45701/99, para 114, ECHR 2001–XII.

128. See *Hasan and Chaush v Bulgaria* [GC] no 30985/96, para 62, ECHR 2000–XI.

While states certainly have a right to ensure that an association's aims and activities conform to the rules made under the legislation, they are required to do so in a manner compatible with their ECHR obligations and subject to the review of the ECHR institutions.[129] Once again the court emphasised the fact that the ECHR embodies, protects and promotes the democratic model and its ideals and values and that it is the only political model envisaged by the ECHR. As a consequence of the wording of the second paragraph of Art 11, and similarly of Arts 8, 9 and 10 of the ECHR, the only necessity capable of justifying an interference with any of rights enshrined in those Arts is one that may claim to arise from 'democratic society' principles which had been considered by the court in *United Communist Party of Turkey v Turkey*[130] and in *Refah Partisi v Turkey.*[131]

[4.042] The court held that the state's power to safeguard its institutions and citizens from associations that might jeopardise them must be used sparingly, since exceptions to the rule of freedom of association are to be construed strictly and only convincing and compelling reasons can justify restrictions on that freedom. Any interference, the court continued, must correspond to a 'pressing social need.'[132] In other words, if the reason for interference is useful or desirable, that is insufficient to justify state interference: the state must be able to prove that it interfered because of a 'pressing social need'. The court noted that prior to the enactment of the new Religions Act in Russia, the applicant had lawfully operated from 1994: that it was unable to acquire 're-registration' as required by the Religions Act and had, by operation of law, become liable for dissolution.[133] Hence, its legal capacity was not equal to that of other religious organisations which

129. Citing *Sidiropoulos v Greece* Judgment of 10 July 1998, Reports of Judgments and Decisions 1998–IV, para 40.

130. *United Communist Party of Turkey v Turkey* Judgment of 30 January 1998, Reports of Judgments and Decisions 1998–1, paras 43–45.

131. *Refah Partisi v Turkey* Nos 41340/98, 41342/98, 42343/98 41344/98, paras 86–89, [2003] ECHR 87: see further *Refah Partisi ILNL* Vol 6, Issue 1, September 2003.

132. Thus, the notion 'necessary' does not have the flexibility of such expressions as 'useful' or 'desirable'. (see further *Gorzelik v Poland* [GC], no 44158/98, paras 94–95, 17 February 2004, with further references).

133. Although this immediate threat was removed later by the Constitutional Court's decision.

had obtained re-registration certificates.[134] Applying the principles in the *Moscow Branch of the Salvation Army v Russia*,[135] the court ruled that there had been interference with the applicant's right under Art 11 of the Convention read in the light of Art 9. It then had to determine whether that interference was 'prescribed by law' and whether it pursued one or more legitimate aims, and was 'necessary in a democratic society'.[136] The court stressed that the restriction on the rights to freedom of religion in Art 9 and freedom of assembly in Art 11 is exhaustive:

> The exceptions to the rule of freedom of association are to be construed strictly and only convincing and compelling reasons can justify restrictions on that freedom. In determining whether a necessity within the meaning of paragraph 2 of these Convention provisions exists, the state have only a limited margin of appreciation, which goes hand in hand with rigorous European supervision embracing both the law and the decisions applying it, including those given by independent courts.[137]

When the court investigates such matters, it does not substitute its own views for that of the national authorities but reviews their decision and the exercise of their discretion reasonably, carefully and in good faith. The court must consider holistically the interference complained of and decide whether it was 'proportionate to the legitimate aims pursued' and whether reasons given by the national authorities are 'relevant and sufficient.' During the process of its investigation the court has to be satisfied that the national authorities applied standards which conformed to the principles enshrined in the Convention and that they grounded their decisions in an acceptable assessment of the germane facts.[138] Applying these principles, the court

134. *Moscow Branch of the Salvation Army v Russia* Application no 72881/01, 23–24 ECHR 2006.

135. *Moscow Branch of the Salvation Army v Russia* Application no 72881/01, 23–24 ECHR 2006.

136. *Moscow Branch of the Salvation Army v Russia* Application no 72881/01, 23–24 ECHR 2006 citing *Metropolitan Church of Bessarabia v Moldova* no 45701/99, para 114, ECHR 2001–XII, para 106.

137. *Moscow Branch of the Salvation Army v Russia* Application no 72881/01, 23–24 ECHR 2006 citing *Gorzelik v Poland* [GC], no 44158/98, paras 94–95, 17 February 2004, para 95: and *Stankov and the United Macedonian Organisation Ilinden v Bulgaria* nos 2922/95 and 29225/95, para 84, ECHR 2001–IX.

138. See *United Communist Party of Turkey v Turkey* 133/1996/752/951, 30 January 1988 and *Paridul Comunistilor (Nepeceristi) and Ungureanu v Romania* No 46626/99, para 49, ECHR 2005–1.

found that the grounds for refusing re-registration of the Church were not consistent throughout the period the applicant sought re-registration. Not alone did this inconsistency deprive the applicant of an opportunity to remedy the alleged defects and to re-submit them, but it ran counter to the specified requirement that any refusal must be reasoned. By failing to state clear reasons for its refusal to re-register the applicant, the Moscow Justice Department acted in an arbitrary manner. Thus, the court found that the ground for refusal was not 'in accordance with law'. Moreover, the court was unable to find that the domestic law was formulated with sufficient precision, which would enable the applicant to foresee the adverse outcome of its submission of copies, and the requirement to include originals was excessively burdensome, or even impossible, to fulfil. Accordingly, the court concluded that the grounds invoked by the domestic authorities for refusing to re-register the applicant had no lawful basis. Because the applicant had lawfully existed and operated in Moscow for three years prior to the re-registration requirement was introduced, the reasons for refusing re-registration should have been 'particularly weighty and compelling',[139] and no such reasons had been put forward by the domestic authorities. In denying registration to the Church of Scientology in Moscow, the court held, the Moscow authorities did not act *bona fide* and they neglected their duty of neutrality and impartiality in regard to the applicant's religious community. The interference with the applicant's right to freedom of religion and association was unjustified and that there had been a violation of Art 11 of the Convention read in the light of Art 9. Refusing the applicant's request for injunctive relief in regard to re-registration, however, the court stated that its judgments are essentially declaratory in character and that in general it is primarily for the state concerned to choose the means to be used under national law to discharge its legal duty under Art 46 of the Convention.[140] Nevertheless, the court ordered the respondent to pay €10,000 (in Russian roubles) in respect of non-pecuniary damage to the applicant together with €15,000 (in Russian roubles) in respect of costs and expenses and any tax that may be chargeable on those amounts plus simple interest until settlement of the total amount due to the applicant. This case has deep implications for minority religions, and for the 'new' religions, particularly those in France, and indeed all the other contracting states in relation to the parity of all religions.

---

139. *Moscow Branch of the Salvation Army v Russia* Application no 72881/01, ECHR 2006, Decision no 7-O of 7 February 2002: *Gorzelik v Poland* [GC], no 44158/98, 17 February 2004.

140. *See Shofman v Russia* no 74826/01, 24 Nov 2005, para 53.

The Right to Education in the ECHR

[4.043] Article 2 of the First Protocol provides:

> No person shall be denied the right to education. In the exercise of any functions which it assumes in relation to education and to teaching, the state shall respect the right of parents to ensure such education and teaching in conformity with their own religious and philosophical convictions.

To a degree, Art 2 of Protocol 1 can be viewed as shielding the right to education which European countries generally perceive as a natural right vested primarily in parents. The word 'philosophical' was added, it appears, to include protection for the parental convictions of non-believing or agnostic parents.[141] During the drafting process many complex legal issues arose for consideration: whether this right to education is vested in the child or in parents and whether that right is sourced in fundamental law or positive law.[142] Further discussions focussed on whether the right of every person to education imposed a corresponding duty on the state to ensure that everyone is educated. Certain member states were reluctant to accept a positive formulation of the right to education lest it would bind them in the future to provide education to each person in the state. A further controversial topic discussed was whether contracting states were to accept that children could be raised as atheists or agnostics. At the heart of the debate was the issue of how and to what degree are the rights of parents to be safeguarded when the state is necessarily assuming major responsibility for education?'[143] Such matters led to a debate of considerable complexity as the Travaux Preparatoires,[144] which run to eight volumes, indicate. When the ECHR was signed into law on the 4 November 1950[145] it contained no article relating to the right to education since it had not been formulated. Because of the difficulties encountered, the right to education was delayed and it did not enter into force until 18 May 1954 as a Protocol to the existing ECHR (Art 2 of Protocol 1).[146] It appears, therefore, that the consensus which finally emerged for the right to education provision was for a limited article only.

---

141. See *Belgian Linguistic Case,* Opinion of the Commission, 'Publications of the Court', Ser B, 379 at 282.

142. ECtHR Decisions and Reports, Volume 2,100.

143. TV Lord Layton, (UK), ECtHR Decision and Reports, Vol 2, 54.

144. Teigten, *Collected Edition of the Travaux Preparatoires of the European Convention on Human Rights* (1985) Council Of Europe.

145. The Convention entered into force on the 3 September 1953.

146. Glendenning, *Education and the Law* (Tottel Publishing, 1999) p 253 *et seq.*

[4.044] The first sentence of Art 2 of Protocol 1 guarantees freedom of education *per se*.[147] As to the meaning of the term 'education', both case law and the use of that term in international treaties indicate the formal kinds of scholastic instruction provided in institutions.[148] The holistic meaning given to the term 'education' as opposed to 'teaching' or instruction was distinguished in *Campbell and Cosans v United Kingdom*,[149] which dealt with the administration of corporal punishment in Scottish schools.[150] Article 2 of Protocol 1 guarantees that certain parental rights (their religious and philosophical convictions) will not be overridden by the state in regard to education and teaching even though the state assumes the major responsibility in education.

Interpreting Article 2 of Protocol 1

[4.045] When interpreting Art 2 of Protocol 1, the Commission and the ECJ have read all three of its components harmoniously. In cases when disagreements have arisen, the court has referred to the extensive preparatory material (*travaux preparatoires*) as a supplementary aid to interpretation.[151] In its first sentence, Art 2 provides that the state shall not deny the right to education to any person. Accordingly, the contracting state may not interfere with or set at nought a persons' exercise of the right to education eg by denying him/her the right to avail of state-provided opportunities in education.[152] In the event of a legal challenge, the state is in a more favourable position than if the obligation was stated in positive terms

147. See De Groof, and Lauwers (eds) (2004), No person shall be denied the right to education: the influence of the European Convention on Human Rights on the right to education and rights in education, pp 19–22.

148. Szabo, *Cultural Rights* (Leiden, 1974): see also the UN Convention against Discrimination in Education.

149. *Campbell and Cosans v UK* (1982) 4 EHRR 165.

150. When the court distinguished between education and instruction, education being 'the whole process whereby in any society adults endeavour to transmit their beliefs, culture and other values to the young, whereas teaching or instruction refers in particular to the transmission of knowledge and to intellectual development.'

151. *Belgian Linguistic Cases* (1967) 1 EHRR 241; (1979) 1 EHRR 252; *James v UK* (1986)8 EHRR 123.

152. *Jordebo v Sweden*, ECHR, Application No 11533/85 decision of 6 March 1987.

as the aggrieved person has the onus of proving that the state has denied him/her the right to education.[153] Clearly Art 2 of Protocol guarantees the right to establish and run a private school, but this cannot be a right without conditions and must be subject to the regulation of the state to ensure a proper educational system as a whole.[154] Although the right to education is formulated in a textually absolute manner, this does not mean that it has to be applied in an absolute manner, a fact which is apparent in a number of cases including the landmark Grand Chamber decision of *Sahin v Turkey.*[155] The applicant's complaint was that a ban on the wearing of religiously inspired headscarves in higher education institutions in Turkey breached her right to education since she had been refused entrance to examinations because she wore such a headscarf. While acknowledging the significance of this right, the court stated that it was not an absolute right, but may be subject to limitations which are permitted by implication.[156]

[4.046] The leading Strasbourg authority dealing with the content of Art 2 is the *Belgian Linguistic Case (No 2)*[157] which addressed the right of French-speaking Belgian parents to have their children educated in French, the language of their choice. The court held that Art 2 enshrines a right to education. Such regulation must not damage the substance of the right to education and the possibility of setting limitations to such access.[158] As to the scope and content of Art 2, the court found that it guarantees the right of access to educational institutions existing at the given time but it imported no linguistic requirements. It did include, however, the right to obtain, in conformity with existing national rules, the official recognition of studies which have been completed. However, there was no guarantee given to parents to have their children educated in a language of their choice. A difference of treatment by the state was not discriminatory provided it could be objectively and reasonably justified. The decision in the *Belgian Linguistic Case (No 2)* has been applied and extended in many later

153. *Campbell and Cosans v UK* (1982) 4 EHRR 165.

154. *Jordebo v Sweden* ECHR, Application no 11533/85 decision of 6 March 1987.

155. *Sahin v Turkey* (2005) 41 EHRR 8.

156. *Sahin v Turkey* (2005) 41 EHRR 8, at para 154.

157. *Belgian Linguistic Cases* (1967) 1 EHRR 241; (1979) 1 EHRR 252.

158. On this latter point see van der Schyff, 'Classifying the Limitation of the Right to Education in the First Protocol to the European Convention', *International Journal for Education Law and Policy,* Vol 2. Issue 1–2, 2006, pp 153–162.

decisions[159] including *Kjelsden, Busk, Madsen and Pederson v Denmark*[160]which is considered later. Art 2 is dominated by its first sentence[161] but that article must be read holistically[162] and not restrictively, which would be inconsistent with its aim.[163] The right to education is not an absolute right,[164] it is subject to regulation by the state, but such regulation must not damage the essence of the right to education or deprive it of its effectiveness[165] nor conflict with other rights enshrined in the ECHR. Such regulation may vary in time and place according to the needs and resources of the community and of individuals. The imposition of disciplinary penalties is an integral part of the process by which a school strives to achieve the object for which it was founded, including the development of the character and mental powers of its pupils.[166] Neither is it contrary to Art 2 for pupils to be suspended or expelled, provided the national regulations do not preclude them enrolling in another institution to pursue their studies[167] but again, this qualification is not absolute.[168] Thus, it appears, the right to education has two dimensions, firstly its scope falls to be considered by the ECtHR and secondly its limitations or restrictions are to be considered and determined.

---

159. *Campbell and Cosans v UK* (1982) 4 EHRR 165: *Sahin v Turkey* (1996) 84 (Application 44774/98), (10 November 2005, unreported), Grand Chamber and *Timishev v Russia* (Application Nos 55762/00 and 55974/00), (13 December 2005, unreported).

160. *Kjelsden, Busk Madsen and Pedersen v Denmark* (1976) 1 EHRR 711.

161. *Kjelsden, Busk Madsen and Pedersen v Denmark* (1976) 1 EHRR 711; *Campbell and Cosans v UK* (1982) 4 EHRR 165.

162. *Campbell and Cosans v UK* (1982) 4 EHRR 165, para 52.

163. *Sahin v Turkey* (2005) 41 EHRR 8, para 137: *Timishev v Russia* (Application Nos 55762/00 and 55974/00), (13 December 2005, unreported) para 64.

164. *Sahin v Turkey* (2005) 41 EHRR 8, para 154.

165. *Campbell and Cosans v UK* (1982) 4 EHRR 165, para 41; *Sahin v Turkey* (1996) 84 (Application 44774/98), (10 November 2005, unreported), Grand Chamber para 154.

166. *Sahin v Turkey* (Application No 44774/98), 10 November 2005, para 156.

167. *Yanaisk v Turkey* (1993) 74 DR 98.

168. *Sulak v Turkey* (1996) 84–A-DR 98.

[4.047] In *Ali v Head Teacher and Governors of Lord Grey School,*[169] Lord Bingham summarised the *raison d'etre* of Art 2 of Protocol 1 with admirable clarity. The basic premise of Art 2 was, he stated, that all existing member states of the Council of Europe and all future member states would have an established system of state education. It was the intention of the drafters to guarantee fair and non-discriminatory access to that system to those persons who lived within the jurisdiction of the respective member states. The fundamental significance of education in a modern democracy was recognised to require nothing less but it was intentionally a weak guarantee, his Lordship considered, by comparison with other ECHR guarantees:

> There is no right to education of a particular kind or quality, other than that prevailing in the state. There is no Convention guarantee of compliance with domestic law. There is no Convention guarantee of education at or by a particular institution. There is no Convention objection to the expulsion of a pupil from an educational institutional institution on disciplinary grounds, unless (in the ordinary way) there is no alternative source of education open to the pupil (as in *Erin v Turkey*, Application No 60856/00 (7 February 2006, unreported). The test as always under the Convention is a highly pragmatic one, to be applied to the specific facts of the case: have the authorities of the state acted so as to deny to a pupil effective access to such educational facilities as the state provides for such pupils?[170]

Nonetheless, the Convention implies a just balance between the protection of the general interest of the Community and the respect due to fundamental rights while attaching particular significance to the latter.[171] If there is a denial of the substance of the right of access to existing educational establishments, however, this would clearly be in breach of Article.[172]

[4.048] While the first sentence of Art 2 of Protocol 1 confers on states considerable discretion in regard to the nature and ambit of their involvement in education, the second sentence requires that, when exercising any functions relating to education and to teaching, the state must respect the religious and philosophical convictions of parents. There are

169. Lord Bingham in *Ali v Head Teacher and Governors of Lord Grey School* [2006] UKLH 14.

170. *Ali v Head Teacher and Governors of Lord Grey School* [2006] UKLH 14, at para 24.

171. *Belgian Linguistic Cases* (1967) 1 EHRR 241; (1979) 1 EHRR 252.

172. *Cyprus v Turkey* (2002) 35 EHRR 30.

certain curricular subjects in which it is difficult to set clear boundaries respecting parental religious and philosophical convictions and sex education is one of these. In *Kjelsden, Busk Madsen and Pederson v Denmark*[173] parents' religious and philosophical objections to the provision of compulsory sex education in state schools in Denmark were rejected by the ECHR on the grounds that they could send their children to private schools or educate them at home and the court further held that there was no breach of Arts 8, 9 or 14 or of Art 2 of Protocol 1 of the ECHR. The Strasbourg institutions considered the scope of the state's duty in the drafting and implementation of a compulsory sex education programme for state schools and it laid down further significant parameters to the right to education. Until the State Schools Act 1970 (the 1970 Act) came into operation, sex education in the Danish State elementary schools was an optional, separate subject. The 1970 Act provided for integrated, and hence compulsory, sex education in these schools. However, state-funded private schools were not required to teach the programme but were obliged to teach factual biological information. Certain parents in the school petitioned the Commission contending that compulsory sex education conflicted with their Christian parental convictions and accordingly breached their rights under the ECHR. The Commission, however, found no breach of Art 2 of Protocol 1[174] and no breach of Arts 8, 9 or 14 but it referred the case to the Strasbourg Court.

[4.049] The ECtHR held that the second sentence of the Protocol, which is an adjunct of the first part, makes parents primarily responsible for the education and teaching of their children[175] and that the second sentence of Art 2 'bound states in the exercise of each and every function that they undertook in the sphere of education and teaching, including the organisation and financing of public education.'[176] The parental right to respect for their religious and philosophical convictions is grafted on to the fundamental right to education in the first sentence and both parts must be read in the light of the whole Convention, particularly Arts 8, 9 and 10.[177]

173. *Kjelsden, Busk Madsen and Pedersen v Denmark* (1976) 1 EHRR 711, paras 54 and 57.

174. By the President's casting vote.

175. *Kjelsden, Busk Madsen and Pedersen v Denmark* (1976) 1 EHRR 711 at 729.

176. *Kjelsden, Busk Madsen and Pedersen v Denmark* (1976) 1 EHRR 711, p 711.

177. *Kjelsden, Busk Madsen and Pedersen v Denmark* (1976) 1 EHRR 711, pp 729–30; *Belgian Linguistic Cases* (1967) 1 EHRR 241; (1979) 1 EHRR 252.

Accordingly, Art 2 of Protocol 1 referred to each of the state's functions and enjoined the state to respect parents' religious or philosophical convictions throughout the entire state education programme both religious and secular. However, the ECtHR recognised the virtual impossibility of a perfect separation of religious and philosophical and secular subjects.

[4.050] Although the court held that the second sentence of Art 2 implies that the setting and planning of the curriculum fall in principle within the competence of the contracting states, it did not set rigid limits to the discretion of the states and it considered that the solution could legitimately vary according to the country and era:

> In particular, the second sentence of Art 2 of the Protocol does not prevent states from imparting through teaching or education information or knowledge of a directly or indirectly religious or philosophical kind. It does not even permit curriculum for otherwise all institutionalised teaching would run the risk of proving impracticable. In fact, it seems very difficult for many subjects taught at school not to have, to a greater or lesser extent, some philosophical complexion or implications. The same is true of religious affinities if one remembers the existence of religions forming a very broad dogmatic and moral entity which has or may have answers to every question of a philosophical, cosmological or moral nature.[178]

In other words, the states have considerable discretion and flexibility in regulating curricular matters touching on religious and philosophical issues and, since that is so, the right of parents to claim respect from the state for their religious and philosophical convictions may be limited in certain circumstances.

[4.051] Nonetheless, the court set certain limits and boundaries to the state's discretion, which may not be crossed. For example the ideals of a democratic society, such as plurality, secularity and equality, must be upheld by the state when regulating education and teaching and the states must take care that information or knowledge contained in the curriculum is conveyed in an '... objective, critical and pluralistic manner'. While it seems legitimate for the state to permit some degree of integration of information or knowledge of a religious or philosophical nature in the curriculum, it may not enjoin a certain ethical or moral view of life and it may not pursue 'an aim of indoctrination.' In other words, the state is forbidden to pursue an aim of indoctrination that might be considered as not respecting parent's religious and philosophical convictions and that is the limit that must not be

---

178. *Kjelsden, Busk Madsen and Pedersen v Denmark* (1976) 1 EHRR 711, at p 730.

exceeded.[179] If, for example, the state were to interfere to a degree that amounted to indoctrination, this would set at nought the objective of the right to protect parents' religious and philosophical convictions and to foster pluralism. Applying these principles to the facts in *Kjelsden*, the court observed that the sex education complained of could not be given without touching upon the religious and philosophical sphere and it declared:

> These considerations are indeed of a moral order, but they are very general in character and do not entail overstepping the bounds of what a democratic state may regard as the public interest. Examination of the legislation in dispute establishes in fact that it in no way amounts to attempt at indoctrination aimed at advocating a specific kind of sexual behaviour.

Accordingly, even though the sex education programme in *Kjelsden* involved considerations of a moral order, and the court found that these, being very general in character, did not overstep the bounds of what a democratic state might have regarded as being in the public interest. Since the aim of the sex-education programme was 'clearly not to impose upon the children a certain ethical or moral view of life',[180] the court concluded that nothing in the challenged statute indicated that the sex education provided would indoctrinate the children in any manner. The court further observed that the Danish State had preserved options for parents who wished to avoid integrated sex education for their children in that it heavily subsidised private schools which were less strictly bound in this regard and that it also permitted home education.[181] Accordingly the court ruled that there was no breach of Art 2 of Protocol 1 either taken alone or in conjunction with Art 14[182] and it unanimously held there was no violation of Arts 8 and 9 read together with the Art 2 of Protocol 1.

[4.052] The relevant Danish legislation was found not to offend the applicants' religious and philosophical beliefs to the extent prohibited by the second sentence of Protocol 1(2) as it was not 'an attempt at indoctrination aimed at advocating a specific kind of sexual behaviour.' Neither did it affect the right of parents to enlighten, advise or guide their children in accordance with their own religious and philosophical convictions. Sex education continues to be an integral and obligatory part of instruction in Danish elementary state schools. A teacher cannot, however, be compelled

179. *Kjelsden, Busk Madsen and Pedersen v Denmark* (1976) 1 EHRR 711.

180. *Kjelsden, Busk Madsen and Pedersen v Denmark* (1976) 1 EHRR 711, p 47.

181. *Kjelsden, Busk Madsen and Pedersen v Denmark* (1976) 1 EHRR 711.

182. By 6:1 votes.

against his or her will to give the more explicit kind of sex instruction referred to in the Danish Executive Order of 1972.[183] Private schools, on the other hand, remain free to decide to what degree they wish to align their teaching, in this sphere, with the rules that apply to state schools.

[4.053] In *Valsamis v Greece*[184] the applicants lodged a complaint that their rights to have their daughter educated in accordance with their religious convictions as Jehovah's Witness had been breached by the state since she was required to attend a National Day parade which they contended had military overtones which conflicted with their religious beliefs. The court held that Art 9 did not confer a right to exemption from disciplinary rules which had been applied generally and in a neutral manner and there had been no breach of the child's right to manifest her religion or belief. While acknowledging that the parent's rights were safeguarded by the second sentence of Art 2 of Protocol 1, the court clarified that democracy does not mean that the views of a majority must always prevail: but must however, on occasion, be subordinated to those of a group. But the court continued, a balance must be achieved which ensures the fair and proper treatment of minorities and avoids any abuse of a dominant position. Having fully considered the facts of the case, the court could discern nothing, either in the purpose of the parade or in the preparatory arrangements, which could offend the applicant's pacific convictions to an extent prohibited by the second sentence of Art 2 of Protocol 1 and it found, therefore, that there was no breach of that sentence. Although the parental religious convictions were interfered with by the state, since this right was not absolute and the state had interfered with this right only to a justifiable degree, the court found that this did not constitute an abuse of a dominant position by Greece.

Sweden's Reservation to Art 2 of Protocol 1

[4.054] In Sweden the different denominations provide religious education for their own children and this tradition was reflected in their legislation. Most children attend the Public Sector School System whose legal basis is the School Act 1962 (the 1962 Act) and the Decree on Schools 1971 (as amended). This legislation permitted parents to educate their children in their own religious creeds but it provided that, if parents did not subscribe to any creed, then the children should be educated according to the state

183. Danish Executive Order of 1972, No 313 of 15 June 1972, s 1(3).

184. *Valsamis v Greece* [1998] ELR 430: see also *Efstratiou v Greece*, decision of 18 Dec 1996, Reports, 1996 VI.

religion. When an exemption under the 1962 Act was granted, the 1971 Decree applied which required a pupil to certify that s/he had received 'other religious instruction.'

[4.055] When faced with the signing of Art 2 of Protocol 1, Sweden entered a reservation so as to avoid conflict with its domestic legislation as it stood at that time. That reservation stated:

> Sweden could not grant to parents the right to obtain, by reason of their philosophical convictions, dispensation for their children from the obligation of taking part in certain parts of the education in the public schools, and also ... the dispensation from the obligation of taking part in the teaching of Christianity in these schools could only be granted for children of another faith than the Swedish Church, in respect of whom a satisfactory religious instruction had been arranged.[185]

Sweden's reservation has withstood two legal challenges. Firstly, in *Karnell and Hardt v Sweden*[186] the applicants[187] contended that this reservation did not apply to them as members of a minority church in Sweden[188] and as they were not listed among those religions meriting an exemption. The applicants petitioned the Commission, on foot of Art 2 of Protocol I, complaining that their request to have their children exempted from the state religion in school had been refused and that their church had also been refused permission to provide alternative religious instruction for the children. The application, in so far as it was brought by a church, was held inadmissible but, to the extent that it was made by four individual applicants, was held admissible. In advance of the Commission's decision, however, the King ordered that the parental requests be granted and that the Religious Instruction in question be separated from other curricular subjects in order to fully facilitate the exemption.[189] On the withdrawal of their application, the applicants were given assurances that pupils affiliated to their church would, following parental requests to that effect, be exempted from

185. See *McCallum v Board of Education* [1948] 333 US 203 in which the US Supreme Court held that no person may be required to attend religious instruction in a state-recognised or state-aided institution.

186. Yearbook of the European Convention 1971.

187. The application was brought by the church initially but four individual parents were joined later.

188. The Evangelical-Lutheran Church.

189. *Karnell and Hardt v Sweden* (No 4733/71), (1971) 14 Yearbook 676.

compulsory religious instruction; that religious instruction would be separate from secular instruction in which exempted pupils participated; and that any exempted pupil would not be disadvantaged by reason of not receiving religious instruction at school.

[4.056] A further challenge to the legality of Sweden's reservation emerged in 1988 in *Angelini v Sweden.*[190] The applicants were a Swedish mother and her daughter. Both were professed atheists. The mother had applied unsuccessfully to the school to have her daughter exempted from participation in the teaching of religious knowledge. Her daughter was not, however, receiving any 'other religious instruction' as required by the 1971 Decree. The applicants lodged an application to the Commission stating that the second applicant was required to participate in the teaching of religious knowledge in breach of Arts 9, 14 and 17 of the ECHR. When a child who is an atheist is obliged to adopt a Christian way of thinking, they argued, freedom of thought guaranteed under Art 9 was violated together with parental freedom of conscience, as the parent holding values other than Christian ones is denied the right to bring up his/her children in an atheistic manner and in accordance with the parent's religious and philosophical convictions. The applicants also referred to Sweden's reservation in respect of Art I of Protocol 2. The Commission, which had already considered this reservation in *Kjelsden v Denmark*[191] in 1979, stated that: 'the reservation gives almost complete freedom to the Swedish government to organise child education regardless of the religious and philosophical convictions of parents.'[192] The Commission found that the exemption could only be granted in cases of children belonging to a religious faith other than the Swedish Church for whom satisfactory alternative religious education could be arranged and children of parents holding particular philosophical convictions could not be granted exemptions. Moreover, the Commission found no indication that Sweden's reservation was contrary to Art 64 of the ECHR and concluded that there had not been a breach of the ECHR or of Art 1 of Protocol 2.[193]

190. *Angelini v Sweden* (1988) 10 EHRR 123.

191. *Kjelsden, Busk Madsen and Pedersen v Denmark* (1976) 1 EHRR 711.

192. *Angelini v Sweden* (1988) 10 EHRR 123 citing *Kjelsden, Busk Madsen and Pedersen v Denmark* (1976) 1 EHRR 711.

193. *Angelini v Sweden* (1988) 10 EHRR 123 at p 128.

[4.057] Since 1980, however, the Act and Decree are supplemented by the compulsory school curriculum which requires that pupils should receive knowledge of different religions and religious views of life including Marxism and Humanism. While Sweden's reservation to Art 1 of Protocol 2 has not been withdrawn, the 1985 Swedish School Law[194] provides for exemption of pupils from religious instruction.

[4.058] Express protection for the religious and philosophical convictions of non-believing or atheistic parents is also provided for in Art 5(1)(b) of the the United Nations Convention against Discrimination in Education 1962 (UNCDE), which also provides that 'no person or group of persons should be compelled to receive religious instructions inconsistent with his or their conviction.'[195] In addition, the ICCPR enshrines the right of parents to ensure that the religious and moral education of their children is in conformity with their own convictions. However, the obligation for a teacher to observe normal working hours, which he or she contends, conflicts with attendance at prayers, may be compatible with the freedom of religion principle.[196] Likewise, the obligation requiring a motorcyclist to wear a crash helmet, which he asserts is incompatible with his religious duties may also be compatible with religious freedom.[197]

[4.059] In summary, with regard to the second sentence in Art 2 of Protocol 1, the state is given the freedom to discern the scope and character of its commitment to education and teaching, but it is not required to guarantee that each person receives the education that he or she wishes to receive nor is it required to provide certain kinds of educational opportunities under this sentence. However, the second sentence guarantees the right of parents in regard to their children's education, to have their religious and philosophical convictions respected by the state when exercising any of the functions it assumes in relation to education or teaching but this right is limited. The right to participate in religious teaching

194. The School Law 1985, chapter 3, s 12: 1100, pars 1, 2 and 3 effected in Government Decree of 1991.

195. United Nations Convention against Discrimination in Education, Art 5(b), 429 UNTS 93, entered into force 22 May 1962. See a copy of this Convention in **Appendix 4** of this book.

196. *X v UK*, No 7992/77, Commission Decision of 12 July 1978, DR 14, p 27.

197. *X v UK*, No 7992/77, Commission Decision of 12 July 1978, DR 14.

was already protected by Art 9 of the ECHR. When religious instruction is provided in state schools, parents must be permitted to make alternative arrangements if they wish to have their children withdrawn from such instruction.

The United Kingdom's Reservation to Art 2 of Protocol 1

[4.060] The UK entered a reservation in regard to the second sentence of Art 2 of Protocol 1 as follows:

> ... in view of certain provisions of the Education Acts in force in the United Kingdom, the principle affirmed in the second sentence of Art 2 is accepted by the United Kingdom only so far as it is compatible with the provision of sufficient instruction and training and the avoidance of unreasonable public expenditure.

In the UK, the Human Rights Act 1998 was passed to enable those persons whose ECHR rights had been violated to have those rights vindicated by the domestic courts.[198] In other words, since 1998 the domestic courts have been called upon to interpret and apply the Convention. However, in *Campbell and Cosans v UK*,[199] the ECtHR pointed out that this reservation must be read as applying only to the legislation in place at the time the reservation was made.

Ireland's Reservation to Art 2 of Protocol 1

[4.061] The Irish Constitution's doctrine of family autonomy in education has influenced the direction of education in Ireland since 1937 and its social function is reflected in its reservation to Art 2 of Protocol 1. Children's rights to education in Ireland have traditionally being viewed as vested in their parents and courts have upheld the primacy of parental choice, subject only to the state's right to require minimum standards of education.[200] While the passage of the Education Act 1998 and other germane legislation has permitted the state to move forward in education, certain constitutional constraints on state action are still apparent in Irish jurisprudence as

198. See further Meredith, 'Incorporation of the European Convention on Human Rights into UK Law, Implications for Education, *European Journal for International Law and Policy* (1998) 2: 7–23, p 7.

199. *Campbell and Cosans v UK* (1982) 4 EHRR 165, para 37.

200. *Re Art 26 and the School Attendance Bill 1942* [1943) IR 334: see further Glendenning, *Education and the Law*, paras [3.70] and [8.65] *et seq*.

chapter 9 illustrates. Ireland's reservation was to the effect that the right to education in the Protocol was not sufficiently explicit in protecting parental choice of schools and the right to educate in the home whether or not such schools were private schools or schools recognised or established by the state.[201]

England's more pragmatic concerns regarding resources contrasts with the more ideological reservations of Sweden and Ireland. It appears that these reservations will be respected under Art 53 of the European Charter of Fundamental Rights which forms part of the Lisbon Treaty which will have full legal effect only when the Lisbon Treaty is accepted and adopted by all 27 member states.

Unequal State Provision for Non-Denominational Schools?

[4.062] One issue which has led to alleged breaches of Art 14 read together with Art 2 of Protocol 1 is the unequal state funding for schools of particular religious denominations as against non-denominational (secular) schools. There is no obligation on the state to subsidise any particular type of education under the Convention, but where it undertakes to do so, it must do so in a non-discriminatory manner. However, because the case law in this sphere has applied a broad approach to justification, challenges on the grounds of Art 14 are difficult to maintain.[202] In *X v UK*[203] a parent from Northern Ireland, who favoured non-denominational or integrated education, challenged the practice of the UK's provision of a grant of 100 per cent to state schools, administered by public authorities, which contrasted with a grant of 85 per cent to private non-denominational schools. As a result of the deficit in funding, parents in the non-denominational schools were required to raise the remaining 15 per cent capital costs themselves.

[4.063] The state's failure to grant a 100 per cent subsidy to the private non-denominational schools, it was argued by the applicants, breached Art 2 of Protocol 1. However, the Commission chose to consider whether the differential in the grant available to the state's schools and that of the private

201. [1954] Ir TS, No 3, see chapter 8 and further Clarke, 'Freedom of Thought and Educational Rights in the European Convention', *Irish Jurist*, 1987, 50–54: and Clarke, 'Freedom of Thought in Schools: a Comparative Study,' in *International and Comparative Law Quarterly*, 35 (1986), 271–301.

202. See further McManus, QC, *Education and the Courts* (Jordans, 2004) p 86–87.

203. *X v UK* No 7782/77, Decision of 2 May 1978, 14 DR 179.

non-denominational schools breached Art 14 which required the state not to discriminate in the allocation of available financial funds. The Commission considered that, by maintaining substantial control in the ownership and management of schools for which it provided a 100 per cent grant, the state acted legitimately and that it was reasonable for the state, in regard to institutions that retain ownership and decisive control in relation to management policy in private schools, to require some degree of financial contribution from them. Accordingly the Commission did not consider the sum of 15 per cent to be an unreasonable or disproportionate requirement in the circumstances and it held that the state had not discriminated under Art 14 in the *X v UK*.[204]

[4.064] The Austrian State allocates subsidies to church schools as a matter of course, whereas non church bodies such as the applicants are required to comply with another condition – that of corresponding to a 'need'. In *Verein v Gemeinsam Lernen*[205] the applicants, which established and administered a non-religious private school, mounted a challenge to the state's provision of more favourable subsidies to the church schools (also private schools) than it did to their non-religious private school which they contended breached Art 2 of Protocol 1 read in the light of Art 14. While the Commission was of the view that Art 14 required that any such subsidies should not discriminate on the specified grounds, it nonetheless held that treating the church schools differently to the applicant body could be justified under Art 14 because the church schools were so widely disseminated that if the educational services provided by them had to be discharged by the state, a considerable extra burden would fall on the state.[206] From a legal perspective, this is a somewhat disquieting decision since arguably it dilutes the legal principle of non-discrimination in Art 14, when taken in conjunction with Art 2 of Protocol 1, and it departs from any legal argument relating to religious freedom and is grounded solely in a contextual argument.

204. *X v UK* No 7782/77, Decision of 2 May 1978, 14 DR 179.

205. *Verein v Gemeinsam Lernen v Austria* N 23419/94, Decision 6 September 1995, 82 DR 41.

206. See McManus, *Education and the Courts* (Jordans, 2004) p 87.

Indoctrination by the State

[4.065] As already noted in *Kjelsden v Denmark*[207] the ECtHR set limitations to the state's remit in regard to indoctrination of students which apply across the full school curriculum and are not restricted to religious instruction or worship classes. However, the court did not elaborate on what it understood by 'indoctrination'. *Cassell's English Dictionary* defines 'to indoctrinate' as 'to instruct in any body of doctrine' or 'to imbue with the distinctive principles of any system'.[208]

[4.066] The Canadian Charter of Rights and Freedoms (the Charter) guarantees certain rights and freedoms subject to such reasonable limitations as are prescribed by law as can be demonstrably justified in a free and democratic society. Among the fundamental freedoms universally guaranteed in the Charter are freedom of thought, belief, opinion and expression.[209] In *Corporation of Canadian Civil Liberties Association v Ontario*[210] the Canadian Court of Appeal devised a comprehensive list of guidelines to be used in its jurisdiction when seeking to establish whether a public school had exceeded the lawful boundaries between religious education and indoctrination:

> (1) that a school may sponsor the study of religion but not the practice of religion;
>
> (2) that a school may expose students to all religious perspectives but may not impose any one particular perspective;
>
> (3) that a school should strive to inform students concerning various beliefs but not seek to conform a student to any one belief;
>
> (4) that a school should promote student awareness of all religions but not press for student acceptance of any one religion;

---

207. *Kjelsden, Busk Madsen and Pedersen v Denmark* (1976) 1 EHRR 711; *Hartikainen v Finland* (Comm No 40/1078) UN Doc A/36–40, decision of 9 April 1981.

208. *Cassells English Dictionary* (Cassells, 1971) p 600.

209. At para 2.

210. *Corporation of Canadian Civil Liberties Association v Ontario* (1990), 71 OR (2d) 341 (CA). See further Clarke, *Church and State: Essays in Political Philosophy* (Cork University Press, 1984) p 215.

(5) that a school should educate about religions, not convert to any one religion;

(6) that a school's approach should be academic and not devotional.[211]

[4.067] More recently in *Ciftci vTurkey*[212] the ECtHR considered allegations of indoctrination against the Turkish State. This case arose from that state's regulatory ban of the teaching of the Koran to pupils in their final years of primary education, on the grounds of limiting the possible indoctrination of minors at a vulnerable stage when they could be readily influenced by Koranic teaching. The ECtHR held that Turkey's legislative ban on such teaching did not constitute an attempt by that state at indoctrination aimed at preventing religious education. Although this decision appears to be tailored to the particular context of Turkey and the various threats to its democratic society, this is, in the opinion of this writer, a potentially dangerous precedent. While the ECtHR requires the contracting states to remain neutral and objective when dealing with religion, and further requires them not to access the legitimacy of any one religion, the court appears to have breached its own recommendations in *Ciftci*. Arguably, the Turkish State did not act neutrally and objectively, since it trespassed on the freedom of religion rights of Muslim parents to educate their children in accordance with their religious and philosophical convictions in breach of Art 2 of Protocol 1 of the ECHR. Unless this case is distinguished by the court and strictly restricted to secularist contexts, what is to prevent the court deciding at a future date that a state party may place a legislative ban on the teaching of the Talmud or the Bible in public schools or in publicly-funded religious schools? Arguably, in the *Ciftci* decision, the ECtHR does not adequately respect the principle of religious freedom which Art 9 of the ECHR has guaranteed to uphold.

[4.068] The ECtHR in *CJ, JJ and EJ v Poland*,[213] confirmed that while Art 9 affords protection from religious indoctrination by the state, it primarily protects the sphere of personal beliefs and religious creeds, ie the area which is sometimes referred to as the *forum internum*. In addition it protects acts which are intimately bound up with these attitudes such as acts of worship or devotion which are aspects of the practice of a religion or belief in a generally recognised form.[214] The *forum externum* embraces outward

---

211. I am grateful to A Mawhinney for drawing my attention to this case.

212. *Ciftci v Turkey* Application No 71860/01, Decision of 17 June 2004.

213. *Ciftci v Turkey* Application No 71860/01, Decision of 17 June 2004.

214. See also ECHR, Application No 11308/84, 3 Dec 1986, DR 46, p 200.

expressions of though, conscience and religion and is subject to limitations. Basic rights safeguarded by the *forum internum* include the right to have a religion or belief, the right not to have a religion or belief and the right not to be involuntarily subjected to preaching or to any form of involuntary indoctrination[215] and the right to hold theistic, non-theistic, sceptical and atheistic beliefs.[216]

The Right to Education: Language Facilities

[4.069] In *Cyprus v Turkey*[217] it was established by the ECtHR that the many issues complained of by Greek Cypriots living in Northern Cyprus fell within the jurisdiction of Turkey by virtue of Art 2 of the ECHR. Among the numerous breaches of their Convention rights which had occurred was an alleged violation of the right to education in Art 2 of Protocol 1. The Turkish authorities had abolished the Greek language facilities in secondary schools, which had been in existence in Northern Cyprus prior to the Turkish invasion of that island. While the court held that the right to education did not specify the language in which education must be conducted, the option open to Greek children, who had previously received their education in Greek, was to continue to receive their secondary education at Turkish- or English-medium schools. The court ruled that, since these Greek children had already received their education in Greek, the actions of the Turkish authorities amounted to a denial of the substance of the right of access to existing educational establishments. In so far as no appropriate secondary school facilities were available to these children, the court ruled that this breached Art 2 of Protocol 1 of the ECHR.

---

215. *CJ, JJ and EJ v Poland* 84-A Eur Comm'n HR Dec & Rep 46 (1996), above; *Kjelsden, Busk Madsen and Pedersen v Denmark* (1976) 1 EHRR 711; *Hartikainen v Finland* (Comm No 40/1078) UN Doc A/36–40, decision of 9 April 1981: *Angelini v Sweden* (1988) 10 EHRR 123 all of which held that Art 9 of the ECHR includes protection against religious indoctrination by the state.

216. *United Communist Party of Turkey v Turkey* judgment of 30 January 1998, Reports of Judgments and Decisions 1998–1, paras 43–45; *Refah Partisi (The Welfare Party) v Turkey* [2003] EHRR 1, see above at p 52; *Moscow Branch of the Church of Scientology v Russia*, Application no 18147/02, judgment of 6 April 2007.

217. *Cyprus v Turkey* (2002) 35 EHRR 30.

Private Schools: a Viable Alternative?

[4.070] Does the existence of highly state-funded private schools reduce the onus on the state in regard to the guarantee of religious freedom in recognised schools?[218] In *Campbell and Cosans v United Kingdom*[219] the Commission rejected the state's contention that its provision for private schools freed it of its duties in regard to the abolition of corporal punishment in state schools. If such schools were expensive or distant from the child's family home, then they would not be viable alternatives for parents, the Commission indicated. However, in *Jimenez and Jimenez Merino v Spain*[220] in which a parent alleged, among other matters, indoctrination by the state aimed at advocating particular sexual behaviour, the ECHR held that the wide network of private schools in Spain, which exist alongside the public sector schools, providing an education better suited to the applicants' faith or opinions, discharged the state's obligation to respect the religious and philosophical convictions of such parents. Since the applicants had chosen a state school, the right to have their beliefs and ideas, as guaranteed by Art 2 of Protocol 1, respected by the state, could not be interpreted as conferring on them 'the right to demand different treatment in the education of their daughter in accordance with their own convictions' in a state school. This important precedent is discussed in considerable detail in **chapter 8** below.[221]

CONCLUSION

[4.071] Now that religious education in Europe is closely related to secular education, human rights are increasingly influencing this sphere of life as is clear from the case law mentioned in this chapter. The jurisprudence of the ECtHR in this area is well-established. In the provision and implementation of a religious education or ethics programme for state schools in a democratic, pluralist society, the state must be impartial, neutral and objective. It may not advance the legitimacy of any one religion over another nor may it indoctrinate in any one faith. The state must respect the liberty of parents or legal guardians to choose for their children institutions other than

218. In *Campbell and Cosans v UK* (1982) 4 EHRR 1653.

219. *Campbell and Cosans v UK* (1982) 4 EHRR 165.

220. *Jimenez and Jimenez Merino v Spain* Application No 51188/99, Reports of Judgments and Decisions 2000–VI.

221. **Para [8.033]** *et seq*.

those maintained by the public authorities but conforming to such minimum education standards as the state lays down or approves. In addition, the state must respect the religious and philosophical convictions of parents and it is required to promote the principles of a democratic society. With regard to teacher training, the state is also required to provide training without discrimination.[222] Religious instruction and worship, however, is not a matter for the state, but a matter for the parents and their churches.

222. Convention against Discrimination in Education, Art 4(d)

Chapter 5

RELIGION, EDUCATION AND LAW IN ENGLAND

Perhaps the greatest challenge we have is that of militant secularism. The West is losing a Christian discourse at the very time it needs it most. Let us pray we are able to recover our Christian nerve and make sure the Gospel is not lost.[1]

INTRODUCTION AND BACKGROUND

[5.001] The United Kingdom (UK) comprises three separate jurisdictions – England and Wales, Scotland and Northern Ireland, each of which has its own distinct legal system. English law and Scottish law have quite distinctive origins and histories, and in some respects Scottish law is quite different from the common law of England. In 1999 Scotland had its Parliament restored after almost three centuries of absence. While modern legislation is frequently enacted separately for each country, certain significant issues are reserved to the UK Parliament,[2] including constitutional issues relating to church and state.[3] The UK is not a secular (laic) state. Neither is it one of those states in which religion is excluded from the state system of education. Rather, the law provides for freedom of religion and the government generally respects this right in practice.[4] Unlike France and the United States (US), there is no principle requiring the separation of religion and state in education in Britain's unwritten constitution, which comprises a collection of laws, institutions and customs

1. Glenhill, 'Bishop says Church's biggest threat is militant secularism' (2008) *The Times,* 25 June, p 3 citing the Anglican Bishop of Rochester, Bishop Michael Nazir-Ali: also see Wynne-Jones at http://www.telegraph.co.uk/news/uknews/1579661/Bishop-of-Rochester-reasserts-no-go-claim.html, accessed on 3 October 2008.
2. McClean, 'State and Church in the United Kingdom', in Robbers (ed), *State and Church in the European Union* (Nomos, 2005) p 553.
3. McClean in Robbers (ed), *State and Church in the European Union.*
4. *International Religious Freedom Report*, 2007, US Department of State, Released by the Bureau of Democracy, Human Rights and Labor.

that govern the country.[5] By contrast with Spain,[6] which imposes a constitutional ban on a state religion, the UK has two established (or state) churches, the Church of England (Anglican) and the Church of Scotland (Presbyterian).

[5.002] The concept of establishment in England, however, is quite distinct from that of establishment in the US, which is embodied in the First Amendment. In England, establishment is not a legal or constitutional tenet but rather a broadly descriptive term referring to the state's special relationship with two specific established churches the Church of England and the Church of Scotland.[7] Neither is there any principle of religious neutrality in the UK system, unlike the position in Belgium (although the neutrality principle in the Belgian Constitution does not preclude the state from funding schools that foster and maintain a particular religious or

---

5. See further Burgess, 'Constitutional Change in the United Kingdom, New Model or Mere Respray?' 40 S Tex L Rev 715, 717 (1999); Harris, *Education and Diversity*, p 429; Fischer and Wallace, 'God and Caesar in the Twenty-First Century: What Recent Cases Say about Church-State Relations in England and the United States' (2006) *Florida International Law Journal*, 18, p 485. This very interesting article is also available at: http://works.bepress.com/judith_fischer/3.

6. Article 6 of the Constitution of Spain 1978 provides: 'There shall be no State religion'.

7. See further Fischer and Wallace, (2006) *Florida International Law Journal*, 18, p 487 and Munro, 'Does Scotland have an Established Church?' (1997) 4 *Ecclesiastical Law Journal*, No 20, 639–645.

8 Article 24(1) of the Constitution of Belgium provides: 'The community organises neutral education. Neutrality implies notably respect for the philosophical, ideological, or religious conceptions of parents and pupils.' See online Federal Belgian Constitution at www.fed-parl.be/constitution_uk.html, accessed 3 October 2008. While Art 10 of the Constitution provides that all Belgians are equal before the law, in practice important juridical distinctions are made between recognised and unrecognised religious groups, with the Catholic Church being *primus inter pares* among the recognised churches (although secularisation is now gradually emerging). In Belgium, Catholic education numerically outstrips state education with 60 per cent of second level pupils attending schools in the state-subsidised Catholic network, while this figure reaches 75 per cent in Flanders. These figures are similar to those in Ireland where approximately 60 per cent of second level students attend schools in the state-funded Catholic network (see **chapter 9** below). Everyone has the right to education with the respect of fundamental rights and freedoms. (contd .../)

philosophical perspective).[8] In England most of the articles[9] of the ECHR have been incorporated by the Human Rights Act 1998. However, as Meredith points out, the government has stopped short of conferring on the courts a power to strike down legislative provisions as being incompatible with Convention rights. Rather the superior courts have a power to issue a declaration of incompatibility which leaves a wide measure of discretion in the hands of the government as to how it should respond, if at all.[10]

[5.003] Education in the UK takes place in one of the most ethnically, culturally and religiously diverse societies in Europe. Nonetheless, certain religious minorities, including the Muslim community, have experienced difficulties when seeking to establish schools in the state system, although that difficulty now appears to be easing.[11] The 2001 census figures for the UK[12] indicate that approximately 72 per cent (41 million) of the population consider themselves Christians,[13] with 1.5 million Muslims, 0.5 million Hindus, 0.3 million Sikhs, 0.25 million Jews and 0.3 million of other faiths, together with 8.5 million of no faith. Because of the distinctions which pertain in the manner in which establishment is interpreted, this chapter will be concerned only with aspects of the interface of religion, education and the law in England.

---

8. (contd) Article 14(3) of the Belgian Constitution provides: 'Access to education is free until the end of obligatory scholarity'. It further provides: 'All pupils of school age have the right to moral or religious education at the community's expense.' See further Torfs, 'State and Church in Belgium,' in Robbers (ed), *State and Church in the European Union* (Nomos, 2005) pp 20 and 32.

9. Note the absence of Art 13, (the right to an effective remedy) for example.

10. Meredith, 'Incorporation of the European Convention on Human Rights into UK Law, Implications for Education' *European Journal for Education Law and Policy,* Vol 2, No 1 p 22.

11. Harris, *Education, Law and Diversity*, p 430.

12. Office for National Statistics, Population Estimates by Ethnic Group Figures, 2001 (experimental) see online at www.statistics.gov.uk/StatBase/Product.asp?vlnk=14238, accessed on 3 October 2008: see further tables and social facts in McClean, op cit 554–557. See further Babbs, Martin and Hazelwindt (eds), *Focus on Social Inequalities*, Table 7.9.

13. Which includes Anglican, Roman Catholic, Presbyterian and Methodist Churches. See Watson, *The Church of England* (Kessinger Publishing, 2004); Mayfield, *The Church of England* (2nd edn, 1963); Lloyd, *The Church of England, 1900–1965* (SCM Press, 1966); Cox, *The English Churches in a Secular Society: Lambeth, 1870–1930* (Oxford University Press, 1982).

Ecclesiastical Law in England: Historical Summary

[5.004] In England, as in other countries, history has left an indelible mark on the structures and evolution of ecclesiastical law. The legislation on this subject dates back to 1688 when the Church of England was then the established church of the land and all other religious denominations were proscribed. In 1688 a measure of tolerance was extended to Protestants who dissented from the established church under the Act of Toleration 1688. This Act permitted such dissenters to meet as a congregation or assembly for religious worship, provided always that their place of meeting was certified to the bishop or to quarter sessions and registered, and provided that the place of assembly was not locked, barred or bolted. Subsequently the same measure of toleration was extended to Roman Catholics by the Roman Catholic Relief Acts of 1791 and 1829.[14] The latter Act repealed the Test Acts 1673 and 1678, which required oaths of supremacy and allegiance, with the aim of restricting civic office to members of the Church of England.[15] Toleration was extended to the Jews by the Religious Disabilities Act 1846. In 1855 toleration was extended to all denominations by the Places of Religious Worship Registration Act 1855 (the 1855 Act), under which all denominations were free to register 'a place of religious worship' provided they discharged the conditions. The 1855 Act applies to 'every place of meeting for religious worship of any other body or denomination of persons'. In accordance with ss 2, 3 and 4 of the 1855 Act, such a place may be certified to the Registrar General and on receipt of the certificate he has to record it as a place of public worship. However, some religions have failed

---

14. These Acts partially removed the Penal Laws, it appears. See further Connolly (ed), *The Oxford Companion to Irish Hist*ory (Oxford University Press, 1999) pp 77–78.

15. The Catholic Relief Act 1829 repealed the Corporation Act 1661, which required that all persons holding civic office be communicants of the Church of England. The object of this latter Act was to restrict all civic office in England to adherents of the Church of England. All the Test Acts were repealed in 1829, including the Test Acts 1673 (requiring all persons holding civic or military office to be communicants of the Church of England and to denounce the doctrine of transubstantiation) and the Test Act of 1678 (extending the 1673 Act to members of both Houses of Parliament). See further Butler's *Historical Memoirs of English, Scottish, and Irish Catholics*. See also his book on *The French Church*, his *The Life of Hugo Grotius* and his book, *The Coronation Oath*.

to obtain registration under the 1855 Act.[16] Active religious discrimination against Catholics was relieved by the various Catholic Reliefs Acts[17] and gradually the discriminations against religious freedom, so apparent in earlier centuries, were repealed. In 1914 the Welsh dimension of the Church of England was separated and disestablished in accordance with the Welsh Church Act 1914.

Relevant Modern Legislation

[5.005] The Crown Prosecution Service reported an increase in prosecutions in 2006 for racist and religiously-motivated incidents. Of these, 43 were categorised as religiously aggravated and 41 defendants were prosecuted. In the 21 cases where the victim's religion was known, 18 were Muslim, 3 were Christians and 1 was a Sikh.[18] It was against this background that the Racial and Religious Hatred Act 2006 (the 2006 Act) was enacted. The 2006 Act[19] makes provision for the prosecution of offences involving stirring up hatred against persons on racial or religious grounds and it amends the Public Order Act 1986. In essence, the 2006 Act seeks to ensure that the criminal law will protect groups of persons defined by their religious beliefs, or lack of religious beliefs, from having hatred intentionally stirred up against them in circumstances covered by ss 29B to 29F of the Act. Accordingly, the Act creates new offences of stirring up hatred on religious grounds and it amends the Police and Criminal Evidence Act 1984,[20] so that the powers of citizens' arrest are not applicable to the new offences created by the 2006 Act. 'Religious hatred' is defined by the 2006 Act as 'hatred against a group of persons defined by reference to religious belief or lack of religious belief.' The Criminal Justice and Immigration Act 2008 abolishes the common law offences of blasphemy and blasphemous libel and introduces a new criminal offence of incitement to hatred on the grounds of sexual orientation.

---

16. For example, the Church of Scientology. *R v Registrar General ex parte Segerdal* [1970] 2 QB 697; [1970] 3 All ER 886 and *Church of Scientology of Moscow v Russia* Application No 18147/02, judgment del 5 April 2007 and *Barralet v AG* [1980] 3 All ER 918 .

17. Catholic Reliefs Acts of 1778, 1793 and 1828.

18. Source: *International Religious Freedom Report 2007*, Released by the Bureau of Democracy, Human Rights and Labor, available at http://www.state.gov./g/drl/rls/irf/2007/90206.htm.

19. Which refers to England and Wales only.

20. Police and Criminal Evidence Act 1984, s 24A.

[5.006] The term 'religious hatred' is broadly defined in line with Art 9 of the ECHR and it embraces, although not definitively, those religions generally recognised in England and Wales including Christianity, Islam, Hinduism, Judaism, Buddism, Sikhism, Rastafarianism, Baha'ism, Zoroastrianism and Janism. Religious hatred directed against branches or sects within a religion and to a group of persons defined by reference to an absence of religious belief, is also covered by the Act, which applies to Humanists and Atheists. However, the 2006 Act does not define 'religion' or what constitutes 'religious belief', leaving such matters to the courts to determine in accordance with the circumstances of each case. Freedom of expression is also protected in s 29J of the Act.[21] It provides:

> Nothing in this Part shall be read or given effect in a way which prohibits or restricts discussion, criticism or expressions of antipathy, dislike, ridicule, insult or abuse of particular religions or the beliefs or practices of their adherents, or any other belief system or the beliefs or practices of its adherents, or proselytising or urging adherents of a different religion or belief system to cease practicing their religion or belief system.

Thus, to constitute an offence under the 2006 Act, an act would have to be threatening and be intended to stir up religious hatred on one of the following grounds: the use of words or behaviour or display of written material;[22] publishing or distributing written material;[23] public performance of a play;[24] distributing, showing or playing a recording;[25] broadcasting or including a programme in a programme service;[26]or possession of inflammatory material.[27] The maximum penalty for stirring up religious hatred under the 2006 Act is seven years' imprisonment or a fine or both.[28] The Act does not apply to prohibited acts which take place inside a private dwelling or to those matters covered by the above-mentioned s 29J (dislike, ridicule etc) of a religious belief.

---

21. In regard to Pt 3A of the Racial and Religious Hatred Act 2006.
22. Racial and Religious Hatred Act 2006, s 29B.
23. Racial and Religious Hatred Act 2006, s 29C.
24. Racial and Religious Hatred Act 2006, s 29D.
25. Racial and Religious Hatred Act 2006, s 29E.
26. Racial and Religious Hatred Act 2006, s 29F.
27. Racial and Religious Hatred Act 2006, s 29G.
28. Racial and Religious Hatred Act 2006, s 29L.

Equality Legislation

[5.007] Under the Employment Equality (Religion or Belief) Regulations 2003, religious discrimination in employment and vocational training is prohibited. In addition, it is illegal under the Equality Act 2006 to discriminate on the grounds of 'religion and belief' or the 'lack of religion and belief', *inter alia*, in the provision of services and education and in the exercise of public functions.[29] Some of these equality provisions have led to ongoing controversy and Christian, Jewish and Muslim leaders have joined forces to complain that the equality rules force them to overturn long-established religious beliefs.

Establishment

[5.008] The Reformation had a profound effect in England, leading to the establishment of the Church of England of which the Queen is the current Supreme Governor on Earth.[30] At a coronation, the English monarch takes an oath to continue to maintain the Church of England.[31] From the Reformation onwards the state formed close links with the Church of England which continue to the present day, although those links appear to have diminished in strength in recent decades.[32] So as to secure the position of the monarch as Supreme Governor of the Church of England at a time of uncertainty, the Act of Settlement 1701 (the Act) prohibits any Roman Catholic, or their spouse, from becoming King or Queen of England or from marrying the heir to the throne. The Act provides:

> Provided always that all and every person and persons, who shall or may take or inherit the said Crown, by virtue of the limitation of this present act, and is, are or shall be reconciled to, or shall hold communion with, the See or Church of Rome, or shall profess the popish religion, or shall marry a papist, shall be subject to such incapacities as in such case or cases are by the said recited act provided, enacted, and established.[33]

---

29. Equality Act 2006, Pt 2, ss 44–45.

30. Act of Supremacy 1534. See also Act of Succession 1534 and Act of Supremacy 1559. For the position in Wales, Northern Ireland and Scotland, see McClean, 'State and Church in the United Kingdom' in Robbers (ed), *State and Church in the European Union* (Nomos, 2005) p 553.

31. The Coronation Oath Act 1688. See also the Bill of Rights Act 1688, the Act of Settlement 1701 and the Accession Declaration Act 1910.

32. Fischer and Wallace, (2006) *Florida International Law Journal*, 18, p 486.

33. 12 & 13 Wm 3 c 2.

This provision is clearly discriminatory, since it applies only to Roman Catholics, and there have been many calls for its removal, given that it now operates in one of the most multicultural, multifaith contexts in Europe.[34] Essentially the law confers on the Church of England the status of establishment and has its genesis[35] in the reign of Henry VIII[36] and his severance of the pre-existing union between the English Churches and Rome.[37] The Church of Scotland too has established status with its own source and distinctive evolution which is beyond the scope of this book.[38] In effect, the UK recognises a distinct body of ecclesiastical law which derives solely from the jurisdiction of these two established churches and significantly this ecclesiastical law is an integral component of the law of England. While it is the Queen, acting on the Prime Minister's advice, who appoints the archbishops and bishops of the Church of England,[39]since 1977 a church-state agreement restricts the Queen's choice to a panel of persons nominated by the church,[40] thereby imposing a substantial constraint on the monarch's powers in that regard.

34. BBC News, 20 November 1999, 'Call for bans by MPs'; also BBC News, Northern Ireland, 'Catholic monarch ban "should end"', citing an interview with Bishop Alan Harper and (2007) *Irish Times*, 18 January, and online at http://news.bbc.co.uk/2/hi/uk_news/northern_ireland/6275011.stm accessed on 3 October 2008.

35. In so far as England is concerned.

36. Henry VIII is described in *O'Keefe v Cardinal Cullen* QB 1873 IR 1873–1874, CL Vol VII, p 319 at 416 as: 'The impetuous Sovereign, Henry 8, declared he would be Lord of Ireland no longer; accordingly, a Statute made him King. Then he said he would not be half a King, but a whole one; and, accordingly, the principles of the old common law and the doctrine of the undivided jurisdiction of the Crown were embodied in the legislation of the Parliament of Ireland.'

37. In 1521 Henry VIII was given the title 'Defender of the Faith' by the Pope. See among others the Act of Succession 1534, the Act of Supremacy 1534, the Act of Supremacy 1559 and the Act of Settlement 1701; and further McClean, in Robbers (ed), *State and Church in the European Union* (Nomos, 2005) pp 553–575.

38. The General Assembly Act 1592 provides the statutory basis of the Scottish Presbyterian Church. See further McClean in Robbers (ed), *State and Church in the European Union* (Nomos, 2005) p 558 *et seq.*

39. Currently standing at 26; Fischer and Wallace, (2006) *Florida International Law Journal*, 18, footnote 21.

40. McClean in Robbers (ed), *State and Church in the European Union*, p 564.

[5.009] The General Synod (the Synod), which has the authority to make alterations to this corpus of law, is the National Assembly of the Church of England,[41] which replaces the earlier Church Assembly[42] and has its genesis in the medieval period. The Synod is empowered to effect change in any matter under its remit, through the passing of Measures, which, if they are approved by the resolution of the two Houses of Parliament, and receive the Royal Assent, become part of the law of England.[43] The Synod also has power to amend or repeal existing Acts and to regulate the relationships between the Church of England and the other churches. Although the Canon law of the Church of England is passed by the Synod without reference to Parliament, formal promulgation of a new Canon remains subject to Royal Assent and Licence.[44] The Synod comprises a House of Bishops, a House of Clergy and a House of Laity – the latter two bodies being elected – and all three Houses must agree to any proposal, thereby facilitating the participation of the Laity in the formulation of Canon law and giving it a democratic input.[45]

Legal Status of Non-Established Churches

[5.010] By contrast with the position of the established churches, the non-established churches in England (the majority of churches, including the Roman Catholic Church, the Protestant denominations and other main faiths) are voluntary associations. In other words, apart from the established Church of England, all the other main churches in England are voluntary associations which have charitable status[46] under the general law of charities and charitable trusts and their 'laws' have the status of contract law between the parties. The property of the non-established churches is usually held in trust by trustees under the secular law or by registered companies under company law, an arrangement which may be supplemented in some

41. Which was established pursuant to the Synodical Government Measures 1969 and came into being in 1970.

42. Church of England Assembly (Powers) Act 1919.

43. *Percy v Church of Scotland Board of National Mission*, 199 SLT 1228 (Employment Appeal Tribunal).

44. McClean, Robbers (ed), *State and Church in the European Union* (Nomos, 2005) p 561.

45. McClean, Robbers (ed), *State and Church in the European Union*, p 560.

46. See Lord M'Naughten's rules of charitable purposes in *Commissioners of Special Income Tax v Pemsel* [1891] AC 531.

instances by a private Act of Parliament.[47] Statutory provision has been made for registration of places of worship[48] and for the formalisation of marriage.

[5.011] When faced with the question of what constitutes a 'church', the English courts have generally interpreted that term conservatively. It has been held, for example, that a humanist association was not entitled to charitable status since it did not exist for the advancement of religion.[49] In *R v Registrar-General ex parte Segerdal*[50] Lord Denning held that Buddhism was a religion for the purpose of being registered as a place of worship under the Places of Worship Act 1855. When the Church of Scientology sought to have a building registered as a place of worship under the same Act, the Court of Appeal ruled that this required the assembly of individuals to worship God or to give reverence to a supreme being or deity and that instruction in a secular philosophy did not qualify as such,[51] a decision which would now fall foul of the ECtHR in the light of its recent decision in *Church of Scientology of Moscow v Russia*.[52] Generally speaking, the courts will not become involved in the internal affairs of churches unless they exceed their jurisdiction or are in breach of the civil law, but there have been some notable exceptions.[53] Undoubtedly the establishment of the Church of England has had a profound impact on church-state relationships in England[54] and consequently on the corpus of ecclesiastical law, as McClean observes:

> The church is closely bound up with the business of the state, many senior church appointments involving Crown patronage and a number of bishops

47. Robbers (ed), *State and Church in the European Union* (Nomos, 2005) p 562.
48. Places of Worship Registration Act 1855.
49. *Barralet v AG* [1980] 3 All ER 918.
50. *R v Registrar General ex parte Segerdal* [1970] 2 QB 697; [1970] 3 All ER 886. See also *Barralet v AG* [1980] 3 All ER 918.
51. *R v Registrar General ex parte Segerdal* [1970] 2 QB 697; [1970] 3 All ER 886.
52. Application 18147/02, judgment delivered 5 April 2007.
53. See *O'Keefe v Cardinal Cullen* 2 QB 1873 CL 7 319 and 1873–1874 IR, Common Law, Vol VII, p 319. Note the position of the courts in Scotland which resolutely insisted on examining every ecclesiastical sentence complained of, as essential to the administration of justice at p 435 of this case.
54. See McClean, 'The Changing Legal Framework of Establishment' (2004) 7 *Ecclesiastical Law Journal*, p 292.

sitting as of right in the House of Lords (though continuing debates as to the further reform of the House may lead to their removal). There can be no 'concordat' or treaty-like relationship between church and state. The ecclesiastical law relating to the Church of England (including its Canon Law) is regarded as an integral part of the law of England. Its continuity with the pre-Reformation church is recognised in the principle that a rule of pre-Reformation ecclesiastical law can be relied upon if it is proved to have been recognised, continued and acted upon in England since the Reformation; if that test is met, the rule is treated as part of the ecclesiastical common law of England.[55] From the 16th to the early 20th century, much legislation affecting the church was passed in the usual way by Parliament.[56]

When Secular Law and Church Law Conflict

[5.012] The fundamental distinction between the legal status of the established Church of England and the non-established churches was discussed in some detail in the Queen's Bench decision *O'Keefe v Cardinal Cullen*.[57] Although this singular precedent was concerned with the suspension of a parish priest from office in Ireland and his effective dismissal, it occurred at a time when Ireland was under English rule. Having been heard in the English courts, this decision manifests clear ideological distinctions[58] between the perspectives of the Crown and the Pope in their respective roles.[59] In the House of Lords, the test of the common law and statute law of England was applied to the distinction the law makes between the 'laws' of the Roman Catholic Church (and accordingly other voluntary associations) and the law of the realm. The net issue was:

> whether and how far the jurisdiction assumed by the Pope, in pursuance of an alleged contract of the Plaintiff, or by virtue of the general discipline of the church, has risen above the level of the law and had infringed upon that long and ancient series of Statutes which assert the principles of the common law and the supremacy of the Crown.

---

55. See Lord Westbury in *Bishop of Exeter v Marshall* (1868) LR 3 HL 17.

56. McClean, in Robbers (ed), *State and Church in the European Union* (Nomos, 2005) p 560.

57. *O'Keefe v Cardinal Cullen* 2 QB 1873 CL 7 319 and 1873–1874 IR, Common Law, Vol VII, p 319.

58. Dating back to the Enlightenment period, the Reformation and indeed much earlier.

59. *O'Keefe v Cardinal Cullen* 2 QB 1873 CL 7 319 and 1873–1874 IR, Common Law, Vol VII, p 319. See in particular p 444.

Following a forensic scrutiny of English common law and statute law, the court[60] concluded:

> No church, no community, no public body, no individual in the realm, can be, in the least above the law, or exempted from the authority of its civil or criminal tribunals. The law of the land is supreme, and we recognise no authority as superior to it. I apprehend that nothing can be recognised as law in the Court but the law of the land. The rules and regulations of a voluntary church may be called 'laws' by way of courtesy or convenience, but they have no force or acceptance here but as the terms of a contract; and the Court could take no notice of them even as such, unless to enforce some civil right or redress some civil wrong, and we can regard them as binding so far only as they are consistent with the laws of the land .... This court has no concern with the private affairs of ecclesiastical bodies not established by law. They may make their own rules of discipline and order, and enforce, and this Court will not interfere; but the moment the temporal rights of a citizen are trenched upon, the Court is bound to enquire into the terms of the alleged contract, how far they are binding and legal, and how far they have been violated.[61]

This contrasts with the approach of the Irish courts to the legal status of Canon law, since the latter consider the Canon law of the Catholic Church to be foreign law and require it to be proved in the same manner as foreign law,[62] an issue which is discussed more fully in **chapter 9**.

Civic Religion

[5.013] Some authors suggest that the Church of England's responsibility to the nation, in making religion present within public life, is in part to be gleaned from expressions of civic religion in that important national events are marked by church ceremonies organised by the Church of England.[63] While these events are conducted in accordance with the Anglican tradition, they are attended by other faiths and religious traditions. A principle of

---

60. *O'Keefe v Cardinal Cullen* 2 QB 1873 CL 7 319 and 1873–1874 IR, Common Law, Vol VII, p 319. Barry J, Fitzgerald J, O'Brien J, and Whiteside CJ.

61. *O'Keefe v Cardinal Cullen* 2 QB 1873 CL 7 319 and 1873–1874 IR, Common Law, Vol VII, p 319, 409 approving *dictum* of Lord Colonsay in *Cardross,* Law of Creeds in Scotland, by AT Innes, p 289.

62. *O'Callaghan v O'Sullivan* [1925] 1 IR 90.

63. McClean, 'The Changing Legal Framework of Establishment', (2004) 7 *Ecclesiastical Law Journal* and Fischer and Wallace, (2006) *Florida International Law Journal*, 18, p 490.

establishment in England is visible in the context of civic religion, which can be perceived as an acknowledgement of the public role of religion, and a certain resistance to religion being viewed as a part of the private sphere.[64] More concrete manifestations of the legal status of the established Church of England, however, can be seen in the statutory requirements that the monarch must be a member of the Church of England, and must take the oath to maintain that church,[65] and the fact that seats within the House of Lords are reserved for a number of bishops of that church. While the bishops frequently participate in Parliamentary debates and influence their outcome, they are generally more concerned with ensuring a place for the spiritual and ethical elements of life, which might otherwise be overlooked.[66] However, there is no gainsaying the fact that a component of the English establishment is that the Canon law of the Church of England constitutes part of the law of the land and can be enforced as such.[67] One of the benefits flowing from establishment, it has been argued, is the maintenance of the Church of England as a moderate, non-dogmatic and pragmatic church, which does not impose religious belief of any form on its citizens.[68] Neither does the concept of establishment in this century permit discrimination against the other main religions and faiths, as Munby J clarified in *Suleiman v Juffali*, which dealt with the status of a Muslim divorce in UK family law:

> Although historically this country is part of the Christian west, and although it has an established church which is Christian, I sit as a secular judge serving a multi-cultural community of many faiths in which all of us can now take pride, sworn to do justice 'to all manner of people.' Religion – whatever the particular believer's faith – is no doubt something to be encouraged but it is not the business of government or of the secular courts. So the starting point of the law is an essentially agnostic view of religious beliefs and a tolerant indulgence to religious and cultural diversity. A secular judge must be wary of straying across the well-recognised divide between church and state. It is not

64. Fischer, and Wallace, (2006) *Florida International Law Journal*, 18.

65. The Coronation Oath Act 1688. See also the Bill of Rights Act 1688, the Act of Settlement 1701 and the Accession Declaration Act 1910.

66. Fischer and Wallace, (2006) *Florida International Law Journal*, 18, p 491.

67. Fischer and Wallace, (2006) *Florida International Law Journal*, 18, p 493.

68. Laws, 'A Judicial Perspective on the Sacred in Society' (2004) 7 *Eccleciastical Law Journal*, 317–327 cited in Fischer and Wallace, (2006) *Florida International Law Journal*, 18, p 491, n 26.

for a judge to weigh one religion against another. All are entitled to equal respect, whether in times of peace or, as at present, amidst the clash of arms.[69]

[5.014] This judicial reasoning is in harmony with the well-established approach to the law of charities which further illustrates the positive approach of the UK system to religion in general, in that it recognises a trust established for religious purposes to be of public benefit and accordingly entitled to charitable status.[70] Once again this positive approach to religion may be deduced from the dual character of the legislative provision made for education from 1870 onwards and from the significant position accorded religion in both denominational and non-denominational education sectors.[71] As in most of Western Europe, the churches played a pivotal role in early attempts to establish a state system of education in England and many of these early schools had a charitable or religious foundation.[72] As one would expect, in these schools there was a long-established tradition of teaching the specific religious doctrine and worship of the foundational church. When the state decided to fund education and to enact legislative measures to provide and support education, other considerations necessarily presented themselves, since education had become a joint church-state enterprise and this included, *inter alia*, denominational education as part of the public system of education. In England there is no requirement for religious groups to register with the government.

Public Funding for Denominational Schools

[5.015] Approximately one-third of state schools in England have a religious character. Of the 6,850 state-funded, faith schools, the majority are Church of England or Roman Catholic: there are 37 Jewish schools, 7 Muslim schools and 2 Sikh schools; and 1 Seventh Day Adventist and 1 Greek Orthodox school.[73] In England faith schools are broadly supported by the

69. *Suleiman v Juffali* 1 FLR 479 at 490 (2002).

70. See *Commissioners of Special Income Tax v Pemsel* [1891] AC 531.

71. Cf Ireland's largely single sector denominational schools discussed at **para [9.005]** *et seq*.

72. McClean, in Robbers (ed), *State and Church in the European Union* (Nomos, 2005) pp 558–561.

73. Meikle, (2007) *The Guardian*, 10 September. Available at http://www.guardian.co.uk/uk/2007/sep/10/schools.faithschools.

government in that they are often schools with particularly high standards of academic achievement and discipline.[74] Provided these schools have been designated by the Secretary of State as having a religious character,[75] they may discriminate in favour of the relevant faith for appointment or promotion of teachers in the school.[76] In addition, discrimination is also permitted in regard to remuneration and in relation to persons who attend religious worship in accordance with the tenets of the germane religion or religious denomination or who are willing to deliver religious education at the school in accordance with those principles. As in Ireland, the faith schools are under pressure to become more inclusive and collaborative. In 1998 the first Muslim school[77] was recognised as part of the state sector and there are more that 80 Muslim schools in the independent school sector.[78] No church or religious body in England receives direct funding from the state, but the government can contribute up to 90 per cent of the total capital costs of the school buildings and 100 per cent of administrative costs in state grants, including teachers' salaries, to the faith schools.[79] This funding has become controversial in what is commonly termed 'the faith school debate', which has achieved a very significant political dimension in recent years. On the one hand, it has been argued that faith schools do not contribute to integration and social cohesion but are divisive and that, accordingly, their control over admissions to their schools should be removed or curtailed by the state.[80] On the other hand, it has been argued that faith schools promote religious freedom, that they contribute to the common good and that they facilitate parental choice of school because of perceptions regarding their

74. Meredith, 'Incorporation of the European Convention on Human Rights into UK Law, Implications for Education' European Journal for Education Law and Policy, Vol 2, No 1 p 13.

75. School Standards and Framework Act 1998, s 69(3).

76. School Standards and Framework Act 1998, s 69(3).

77. Islamia Primary School in Kent.

78. Assocation of Muslim Social Scientists *et al, Muslims on Education: a Position Paper (*Assocation of Muslim Social Scientists, 2004) p 2.5.2.

79. Meikle, (2007) *The Guardian*, 10 September. Available at http://education.guardian.co.uk/faithschools/story/0,,2166017,00.html.

80. Stewart, 'Control Admissions Call' (2006) *Times Educational Supplement*, 10 March. Richard Garner, 'New fears over school selection' (2006) *Independent*, 18 April, which expresses fears that allowing schools control over their own admissions will increase levels of covert selection, BBC Online, 14 February 2006.

high standards of academic achievements and discipline.[81] With the specific aim of advancing social cohesion, Lord Baker tabled an amendment to the Education and Inspections Bill that quotas be imposed on all new faith schools which would oblige them to fill up to 30 per cent of their school placements with pupils from different faiths or non-faith backgrounds. In the first debate of its kind since the Education Act 1944, the peers in the House of Lords discussed the impact of modern faiths on contemporary English society and the potential impact of Lord Baker's proposed amendment. However, the House of Lords rejected the proposed amendment by 119 votes to 37. By way of reply, Lord Baker stated that the real beneficiaries of the government removing its quotas plan would be the 120 Muslim private schools wishing to gain entry to the state sector.[82]

[5.016] The current position is that there are no formal quotas[83] for admission of 'other faith' or 'no faith' pupils to faith schools, but this topic remains controversial. In other words, if a faith school is over-subscribed, it can favour the children of the foundational faith when admitting or enrolling pupils, a position which was affirmed by the House of Lords in *Choudbury v Governors of Bishop Challoner Roman Catholic Comprehensive School*,[84] a matter which is discussed later.[85] However, if a faith school is undersubscribed, then it cannot lawfully refuse to admit 'other faith' or 'no faith' pupils.

Education and Religion: Relevant Statutory Framework

[5.017] Education in England, by contrast with Ireland, has an established tradition of legislative provision, which comprises an important component

81. Meredith, 'Incorporation of the European Convention on Human Rights into UK Law, Implications for Education' European Journal for Education Law and Policy, Vol 2, No 1 p 13.

82. See 'Peers reject faith school quotas', BBC News, 30 October 2006 at http://news.bbc.co.uk/2/hi/uk_news/politics/6099156.stm.

83. Quotas may, of course, be agreed between the parties in education and the government.

84. *Choudbury v Governors of Bishop Challoner Roman Catholic Comprehensive School* [1992] 3 All Eng 277.

85. At **para [5.016]**.

of secondary legislation.[86] This complex statutory system can be traced to the Factories Act 1833, which made provision for two hours of compulsory education for all classes of children for the first time. Furthermore, there is a well-established tradition in England of including religious education as part of the basic curriculum in state schools but this is not part of the National Curriculum which provides for secular subjects only. While the Education Act 1944 required every LEA to devise an 'agreed syllabus' for religious education, it did not prescribe the content of that latter syllabus but left this to local level as part of the basic curriculum. While non-denominational education has been provided in English state schools since 1870,[87] religious instruction, however, is a matter for the churches and religious denominational school authorities in both England and Ireland.

A Dual System

[5.018] When the state became formally involved in the establishment of elementary schools in England, it decided, unlike France and the US, not to separate church and state. Rather, a decision was taken to permit the existing church or denominational schools to continue to exist and to fund them at least partially. However, it was decided that a separate stream of state-funded, non-denominational schools would run parallel to the denominational schools and these were established under the Elementary Education (England) Act 1870 (the 1870 Act or the Foster Act). While the church schools would be permitted to continue to teach religious education according to their own tenets and doctrines, the non-demoninational schools were bound by the 'Cowper Temple clause' which was inserted into the 1870 Act. This clause provided: 'No religious catechism or religious formulary which is distinctive of any particular denomination was to be taught.' In this manner the dual nature of the elementary schools in England, and the duality of religious education delivered in the schools, was established and has continued to exist. Under the 1870 Act school boards were set up nationwide to enable the provision of elementary education to children from 5–12 years, inclusive.[88] School boards were abolished by the

86. But the common law duty of care also has a significant bearing on some spheres of educational practice. See 15(1) *Halsbury's Laws of England* (Lexis Nexis/ Butterworths, 2006), *EDUCATION*, p 20.

87. Note, however, the impact of the Education Reform Act 1988.

88. The Education Act 1880 made school attendance compulsory for children up to 10 years of age. This was extended to 14 years of age by the Education Act 1918.

Education Act 1902 (the Balfour Act) and powers in education were devolved to the Local Education Authorities (LEAs)[89] whose remit included secondary education and vocational education for the first time. Significantly, the Balfour Act also assimilated the denominational schools into the state sector and required that they be supported by public taxation, thus conferring on the state a greater measure of control over these schools.

Post-War Educational Provision: Religious Education

[5.019] For many decades, the principal post-war legislative measure was the Education Act 1944 (the 1944 Act), which provided many elements still present in contemporary education law.[90] The 1944 Act, which became one of the most significant advances in the history of English education, required that religious education be provided in all schools within the state system.[91] This landmark legislation also made provision for compulsory prayer in all state-funded schools and it required that the school day 'begin with collective worship on the part of all pupils in attendance at the school.'[92] In addition, the 1944 Act introduced the provision that every LEA must devise 'an agreed syllabus' for religious education (RE)[93] or use one devised by another LEA. Such a syllabus was to be drawn up in accordance with the decision of a representative conference of the various religious denominations, the LEA and the teachers' organisations. Moreover, the LEA was empowered to establish a Standing Advisory Council for Religious Education (SACRE) to advise it and its teachers on issues relating to RE. From 1944 onwards, the statutory requirement for the delivery and inspection of RE in English schools has been determined at local level

89. See the position in Ireland which has remained, to a considerable degree, a centralised system with free secondary education being introduced some 23 years later. See further **para [9.067]** *et seq* below.

90. Among its many ground-breaking initiatives, the Butler Act provided for free secondary education in state schools for children up to 15 years of age and this limit was raised to 16 years in 1972. The Act also provided for the 11 plus examination and community colleges for children and adults. Cf the position in Ireland where free secondary education was introduced informally some 23 years later, in 1967.

91. Education Act 1944, s 25(2) provided there is suitable accommodation for meeting with the whole school (s 25(1)).

92. Education Act 1944, s 25(1). See further Dunford and Sharp, *The Education System in England and Wales*, 17–24.

93. See Education Act 1944, Sch 5.

through the ingenuous mechanism of the 'agreed syllabus.'[94] The 1944 Act was amended and supplemented by numerous other Acts[95] and was finally repealed by the consolidated Education Act 1996 (the 1996 Act) which, in its amended form, is now the major legislative measure relating to education.[96] Local control over RE survived the Education Reform Act 1988 (the 1988 Act), which made provision for the secular subjects in the National Curriculum of England and for the basic curriculum of a school, which included RE. The main provision for the agreed syllabus is currently to be found in the 1996 Act.[97]

Current Categories of School

[5.020] The long-established pattern of state support for RE in a dual system of schools continues in contemporary England in, firstly, the state schools (non-denominational sector) and, secondly, the church schools (the denominational sector), both of which form part of the state education system. The main categories of schools in England currently are:

(a) Community schools (comprising the earlier 'county schools') in which religious education is required to be taught in accordance with the agreed syllabus of the governing Local Education Authority (LEA) made under the Schools Standards and Framework Act 1998.

(b) Foundation schools (comprising the earlier county schools and the earlier voluntary controlled schools), many of which were grant-maintained schools. In these schools religious education is required to be taught in accordance with the LEA agreed syllabus, unless the school is designated as having a religious character, in which case RE is taught in accordance with their trust deed.

---

94. The Education Acts 1944 and 1981; Education (Schools) Act 1992; Education Acts 1993, 1996 and 2002.

95. By the Education Act 1946; Education (Miscellaneous Provisions) Acts 1948 and 1953; Education Acts of 1959, 1962, 1964, 1967, 1968, 1973, 1975, 1976, 1979, 1980 and 1981; Remuneration of Teachers Act 1965; Education (No 2) Act 1968; Education (Work Experience) Act 1973; Education (School Leaving Dates) 1976 and Education (Grants and Awards) Act 1984.

96. With regard to the Agreed Syllabuses under the Education Act 1996, see Sch 31, s 375.

97. Education Act 1996, Pt 1, Ch 3, s 375 and Sch 31. See also Sch 19 of the School Standards and Framework Act 1998 and the Education Act 2002, s 80.

(c) Voluntary-aided schools are those schools originally established by voluntary organisations but which are in receipt of public funding. In this type of school the majority of governors are foundation governors and religious education[98] is taught in accordance with their trust deed.

(d) Voluntary controlled schools were originally established by voluntary bodies but are currently controlled and entirely funded by the LEA. The voluntary body is entitled to appoint a minority of foundation governors in order to preserve the character and ethos of the school. In these schools religious education is required to be taught in accordance with the agreed syllabus of the relevant LEA, but parents may request that religious education be provided in accordance with the trust deed.

[5.021] Every maintained (state) non-denominational school is required to follow the basic curriculum, which includes RE for all pupils,[99] and the National Curriculum for England, comprising secular subjects. The Cowper-Temple clause is incorporated in Sch 19 of the Schools Standards and Framework Act 1998, para 2(5) and provides that no agreed syllabus may provide for RE to be given to pupils at such schools by means of any catechism or formulary which is distinctive of a particular religious denomination, but this is not to be taken as prohibiting provision in such a syllabus for the study of such catechisms or formularies. In other words, RE in maintained schools must not be denominational, but it may include teaching about the denominations. Although such RE is not subject to national attainment targets or assessment, it is subject to inspection.[100]

[5.022] Within the legislative framework, the churches remain free to establish their own independent schools and in these schools they may teach RE and worship according to their own principles and dogma.[101] The independent schools in England are exempted from the general statutory requirements on the curriculum, but prescribed standards have been

98. What is considered in some other countries (eg in Ireland) religious instruction and worship or RI.

99. Education Act 1996, Ch 111, ss 375–381; School Standards and Framework Act 1998, Ch VI, ss 69–71 and Sch 20; Education Act 2002, s 80.

100. Education (Schools) Act 1992.

101. McClean, in Robbers (ed), *State and Church in the European Union* (Nomos, 2005) p 566.

introduced pursuant to the Education Act 2002, Pt 10. These standards are a response to concerns that not enough has been done to force the improvement or closure of the weaker independent schools.[102] Moreover, the curriculum content or aims for these schools have not yet been prescribed in law, although the Department for Children, Schools and Families (DCSF) has provided informal guidance. There are official concerns regarding a minority of independent schools with a religious character that insufficient time is allocated to the secular curriculum,[103] a concern which is discussed later in the context of some recognised schools in Ireland (**chapter 9**).

Parental Choice of School

[5.023] The right to parental choice of school in England is a statutory right[104] with its origins in the Education Act 1944, s 76, which required the Secretary of State and the LEAs merely 'to have regard to the principle ... that children are to be educated in accordance with the general wishes of their parents.' This obligation is now found in s 9 of the 1996 Act, but the obligation that adherence to the wishes of parents must be 'compatible with the provision of efficient instruction and training and the avoidance of public expenditure'[105] has generally diluted the parental right. It is widely acknowledged that religious and denominational factors may add a significant element to the nature and quality of choice of school for many parents[106] where denominational or faith schools exist. It should be noted, however, that the law does not guarantee parental choice of school grounded on religious or denominational considerations even where denominational

102. See further Harris, *Education, Law and Diversity*, p 441, citing Bell HMCI, 'Standards and Inspections in Independent Schools', Address to the Brighton College Conference on Independent Schools, 29 April 2003 and generally 'The Independent Sector', pp 441–6.

103. Office for Standards in Education, *Annual Report of Her Majesty's Chief Inspector of Schools: Standards and Quality in Education 2001/2* (Ofsted, 2003).

104. See, for instance, the position in Ireland where it is a constitutional right, Art 42.3.1°.

105. School Standards and Framework Act 1998, s 86(3)(a); EA 1996, Sch 27 para 3.

106. Meredith, 'Incorporation of the European Convention on Human Rights into UK Law, Implications for Education' *European Journal for Education Law and Policy,* Vol 2, No 1 p 13 and Meredith, 'Judicial Review and Education', chapter 3 of Hatfield (ed), *Judicial Review: a Thematic Approach* and in particular pp 88–91.

schools exist. However, the Schools Standards and Framework Act 1998, s 86 (SSFA), as amended,[107] facilitates parental choice of school, to some degree, and this may include, *inter alia*, religious or denominational reasons.

[5.024] When it comes to denominational education, the issue of parental choice becomes more significant because of the freedom of religion principle which has been embodied in the Education (England) Act 1870, Education Act 1944, Education Act 1996 and in the ECHR,[108] but it is a general principle only, and the relevant personnel must have regard to the principle when exercising or performing their powers and duties. Yet they are not precluded from taking account of other factors and may make exceptions to the general principle if they see fit. Thus, when a grammar school in the vicinity was not provided by the LEA and a Catholic father did not wish his two children to attend the independent school provided, he failed in his attempt to compel the LEA to fund his children's attendance at a Roman Catholic boarding school.[109] Provision for school places at state-funded faith schools within any given area is variable and places may be denied to parents simply on account of a lack of suitable places.

[5.025] This position may be exacerbated by the fact that faith schools are often heavily over-subscribed, and are much sought after by parents, who, although not adherents of the foundational faith of the school, value their perceived high standards of academic achievement and discipline.[110] If denominational schools exist in an area, however, parents must have the right to select them, particularly where they comprise part of the state-funded system of education.[111] Although most of the denominational schools have voluntary-aided status and receive most of their funding from the state, the school authority retains the right to control admissions to the

107. By the Education Act 2002 and the Education and Inspections Act 2006.

108. Particularly Art 9 and Art 2 of Protocol 1.

109. *Watt v Kesteven* CC [1955] 1 QB 408, 1 All ER 473, CA; *Darling v Minister of Education, Jones v Minister of Education* (1962) *Times*, 7 April; *Wood v Ealing* BDC [1967] Ch 364, [1966] 3 All ER 514. See further Harris, Education, Law and Diversity, pp 307 *et seq* with regard to interviewing for admission to these schools.

110. Meredith, 'Incorporation of the European Convention on Human Rights into UK Law, Implications for Education' *European Journal for Education Law and Policy,* Vol 2, No 1 p 11.

111. Harris, *Education and Diversity,* pp 6, 304–308 and generally chapter 3.

school.[112] Similarly, when admitting students, denominational schools in Ireland may confer priority on adherents of their own religion to a degree that is yet uncertain, because the Equal Status Act 2004, s 7(c) has not yet been judicially considered.[113] Since Ireland lacks a full public sector school system, however, the impact of the denominational school's right to confer priority on adherents of their own religion[114] has a much more severe impact than the corresponding right has in England, where a full public school system exists. For this reason, the denominational school's right in this regard has been highly controversial in Ireland, as will be seen in **chapter 9** below.

[5.026] One of the relevant issues which arises in relation to the provision of school transport is the right of parents to have their preferences taken into account were they desire to have their child attend a school at which the RE provided is that of the religion to which the parent adheres. Section 509(4) of the Education Act 1996[115] provides that parental preference is a factor to be considered if a parent wishes their child to attend a school at which the religious education provided is that of the religion to which the parent adheres. It is notable that the preference here is limited to the RE preference and does not adhere to other preferences.[116] Even though the amendment clearly confers greater rights on parents where religious preferences are

112. *Choudhury v Governors of Bishop Challoner Roman Catholic Comprehensive School* [1992] 3 All ER 277.

113. Although the right in Ireland is qualified by s 7(c) of the Equal Status Act 2000, but this has been interpreted as an absolute right in many denominational schools, it appears. See further **para [9.077]** below. For the position in Northern Ireland, see Lundy, 'Education Law under Devolution: the Case of Northern Ireland, (2000) 1 *Education Law Journal*, 81; L Lundy, 'From Act to Order: The Metamorphosis of Education Legislation' (1998) XXI, *Liverpool Law Review*, 63.

114. Which derives from a constitutional right; Art 44.5 of the Constitution of Ireland. See further **para [9.031]** *et seq* below.

115. Which amends Sch 9, para 15 of the Education Act 1993 and s 55(3) of the Education Act 1944.

116 Cf *R v Bedfordshire ex parte WE*, (8 November 1996, unreported) cited in McManus, with contribution by Lewis, Sharland and Moffat, *Education and the Courts*, p 15, fn 4. See also *R v East Sussex County Council ex parte D* [1991] COD 374, 15 March 1991 cited in Liell (ed), *The Law of Education* (9th edn, Butterworths, 1984), at p 806, which held that there was no obligation to provide free school transport where a pupil is outside the statutory walking distance where this arises solely from the exercise of parental preference. (contd .../)

being exercised, such preferences are nonetheless merely a factor to be considered and not an overriding one.[117] However, the coming into force of the Human Rights Act 1998 adds a new dimension to such matters and it is now likely that the courts, in construing s 509(4), would consider that the parental preference for a child to attend a school in which the RE provided is different from the kind of RE to which the parent adheres, would be taken into account by a court, since to do otherwise would be discriminatory on the face of it.[118] In addition, admissions arrangements must take account of Art 2 of Protocol 1 of the Convention, so that there is no denial of the right to education, and respect must be accorded the parent's religious and philosophical convictions as regard the teaching and education of their child. Accordingly, any religious or philosophical conviction grounding the parents' choice of school must be considered by the school.[119] It would be incorrect, for example, to deduce parental preference for a single-sex school for their child rather than to provide an opportunity for the parents to set down their (religious) reasons for their choice of school.[120]

[5.027] The compatibility of admissions arrangements with the ECHR has been considered in a number of cases. While sibling preference[121] as a priority criterion has been held to be lawful *per se*,[122] if it comes lower down on the priority ladder, so to speak, than a residence criterion, the outcome could be that siblings would be separated in the case of over-subscription of the school.[123] In *R (O) v St James RC Primary School Appeal Panel*[124] the

---

116. (contd) The latter case was followed in *R v Essex CC ex parte C* [1994] ELR 54 at 63 G and 65G.

117. McManus, with contribution by Lewis, Sharland and Moffat, *Education and the Courts*, p 15.

118. McManus, with contribution by Lewis, Sharland and Moffat, *Education and the Courts*. It would not be so if Art 14 (discrimination) was solely relied upon, but if another article could be prayed in aid, such as Art 8, 9 or Art 2 of Protocol 1, since Art 14 is not a stand alone provision, so to speak.

119. *Valsamis v Greece* [1998] ELR 430.

120. *R (K) v London Borough of Newham* [2002] ELR 390 *per* Collins J.

121. Giving preference to a child on the grounds that a brother or sister is already a pupil in the school.

122. *R v Greenich London Borough Council ex parte Governors of John Bull Primary School* (1990) 154 LGR 678 CA.

123. See further Harris, *Education, Law and Diversity*, p 267.

124. *R (O) v St James RC Primary School Appeal Panel* [2001] ELR 469, para 36 *per* Newman J.

court accepted, without deciding that Art 8 of the ECHR (right to respect for private and family life) could be at issue in school admissions decisions, especially in the case of admission to a religious school, that Art 8 conferred no absolute right to have a child admitted to a school already attended by a sibling. A later decision, however, gives more weight to the sibling criterion considered in the light of Art 8 which makes it all the more necessary to consider this 'very important criterion'.[125]

[5.028] In the case of over-subscription of a school, however, religious considerations can lawfully be employed for determining priorities in a denominational school, as was held in *R v Governors of Bishop Challoner Roman Catholic Comprehensive Girls School ex parte Choudhury.*[126] In that case the House of Lords upheld the policy of a single-sex Roman Catholic school which, in the case of over-subscription, conferred priority on Roman Catholic students, thereby denying a place to a Muslim and a Hindu student. Lord Browne-Wilkinson expressed the view that the school's policy was rational and that it provided a legitimate ground on which a denominational school could prioritise applicants. In determining criteria for admissions to a denominational school, however, the court indicated that requirements for commitment to the germane religion should be more precise, referring, for example, to 'weekly worship' or attendance at church fortnightly rather than 'regular worship' or 'regular attendance'.[127] Furthermore, the criteria on which the school will rely should be stipulated in the admissions policy, eg Baptismal Certificate.[128] Moreover, faith criteria in the selection process should be as transparent, fair and straightforward as possible.[129]

125. *R (K) v London Borough of Newham* [2002] ELR 390 *per* Collins J.

126. *R v Governors of Bishop Challoner Roman Catholic Comprehensive Girls School ex parte Choudhury* [1992] 3 All ER 277.

127. *R v Governors of Bishop Challoner Roman Catholic Comprehensive Girls School ex parte Choudhury* [1992] 3 All ER 277.

128. See further *R v Governors of La Sainte Union Convent School* [1996] ELR 98 in which Sedley J gave leave to take judicial review proceedings on the grounds that a baptism certificate constituted evidence that at least one of the parents was a practicing Roman Catholic. See now the Code of Practice which requires that the admissions arrangements must clarify whether a statement of religious affiliation or commitment is to be sufficient, whether this is to be tested by the school, and if so, how is this to be done; also whether references are to be required and how they are to be used in deciding the application.

129. *Governing Body of the London Oratory School; Adams, Goodliffe and Lindsay v The Schools' Adjudicator* [2003] EWHC; [2005] ELR 162.

[5.029] Since 1999, objections to a school's admission procedures for any year have had to be referred to an adjudicator.[130] When the admissions criteria apply to 'a person's religion, religious denomination or religious practice', the adjudicator must refer the issue to the Secretary of State for a determination[131] and the decision of the Secretary of State is binding.[132] In 2004 objections were lodged to the over-subscription admissions criteria applied by the London Oratory School. Under those criteria, the first priority referred to the requirement that the prospective student and his or her parents be practising Catholics, while the second criterion required their commitment to the Catholic Church, the life of the parish, 'the ethos and expectations' of the school and their Catholic education. When the objections to these criteria were referred by the adjudicator to the Secretary of State, and the latter deleted the reference to 'the ethos and expectations' of the school, a legal challenge ensued against the adjudicator's separate determination on the interview that took place with the parent and the child which was part of the admission's process.[133]

The Challenge of Diversity

[5.030] Harris and others point to the significant challenges which arise in England, not only from inherent social disadvantage and exclusion, but also from the need for education to respond to diversity by devising inclusive policies and practices that recognise the cultural and religious rights of all groups and foster values of mutual respect so as to enable pluralist societies to live peacefully and cohesively.[134] The overall thrust of human rights law,

---

130. School Standards and Framework Act 1998, s 90. See the Education (Objections to Admission Arrangements) Regulations 1999 (SI 1999/125) as amended. For a discussion on the role of the adjudicator see Harris, *Education, Law and Diversity*, pp 261–265.

131. School Standards and Framework Act 1998, s 90(3)(b) and SI 1999/125, reg 7(1).

132. School Standards and Framework Act 1998, s 90.

133. *Governing Body of the London Oratory School; Adams, Goodliffe and Lindsay v The Schools' Adjudicator* [2003] EWHC; [2005] ELR 162: See further Meredith, 'An end to Interviewing? The London School Oratory Case and Reform of School Admissions Practices,' 7(4) *Education law Journal* 233.

134. Harris, *Education, Law and Diversity*, p 5, and further Cole, *Education, Equality and Human RIghts: Issues of Gender, 'Race', Sexuality, Disability and Social Class* (Routledge Falmer, 2006).

Harris states, requires that in regard to education, the state is mindful of the autonomy of these distinct communities and of the cultural rights and religious freedoms within a pluralist society.[135] With regard to education, these state obligations include matters relating to the provision of schools, admissions policies, the curriculum, the provision of religious education and dress codes etc. The significance of these multifaceted dimensions of education has moved to the fore since the enactment of the Human Rights Act 1998, which incorporated into UK law many of the main provisions of the ECHR. Notably, s 13 (the right to a legal remedy) has not been incorporated into English law.[136]

[5.031] In *R v Secretary of State for Employment ex parte Williamson*,[137] the House of Lords was recently called upon to decide whether the statutory prohibition on the sanction of corporal punishment breached the human rights of parents in a Christian Fellowship school who wished, as a matter of Christian belief, to retain that particular sanction. Until s 548 of the Education Act 1996 was amended, by the School Standards and Framework Act 1998, parents and teachers in private schools in England were at liberty to manifest their belief in corporal punishment by imposing that sanction. The net issue in *Williamson*[138] was whether the 1998 amendment of the law interfered materially with the claimant's freedom to manifest their beliefs in regard to corporal punishment, in the context of a Christian Fellowship school in the light of Art 9[139] of the ECHR. While corporal punishment and its infliction were held to be manifestations of belief, the House of Lords held that s 548 (as amended) did not violate the rights of parents or teachers under Art 9 of the ECHR. However, the court approved the dictum of Richards J in *R (Amicus) v Secretary of State for Trade and Industry*[140] that it would be inappropriate for a court to adjudicate on the seriousness, cogency and coherence of theological beliefs since that would take the court beyond its legitimate

135. Harris, *Education, Law and Diversity*.

136. Cf the position in Irish law.

137. See *R (Williamson) v Secretary of State for Employment* [2005] UKHL 15; [2005] ELR 291; [2005] 2 AC 246.

138. *R (Williamson) v Secretary of State for Employment* [2005] UKHL 15; [2005] ELR 291; [2005] 2 AC 246.

139. Freedom of thought, conscience and religion.

140. *R (Amicus) v Secretary of State for Trade and Industry* [2004] IRLR, pp 436–7.

role.[141] On the other hand, the court stated that it was only in clear and extreme cases that a claim to religious belief could be disregarded by a court; for example, in *X v United Kingdom* in which there was no evidence whatever before the court that the 'Wicca' religion existed.[142]

Legal Framework for Religious Education

[5.032] The current legal framework for the provision of religious education and for collective worship in state schools in England and Wales was laid down in the Education Reform Act 1988 (the 1988 Act) and is currently to be found in the consolidating Education Act 1996 (the 1996 Act). The 1988 Act made provision for a mandatory National Curriculum comprising ten subjects. Religious education, not being part of the National Curriculum, was determined locally under the Act as part of the school's basic curriculum, which allows for flexibility and local input that would be difficult to achieve under statutory provisions. A fundamental change to the provision made in the Act of 1944 for collective worship was effected by the Education Reform Act 1988, which provided that 'the collective worship required in the school … shall be wholly or mainly of a broadly Christian character', a provision which has been carried over into the 1996 Act.[143] However, it is not necessary that every collective act of worship be broadly Christian but the majority of such acts in any one term must be so.[144] Moreover, in determining the substance of collective worship, schools are required to have regard to particular circumstances regarding the family background of the pupils, which will obviously take account of the character and diversity of religious beliefs within the school enrolment.[145] However, the legislation permits the collective act of worship to be disregarded entirely with regard to a particular school or to a group of pupils in the school by the determination of the LEA's Standing Advisory Council on

141. This view was also upheld in House of Lords case *R (Williamson) v Secretary of State for Employment* [2005] UKHL 15 at para 57. On this point, see somewhat similar views expressed by the Supreme Court of Canada in *Syndicat Northcrest v Amselem* [2004] 2 SCR 551, and in the US Supreme Court in *Employment Division, Department of Human Resources of Oregon v Smith* 494 US 872 (1990) pp 886–7.

142. *X v United Kingdom* Application No 7291/75, admissibility decision of 4 October 1977.

143. Education Act 1996, s 386(2).

144. Education Act 1996, s 386(4).

145. Education Act 1996, s 386(5) and (6).

Religious Education (SACRE).[146] At first glance, the requirement for a collective act of worship in state schools, which is wholly or mainly of a broadly Christian character, sits uneasily in racially and religiously diverse modern England. On deeper reflection, however, the fact that considerable flexibility is conferred on schools in regard to its implementation suggests that the aim of the collective act of worship is clearly not indoctrination, but rather an attempt to secure a form of civic religion in schools and in the wider society. Furthermore, this requirement is subject to an express right of withdrawal of pupils.[147] Meredith states that there is considerable evidence that parents are disinclined to exercise this right on account of the inconvenience or embarrassment it may cause.[148] Meredith is also of the view that it cannot be said with certainty that the mere provision of a parental right of withdrawal will *per se* meet the parents' ECHR rights under Art 2 of Protocol 1. However, given the applicility of the margin of appreciation doctrine in this sphere, it is likely to be highly persuasive provided it is a full withdrawal.[149]

[5.033] There is a duty on each LEA and governing body, with regard to community, foundation or voluntary schools, subject to certain exceptions and special arrangements, to exercise their functions with a view to ensuring that RE is given in accordance with the provision for such education included in the school's basic curriculum.[150] Furthermore, the head teacher must ensure that religious education is given in the school.[151] The agreed syllabus is to be drafted by local representatives (at Agreed Syllabus Conferences) which may delegate to a committee the power to draw up, in general terms, a special syllabus for religious education in the LEA's area or, alternatively, they may adopt a syllabus drafted by another LEA. So as to ensure local consultation with teachers, faith communities and elected councillors and to discharge the statutory requirements, the SACRE

146. Education Act 1996, s 387.

147. Education Act 1996, s 389(1).

148. Meredith, 'Incorporation of the European Convention on Human Rights into UK Law, Implications for Education,' (1998) *Journal of the European Assosiation for Education Law and Policy*, vol 2, no 1, p 13.

149. See *Leirvag v Norway*, Communication no 115/2003, CCPR.

150. See *The RE Directory*, Overview, at http://www.theredirectory.org.uk/overview.php.

151. As amended by the Education Act 2002, s 215(1), Sch 21, para 104(1), 2.

Conference's composition, which is similar to that required for SACRE itself, must comprise the following parties:

(a) a committee of persons who represent, in the opinion of the LEA, Christian denominations and religions, and denominations of such religions as reflect the principal religious traditions of the area;[152]

(b) a committee of persons who represent the Church of England;[153]

(c) a committee of persons who, in the opinion of the LEA, represent teachers who ought to be represented given local circumstances;[154] and

(d) a committee of persons representing the LEA itself.[155]

Surprisingly, no specific provision is made for the election of parents, although persons elected to other categories may well be parents of pupils in the school. Nonetheless, this is a significant omission since parents are usually considered as the primary educators of their children and questions need to be asked concerning the constitutionality of this position. Moreover, by omitting parents as a category for SACRE and the Agreed Curriculum Conferences, arguably the state fails fully to respect the right of parents to ensure education and teaching in conformity with their own religious and philosophical convictions.[156]

In addition, the agreed syllabuses must reflect the reality that the religious traditions in Britain are predominantly Christian, but they must also take account of the teaching and practices of the other main religions represented in Great Britain.[157] Although the Church of England has a veto in regard to the agreed syllabuses, it may not insist on any component to which the other groups object and it cannot achieve anything close to 'confessional' religious teaching in these schools.[158] Indeed, it is expressly prohibited from doing so by s 376(2) of the 1996 Act, which re-enacts 'the Cowper-Temple clause' requiring that in maintained schools the character of the religious

152. Subject to prescribed exceptions; see the Education Act 1996, s 579(1).

153. The Education Act 1996, s 397(2)(b).

154. The Education Act 1996, s 397(2)(c)(i).

155. The Education Act 1996, s 397(2)(c)(ii).

156. Art 1 of Protocol 2 of the ECHR.

157. The Education Act 1996, s 375(3).

158. See generally McClean, in Robbers (ed), *State and Church in the European Union* (Nomos, 2005) p 564 *et seq*.

education given to pupils must be non-denominational.[159] Notably, there is no provision in the 1996 Act requiring any pupil to attend Sunday school or any other place of worship and such a practice is expressly prohibited.[160] Presumably this is envisaged as a safeguard to ensure religious freedom and to prevent religious indoctrination or proselytising of pupils taking place in the non-denominational sector.

[5.034] Teachers, as well as pupils, have the right of withdrawal from religious education and every LEA is required by the Education Act 1993 to review its agreed syllabus every five years.[161] The 1996 Act carried over any agreed syllabus in force prior to its commencement and it also made provision for new agreed syllabuses of religious education.[162] In 2004, the Department for Education and Skills, as it was then, and the Qualifications and Curriculum Authority jointly published a Non-Statutory National Framework for Religious Education following extensive consultation. While the document is intended mainly for the SACREs and Agreed Syllabus Conferences, it will clearly be of influence nationwide as the LEAs review their agreed syllabuses.[163] However, the legal document for use in schools continues to be the locally agreed syllabus, except in the case of a voluntary-aided or special agreement school where RE will be arranged in accordance with the faith tradition indicated in the trust deed.

Reserved Teachers

[5.035] With reference to voluntary or church schools, s 28 of the School Standards and Framework Act 1998 requires that when two or more teachers are employed in a school, at least one of these teachers (reserved teachers) must have the competence to teach RE in accordance with the doctrines of

159. With reference to access to any convened conference and any standing advisory council on religious education, see further 15(1) *Halsbury's Laws of England* (Lexis Nexis/Butterworths, 2006), *EDUCATION*, para 967, pp 326–7.

160. The Education Act 1996, s 398(1)(a) renumbered by the Education Act 2005, s 98. Sch 14, para 16 (1), (3).

161. See Ofstead, Making Sense of Religion, 2007 which is the Ofstead report on religion in maintained community schools in England.

162. Accordingly, the term 'agreed syllabus' now means a syllabus of religious education prepared, before 1 November 1996, under the Education Act 1944, Sch 5 or, after that date, in accordance with Sch 31 of the 1996 Act and adopted by an LEA under that Schedule, s 375(2). See Ch 111 of the 1996 Act.

163. *The RE Directory*, Overview, at http://www.theredirectory.org.uk/overview.php.

the relevant church.[164] Provision is also made for the numbers of such teachers to be increased in proportion to the staff to reach a ceiling of one-fifth of the relevant staff.[165] Moreover, the appointment of any teacher in a voluntary-aided school may take account of religious opinions, observance and willingness to give RE in accordance with the principles of the relevant church, and any conduct which is not compatible with such principles may be a ground for dismissal.[166] Likewise, when appointing the head teacher of a voluntary school that has 'a religious character', account may be taken of the candidate's ability and fitness to preserve and develop the religious character of the school.[167] When reserved teachers are being appointed, the foundation governors must be consulted and be satisfied as to the fitness and competence of these teachers to give such religious education and, if they are not so satisfied, they may require the appropriate body to dismiss them without the consent of the relevant LEA.[168] It is notable, however, that in non-denominational schools, by contrast, it is provided that religious opinion or attendance or non-attendance at religious worship may not affect employment, salary or promotion of a teacher.[169]

Dress Codes and Uniforms

[5.036] The influence of human rights on school rules is well illustrated in the well-known case of *R (Begum) v Head Teacher and Governors of Denbigh High School* which was considered in the High Court, the Court of Appeal and the House of Lords.[170] That case arose out of the exclusion from a community school – in which approximately 80 per cent of the pupils were Muslim – of a female Muslim student for failing to comply with the school rule relating to school uniform. Unlike many dress code cases in other European countries, the grounds of the exclusion arose, not from a rule banning Muslim dress in the school so as to secure or promote a secular or other ethos, but rather from the decision of an individual student, on the

164. School Standards and Framework Act 1998, s 28.

165. School Standards and Framework Act 1998, s 28.

166. School Standards and Framework Act 1998, s 60(5).

167. School Standards and Framework Act 1998, s 60(4).

168. School Standards and Framework Act 1998, s 58(7).

169. School Standards and Framework Act 1998, s 59.

170. *R (Begum) v Head Teacher and Governors of Denbigh High School* [2004] EWHC Admin 1389, [2004] ELR 374 (QBD), [2005] EWCA, Civ 199, [2005] ELR 198 (CA), [2006] UKHL 15, [2006] 2 WLR 719.

grounds of religious belief, to wear a more conservative choice of clothing than that which the school permitted.[171] Having gone to unusual lengths to acquire consensus on its uniform, the school required female pupils to wear a shalwar kameez (the shalwar comprising loose trousers tapering at the ankles and the kameez being a sleeveless, smock-like dress with a square neckline). This mode of dress was seen as meeting the religious requirement that Muslim girls must wear modest dress and it was acceptable to the majority of Muslim, Sikh and Hindu parents and to the local mosque which had been consulted. Having worn the shalwar kameez for almost two years without complaint, the claimant, a devout Muslim, contended that when she reached puberty, the wearing of the shalwar kameez no longer met the requirements of Islamic Sharia law which required mature women to wear the jibab, a form of capacious dress, which covers the arms and legs when in public. In September 2002 the claimant attended the school wearing the jibab and was told to go and change into proper school uniform, but she did not return to school. No compromise was reached and the student, who missed almost two years of schooling, finally took a case against the school claiming that she had been unlawfully excluded from the school, which had unjustifiably limited her right under Art 9 of the ECHR to manifest her religion or beliefs, and violated her rights not to be denied education under Art 2 of Protocol 1 of the ECHR. Bennett J, ruling on the claimant's application for judicial review at first instance, rejected all three claims.[172]

[5.037] However, the Court of Appeal[173] reversed Bennett J's decision and accepted all three of the claimant's contentions. Having considered the facts of the case, the court identified the chief sources of the Muslim religion as: the Holy Quran, which for Muslims represents the word of Allah;[174] the Hadiths or sayings of the Prophet Muhammad on various topics; and the Sunnah, a secondary source of authority which comprises a canon of practices and sayings ascribed to Muhammad. The court noted that, although there is some debate among scholars as to the authority of the Sunnah, it is generally accepted that the above three documents form the basis for the Islamic law known as the Sharia. It also accepted that all

171. See further Dr Paul Meredith, 'Islamic Dress in English Schools: Reconciling Conflicting Interests', *International Journal for Education Law and Policy,* [2006] 2(1–2), 164.

172. [2004] EWHC 1389 (Admin); [2004] ELR 374.

173. Lords Brooke, Mummery and Scott Baker.

174. See Dawood (trans), *The Koran* (Penguin Classics, 1990).

Muslims strive to follow the teachings of the Holy Quran, which include the following statements on women's dress code:

> And tell the believing women to lower their gaze and guard their sexuality, and to display of their adornment only what is apparent, and to draw their head-covering over their bosoms … O prophet, tell your wives and daughters and the believing women to draw their outer garments around them when they go out and are among the men.

On the other hand, evidence was heard on the mainstream modern consensus view of Muslim scholars on an appropriate dress code for Muslim women in England,[175] which found no anti-Islamic act in the wearing of the shalwar kameez. The matter of importance, they pointed out, was that women's attire must be within the Islamic guidelines and that whatever was worn must be a full and honest Islamic hijab which clearly reflected the wearer's identity. Having balanced the claimant's right to religious freedom against the collective right of the school to impose the rule, the court found for the claimant, holding that religious freedom involved the individual conscience rather than the obligation to take part in a specific collectivity. The court held that the school had breached the Human Rights Act 1998 since it did not approach the matter from the right direction but started from the premise that its uniform policy was there to be obeyed and if the claimant did not accept that she could go to another school.[176] Thus, it failed to consider whether the claimant's right under Art 9 of the ECHR would be, or had been, violated and whether the interference with the manifestation of the claimant's religion could be justified under Art 9(2).

[5.038] On appeal to the House of Lords, the court upheld the school's appeal. At the outset, the court made it clear that it was not and could not be invited to rule on whether Islamic dress or any of its features, should or should not be allowed in England's schools and that this decision fell to be decided solely on its own facts.[177] The court accepted that Art 9(1) was engaged or applicable in this significant case and that any sincere religious belief must command respect, particularly when it derives from an ancient and respected religion. The court focussed first on the question of whether the claimant's right pursuant to Art 9 had been violated by the school

175. Evidence given by Dr Anas Abushudy, deputy Director General of the London Central Mosque Trust and Chairman of its Religious Affairs Dept.

176. *R (Begum) v Head Teacher and Governors of Denbigh High School* [2004] EWHC Admin 1389, [2004] ELR 374.

177. At para 2 of the judgment, *per* Lord Bingham of Cornhill.

authorities.[178] The main issues for consideration were whether the respondent's freedom to manifest her religion by her dress was subject to limitations or interference within the meaning of Art 9(2) and, if that were the case, whether such interference was justified under that provision. The court noted that Art 9 protects both the right to hold a belief, which is absolute, and a right to manifest a belief, which is qualified.[179] Holding that Art 9 is concerned with substance and not procedure, it examined the result of the school's decision rather that the steps taken by it in reaching that decision. Applying the principle of justification, the court concluded that the school's decision was justified under Art 9(2) of the ECHR in that some limitations on school dress were necessary to protect the freedoms and rights of other pupils in the school. But had that point been reached in this case? The court noted that the school had gone to unusual lengths in devising the uniform policy and in building that policy on consensus and that it had a legitimate aim of striving for religious and ethnic harmony. The court found no violation of Art 2 of Protocol 1 since it does not guarantee the right to attend any particular educational institution.[180]

[5.039] A different approach to the accommodation of religious minorities, and a different standard is evident from Canada's jurisprudence, although Canada remains close to the UK in its laws and legal traditions.[181] This distinction arises out of the Constitution of Canada, the Charter of Human Rights and Freedoms (the Charter) and other human rights instruments[182] and from the fact that religious tolerance is a very significant value in Canadian society which is one of the most diverse in the Western world. The

178. Three of the Lords found that there had not been an interference with the right under Art 9(1).

179. Citing with approval Lord Nicholls of Birkenhead in *R (Williamson) v Secretary of State for Education and Employment* [2005] UKHL 15, [2005] 2 AC 246, paras 15–19 and also the South African Constitutional Court in *Christian Education South Africa v Minister for Education* [2001] 1 LRC 441, para 36.

180. Approving the House of Lords decision in *Ali v Headteacher and Governors of Lord Grey School per* Lord Hoffman at para 69, [2006] UKHL 14; [2006] 2 WLR 690, a decision made on the same day as *Begum.*

181. Boonstra, 'Of Kirpans and Jilbabs', Liberty, a Magazine for Religious Freedom, available online at http://www.libertymagazine.org/article/articleview/683/1/100/ Mr Boonstra is a partner in the law firm Kuhn & Company, practising in Vancouver and Abbotsford, British Columbia.

182 The Universal Declaration of Human Rights has been incorporated into Canadian law. (contd .../)

Charter guarantees the rights and freedoms set out in it subject only to such reasonable limits prescribed by law as can be demonstrably justified in a free and democratic society. Section 2(a) of the Charter provides: 'everyone has … freedom of conscience and religion.' This right includes the right to manifest religious belief by worship and practice or by teaching and dissemination[183] subject only to such reasonable limits prescribed by law as can be demonstrably justified in a free and democratic society.

[5.040] In *Multani v Commission Scolaire Marguerite-Bourgeoys*[184] the plaintiff was an orthodox Sikh student who had been prohibited by his Canadian school from wearing his kirpan (a 20 cm knife with a metal blade required to be worn by his religion) to school. However, the school had suggested that a pendant or a kirpan made of another substance would be an acceptable alternative. This alternative was unacceptablc to the plaintiff on religious grounds and he then applied to court seeking permission to wear the kirpan to school if it were sealed in a wooden sheath and wrapped and sewn securely in a sturdy cloth envelope inside his clothing, which he contended would be a reasonable accommodation of his religious freedom. Having been successful in the lower court, the plaintiff lost on appeal. However, he then appealed to the Supreme Court which held that the school authority, by failing to accommodate the plaintiff's religious practice, contravened the constitutional guarantee of religious freedom. There was, it should be noted, no evidence that the plaintiff had any disciplinary problems in school and the probability that the kirpan would ever be used for violent purposes was very low, the court considered. This decision strongly indicates that, by contrast with England, Germany (in certain Länder) and France, efforts to prevent the wearing of religious clothing in Canadian schools will not be acceptable as this case is in line with Canadian human rights jurisprudence in which reasonable accommodation of religion is a well established principle.[185] It is also interesting to observe that the

182. (contd) The four key mechanisms for the protection of human rights in Canada are: the Canadian Charter of Rights and Freedoms 1982; the Canadian Human Rights Act 1978; the Human Rights Commissions and the Provincial Human Rights laws and legislation.

183. *R v Big M Drug Mart* [1985] 1 SCR, p 295.

184. *Multani v Commission Scolaire Marguerite-Bourgeoys* [2006] 1 SCR 256.

185. See *R v Big M Drug Mart Ltd* [1985] 2 SCR 295 at 336: *Syndicat Northcrest v Amselem* [2004] 2 SCR 551 at 256: *Law v Canada* [1999] 1 SCR 497: *Bruker v Markovitz* [2007] SCC 54.

approach of the US to this issue is much closer to that of Canada, a matter which is discussed in **chapter 10** below.

CONCLUSION

[5.041] A principle of establishment of religion is apparent in the context of civic religion in England, which may be viewed as an acknowledgement of the significance of the public role of religion and a certain resistance to religion being relegated to the private sphere of life as, for example, in France. As in Germany and Ireland, religion in England is viewed as a societal benefit, generally speaking, as is evident, *inter alia*, from the carefully crafted, broad, legislative measures for the provision and maintenance of religious education in schools within the State system. It will, however, be increasingly difficult for Christianity to continue to be the nation's public religion in the context of England's growing multi-culturalism and multi-faith societies. The system itself has retained a number of features, which seem out of alignment with the concepts which uphold a democratic society and these features are likely to be the target of EU's Directives on equality and non-discrimination in the not too distant future.

[5.042] Indeed, the concept of Establishment, for example, is becoming something of an anachronism in Europe. In particular, it can be argued that one of the benefits deriving from Establishment is the maintenance of the Church of England as a moderate, tolerant non-dogmatic church which does not impose religious belief on its citizens and that civic religion operates as a cohesive factor in England's highly diverse multi-faith society. That said, the distinction made between the legal status of the established Church of England and the other churches sits uneasily with the principle of equality and non-discrimination which underpins English law, European law and human rights law. Moreover, the fact that England recognises a distinct body of ecclesiastical law, which emanates solely from the jurisdiction of its two established churches, as an integral component of the law of the realm, also raises questions of unequal treatment of the churches. The right of one religion to appoint its bishops and archbishops to the House of Lords appears discriminatory. Furthermore, the provision in the Act of Settlement 1701[186] prohibiting a Roman Catholic, or their spouse, from becoming King

186. Act of Settlement 1701 12 & 13 Wm 3 c 2.

or Queen of England or from marrying the heir to the throne is blatantly discriminatory as against the Catholic faith.

[5.043] Despite the above criticisms, the conclusion is drawn that England has set up and maintained a broad ecclesiastical legal framework within which considerable flexibility and fairness for the minority religions has been achieved generally speaking. Church and denominational schools are part of the state system of education although religious education is provided as part of the basic curriculum of the school rather than as a component of the National Curriculum. This unique system facilitates local input for the provision and content of religious education and its delivery in publicly-funded schools adds a distinctive democratic and uniquely flexible element to the process. Within that legal framework, the churches remain free to establish their individual schools in which they may teach religious education and/or instruction and worship according to their principles and doctrines and the state provides generously for faith schools (schools with a religious character) which comprise approximately one third of all state schools.

[5.044] Non-denominational religious education has been provided in England's state schools since 1870. When the state became more fully and formally involved in elementary schools in 1902, unlike France, Turkey and the US, it decided not to separate church and state. Rather the denominational schools were assimilated into the state sector and they were supported by public taxation thus enabling greater State control of these schools. In this manner a dual system of schools was established in the State sector in which the state-funded non-denominational school system ran alongside a separate stream of state-funded denominational schools which was regulated to some degree by the state. The Education Act 1944 required that religious education be provided in all schools within the statutory system and it also provided for compulsory prayer in such schools, a feature which contrasts with the position in US state schools in which the recitation of prayers is prohibited by the First Amendment. Local control over religious education, introduced by the 1944 Act, remains a feature of the English state system to date and it has contributed in no small way to the democratic spirit and flexibility of this unique system.

Chapter 6

RELIGION, EDUCATION AND THE LAW IN GERMANY

> *[T]he state could never be in safety, where there was toleration of two religions. For there is no enmity so great as that of religion, and they that differ in the service of God, can never agree in the service of their country.*[1]

INTRODUCTION

[6.001] The Federal Republic of Germany (Germany) has a population of in excess of 80 million. Indeed, Germany is a living contradiction of the above quotation for it accommodates approximately equal numbers (26 million) of Roman Catholics and Protestants,[2] together with an estimated population of 3 to 3.2 million persons of the Islamic faith, approximately 100,000 Jewish people and 22 million persons who profess no religion.[3] The last category was significantly increased at the time of the reunification of Germany (1990)[4] as many persons from the former German Democratic Republic (GDR) had no religious affiliation because the political system of the former East Germany was hostile to the churches.[5] Germany is among those countries which have retained certain conservative elements in their education systems, which are supportive of religion generally[6] and of the

1. Hylson-Smith, *The Churches in England from Elizabeth I to Elizabeth II* (Canterbury Press, 1996–1998), chapter 4 quoting Elizabeth I's chief Minister Sir William Cecil.
2. Mainly Lutheran and Reformed Churches. In the Religious Peace of Augsburg (1555), the Catholic and Lutheran religions were recognised as being of more or less equal status.
3. Robbers, 'State and Church in Germany', in Robbers (ed), *State and Church in the European Union* (Nomos, 2005) p 77.
4. By the Unification Treaty of 31 August 1990 and Federal Statute of 23 September 1990.
5. Robbers, 'State and Church in Germany', p 77.
6. For example, see the Basic Law and in particular Art 4 (Freedom of faith, conscience and creed) and Art 7 (School Education).

role of the churches in society. Among Europe's church-state systems Germany adopts a centralist approach between an established religion, on the one hand, and a strict separation of church and state, on the other. As in many countries of Northern Europe, the position of religion in Germany is strongly marked by the Reformation of 1517 and by subsequent epic battles between the churches and the temporal powers. Finally, in the Religious Peace of Augsburg (1555)[7] the Lutheran and Catholic Churches were given recognition, to a large degree, on an equal basis, although no victors emerged. The conclusion of the Thirty Years War (1618–1648), however, brought victory to neither religion but it strongly influenced subsequent events and the distribution of the churches.[8] With the passage of the centuries, the two main religions learned to live together. In 1919 the Weimar Constitution was adopted by the people. This constitution embodied a separation of church and state (albeit not a strict separation), since it provided for a co-operative church-state approach in such matters as religious instruction in public schools,[9] the church tax,[10] and the provision of chaplains in the army, hospitals and in prisons, if such were required.[11] The following compromise arrangements were inserted in the Weimar Constitution: religious instruction would be a regular school subject, regulated by legislation, and taught in accordance with the principles of the respective communities, notwithstanding the state's right of supervision.[12] Articles 136, 137, 138, 139 and 141 of the Weimar Constitution were transposed by Art 140 of the Grundgesetz (Basic Law), thereby an integral part of the modern constitutional framework.

7. Reich (ed), *Select Documents Illustrating Medieval and Modern History* (PS King, 1905) pp 230–232.

8. Bonney, *The Thirty Years War 1618–1648* (Osprey Publications, 2002).

9. The Reich Constitution of 11 August 1919 (Weimar Constitution) with Modifications (1), Art 149, accessible online at www.bwbs.de/bwbs_biografie/weimar_constitution_B723, accessed on 6 March 2008.

10. The Reich Constitution of 11 August 1919 (Weimar Constitution) with Modifications (1), Art 137.

11. The Reich Constitution of 11 August 1919 (Weimar Constitution) with Modifications (1), Art 141.

12. The Reich Constitution of 11 August 1919 (Weimar Constitution) with Modifications (1), Art 149.

BACKGROUND

[6.002] Since the gradual introduction of compulsory schooling in Germany in the eighteenth century, schools have been perceived as the most important agencies for socialisation of young people.[13] Avenarius points out that this was due to the assumption that whoever controls the school also controls the young generation, and, therefore, the future of society: 'So educational policy became a battlefield in which diverse and controversial beliefs, ideas and ideologies struggled with one another in order to determine the value orientation of schools in general and particularly of state schools.'[14] As in other countries, this ultimately became a church-state struggle for the dominant role in education.

[6.003] At first, the churches were successful in retaining their influence. From the early nineteenth century, the school normally attended by most children, the 'Volksschule', was a denominational school ('Bekenenntnisschule'), whether Protestant or Catholic.[15] The denominational structure survived in most of West Germany until the 1970s, with the exception of the Nazi period and the four decades of the German Democratic Republic (GDR), with many *Länder* guaranteeing the existence of the denominational school in their constitutions. However, following the massive displacement which took place after the Second World War, the denominational schools were no longer seen as capable of meeting the needs of a rapidly-changing, diverse society. After a period of conflict and litigation in the 1970s, the majority of the *Länder* in West Germany amended their constitutions and introduced the Christian Communal School ('*christliche Gemeinschaftsschule*' CGS hereafter) as the norm for compulsory schooling. Although not bound by a specific creed,[16] the CGS is grounded in Christian cultural traditions as it is open to Christian religions while excluding, as far as possible, ideological or

13. Avenarius, 'The case of Germany,' *Religious Education in Public Schools: Study of Comparative Law,* pp 143–169, 143–4. Religious Education in Public Schools, pp 143–167, at pp 143–4.

14. Avenarius, 'The case of Germany,' *Religious Education in Public Schools: Study of Comparative Law*, p 144.

15. Avenarius, 'The case of Germany,' *Religious Education in Public Schools: Study of Comparative Law.*

16. Cf the concept of the Community Schools in Ireland discussed later in **para [9.019]** *et seq*.

religious pressures.[17] A number of the Constitutional Court's decisions have found that the CGS is in harmony with the Basic Law[18] since this school model does not impose a constitutionally unreasonable conflict of faith and conscience on parents or on students who prefer a denominational education, nor on parents and students who reject such an education and prefer a secular education.[19] In other words, the court concluded that a pragmatic and reasonable balance had been struck in these schools between parents and student preferences for denominational schools on the one hand, and their preferences for secular schools on the other.

CHURCH-STATE RELATIONS

Main Constitutional Structures

[6.004] The Basic Law lays down the structural principles of political order and the upholding constitutional principles for Germany.[20] As already noted, a number of articles from the Weimar Constitution relating to the freedom to practice religion or to practice no religion, and to the freedom of religious bodies to organise and administer their own affairs[21] were carried over into the Basic Law which confer on citizens liberty, democratic self-governance and personal responsibility protected by law and justice.[22] Article 4 guarantees freedom of faith and of conscience and freedom to profess a religion or philosophical creed and the undisturbed practice of religion.[23]

17. **Chapter 9**.

18. See the decision of the Federal Constitutional Court of 17 December 1975, BVerfGE 41,29; 42,65 and 41,88: also see the role of the community and comprehensive schools in Ireland established about the same time and the legal challenge to the public funding of chaplains in *Campaign to Separate Church and State v Minister for Education* [1996] 2 ILRM 241; [1998] 2 ILRM 81 which is discussed in **para [9.036]**.

19. 17 December 1975, BVerfGE 41,29; 42,65 and 41,88.

20. Kommers, 'The Basic Law: a Fifty Year Assessment', in Conference Report, *Fifty Years of German Basic Law*, American Institute for Contemporary German Studies (The Johns Hopkins University), November 1999.

21. Articles 136–139 and 141.

22. See Kommers, *The Constitutional Jurisprudence of the Federal Republic of Germany.*

Freedom of expression is guaranteed by Art 5, which expressly prohibits censorship.[24]

Essentially, the constitutional foundation of the church-state system in Germany builds on the principles of neutrality, tolerance and parity.[25] Broadly speaking, the principle of neutrality equates with non-intervention as indicated by Art 137(3) of the Weimar Constitution 1919, which was transposed into the Basic Law by Art 140. Article 137(3) provides:

> Every religious community regulates and administers its own affairs independently but within the framework of the general law. This right of self-determination is valid, regardless of the legal status of the religious congregation.[26]

Article 137(1) prohibits the establishment of a state church. The State may not assess the legitimacy of any one religion or make decisions relating to the affairs of religious communities who are independent in that regard, provided they act lawfully.[27] Associations whose purpose is to foster a philosophical creed (eg humanism) have the same status as religious societies in Germany.[28] Although the constitutional neutrality principle – which obliges the state not to identify with any particular church – is a well-founded constitutional principle arising from the prohibition on having a state church,[29] the Basic Law provides for a system of church-state co-operation which applies to a wide area of life in order to meet the needs of

---

23. Arts 4.2 and 4.3 of the Basic Law (*Grundgesetz*) for the Federal Republic of Germany (Promulgated by the Parliamentary Council on 23 May 1949) as amended by the Unification Treaty of 31 August 1990 and Federal Statute of 23 September 1990. The translation used by this author was provided by General Electric's Germany and Europe Round Table for which I am grateful.
24. As is the position in Ireland where the Censorship of Public Acts 1929–1967 remain on the statute book although these powers are seldom used in modern Ireland.
25. Robbers, State and Church in Germany', in Robbers (ed), *State and Church in the European Union* (Nomos, 2005) p 80.
26. Robbers, 'State and Church in Germany', in Robbers, *State and Church in the European Union*, p 78.
27. Art 137(3) of the Basic Law which was transposed into the Basic Law by Art 140.
28. Art 138 which was transposed into the Basic Law by Art 140.
29. The Weimar Constitution (1919) rejected that concept in Art 137(1) which was transposed into the Basic Law by Art 140.

the people co-operatively.[30] The right to establish private schools is also constitutionally guaranteed in Germany but this right requires state approval and is subject to the laws of the *Länder*.[31]

Main upholding principles

[6.005] The principle of tolerance, which includes positive tolerance for the religious needs of the people, requires the state to be impartial when dealing with religious faiths and perspectives and also with those persons who profess no faith. This may be deduced from the provisions of Art 4 (Freedom of faith, of conscience and of creed) of the Basic Law which guarantees freedom of religion for each individual no matter what his belief. Article 4 provides, *inter alia*:

> (1) Freedom of faith and of conscience, and freedom of creed, religious or ideological, are inviolable.
> (2) The undisturbed practice of religion is guaranteed …

Robbers posits the view that it is freedom of faith, in the sense of positive tolerance, which permits the state to offer in public schools the opportunity for interdenominational school prayer, provided participation is a part of the existing social attitude and is entirely voluntary.[32] In certain circumstances, he continues, such as when a person is required to attend school, the state is obliged to provide for the religious needs of that pupil.

[6.006] The parity principle in Germany's Basic Law requires the state to treat all religious communities equally. However, Robbers refers to 'a constitutional differentiation of legal status, a sort of graded parity … that provides an adequate basis for dealing with the various social phenomenon.' But, if parity is 'graded' so as to facilitate 'a constitutional differentiation of legal status', this could result in a form of Orwellian equality,[33] which sits uneasily with the constitutional tenet of parity of state treatment of churches in the Basic Law. As will be seen, it is difficult to reconcile the parity principle with the unequal provision made in practice for the various churches in Germany.

---

30. Robbers, State and Church in Germany', in Robbers (ed), *State and Church in the European Union* (Nomos, 2005) p 80.

31. Article 7(4).

32. Robbers, 'State and Church in Germany', in Robbers (ed), *State and Church in the European Union* (Nomos, 2005) p 77–94.

33. George Orwell, *Animal Farm* (Harcourt, Brace, 1946). The 7th commandment of Animalism by which the Animals in *Animal Farm* are governed: 'All animals are equal but some are more equal than others'.

[6.007] Another important foundational principle, *inter alia*, of German constitutional law is that of subsidiarity,[34] which is reflected in education law. The concept of subsidiarity, which is also found in EU law (being enshrined in the Maastricht Treaty),[35] derives from Catholic social principles that were promulgated by Pope Pius XI in his *Encyclical Quadragesimo Anno* (1931). In that context it means that it is unjust if the higher community acts in spheres of activity in which the smaller and subordinated community can act successfully.[36] This doctrine viewed state activity in education with suspicion and advocated the principle of subsidiarity, which envisaged the state playing a limited role in family life and in education. A large part of church-state affairs in Germany has been delegated to the 16 *Länder*, which are also in charge of the public school sector.[37] The principle of subsidiarity is applicable to the devolution of educational responsibility to the *Länder*. In German educational law a distinction is made between 'vertical subsidiarity', ie the distribution of powers between the central state (the 'Bund') and the *Länder* and the local communities, and 'horizontal subsidiarity', ie the distribution of powers between the state and society or citizens.[38] Many of the upholding regulations are to be found in legal provisions and regulations of lesser status than the Basic Law. Like Spain, Germany and its *Länder* have negotiated many treaties and concordats with the churches thereby facilitating church-state co-operation in many spheres of public life, such as the provision made for military chaplains, faculties of

---

34. See further Anheier, 'An Elaborate network: Profiling the Third Sector in Germany', Gidron (ed), *Government and the Third Sector: Emerging Relationships in Welfare States*. This principle later became a political doctrine and one of the principles in the EC legal system. The principle of subsidiarity also underpins education in Ireland and in particular Art 42 (Education) of the Constitution. See further Glendenning, *Education and the Law*, p 51.

35. See Art 126, paras 1–3 inclusive. See further Postma, 'The Principle of Subsidiarity in the Treaty of the European Union', in de Groof (ed), *Subsidiarity in Education*, pp 151–153, and in the same book see, Keukeleire, 'The Principle of Subsidiarity between Words and Deed. The operation of Art 3B of the Maastricht Treaty', pp 155–179.

36. See further Fussel, 'The Attribution of Powers as to Education in Germany', in de Groof (ed), *Subsidiarity and Education: Aspects of Comparative Educational Law*, p 267.

37. In accordance with Art 7(3) of the Basic Law.

38. Fussel, 'The Attribution of Powers as to Education in Germany', in de Groof (ed), *Subsidiarity and Education: Aspects of Comparative Educational Law*, p 267.

theology and matters surrounding the teaching of religious education in public schools.[39] Accordingly, each religious community regulates and administers its own affairs independently within the framework of the general law and this applies to all religious communities regardless of their legal status.[40] Having set down the constitutional provisions which bind all Germans, the Basic Law has chosen a decentralised school system,[41] delegating to the *Länder* the responsibility for education subject to the provisions of the Basic Law. Although the remit of the *Länder* in education is without the supervision of the Federal Executive, the courts, including the Federal Constitutional Court, will guarantee and vindicate the enforcement of these constitutional provisions nationwide.[42]

The Principle of Neutrality: The Crucifix Case

[6.008] The principle of state neutrality derives mainly from the policy of non-intervention[43] and arguably from Art 33, while the principle of religious neutrality derives from Art 4(1), which guarantees freedom of faith and conscience and religious and ideological beliefs. Accordingly, there is a guarantee of free intellectual life in which the state may not lawfully interfere.[44] Catholic Bavaria, one of the first states in Germany to ban the Muslim headscarf from its public schools, fought an unsuccessful battle to retain the right to display the crucifix in each classroom in 1995.[45] This controversial legal challenge, which finally reached the Federal Constitutional Court, has come to be known as 'the *Crucifix Case*'. The case was taken by the theosophist[46] parent[47] of a public school pupil in Bavaria who objected, on ideological grounds, to the custom and legal requirement

39. Robbers, 'State and Church in Germany', in Robbers (ed), *State and Church in the European Union* (Nomos, 2005) p 79.

40. Article 137(3) of the Weimar Constitution carried over by Art 140 of the Basic Law.

41. As with Ireland's centralised system in **chapter 9** below.

42. Lambert, 'School legislation in Germany', de Groof, *Subsidiarity and Education: Aspects of Comparative Educational Law*, pp 259–266 at p 260.

43. Embodied in Art 137(1) and (3) as transposed by Art 140 of the Basic Law.

44. Avenarius, 'The case of Germany,' *Religious Education in Public Schools: Study of Comparative Law*, p 149.

45. BVerfGE 93,1.

46. A follower of Rudolph Steiner (1861–1925).

47. Seler, a Bavarian artist and composer.

in Christian communal schools ('Volksschulen') of displaying a crucifix in every classroom. In a 5:3 decision, the Federal Constitutional Court in 1995 held that the Bavarian regulation was in breach of state neutrality as enshrined in Art 4(1) of the Basic Law.[48] The court held that since the obligation to attend school was generally required by law, crosses in classrooms mean that the state confronts pupils with this symbol during their lessons, leaving them no alternative to 'learning under the cross'. Accordingly, the court ruled that the Bavarian regulation was unconstitutional.[49]

Teacher Rights

[6.009] In German public schools, teachers are full civil servants employed by the state since their status is governed by public law and specifically provided for in Art 33 of the Basic Law:

(1) Every German has in every *Land* the same civil rights and duties.

(2) Every German is equally eligible for any public office according to his aptitude, qualifications and professional achievements.

(3) Enjoyment of civil and civic rights, eligibility for public office, and rights acquired in the public service are independent of religious denomination. No one may suffer disadvantage by reason of his adherence or non-adherence to a denomination or ideology.

(4) The exercise of state authority as a permanent function shall as a rule be entrusted to members of the public service whose status, service and loyalty are governed by public law.

(5) The law of the public service shall be regulated with due regard to the traditional principles of the permanent civil service.

[6.010] In addition, Art 7(3) of the Constitution, *inter alia*, provides: 'No teacher may be obliged, against his will to give religious instruction.'[50] The position of teachers in Germany contrasts with the position of teachers in Ireland, since the latter are, for the most part, [51] public servants employed by

48. BVerfGE 93, 1 (18 ff)

49. BVerfGE 93,1.

50. Art 7(3).

51. The main exception to this rule are the teachers employed by the vocational education committees pursuant to the Vocational Education Acts 1930–2001. See further **para [9.062]** below.

a denominational school board, and they are usually required to teach religious instruction in primary schools.[52] Fussel states, however, that the rights of public school teachers in Germany are limited by virtue of their special status as civil servants and even if their pedagogical freedom is recognised by school legislation, this does not amount to a real freedom for the individual teacher.[53] Teachers may express their religious convictions in school incidently through history or social studies, but not in an aggressive or missionary manner, and they may not utilise their religious freedom for the purpose of indoctrination.[54]

While freedom of teaching is guaranteed by Art 5.3, this does not absolve teachers from loyalty to the Basic Law. Essentially, teachers have the same basic rights as any other citizen guaranteed under the law of the particular *Land* in which they reside and by the Basic Law. Thus, the freedom of faith and of conscience and freedom enshrined in Art 4(1) applies to their lives generally and to their professional work and is not delimited by legislation.[55] But teacher rights have to be balanced against competing rights such as the state's educational mandate,[56] the religious freedoms of students and parents, the principle of state neutrality in schools[57] and children's rights. Avenarius (2006) refers to the provisions of the Religious Education of Children Act 1921[58] which embodies principles which show that even minor children have their own rights in this matter and that, when a child reaches the age of 13 years, they may decide for themselves whether they wish to have religious instruction or not.[59] Concerns regarding the numbers of students opting out

52. It has not been established in law whether or not this obligation arises from the contract of employment or otherwise.

53. Fussel, 'Freedom in the German School System', *European Journal for Education Law and Policy,* 2: 53–57, (Kluwer Law International, 1998): this article was also published by Professor Jean Raux, Universite de Rennes 1, Faculte de Droit at de Science Politique, 1998.

54. Which would breach international law principles, *Kjelsden, Busk Madsen and Pedersen v Denmark* (1976) 1 EHRR 711.

55. Avenarius, 'The case of Germany,' *Religious Education in Public Schools: Study of Comparative Law,* p 149.

56. Art 7(1) of the Basic Law.

57. Avenarius, 'The case of Germany,' *Religious Education in Public Schools: Study of Comparative Law,* p 149.

58. Ibid, which is still in force.

59. Avenarius, The Case of Germany, loc cit, *Religious Education in Public Schools,* p 145.

of religious instruction, however, have led most *Länder* to introduce a new subject called 'Ethics' for those students who have been exempted from religious instruction, a topic to which I will return later. While it seems clear that a Muslim female student in a state school in Germany is permitted to wear a headscarf in the school because of her constitutional right to religious freedom, the guarantee of state neutrality would require a ban on female teachers wearing a headscarf, since teachers represent the state in the public school. Such teachers would be required to act in accordance with the principle of religious neutrality.[60]

THE HEADSCARF CASE

[6.011] In Germany, as in many other European countries, the conflict between religious freedom for the individual and the right of pupils to have a religiously neutral education has been controversial for years. More recently, the issue of German law regulating the rights and duties of a teacher in a public school, in what is generally known as 'the headscarf case',[61] achieved a significance which far outweighed its practical significance in purely legal terms.[62] Perhaps the 'headscarf issue' more than any other illustrates the tensions at the intersection of religious freedom and determined secularism and the principle of state neutrality against a background of increasing Muslim immigration in predominantly Christian countries. In the so-called 'Headscarf case' the German Federal Constitutional Court was called upon to find a *via media* between the constitutional principle of religious freedom for the individual teacher on the one hand, and religious neutrality in public education[63] on the other. The court's decision gave rise to considerable global debate on the wider issues of state neutrality on religious matters, the boundaries of religious freedom for individuals and the difficulties of accommodating these tenets due to the increasing plurality of religions in modern society and in particular where the ideologies of the West and the East meet and are called upon to peacefully co-exist.

---

60. Avenarius, The Case of Germany, *Religious Education in Public Schools*, p 151.

61. BVerfG, 2 BvR 1436/02, 24 September 2003 available at http://www.bverfg.de.

62. For an interesting analysis of this case, see Mahlmann, 'Religious Tolerance, Pluralist Society and the Neutrality of the State: The Federal Constitutional Court's Decision in the Headscarf Case' in (2003) 4 *German Law Journal*, No 11 (1 November), Public Law.

63. Pursuant to Art 33 of the Basic Law.

[6.012] At issue in the Headscarf case were the rights of a 31-year old, Kabul-born German citizen, Fereshta Ludin, who was refused a position teaching English and German in a Baden-Württemberg public school because she insisted on wearing, for stated religious reasons, a headscarf or hijab in the classroom. The state board of education in this mainly Roman Catholic state considered that the wearing of the hijab breached Germany's religious neutrality principle and this was upheld by the Administrative Courts, which ruled that teachers in public schools must refrain from openly displaying religious symbols in the classroom, since as civil servants they are representatives of the state and they also function as role models for their students. When the Federal Constitutional Court was called upon to decide the matter on constitutional principles, Ms Ludin relied in particular on the constitutional guarantee of religious freedom in Art 33.2 of the Basic Law. The state, on the other hand, contended that the wearing of the headscarf would infringe Germany's constitutional religious neutrality principle.[64] The court emphasised that the German state's neutrality on religion should not be interpreted as a strict separation of church and state, and that if federal states did not wish to employ teachers who wore headscarves, they would need to have unambiguous legislation in place which would expressly forbid such religious symbols in the classroom. Since no such ban was in place in Baden-Württemberg, where Ms Ludin was employed, she was entitled to wear her Islamic headscarf, the court concluded. In addition, the court distinguished between symbols that the state or a public authority employs of its own initiative and those which are simply tolerated by the state or public authority when worn by individuals. The latter position is a personal statement of the individual, the court considered, and cannot or may not be taken as a statement of the state; neither did the headscarf in principle impede the teaching of the values inherent in the Constitution, the court considered. Having evaluated the relevant constitutional principles on the rights and obligations of civil servants, the court concluded that none of these tenets constituted sufficient grounds for the administration not to appoint Ms Ludin to the teaching post. The Constitutional Court ruled in a 5:3 decision that since Baden-Wurttemberg had not banned religious symbols by legislative measures, then under current laws Ms Ludin could wear the headscarf. Furthermore, the court recommended that the *Länder*, which have responsibility for education in their own jurisdiction, should strive to find an acceptable balance between religious freedom and neutrality in schools.

64. Art 33.

[6.013] However, Baden-Wurttemberg moved almost immediately to pass legislation banning the headscarf in public schools, and many of the *Länder*, including Bavaria, have passed legislative measures prohibiting the wearing of headscarves in state schools. In Catholic Bavaria, however, the wearing of Christian clothing, such as nuns' habits, crucifixes and Jewish clothing, are excluded from the ban and the Bavarian Constitutional Court has recently upheld the legality of that practice. Although Christian symbols are closely linked to culture, religion and national identity, a ban which permits religious symbols of some faiths in public schools but denies that right to other faiths appears to conflict with the freedom of religion guaranteed in Art 4 of the Basic Law, and with the guarantees of equality in Art 3. In particular Art 3(3) provides: 'No one may be prejudiced or favoured because of his … his faith or his religious or political opinions.' If the headscarf is a religious symbol, then Arts 4(1) and 4(2) of the Basic Law would appear to guarantee a teacher's right to wear it as part of her religious freedom guarantee unless it violates the constitutional rights of others. In *Ludin* Germany's Federal Constitutional Court held that the wearing of the headscarf did not impede the teaching of the values inherent in the constitution. Moreover, from the perspective of international human rights law, a decision to deny the right to Muslims to wear a headscarf in public schools would seem to lack that tolerance, pluralism and non-discriminatory approach that is usually the norm in democratic societies in which the state itself is meant to be neutral and objective towards religion. One would also have to question whether the legislative ban on the wearing of the headscarf in public schools is a breach of the well-established international human right to manifest religion in community with others and whether the state's legislative ban on the headscarf in these circumstances violates the human rights principle that the state itself may not access the legitimacy of any one religion. Unlike other headscarf-banning *Länder*, which perceived the Muslim headscarf as a threat to Christian values, Berlin, which enjoys a unique historical status, decided that a ban on all religious symbols in public schools was more in line with the constitutional principles of parity between the religions and state neutrality towards religion generally[65] and there is much to be said for Berlin's approach in that it treats all religions equally.

[6.014] Having set down the constitutional provisions which bind all Germans, the Basic Law has chosen a decentralised school system, which

65. Gallala, 'The Islamic Headscarf: An Example of Surmountable Conflict between *Shari'a* and the Fundamental Principles of Europe,' *European Law Journal,* Vol 12, No 5, September 2006.

delegates to the *Länder* the responsibility for education subject to the provisions of the Basic Law. Although the remit of the *Länder* in education is without the supervision of the Federal Executive, the courts up to the Federal Constitutional Court will guarantee and vindicate the enforcement of these constitutional provisions nationwide.[66]

RELIGIOUS FREEDOM

[6.015] In Germany as in Ireland, the scope of religious freedom extends the right of self-determination into wider social spheres which are rooted in religious objectives, such as the administration of hospitals, retirement homes, universities and private schools. In other words, while the Basic Law prohibits the secular government from establishing a state church, it facilitates co-operation between church and state particularly in social spheres. Furthermore, the Basic Law empowers the Federal Constitutional Court, as guardian of the Basic Law, to ban political parties that seek to overthrow or endanger the democratic principles, civil rights and the rule of law.[67] Moreover, the state collects taxes for the Catholic Church, the Jewish Church and the many Protestant communities and it enters into tax agreements with these churches which have a special legal status. With regard to the Jewish population, Robbers states: 'Taking responsibility for the murder of millions of European Jews by Nazi Germany in the 1940s has led Germany to give to the Jewish religious communities, thought still small in numbers, a very visible role in society.'[68] Kommers points out that the German government must maintain a 'militant' protection of 'the free democratic basic order' which requires officials to monitor, and if necessary move against, anti-democratic organisations who operate in the country, short of breaching human rights agreements which Germany has ratified.[69]

---

66. Lambert, 'School legislation in Germany' in de Groof (ed), *and Education: Aspects of Comparative Educational Law*, pp 259–266.

67. Which is facilitated by Art 137(6) which was transposed into the Basic Law by Art 140.

68. Robbers, 'State and Church in Germany', in Robbers (ed), *State and Church in the European Union* (Nomos, 2005) p 78.

69. Kommers, *The Constitutional Jurisprudence of the Federal Republic of Germany* (2nd edn, Duke University Press, 1997).

Legal Status of the Churches

[6.016] In practice, those religious communities in Germany with a large membership – such as the Catholic and Protestant communities together with the Jewish community and a number of other smaller religious communities[70] – have achieved the status of 'public law corporations'. These religions have considerable independence and tax concessions which accrue to them as a result of this legal status, eg relief from gift tax, corporate tax and inheritance tax. Other religious denominations fall under private law but they too may acquire public law status provided they meet the 'public benefit purposes' requirement in the German Fiscal Code.[71] Otherwise, they may achieve the status of 'registered associations' (*eingetragener Verein*).

Kirchensteuer (Church Tax)

[6.017] The payment of church tax is not uncommon in certain European countries.[72] Each *Land* has separate contracts with the two main Christian churches. Some contend that the relationship between the state and the two main churches is too close and too powerful, a fact which they allege is axiomatic in the Church Tax arrangements. Members of the Lutheran, Catholic and Jewish religions are required by law to pay 'church tax' (*kirchensteuer*). In other words, churches which have acquired the status of public law corporations are entitled to levy (church) tax on their members[73] and they also have the right to employ officials. The deductible church tax, which has an ancient lineage,[74] is a feature of the revenue laws in

70. That status has also been conferred on the Salvation Army, Mormons, Christian Scientist, Adventists and the New Apostolic Church.

71. German Fiscal Code, ss 51–68.

72. Members of certain religions are required to pay church tax, for example, in Spain, Denmark, Sweden, Finland, Austria and in parts of Switzerland.

73. Pursuant to Art 140 of the Basic Law in conjunction with Art 137(6) of the Weimar Constitution.

74 The '*Kirchensteuer*' dates back to the early nineteenth century, at least, when the churches were granted the right to levy taxes by Prussia partly as a means of compensating them for property which was alienated from them by the state to assist in payment for the Napoleonic wars. However, church taxes date back for many centuries. Judaism's early *di-drachma* tax was payable by every Jew for the upkeep of the Temple; the Roman Empire later levied this tax payable to her own Treasury and dedicated it to the temple of Jupiter Capitolinus. (cont \....)

Germany.[75] This tax was enshrined in the Weimar Constitution, which conferred on religions that had achieved the status of public law corporations the right to levy church tax.[76] This right was carried over from that Constitution into the Basic Law by Art 140 and extended to the former GDR by the Unification Treaty in 1990.[77] Although church members carry the main financial responsibility for supporting the churches in Germany, the state collects the tax for the two main Christian Churches and retains approximately 3 per cent for administration. However, only about 30 per cent of the total number of Catholics actually pay church tax, it appears. For example, young persons without income, the elderly with small pensions and the unemployed do not pay such tax. Church tax is collected on the basis of income tax by the public tax office and is then transferred to the churches. In practice, this means that if a Protestant or Catholic citizen declares a religion on his or her tax form, the revenue authorities levy an 8–9 per cent tax as a payroll deduction on their income. This church tax funds the two main Christian denominations annually and it also funds religious education in state schools as well as the education of priests and theologians at third-level institutions. In addition, this general taxation funds, *inter alia*, 'pastoral care' in the army and in prisons and church media broadcasts. Moreover, the churches maintain their own pre-schools, hospitals and homes for the elderly, which are largely state funded.

[6.018] The practice of conferring a different legal status on the churches, which advantages some churches over others, sits uneasily with the guarantees of freedom of faith, conscience and religious of philosophical expression in Art 4(1) which are described as 'inviolable'. Furthermore, the fact that the state collects the tax for the two main Christian churches is not without its critics even in Germany. It is regarded by some as discriminatory and in breach of the principle of state neutrality enshrined in Art 33 of the

---

74. (contd) The majority of Jews continued to support the expenses of the Patriarch by another special tax – the *aurum coronarium, a* name conferred on it by the Theodosian Code which recognised this tax's legality. See Vincent, Scanlan (trans), *Judaism* (Sands & Co, 1934) pp 14 and 24, citing Bell Jud Iv, iii, 8; Antt x, 23. See further Josephus, *The Works of Josephus*; *Jewish Enclyclopedia*, vol 1-X11 and Margolis and Marx, *A History of the Jewish People* (Atheneum, 1927).

75. Barker, 'Church and State Relationships in German "Public Benefit" Law', 3 *International Journal of Not-for-Profit Law,* issue 2 (December 2000).

76. Art 136(6) of the Weimar Constitution.

77. Art 136(6) of the Weimar Constitution.

Basic Law. In particular Art 3(1)(3) provides: 'No one may be disadvantaged by reason of adherence or non-adherence to a particular religious denomination or philosophical creed.' Furthermore, critics of the church tax system allege that the main churches are compromised in their mission by the fact that the state collects tax on their behalf. Opponents of church tax and of the major role played by the two main Christian churches in social welfare provision, have proposed dispensing with church tax entirely and replacing it with freewill contributions from church members to be collected by the churches themselves. Others recommend the system which operates in Italy in which the state deducts eight per cent of income from each tax payer, who can choose whether that contribution goes to their chosen church or to the state to be used for social, humanitarian or cultural purposes.[78] As will be seen in **chapter 9**, there have been some recent reforms in regard to a similar church tax by the socialist government in Spain. On the other hand, the churches in Germany support the *status quo* contending that the church tax system is both fair and effective, with benefits accruing to both church and state, since the state stands to gain from the many social welfare church-related activities which it would otherwise have to fund, and also from the private education which the church provides and administers. The desire for a more distinct separation between church and state is consistently raised in arguments for abolishing the church tax,[79] particularly when a state law compels a link between church membership and the collection of taxes by the state.

[6.019] As to the legality of the church tax under national law, that was placed beyond doubt in 1994 when a legal challenge was taken against the levying of the tax in the Federal Administrative Court which confirmed its legality.[80] Such tax was entitled to be deducted from the income of taxpayers, the court held, in the same way as deductions for health insurance, pension and unemployment insurance. This legal challenge arose from the fact that a huge decrease in average church-membership in Germany followed upon German unification, because a considerable percentage of the population in the GDR were not affiliated to any church.[81]

78. Art 136(6) of the Weimar Constitution.

79. Church and State Relationships in German 'Public Benefit' Law, *International Journal for Not-for-Profit Law,* Vol 3, issue 2, pp 1–8.

80. (1994) file no 1 BvL 8/85.

81. (1994) file no 1 BvL 8/85.

[6.020] The right to opt out of paying the church tax is available to everybody by relinquishing their church membership. However, this requires a formal declaration and formal legal certification from a state authority which is documented in civil and church registers. Nonetheless, this is a step which increasingly many people are taking especially the young.[82] Critics of the church tax declare that it should be transformed into a levy on every individual to benefit culture in general possibly with the requirement that the taxpayer can designate which statutory body is to receive the money.[83] Given the current demographic structure in Germany, the growing harmonisation of laws in the member states, and the advance of human rights in Europe generally, tax privileges conferred by the state on particular religions under the Basic Law which guarantees religious freedom will inevitably come under pressure. In view of the fact that EU regulators are now asking Italy to explain state subsidies for Catholic Church clinics and hostels, fearing that they confer an unfair competitive advantage over its rivals, further pressure is likely to emerge from the European Commission in regard to the church tax in Germany.[84] In 2005 EU regulators also requested Spain to discontinue a sales tax exemption that had previously cut the price of goods the church had purchased.

RELIGIOUS INSTRUCTION IN PUBLIC SCHOOLS

[6.021] Article 7(1) of the Basic Law provides:[85]

> (1) The entire school system shall be under the supervision of the state.
>
> (2) Parents and guardians shall have the right to decide whether children shall receive religious instruction.
>
> (3) Religious instruction shall form part of the regular curriculum in state schools, with the exception of non-denominational schools. Without prejudice to the state's right of supervision, religious

82. (1994) file no 1 BvL 8/85.

83. Dw-world.de Deutsche Welle, 'Quelling the Flight from the Church (Tax)', 13 April 2004.

84. 'EU Regulators ask Italy to explain tax breaks for Catholic Church Property', (2007) *International Herald Tribune,* 28 August, www.iht.com/articles/ap/2007/08/28europe/EU-GEN-EU-Italt-Tax-Breaks.php accessed 7 March 2008.

85. Federal Constitution Court 47, 46 (80). See further Jasch, 'Educational policy of the German Bundesverfassungsgericht', (1999) *European Journal for Education Law and Policy,* 3: 81–87, Kluwer Law International.

instruction shall be given in accordance with the tenets of the religious community concerned. Teachers may not be obliged against their will to give religious instruction.

[6.022] In the case of state schools, Art 7(1) indicates the state's absolute right with regard to organisation, planning, control and supervision of the entire curriculum including religious instruction.[86] Thus, the state's overarching right of supervision of the entire school system, which includes the supervision of religious instruction and/or religious education, appears wider than that conferred by the state in Ireland under the Irish Constitution.[87] In accordance with Art 7(3) of the Basic Law, religious teaching, in the majority of the *Länder*, is part of the standard curriculum and usually the denominational religious instruction in public schools is given by religious communities under the supervision of the *Länder.*

[6.023] While religious instruction forms part of the regular curriculum in state and in municipal schools, with the exception of non-denominational schools[88] and those *Länder* exempted under Art 141,[89] the right to decide whether a child receives religious instruction or not vests in the persons entitled to bring up the child.[90] Although religious instruction has

86. Federal Constitution Court 47, 46 (80): see further Jach, 'Educational policy of the German Bundesverfassungsgericht', *European Journal for Education Law and Policy,* 3: 81–87 (1999), Kluwer Law International.

87. In this regard see **para [9.031]** *et seq*.

88. Art 7(3).

89. For example Bremen and Berlin. Art 7(3) does not apply in Bremen and Berlin for historical reasons. Art 7(3) is not applicable to Länder in which a different regulation had been operational on the 1 January 1949. Religious instruction was carried out in the past in these Länder by the Christian Churches and by the Jewish community remunerated by the state and given by state teachers. This exception was recognised in the Wiemar Constitution (1919) and carried over into the Basic Law by Art 140. Brandenburg, however, has claimed this exemption also, and did not introduce religious instruction as a regular teaching subject, so the churches normally offer religious instruction themselves. Note the controversy surrounding this topic in the so-called new Länder in East Germany, which were not part of the GDR on the 1 January 1949, but were re-established in 1990. Constitutional questions surround this issue. These matters are discussed in Avenarius, The Case of Germany, *Religious Education in Public Schools*, pp 146–7.

90. Art 7(2) of the Basic Law.

constitutionally the same academic status as other subjects of the curriculum, this does not mean that marks gained by student in religious instruction necessarily go towards his/her final calculation of marks for a career.[91] Rather, the *Länder* parliaments remain free to regulate whether such marks are to be taken into account or not for the student's final examination. Since religious instruction is part of the state school curriculum, it is the responsibility of the state and is subject to state supervision.[92] Accordingly, the state defrays the cost of personnel and materials for religious instruction.[93]

[6.024] Since religious instruction must be taught 'in accordance with the tenets of the religious community concerned',[94] the churches generally decide the content of the religious instruction programme[95] and the state pays for such instruction to be taught to students.[96] This guarantees the churches the right to co-operate with the state in designing syllabuses, in choosing textbooks and in inspecting quality and compatibility of the religious instruction taught.[97] Most significantly, the churches retain the right to co-operate with the state in the selection and appointment of teachers for religious instruction.[98] By contrast with Ireland, the German state generally provides a mandatory 'replacement' class for those students whose parents decide that they are to be withdrawn from religion.[99] While religious instruction (unlike the broad programme of religious education or ethics) is to be given in accordance with the tenets of the religious communities, this position is expressly stated to be 'without prejudice to the state's right of supervision' which embraces the entire curriculum.[100]

91. Avenarius, The Case of Germany, *Religious Education in Public Schools*, p 145.
92. Avenarius, The Case of Germany, *Religious Education in Public Schools*, p 145.
93. From the Church tax fund.
94. Art 7(3) of the Basic Law.
95. Note the exceptions for Berlin, Bremen and Brandenburg.
96. As in Ireland.
97. Avenarius, The Case of Germany, *Religious Education in Public Schools*, p 145.
98. Avenarius, The Case of Germany, *Religious Education in Public Schools*.
99. See 'Religion in Europe: Powerful Churches, but few believers', lecture given by Rene Hartmann at the Atheist Alliance International Annual Convention 2002, Dallas, Texas. Published in *Secular Nation*, No 3, 2002.
100. Art 7(1) of the Basic Law.

[6.025] Thus, the German state retains its supervisory power even over religious instruction, a position which contrasts with the position in Ireland where the responsibility for religious instruction appears to rest with parents and the churches who act on their behalf but within the legal structures provided by the state. If teachers in Germany wish to teach religious instruction, they must acquire a specific mandate from the relevant church, which is termed a '*vocatio*' for Protestant teachers and a '*missio*' for Catholic teachers.[101] The German Constitutional Court has determined that a church may not be compelled to take a student from another denomination into its religious instruction class.[102] On the other hand, the state may not prevent a church from admitting students of another faith, or of no faith, to attend its religious instruction class, as this right is reserved to the germane Church.

[6.026] In Germany, the ideological-religious element of education is also an essential component of parental rights, which when read together with Art 4(1) of the Basic Law includes the right of the parents to convey to their children their own religious and ideological convictions,[103] but in public schools that right is clearly not absolute. The Federal Constitutional Court has pointed out that in a pluralistic society, it is impossible to fully accommodate all parental wishes regarding the ideological orientation of public compulsory schools,[104] and consequently parents do not have any claim against the state to educate the children in any specific ideological form which they desire for their children.[105] Hence the remit of the German public school to instruct and educate its students is not perceived as being subject to parental rights but rather as running parallel to parental rights.[106] Neither the educational jurisdiction of the state, nor parental educational

101. In the Constitution of Ireland 1937, no express powers in regard to the teaching of religious instruction were reserved to the State.

102. BVerfGE 68, 16 (19f); 74,244 (253 ff).

103. Which is in line with Art 2 of Protocol 1 of the ECHR.

104. See the three decisions of the Federal Constitutional Court of the 17 December 1975, BVerfGE 41,29;41,65 and 41,88.

105. This approach is in line with the ECHR's finding in *Jimenez* Application No 51188/1999, Reports of Judgments and Decisions 2000–VI. in regard to Spain's programme of 'Natural Sciences'.

106. Federal Constitutional Court 27, 195 (201). Compare this with the position in the Constitution of Ireland (Art 42.1) in which the primary and natural educator of the child is the Family.

rights can claim absolute priority in this regard, but the German state can follow its own educational objectives in public schools relatively independently of parents from a constitutional viewpoint.[107] This arises from the express constitutional jurisdiction of the state over the entire curriculum in Art 7(1). While the ideological-religious element of education is clearly an essential component of parental rights, which includes the parental right to convey to their children their own religious and ideological convictions,[108] parents have no claim against the state to 'educate the children in the desired ideological form'.[109] Germany's express over-arching supervision of the entire curriculum contrasts with the more restricted powers vested in the Irish state in this regard, a matter discussed later in **chapter 9**. The apparent limitation on state powers in Ireland, in this regard, arose mainly from the fears of the constitutional drafters and church bodies that the conferring of over-arching powers on the state could conceivably lead to an unfettered state regime in education and to the rigid imposition of a state ideology in education ('statism').[110]

Religious Freedom for the Muslim Community

[6.027] Since Art 7(3) of the Basic Law makes provision for religious instruction as part of the regular curriculum and for religious instruction to be given in accordance with the tenets of the religious community concerned (albeit without prejudice to the states's right of supervision), persons of the Islamic faith, *inter alia*, have a fundamental right to have religious instruction provided in state schools in Germany. Nevertheless, difficulties have been encountered in organising such religious instruction in state schools in the past, a problem which is common to many European countries primarily because of the lack of a central Islamic religious

107. Federal Constitutional Court 47, 46 (72): Federal Constitutional Court 27, 195 (201).

108. Federal Constitution Court 41, 29 (47f).

109. Federal Constitution Court 41, 29 (48).

110. These fears were later expressed almost 30 years later by O'Rahilly when he stated: '... for when the State starts to be schoolmaster, it ceases to be neutral and liberal, it begins to inculcate a creed and to suppress all cultural rivalry and diversity, it becomes a monopolistic Church backed by physical force and overwhelming economic pressure. We in Ireland-Catholic, Protestant, or Jew-are determined to resist any State imposed ideology.' See further Glendenning, Education and the Law, pp 28–29.

community to negotiate with the state in each country. Writing in 1999, Fussel observed that the problem is wider than perhaps generally acknowledged:

> Despite German politicians making regular complaints about the lack of religious authority for the Muslims in Germany and outlining the necessity for religious instruction in schools in order to integrate Islamic pupils into Germany, they also seemed quite happy with that situation: many people in Germany are afraid of Islam as a political power in Germany ....[111]

As will be seen, however, in recent years, this problem has been addressed in Germany by establishing a state body to facilitate liaison between the representatives of the Muslim faith and the state. Similar initiatives have been undertaken by other countries to address specific integration problems with the Muslim communities, for example, in Spain (1992), in England (1996); in Belgium (1998), in Italy and in the Netherlands.[112] Issues which have arisen for discussion in these countries include dialogue in relation to the building of mosques, the education of Imams and religious education and instruction for persons of the Islamic faith.[113]

[6.028] However, the majority of the Muslim community in Germany are perceived as religious moderates who have not traditionally been attracted to extreme forms of Islam and many, it appears, are not attached to any formal religious organisation.[114] Those associations which claim to represent Muslim interest are classified as 'registered associations' and they have, therefore, a lesser legal status than Jews, Protestants and Catholics which have achieved the status of public law corporations. Clearly, the

---

111. Fussel, "Country report: Religious instruction for Islamic pupils-a german discussion', European Journal for Education Law and Policy, 3: 139–140, Kluwer, 1999, p 139.

112. Jasch, 'Dialogue with Islam and integration of Muslims in Italy and Germany-a comparison of the political conditions and the legal framework for mechanisms of dialogue with the Islamic faith communities in both countries,' Part 1 of 11, 8 *German Law Journal*, no 4 (1 April 2007). This excellent article was assessed by the author on 14 October 2008 and is available in PDF form http://handle.dtic.mil/100.2/ADA476044.

113. Jasch, 'Dialogue with Islam and integration of Muslims in Italy and Germany - a comparison of the political conditions and the legal framework for mechanisms of dialogue with the Islamic faith communities in both countries,' Part 1 of 11, 8 *German Law Journal*, no 4 (1 April 2007).

114. Jasch, 'Dialogue with Islam and integration of Muslims in Italy and Germany', p 368.

principle of religious freedom and non-discrimination acquires a new dimension and a fresh urgency when looking at Islam as a religion of growing significance in Germany.

[6.029] The fact that the public schools do not cater for Islamic religious instruction has become in recent years a matter of official concern since it could serve to shape Muslim identity and contribute to greater intercultural dialogue and social integration. But this is a complex issue, perhaps requiring diverse responses in the *Länder*, since there are many Islamic denominations in Germany including the Sunni, the Shiites, the Alevis and the followers of the South-Asian Ahmaddiyya.[115] With such a broad spectrum of beliefs, it would be difficult to devise a single comprehensive course, as the experience in Austria has proven, since the smaller denominations may be overlooked in such a system. Nonetheless, it is a significant issue which in now being addressed by the German government. Some of the *Länder* have negotiated agreements with Islamic representative groups regarding the teaching of religious instruction in the public schools.[116] In Berlin, where religious education is not taught as a standard school subject,[117] an Islamic association has won a protracted legal challenge against the *Land*, which permits it to provide religious Islamic education in Berlin's public schools,[118] but in the other *Länder* the matter remains inconsistent and frequently controversial.

[6.030] The most common approach is a type of state-aided foundation of Islamic religious communities. These communities would then be recognised as the negotiating 'partners' with the *Land* for religious

---

115. Ripperger, 'Teaching of Islam in German Schools Gains Ground', (2007) *Deutche Welle,* 27 May; Amel Al-Ariqi, 'Muslims in Germany: Obstacles prevent integration,' (2007) *Yemen Times*, 20 May.

116. See further Zacharias, 'Access of Muslim Organisations to Religious Instruction in Public Schools: Comment on the Decision of the Federal Administrative Court of 23 February 2005,' 6 *German Law Journal* 1319 (2005), available at www.germanlawjournal.com/pdf/Vol106No10/PDF_Vol_06_No_10_1318–1337_Developments_Zacharias.pdf, accessed 5 March 2008.

117. Due to its historical exemption under the so-called 'Bremen Clause', Art 141 which was transposed from the Weimar Constitution (1919) by Art 140 of the Basic Law.

118. BVerwG, Federal Administrative Court, 23 February 2000 and BVerwGE 326.

instruction. In Lower Saxony, for example, a group of Muslim organisations have come together to form a 'shura' or council to assist authorities to define the fundamental tenets to be included in courses on Islam in state schools. Bavaria and North-Rhine Westphalia are adopting a somewhat similar approach while Baden-Wurttemberg has decided to offer two courses: one for Shiites and Sunni students and another for Alevis.[119] Berlin has been providing Islamic studies to considerable numbers since 2003[120] and Northrhine-Westphalia has been making some provision in this sphere since the 1980s.[121] The difficulties the Muslim communities are currently experiencing, however, are exacerbated by the fact that the Islamic churches are not recognised as public entities in Germany. In order to avoid further controversy, teaching concerning Islam is generally included as part of comparative programmes of religious education in public schools, but the practice may vary from one *Land* to another.[122]

[6.031] Following the 9/11 terrorist attack in the US, Germany, aware that three of the attackers had previously lived in Hamburg, tightened its anti-terrorist laws considerably.[123] Conscious of the fact that repressive measures alone were inadequate to deal with extremism and radicalisation, it turned the focus of its attention to integration and participation and to the training of Muslim clerics.[124] As in many other member states, formal training and education for imams has been overlooked in the past and most imams in Germany traditionally received their training in Turkey or Saudi Arabia.

119. Ripperger, 'Teaching of Islam in German Schools Gains Ground', (2007) *Deutche Welle,* 27 May ; Amel Al-Ariqi, 'Muslims in Germany: Obstacles prevent integration,' (2007) *Yemen Times*, 20 May.

120. Ripperger, 'Teaching of Islam in German Schools Gains Ground', (2007) *Deutche Welle,* 27 May ; Amel Al-Ariqi, 'Muslims in Germany: Obstacles prevent integration,' (2007) *Yemen Times*, 20 May.

121. Jasch, 'Dialogue with Islam and integration of Muslims in Italy and Germany,' p 370, n 109.

122. Jasch, 'Dialogue with Islam and integration of Muslims in Italy and Germany,' p 370.

123. Jasch, 'Dialogue with Islam and integration of Muslims in Italy and Germany,' p 372 referring to the relevant legislation approved in November 2001.

124. Jasch, 'Dialogue with Islam and integration of Muslims in Italy and Germany,' p 372 referring to the relevant legislation approved in November 2001.

With increasing fears that students who do not attend supervised religious programmes may be open to extreme views in unsupervised Koran classes, the German state established two official programmes in 2004 for the education and training of teachers of Islam: one in the University of Münster and the other in Frankfurt/Main.[125]

[6.032] Another positive sign was the establishment of the German Islam Conference (Deutsche Islam Konferenz – DIK) in 2006 which will facilitate liaison and negotiation between the German state and Muslim community representatives. The DIK, like its counterpart in Italy, has no decision-making powers but rather elaborates recommendations grounded in a broad consensus.[126] Jasch states:

> With the DIK the Federal Minister of the Interior intends – in cooperation with the German States/*Länder* – to alleviate existing integration problems and create a forum for dialogue with the Muslim Communities which is to develop concrete recommendations on central issues such as Islamic education, training of imams, use of the hijab etc. In the course of this conference – process representatives of the state and the Muslim communities are also to explore ground for improving the integration of Islam – as a 'religion without church'-into the constitutional framework of Germany. The proclaimed objective of the DIK though is not only to involve representatives of the Muslim communities in dialogue with the state but explicitly also containing Islamic extremism.[127]

These are positive signs of progress. Questions have been raised, however, as to the appropriateness of such communities since they may not be acceptable to the Muslim people as their own communities. Arguably, neither would they accord full religious freedom to the Muslim people. Perhaps, it would be preferable that the Muslim people devise their own programmes of religious instruction and that these be assessed and supervised by the German state, which has the right of supervision of the full education system which can be delegated to the *Länder* which have generally the control of education in their own jurisdiction.

125. Jasch, p 371 and n 112.

126. Jasch, p 374.

127. Jasch, p 374.

Religious Instruction in Public Schools

[6.033] Religious instruction is generally part of the regular curriculum[128] and, subject to the supervision of the *Länder*, it is provided by the religious communities in public schools. In that regard, Art 7(3) of the Basic Law is quite clear: 'Religious instruction shall form part of the regular curriculum in state schools with the exception of non-denominational schools.' Moreover, such instruction has to be delivered 'in accordance with the doctrine of the religious community concerned'[129] but the state reserves the right of supervision. In accordance with Art 4 of the Basic Law, parents or pupils may decide children are to participate in such instruction or they may withdraw their children if they so wish.

Religious Instruction v Religious Education

[6.034] The growing secularisation of German society is reflected in the increasing numbers of students who are opting out of religious instruction, a fact which has caused administrative and church concerns, principally because moral education was no longer available to those who opted out of religious instruction classes. New comparative programmes of religious education have been introduced by many of the *Länder*. Despite many protests from the churches, Brandenburg passed controversial legislation in 1996 making provision for the senior schools in that state to introduce a mandatory comparative course on world religions and philosophies. In view of the fact that Art 7(3) of the Basic Law mandates that religious instruction forms part of the ordinary curriculum as a compulsory subject, it is not surprising that its replacement with the new programme (religious education) faced a legal challenge. In 1998 the Federal Administrative Court in Berlin ruled that the state had a right to make this new subject, 'ethics', obligatory for those students who did not participate in religious instruction classes.[130] One year later the Federal Constitutional Court rejected any further appeals from the earlier decision of the Federal Administrative

128. As is the position in Ireland where religious instruction is not part of the state curriculum under the Education Act 1998, s 30 but is a matter for the religious denominations and their religious inspectorates. In this regard, note also the distinction made in England between the National Curriculum and the Basic Curriculum, provision for religious education being made under the latter.

129. Art 7.3.

130. Decision of 17 June 1998, *Deutsches Verwaltungsblatt* 1998, p 1344 ff.

Court.[131] The state's right to educate pupils in state schools, the court ruled, extended to questions of morality and was grounded in a wide interpretation of the provision that states: 'the entire school system shall be under the supervision of the state' (Art 7, para 1 of the 'Basic Law'). In addition, the court held that the state and the public school administration might lawfully introduce a new compulsory subject such as ethics and, furthermore, the state had the discretion to decide whether this subject was compulsory for all students or solely for those who did not attend religious instruction. However, the court issued one *caveat* in this regard – that complete equality must be maintained between religious instruction and the ethics programme in the school curriculum and in the assessments of schools. Similarly, in Ireland, the way was paved for the state to introduce a programme of religious education, as opposed to religious instruction, by the Supreme Court case *Campaign to Separate Church and State v Minister for Education*[132] which is discussed in **chapter 9** below. However, no legal challenge ensued in regard to the introduction of that programme, which is now part of the state examinations programme in Ireland. Following the Federal German Constitutional Court's decision, most of the *Länder* have introduced a new subject into the curriculum of the state schools, described as 'ethics', 'philosophy' or 'values and norms'.[133] This new subject has become mandatory for all students who do not attend religious instruction in the state schools. However, this provision has continued to be controversial and some students and their parents have initiated constitutional challenges in a number of *Länder*.[134] As has been seen, while the ECtHR has upheld the right of a public school in Spain to prescribe in the curriculum objective and scientific information on the sex life of humans, venereal diseases and Aids in *Jimenez and Jimenez Merino v Spain*,[135] it has recently ruled that a programme of religious education, which is biased in favour of one religion (Sunni Islam), breached Art 2 of Protocol 1 of the ECHR in regard to the

131. Decisions of 17 and 18 February 1999 (1 B v R 1840/98), NV wZ 1999, p 756.

132. *Campaign to Separate Church and State v Minister for Education* [1996] 2 ILRM 241; [1998] 2 ILRM 81. See also *McGrath v Trustees of Maynooth College* [1979] ILRM 166. See further Glendenning, *Education and the Law*, p 67 *et seq*.

133. Fussel, 'Country Report: Germany, "Ethics" and "Religious Instruction", "Ethics" or "Religious Instruction"'? (1999) *European Journal for Education Law and Policy*, Kluwer Law International, p 59.

134. Fussel.

135. Application No 51188/99, Reports of Judgments and Decisions 2000–VI.

applicants who were of the Alevi faith.[136] No doubt the court's jurisprudence in this significant sphere of education will continue to evolve.

CONCLUSION

[6.035] While France's ecclesiastical law was forged in the furnace of societal revolt and revolution, so to speak, Germany's church-state relations have been deeply marked by the Reformation and by the many compromises that have emerged over the centuries. Nonetheless, Germany has managed to accommodate its two main churches in relative harmony while retaining certain conservative ecclesiastical law elements generally supportive of religion, but more specifically supportive of the two main religions. Unlike France, which maintains a strict separation of church and state, Germany has adopted a centralist approach which it enshrined in the relevant provisions of the Weimar Constitution (1919), and later transposed into the Basic Law. Accordingly, provision is made for a system of church-state cooperation applying to a wide sphere of life so as to meet the needs of the people.

[6.036] Broadly speaking, the principle of constitutional neutrality towards religion equates to non-intervention, and the main churches, in practice, have been accorded considerable autonomy within the general legal framework. Like Spain, Germany and its *Länder* have negotiated various treaties and agreements with the churches relating to areas of mutual concern, for example, faculties of theology in universities and colleges, military chaplains and religious education in schools. The principle of subsidiarity is reflected in the fact that a considerable part of church-state affairs, including education, has been devolved to the 16 *Länder*, which have separate contracts with the two main churches, indicating a closer ecclesiastical law relationship in regard to some religions than to others.

[6.037] Although the parity principle requires the state to treat all religions equally, significant distinctions are made in practice between the legal status of three churches (Lutheran, Catholic and Jewish) and all other churches, in that the former have the status of public law corporations while the latter are accorded the status of religious associations. Thus, fiscal and other advantages accrue to public law corporations which are not available to religious associations. This appears discriminatory since it breaches the parity principle. Of course, the practice of conferring a different status on certain churches is not unique to Germany and is to be found in England,

136. *Xengin v Turkey* Application no 1448/04 (2008), judg del 9 Jan 2008.

France, and Spain. Although these church-state arrangements have survived a constitutional challenge in Germany, they are unlikely to survive a challenge in the ECJ. As already noted, the Commission has already questioned analogous church-state arrangements in Italy, Spain and Ireland relating to equality and non-discrimination principles in EU law and this process is likely to intensify as the Union integrates and harmonises. With regard to international human rights law, can the state be considered to be neutral and objective if it collects tax for two or three different churches but not for others? Nonetheless, in Germany each religious community is free to administer its own affairs independently within the existing legal framework, regardless of its legal status.

[6.038] As in many other EU countries, particular difficulties are being experienced by Muslims because of the lack of a central Islamic body to negotiate as a 'partner' with the state. However, Germany has taken this problem seriously and has adopted a number of approaches to remedy this omission. In particular, the establishment of the state-aided foundation, the German-Islamic Conference, has shown real initiative in attempting to solve this complex problem, and, among others, the problems faced by adherents of Islam in attempting to secure religious instruction in publicly funded schools in some *Länder*.

[6.039] While provision is made in the Basic Law (as amended) for the teaching of religious instruction as part of the regular curriculum, practice has evolved to meet modern day needs and developments. With many students withdrawing from the religious instruction classes, the state has moved to provide an alternative broad programme of moral or ethical education and has won the right under national law for this initiative. However, the compulsory attendance of students at these religious education programmes continues to be controversial among both students and parents in Germany. With regard to religious values in state schools, two somewhat conflicting trends are apparent. On the one hand, there is evidence of a movement towards secularisation that is reflective of the wider society, which has been influenced by the disintegration of the GDR. On the other hand, there is evidence of an increasing demand from the Muslim community for respect and parity for their faith and its manifestation in state schools.[137] Some are of the view that a growing process of secularisation and pluralisation has permeated all strata of German society and that religious

137. Avenarius, 'The case of Germany,' *Religious Education in Public Schools: Study of Comparative Law.*

values and traditions have lost to a great extent their vital influence in German schools.[138] As public schools cater for a growing population of students of the Islamic faith, they will, undoubtedly face the challenges of equitably accommodating a religion which is unlikely to be affected by the process of secularisation.[139] Thus, the interface of religion with education in Germany is entering a new and challenging phase of development.

138. Avenarius, 'The case of Germany,' *Religious Education in Public Schools: Study of Comparative Law.*

139. Avenarius, 'The case of Germany,' *Religious Education in Public Schools: Study of Comparative Law.*

Chapter 7

RELIGION, EDUCATION AND THE LAW IN FRANCE

Above the nation, in France, there is humanity. Above the society, in America, there is God.[1]

INTRODUCTION

[7.001] Not only is the French Republic (France) perceived internationally as a champion of human rights, it is the source of the Civil Code of 1804, the cradle of the Enlightenment and the creator of the separate system of administrative jurisdiction and administrative law[2] which has been adopted by most countries of Western Europe.[3] The formation of the state in France, which does not recognise any religion, has been achieved in quite a distinctive manner from the European norm arising from the fact, *inter alia*, that religion has been problematic there for centuries.[4] In particular, the Catholic Church has been identified as an institution which can place limitations on the state's power, so the tradition has emerged of controlling the churches/religion through legislative measures so as to protect the

1. Debray, 1992 'Rebublique ou democracie [Republic or Democracy].' Debray (ed) *Contretemps: Eloges des idéaux perdus* (Gallimard, 2004) [Inconvenience: Praise for the Lost Ideas] (Gallimard, 1992).
2. Established by the Conseil d'Etat in the nineteenth and twentieth centuries. See Rudden, *A Source Book on French Law* (3rd edn, Clarendon Press, 1991); Jacobs, 'The Principle of Legality – towards a European Standard', in Hand and McBride, *Droits sans Frontieres: Essays in Honour of L Neville Brown* (Holdsworth Club, 1991), 235; Flaus in Schwarze (ed), *Administrative Law under European Influence* (Sweet & Maxwell, 1996), 113; Brown and Bell, with assistance from Galabert, French Administrative Law (5th edn, Clarendon Press, 1998) p 304.
3. Including the Netherlands, Italy, Belgium, Luxembourg, Spain, Portugal and Greece.
4. On 26 December 1790 King Louis XV1 acceded to the pressure of the National Assembly and gave his public assent to the law of the Civil Constitution of the Clergy, which became operational. This resulted in a schism between the French clergy, which was firmly condemned by Pope Pius VI.

people from excessive power and to ensure their equality and religious freedom.[5] France aims to integrate all minorities into society as individual citizens rather than as religious or ethnic groups, including all immigrants who are required to respect the secular principle and the French way of life.[6] After Algeria achieved its independence in 1962, for example, it was declared an extension of the French soil, so its residents became French citizens who were expected to assume French identity.[7]

Separation in France and the United States

[7.002] Davies points to the fundamental distinction which exists between the principle of separation in France, where any religious activity in 'the public space' is a threat to society's commitment to *laïcité* and the principle of separation in the US, where religious activity in 'the public space' is proscribed only when government is sponsoring or promoting the activity.[8] Regis Debray, the French philosopher, also emphasises the distinction between France and the US's perspectives on religion in the public sphere of life:

> Above the nation, in France, there is humanity. Above the society, in America, there is God. The President in Paris takes an oath on the Constitution voted by the people from the world, and in Washington on the Bible, which came from the heavens. The first one, after saying 'Long live the Republic, long live France,' will be painted in his library with the Essays of Montaigne in his

5. Davies, 'Reacting to France's ban: headscarves and other religious attire in American Public Schools,' (2004) *Journal of Church and State*, Spring.

6. Replying to his party's nomination in January 2007, Nicolas Sarkozy stated that it was unacceptable to wish to live in France 'without respecting and loving France and learning the French language .... If you live in France then you respect the laws and values of the Republic.' Sciolino, 'French Governing Party endorses Sarkozy for President' (2007) *International Herald Tribunal*, 14 January.

7. Alba and Silberman, 'Decolonization, Immigrations and the Social origins of the Second Generation: The Case of North Africans in France' 36 *International Migration Review* 2002, 4, 1169, 1174.

8. Davies, 'Reacting to France's Ban: Headscarves and Other Religious Attire in American Schools,' 46 *Journal of Church and State*, Spring 2004, No 2. See also Debray, 'Republique ou democracie' in Debray (ed) *Contretemps: Eloges des idéaux perdus* (Gallimard, 2004) pp 22–23.

hands. The other will end his discourse on 'God Bless America' and will be photographed in front of the starred flag.[9]

As we have seen, the meaning of the word 'God' in this context is controversial and many share the view that it was the God of the deists that was intended by the founding fathers.[10]

The Contemporary Challenge

[7.003] While the inherited tradition of rigorous separation in France derived from the premise that Roman Catholicism and democratic republicanism are fundamentally antipathetic, the contemporary challenge arises from difficulties relating to the integration of the growing population of Muslim immigrants.[11] The Parisian riots of October 2005 are but one episode in the continuing struggle to secure a place for the Muslim community in French society. When conducting their recent research on Muslims in three EU countries, Fetzer and Soper found that the way in which states responded to the religious needs of Muslims seemed linked to the particular church-state institutions in that country.[12] They concluded that the French state has a more negative attitude towards Muslims than their counterparts in England and Germany.[13] Kuru also found that Muslims have faced a greater number of bureaucratic barriers in the course of learning and practising Islam in France than their counterparts have faced in other EU

9. Davies, 'Reacting to France's Ban: Headscarves and Other Religious Attire in American Schools,' 46 *Journal of Church and State*, Spring 2004, No 2 cited by and translated by Kuru, 'Muslims and the Secular State in France', online at http://europe.byu.edu/islam/pdfs/Kuru-paper.pdf accessed on 5 October 2008.

10. Dershowitz, *America Declares Independence*, 'Who is the God of the Declaration?', chapter 1, p 8, Wiley.

11. Saxena, 'The French Headscarf Law and the Right to Manifest Religious Belief', p 7 in The Selected Works of Mukul Saxena, available at http://works.bepress.com/mukul_saxena/2 accessed on 5 October 2008 Also, see Lee, 'Expulsion over Veil Intensify French debate on Secularity' (2003) *International Herald Tribune*, 21 October, 19.

12. Fetzer and Soper, *Muslims and the State in Britain, France and Germany* (Cambridge Press, 2005), Preface.

13. Fetzer and Soper, *Muslims and the State in Britain, France and Germany* (Cambridge Press, 2005), Preface.

countries.[14] Among such barriers he mentions instruction on Islam in public schools; state funding of Islamic schools; and the construction of mosques.[15]

[7.004] It is against this background that the *affaire des voiles*, or the headscarf issue as it has come to be known, has acquired considerable social and political significance. In March 2004, President Chirac caused international consternation when he approved a legislative prohibition on the wearing of 'conspicuous religious symbols' in public schools,[16] a measure which received enthusiastic approval in the French Assembly[17] and indeed across the political spectrum in France.[18] Despite significant efforts made by the government to foster interfaith understanding and to condemn crimes of a 'racist, anti-Semitic, or xenophobic' character,[19] anti-Semitic acts in France increased by approximately 6 per cent in the year 2006.[20]

---

14. Kuru, 'Muslims and the Secular State in France', p 1, online at http://europe.byu.edu/islam/pdfs/Kuru-paper.pdf pdf.

15. http://europe.byu.edu/islam/pdfs/Kuru-paper.pdf.

16. *Loi No 2004–228 du 15 Mars 2004 encadrant, en application du principe de laïcité, le port de signes ou de tenues manifestant une appartenance religieuse dans les ecoles, colleges et lycées publics*: *Journal Officiel* No 65, 17 March 2004, p 5190.

17. With votes of 494 to 36 in the Assembly and 276 to 20 in the Senate, see Beller, 'The Headscarf Affair: The *Conseil d'État* on the Role of Religion and Culture in French Society' 39 *Texas International Law Journal* 581 (2004).

18. Beller, 'The Headscarf Affair: The *Conseil d'État* on the Role of Religion and Culture in French Society' 39 *Texas International Law Journal* 581 (2004) and further Boustead, 'The French Headscarf Law before the European Court of Human Rights' (16) *Journal of Transnational Law and Policy,* Florida State University, Spring 2007, No 2, pp 167–196 at 168 and further Gey, 'Free Will, Religious Liberty, and a Partial defence of the French Approach to Religious Expression in Public Schools' 42 *Houston Law Review* 1, 13 (2005).

19. Through the passing of strict anti-defamation legislation which bans religiously motivated attacks. Under the Gayssot Act (Loi Gayssot 1990) it is a crime to question the existence of this category of crimes against humanity as set down by the London Charter, 1945. In 2003 legislation was enacted prohibiting crimes of a 'racist, anti-Semitic or xenophobic' nature and a law in 2004 further increased the sanctions against 'hate' crimes. These laws are frequently implemented in practice. Source: US Dept of State, International Religious Freedom Report 2007, p 3.

20. US Dept of State, International Religious Freedom Report 2007.

[7.005] While the Constitution of 1958 provides for freedom of religion and the government generally respects this right in practice,[21] it has been alleged that the government's anti-sect policies have led to discrimination and intolerance against minority religions and belief groups.[22] In particular, the provisions of the About-Picard Law of 2001 have been the subject of criticism by human rights groups and others, as will be seen. This chapter considers whether, in the light of its current international law obligations, France can justify such a restrictive interpretation of *laïcité* in the context of its religiously and culturally diverse population. At the outset, it should be stated that a distinction between the terms 'sect' and 'cult' does not exist in the French language.[23] However, 'sect' is employed in parliamentary documents on this topic and also by the media and in society generally, but scholars usually prefer the term 'new religious movement' or 'new religions'.[24]

Public Education

[7.006] Public education is perceived as the primary instrument for the inculcation of republican values in France. It is in public school that the citizens of tomorrow, called to live together within the Republic, are prepared for their lives as citizens.[25] The education system itself is grounded on broad principles, some of which draw their inspiration from the Revolution of 1789, from laws enacted between 1881 and 1889 and under the Fourth and Fifth Republics, and from the Constitution of 4 October 1958.[26] Public service education co-exists alongside private institutions, all of which are under the control of the state. Private schools, the majority of

21. US Dept of State 2007, International Religious Freedom Report 2007, released by the Bureau of Democracy, Human Rights, and Labor, available online at http://www.state.gov/g/drl/rls/irf/2007/90175.htm, accessed on 8 June 2008.

22. At the Implementation Meetings on Human Dimensions Issues of the OSCE in 1998, 1999 and 2000. See further Fautre, *Human Rights without Frontiers*, 'The Sect Issue in France and Belgium,' available at http://willyfautre.com.

23. Fautre, *Human Rights without Frontiers*.

24. Fautre, *Human Rights without Frontiers*.

25. Lee, 'Expulsion over Veil Intensify French debate on Secularity' (2003) *International Herald Tribune*, 21 October, p 23.

26. The French Ministry for Education's website at http://www.education.gouv.fr, 'Le Systeme Educatif' and note 'The Main Principles' upholding the education system are 'Neutrality' and 'Secularism', including a secular staff and a ban on proselytising.

which are Catholic, are within the remit of public service education, and are eligible for public funding, provided they have signed a contract with the state.[27] Both philosophical and political neutrality is required of teachers employed in the public schools and of the public school students also.[28] Another foundational tenet of the state is secularity, which was mandated by the Laws of 28 March 1882 and 30 October 1886, and this tenet is also reflected in the public education system.[29] The significance of secularism in school republican values was buttressed by the Law of 9 December 1905 which established the secular government in France and sections of this law are still in force.[30]

[7.007] The public school teacher plays a pivotal role and, as a full civil servant of the state, is the chief inculcator of these republican values. In these schools, the state promotes its own ideology which is secular. By contrast, the relevant church is the employer of the teacher in the denominational school which is regulated by the State.

With regard to the promotion of a state ideology, some months prior to the revolution of 1848, Hippolyte Carnot, the Minister for Public Instruction and Religion from 1832 to 1836, advised the administrators of public instruction to encourage their teachers to prepare manuals on the lines of the Catholic catechism to teach pupils the rights and obligations of citizens under the Republic and 'guarding against ignorance'.[31] Although Rousseau's concept of 'moulding' man in a particular way was acknowledged at this juncture, it was only during the Third Republic, founded in 1871, that these

27. The French Ministry for Education's website at http://www.education.gouv.fr, 'Le Systeme Educatif'.

28. The French Ministry for Education's website at http://www.education.gouv.fr, 'Le Systeme Educatif'.

29. The French Ministry for Education's website at http://www.education.gouv.fr, 'Le Systeme Educatif'.

30. For a translation of the more general sections of the Law of 1905 by Fraser, National Secular Society; see 'Law separating Church and State (1905): Excerpts' at: http://www.concordatwatch.eu/showkb.php?org_id=867&kb_header_id=849. This is a consolidated version of 29 July 2005.

31. Harrigan, 'France: Education, extracted from Encyclopedia of 1848 Revolutions,' Chastain, available at http://www.ohiou.edu/~chastain/dh/franedu.htm and revised at http://www.cats.ohiou.edu/~chastain/dh/franedu.htm. See list of contributors on final page of this document.

citizenship manuals emerged, in which religious norms and values were replaced by secular and republican principles.[32]

[7.008] In post-1905 France, therefore, not only did the state replace the role and function of the Catholic Church in its network of confessional schools nationwide, but it substituted a civic ideology for the spiritual mission of the churches,[33] an ideology grounded in the principles of equality, neutrality and a more assertive species of secularity (*laïcité*).[34] It appears that in modern France the Jacobin ethos of a Republic, which is considered 'one and indivisible', has been revived, together with its assumptions that a national, republican identity must be accorded priority over other aspects of an individual's life, whether they are religious, linguistic or ethnic.[35] Ironically, France frequently refers to its 2,000 years of Christian heritage,[36] now that the focus of its concern has moved to a fresh challenge with a new religion and culture at its core: that of integrating many millions of immigrants who are of the Muslim faith as French citizens in accordance with its state ideology.

Social Facts and Background

[7.009] The French government does not retain statistics on religious affiliation in recognition of its church-state principle of separation,[37] and the law prohibits a census based on religious trends. However, it is estimated that approximately 80 per cent of the population in France declare themselves Catholic, although less than 15 per cent attend Mass

32. Harrigan, 'France: Education, extracted from Encyclopedia of 1848 Revolutions,' Chastain, available at http://www.ohiou.edu/~chastain/dh/franedu.htm.

33. See Parker, 'Civic-Moral Teaching in French Secular Schools,' Pt 1, in 20 *The Elementary School Journal,* No 7 (March 1920) pp 520–529.

34. See the French Ministry for Education's website at http://www.education.gouv.fr, 'Le Systeme Educatif'.

35. Hollifield and Ross, 'Searching for the New France', Routledge, 1991, 113–114: axena, 'The French Headscarf Law and the Right to Manifest Religious Belief', p 7 in The Selected Works of Mukul Saxena, available at http://works.bepress.com/mukul_saxena/2 accessed on 5 October 2008 Also p 7.

36. Including President Sarkozy in his reply to his party's nomination in January 2007; Sciolino, 'French Governing Party endorses Sarkozy for President', (2007) *International Herald Tribunal*, 14 January.

37. Embodied in the Law of 1905, sections of which are still in force.

regularly.[38] Thus, although it has a population of more than 60 million, comprising six major religious groups, France remains a country in the Catholic tradition.[39] Nevertheless, France is the advocate *par excellence* in Europe for a clear separation between state and church, with a tradition in this regard which can be traced to the fifteenth century.[40] The growth of the Muslim Community, now estimated at between 5–6 million, means that Islam is now France's second largest religion and this presents new challenges of integration which are unlikely to diminish.[41] The National Council of the Muslim Faith and its 25 linked regional councils operate as interlocutors for the Muslim community with the state on matters of mutual interest.[42] Accordingly, it is the central body for the training of imams and for the funding of mosques and related matters of mutual church-state concern. Essentially, France is a secular country in which virtually all religious faiths and denominations, including 'the new religions,' are represented, but 'sects' are monitored and controlled by the state authorities in accordance with legislation[43] and government policy.[44]

---

38. Basdevant-Gaudemet, 'State and Church in France' in Robbers (ed), *State and Church in the European Union* (Nomos, 2005) p 157 *et seq*.

39. Approximately Protestants (750,000); Jews (650,000); Orthodox (200,000); and Muslims (6,000,000), according to Basdevant-Gaudemet in Robbers (ed), *State and Church in the European Union* (Nomos, 2005).

40. The Pragmatic Sanction of Bourges (1438) which terminated the Pope's right to name candidates for vacant dioceses and eliminated his entitlement to collect the Annate tax; also the Concordat of Bologna (1516) which copper-fastened the French monarch's control over church revenues and appointments.

41. Astier, 'Tense Anniversary in French Suburbs', BBC News, 26 October 2006 citing the Deputy Mayor of Clichy-sous-Bois who is quoted as saying: 'The pow[d]er keg is still here, and a new spark could trigger another blast.' http://news.bbc.co.uk/2/hi/europe/6083790.stm.

42. US Dept of State, International Religious Freedom Report 2007, p 3.

43. The About-Picard Law 2001, *La Loi n 2001–504 du 12 juin 2001*.

44. See Report of 22 December 1995 (Rap Gest Guyard), *La Rapport de la commissione d'enquete sur les sectes* (dixieme legislature, Decembre 1995). The long list of sects set out in this report includes some unlikely ones, eg Jehovah Witnesses, Transcendental Meditation and the Queen of Peace – Order of the Immaculate Heart of Mary and St Louis de Montfort. For the full list in English, see http://www.cftf.com/french/Les_Sectes_en_France/cults.html see 'Freedom of Religion and Sects', http://www.info-france-usa.org/atoz/religion.asp and also Fautre, 'Human Rights without Frontiers Int', online at http://willyfautre.com.

Historical Outline

[7.010] By contrast with other countries in which the separation of church and state occurred as a result of evolution, reformation and other historical developments, the separation in France arose out of the tumult of a revolution which was deeply influenced by the positivist ideology of the humanist Renaissance of the sixteenth century and the Enlightenment of the eighteenth century, including the writings of Voltaire, Montesquieu, Rousseau, Diderot and others. Indeed, the history of church-state relations in France includes episodes of acrimony seldom experienced elsewhere. For centuries, close ties had existed between the monarchy and the Catholic Church in a relationship which was mutually beneficial, it appears. However, the concepts of deism, rationalism, empiricism and anti-clericalism, inspired by the Enlightenment writers, found fertile ground in the grossly unequal society of the eighteenth century, which had become increasingly disenchanted with both monarchical rule and with the institutional Catholic Church. The concept of deism posited the belief that the world was created by a supreme power (god), but that it was governed by natural laws revealed to man through his reason, logic and observation. Unlike the functions of faith, divine revelation and tradition, which are fundamental to Christianity, reason became the kingpin of the ideological edifice, so to speak, and supported by scientific enquiry, logic and progress, it became the philosophical inspiration for the 'new'[45] version of natural law ('the natural rights philosophy'), which would become the foundation of the law in France. This ideology aimed to overthrow *l'ancien regime* with its established monarchy and religion and it called for 'a new way forward' (progress) which would affirm freedom of religious belief while, at the same time, establishing a regime of strict separation of state and church. The philosophy posited by the Enlightenment writers had, over time, a profound impact in France and on the legal and political structures which subsequently emerged there and ultimately on international human rights law.

45. To the ancient Greeks, the natural law meant a universe governed by an eternal immutable law. See Plato, *The Laws*. To Plato the rule of law meant that every authority in the state was exercised under a code of laws which was definitively established and which was fundamental. See Plato, Pangle (trans), *The Laws of Plato* (Basic Books, 1980).

Legal Sources

[7.011] When the Third Republic was founded in 1871, the Catholic Church, with its foreign jurisdiction and nationwide network of religious schools, was considered to be a major obstacle to the attainment of the Republic's objectives. As in other countries, it was through the schools that the church educated, evangelised and transmitted its doctrines, values and facilitated worship from one generation to the next. If the church could be removed from the sphere of public education, and its role and function were assumed by the state, then teachers would become civil servants of the state and 'progress' would be achieved. Accordingly, the Third Republic envisaged a 'sacrosanct' area of public space in public life which would not permit trespass by any religion and the concept of public schools was perceived as central to the achievement of that plan. Such an ideal could only become permanent, however, if it was accepted by the majority of the people and was enshrined in legislation. The concept of assertive secularity (*laïcité*), it was posited, would preclude religious bodies from invading the public sphere and would safeguard the people from the excesses of religion and from religious domination.

[7.012] The Declaration of the Rights of Man and of the Citizen (1789)[46] declared that no one shall be disquieted on account of his opinions, including his religious opinions, provided their manifestation did not disturb the public order established by law.[47] For the first time, it was formally acknowledged that religious opinions fell into the private sphere of life.[48] Having guaranteed freedom of belief and its manifestation subject to public order, the decree of 2 November 1789 provided for the confiscation of church lands by the state and, as a *quid pro quo*, the state undertook responsibility for the church's administrative expenses and clerical maintenance. One year later the Civil Constitution of the Clergy of 12 July 1790 (the Civil Constitution)[49] unilaterally drew up decrees to control and reorganise the clergy nationwide and effectively to subordinate the church to

46. A copy of the Declaration is in **Appendix 2** of this book.

47. Article 10.

48. Troper, 'French Secularism or *Laïcité*' 21 *Cardozo Law Review* 2000, 1267.

49. The Law of the Civil Constitution of the Clergy ('*Constitution Civile du Clerge*') passed on 12 July 1790, during the French Revolution. See further Robinson (ed), *Readings in European History* (Ginn, 1906), 2 at 423–427, 2 vols.

the state.[50] The decrees of the Civil Constitution were declared as constitutional articles, thus raising their status to fundamental principles. The restructuring of the Catholic Church, which ensued on the confiscation of its considerable possessions, demonstrated the determination of the National Assembly to reform the church and to bring it under the regulation of law. As a result of the Civil Constitution, all existing Roman Catholic bishoprics and parishes, and their attendant titles and offices, were abolished. Henceforth, bishops and parish priests would be elected by the people[51] and they would be supported by the nation[52] and remunerated by the district treasurer.[53] Furthermore, they would be bound by an oath of loyalty to the state.[54] In this manner, the Civil Constitution consolidated and extended what earlier legislation had initiated.[55]

[7.013] As a result of the regulation of the status of the ministers of religion, the majority became paid employees of the state and virtual public servants. No church, parish or citizen could lawfully acknowledge the authority of an ordinary bishop or archbishop acting under the supremacy of a foreign power, nor that of his representatives residing in France or elsewhere.[56] New bishops were prohibited from applying to the Pope for any form of confirmation but they were required to write to him as a testimony to the unity of faith and communion maintained with him.[57] The decree of 21 February 1795, while supporting the freedom of religion principle, set up a

---

50. See Burke, *Reflections on the Revolution in France, 1790* (Harvard Classics, Collier & Son 1909–1914 and Bartley.com, 2001): See Paine, *The Rights of Man* (Penguin Classics, 1984), rendered into HTML on 9 April 1998 by Steve Thomas for the University of Adelaide Library Electronic Texts, available online at ebooks.adelaide.edu.au/p/paine/Thomas/p147r/ Paine gave his support to the French Revolution. Kagan, Ozment and Turner, *The Western Heritage* (7th edn, Prentice Hall, 2001).
51. The Civil Constitution of the Clergy, Title 11.
52. The Civil Constitution of the Clergy, Title 11.
53. The Civil Constitution of the Clergy, Title 11.
54. The Civil Constitution of the Clergy, Title 11, Art XX1.
55. See the *Declaration of the Clergy in France* (1682) pursuant to which the French monarch had the right to assemble church councils and to make laws and regulations concerning ecclesiastical matters. Papal authority was also severely constrained by the necessity of obtaining royal consent.
56. The Civil Constitution, Title IV.
57. The Civil Constitution, Title IV, Art X1X.

mechanism for separating church and state but it did not recognise any clergy and did not pay salaries, with the result that the church suffered severely during this period.[58] While the 1795 law affirmed the tenet of free worship, it permitted state control over the display of certain religious symbols by formulating a 'decision in principle', during the Constituent Assembly of 1792, that priests must not wear religious attire in public.[59] Thus, the prohibition on the wearing of religious symbols in public derives from a firmly-rooted tradition in France being aligned to secularism, anti-clericism and national cohesion.

Public Education Emerges

[7.014] Like Prussia, France recognised the significance of public education in nation-building quite early. Napoleon affirmed that principle when he made public education generally and second level education specifically the focus of his monumental reforms:

> Of all the institutions public education is the most important. Everything depends on it, the present and the future. It is essential that the morals and political ideas of the generation which is now growing up should no longer be dependent on the circumstances of the moment. Above all we must secure unity: we must be able to cast a whole generation in the same mould.[60]

Indeed, Napoleon astutely encapsulated the essence of France's ideal of nation building: '… we must be able to cast a whole generation in the same mould' together with the instrument for its advancement-public education. This official objective was pursued with nothing short of missionary zeal and the tenet of *laïcité* facilitated its progress. As in the United States,[61] the unified public school system became the instrument *par excellence* for building social cohesion and national solidarity in France.

58. Brigitte Basdevant-Gaudemet, State and Church in France, in Robbers (ed), *State and Church in the European Union* (Nomos, 2005) 119, 122 p 159.

59. Higonnet, 'Goodness Beyond Virtue: Jacobins during the French Revolution', 235, *Harvard University Press*, 1998.

60. Molé, *The Life and Memoirs of Count Molé,* Marquis de Noailles, (ed), London, 1923, p 61 cited in Research Subjects: Nineteenth century Society, The Napoleonic Series, Markham, International Napoleonic Society, '*The Revolution, Napoleon and Education*', p 8, available online at http://napoleon-series.org/research/society/c_education.html and accessed by the author on 2 June 2008.

61. See **[10.008]** *et seq*.

[7.015] On 1 May 1802 a decree was promulgated that a new system of education was to be established, which became in time the foundation of the contemporary system of education in France.[62] Meanwhile Napoleon's Concordat with the Pope in 1801 had resolved, in part, the difficulties between religion and primary education. Although these schools were placed under the control of the local municipalities, the religious schools generally shared responsibility with the state. By contrast, the second level schools, many of which were established by private initiative, were all placed under the central authority of the state.[63] Likewise, the 30 *lycées* established for boys aged 16 and upwards[64] were under state control. Although Napoleon's curriculum was replaced by the Law of 1905, and the teaching of religion was removed from the public school curriculum, some characteristics of his system are still evident in the modern French system, such as centralised control in the Ministry for Public Instruction, the *lycées* and school chaplains.[65] During the whole nineteenth century, the main churches, although they were afforded some advantages, particularly financial, were subject to the continuous supervision of the public authorities.[66] Possibly one of the severest critics of the Revolution and its aftermath was Edmund Burke who considered the changes wrought by the National Assembly as 'superficial' and their errors as 'fundamental.' Burke predicted a dire outcome for post-Revolutionary France, which is encapsulated in the celebrated phrase: 'The age of chivalry is gone .... That of sophisters, economists and calculators has succeeded; and the glory of Europe is extinguished forever.'[67]

[7.016] France's contemporary public education system has its origins in the Third Republic when in the 1880s Jules Ferry (1832–1893), Minister of Public Education, introduced free, compulsory, secular primary education

---

62. Lefebvre, 1969, Correspondence VII, 5874, *Exposé de la Situation de la Republique,* 20 November 1801. In part in Herold (ed), *Napoleon 1, Emperor of the French, The Mind of Napoleon: A Selection from his Written and Spoken Words* (Columbia University Press, 1955), p 116.

63. Markham, '*The Revolution, Napoleon and Education*'.

64. And currently 16–18 years for girls and boys.

65. Markham, '*The Revolution, Napoleon and Education*'.

66. Markham, '*The Revolution, Napoleon and Education*' p 159.

67. Burke, 'The Works of the Right Honourable Edmund Burke' vol 2, London (1864), Henry G Bohn, 1864, pp 515–6.

for all boys and girls under 15 years.[68] As a consequence of this initiative, the state's strategy to forge national identity and social cohesion was advanced considerably. Moreover, the education laws enacted between the years 1882 and 1886 (the Ferry Laws) cast an even greater obligation on the state to promote republican values and norms and to mould national sentiments[69] through public education[70] in which the principle of *laïcité* was guaranteed, not just to secure the separation of church and state, but to ensure equality between all citizens as well a harmonious interfaith co-existence.[71] Thus, the view that religion should be excluded from public life, and public education, is not just enshrined in legislation[72] and the institution and curricula of the public schools, but it is enshrined in the ideological and pedagogical education of public school teachers.[73] Accordingly, no religious instruction is taught in France's public schools, as is the case with the public schools in the US, by contrast with the other European countries in this study (Germany, Spain, England and Ireland).

The Law of 19 December 1905

[7.017] In France, following the severing of diplomatic relations with the Holy See in 1904, the Law of 19 December 1905 made provision for the separation of church and state. Article 1 provides:

> The Republic assures the freedom of conscience. She guarantees the free exercise of religion subject only to the restrictions mentioned hereafter in the interests of the public order.

---

68. See the introduction of universal free primary education in Ireland, by the English, in 1831 by informal methods in **para [9.025]** *et seq* below.

69. Weber, *Peasants into Frenchmen*, 303.

70. Saxena, 'The French Headscarf Law and the Right to Manifest Religious Belief' in The Selected Works of Mukul Saxena, available at http://works.bepress.com/mukul_saxena/2 accessed on 5 October 2008 p 6.

71. Consulat Generale de France a Londres, www.consulfrance-Londres.org/spip.php?article384–76k accessed on 5 October 2008.

72. And in particular the Law of 1905, see prohibition on the teaching of religious instruction in state schools in Art 30 which was abrogated by Ordinance No 2000–549 of 15 June 2000, Art 7 (JORF 22 June 2000).

73. Ordinance No 2000–549 of 15 June 2000, Art 7 (JORF 22 June 2000).

[7.018] Article 2 provides:

> The Republic does not recognise, fund or subsidise any religion …. Nevertheless there can be included in these budgets (of the state or public entities) the expenses in relation to chaplaincy services designed to assure the free exercise of religion in public establishments such as secondary schools, colleges, schools, nursing homes, asylums and prisons.

[7.019] In effect, the Law of 1905 excluded the church from public education and influence, relegated religion to the private sphere and effectively subjugated the church to the state. This law terminated the traditional status of the 'recognised Churches' so that they were, generally speaking,[74] no longer public institutions but part of the private sector. The Law of 1905 further empowered the state to complete the divestment of the Catholic Church's considerable lands and acquisitions and to negate its former influence in many aspects of public life. Most significantly, the Law blocked the church's on-going influence on future generations by providing for the establishment of a nationwide network of public schools in which no religion could be taught. It was still possible for the churches to operate private schools, following the enactment of the Law of 1905, but this became much more difficult since there was no state funding available to them at that time. On the broader front, the assertive secular principle (*laïcité*), at the core of the 1905 Act, facilitated the cohesion of the various regions, and it became in time one of the foundational pillars of France's national identity and part of its accepted social model, which is reflected in public education. In addition, public regard for the *laïcité* principle increased and it came to be perceived as a component of the social contract[75] or bargain between the various religions and the state in the interest of national cohesion and solidarity. Essentially, *laïcité* may be considered to be a principle of religious neutrality which aims to strike a balance between religious freedom and public order so as to create the conditions for religious freedom in a secular society. As a species of secularism which removes religion from the public sphere, laïcité has emerged as an elemental

74. Ordinance No 2000–549 of 15 June 2000, Art 7 (JORF 22 June 2000) p 160, with the exception of Alsace Moselle which retains the system of 'Recognised Churches', since the law.of 1905 is not applicable there. Civil rights were achieved for Protestants in 1787 but not for Jews.

75. See further Rousseau, *The Social Contract or the Principles of Political Right* (New American Library, 1974) which influenced much political philosophy in Western Europe including the French Revolution. It held that people must establish institutions of law or perish, see further Wokler, Rousseau (Altýn Kitaplar Yayýnevi, 2003).

part of France's national identity, representing core values of equality, neutrality and freedom of conscience.[76]

Constitutional Provision

[7.020] With regard to constitutional provision, the secular principle was carried over and embodied in constitutional law. Section 2 of the Preamble of the Constitution of 4 October 1946 provides: '*la France est une Republique ... laique*.' It is notable that the Constitution does not determine the status of the churches and it makes only two references to religion or faith: firstly in the Preamble, which refers to the Declaration of the Rights of Man and of the Citizen of 1789, which in turn guarantees the freedom of belief, and secondly in Art 1. Article 1 of the Constitution of the French Republic 1958 provides: 'France shall be an indivisible, secular, democratic and social republic. It shall ensure the equality of all citizens before the law, without distinction of origin, race or religion. It shall respect all beliefs.' These two brief but fundamental provisions, ensure the neutrality of the state. As has been seen, the Law of 1905 lays down the fundamental tenets in regard to religion: freedom of religion and the principle of non-recognition and non-subsidisation of religion. But constitutional case law has determined that these provisions must now be considered in the light of another fundamental principle: freedom of education. Article 9 of the Constitution of 1848 recognised freedom of education. Despite the fact that this latter principle is not expressly declared in the Constitutions of 1946 or 1958, the Conseil Constitutionnel, in its landmark decision of 23 November 1977, determined that freedom of education is one of the fundamental principles recognised by the laws of the Republic[77] and this principle had accordingly acquired constitutional status.[78] It was this landmark finding of the Conseil which enabled France to make state funding available to the private schools, a pragmatic compromise which would, of course, be precluded in the USA by the First Amendment of the Constitution, an issue which is considered at **[10.007]**.

---

76. Gunn, *Religious Freedom and Laïcité: a Comparison of the United States and France,* 2004 BYU Law Rev 419, 466 (2004).

77. *Conseil Constitutionnel,* 23 November 1977, AJDA 1978, p 565; *Conseil Constitutionnel* 18 January 1985, 5, p 633.

78. Reaffirmed in the Preamble of the 1946 Constitution and given constitutional status in the 1958 Constitution, *Conseil Constitutionnel,* 16 July 1971.

The About-Picard Law

[7.021] During the 1990s, the world was shocked by a number of collective suicide-homicides and other attacks which took place in the US, Canada, Europe and Japan at what appears to have been the instigation of leaders of so-called religious movements.[79] In the wake of these tragedies, the Council of Europe investigated these matters and concluded that 'sects' do not damage the individual, family, society or democratic institutions to the degree that requires advocating major legislative measures to combat them.[80] Problems presented by such 'sects', they considered, could be resolved by the implementation of existing legislation or other normal legal mechanisms, by prevention and by education.[81] Accordingly, they did not recommend any legal or political interventions, which they feared might trespass on international human rights in regard to religious freedoms or beliefs such as those protected by Art 9 of the ECHR,[82] or Arts 18(3)[83] or 4(2)[84] of the International Covenant of Civil and Political Rights. Nonetheless, four of the member states (Austria, France, Germany and Belgium) decided to implement their own national protective measures in this regard.[85] New movements in France, many of which were religious, were increasingly demanding the protection and benefits accruing to mainstream religions and they failed to conform to the accepted norms and values of French society. Such movements, it appears, were regarded as a

---

79. In Waco, Texas, approximately 88 Davidians died in a battle with the police on 19 April 1993; in or about 18 months later 53 members of the Order of the Solar Temple (New Age) took part in a mass suicide-homicide in Switzerland while a suidide-homicide of 16 members of the Solar Temple Order took place in France in 1995. Five others died in a ritual suicide outside Ottawa in 1994. Fautre, 'Human Rights without Frontiers Int', online at http://willyfautre.

80. See 'Illegal Activity of Sects Report', Council of Europe on Sects and Cults, 22 June 1999, Commission on Legal Affairs and Human Rights.

81. Fautre, *Human Rights without Frontiers*, 'The Sect Issue in France and Belgium,' available at http://www.willyfautre.com.

82. Which guarantees freedom of thought, conscience and religion.

83. Which sets down the extent and ground of permissible limitations.

84. Which makes freedom of religion a non-derogable right.

85. Germany established a parliamentary commission while Austria set up an information and documentation centre about sects, Fautre, *Human Rights without Frontiers*, 'The Sect Issue in France and Belgium,' available at http://willyfautre.com p 2, in this interesting paper, the author analyses and compares the anti-sect policies in France and Belgium and the results of such policies.

potential threat to neutrality, *laïcité* and the French way of life, as well as to the welfare of certain young people.

[7.022] The French government closely monitors potentially 'dangerous' cult activity[86] and certain groups allege that this has led to some public distrust of minority religions.[87] In December 1998, a Parliamentary Commission to enquire into the finances, property and fiscal position of sects, together with their economic activities, was established and it reported within the requisite six-month period.[88] The Report of the Parliamentary Commission of June 1999 recommended continued state monitoring on cults and further discussion as to whether 'an anti-brain-washing statute' should be proposed.[89] Fautre traces in detail, *inter alia*, the development of anti-sect policies in France that culminated in the About-Picard Law of 2001[90] (the Law of 2001), which aimed to strengthen prevention and repression of sectarian groups liable to undermine human rights and fundamental freedoms.[91] The Law of 2001 increased restrictions on associations and had provisions dealing with:

1. the dissolution of organisations, including certain religious organisations;
2. placing minors at mortal risk;
3. the illegal practice of medicine or pharmacology;
4. false advertising;
5. violation of another individual's freedom, dignity, or identity; and
6. fraud or falsification.[92]

The law is applicable only to religious and philosophical groups.

---

86. Through the aegis of the *Inter-Ministerial Monitoring Mission against Sectarian Abuses*. This official body observes and examines 'sect.cult' movements, which may constitute a threat to public order, or that break the law and it informs the public of possible risks arising therefrom. It also assists victims to receive aid.
87. US Department of State, International Religious Freedom Report 2007, p 1.
88. This followed an earlier investigation and report in 1995.
89. The text of this report may be assessed on Cesnur's website http://www.cesnur.org/testi/fr99/fr_summary.htm.
90. *Loi No 2001–504 du 12 juin 2001.*
91. *Loi No 2001–504 du 12 juin 2001.*
92. *Loi No 2001–504 du 12 juin 2001.*

[7.023] Essentially, the About-Picard Law[93] permits the government to prosecute or dissolve any organisation that appears to establish a condition of physical or psychological reliance that causes a follower to behave differently from the way he or she behaved in the past, and it makes illegal any species of proselytising that constitutes 'abuse of a person's state of weakness'[94] which was previously termed 'mental manipulation' but was later removed following considerable international criticism.[95] The Law of 2001 creates broad new spheres for potential discrimination and violations of human rights and religious freedoms. For example, it could criminalise those who practice faith healing or healing through prayer, or those who refuse to submit to blood transfusions. In addition, innocent members of various religious groups could be denied the right to worship. Although the Law of 1905 and the Constitution of 1958 guarantee freedom of conscience[96] and the free exercise of religion subject only to public order requirements,[97] the Law of 2001 imposes questionable new restrictions on certain minority religions. Furthermore, the Constitution guarantees the neutrality of the state and the equality of the citizen without discrimination, *inter alia*, on the grounds of religion.[98] Not only do the provisions of the Law of 2001 sit uneasily with these express guarantees in national law, but, they may trespass on certain well-founded rights in international human rights instruments to which France has acceded. Such instruments include Art 9 of the ECHR, Arts 2(1), 4(2) and 18 of ICCPR 1966 and a number of relevant provisions of the Declaration on the Elimination of all Forms of Intolerance and of Discrimination based on Religion or Belief (1981).[99]

93. Which bears the names of its authors Senator Nicholas About and Catherine Picard.

94. Grieboski, 'The French Model', The Threat of France's Anti-Sect laws to Religious Liberty in Europe and Beyond, Touchstone Archives: The French Model, Joseph K Grieboski is founder and president of the Institute on religion and Public Policy in Washington DC, this article is available online at http://www.touchstonemag.com/archives/print.php?id=17-02-041-f.

95. Fautre, p 4.

96. Art 1.

97. Art 2.

98. Art 1.

99. A copy of this significant Declaration is included in **Appendix 8**. Art 7 provides that the rights set down in this Declaration shall be accorded in national legislation so that everyone shall be able to avail himself of such rights and freedoms in practice.

There has been, at least, one prosecution under the Law of 2001, that of Arnaud Mussy, leader of the New Lighthouse Cult (Neo-Phare). Mussy asserted that he was 'the Christ' and that the Apocalypse was drawing near. It was alleged that one of his followers committed suicide and two others attempted suicide. Eventually the Criminal Court in Nantes sentenced Mussy to three years for fraudulent 'abuse of a person's state of weakness' when that person was in a state of bodily or mental dependence. On appeal, a higher court in Rennes affirmed the lower court's decision. Concerns have been expressed regarding the constraints placed by the About-Picard Law on religious freedoms relating to unconventional religions[100] and in 2002 the Council of Europe[101] passed a resolution which was critical of this law. The Council invited the government to reconsider this law but no further action was taken by France.[102] The US Department of State's International Religious Freedom Report 2007 was also critical of the Law of 2001, alleging that it had contributed to intolerance and bias against a number of minority religions, allegations which are strongly refuted by France.

The Law of 15 March 2004

[7.024] The Stasi Report, published in December 2003, favoured the banning of political and religious expression in public schools and this report was to become central to the legal ban on conspicuous symbols in France. Former President Chirac praised this report and indicated that his government would implement its recommendations.[103] A circular from the education authorities, issued later in 2004, clarified that not all religious symbols were prohibited, but only those 'signs ... such as the Islamic headscarf, however named, the kippa or a cross that is manifestly oversized which make the wearer's religious identity immediately identifiable.'[104] The Law of 2004 inserted a new Art in the Education Code (L 141–51), which provides:

> In State primary and secondary schools, the wearing of signs or dress by which pupils overtly manifest a religious affiliation is prohibited. The school rules

100. See further Palmer, France's 'War on Sects': A Post 9/11 Update, *Nova Religio,* February 2008, vol 11, No 3, pp 104–120, Univ of California Press.

101. Whose powers are merely advisory.

102. US Department of State 2007, International Religious Freedom Report 2007, p 2.

103. US Department of State 2007, International Religious Freedom Report 2007, p 2.

104. US Department of State 2007, International Religious Freedom Report 2007, p 2.

shall state that the institution of disciplinary proceedings shall be preceded by dialogue with the pupil.

This Law prohibits, *inter alia*, Sikh students from wearing turbans, Islamic students from wearing headscarves, Christian students from wearing large crucifixes and Jewish students from wearing skullcaps (kippa) in French public schools. Since by far the largest group affected by the legal ban is female Muslim students, it is commonly believed that the main objective of this law is to regulate Muslim dress in public schools, so as to enforce integration. However, the issue is more complex than that. As is clear from the huge majorities which supported it in the National Assembly and the Senate, the Law of 2004 has strong backing.[105] The legislative ban applies to state schools, educational institutions and post-*baccalaureate* courses. However, the ban does not apply to private schools or to state universities, by contrast with the position in Turkey, Albania and Azerbaijan, where the issue is not so much identified with individual liberty or religious freedom, but with the political meaning of the wearing of the headscarf in universities.[106] Nonetheless, the enactment of the Law of 2004 aroused intense global debate on the meaning of secularity[107] and on the place of religion and religious symbols in public schools and in public life generally. Moreover, it led many to question France's motivation in introducing this measure in the light of its policies implemented between 1989 and 2004.

[7.025] The public controversy over the banning of the headscarf commenced in Criel, a Paris suburb, in 1989 when a headmaster of a high school expelled three Muslim pupils for wearing Islamic headscarves to school.[108] When this issue was referred to the *Conseil d'Etat,*[109] it determined that freedom of conscience was one of the fundamental tenets

105. In the National Assembly (494–20 votes in favour of the ban) and in the Senate (276–20 votes in favour).

106. See further *Sahin v Turkey* (2005) 41 EHRR 8.

107. Barbier, *La laïcité (The secular principle)*, (L'Harmattan, 1995): Durand-Prinborgne, *La Laïcité*, (Dalloz, 1996): See also Jean Bauberot, Professor at *L'École des Hautes Etudes en Sciences Sociales*, 'The Secular Principle' at http://ambafrance-us.org/IMG/html/secularism.html: source, Images de la France (SIG), Embassy of France in the USA, 15/3/2001.

108. DeBula Baines, '*L'Affaire des Foulards-Discrimination*, or the Price of a Secular Public Education?' 29 *Vand J Transnational* 3304, 1996.

109. The Council of State, which advises the Government, being the highest court for administration.

recognised by the laws of the Republic, which applied equally in education – one of the state's primary responsibilities. It held that the expression by students of their religious beliefs in school was not by itself incompatible with the principle of *laïcité*.[110] As late as 2003, both legal and executive decisions upheld the decision followed by the *Conseil d'Etat* in 1989. Saxena questions the rationale behind the drastic change of policy which culminated in the Law of 2004–228 and concludes:

> The most obvious explanation for this reversal of policy is that law 2004–228 serves a political dimension, attempting to find ways to balance France's secular identity with the integration of the five million-strong population of Muslims in France in the light of three trends: the new wave of anti-Semitism in Western Europe[111], the strong Islamophobia in those cultures post September 11, 2001, and the expansion of the European Union with its greater religious, ethnic, linguistic and cultural diversity .... On the other hand, law 2004–228 in effect creates conditions in which minority groups are required to surrender their distinctive characteristics for the sake of assimilation, a surrender dressed in the garb of the constitutional requirement of Laïcité.[112]

In Belgium there is no overall prohibition on the wearing of religious symbols at school but a headscarf ban on the wearing of religious or political symbols for certain city personnel (eg librarians, child care workers) has been introduced in the city of Ghent. This ban, however, does not extend to teachers or to police officers.[113] In the Flemish community, a decree of neutrality of 13 March 1994 provides that education shall be neutral within the community.

The Law of 2004 and Human Rights

[7.026] The French government points out that the Law of 2004 is one of a set of measures which were implemented by the state to promote better

110. Avis du Conseil d'Etat No 346893 (27 November 1989), reprinted in Jeuffroy, Tricard and Durand, *Liberté religieuse et régimes des cultes en droit francais* 1031–1034 (Editions du Cerf 1996).

111. See European monitoring centre on Racism and Zenophobia (EUMC) *Manifstation of Anti-Semitism in the EU 2002–2003, 2004* (available at: http://eumc.eu.int/eumc/index.php?fuseaction=content.dsp_cat_content&catid=449677441f3f3.

112. Saxena, 'The French Headscarf Law and the Right to Manifest Religious Belief', in The Selected Works of Mukul Saxena, available at http://works.bepress.com/mukul_saxena/2 accessed on 5 October 2008 pp 2–3.

113. See 'Headscarf ban for employees in Ghent', 17 November 2007, available at http:www.expatica.com/be/articles/news/headscarf-ban-for-employees-in-Ghent–46398.html.

integration and to fight economic and social discrimination.[114] Generally speaking, each individual is free to choose his or her religion and to practice that religion without restriction provided that right is exercised in compliance with the rule of law and that it respects the rights of others. However, the right to manifest religion or religious faith and belief is restricted so as to comply with the traditional model of secularity, as outlined above, which is an established legislative and constitutional principle promoted by the French state. Article 9(2) of the ECHR lays down certain justifiable limitations on the freedom of religious expression:

> Freedom to manifest one's religion or beliefs shall be subject only to such limitations as are prescribed by law and are necessary in a democratic society in the interests of public safety, for the protection of public order, health or morals, or for the protection of the rights and freedoms of others.

If the headscarf ban of 2004 was intended to enforce integration, quite the reverse seems to have happened (as Muslim communities had predicted), because four new private confessional schools had been opened in France by 2007, an increase which is likely to continue.[115] What were the origins of the distinctions made between religious instruction and moral education in the early public school system in France?

Religious Instruction and Moral Education

[7.027] When establishing the public school system,[116] Jules Ferry clarified the distinction between the domain of religious instruction and moral education in a letter which he sent to schoolteachers in 1883:

> Religious instruction belongs to the home and to the church; moral instruction belongs to the school. The first goal of the law is to separate school and church, to assure freedom of conscience for both masters and pupils, to make a distinction between two domains too long confused, that of beliefs, which are

114. *Consulat Géneralé de France a Londres.*

115. International Religious Freedom Report, 2007, Bureau of Democracy, Human Rights and Labor, USA: Boustead, 'The French Headscarf Law before the European Court of Human Rights' (16) *Journal of Transnational Law and Policy,* Florida State University, Spring 2007, No 2, pp 167–196 at 168: Bussy, 'Recognising Religion in a Secular Society', *Journal of Church and State,* 2007, edited by Farrow, McGill (Queen's University Press, 2004): Beller, *The Headscarf Affair: The Conseil d'Etat on the Role of Religion and Culture in French Society,* 39 TX INT'LJ581 (2004).

116. Law of 15 March 1882 (*Loi Ferry*).

personal, free and variable, and that of knowledge, which is common and essential to all.[117]

Both citizenship and 'ethical character' were required subjects in the curriculum of the elementary schools under the Law of the 15 March 1882 (*Loi Ferry*)[118] and religion was formally excluded since the law contained 'no obligations to God'. The introduction of subjects such as 'ethics' and 'citizenship' in the curricula of modern European schools is not a novel idea, it can be argued, but a return to the nineteenth century ideology and pedagogy of Jules Ferry. At that time Ferry's Director of Elementary Education, Ferdinand Buisson, presciently declared that Ferry's laws of 1881–2 relating to education constituted the whole base or the whole edifice on which human culture would henceforth rest in France. It was an edifice which omitted 'the pillar' of religion, so to speak, and religion was relegated to the private sphere of life.

[7.028] In keeping with the Law of 1905 and its constitutional provisions, France's current public education system is secular. Accordingly, with the exception of three *départments* in the east of the country,[119] there is no religious instruction in the public schools, but 'moral and civic' education is taught and facts about religion are taught as part of the history curriculum.[120]

[7.029] In common with religious instruction generally, Islamic instruction is not part of the public school curriculum in France. Few Islamic schools exist in France and these, it appears, have not achieved state funding.[121] Because of insufficient places of worship (mosques) in France, Kuru found in his recent research that some people conduct their Friday prayer in the streets of Paris[122] and he argues 'that the main reason for the French state's

---

117. Cited in France Diplomatie, 'Society and Environment', No 60 'One Hundred Years of French Secularism' available online at http://www.diplomatie.gouv.fr/en/.

118. The first of Ferry's laws on education was introduced in 1881 which introduced free elementary education and the Law of 1882 made such education mandatory and *laic*.

119. Haut-Rhin, Bas-Rhin and Moselle where the local law of Alsace-Moselle still applies.

120. International Religious Freedom Report, 2007, p 2.

121. Kuru, 'Muslims and the Secular State in France', online at http://europe.byu.edu/islam/pdfs/Kuru-paper.pdf accessed on 5 October 2008.

122. Kuru, 'Muslims and the Secular State in France', online at http://europe.byu.edu/islam/pdfs/Kuru-paper.pdf accessed on 5 October 2008 citing field-work conducted by him in October-December 2004.

exceptionally restrictive policies towards Muslims is the dominant secular ideology in France,' which he calls 'combative secularism.'[123] Religious instruction is taught, however, in the publicly-funded private schools which are predominantly Catholic.

[7.030] As the documentation of the French Ministry indicates, *laïcité* is one of the foundational principles ('*les grands principes*') upholding the system of public education being inspired by the Revolution of 1789, embodied in the laws,[124] enshrined in the Constitution of 1958 and supported by the Fourth and Fifth Republics.[125] Such education is officially described as being '*laic*' in character.[126] Emphasis is placed upon the importance of *laïcité* as expressed in the Law of 1905 which, as has been seen, established the secularity of the state (*laïcité de l'état*) beyond all doubt. Respect for students and their parents is implied, it is stated, by the absence of religious instruction in the public school's programme,[127] by the *laïcité* of the personnel delivering that programme and by the prohibition on proselytism in the public schools.[128] Significantly, the Ministry also points out that schools have the discretion to leave one day a week free so that parents, if they wish, may make arrangements for religious education outside of school in compliance with the Law of 28 March 1882, which made express provision for this. Arrangements may vary at the different levels of education but, generally, primary school pupils do not have classes on Wednesdays, it appears.[129] Thus the significance of religion in the children's formation is acknowledged, although it is clearly seen as the domain of parents and the churches.

[7.031] For historical reasons, in the three *départments* in the east (Haut-Rhin, Bas-Rhin and Moselle), religion comprises part of the general curriculum at first and second level, the teachers being paid by the state, as

123. Kuru, 'Muslims and the Secular State in France', online at http://europe.byu.edu/islam/pdfs/Kuru-paper.pdf accessed on 5 October 2008.

124. And in particular the law of 28 March 1882 and the law of 30 October 1886, the Law of 1905 and the Law of 2005.

125. The French Ministry for Education's website at http://www.education.gouv.fr.

126. http://www.education.gouv.fr.

127. http://www.education.gouv.fr.

128. http://www.education.gouv.fr.

129. Basdevant-Gaudemet, 'State and Church in France' in Robbers (ed), *State and Church in the European Union* (Nomos, 2005) p 171–2.

in Ireland, and these classes are voluntary for students. At the end of the Franco-Prussian war, in or about 1870, these three *départments* fell under German rule. As a result of an agreement between the German Emperor and the Holy See, the French religious law, which was operational at that time in the dioceses of Metz and Strasbourg, was permitted to continue in these areas. When these territories were returned to France, following the First World War, in 1918 politicians and the local population wished to preserve the *status quo* in these territories and this was permitted. Hence the Law of 1905 does not apply to these *départments*, but rather the local law of Alsace-Moselle. In other words, the system of recognised churches still applies in these three departments and their churches are still supported financially by the French state.[130] There is freedom of education since parents may choose either public or private, religious or non-religious schools for their children, which are generously subsidised by the state albeit under strict conditions.

Private Schools: Public Funding

[7.032] As has been seen, public service education includes private schools under the control of the state and these schools are entitled to public funding provided they have signed a contract with the state.[131] Currently, approximately 17 per cent of pupils in France attend private schools (94 per cent of which are Catholic), in which the teachers are remunerated by the state. The freedom to organise and provide education is perceived as a manifestation of freedom of expression.[132] Thus, despite the fact that the Law of 1905 provides: 'The Republic does not recognise, fund or subsidise any religion' and that the *laïcité* principle is enshrined in the Constitution, private schools are subsidised by the State on strict conditions. In order to permit this to happen, special legal rules have been devised by the state[133] which apply to a complex network of bodies (associations for the

130. Basdevant-Gaudemet, 'State and Church in France' in Robbers (ed), *State and Church in the European Union* (Nomos, 2005) p 160 and 172.

131. Le Systeme Educatif, http://education.gouv.fr: Ministere Education Nationale, 'The main principles', available at http://www.education.gouv.fr.

132. Le Systeme Educatif, http://Education.gouv.fr: Ministere Education Nationale, 'The main principles', available at http://www.education.gouv.fr.

133. Under the Laws of 1901, 1905 and 1907. In particular the law of 1 July 1901, which it still in force, embodies the tenet of freedom of association of all who share their knowledge or activity for non-profit making purposes.

purpose of a church) which Basdevant-Gaudemet has categorised into three main groups: Religious Associations (*associations culturelles*);[134] Diocesan Associations (*associations diocesaines*);[135] and the Religious Orders.[136] Certain compromises emerged over time, in the case of the Catholic Church, when relations with the Holy See were restored. During the 1940s France's political leaders had to decide whether to permit the system of private schools (predominantly Catholic) to decline, thereby eliminating the preferred option of approximately one sixth of French parents, or to grant them some degree of public funding which would ensure their survival. The state opted for the latter approach.[137]

[7.033] Thus, supporters of public funding for private schools succeeded under the Fifth Republic to acquire passage of the *Loi Debré* by a huge majority.[138] Prime Minister Michael Debré stated in parliamentary debates that the private sector (with approximately 1,797,000 students) brought to the education of French youth a cooperation which it would be unjust to fail to recognise.[139] This law, which is still in force, provides that: 'the State proclaims and respects educational freedom.' Under the Debré Law[140], a

---

134. Basdevant-Gaudemet, 'State and Church in France' in Robbers (ed), *State and Church in the European Union* (Nomos, 2005) pp 162–163. From 1905 onwards Protestants and Jews have established *associations cultuelles* which are still operational in accordance with the Law of 1905. Because of its determined opposition to the Law of 1905, the Catholic Church did not establish any *associations cultuelles.*

135. Basdevant-Gaudemet, 'State and Church in France' in Robbers (ed), *State and Church in the European Union* p 163. Since 1924 the bishops in France have established *associations diocesaines* in compliance with the Laws of 1901 and 1905. After 1924 it was encumbent on the Catholic Church to fund the construction of new churches and to maintain them. Furthermore, the flexibility conferred by the freedom of association provision in the Law of 1901 facilitated the growth of numerous cultural associations with educational purposes established out of religious faith or conviction. This latter form is used, *inter alia,* by the Muslims to establish their Koranic schools.

136. Basdevant-Gaudemet, 'State and Church in France' in Robbers (ed), *State and Church in the European Union* (Nomos, 2005) p 165–6.

137. Healey, *The French Achievement: Private School Aid - A Lesson for America* (Paulist Press, 1974).

138. The vote being 427–71, see further Glenn, *Religious Education in Public Schools,* 277 at 284.

139. Visse, *La question scolaire,* 1975–1984 (Septentrion, 1995), 62.

140. Debré Law, no 59–1557 of 31 December 1959.

pilot programme of public aid for private schools was initiated and, evaluated over an eleven-year period, and this initiative was finally adopted. This compromise was found not only to improve the quality of education but also to mitigate the harsh divisions that had emerged over the church-state issue.[141] What was the legal and constitutional rationale that upheld the public funding of private schools?

The *Conseil Constitutionnel* determined on the 23 November 1977 that the Freedom of Education principle was one of the fundamental principles recognised by the laws of the Republic, reaffirmed in the Preamble of the 1946 Constitution and embodied in the Constitution of 1958, thought not expressly.[142] Under this principle, the French state recognises and justifies the co-existence of public and private schools within the French education system together with the provision of state funding to private education on the terms defined by law.[143] Currently, private education largely comprises schools under contract to the state in the context of the Debré law. In addition, private individuals may organise and finance other schools. The legal status of private educational establishments set up and operated by private individuals, groups, and legal entities is to be found in three basic laws reflecting the three levels of education: the Goblet law of 30 October 1886 (primary education); the Falloux law of the 15 March 1850 (general education classes in colleges and lyceé) and the Astier law of the 25 July 1919 (technical education).[144] Any French citizen or EU citizen may establish a private school provided they comply with the law and the conditions laid down by the state.[145] All private schools are entitled to receive public funding in accordance with the above-mentioned laws, and

141. Healey, 'Religious Freedom or "Catch-22"? The Private School Aid Issue', *The Christian Century* (The Christian Century Foundation, 23 April 1975) pp 413–16, www.christiancentury.org.

142. FRANCE 2000, 'Private Education in the European Union', Organisation, administration and the public authorities' role, Socrates, EURYDICE. This document sets out in detail the arrangements for the provision of private education in France in the year 2000: For an interesting discussion on some of this legislation, see further Gardner, Lawton and Cairns, *Faith Schools: Consensus or Conflict*? (Routledge, 2005) p 181.

143. FRANCE 2000, 'Private Education in the European Union', Organisation, administration and the public authorities' role, Socrates, EURYDICE p 80.

144. FRANCE 2000, 'Private Education in the European Union', Organisation, administration and the public authorities' role, Socrates, EURYDICE.

145. FRANCE 2000, 'Private Education in the European Union', Organisation, administration and the public authorities' role, Socrates, EURYDICE.

schools under contract can receive additional public aid on the basis of the Debré law. [146] With regard to the private schools under contract, the state and local organisations provide public funds for private schools jointly in accordance with the Debré law.[147] The state undertakes responsibility for payment of salaries, the employer's social security and fiscal contributions and the expense of initial and on-going teacher training.[148] Local municipalities contribute to the running costs of classes under contract by paying a lump sum (*forfeit*) to the schools and in certain instances this is an optional payment.[149]

Chaplains in Schools

[7.034] When Napoleon established the *lycées* for boys, he made provision for chaplains as an integral element in the schools at second level. Some time later, *lycées* for girls made provision for church teachers in these schools, but the Third Republic later abolished them.[150] From 1905 onwards, chaplaincies were permitted but the state did not fund them.[151] Such posts are established by the school head, following parental requests, and on foot of the nomination of the relevant religious body, and these posts are jointly funded by the diocese and by parents. They operate either within the school

146. FRANCE 2000, 'Private Education in the European Union', Organisation, administration and the public authorities' role, Socrates, EURYDICE, p 81.

147. FRANCE 2000, 'Private Education in the European Union', Organisation, administration and the public authorities' role, Socrates, EURYDICE. The appointment, status, terms and conditions of service of teachers is complex and these are set down at para 7 of the EURYDICE paper.

148. FRANCE 2000, 'Private Education in the European Union', Organisation, administration and the public authorities' role, Socrates, EURYDICE, in classes under a contrat simple or a contrat d'association.

149. FRANCE 2000, 'Private Education in the European Union', Organisation, administration and the public authorities' role, Socrates, EURYDICE.

150. FRANCE 2000, 'Private Education in the European Union', Organisation, administration and the public authorities' role, Socrates, EURYDICE, pp 171–2: also Markham, 'The Revolution, Napoleon and Education', op cit.

151. FRANCE 2000, 'Private Education in the European Union', Organisation, administration and the public authorities' role, Socrates, EURYDICE, these matters are governed by a decree of 22 April 1960, an order of 8 August 1960 and a ministerial Circular of 22 April 1988.

or, in some instances, outside the school.[152] By contrast, the Irish state funds chaplains in community and comprehensive (second level schools established by deeds of trust) schools and this practice has survived a constitutional challenge,[153] while the German state funds chaplains in hospitals, prisons and the army from the church tax, as was seen in **chapter 6** in this book.

Citizenship Programmes

[7.035] Towards the end of the 1990s both the French and English governments, among others, placed a new focus on citizenship education. However, ethics and citizenship education is not new to French education since these subjects were taught under the Jules Ferry law of 1882. Starkey concludes that, while the English curriculum aspires to create a diverse society grounded on multicultural citizenship, the French syllabus on citizenship focuses on commitment to anti-racism, human rights and civil action against injustice and that its commitment to individual equality without distinction, denies any recognition of social groups grounded in culture or ethnicity:

> This blindness to difference also tends to undermine citizenship education as a social project intended to promote integration in schools. Whereas French citizenship education is intended to integrate individuals into a predetermined, existing republican framework, English citizenship education apparently aims to create a new society and a new national identity.[154]

[7.036] The broader potential difficulty with citizenship education is that it is intrinsically value-laden since a pupil is presented with a model of civic virtue that accords with certain norms and values that underpin citizenship.[155] Accordingly, there is a risk of state indoctrination,[156] regardless of the fact that it may be unintentional.[157] Some of the concepts

---

152. FRANCE 2000, 'Private Education in the European Union', Organisation, administration and the public authorities' role, Socrates, EURYDICE.

153. *Campaign to Separate Church and State* [19968] 2 ILRM 241, HC; [1998] 2 ILRM 81 Supreme Court.

154. Starkey, 'Citizenship Education in France and Britain: evolving theories and practices', *Curriculum Journal,* vol 11, Issue 1, 1 March 2000, pp 39–54.

155. Harris, *Education Law and Diversity,* op cit, p 380 *et seq.*

156. Bell, HM Chief Inspector of Schools, Hansard Society/Ofstead lecture, 17 January 2005.

157. Harris, *Education Law and Diversity,* op cit, p 380, see n 998 above.

presented in certain citizenship, ethics and religion education programmes (secular programmes) may conflict with the religious or philosophical convictions of parents or guardians as is clearly illustrated in *Jimenez v Spain*[158] and in *Zengin v Turkey*[159] and in *Leirvag v Norway*.[160] Thus, problems tend to arise where the states' programmes of religious education/ citizenship are compulsory on all students.

Status of Teachers

[7.037] The status of a public school teacher in France is that of a civil servant of the state. Such teachers are expected to respect and promote state policies, which are set down in the Education Codes, including those of equality and *laïcité*.[161] By contrast, the teaching staff in non-contract private schools (independent schools) are private-sector employees and their appointment, remuneration and job security are regulated by the labour laws and any collective agreements to which their employers subscribe. These teachers have no contractual agreement with the state, unlike their public school counterparts.

With regard to the legal status of teachers in private schools, this depends on whether they are employed in schools which have a '*contrat simple*' or a '*contrat d'association*' with the state.[162] If the teacher works in a school which falls into the first category, they are appointed by the private school authority and approved by the state. Thus, they are private sector employees remunerated by the state, who are expected to uphold the denominational school's ethos. However, if private school teachers are employed by schools under a *contrat d'association*, the district school authority, in consultation with the school administration, appoints them and they become temporary civil servants.[163] The distinctions between the legal status of public school

158. Application 51188/99 EHRR.

159. Application 1448/04 EHRR, judg del 9 January 2008.

160. Communication No 1155/2003 CCPR.

161. See Ministere des Affaires Etrangeres/French Ministry of Foreign Affairs, 2007, Education Code: Arts L141–1 and Arts. L151–6, Secular Public Education and also Education Code: freedom of education, Arts L151-L151–6, available at Legifrance.gouv.fr.

162. See Ministere des Affaires Etrangeres/French Ministry of Foreign Affairs, 2007, Education Code, p 82.

163. FRANCE 2000, 'Private Education in the European Union', Organisation, administration and the public authorities' role, Socrates, EURYDICE.

teachers, and their private-school counterparts, caused considerable controversy some years ago, when the former were transferred to private schools, where they had to comply with certain ethos-related constraints having come from the public school sector where they were required to uphold the *laïcité* principle. Not surprisingly, in their new situation, these teachers felt somewhat conflicted.

[7.038] Inspection of teaching takes place so as to ensure that it upholds standards of morality, the laws and the Constitution and the provisions governing compulsory education. Inspection of non-contract schools is confined to the qualifications required by teachers and head teachers, public order, moral standards, and social and health regulations.[164] Inspections are designed to ensure that these schools comply with curricula, timetables and respect for pupils' freedom of conscience in accordance with the Debré Law, which guarantees access to these schools without discrimination on the grounds of origin, opinion or faith.[165] The state examinations are under the control of the state nationwide.

Is the Headscarf Ban Symbolic of Deeper Problems?

[7.039] Arguably the ban on the wearing of the Islamic headscarf in public schools in France is symbolic of more fundamental problems surrounding issues of the integration of many millions of citizens of diverse cultures, races and religions. Is the passing of the law of 2004 an example of what Istvan Bibo, the Hungarian historian and social scientist, calls 'political hysteria', which impels the given society to take the wrong developmental direction and distorts its mentality and structures?[166] Bibo believed that there were analogies that could be drawn between individual reactions and those of communities. When communities are faced with problems which seem insurmountable, as a result of shock, he contends, they substitute a fictional problem which can be mediated through words and symbols for the real problem and, having resolved the former, the society can convince itself that

164. FRANCE 2000, 'Private Education in the European Union', Organisation, administration and the public authorities' role, Socrates, EURYDICE.

165. FRANCE 2000, 'Private Education in the European Union', Organisation, administration and the public authorities' role, Socrates, EURYDICE.

166 Bibo (1911–1979) explored the concept of 'political hysteria' in his book '*On European Balance and Peace*' written in 1942–3. He posited the view that (a) the society which sustained a shock rejects the reality of the existing world and its problems; (contd .../)

it has resolved the latter.[167] Indeed, the legal ban on the wearing of the hijab in public schools may be symptomatic of a deeper malaise in French society. The serious rioting in the *banlieues* of Paris in 2005 indicates that creative political engagement, requiring some degree of compromise on both sides, is necessary if France is to resolve its serious social problems arising from immigration on a massive scale. Although the principle of laïcité has served the nation well for more than a century, the context has changed and it may now be necessary to adapt that principle to the realities of contemporary life.

Feared Erosion of Secular Tradition

[7.040] Recently, France reacted with shock and outrage to a decision of the High Court in Lille to annul a marriage because the bride was not a virgin. It appears that, prior to their marriage, a French Muslim lady assured her fiancé, who was also a Muslim, that she was a virgin, but she later admitted that she lied to him.[168] The newly-married husband made application to a French court in Lille for an annulment under French law and his wife supported that application. The judge decided that there had been an error as to one of the 'essential qualities' or capacities of one of the parties and he granted the annulment. This case was grounded in Art 180 of the French Civil Code of 1804 which provides *inter alia*: 'Where there was a mistake as to the person, or as to the essential capacities of the person, the other spouse

166. (contd) (b) the society becomes incapable of solving its problems; (c). the society builds up an illusory world which fails to face the problems of the real world; (d) the nation's self-evaluation becomes uncertain; (e) the reactions of such a nation to the outer world's challenges become unrealistic and exaggerated. As a result of the above factors, the society deals with the illusory problem, but the real problems persists. See further Kovacs Gabor, 'Can Power Be Humanised', Pt 1, http://www.fil.hu/intezet/kg01_p.htm, this research was supported by the Research Support Scheme of the Central European University. I am indebted to Brian Coll, whose thesis in Cambridge University deals with French secularism, for drawing my attention to Bibo's concept of 'polititial hysteria' and to Lara Marlowe for her reference to Mr Coll's research in 'French-style secularism has no room for Muslims' (2005) *Irish Times*, 11 December.

167. Bibo,'*On European Balance and Peace*'.

168. Berlins, 'A French judge annulled a marriage because the wife lied about her virginity. Could it happen here?' (2008) *The Guardian,* 4 June available to download at http://www.guardian.co.uk/commentisfree/2008/jun/04/relationships.women.

may apply for annulment of the marriage.'[169] However, this case has renewed fears that France's second religion is now eroding the country's secular tradition and there is a liklihood of a Supreme Court challenge.[170] Granting the annulment was perceived by some as permitting Sharia law to enter French law surreptitiously.[171] Realistically speaking, in view of the fact that there are approximately five or six million Muslims in France, it is inevitable that the Muslim community will effect some changes in French society.

Addressing Racial and Religious Issues

[7.041] Racial and religious issues are now being addressed at government level. In 2004 the government released the Ruffin Report, which concluded that racism and anti-Semitism were threats to democracy. The Report recommended, among other matters, reform of the press law and the introduction of measures for countering intolerance in primary schools.[172] In June 2007, the Interior Minister, Michele Alliot-Marie, met leaders of France's major religious confessions (Catholic, Protestant, Muslim and Jewish) to enter into dialogue with them on the public policy of secularism in the public sphere and to elicit their thinking on the role of religion in the life of the community, especially with regard to the youth. Some of the impetus for this meeting was the announcement by President Sarkozy of a plan to debate the findings of an earlier report from the Commission of Judicial Consideration on the Relations of Religions and Public Authority (the Commission).[173] Sarkozy stated that he wished to initiate 'a debate without taboos' about the merits of legal reform concerning religion. The Commission, set up by Sarkozy in 2005, recommended that the Law of 1905 separating church and state be reformed, that local communities be permitted to fund the construction of places of worship and that more flexible criteria be devised for a religion to acquire the legal status of an *association cultuelle*.[174] The Report also supported Sarkozy's suggestion,

---

169. Berlioz Consulting, French Civil Code of 1804 (English version), with links to Legifrance. Note the French version is the official version.

170. Berlioz Consulting, French Civil Code of 1804 (English version), with links to Legifrance.

171. Berlioz Consulting, French Civil Code of 1804 (English version), with links to Legifrance.

172. International Religious Freedom Report 2007.

173. International Religious Freedom Report 2007.

174. International Religious Freedom Report 2007.

made in 2002, that the French state should encourage a public form of Islam, moderated by social recognition and open practice.[175] In addition, the government has established a commission of Muslim and non-Muslim scholars to examine methods by which the provision of imam training can be broadened.[176] Currently, approximately 90 per cent of imams in France come from North Africa.[177] At present, there are no indications of any change in regard to the above-mentioned Laws of 2001 and 2004, however.

[7.042] The historian, Jean Bauberot, who was the single dissenting member of the Stasi Commission opposed to the legislative ban on the Islamic headscarf, distinguishes between the democratic model of *laïcité* and the republican model of *laïcité* which is currently being pursued in France, he asserts. In the democratic model of laïcité, which he believes has been applied to Christians and Jews in France, Bauberot sees it as the conscience of democracy, which manifests an effort to 'contain religion within its limits without denying its immense cultural significance.' He views the school as the cradle of democracy in which differences are mediated and negotiated and in which established practices are critically revised and debated in the absence of dogmatic assertions of immutable truth.[178] If France applied the democratic model of secularity to the present-day context, rather than the Republican model, then substantial progress could be made towards the accommodation and integration of the various religions and races in that country.

CONCLUSION

[7.043] Among the European countries considered, France's approach to religion in the public sphere is by far the most restrictive. That approach

175. International Religious Freedom Report 2007, p 3.

176. BBC NEWS, Tim Whewell, 'State training for Europe's imams', BBC Radio 4's Crossing Currents, broadcast on 17 June 2004 at 11000BST and was repeated on 21 June 2004.

177. BBC NEWS, Tim Whewell, 'State training for Europe's imams', BBC Radio 4's Crossing Currents, broadcast on 17 June 2004 at 11000BST and was repeated on 21 June 2004.

178. Scott, 'Forced to be Free', *New Humanist,* vol 123, Issue 2, March/April 2008 citing Bauberot: See further Bauberot, 'Two Thresholds of Laicization'. Bhargava (ed), *Secularism and its Critics* (Oxford University Press, 1999): *La Laïcité, Une Chance Pour le XXIe Siecle*, Bauberot (ed), *La Laïcité a l'epreuve: Religions et Liberte dans le monde*, 2004c.

contrasts sharply with that of Germany, Spain, England and Ireland, where religion, generally speaking, is perceived as a societal benefit and is accommodated in publicly-funded schools generally. Unlike the position in the other countries, there is no religious instruction in the public schools in France but it is taught, however, in public universities and in private schools. At a time when fear of radical Islam is pressing governments across the EU into ambitious plans to foster loyalty and moderation in their Muslim citizens, France's approach is unique. It appears that the Muslim community in France experiences difficulties in funding a sufficient number of mosques, in establishing publicly funded Islamic schools, in securing Islamic instruction in schools and in relation to the wearing of Islamic headscarves in public schools. Confessional Muslim schools are few. France has, however, a central institute (the Council of French Muslims) for the training of imams and for the funding of mosques. In England, the approach appears to be more sensitive, and some Muslims welcome the possibility of public funding for certain training initiatives in which they have a contributing role.

[7.044] A more assertive species of secularity, '*La Laïcité*', keeps watch over the secular character of public education in France. This ideological and doctrinal principle, distilled over the centuries in the crucible of church-state struggles, embodies certain elements of anti-clericism, deriving from France's fraught history, which has carried over into contemporary times. France tends to deal with any threats to its cherished tenet of *laïcité* defensively, for example, through direct legislative measures. In other words, it employs the law to control religion in a top-down manner, so to speak, and to sequester it in the private sphere. It is as though, having experienced the dominance of one religion, France is suspicious of others and is defensive of new arrivals, be they Muslim, new religions or sects. Nonetheless, France has made a very significant compromise with the churches under the *Debré* law relating to the public funding of its private schools, which would be unthinkable and indeed unconstitutional in the US because of the Establishment Clause. In the wake of the French Revolution of 1789, the concept of '*laïcité*' emerged and was promoted by the State until it became part of a dominant ideology which was enshrined in the Law of 1905. Since then, the laic principle has retained its position in French society through the process of public education, ideological indoctrination, and cultural assimilation, despite opposition from certain quarters and a not inconsiderable element of global criticism. Nevertheless, *laïcité* is not universal throughout all departments, and strong bonds still exist with the publicly-funded main churches in Alsace-Moselle, for historical reasons, and with the dominant Catholic culture of the nation, which may not be, *prima facie*, apparent.

Despite its history and its well-established separation doctrine, France has accommodated private education as part of the public service of education within strict limits in quite a remarkable manner. Although the laic principle continues to be a constitutional and legislative tenet, the freedom of education and freedom of religion principles, when read together, have enabled the state to reach a compromise with the churches and with that part of its population (approximately one-sixth) who desire private education for their children.[179]

President Sarcozy is acutely aware of the significance of religion in France and in the rest of the EU. There are now some indications that France may reform its Law of 1905 so as to facilitate a less defensive approach to the mainstream churches and to the new religions. This could conceivably be achieved, without undue damage to the cherished *laïcité* principle, through the application of the freedom of religion, and freedom of education principles so as to meet the new social realities. In 2005 France's former President, Jacques Chirac, posed a question to the French people which summarised their contemporary dilemma: 'With, in the background, a globalisation question: how can we stay ourselves in a world of accelerating change?'[180] The reality is that France, no more than any other country, will be unable to remain unchanged but it can adapt reasonably to the new social realities it now faces, while still retaining what is best in its greatly admired culture and traditions.

179. Healey, 'Religious Freedom or "Catch 22"? The Private School Aid Issue'.

180. Former President Jacques Chirac in a New Year's Eve broadcast to the Nation, Paris, 31 December 2005: see also Michael Gurfinkiel, 'Islam in France: The French Way of Life is in Danger', *The Middle East Quarterly,* March 1997, vol 4, No 1.

Chapter 8

RELIGION, EDUCATION AND THE LAW IN SPAIN

INTRODUCTION

[8.001] The secularisation of modern society is particularly evident in the kingdom of Spain, which was formerly a socially conservative, Catholic nation, deeply influenced by a bitter civil war[1] and by more than three decades of General Franco's dictatorial regime.[2] Arguably, Spain has experienced more profound political, economic and social change than any other country in Western Europe in the past 25 years.[3] After the demise of Franco in 1975, a transformation in Spanish society gradually took place over the ensuing decades, which culminated in Spain becoming a parliamentary monarchy and one of the most liberal societies in Europe. An increasing transfer of power from the central government to regional and local government has been apparent in Spain in recent years and this is also reflected in education in Spain, which has been striving to promote EU standards and guidelines to improve the quality of education and to devolve greater responsibility for financial, administrative and curricular matters to the regional governments.[4] The Catholic Church, which traditionally claims the spiritual adherence of approximately 82 per cent of Spain's estimated 43.9 million inhabitants, [5] has been particularly critical of the latest phase of

---

1. Borkenau, *The Spanish Cockpit* (Osprey Publishing, 2002); Brenan, *The Spanish Labyrinth: an Account of the Social and Political Background of the Spanish Civil War.*

2. See Mitchell, 'Men and Women under Franco' in Mitchell, *Betrayal of the Innocents: Desire, Power, and the Catholic Church*; 'A Survey of Spain', *The Economist*, 24 June.

3. Rowling, 'Spanish Education Reshaped by Political Changes, Economic Realities', (10)2 *World Education News and Reviews*, Spring 1997.

4. Rowling, 'Spanish Education Reshaped by Political Changes, Economic Realities', (10)2 *World Education News and Reviews*, Spring 1997, p 20.

5. In 2005 the population was approximately 43,398; source OECD Report, *Education at a Glance* (2005).

secularism in Spanish society.[6] When Pope Benedict XVI spoke publicly in June 2005 of the erosion of marriage, free unions, trial marriages and 'pseudo marriages between people of the same sex', he most likely was referring to the Bill then passing through the Spanish Parliament which proposed to enact a law permitting same-sex couples to marry and adopt children.[7] As part of the social reforms under Jose Luis Rodriguez Zapatero's socialist government, that law was enacted on 30 June 2005 and came into force on 3 July 2005, making Spain the third country in Europe to recognise same-sex marriage after the Netherlands (2001) and Belgium (2003).[8] The striking economic and social evolution in Spain in recent decades has led to the enactment of new laws on no-fault divorce and plans to introduce stem cell research. Zapatero has also introduced major educational reforms. After he took up office in 2004, he repealed the Education Bill, which, if enacted, would have made religious education a compulsory subject for Spanish school children.[9] Then Zapatero brought forward his own plans for educational reform, including a decrease in the academic status of voluntary religious education, limits on parental freedom to choose a school and the introduction of a compulsory course entitled 'Education for Citizenship' to teach democratic values. These plans were staunchly opposed by the Muslim community, the Catholic Church, the People's Party and the Catholic Confederation of Parents' Associations. In particular, the Catholic Church claimed that the introduction of 'civic education' into all Spanish schools would impinge on the rights of parents to shape their child's moral vision,[10] an issue that has troubled parents in Spain and Germany. The church claims that Zapatero is determined to erase Spain's past and that he is sacrificing Spanish national identity and

---

6. Luxmore, 'Bishops call for "healthy collaboration"', (2007) *The Universe*, 23 Sept, p 1.

7. Graham and Labanyi (eds), 'Catholicism and Social Change', in *Spanish Cultural Studies: An Introduction: The Struggle for Modernity* (Oxford University Press, 1995), 276–82.

8. Compare with 'The Canadian Earthquake: same sex marriage in Canada', (38)3 New England Law Review, 2004.

9. See Tremlett and Hooper, (2004) The Guardian, 26 October; McLean, 'Zapatero answers religious protest', (2005) International Herald Tribune, 13 November; Burnett, 'Zapatero hopes to ease Tensions between Government and the Catholic Church', (2008) International Herald Tribune, 13 February.

10. Burnett, 'Zapatero hopes to ease Tensions between Government and the Catholic Church', (2008) International Herald Tribune, 13 February.

demonstrating that he does not understand the distinctiveness of Spain's unique domestic and security needs.[11]

Following three years of disputes with Zapatero's socialist-led government, the head of Spain's Catholic Bishops' Conference, Bishop Ricardo Blazquez of Bilbao, has appealed for a 'healthy Church-State co-operation.' Speaking at a Madrid conference on the moral foundations of Spanish democracy, he stressed that the church is not looking for a confrontation but that it reserves the right to caution against problems so that trends which seem dangerous can be corrected.[12] Furthermore, he emphasised that the government should remember that Catholics were part of a solution to current problems and not an impediment, and that the church would continue to oppose, what he described as, the destruction of 'Spain's constitutional heritage.'[13] The Catholic Church has been in almost continuous dispute with the socialist government since it came to power in 2004, concerning, *inter alia*, certain educational reforms and family life issues. Since Franco's death in 1975, Bishop Blazquez stated that church-state relations had been grounded in 'mutual independence and healthy co-operation' and the Catholic Church had not assumed state privileges, while the state recognised the rights of personal conscience.[14] Despite the latest phase of secularism, the bishop made it clear that the church would continue to seek to foster a healthy church-state collaboration and strive to ensure Spain's democracy gains ever greater value and that social life becomes more peaceful and equitable for all.[15]

Background

[8.002] Generally speaking, amicable relationships prevail among religious bodies in Spanish society – a factor which contributes to religious freedom

11. Ho, 'Spain no More', 27(3) Harvard International Review, Fall 2005. See further Loewenberg, 'As Spaniards Loose their Religion, Church Leaders struggle to Hold On', (2005) New York Times, 26 June.
12. Luxmore, 'Bishops call for "healthy collaboration"', (2007) *The Universe*, 23 Sept, p 1.
13. Luxmore, 'Bishops call for "healthy collaboration"', (2007) *The Universe*, 23 Sept, p 1.
14. Luxmore, 'Bishops call for "healthy collaboration"', (2007) *The Universe*, 23 Sept, p 1.
15. Luxmore, 'Bishops call for "healthy collaboration"', (2007) *The Universe*, 23 Sept, p 1.

nationwide.[16] Discrimination on the grounds of religious beliefs or faith is unlawful and there is no state religion in Spain, although distinctions are made in practice between the treatment of the principal religions and other religions. Although Spain has all the social hallmarks of a secular state, religion is still perceived by a considerable percentage of the Spanish population as an important element of social life, firmly anchored within the private domain, rather than as a force under the dominion of any legal or civil institution.[17] Although the only strong religious presence in Spain is Catholicism, this needs to be viewed against the background of an increasingly secular society which asserts that standards of conduct should not be determined by any one specific religion.[18] Marriage too, it appears, has shed much of the traditional religious influence of the Catholic Church and is now effectively a civil institution that is accessible to all, regardless of gender or sexual orientation.[19] Current socialist government reforms indicate that religious instruction is to lose its position in the curriculum of state schools and that the Catholic Church will be required to become much more self-financing and independent.[20] While such reforms may be welcomed by many Spanish voters, they are anathema to religious and conservative interests and are being steadfastly opposed by them.

[8.003] The Constitution of 1978 (the Constitution) makes provision for freedom of religion and this right is usually respected by the government.[21] As the dissenting judge stated in the Constitutional Court in *Unification Church v Spain*,[22] Art 16 of the Constitution ensures the freedom of religion for both individuals and communities. However, a laic state was not

16. Luxmore, 'Bishops call for "healthy collaboration"', (2007) *The Universe*, 23 Sept, p 1.

17. Merino-Blanco, *Spanish Law and Legal System* (2nd edn, Sweet and Maxwell, 2006) vii.

18. Iban, 'State and Church in Spain' in Robbers (ed), *State and Church in the European Union* (Nomos, 2005) p 139 at 140.

19. To believing Catholics, of course, marriage remains primarily a sacrament with all that entails.

20. See Mitchell, *Betrayal of the Innocents: Desire, Power and the Catholic Church in Spain* (University of Pennsylvania Press, 1998) pp 124–125.

21. United States, Department of State, International Religious Freedom Report (2006), released by the Bureau of Democracy, Human Rights and Labor, p 1, available at http://www.state.gov/g/drl/rls/irf/2006/71409.htm.

22 *Unification Church v Spain*, judgment of 15 February 2001, citing Mr Justice Manuel Jimenez de Parga y Cabrera published in the Official Gazette, (contd .../)

established in Spain[23] within the French meaning of the term (ie a legal-political organisation devoid of any religious credo as was characteristic of the Third Republic). According to the Spanish Constitution, all beliefs, as a manifestation of the intimate conscience of the individual, are equal and have identical rights and duties.[24] While the collaboration of the state with churches and religious confessions is accepted in the Constitution,[25] a confessional state was not established by the Constitution. Paragraph 3 of Art 16 provides: 'No confession shall have a State nature'. Moreover, the freedom of religion principle is guaranteed: 'The freedom of religion is not only a fundamental right, but it must be understood as one of the constitutional principles where the religious fact is a basic component.'[26] Thus, the right to freedom of religion cannot be compared to, for instance, the right to collective bargaining inherent to trade union freedom. Although the latter is a fundamental right in the Constitution, it is not a constitutional principle such as freedom of religion, which pre-dates the Constitution of 1978.

[8.004] Furthermore, public authorities are required to take into account the religious beliefs of Spanish society.[27] In *Unification Church v Spain*,[28] the Constitutional Court, which vindicated the applicant's right to official registration in the Registration of Religious Institutions of the Ministry of Justice, emphasised that all beliefs have identical constitutional rights and duties. Yet the Organic Act on Freedom of Religion 1980 (OAFR) provides for three levels of state protection – for churches, confessions and religious communities – a distinction which sits uneasily with the constitutional guarantee of equality between the churches. The highest level of protection is afforded the Catholic Church, which is the only religion expressly mentioned in the constitutional text.[29] A second level of state protection is conferred on the confessions who have signed Agreements of Collaboration

22. (contd) also available at Centre for Studies on New Religions Library (Texts and Documents), http://file://G:\Constitutional Court-Unification Church.htm, accessed on 12 Nov 2007.

23. See Arts 16 and 14 of the Constitution.

24. Articles 16(1) and 14.

25. Articles 16(1) and 14.

26. *Unification Church v Spain*, judgment of 15 February 2001.

27. *Unification Church v Spain*, judgment of 15 February 2001, citing Art 16(3).

28. *Unification Church v Spain*, judgment of 15 February 2001.

29. Article 16(3).

with the state, including those approved by legislation in 1992: the Federation of Evangelical Religious Institutions in Spain, the Federation of Israel Communities and the Islamic Commission in Spain. In the third category, one finds the religious institutions recorded in the appropriate public register of the Ministry of Justice. In addition, public authorities also recognise and protect the freedom of religion of individuals and communities existing in Spain, although these are not recorded in the Register of the Ministry of Justice.[30]

[8.005] The Constitution formally establishes a separation of state and church and Art 14 guarantees equality and non-discrimination on the grounds of religion. However, the state has traditionally funded the Catholic Church, under Agreements (concordats) with the Holy See which have been controversial, and these have recently been the subject of a new accord.[31] As in Ireland, the contribution of the Catholic Church in Spain to education has been immense, but that contribution is not without its critics, some of whom are harsh. Writing in the early 1990s, Gonzalo Ojea Puente,[32] political scientist and intellectual, claimed that Spain's much-heralded transition to democracy in the 1970s was engineered from on high, with minimal input from the people and maximum regard for the ongoing interests of the Catholic Church who, together with the socialist leaders of the time, he alleged, sought to lobotomise the national memory in the matter of past abuses. Puente identified education as holding the key to change and he was critical of what he termed 'the Catholic straitjacket on education' in Spain and 'the traditional terrain of the national custody battle, the educational system.' Indeed, it is quite remarkable that among the eight measures Puente recommended to achieve a true separation of church and state in Spain, five related to the education system, illustrating his firm conviction that education was the pivot on which societal change turned,[33] a view which is not unique to Spain, as this book illustrates. However, secularisation in

---

30. *Unification Church v Spain*, judgment of 15 February 2001.

31. See below at **[8.005]**.

32. Gonzalo Ojea Puente's, *Ideologia e historia: La Formation del cristianismo como fenomeno ideologico* (6th edn, España Editores, SA, 1993) and *Fe cristiana, Iglesia*, poder, Madrid, trans by Timothy Mitchell, Professor of Spanish at Texas A & M University.

33. Mitchell, *Betrayal of the Innocents: Desire, Power and the Catholic Church in Spain* (University of Pennsylvania Press, 1998), citing Puente at pp 124–5.

Spain has accelerated dramatically since Puente penned those criticisms of the Catholic Church.

[8.006] Since Zapatero took office, he has adopted a distinctive model of social democracy.[34] In particular, he introduced his own educational reforms in 2005, which have been opposed by the Catholic Church, the People's Party and the Catholic Conference of Parents for a variety of reasons. Objections have been raised, for example, to the recent restrictions imposed on parental choice of schools, the introduction of a mandatory civics education programme (Education for Citizenship),[35] the lessening in academic status of voluntary religious education and the weakness of the reforms to effectually address the poor educational performance of Spanish schools. Among developed countries, Spain has not ranked as highly as one would expect in terms of the quality of its education[36] and this is an ongoing challenge.

Social Background

[8.007] Article 16(2) of the Constitution prohibits the collection of census data grounded on religious belief. It provides: 'Nobody may be compelled to make statements regarding his religion, beliefs or ideology.' For this reason, no firm statistics exist for the breakdown of the various religions in Spain. However, an autonomous state agency, the Centre for Sociological Investigation (CSI), collates statistics on societal religious trends. A CSI survey (February 2006) indicates that almost 77 per cent of citizens consider themselves Catholic, with approximately 46 per cent stating that they never attend Mass. Approximately 13 per cent of the population stated that they were agnostics, while 6 per cent considered themselves atheists. Furthermore, only 22 per cent of the voting population believe that religious instruction should be mandatory in schools.[37] Yet, despite the country's rapid move towards secularism, Roman Catholicism exerts a strong social presence, being closely intertwined with Spain's national, cultural and

34. See further Mathieson, 'Spanish Steps: Zapatero and the Second Transition in Spain', e-pamphlet, Policy Network, 26 March 2007, http:www.progressive-governance.net/publications/?d=1142.

35. See further the recent English publication, Routledge, Taylor and Francis, (11)2 Citizenship Beyond the State (2007).

36. See comparisons in OECD Report, Education at a Glance (2004), and the PISA Report (2003) and www.oecd.org/spain.

37. www.oecd.org/spain.

linguistic identity, and with its history and unity – a fact which is reflected in the distinctive treatment accorded the church, particularly in church-state revenue arrangements which are discussed later. Although the statistics vary considerably, it is estimated that approximately one million Muslims, comprising both legal and illegal immigrants,[38] live in Spain, but these figures may be much higher. Statistics estimate the Jewish population at 30,000–40,000; practising Buddhists at 9,000 persons; and evangelical Christians at approximately 400,000.[39] The influence of Catholicism in Spain's contemporary society can only be understood in the light of history. While the history of Spain as a political entity is beyond the scope of this book, because its national identity is closely linked to religious unity, some historical landmarks must necessarily be considered.

HISTORICAL OUTLINE

[8.008] By contrast with many of its European neighbours, Spain was scarcely touched by the Reformation, but it was a pivotal influence in Europe and led to the identification of the nation (and later the state), with one specific church and to the establishment of national churches and established churches.[40] Spain's close identity with Catholicism has an ancient lineage. As far back as the Third Council of Toledo (589) the official religion of Spain was proclaimed to be Catholicism. The internecine struggles which took place over the centuries on the Iberian Peninsula between Catholicism, Islam, and Judaism, have been well documented elsewhere.[41] However, Iban is of the view that while Christianity, Judaism and Islam had cohabited the Ibernian Peninsula for centuries, the most significant step towards the full unity of Spain (1492) coincided with the military defeat of Islam and the expulsion of the Jews.[42] Accordingly, national identity is based to a large degree on religious unity.[43] In a mutually,

38. The Federation of Spanish Islamic Entities (2006).

39. The Federation of Spanish Islamic Entities (2006).

40. Iban, 'State and Church in Spain' in Robbers (ed), *State and Church in the European Union* (Nomos, 2005) p 140.

41. See Pierson, *The History of Spain*; Carr, *Spain 1808–1975: A History* (Oxford University Press, 1982); Carr and Fusi, *Spain: Dictatorship to Democracy*; Esdaile, *Spain in the Liberal Age: From Constitution to Civil War, 1808–1939*.

42. Iban in Robbers (ed), *State and Church in the European Union* (Nomos, 2005) p 140.

43. Iban in Robbers (ed), *State and Church in the European Union* (Nomos, 2005) p 140.

beneficial arrangement, the Catholic monarchy succeeded in gaining considerable control over the Catholic Church within its jurisdiction, while in turn the Catholic Church achieved a degree of social control, beyond the ambit of its inherent religious jurisdiction, which enabled it to move gradually into the political sphere.[44] The operation of the Inquisition in Spain, Iban believes, is the clearest example of this.[45] For the purposes of this book, it is sufficient to note that following centuries of religious strife in which Christians strove to expel Muslims from Europe, the Inquisition aimed to continue that struggle by expelling Jews, Protestants, and other non-believers from the Iberian Peninsula. Even after the Inquisition ended,[46] religious freedom was still denied in practice in Spain. Iban observes how the Spanish monarchy used the Catholic religion as an instrument of social control, most notably in the eighteenth century, but indeed much earlier and continuing into contemporary times, with the tacit approval of Rome, and that the monarch operated strong control over the Catholic Church in its sovereign territory, without Rome's approval.[47] A public school system was established by Spain in 1857 but the educational system remained deficient, it appears.[48]

[8.009] Among the many constitutions, ranging from conservative to liberal, approved in the nineteenth century, the Constitution of Cadiz (1812) stands apart in that it provided that Catholicism was the official religion of Spain and it prohibited the practice of any other religion.[49] It was not until 1931, when the secular Constitution of the Second Republic was proclaimed, that

---

44. Iban in Robbers (ed), *State and Church in the European Union* (Nomos, 2005), p 40.

45. Coulton, *The Inquisition* (Ernest Benn, 1929); Hauben (ed), *The Spanish Inquisition*; Kamen, *The Spanish Inquisition and Society in Spain in the Sixteenth and Seventeenth Centur*ies (Indiana University Press, 1985); Langdon-Davies, *The Spanish Inquisitio*n; Lea, *A History of the Inquisition in the Middle Ages* (1988, Harbor Press, 1955); Bray (trans), Montaillou: *The Promised Land of Error* (Vintage Books, 1979); Monter, *Frontiers of Heresy: The Spanish Inquisition from the Basque Lands to Sicily* (Cambridge University Press, 2003); O'Brien, *The Inquisition*; Peters, *Inquisition*; Roth, *The Spanish Inquisition*; Wakefield, *Heresy, Crusade, and Inquisition in Southern France, 1100–1250.*

46. In 1821 in Portugal and in 1834 in Spain.

47. Iban in Robbers (ed), *State and Church in the European Union* (Nomos, 2005) pp 140–141.

48. Taus-Bolstad, *Spain in Pictures*, p 38.

49. Iban in Robbers (ed), *State and Church in the European Union*, pp 140–141.

the initial formal severing of the links binding the legal-political framework and the Catholic Church came about. Article 3 of that Constitution provided: 'the Spanish State has no official religion.' Among other changes, state funding of the Catholic Church was discontinued and religious teaching was prohibited. However, these reforms proved to be short-lived and the anti-clerical proposals, which threatened the very existence of the Catholic Church in Spain, became one of the most contentious elements in the sequence of events leading up to the bitter civil war that took place between 1936 and 1939.

The political regime that succeeded the civil war reverted to the traditional model, with close church-state ties being re-established by the Franco regime. During this period, which lasted for approximately four decades, the Catholic Church had a virtual monopoly in first- and second-level education, together with considerable political influence; furthermore, a concordat with the Holy See secured many privileges.[50] Among those privileges were an exemption from state taxation, grants for new building works, the power to censor materials the church considered offensive, the right to establish universities, the right to publish newspapers and magazines and the exemption of clergy from military service. Laws were enacted that abolished divorce and prohibited the sale of contraceptives. Catholic religious instruction became mandatory, even in public schools. As a *quid pro quo*, Franco achieved considerable social control over the Catholic Church, including the right to nominate the bishops and a veto power over appointments of clergy right down to parish priest level.[51] In 1966, however, the Franco regime passed a law that freed other religions from many of the earlier restrictions, but it also confirmed the privileges of the Catholic Church. Any attempt to revise the 1953 Concordat was met with Franco's determined resistance.[52]

The Establishment of a Democracy

[8.010] The emergence of democracy in Spain followed closely on the demise of Franco in 1975. In 1976, King Juan Carlos de Bourbon renounced the right to name bishops. Spain and the Holy See signed a new concordat in 1976 which, *inter alia*, formally returned to the church the power to name its bishops. For its part, the Catholic Church agreed to a phasing out of

---

50. Robbers (ed), *State and Church in the European Union*, pp 140–142.

51. US Library of Congress, 'Religion in Spain', available at file://E:\Enter Spain, learn more about Spain-Religion in Spain.htm.

52. US Library of Congress, 'Religion in Spain'.

financial support from the state, since this support was being strenuously contested by sections of the public. Church property that was not being utilised specifically for religious purposes would be made answerable to revenue laws and, incrementally, the church's reliance on state funding would be diminished. The timetable for this reduction was not adhered to, however, and the church continued to receive the public subsidy up to 1987.[53] By the close of 1987, state funding and education matters had not been fully resolved and the revised concordat still had not been concluded, even though the 1953 concordat had expired in 1980.[54]

When defending its position, the church reminded Spanish society that, in return for state funding, the people had benefited by receiving social, health and educational services from large numbers of dedicated religious people who discharged vital functions that the state was unable to provide, and the state subsidy continued to be discharged albeit somewhat reluctantly, it appears. In 1985 taxpayers were allowed to deduct up to 10 per cent of their taxable income for donations to the Catholic Church. However, representatives of Spain's other religious groups continued to protest against this practice, and in 1987 the tax laws were changed so that taxpayers could choose between: (a) giving 0.52 per cent of their annual income tax to the church; and (b) allocating it to the government's welfare and culture budgets. For three years, the government stated that it would continue to give the church a gradually-reduced subsidy, but after that the church would have to subsist on its own resources. The government would, in the interim, continue to fund Catholic schools and pay the teachers.[55] Government financial aid to the Catholic Church has continued to be a controversial issue up to the present time. However, a new accord has recently been agreed between Spain and the Catholic Church but the church-state controversy in this sphere of life has not abated.

The New Church-State Accord

[8.011] Until recently, the Catholic Church had two sources of public funding:

(a) an allowance paid directly by the government to the church annually; and

---

53. Amounting to US$110 million in that year alone.

54. US Library of Congress, 'Religion in Spain'.

55. US Library of Congress, 'Religion in Spain'.

(b) voluntary donations made by taxpayers to the Tax Office, which then paid it over to the church.[56]

The state has recently discontinued its direct annual allowance to the church but, by way of compensation, the individual taxpayer, if they choose to do so, may pay 0.7 per cent (formerly 0.52 per cent) of their income tax to the Catholic Church instead of to the Tax Office. The Spanish government has made it clear that it will strive to ensure that the church will become self-financing. When announcing the new accord, the socialist deputy Prime Minister at that time, Maria Teresa Fernandez de la Vega, made it clear that henceforth the church in Spain would be required to pay value added tax on the sale or purchase of goods and property, as this was required by the EU, she stated. In the discharge of accountability for public funding, she further stated that the church would be required to send an annual report to the government on how it spent the money it received from taxpayers.[57] One may conclude from these developments that the position of the Catholic Church in Spain is under serious pressure from the socialist government.

Legal Framework

[8.012] Spain has a complex constitutional history that dates back to the Constitution of 1812.[58] Modern Spain is a social and democratic constitutional state and its form of government is a parliamentary monarchy.[59] The Spanish nation comprises a coalition of several states with distinctive cultures, histories, boundaries and, in some instances, languages, and consequently integration has been, and continues to be, a prime national objective. During the Reconquest and following a struggle of approximately 800 years, Spain recovered the territories taken from it and established one nation through the fusion of the Hispano-Roman, Latin, Celtic and Gothic elements of the country.[60] In Spain, as in Ireland, the Catholic Church became identified with this protracted struggle, leading to that unique fusion

---

56. Iban in Robbers (ed), *State and Church in the European Union* (Nomos, 2005) pp 152–3.

57. 'Spain reaches new accord on financing Catholic Church', (2006) *International Herald Tribune*, 22 September.

58. Merino-Blanco, *Spanish Law and Legal System*, p 16 *ff.*

59. Article 1(3) of the Constitution of 1978. Spain has a bi-cameral Parliament. On the role of Parliament, see further Merino-Blanco, *Spanish Law and Legal System*, Ch 3, p 25.

60. Catholic Encyclopedia, available at http://catholic.org/encyclopedia/.

of Catholicism and patriotism (faith and fatherland) which is a striking characteristic of both countries. At the close of the 1960s, the Spanish education system was deemed out of date, lacking in quality and efficiency, and patently discriminatory.[61] The Education and Educational Reform Financing Act 1970 (the Act of 1970) was an attempt to ensure universal educational provision and to vindicate the right to education in the interests of a more equitable society. The Act of 1970 standardised free compulsory education up to the age of 14 years, making equality of access and equality of opportunity its upholding principles.

[8.013] In 1977, two years after Franco's death, a general election was held. The 1978 Constitution was drafted by a constitutional committee representative of the main victorious political parties. At first, the Constitution envisaged a mainly unitary state, with the exception of Catalonia, Galicia and the Spanish Basque country which became autonomous regions under Art 143 of the Constitution. Clearly, the categories under Art 143 were not closed, since Spain now comprises 17 Autonomous Communities and two enclaves, with varying degrees of autonomy. In December 1978, a Constitution was approved by referendum and it was sanctioned by the King a few weeks later. Although the Constitution does not formally declare so, Spain is now a federation in practice.[62] Among the pivotal issues determined in the Constitution were the form of government (a parliamentary monarchy) and the relationship between church and state, which proved to be quite a controversial issue. Left-wing political parties argued for the complete separation of church and state,[63] while the more conservative parties sought to retain, to some degree at least, the traditional powers of the Catholic Church. One of the main challenges facing the drafters of the Constitution was to strike a balance between these two sets of competing rights.

---

61. Casamayor, The Administration of Remedial Education in Spain, 2(2) *Journal of the European Association for Education Law and Policy* (Kluwer Law International, 1998) pp 171–183 at 181, fn 36.

62. Casamayor, The Administration of Remedial Education in Spain, 2(2) *Journal of the European Association for Education Law and Policy* (Kluwer Law International, 1998) pp 49–52, 204–6, 220.

63. As was the case in the Constitution of 1931.

THE CONSTITUTION OF 1978

[8.014] Article 16 provides for freedom of ideology, religion and worship (of individuals and communities) and for freedom of expression, subject to the maintenance of public order as protected by law.[64] Article 16 lays down the framework of the law as it relates to the system of ecclesiastical law and it provides:

1. Freedom of ideology, religion and worship of individuals and communities is guaranteed, with no other restriction on their expression than may be necessary to maintain public order as protected by law;
2. Nobody may be compelled to make statements regarding his religion, beliefs or ideology;
3. There shall be no State religion. The public powers shall take the religious beliefs of Spanish society into account and shall in consequence maintain appropriate co-operation with the Catholic Church and the other religious Communities.

[8.015] Article 14 is also relevant to church-state matters since it prohibits discrimination: 'Spaniards are equal before the law and may not in any way be discriminated against on account of birth, race, religion, opinion or any other personal or social condition or circumstance.'

[8.016] In addition, Art 27(3) guarantees parental rights in relation to religious and moral instruction and it respects international law.[65] The position conferred on international law is of great significance in that Art 10(2) enshrines it as a source of law:

> The rules relating to the fundamental rights and liberties recognised by the Constitution shall be interpreted in conformity with the Universal Declaration of Human Rights and the International Treaties and agreements thereon ratified by Spain.

At first it was not at all clear whether the Constitution would opt for a unitary state or a federal state. Finally, a unitary but decentralised model was enshrined in the Constitution, enabling the various historical territories to acquire differing levels of autonomy in accordance with a specified procedure.[66] Arguably the single most controversial church-state issue was education. As in France, the Catholic Church was reluctant to lose its

64. Article 16.
65. See Art 10(2), which buttresses the position of international law in Spain.
66. Set down in Title VIII.

ideological and economic monopoly on private education and the representative political parties safeguarded that right in Art 27 of the Constitution.[67]

[8.017] The Preamble of the Institutional Law 1/1999 of 3 October on the General Planning of the Educational System (the Act of 1999) confers on all Spaniards a right to education. It also guarantees freedom of teaching, the establishment of schools and the right to receive religious and moral instruction in accordance with personal convictions. Moreover, the Preamble recognises the right of parents, teachers and pupils to participate in the supervision and management of publicly funded schools.

[8.018] As in France, within the above constitutional and legislative framework, there is a wide network of state-subsidised private schools. With regard to education, Art 27 of the Constitution provides:

> 1 Everyone has the right to education. The freedom of teaching is hereby recognised;
>
> 2 The purpose of education is the full development of the human personality in a manner consistent with the democratic principles of coexistence and fundamental rights and freedoms;
>
> 3 The public authorities shall guarantee the right of parents to provide their children with a religious and moral education in accordance with their own convictions;
>
> ...
>
> 6 Natural and legal persons shall have the right to set up teaching institutions in a manner consistent with constitutional principles;
>
> ...
>
> 9 The public authorities shall assist teaching institutions satisfying the conditions established by law.

[8.019] The right to education is featured as a fundamental right. This means, in the Spanish context, that its development is required to be made law, to be passed with a simple majority and that such a right is amply protected: it is also possible to sue for violation of such a right and to take an action in the Constitutional Court.[68] Article 27 also makes provision for the right of

67. See further, Merino-Blanco, *Spanish Law and Legal System*, p 25.

68. Casamayor, The Administration of Remedial Education in Spain, 2(2) *Journal of the European Association for Education Law and Policy* (Kluwer Law International, 1998) p 182, fn 38, citing Embid Irujo, *El Tribunal Constitucional y la proteccion de la libertades publicas en al ambitio privado, en El Tribunal Constitucional*, p 903.

individuals and groups (and hence the Catholic Church) to create or establish educational centres. This constitutional structure has enabled the government to make arrangements whereby public financing benefits accrue to the Catholic Church which are not accorded to the other religious bodies. These arrangements became effective through the mechanism of four *Concordato* or accords signed by Spain with the Holy See in 1979, covering economic, religious education, military and judicial matters.[69] The Catholic Church has been traditionally funded by way of voluntary tax contributions and other direct annual funding from the state. However, revenue forms now allow taxpayers to pay up to 0.5 per cent of their taxes to the Catholic Church. In 2004, individual taxpayers contributed approximately €105.9 million to the Catholic Church, while, in addition, the state contributed €32.8 million. This latter sum did not take into account state funding for teachers of religion in public schools, military and hospital chaplains and other indirect benefits.[70] As has been noted, the state has recently discontinued its direct annual allowance to the church but, by way of compensation, the individual taxpayer may opt to pay 0.7 per cent of their annual income tax to the Catholic Church instead of to the tax office, a procedure which contrasts with the much more restrictive requirement in German law to pay church tax considered in **chapter 6**.

Concordats with the Holy See

[8.020] Traditionally, relations between the Catholic Church and the state in Spain have been regulated by various *Concordato* with the Holy See that date back to the eighteenth century.[71] These formal agreements were negotiated between the parties with a view to avoiding dissention between the civil and ecclesiastical powers in regard to certain church-state issues of mutual concern. The substance of these *Concordato* related to spiritual and temporal matters and they had a status akin to treaties signed in international

69. United States, Department of State, *International Religious Freedom Report* (2006) p 2.

70. United States, Department of State, *International Religious Freedom Report* (2006).

71. Fink, *De Concordatis* and Catholic Encyclopedia.

72 The main early concordats with Spain are: the Concordats of 1737 (Clement XII and Philip V), 1752 (Benedict XIV and Ferdinand VI), and 1851 (Pius IX and Isabel II). The 1851 concordat was intended to provide for the new conditions of the Catholic Church in Spain following confiscation of church property. According to this concordat, the Catholic religion is the only religion of the Spanish people. (contd .../)

law,[72] as similar agreements had in Germany. Despite the fact that significant constitutional, political and social changes have occurred in latter decades, the system has continued, although the content of recent *Concordato* differs from that of earlier models.[73] Five *Concordato* have been signed with the Holy See[74] and their international law status is apparent from parliamentary procedure and decisions of the Supreme Court and Constitutional Court in Spain.[75] One outcome of the concordat signed in 1851 (still in force in 1931) was that the Catholic religion effectively became the state religion in Spain. In addition, the state had consented to pay for the maintenance of churches and to pay the salaries of the clergy of the Catholic Church.[76] Catholicism was re-affirmed as the sole legal religion in Spain and the guiding moral force in education.[77]

[8.021] When the secular constitution of the Second Republic imposed a series of anti-clerical measures, this fostered the Catholic Church's support for the Franco uprising some years later and the advent of the Franco regime led to the restoration of the church's privileges. The 1953 *Concordato* ratified arrangements which had been in existence from 1853 and it was to replace the 1851 document that the Republic abrogated. Catholicism was again declared the official religion of Spain and other religions were not recognised by the Spanish state. Full Church recognition was accorded Franco's government which re-affirmed the confessional character of the Spanish state. The position of the Catholic Church within the Spanish system was recognised and the public practice of other religions was not permitted.[78] Furthermore, religious instruction in public schools was

72. (contd) Public instruction is under the inspection of the bishops and other diocesan prelates and state remuneration of the clergy and maintenance of church buildings is fixed. Source, Catholic Encyclopedia.

73. Iban in Robbers (ed), *State and Church in the European Union* (Nomos, 2005) p 143.

74. The four concordats signed since 1979 cover legal issues, education and culture, the armed forces and economic issues.

75. Iban in Robbers (ed), *State and Church in the European Union* (Nomos, 2005) p 143.

76. See further Mitchell, *Betrayal of the Innocents: Desire, Power and the Catholic Church in Spain* (University of Pennsylvania Press, 1998) p 73.

77. Mitchell, *Betrayal of the Innocents: Desire, Power and the Catholic Church in Spain* (University of Pennsylvania Press, 1998).

78. US Library of Congress, Country Studies, Spain, Foreign Policy under France, 1988.

mandatory. During this period, the church and its clergy received preferential treatment in regard to, *inter alia*, revenue matters, state financing and judicial immunity, together with control and censorship of the press, the theatre and books.[79] In particular, the church exerted an immense influence on education and even achieved a political decision-making role in some instances.[80] Matters began to change in the following decades, however, when society began to liberalise and matters such as divorce and abortion became more acceptable in Spanish society.

The Concordat on Education 1979

[8.022] According to the 1979 *Concordato* on Education, 'the State recognises the fundamental right to religious education and has ratified international agreements that guarantee the exercise of this right.' Meanwhile the church is required to harmonise its mission in education with the principles of civil liberty in religious affairs and with family rights, individual teacher rights and student rights, so as to avoid any discrimination or inequality. Four concordats were signed with the Holy See in 1979. One of these agreements is entitled Instrument of Ratification of the Agreement of 3rd January 1979 between the Spanish state and the Holy See, concerning Education and Cultural Affairs.[81] That document opens with both parties acknowledging the pivotal significance of educational matters. This *Concordato* recognises the fact that the church's historical, artistic and documental patrimony continue to be an extremely significant part of Spain's cultural heritage. The conserving and placement of this heritage before society for its enjoyment, the *Concordato* states, justifies church-state collaboration. It is agreed between the parties, *inter alia*, that they will respect in schools the fundamental right of parents concerning the moral and religious education of their children and that public school education will be respectful towards Christian values. With regard to educational plans at pre-school, elementary, high school and technical levels:

(a) the state is required by the agreement to include the teaching of the Catholic religion in all educational centres in conditions which are on an equal footing with other curricular subjects;

---

79. Mitchell, *Betrayal of the Innocents: Desire, Power and the Catholic Church in Spain* (University of Pennsylvania Press, 1998) p 104.

80. Mitchell, *Betrayal of the Innocents: Desire, Power and the Catholic Church in Spain* (University of Pennsylvania Press, 1998).

81. BOE N1 300, 15 December.

(b) the right to receive religious education is guaranteed but, respecting the freedom of conscience doctrine, it is not mandatory on the individual;

(c) academic authorities are required to ensure that students are not discriminated against by reason of their attending or refusing to attend religious instruction at school;

(d) teachers of religion are to be, for all purposes, part of the faculty of their respective schools;

(e) no person is to be compelled to teach religion;

(f) the diocesan Ordinary (bishop) puts forward the names of those teachers and persons considered competent to give religious instruction to the academic authority who then makes the appointment; and

(g) the state guarantees that the Catholic Church may organise voluntary teaching courses and other religious activities in public universities using the premises and resources of these institutions.[82]

Thus, despite the constitutional guarantees of non-discrimination expressed in Art 14 of the Constitution, in practice the *Concordato* govern the ecclesiastical law relationship between the state and the Catholic Church in Spain, and they have a status analogous to international law treaties, while different arrangements have been made for the other main churches.

Registration of Religious Organisations

[8.023] The Act of Religious Freedom was enacted in 1980 (the Act of 1980) with a view to declaring individual and collective religious freedom and defining the ambit and content of that right in so far as possible. A crucial objective of the Act of 1980 was to fix the status of the (non-Catholic) religious communities within the legal system. With these objectives in mind, a new mechanism was introduced into Spanish ecclesiastical law, whereby provision was made for co-operation agreements or conventions with the churches, faiths or religious communities who were registered with the state.[83] Since the legal status of the Catholic Church has already been determined by the *Concordato*, Catholic dioceses and parishes are not

82. BOE N1 300, 15 December.

83. Article 7(1) of the Act of 1980.

required to register under the Act of 1980 in order to achieve benefits under the Act. However, Catholic monasteries, religious communities, associations and foundations may volunteer to register so as to participate in the legal scheme.[84]

[8.024] Three agreements were formulated in 1992 under the statutory scheme established by the Act of 1980 with the Protestant churches, the Islamic community and the Jewish community. However, the exact status of these agreements is uncertain. The 1980 Act established a system which confers certain entitlements on religious organisations in accordance with the constitutional guarantees:[85] in practice, the Ministry of Justice maintains a Register of Religious Entities and if a religion seeking registration is refused registration, an appeal lies to the courts. The 1980 Act, through the mechanism of registration, regulates the right of association and confers legal status as authorised by law. If a religious entity is not registered, it is generally classified as a cultural association. For example, the Church of Scientology in Spain had been refused registration by the Ministry of Justice since its initial application in 1983, but it has been accorded the status of a cultural association.[86] Since the Act of 1980 places the main religions (Muslim, Jewish, Buddhist and Protestant) in a position which is of lesser status in legal terms than that accorded the catholic church under the *Concordato* (a status akin to international law having constitutional protection), this arrangement appears to discriminate under Art 14, which offers guarantees of equality and of non-discrimination between the religions. Moreover, these arrangements sit uneasily with the principles of equality and non-discrimination in EU law.[87] However, under Art 307 EC, the rights and obligations created by international treaties made by member states and a third state, before the EC Treaty became effective, are not affected by the Treaty, but nonetheless, member states are obliged to remedy any incompatibilities in these treaties. It remains to be seen how this sensitive sphere will be harmonised in the member states. Following a successful application for registration by the Unification Church, on foot of its successful challenge in the Constitutional Court, the Church of

---

84. United States, Department of State, *International Religious Freedom Report* (2006) p 3.

85. See in particular Arts 16(3) and 14(2).

86. United States, Department of State, *International Religious Freedom Report* (2006).

87. Discussed in **[3.003]** *et seq*.

Scientology again applied for registration as a religious entity in 2004. This was refused once again by the Ministry in 2005, which stated that it did not possess the authority to act contrary to the 1990 decision of the Supreme Court through an administrative action. A Notice of Appeal was filed by the Church of Scientology to this decision. However, the Ministry officials held that the 2001 decision applied only to the Unification Church, and that the Church of Scientology must pursue the case through the court system. The Spanish authorities stated that the government would not interfere in any way with the activities of the Church of Scientology. The ongoing difficulties between the Scientologists and Spain are considered by some as symbolic of a clash between the old Spain and the new democratic Spain whose Constitution of 1978 is only now vindicating its constitutional guarantees of freedom of religion, thought, conscience and expression.[88] From the human rights perspective, the epic battle against the Church of Scientology in a number of European countries is over, since the unanimous decision of a chamber of the ECtHR has held in *Church of Scientology Moscow v Russia*[89] that the refusal of the Russian Federation to re-register the Church of Scientology Moscow as a legal entity under new legislation violated Arts 9 and 11 (freedom of association and expression) of the ECHR. While this decision is binding only on Russia, it has application for all the other contracting states.

Recent Educational Reforms

[8.025] Despite the economic and social reforms of the past decades, up until recently it was generally accepted that Spain was still fragmented across cultural, social, economic and political lines and that the education system was not sufficiently assisting in resolving these difficulties. Furthermore, considerable public concern was being expressed in Spain regarding public

88. See 'Spanish Court ends 14 years of Prosecutor's Harassment of American Religious Leader', *Scientology Press Office*, referring to the dismissal of a 14-year-old case against Rev Heber C Jentzsch, president of the Church of Scientology International, by the Madrid Provincial Court in 2002. This decision followed a 7-month trial and the unconditional acquittal of 12 members of the church who had been accused of conspiring with Rev Jentsch. See further http://www.scientologytoday.org/News/2002/0240411.htm.

89. *Church of Scientology Moscow v Russia* Application no 18147/02, judgment of 5 April 2007, which held there was also a breach of Art 11 (freedom of assembly and association).

funding for the private school sector, allegedly to the detriment of the poorer members of society. Consequently, educational reforms were urgently needed to integrate these specific spheres of life and to bring participation rates in education up to the standards of other Western European countries. As late as 1965, only 38 per cent of Spain's children were enrolled in second level schools and only 29 per cent of females were enrolled in secondary grades.[90] When the socialist government came to power in 1982, it resolved to eliminate the divisions which had arisen between the private (mainly Catholic) schools and the public school sector by subsuming, in so far as possible, the private school system into Spain's national education system. With this objective in mind, three major educational reforms were implemented, largely through three separate legislative measures:

(1) Law of University Reform 1983 (*Ley de Reforma Universitaria* 1983);[91]

(2) Organic Law on the Right to Education 1985 (*Ley Organica del Derecho a la Educatión*); and

(3) Organic Law on the General Organisation of the Educational System 1990 (*Ley Organica de Ordenación General del Sistema Educativo* 1990).

[8.026] The 1985 Act made provision for three types of school:

(a) Free public schools under the Minister for Education and Science or under the Autonomous Communities. Instruction in these schools was to be ideologically neutral and it was required to safeguard diversity and comply with constitutional principles;

(b) Private schools, which could be established by any individual provided they complied with constitutional principles. These schools received no state funds and were totally dependent on private funding;

(c) Mixed schools (generally religious). These schools were state funded but democratic; both the Director and the faculty were

---

90. At approximately the same time (1967), Ireland was introducing free universal second level education, which had been brought in by England in 1944.

91. See further Rowling, 'Spanish Education reshaped by Political Changes, Economic Realities', 10(2) *World Education News Review*, Spring 1997, p 21. Mr Rowling is an Assistant Director at World Education Services.

selected by a school council comprising representatives of the school communities including parents and faculty.

The Act of 1985 (LODE) elaborated the constitutional principles relating to education by establishing the right to free compulsory education, ensuring respect for Spain's various languages and cultures, restoring the management of schools to the local communities, requiring the establishment of democratic school management boards and ensuring that private schools met certain conditions as a condition of receiving public funding.[92]

[8.027] The Act of 1990 made further provision by laying down a new structure for the organisation of the system of education in primary and secondary education in Spain and it also made provision for a new curriculum. Compulsory education was extended from eight to 10 years in duration and became compulsory for children aged six to 16. Provision was also made for the teaching of one foreign language from age eight upwards by specialist teachers. Class size has been restricted to 25 pupils and specialist teachers have been employed to teach music and physical education.[93] The above reforms in education have combined to bring about greater democracy and decentralisation in the Spanish education system and greater equity in the funding of schools. With the restoration of democracy in Spain, education has become and remains a central instrument for the restoration of social integration, economic integration, cultural integration and political integration.

[8.028] In Spain there are religious schools for Protestant, Catholic, Jewish and Muslim students and parents are free to give religious training or education in the home or in private schools. In public schools, however, religious education is not compulsory for children whose parents do not wish them to attend religious classes and such children have a right to participate in alternative activities at this time. Furthermore, Muslim students have a right to receive religious education based on Islam in public schools if their parents request that this be done. With regard to Muslim students' right to be given Islamic religious instruction in public schools, the European Commission against Racism and Intolerance (ECRI), in 2006

---

92. Rowling, 'Spanish Education reshaped by Political Changes, Economic Realities', 10(2) *World Education News Review*, Spring 1997, p 22.

93. Rowling, 'Spanish Education reshaped by Political Changes, Economic Realities', 10(2) *World Education News Review*, Spring 1997.

considers this development 'a very significant step forward in ensuring the religions have the same rights as Catholicism as regards religious instruction in schools.'[94] In its 2006 report, the ECRI encouraged Spain to ensure that this right conferred by Spanish law to Muslim pupils is implemented in practice. Moreover, the ECRI encouraged Spain in its efforts to introduce human rights as a compulsory part of primary and secondary education, with an emphasis on non-discrimination and the need to respect differences. The ECRI also noted that non-discrimination and respect for differences was not imparted in Spanish schools as a separate subject, but only as a cross-curricular subject, and it encouraged Spain to introduce a new compulsory subject on education in values and citizenship, including specific human rights education. Furthermore, it recommended that pre-service and in-service programmes in intercultural education be provided for Spanish teachers so that they would be better prepared to cope with immigration and intercultural difference.[95]

[8.029] In recent years, all the minority religious communities have petitioned the government to revise the national income tax form so as to facilitate taxpayers to designate a certain percentage of their taxes to non-Catholic religious entities.[96] In 2004, the Protestant, Muslim and Jewish communities debated issues of common interest with the Office of Religious Affairs in the Ministry of Justice, including tax benefits, the quality of religious education and the opening of new places of worship. They requested treatment on a par with that accorded the Catholic Church. In addition, the Muslim and Protestant churches have requested that the government makes state funds available for public religious education in each of their faiths.[97] By way of response, in 2004, legislation providing for public funding of teachers of Islamic, Catholic, Jewish and Evangelical/Christian studies (for classes of ten or more students) was passed. Such courses are not mandatory for any student but if a student does not choose to take a confessional (religious) course, then they must take an alternative course which includes general social, cultural and religious themes.[98]

---

94. ECRI, *Third Report on Spain*, made public on 21 February 2006.

95. ECRI, *Third Report on Spain*.

96. United States, Department of State, *International Religious Freedom Report* (2006).

97. United States, Department of State, *International Religious Freedom Report* (2006).

98. United States, Department of State, *International Religious Freedom Report* (2006).

[8.030] There are many indications that the government has, in recent years, decided to foster interfaith understanding through supporting or sponsoring programmes on interfaith dialogue, but there is clearly some way to travel before full interfaith reconciliation in Spain comes about. In 2004, the Spanish government decided to fund 20 Muslim teachers who would teach courses on Islam to public school students in four centres.[99] It was a requirement, however, that such teachers would be graduates of a Spanish university, be trained in Spanish law and be fluent in Spanish. In September 2005, a total of 37 teachers were providing Islamic instruction in various parts of Spain. By way of response to a number of anti-Semitic attacks in Spain, the Council of Ministers approved a proposal from the Justice Ministry in 2004, seeking the establishment of a 'Foundation for Pluralism and Co-existence' and the government designated 27 January as Holocaust Remembrance Day.

[8.031] It is, however, the socialist government's attempt to introduce a new secular programme entitled Education for Citizenship and Human Rights into public schools which has ignited the anger of the churches and led to a bitter church-state dispute as thousands of families have boycotted this new course.[100] The president of the Autonomous Community of Madrid, Esperanza Aguirre,[101] has labelled this programme 'indoctrination'. The programme's guidelines advise that children are to be taught to reject 'existing discrimination for reasons of sex, origin, social differences, affective-sexual, or whatever other type' and to exercise a critical evaluation of the social and sexual division of labour together with racist, xenophobic, sexist and homophobic social prejudices. In addition, these guidelines also instruct teachers to 're-visit the students' attitude to homosexuality'. It is reported that the Catholic Bishop of Toledo has denounced the programme, alleging that the government is acting unconstitutionally since it is now imposing morals. He encouraged Spaniards to resist the programme with the means available to them.[102]

---

99. United States, Department of State, *International Religious Freedom Report* (2006). These four centres were Madrid, Catalonia, Andalucia and Valencia.

100. *The Brussels Journal: The Voice of Conservatism in Europe*, in a quote for lifesite.net, 5 September 2007; see http://debainlinux.net/empire/archive/20070907.html.

101. And the first woman to have been President of the Senate and Minister for Education and Culture in Spain's democracy.

102. *The Brussels Journal: The Voice of Conservatism in Europe*.

[8.032] The legal issues at the heart of the 'Education for Citizenship and Human Rights' programme dispute have been well settled in Spain since the late 1990s, however, and were settled in the ECtHR in *Jimenez and Jimenez Merino v Spain*.[103] This case clarifies the role the state may lawfully assume when devising and implementing such a programme in state schools in Spain and in accordance with international human rights law. The applicants were both Spanish nationals. During the school year 1996–97, Pilar (aged 13–14) was in the eighth year of compulsory education in a state school in Cantabria. Her father was a teacher in the same school and he was the first applicant in the case, having been her personal tutor during that school year. In 1997, the Natural Science teacher taught classes on human sexuality as an element in the 'Vital Functions' syllabus and, as a teaching aid, she gave to her pupils a 42-page booklet published by the Department of Education of the Autonomous Government of the Canary Islands. This booklet included chapters entitled: 'Concept of sexuality', 'We are sexual beings', 'Body awareness and sexual development', 'Fertilisation, pregnancy and childbirth', 'Contraception and abortion', 'Sexually transmitted diseases and Aids', as well as comprehension questions and basic terminology. In the first applicant's opinion, the contents of the booklet went well beyond the ambit of 'Natural Sciences' and included actual guidelines on sexuality, which he considered contrary to his moral and religious convictions. Accordingly, he informed the headmaster that his daughter would not be attending the sex education classes in the light of his constitutional right to choose his daughter's moral education. The second applicant absented herself from the classes in question and failed to answer the questions when sitting her final examination in the subject, with the result that she failed the examination and was required to repeat the whole school year.

Following an unsuccessful administrative application to the Ministry of Education and Culture, the first applicant lodged a special appeal for the protection of fundamental rights to the High Court of Justice (Administrative Division) of Cantabria. Among other matters, he complained of the lack of consultation with parents concerning the content of the sex education classes; of the explicit moral component of the course; of an infringement of his right to freedom of choice of education guaranteed by Art 27(3) of the Constitution; of a breach of the principle of non-discrimination pursuant to Art 14; and of a breach of the right to freedom of religion and thought guaranteed by Art 16 of the Constitution. The High Court of Justice of Cantabria dismissed the appeal, holding that the

103. *Jimenez and Jimenez Merino v Spain* Application no 51188/99, Reports of Judgments and Decisions 2000–VI.

Ministry's decision was in conformity with the fundamental rights in the Constitution and with the case law of the Constitutional Court. In addition, the court referred to a number of international human rights provisions including Protocol 1 of the ECHR, the UNESCO Convention on Discrimination in Education 1960 and the Convention on the Rights of the Child 1989 and it held, *inter alia*:

> The right of parents to provide their children with an education in accordance with their convictions presupposes, in a pluralist society, the right to choose, that right being linked to the freedom to establish schools so that parents can choose one adapted to their belief and ideas. However, that does not presuppose, nor can it presuppose, the right to impose one's personal convictions on others or to request different treatment in accordance with such convictions.
>
> ... The enunciation of respect for personal convictions, in the form of a right to freely choose a school, derives from and is based on certain legal provisions and statements of the Constitutional Court and the Supreme Court.

[8.033] The court referred to s 4 of the Institutional Act 8/1985 of 3 July on the right to education, which provides that parents or guardians shall be entitled, in accordance with the legal provisions:

> (a) to provide their children ... with an education in conformity with the aims laid down in the Constitution and the present Act;
>
> (b) to choose a different school from those set up by the public authorities;
>
> (c) to provide their children with religious and moral education in conformity with their own convictions.

The court held that the right of parents to educate their children according to their own moral, religious and philosophical convictions is not an absolute right. Rather, that right must be determined in relation to the rights the Constitution guarantees to the other partners in the educational community. Furthermore, the court continued, parents such as the applicant have the right to choose a specific type of education provided in private schools, which can offer a special curriculum, unlike the position in state schools in a pluralist society.

[8.034] The first applicant lodged an *amparo* (appeal) to the Constitutional Court, relying on Art 27(3) (right of parents to choose their child's religious and moral education), Art 14 (principle of non-discrimination) and Art 24 (right to a fair trial) of the Constitution, but the Constitutional Court declared the appeal inadmissible and manifestly unfounded on the following grounds:

> Article 27 of the Spanish Constitution recognises rights in favour of all those who participate in the education system, which presupposes that, in the event of dispute, a balance has to be struck between the different interests in issue. In the instant case the trial court adequately weighed the various conflicting interests while stressing that state education was involved. In the context of that type of education, ideological neutrality has to be preserved, as the court affirmed .... In the instant case, neutrality was preserved, with the result that the trial court's decision was neither arbitrary or absurd and thus cannot be reviewed in *amparo* proceedings ... Nor has there been an infringement of the principle of equality laid down in Article 14 since no relevant term of comparison has been submitted in support of the appeal.

The applicants appealed to the ECtHR, complaining that the administrative and judicial decisions dismissing their appeals against the school's decision to fail the second applicant in the Natural Sciences examinations because of her refusal to attend the sex education class, breached Art 2 of Protocol 1 of the ECHR. Furthermore, the applicants also complained that, despite having passed all her mid-term examinations, the second applicant was required to sit an end-of-term examination in Natural Sciences, while no other pupil in her class was obliged to sit it and that his was an infringement of the principle of non-discrimination guaranteed by Art 14 of the Convention. Finally, the applicants submitted that they had not been afforded a fair hearing by the domestic courts.

[8.035] The ECtHR reiterated the principles of international human rights law, as established, *inter alia*, in *Kjelsden v Denmark*,[104] that the second sentence in Art 2 is binding on the contracting states in the exercise of every function they undertake in relation to education and teaching, including the organisation and financing of public education, and that the second sentence of Art 2 must be read harmoniously with the first, which enshrines everyone's right to education. Furthermore, the court stressed that the second sentence of Art 2 essentially aims to safeguard the possibility of pluralism in education, which is necessary for the preservation of the 'democratic society' envisaged by the Convention. In view of the power of the modern state, the court continued, it is above all through state teaching that this aim must be realised. The court re-stated that the setting and planning of the curriculum fall in principle within the competence of the contracting states, which mainly involves questions of expediency that it is

104. *Kjelsden, Busk Madsen and Pedersen v Denmark* (1976) 1 EHRR 711 at 712.

not for the ECtHR to rule on and whose solution may lawfully vary from country to country and according to the era. Once again, the court confirmed that the second sentence of Art 2 does not prevent the state from imparting through teaching or education information or knowledge of a directly or indirectly religious or philosophical kind. Nonetheless, in discharging the functions assumed by it in regard to education and teaching, the state must take care to ensure that information or knowledge included in the curriculum is conveyed to students in an objective, critical and pluralist manner, but it is forbidden to pursue an aim of indoctrination that might be considered as not respecting parents' religious and philosophical convictions, that is the limit that must not be exceeded.[105]

[8.036] In *Jimenez*, the ECtHR stated that the sex education class was drawn up to provide students with objective and scientific information on the sex life of humans, venereal diseases and Aids. Thus, the booklet sought to alert the pupils to unwanted pregnancies, the risk of pregnancy at an increasingly young age, methods of contraception and sexually transmitted diseases. Hence, the court considered that it was information of a general character which did not in any manner constitute an attempt at indoctrination aimed at advocating particular sexual behaviour. Neither did that information work against parents' entitlement to enlighten and advise their children, to exercise natural parental functions as educators or to guide their children on a path in line with their own religious and philosophical convictions.[106] The court noted that the Spanish Constitution guarantees to all natural and legal persons the entitlement to establish schools in accordance with constitutional principles and the universal right to receive a religious and moral education in accordance with their own convictions. However, the court observed that, in accordance with constitutional provisions, in Spain there was 'a wide network of private schools which coexist with the State-run system of public education', and that parents are free to enrol their children in private schools, providing an education better suited to their faith or opinions. Furthermore, it noted that the applicants did not indicate any obstacle which would prevent the second applicant from attending such a private school. Since the applicants had chosen a state school, however, the right to have their beliefs and ideas, as guaranteed by Art 2 of Protocol 1, respected by the state, could not be interpreted as conferring on them 'the

105. *Jimenez and Jimenez Merino v Spain*, Application no 51188/99, Reports of Judgments and Decisions 2000–VI, pp 26–27, para 53.

106. *Jimenez and Jimenez Merino v Spain*, Application no 51188/99, Reports of Judgments and Decisions 2000–VI, pp 27–28, para 54.

right to demand different treatment in the education of their daughter in accordance with their own convictions'. In the light of the above findings, the court considered that part of the application as manifestly ill-founded under Art 35, para 3 of the ECHR. The court also found that the fact that the second applicant was required to sit an examination in a curricular subject (Natural Sciences), because of her deliberate absence from a component of the course, did not *per se* constitute discrimination under Art 14 of the ECHR, and that it too was manifestly ill-founded under Art 35, para 3 of the ECHR. In addition, the applicants relied on Art 6, para 1 (a fair hearing). The court stated that it is not its function to deal with errors of fact or of law made by a national court unless and in so far as they may have infringed on rights and freedoms protected by the ECHR. Moreover, it declared that the issue of admissibility of evidence and of its probative weight is primarily a matter for regulation under national law.[107] In that regard, the court observed that the applicants' case had been considered by a number of domestic courts which had deliberated upon the complaints and the germane grounds of defence in adversarial proceedings. Accordingly, the applicants' complaint under Art 6(1) was also rejected as being manifestly ill-founded.

[8.037] Having exhausted all available remedies, the applicant was left with the option of attending the state school and accepting its secular programme for his daughter or of transferring her to a private school, provided he could afford it. This decision is a striking example of the 'tyranny of the majority', of which de Tocqueville warned, since it avoids any attempt at reasonable accommodation of the minority right in the public school. Not only does it fail to balance equitably the two competing rights, but it substitutes a right for the minority that is totally inadequate, since only the prosperous classes can vindicate this right on behalf of their children. Arguably, this introduces a new form of inequality into the equation since the decision disregards the religious and philosophical convictions of the minority to religious instruction in the public school, who have no option but to choose between the public school's secular programme for their children or private education. In the opinion of this author, this decision downgrades the principle of religious freedom by fettering its manifestation and expression, since it presses those children whose parents wish to avail of public education, while still having their religious and philosophical beliefs respected there, into the private schools. Although the ECtHR has

---

107. See *K v Sweden, Application no 13800/88*, Commission Decision of 1 July 1991, Decisions and Reports 71, p 94.

consistently declared that pluralism is 'indissociable from a democratic society',[108] it fails to accommodate that principle in the public school, but relies on the secular principle which is inimical to religion *per se* and to religious freedom.

CONCLUSION

[8.038] Spain's transformation from a highly conservative country into one of the most liberal countries in Europe has taken place over a 30-year period of profound economic, political and social change. Internal tensions are apparent between its current socialist government and the Catholic Church as the latter strives to hold its special place in Spanish society. As a result, the status of the Catholic Church in particular, is now under severe threat, although that Church is still closely bound up with nationality, culture, history and unity, as is also the case in Ireland. In both countries, the church is under pressure from growing materialism, from the inexorable advance of democracy, from the processes of harmonisation in Europe and from international human rights law. Although the Spanish Constitution guarantees that all Spaniards are equal, that there will be no discrimination, *inter alia*, on religious grounds, and that there is no official religion, the Catholic Church retains a number of advantages which indicate that, in practice, it is still *primus inter pares*. It is, for example, the only religion mentioned in the Constitution, which also makes special provision for concordats between the Catholic Church and the Holy See which have been accorded the status of international law. Furthermore, as outlined in this chapter, the Catholic Church has a privileged position in revenue law and, unlike other religions, it is not required to register with the Ministry of Justice under the 1980 Act. Since these special arrangements for the Catholic Church are not in harmony with Spain's constitutional guarantees of equality and non-discrimination in Arts 14 and 16, they are likely to be targeted by the EU's Framework Directive (Council Directive 2000/78/EC) in the future.

President Zapatero and his party (the Spanish Socialist Worker's Party) have devised a distinctive model of social democracy which is determined to effect change, not least regarding the special position of the Catholic

108. *Metropolitan Church of Bessarabia v Moldova*, Application no. 45701/99, para 114, ECHR 2001–XII. In the context of freedom of association, the restriction of which necessitates justifications akin to Art 9, the ECHR stated, 'The autonomy of religious communities is in fact indispensable to pluralism in a democratic society.' See also *Kokkinakis v Greece* (1994) 17 EHRR 397, 418.

Church. While the government's plans for social reforms are popular among the young, the churches are, generally speaking, staunchly opposed to these reforms. In particular, the educational reforms of 2005 have met with strenuous opposition, especially those relating to parental choice of school, the mandatory 'civics education' programme in state schools and the lessening of the focus on religious instruction in schools. As in Germany, if a student refuses to take the religious instruction option in school, they must take an alternative general course that includes general, social and religious themes (civics education). It is with the content of this latter course that parents are mainly concerned since they consider that it invades that sacrosanct sphere which has been traditionally within the exclusive remit of parents. However, that battle has already been lost in the national courts and in the ECtHR. Nonetheless, many Spanish parents are unhappy, since they fear that a state ideology is being imposed on their children in public schools – an ideology to which they are staunchly opposed. If such parents wish to avoid having their children 'indoctrinated' by the state in this manner, then the only choice left to them is to opt for private education. Yet, as in Germany, England and Ireland, there are concerns in Spanish society that the substantial public funding of the private sector schools is working to the detriment of poorer members of society. In such circumstances, it would appear more expressive of religious and educational freedoms to ensure that students of all religions and none be reasonably accommodated in the public school sector.

With regard to the accommodation of the Islamic faith, its adherents have a right to receive religious education grounded in that faith if parents request it and Spain is to the fore in this regard. This is a very significant step forward since it places the Islamic faith on the same level as religious instruction for the Catholic Church, thus respecting religious freedom. Furthermore, a number of hopeful initiatives have been instigated in Spain, which indicates that the government is now determined to secure more equitable treatment for the Muslim community. There are many indications that the government has, in recent years, decided to promote interfaith understanding through supporting or sponsoring programmes on interfaith dialogue, but there is clearly some way to travel before full interfaith reconciliation in Spain comes about.

Chapter 9

RELIGION, EDUCATION AND THE LAW IN IRELAND

Being a democrat means, primarily, not to be afraid ....[1]

INTRODUCTION

[9.001] Although the Constitution of Ireland 1937 reflects a firm conviction that the Irish are a religious people,[2] this now needs to be considered in the context of recent unprecedented social, cultural and economic changes in Ireland which indicate a nation in a state of flux.[3] As one writer observes, the Irish have become the same as their Western counterparts in their immersion in the material world, their pursuit of pleasure, search for excitement, fulfilment of desire, obsession with consuming and obsession with self.[4] Such changes have combined to fragment the relative homogeneity of Ireland's religious affiliation. Another commentator claims that Ireland has made the transition to the first phase of secularism following 'the painful experience of church domination from the 1920s to the 1960s',[5] and he further contends that the transition to the second phase of secularism[6] is well under way as church-state relations face changing times.[7] Although

1. István Bibó, Hungarian historian and political scientist. See Nagy (ed), Boros-Kazai (trans), *Democracy, Revolution, Self Determination* (Columbia University Press, 1991); also Bibo, *On European Balance and Peace*.
2. *Quinn's Supermarket v Attorney General* [1972] IR 1, *per* Walsh J and *McGrath and O'Ruairc v Trustees of Maynooth College* [1979] ILRM 166.
3. See further Cruise O'Brien, *Ancestral Voices, Religion and Nationalism in Ireland* (University of Chicago Press, 1995).
4. Inglis, *Global Ireland: Same Difference* (Routledge, 2007) pp 189–190. Inglis further states: 'They [the Irish] have moved from being quiet poor Catholic Church mice embodying a discourse and practice of piety and humility, to becoming busy, productive, self-indulgent rats searching for the next stimulation.'
5. Gillespie, 'Church-State relations face changing times', (2008) *Irish Times*, 29 March, p 13.
6. On the issue of secularism in Ireland, see Girvin, 'Church, State and the Irish Constitution: The Secularisation of Irish Politics', 49(4), *Parliamentary Affairs*, 1996, pp 599–615, p 614.

religion is not marginalised in the public sphere, Ireland has become much more pluralist and open to foreign influences than formerly, as Irish Catholics no longer accept unquestioningly the teachings of their church.[8] Reflecting the changes in the wider society, the church-state relationship too is in transition, particularly in education where considerable powers, formerly vested in the churches, are moving inexorably towards the state. As the forces of democracy permeate this sphere of Irish life, more than a century later than the European norm, certain church-state tensions are now becoming apparent in educational matters.[9] Ireland's education system is also being affected, *inter alia*, by globalisation, by the influence of ideas from Europe, by the harmonisation of laws in the EU and by the impact of international human rights law.

CHURCH-STATE RELATIONS

[9.002] The economic prosperity and social cohesion Ireland experienced between 1993 and 2007 is frequently attributed to the quality of education delivered in its predominantly denominational school system.[10] As Kiernan points out, however, it is possible to interpret the influential and long-established tradition of Catholic involvement in education in radically different ways.[11] The Report of the Constitutional Review Group (1996) concluded that: 'The State and its citizens clearly owe a huge debt of

7. Girvin, 'Church, State and the Irish Constitution: The Secularisation of Irish Politics', 49(4), *Parliamentary Affairs*, 1996.

8. Penet, 'From Modernity to Ultramodernity: The Changing Influence of Catholic Practice on Political Practice in Ireland', in Littleton and Maher (eds), *Contemporary Catholicism: a Critical Appraisal* (Columba Press, 2008) pp 69–87, 85.

9. See McGee and McGarry, 'Department of Education says it will consider Bishop's Criticism', (2008) *Irish Times,* 14 August, p 1. In an outspoken defence of the Catholic Church's role in education, Bishop Leo O'Reilly, Chairman of the Irish Bishops' Conference on Education, stated that 'there seemed to be a policy assumption in the Department of Education that every new school at second level should be multi-denominational. We don't accept that that should be the case'.

10. Fuller, Irish Catholicism since 1950, generally and in particular **chapter 11**.

11. Kiernan, 'Embracing Change: The remodelling of Irish Catholic primary schools in twentyfirst century', in Littleton and Maher (eds), *Contemporary Catholicism: a Critical Appraisal* (Columba Press, 2008) pp 43–68 at 44.

gratitude for the tireless and selfless work of the religious institutions who provided such education and healthcare.'[12] However, a number of studies have been critical of the character of the relationship which was forged between church and state on education policy in post-independent Ireland. [13] While recognising the immense contribution made by religious men and women in expertise, time and resources, these authors perceive the climate which existed to have had many stultifying, narrow influences. Although the principle of the separation of church and state had been accepted in Irish law since the disestablishment of the Church of Ireland in 1871, education remained an exception to the general rule.[14] In his seminal work *Church and State in Modern Ireland, 1923–70*, John H Whyte notes the closeness of church-state relations in education and the deference paid to the church's role in educational policy and practice in the past:

> Over most of the period since independence, the remarkable feature of educational policy in Ireland has been the reluctance of the state to touch on the entrenched positions of the church. This is not because the church's claims have been moderate; on the contrary, it has carved out for itself a more extensive control over education in Ireland than in any other country in the world. It is because the church has insisted on its claims with such force that the state has been extremely cautious in entering its domain.[15]

O'Buachalla believes that during the first six decades of independence (1922–1982), defence and consolidation were frequently the objectives of policy and that the structural *status quo* and the dominant role of the church in education were to be defended: 'The position was to be consolidated by the removal of surviving structural features which were not favoured and the

12. Government Publications, p 377.
13. Akenson, *A Mirror to Kathleen's Face: Education in Independent Ireland 1922–60* (McGill-Queens, 1975); Titley, *Church-State and the Control of Schooling in Ireland* (McGill-Queens, 1983); O'Donoghue, *The Catholic Church and the Secondary School Curriculum in Ireland 1922–62* (1999); O'Buachalla, *Education Policy in Twentieth Century Ireland*; Coolahan, 'Church-State relations in Primary and Secondary Education' in Mackey and McDonagh (eds), *Religion and Politics in Ireland at the Turn of the Millennium* (Columba Press, 2003) pp 132–151.
14. Casey, 'State and Church in Ireland', in Robbers (ed), *State and Church in the European Union* (Nomos, 2005) pp 18–208 at 191.
15. Whyte, *Church and State in Modern Ireland, 1923–70* (Gill & Macmillan, 1971). Note the second edition goes up to 1979, p 21.

assimilation into favoured structures of any new institutions established.'[16] Nonetheless, it has to be acknowledged that members of religious orders and priests have provided the main support for Catholic education in Ireland during the past two centuries[17] and they provided a cost-effective system of education when the state could not find the resources to do so. Nevertheless Littleton and Maher conclude: 'There can be no denying that in the past the Catholic Church in Ireland exerted an undue influence on the affairs of state.'[18] However, the main threat the Church now faces is the ongoing decline in religious vocations[19] and the advance of what has been described as 'an aggressive form of secularism that is intolerant of opinions that do not coincide with the widely embraced "liberal agenda".'[20]

[9.003] In multiracial and multicultural Ireland, it is now generally accepted that there is an urgent need for reasonable and practical interfaith relations grounded in dialogue and in the shared features of each faith[21] and for ongoing church-state dialogue. Former Taoiseach Bertie Ahern was one of the first European heads of government to establish an official forum with the churches and faith communities, including those of the humanist tradition.[22] These formal church-state meetings have laid the foundations for cordial negotiations in this important sphere,[23] but Ahern has observed the

16. O'Buachalla, *Education Policy in Twentieth Century Ireland* (Merlin Publishing, 1988) p 221.
17. Fuller, Irish Catholicism since 1950: The Undoing of a Culture, p 259 and generally.
18. Littleton and Maher, (eds), Preface to Contemporary Catholicism in Ireland: A Critical Appraisal, p 8.
19. *Vocations in Ireland,* 1989, Council for Research & Development, Maynooth, 1989. See *Trends in Irish Church Personnel*, 1990–1994, Council for Research & Development, Maynooth 1995: and further Flannery, *The Death of Religious Life* (Columba Press, 1997).
20. Littleton and Maher (eds), *Contemporary Catholicism: a Critical Appraisal* (Columba Press, 2008) Preface, p 7.
21. Selim, 'Urgent need for interfaith dialogue based on mutual trust', (2008) *Irish Times,* 22 April. Ali Selim is a Muslim theologian and secretary to Imam Halawa of the Islamic Cultural Centre, Clonskeagh, Dublin.
22. McGarry, 'Ahern "upset" by hesitation to publicly debate faith', (2008) *Irish Times*, 23 April.
23. Cooney, '"Blessed Bertie" hailed for putting religion on agenda', (2008) *Irish Independent,* 23 April.

reluctance of the Irish people to debate publicly matters of faith.[24] A church-state forum took place in June 2008, which assembled all the patrons of recognised schools nationwide[25] with a view to formulating a consensus on a way forward for the management of schools in a multicultural and increasingly secular society.[26] This forum considered the challenges that a changing society presents to both existing and newly recognised schools: the position of religious education in schools in a diverse society; the need to ensure that all schools are inclusive; and the development of 'admissions and participation policies' that are accessible to all children.[27] While some expect a reduction in the influence of the Catholic Church in primary education in the future,[28] it is clear from the pastoral letter (Vision 08)[29] that the church is not moving out of education, but is rather redefining its vision and philosophy of education for the future.[30]

[9.004] One insidious aspect of modern Irish society which has militated against church interests is the loss of respect for authority in many forms, including the moral authority of the Catholic Church: a loss contributed to by the Church's handling of the scandal of child sex abuse.[31] As a consequence of these and other factors, the unique church-state relationship which has upheld Irish education for centuries is under pressure both internally and externally. Indeed, there seems little doubt that Matthew Arnold's famous lines, penned with regard to Victorian England, apply equally to contemporary Ireland; that 'the Sea of Faith' which was once 'at the full' is retreating.[32] Yet, by contrast with other traditionally Catholic European countries, where a large percentage of the population is nominally

---

24. Deere, 'Ahern upset as debates fail faithful.' (2008) *The Universe,* 4 May, former Taoiseach, Bertie Ahern speaking at an official reception for faith communities.
25. Recognised by the Minister for Education under s 10 of the Education Act 1998 which gives access to state funding under s 12 of that Act.
26. Flynn, Education Editor, (2008) *Irish Times,* 25 March.
27. Flynn, Education Editor, (2008) *Irish Times,* 25 March.
28. Flynn, Education Editor, (2008) *Irish Times,* 25 March.
29. Published on 12 May 2008, accessed online on 24 May 2008 at http://www.catholiccommunications.ie/vision08/vision08-pressrelease.htm.
30. http://www.catholiccommunications.ie/vision08/vision08-pressrelease.htm.
31. See 'Church and moral chaos', Editorial, (2006) *Irish Independent*, 8 December.
32. Matthew Arnold's delightful poem is available online at http://www.island-of-freedom.com/oldiof/ARNOLD.HTM; see further Claffey, 'Ignoring voice of faith harms national debate', (2007) *Irish Times,* 4 September.

Catholic, it is estimated that in Ireland 45 per cent of the population attends a Sunday service and over 80 per cent still pray.[33] Surveys from the 1990s onwards, however, have indicated a decline in religious practice particularly among the young.[34]

Respecting Diversity: Headscarves and Turbans

[9.005] Many believe that the 2006 census, which recorded 32,500 members of the Islamic faith in the Republic, underestimates the true figure.[35] Assuming the 2006 census figures are accurate, these figures indicate a 70.2 per cent increase on the 19,100 total for Muslims given in the 2002 census. Ireland's, predominantly Sunni, Muslim community comprises mainly professional or business people and they appear to have integrated well despite their relatively recent arrival in Ireland.[36] Muslim children generally attend Ireland's mainly denominational schools, while two separate Muslim schools have been established in Dublin and others are planned.

With regard to the wearing of the Islamic headscarf in schools, the Minister for Integration Policy (Mr Connor Lenihan TD), having consulted with school principals nationwide, stated recently that the government saw no reason currently for 'regulatory zeal' and that the overwhelming evidence is that the wearing of the hijab is not an issue in schools.'[37] However, Mr Lenihan and the Minister for Education and Science (Mr Batt O'Keefe

33. Figures taken from a poll in (2008) *Irish Examiner*, 20 March. 41% disagreed with the Catholic Church's opposition to abortion, 50% disagreed with the Church on same-sex unions (31% agreed), 57% disagreed with the church on divorce, while two-thirds rejected its views on contraception.

34. Fuller, *Irish Catholicism since 1950: The Undoing of a Culture*, p xiii. See also INTO, *Teaching Religion in the Primary School: Issues and Challenges*, Ch 8, p 133, which notes a perceived decline in religious practice in primary schools; *NCB Stockbrokers, 2020 Vision: Ireland's Demographic Dividend* (2006) p 13 and generally chapter 5.

35. The chairperson of the Irish Council of Imams and the Imam of the Islamic Cultural Centre in Clonskeagh, Imam Husein Halawa, indicates that the true figure is in or about 45,000 comprising approximately 50 nationalities; McGarry, 'Muslims have integrated well despite recent arrival', (2008) *Irish Times*, 14 May, citing the Imam.

36. 'Muslims have integrated well despite recent arrival', (2008) *Irish Times*, 14 May.

37. Speaking at the Parnell Summer School in Avondale, Co Wicklow, in Summer 2008 McGarry, 'No directive for schools on use of Islamic scarf.'

TD), following consultation with the key stakeholders in education,[38] have now agreed general recommendations on school uniform policy which will shortly be formally conveyed to schools.[39] The recommendations were formulated on the basis of feedback from all relevant stakeholders in education and they are as follows:

1. The current system, whereby schools decide their uniform policy at a local level is reasonable, works and should be maintained;
2. In this context, no school uniform policy should act in such a way that it, in effect, excludes students of a particular religious background from seeking enrolment or continuing their enrolment in a school. However, this statement does not recommend the wearing of clothing in the classroom which obscures a facial view and creates an artificial barrier between pupil and teacher. Such clothing hinders proper communication;
3. Schools, when drawing up uniform policy, should consult widely in the school community;
4. Schools should take note of the obligations placed on them by the Equal Status Acts before setting down a school uniform policy. They should also be mindful of the Education Act, 1998. As previously mentioned, this obliges boards of management to take account of 'the principles and requirements of a democratic society and have respect and promote respect for the diversity of values, beliefs, traditions, languages and ways of life in society.[40]

Minister O'Keefe stated:

> 'While 92 per cent of schools in the country are under the patronage of one religion, it is clear that this fact has not operated to exclude pupils of different religions from these schools or from schools operating under other patronage arrangements. It seems clear that, where schools have permitted the wearing of the hijab in a colour similar to the school uniform, no problems have been

38. Including management bodies, parent associations, teacher bodies etc.

39. See 'Ministers agree recommendations on school uniform policy' at http://www.education.ie/robots/view.jsp?pcategory=10861&language=ENG&ecategory=10876&link=link001&doc=42160.

40. http://www.education.ie/robots/view.jsp?pcategory=10861&language=ENG&ecategory=10876&link=link001&doc=42160 and further UN Convention on the Rights of the Child, Art 29(c) and Art 18(4) of the ICCPR, the latter being non-derogable.

encountered. The important consideration here is that all parties involved are clearly aware of the position.'[41]

However, this issue is wider than domestic law. Under international human rights law, states may set limitations to the right to manifest a belief or faith on certain specified grounds and they must show that any such limitations were 'prescribed by law' and necessary to protect public safety, order, health, or morals or the fundamental rights and freedoms of others.[42]

The UNHCR have clarified that the right to manifest religion includes the 'wearing of distinctive clothing or head coverings', but that states may limit this right solely in the interests of morality health, public safety and public order and the fundamental rights and freedoms of others, provided it is 'prescribed by law'. If Ireland is to comply with its international human rights obligations, then its recommendations on the wearing of the hijab in recognised schools must be statutory, or derive from statute. Furthermore, the information conveyed must be accessible, foreseeable, precisely formulated and it must afford a measure of legal protection against arbitrary interference by public authorities and school authorities with the rights protected by the ECHR.[43]

In addition, any such law is required to indicate with sufficient clarity the scope of any discretion conferred on the competent authorities (school authorities and public authorities) and the manner of its exercise.[44] Furthermore, in the opinion of this writer, it would be imprudent to introduce any requirement relating to colour in regard to the wearing of any 'conspicuous religious clothing' in recognised schools in Ireland as this sphere is already sufficiently complex.

[9.006] At secondary level, the dominance of voluntary or confessional schools is an unusual and historical feature.[45] The majority of these schools are Catholic and they were established in the eighteenth century with the

---

41. http://www.education.ie/robots/view.jsp?pcategory=10861&language=ENG&ecategory=10876&link=link001&doc=42160.

42. ICCPR, Art 18.3 and ECHR Art 9.2.

43. *Metropolitan Church of Bessarabia v Moldova* (2002) 35 EHRR, 13, 333.

44. *Metropolitan Church of Bessarabia v Moldova* (2002) 35 EHRR, 13, 333.

45. *International Review of Curriculum and Assessment Frameworks: Ireland*: Organisation/control of education system, available online at http://www.inca.org.uk/ireland-organisation-mainstream.html: (Eurydice, 1999), European Unit Summary Sheets on Education Systems in Europe, available online at http://eurdice.org.

objective of providing Catholic children with a Catholic education. The schools' trustees (the legal representatives of the owners) undertake to ensure that the school will be administered in accordance with Catholic ideals and the school's foundational philosophy. Voluntary secondary schools (approximately 57 per cent of all schools),[46] respect the diversity of cultures and traditions and the only issue with the Islamic headscarf appears to be 'in relation to colour to complement uniform colour.'[47]

[9.007] Despite the diversity of their geographical and ethnic origins, the Muslim community in Ireland do not appear to have experienced the same difficulties relating to integration as their co-religionists in some other Western European countries. Rather, they have achieved, over five decades or so, a considerable degree of integration, religious freedom and representation in practice. Representation has been achieved, for example, on the Three Faiths Forum, which considers common matters relevant to Judaism, Christianity and Islam; on The Structured Dialogue which discussed spheres of mutual interest between the various religions and the state; and on the Irish Council of Imams, which was established in 2006 to discuss matters germane to the Muslim community in Ireland.[48] One likely reason for what appears to be the greater accommodation of the Muslim community in Ireland arises from the fact that the Constitution includes a number of protective provisions relating to religious denominations and denominational education, which are discussed later.

[9.008] Fully-private schools, which are provided and controlled by non-government bodies, do not receive any public funding and this sector is not highly developed in Ireland. In 2001–2002, only about 2 per cent of all students attended private schools, with 98 per cent attending publicly-funded regulated schools.[49]

---

46. Lodge and Lynch, *Diversity at Schoo*l, p 47 available at www.equality.ie/index.asp?docid=255.

47. Lodge and Lynch, *Diversity at Schoo*l, p 47 available at www.equality.ie/index.asp?docid=255, quoting Ferdia Kelly, Secretary of the Joint Managerial body for Secondary Schools (JMB).

48. Lodge and Lynch, *Diversity at Schoo*l, p 47 available at www.equality.ie/index.asp?docid=255.

49. (Eurydice, 1999), European Unit Summary Sheets on Education Systems in Europe, available online at http://eurdice.org.

Definition of Terms

[9.009] In this chapter, the term 'religious denomination' will mean the various churches, religious societies or religious congregations,[50] while the term 'primary schools' will mean first-level schools, which are also frequently referred to as 'national schools', despite the fact that they are neither owned by the state nor established by the state, but are regulated, funded and supervised by the state. The terms 'secondary schools' or 'voluntary secondary schools' will mean second-level schools owned and managed by the religious denominations or the diocese and recognised by the Minister for Education and Science and regulated under Irish legislation. 'Religious instruction' will mean instruction in the doctrine and worship of one religion or religious denomination, while 'religious education' will mean a secular subject which is part of the state curriculum, which may now be taken voluntarily by students in the state examinations (Junior and Leaving Certificates).

LEGAL AND CONSTITUTIONAL STRUCTURES

[9.010] Ireland is a country with a common law tradition. However, it has a written Constitution which includes judicial review of legislation and in this respect it resembles Spain, Germany, Italy and Portugal, but, unlike these countries, it has no specialised constitutional court.[51] Rather, judicial review is within the High Court's jurisdiction and, on appeal from the High Court, to the Supreme Court. Since the disestablishment of the Church of Ireland in 1871, Irish law has accepted the principle of the separation of church and state with the exception of education in which church and state have co-operated closely and continue to do so, although the balance of control in education has moved towards the state in recent decades[52] largely as a consequence of a body of legislation. One unique feature of Ireland's system of education is that it evolved without a supporting framework of substantive legislation until 1998.[53] This feature contrasts with the European norm in which legislation has played a central role for more than a century. However,

50. *Employment Equality Bill 1996* [1997] 2 IR 321 at 354, SC, per Hamilton CJ.

51. Casey, 'State and Church in Ireland' in Robbers (ed), *State and Church in the European Union* (Nomos, 2005) pp 18–208 at 187.

52. Casey, 'State and Church in Ireland' in Robbers (ed), *State and Church in the European Union* (Nomos, 2005) pp 18–208 at 187.

53. When the Education Act 1998 was enacted.

despite the theistic natural law origins of its Constitution,[54] the liberalisation of Irish society is reflected in a number of its Supreme Court decisions from the 1970s onwards.[55]

[9.011] Article 5 of the Constitution of Ireland 1937[56] (the Constitution) provides: 'Ireland is a sovereign, independent, democratic state', which is both a statement of political belief and of law.[57] Although the Constitution included two interlinked Arts, Art 42 (Education) and Art 44 (Religion), constitutional litigants were few in the past and, despite the fact that Art 44.4 envisaged that legislation would be passed for educational provision, the informal character of education was permitted to continue until 1998.[58]

[9.012] Following the advent of free second-level education in 1967,[59] parents became gradually more assertive of their lawful position in education[60] and by 1998 a consensus had emerged which enabled the enactment of substantive educational legislation, the Education Act 1998

54. The Constitution of Ireland 1937 (Bunreacht na h-Éireann), Preamble and Article 6.1 of the Constitution of 1937, which provides: 'All powers of government, legislative, executive and judicial, derive under God from the people ...'.

55. See *McGee v Attorney General* [1974] IR 284 and in particular *Re Article 26 of the Constitution and in the Matter of the Reference to the Court of the Regulation of Information (Services outside the State for Termination of Pregnancies) Bill 1995* [1995] 2 ILRM 81, which indicates a serious shift in direction for the Irish courts in recent decades, a case which some suggest indicates the death of natural law. See further Whyte, 'Natural Law and the Constitution' (1996) *ILTR* 14 ILT (ns) 8 and Twomey, 'The Death of the Natural Law', (1995) *ILT* (ns) 270. Others, however, believe that natural law it is so embedded in Irish jurisprudence that it would take 'a shift of massive proportions to dislodge it', de Blacam, 'Justice and Natural Law' (1997) Irish Jurist Vol 32,335.

56. Bunreacht na h-Éireann 1937.

57. *In re Article 26 of the Constitution and the Criminal Law (Jurisdiction) Bill 1975* [1997] IR 129, SC, *per* O'Higgins CJ; Arts 5 and 15 of the Constitution of Ireland 1937.

58. And the enactment of the Education Act 1998.

59. Compare with the position in England where the Education Act 1944 made provision for free second level education for all.

60. By virtue of Arts 6, 42 and 44 of the Constitution of Ireland 1937.

(the 1998 Act). Despite its broad constitutional base,[61] educational provision has remained remarkably narrow in practice. At the time of writing (August 2008), no permanent public school sector exists for first-level education,[62] although that is now beginning to change,[63] and only a limited public sector has been established at second level.[64] This means there is still no alternative to denominational education for a large number of parents and their children, especially for those who live outside the small number of urban centres where most multidenominational schools are located.[65] But, with the rapid growth of multidenominational schools and other school types, that situation too is changing. Some writers contend that the religious control of schools in a publicly-funded system presents serious challenges to the pursuit of equality for particular minorities in education, and to the accommodation of differences surrounding disability, ethnicity and beliefs.[66]

Absence of Public Sector Schools: Primary Level

[9.013] The lack of a public schools sector at primary level has proved particularly problematic for the immigrant population (who in 2006 comprised 14 per cent of the total population of 4,239,848 persons).[67] However, if the immigrants profess a different religion to a denominational primary school, or no religion at all, they may find their children excluded by the school's admission policy, since religious schools have been afforded a limited statutory exemption[68] in this regard which is discussed later.

61. Arts 42.2 and 42.3.1°.

62. With the exception of nine model schools, which are a relic of the nineteenth century, no state primary schools have been established.

63. With the establishment of a new type of school, a community national school, which is currently being piloted. These will be the first public schools established by the Irish state since 1922.

64. The schools established pursuant to the Vocational Education Acts 1930–2001.

65. Lodge and Lynch (eds), *Diversity at School*, p 3.

66. Lodge and Lynch (eds), *Diversity at School*, p 3: Coolahan observes that the state project of political and cultural cohesion was realised in Ireland in great part through education, which led to the neglect and even negation of difference in educational life; Coolahan, *Irish Education: History and Structure.*

67. Census 2006, Commentary – a Summary of Results (Government Publications) p 11.

68. The Equal Status Act 2000, s 7 (3)(c).

[9.014] The Catholic Church accepts that for historic reasons it is overrepresented in school patronage and it reiterates that it has no desire to monopolise educational provision,[69] but it wishes to retain the *status quo* in the schools it owns.[70] While calls for the church to give up running schools have been made by individuals,[71] some from unexpected quarters,[72] to date there has been no concerted demand from representative parent bodies in education that such a step be taken. Figures from a recent survey indicate that parents of children in Catholic primary schools, north and south of the border, back a continued strong role for the church in education, with 63 per cent believing the church should continue to have a prominent role in the provision of primary education.[73] On the other hand, a recent small-scale poll indicates that the majority of parents favour state-run schools,[74] so it is extremely difficult to glean an accurate and objective picture in this regard.

[9.015] The Catholic Cardinal of Armagh, Dr Sean Brady, has strongly defended Catholic education stating that there is an enduring need for the Church to continue to be involved in education and that in an age of moral confusion, the Church offers 'a clear and unapologetic set of values based on the Gospel.' Furthermore, he denies the contention that Catholics are seeking to retain a monopoly in Irish education or that these schools are sectarian and he concludes: 'It is time to recover a balance of respect in our society between those who exercise legitimate authority for the common good and the important freedoms of the individual.'[75] It is this very balance

---

69. O'Brien, 'Lack of School Places Indicates Greater Problems', (2007) *The Irish Catholic*, 13 September, p 12, citing the Catholic Archbishop of Dublin.
70. O'Brien, 'Lack of School Places Indicates Greater Problems', (2007) *The Irish Catholic*, 13 September, p 12.
71. Bacik, 'Call for church to quit schools', (2007) *Irish Times*, 27 September. In this letter, Senator Bacik concludes, 'It is time for religion to be left outside the school door.'
72. Mac Cormaic, 'Nun urges church to give up running schools', (2007) *Irish Times,* 19 September.
73. Flynn, (2008) *Irish Times*, 9 April, citing a survey conducted by the Council for Research and Development of the Irish Bishops, Conference, 2007.
74. Flynn, 'Majority of parents favour State-run schools, poll finds', (2008) *Irish Times*, 30 June. This RedC poll was commissioned by the Irish Principals' Network (IPPN). This telephone poll used a sample of 350 parents.
75. Keenan, 'Archbishop defends Catholic schools', (2007) *Irish Times*, 22 September.

that Ireland is attempting to achieve as it strives to ensure that its meets the needs of all religions and none. Clearly, the contribution of the churches in education is still valued in Ireland and the churches will retain a key role in education in Ireland as long as parents continue to support them in that role.[76]

Growing Democracy in Education

[9.016] The Act of 1998, which brought about the main substantive changes in first- and second-level education was preceded by almost a decade of public debate[77] which indicated that the old model of 'patron acting on behalf of parents' was coming under pressure.[78] Once the genie of democracy had escaped from the bottle, so to speak, other legislative measures in education followed in quick succession: the Education (Welfare) Act 2000, Education for Persons with Special Needs Act 2004[79] and the Education (Miscellaneous Provisions) Act 2007. Cumulatively, these legislative measures caused a seismic shift of control in education from church to state, transforming the ecclesiastical law relationship in Ireland in modern times. However, school ownership, for the most part,[80] and the employment of teachers to a considerable degree,[81] has remained with the churches and religious denominations. At the time of writing, approximately 98 per cent of all first-level schools are regulated, denominational (religious or confessional) schools, while in or about 57 per cent of all second-level

76. Walshe, 'Bishops pin school hopes on parents: New blueprint to outline Church role in education', (2008) *Irish Independent,* 12 May and 'Church relaxes grip on education', p 8.

77. See Coolahan (ed), *Report on the National Education Convention. Ireland: The National Education Convention Secretariat* (Government Publications, 1994) p 25. This convention included a week of televised public debate in Dublin Castle and is available from the National Archives, Bishop Street, Dublin.

78. Coolahan (ed), *Report on the National Education Convention. Ireland: The National Education Convention Secretariat* (Government Publications, 1994) p 25.

79. Not fully commenced at the time of writing (November 2008).

80. A new option of school ownership has been introduced in which the state will, if the school founder (the patron) wishes, own the newly founded school.

81. Exceptions being the vocational schools (second level) and the 6–7 model schools (primary level), which are owned by the state.

schools are voluntary secondary schools (denominational), being either free-scheme or fee-paying privately-owned schools.[82] Most denominational primary schools (approximately 94 per cent) are Roman Catholic in ownership and management, the remainder being owned mainly by the Protestant churches. Nonetheless, it is generally acknowledged that public education is provided in these privately owned, publicly-funded, recognised[83] schools. Responsibility for the characteristic spirit of the religious school, and control over religious instruction and worship, in these schools is vested in the churches or religious denominations (acting on behalf of parents) under the Constitution and pursuant to the Act of 1998 and this sphere is not supervised or inspected by the state.[84] This position contrasts with that of the German state whose Basic Law expressly retains control over the entire education system as was seen in **chapter 6**.

MEETING THE NEEDS OF A DIVERSE SOCIETY

[9.017] In recent decades, Ireland has faced the challenge of integrating diverse cultures, languages[85] and religions in an education system that is almost entirely denominational.[86] A small but rapidly-growing body of multidenominational schools (approximately one per cent of all schools currently)[87] has also been established, mainly in urban and suburban settings, under the aegis of 'Educate Together'.[88] These schools were established by parental initiative and they faced many obstacles, especially

82. Lodge and Lynch (eds), *Diversity at School*, p 47.

83. Recognised by the Minister for Education and Science under the Act of 1998, s 10.

84. See Deeds of Variation for Catholic Primary Schools, Management Board Members' Handbook, (Catholic Primary School Managers' Association, 2004) pp 10–14.

85. O'Brien, 'From Acholi to Zulu, Ireland a land of over 167 languages', (2006) *Irish Times*, 25 March. A number of these, it appears, are dialects.

86. Glendenning, 'Denominational Primary Schools in the Republic of Ireland and the Challenge of Democracy', (2006) *International Journal for Education Law and Policy*, vol 2, Issue 1–2, p 41.

87. Comprising 42 schools. There are 3,032 Catholic primary schools, 183 Church of Ireland schools, 14 Presbyterian schools, 5 interdenominational schools and 1 Religious Society of Friends (Quaker) school.

88. A company limited by guarantee without share capital. Some of these schools operate under the patronage of 'Educate Together', while others are under the patronage of various dioceses (the local Bishop).

in the early years.[89] Parental demand for multi-denominational education is increasing annually, a fact which is indicated by the recognition by the Minister of twelve more Educate Together schools in September 2008, which is the largest annual increase in the Educate Together network in its 30-year history.[90] Unlike the traditional national schools, these schools do not teach religious instruction during the course of the school day. These schools teach a programme of ethical education called 'the Learn Together Programme',[91] which is allocated the same amount of time within the school day as similar programmes in Catholic[92] or Protestant[93] schools.[94] Educate Together's programme of ethical education has four components: moral and spiritual development, equality and justice, belief systems, and ethics and environment.[95] Religion is explored in the belief systems component, including the great world religions and the humanistic and non-religious outlooks, while the school promotes 'a respectful interchange between these viewpoints while carefully declining to promote any one.'[96] In addition, the boards of management in the Educate Together schools make their facilities available to any parental group which wishes to run specific faith-formation classes, which take place outside the compulsory school day.[97] In this manner, Catholic parents, for example, organise sacramental preparation classes and many pupils are prepared for the sacraments in after-school services organised by parents through their local parish.[98]

---

89. See Hyland, 'The multi-denominational Experience', 8(1) *Irish Educational Studies*, p 1.
90. Electronic Newsletter from Educate Together, 'Twelve New Educate Together Schools to open September 2008', Vol 8, no 2, 24 April 2008.
91. Rowe, Chairperson of Educate Together, 'Making an article of faith', (2008) *Irish Times*, 15 April.
92. The Alive O Programme.
93. The Follow Me Programme.
94. Rowe, Chairperson of Educate Together, 'Making an article of faith', (2008) *Irish Times*, 15 April
95. Rowe, Chairperson of Educate Together, 'Making an article of faith', (2008) *Irish Times*, 15 April
96. Rowe, Chairperson of Educate Together, 'Making an article of faith', (2008) *Irish Times*, 15 April
97. Rowe, Chairperson of Educate Together, 'Making an article of faith', (2008) *Irish Times*, 15 April
98. Rowe, Chairperson of Educate Together, 'Making an article of faith', (2008) *Irish Times*, 15 April.

SCHOOL MODELS

[9.018] As has already been noted, Ireland has two Muslim primary schools, one Jewish school, one Jehovah Witness school and one Quaker school. In addition a new primary school for County Kildare is being piloted under the joint patronage of Jewish, Muslim and Catholic patronage and the outcome is awaited with interest.[99] There are also plans (and pilot programmes) to establish 'community national schools' which will extend the remit of the existing vocational school sector, (local authorities which administer the second-level public sector vocational schools),[100] representing the first venture by that sector outside its traditional remit of second-level and further education.[101] Approximately 26 per cent of second-level students are currently educated in the vocational school sector (the public sector), which will also administer the new community national schools at primary level.

Community National Schools

[9.019] The two 'community national schools' now being piloted[102] are the first primary schools founded directly by the Irish state and there has been a lively debate as to the character of the religious programme to be provided in them. Remarkably, there has been little public debate on the possibility of presenting non-denominational education in these schools, should parents wish to avail of this form of education. When establishing the 'community national schools', Catholic primary school representatives were opposed to a 'one-size-fits all' common programme of religious education, while the vocational school authorities, who administer these schools, were demanding a 'faith-neutral' programme in accordance with their upholding secular legislation, the Vocational Education Acts 1930–2001. Meanwhile, the Irish National Teachers' Organisation (INTO)[103] proposed that a

99. Downes, 'Religious faiths may co-operate to run school', (2008) *Irish Times,* 12 January.

100. Under the Vocational Education Acts 1930–2001.

101. Donnelly, 'VEC makes historic bid for primary schools', (2006) *Irish Independent*, 28 February.

102. Scoil Gráinne in Phibblestown near Clonee, Co Meath and Scoil Choilm in Porterstown, Co Dublin; see Carbery, 'A big first as two State-run community schools open', (2008) *Irish Times,* 2 September.

103. The main representative body for teachers at first level, which operates throughout the whole island of Ireland.

common programme of religious education be taught on four days weekly, with the various faiths coming in on the fifth day to teach their individual religion.[104] With regard to religion, Scoil Gráinne, Phibblestown, now runs a newly developed pilot programme for religion taught during school time for children from 23 countries of whom approximately 85 per cent are first generation Irish citizens. According to the principal, David Campbell, it will be 'multi-faith religious education instead of a Catholic programme … the commonalities shared by faiths, rather than separating them into different religions.' The only situation where children might be separated for religion classes at some stage would be one class per week, to prepare for First Holy Communion, he continued.[105] If a facility for religious instruction is afforded one denomination on the fifth day, then it must be afforded to all denominations on equal terms, because of the state's guarantee in Art 44.2.3° not to impose any disabilities or make any discrimination on the ground of religious profession, belief or status. From an administrative perspective, this could be difficult, given a schools' multiethnic, multireligious enrolment composition.

Since the religion programme to be taught in vocational schools and colleges is a pivotal issue for the family under the Constitution, this matter requires a broadly-based public debate leading to the formulation of a national consensus and the Vocational Education Acts 1930–2001 should be amended to incorporate this provision.

[9.020] In July 2008, the UN Human Rights Committee, having considered Ireland's reports under the ICCPR, noted with concern Ireland's failure to provide non-denominational primary education 'in all regions of the state party'. This committee called on Ireland to open up its largely Roman Catholic primary school system to secular education on the grounds that people have a human right to such education in a diverse society. As Ireland debates the character of its 'community national schools' now being piloted, it needs to take account of this significant recommendation since it is one of the 161 states parties and 70 signatories of the ICCPR.

[9.021] It has been alleged that there is 'profound and embedded institutionalised religious discrimination' throughout the education

---

104. See further Quinn, 'Clash over RE class at school', (2007) *The Irish Catholic,* 24 May.

105. Carbery citing Campbell, 'A big first as two State-run community schools open', (2008) *Irish Times,* 2 September.

system,[106] but no firm evidence of institutional racism had emerged to date.[107] It is remarkable, however, that the overwhelming majority of a recent multidenominational school's enrolment in County Dublin were from Irish ethnic minorities of African origin. In a rapidly-growing area, these children had failed to gain admission to any existing primary school and it was necessary to establish 'an emergency school' to accommodate them.[108] This development requires ongoing monitoring by state authorities in Ireland lest a two-tier system emerges at primary level.

HISTORICAL LEGACY

Centrality

[9.022] Some of the historical features of Ireland's system of education have not changed. Unlike England,[109] Scotland[110] and Northern Ireland,[111] Ireland did not devolve to the local authorities the control of general education,[112] which it entrusted to the churches and religious denominations under the centralised administration of the state.[113] What emerged was a unique church-state educational enterprise in which the state generally funded ('provided for') the churches and religious denominations who provided education. The exception to this general rule was the vocational sector in which, from 1930 onwards, the state provided public sector education through the local authorities (Vocational Education Committees). With the establishment of comprehensive and community schools at second level, the scope of educational provision broadened from the 1960s onwards, but the centrality of the system remained unchanged.

---

106. 'Balbriggan school opens', (2007) *Irish Times*, 25 September, citing Paul Rowe, Chief Executive Officer of Educate Together Schools.

107. Any segregation along racial lines constitutes discrimination under the Equal Status Acts 2000–2004. Discrimination on the grounds of race (including colour, nationality, national or ethnic origins) is prohibited by s 6 of the 2004 Act.

108. 'Balbriggan school opens', (2007) *Irish Times*, 25 September, citing Paul Rowe, Chief Executive Officer of Educate Together Schools

109. Elementary Education Acts (England) 1870–1909.

110. Elementary Education Act (Scotland) 1872.

111. Education Act (NI) 1923.

112. *Reviews of National Education Policies: Ireland*, (OECD, 1991), which considered Ireland's education system to be one of the most centralised in Western Europe.

113. Currently under the Department of Education and Science, Dublin.

[9.023] All three attempts to decentralise the system of general education have failed to date. Gladstone had plans for the devolution of Irish education, but by 1873 he had abandoned them because of the strong opposition of the Catholic bishops.[114] A further controversial attempt to legislate for the 32 counties in the Education Bill 1919 was defeated, due to the opposition of the Catholic bishops,[115] and this initiative was also overtaken by political events as Ireland moved towards independence.[116] Once again the challenge of devolution in Ireland, which McCarthy refers to as 'the distasteful challenge',[117] was resisted when the Education Bill 1997, which proposed to legislate for ten regional education boards nationwide, failed to pass into law. Despite this consistent reluctance to devolve education to local bodies, the proposed establishment of 'community national schools' indicates that public schools at primary level will emerge incrementally under the control and management of the vocational education sector provided parents support this initiative.

[9.024] Many of the distinctive features in the contemporary system can only be understood in the light of history,[118] which records a century-old battle of epic proportions for control of education between the English authorities in Ireland and the Irish churches. Ireland's antipathy to legislative measures in education may have originated in the remarkably repressive legislation of the seventeenth and eighteenth centuries commonly known as 'the Penal laws'.[119] This legislation was imposed by English authorities in Ireland, which targeted four main areas of Catholic life: property, religion, personal

---

114. See Hyland and Milne (eds), *Irish Educational Documents*, p 133 in which Dr Hyland refers to a letter from Gladstone to Bishop Cullen in February 1872 indicating his intention to legislate for Ireland.

115. Hyland and Milne (eds), *Irish Educational Documents*, pp 21, 186–189 and O'Buachalla, *Educational Policy in Twentieth Century Ireland*, p 52.

116. O'Buachalla, *Educational Policy in Twentieth Century Ireland.*

117. McCarthy, *The Distasteful Challenge*.

118. Akenson, *The Irish Education Experiment*; Coolahan, *Irish Education: History and Structure*; Auchmuty, *Irish Education: a Historical Study* (Hoggis Figgis, 1937).

119. See An Act for the English Order, Habite and Language 1537 (28 Henry viii c 6); An Act to Restrain Foreign Education 1695 (7 William 3 c 4); An Act for the Uniformity of Public Prayers and Administration of Sacraments 1665 (17 and 18 of Charles 2 c 6); An Act to Prevent the Further Growth of Popery 1703 (2 Anne c 6); An Act for Explaining and Emending an Act entitled An Act to Prevent the Further Growth of Popery 1709 (8 Anne c 3).

disabilities and education. While the more prosperous classes travelled to Europe to acquire an education, the poorer classes generally achieved a basic education secretly in the primitive schools ('hedge schools')[120] frequently run by Catholic priests and like-minded teachers. This priest-teacher educational initiative evolved over time and it eventually transformed the non-denominational state initiative that was introduced by English authorities in 1831, officially described as 'a system of national education in Ireland'.[121] Under English dominion, Ireland, as part of a social experiment, had one of the earliest state-supported, non-statutory systems in Europe providing universal elementary education.[122] The relaxation of the Penal laws towards the end of the eighteenth century under the various Catholic Relief Acts resulted in the emergence of secondary schools established by the dioceses and religious bodies and these schools were under ecclesiastical control.[123] These schools were the antecedents of the existing voluntary schools, which are now regulated, recognised schools comprising approximately 57 per cent of second-level schools.

The 1831 Stanley Plan for National Education

Informality

[9.025] When the English authorities in Ireland decided to fund free elementary education in 1831, in accordance with the Stanley plan, this initiative was grounded in 'the mixed education principle', ie that all creeds would be educated together in the same school in secular subjects, with separate religious instruction being provided in accordance with the tenets

120. Glendenning, *Education and the Law*, Ch 2; Fitzgerald, 'Education in from the hedge', (2008) *Irish Times*, 15 March.

121. The Chief Secretary for Ireland, EG Stanley, in his letter to the Duke of Leinster invited him to become president of a new state board which would administer public funds for education on an informal, non-sectarian basis so as to obviate problems relating to religious beliefs (referred to in this book as 'Stanley's letter'). A copy of Stanley's letter, which contained the Stanley Plan for mixed education, is included in Hyland and Milne (eds), *Irish Educational Documents*, p 98 *et seq*. See also Glendenning, *Education and the Law*, Appendix F.

122. O'Buachalla, *Education Policy in Twentieth Century Ireland*, p 19; Jarman, *Landmarks in the History of Education*, p 256; Hyland, 'National Education' in Hyland and Milne (eds), *Irish Educational Documents*, pp 98 and 13.

123. Coolahan, 'Church-State relations in Primary and Secondary Education' in Mackey and McDonagh (eds), *Religion and Politics in Ireland at the Turn of the Millennium* (Columba Press, 2003) p 134.

of the various denominations.[124] Clearly this government plan was for a non-denominational system of education, which one contemporary Catholic bishop uniquely described as a plan 'well suited to the special circumstances of this distracted country.'[125] Despite the fact that the Stanley plan ran counter to the objectives of the main churches, the churches generally participated in the system, adapting it gradually to meet their own objectives. With the passage of the century, the people perceived or, as one writer puts it, were persuaded to perceive,[126] elementary education in denominational terms. However, the very flexibility of this informal system became its Achilles heel and 'the mixed education principle' was gradually abandoned as the century progressed. By the close of the nineteenth century, following many decades of internecine church-state struggle, each religious denomination owned its parish school(s), in which religious instruction was taught according to its own tenets and the manager (usually a clergyman) was the employer of the teachers who were remunerated and supervised by the state. This system of education continued in the twentieth century with no significant structural changes. In independent Ireland, the existing denominational system of education, which was highly cost-effective, was adopted by the under-resourced Free State in 1922 with no substantive structural change. However, as the decades moved on, the church-state relationship became closer,[127] particularly in education.

Conscience Clauses

[9.026] In order to ensure the free practice of religion, in Ireland, as in England,[128] the concept of the 'conscience clause' became a feature of educational provision. The conscience clause has an ancient lineage which can be traced from the Stanley plan for primary education (1831) down

124. A copy of this letter is included in **Appendix 10** of this book.

125. Hyland and Milne (eds), *Irish Educational Document*, p 107, citing a circular (dated 26 December 1931) sent by Bishop Doyle of Kildare and Leighlin to his clergy when the national system of education was first announced.

126. Osborough, 'Irish Law and the Rights of the National Schoolteachers', (1979) *Irish Jurist* ns 36 at 37.

127. Fuller, *Irish Catholicism since 1950: The Undoing of a Culture*, p 3 and generally chapter 1. Coolahan, 'Church-State relations in Primary and Secondary Education' in Mackey and McDonagh (eds), *Religion and Politics in Ireland at the Turn of the Millennium* (Columba Press, 2003) p 140, where the author describes this church-state relationship as 'a cosy partnership'.

128. See **para [5.018]** above in which the Cowper Temple Clause is discussed.

through various measures such as: the Intermediate Education (Ireland) Act 1878, s 7; the Government of Ireland Act 1920, s 5; the Irish Constitution of 1922, Art 8; the Constitution of Ireland 1937, Art 44.2.4° and the Education Act 1998, s 30(2)(e). Section 30(2)(e) of the Education Act 1998 provides under the various Catholic Relief Acts provides:

> Without prejudice to the generality of subsection (1), the Minister ...
>
> (e) shall not require any student to attend instruction in any subject which is contrary to the conscience of the parent of the student or in the case of a student who has reached the age of 18 years, the student.

This latter provision gives effect to the liberal guarantee in Art 44.2.4° of the Constitution but it is considerably wider in scope since it applies, not just to religious instruction but, to 'any subject'.

Developments up to 1937

[9.027] In order to respect the freedom of religion principle in the informal provision of education from 1831 onwards, periods of religious instruction in national schools required strict timetabling[129] while periods of secular instruction were to be provided separately so as to ensure that they were free from all forms of religious worship.[130] This principle was 'regulated' by Rule 90 of the informal Rules of the Commissioners of National Education, the antecedent of the non-statutory Rules for National Schools (the Rules hereafter), which are still operational.[131] Thus, the right of parents or guardians to withdraw their children from religious instruction, if they so wished, was facilitated.[132] Files in the National Archives indicate that the implementation of Rule 90[133] in national schools was strictly monitored by

---

129. Facilitated by a blackboard marked 'Secular Education' on one side and 'Religious Instruction' on the other. It was required that the blackboard be changed around in accordance with the instruction being given to students, thus emphasising the separateness of these two bodies of knowledge.

130. See Rules and Regulations of the Commissioners of National Education in Ireland with Appendix (HMSO, 1898), s 111, pp 13–15 and later Rule 69 and Rule 90 of The Rules for National Schools (Government Publications, 1965).

131. *The Rules for National Schools* (Government Publications, 1965).

132. See further Hyland and Milne (eds), 'National Education, 1831–1922' in *Irish Educational Documents,* Vol 1, pp 98–193 at p 124.

133. See *Fifth Report of the Commissioners of National Education in Ireland,* Vol 1, s 11, p 67, which covers 1834–1851; Vol 2 covers 1852–1865, inclusive.

the Commissioners of National Education,[134] and the files include reports of the indoctrination of pupils.[135] Rule 13 of the 1890 Rules state: 'No emblems or symbols of a denominational nature shall be exhibited in the school-room during the hours of united instruction.'

[9.028] When the Irish Free State was established in 1921, no substantial changes were made in the administrative system of national education but radical curricular reform was introduced in 1922 following the recommendations of the First National Programme Conference.[136] A second committee was established in 1925 to review the curriculum, and the report of this committee,[137] under the Second National Programme Conference, was published in 1926.[138] That report concluded:

> Of all the parts of the school curriculum Religious Instruction is by far the most important, as its subject matter, God's honour and service, includes the proper use of all man's faculties, and affords the most powerful inducements to their proper use. We assume therefore, that Religious Instruction is a fundamental part of the school course. Though the time allotted to it as a specific subject is necessarily short, a religious spirit should inform and vivify the whole work of the school. The teacher – while careful in the presence of children of different religious belief, not to touch on matters of controversy – should constantly inculcate, in connection with secular subjects the practice of charity, justice, truth, purity, patience, temperance, obedience to lawful authority and all the other moral virtues. In this way, he will fulfil the primary

134. Not to be confused with the post-1922 National Commissioners of Education.

135. National Archives, Bishop Street, Education File, 9, No 2690, complaint against King's Inn Convent NS, Dublin 1884–5 for failing to remove crucifix during secular instruction; File No 4349, Co Down, 1887, pupils given secular instruction during religious instruction time; File No. 4593, Co Antrim, 1887/88, violation of Rule 90, Roman Catholic pupils were present in Religious Education class in Protestant school thus violating Rule 90. Such reports are numerous and very interesting, both socially and historically.

136. National Programme Conference, *National programme of primary Instruction,* Browne and Nolan, Dublin 1922: see further Hyland, 'The Multi-denominational experience', *Irish Educational Studies,* 8, 1:1, available online at http://www.esatclear.ie/~dejames/CRGHyland.htm accessed by this author on 20 Oct 2008.

137. Under the chairmanship of Rev J McKenna, SJ: Hyland, 'The Multi-denominational experience.'

138. National Programme Conference, Report and Programme, Stationary Office, 1926.

> duty of an educator, the moulding to perfect form of his pupils' character, habituating them to observe in their relations with God and with their neighbour, the laws which God both directly through the dictates of natural reason and through Revelation, and indirectly through the ordinance of lawful authority, imposes on mankind.

Since the prescription of the subject-matter of Religious Instruction, the examination, and the supervision of its teaching are outside the competence of the Department of Education, no syllabuses of religious instruction are set forth of it are set forth.[139]

Although the ecclesiastical law relationship in educational affairs became closer after 1922,[140] the Rules for National Schools 1926, which governed the administration of national schools, required that teachers exercise 'due regard' for the right of children of minority religions when dealing with matters of religious sensitivity. However, the practice of issuing annual reports, as followed by the Commissioners of National Education, was discontinued in the under-resourced Free State. Informal methods of administration were favoured which facilitated changes in education policy with a minimum of attention. Certain safeguards for minority religions in schools were retained in the 1947 Rules,[141] however, such as the Certificate Book, introduced in the 1889 Rules.[142] In the Certificate Book a parent could consent to his or her child receiving religious instruction from a teacher of a different denomination to the child, or from a teacher giving any religious instruction to his or her child. The Certificate Book, as its name suggests, had to be certified both by the teacher and the inspector and it safeguarded minority religious interests to some degree. However, the Certificate Book was dropped from the 1965 Rules as well as the 'due regard' requirement for religious minorities, indicating less rigorous

---

139. National Programme Conference, Report and Programme, Stationary Office, 1926; and further Hyland, 'The Multi-denominational experience',

140. Coolahan, 'Church-State relations in Primary and Secondary Education' in Mackey and McDonagh (eds), *Religion and Politics in Ireland at the Turn of the Millennium* (Columba Press, 2003) p 140.

141. See, for example, Rule 65(16) on prayer, religious exercises and religious instruction.

142. *Rules and Regulations of the Commissioners of National Education in Ireland with Appendix*, (HMSO, 1989), s 111, pp 13–15. See further Glendenning, 'The Role of the State in First and Second level Education in Ireland: Retrospect and Prospect', Unpublished Thesis (Ph D) (Trinity College, Dublin, Law School, 1996) p 37.

implementation of protections for religious minorities in schools. Rule 69.1 of the Rules still requires the religious denomination of each pupil to be entered in the school register and roll book.[143] Moreover, Rule 69(2)(a) states: 'No pupil shall receive, or be present at, any religious instruction of which his parents or guardians disapprove.' While part (b) of the same Rule requires the periods of formal religious instruction to be fixed so as to facilitate the withdrawal of pupils whose parents or guardian disapprove of such instruction.[144] Further, Rule 69(3) provides:

> Where such religious instruction as their parents or guardians approve is not provided in the school for any section of the pupils, such pupils must, should their parents or guardians so desire, be allowed to absent themselves from school, at reasonable times, for the purpose of receiving that instruction elsewhere.

In addition, the periods of formal religious instruction are required to be indicated on the time-table[145] and no visitor may be present at such instruction without the express approval of the school manager.[146]

THE CONSTITUTION OF 1937

Religion and Education

[9.029] Larkin asserts that it was left to de Valera, the main architect of the Constitution of 1937, to make the state confessional in practice.[147] In 1937, with approximately 95 per cent of the population Roman Catholic, there was little demand for non-denominational education and so the existing system of denominational education was embodied in Arts 42 (Education) and 44 (Religion).[148] Catholic social principles were enshrined in Arts 42 and 44 of the Constitution,[149] which included the doctrine of state subsidiarity. Accordingly, the tenet of parental supremacy in education was prioritised

143. Rule 69.1.

144. Rule 69.2(b).

145. Rule 69.5.

146. Rule 69.4.

147. See further Larkin, 'Church State and Nation in Modern Ireland', (Dec 1975) *American Historical Review,* LXXX/5, 1267.

148. The Employment Equality Bill 1996.

149. And further Glendenning, *Education and the Law,* ch 3.

and the churches, through the agency of parents and with the tacit consent of the state, assumed a central role in education. Anxious to avoid full responsibility for education, the Secretary of the Department of Education, Seosamh O'Neill, suggested a state-aiding system of education be incorporated in the Constitution, rather than a state system. From O'Neill's letter, it is clear that the state was mainly concerned with resource implications. If a constitutional duty was imposed on it 'to provide education' rather than 'to provide for' education, the state could be compelled to fund school transport, school buildings, equipment, free books and requisites for children, as well as the full maintenance of recognised schools.[150] Accordingly, de Valera, under pressure from state departments, personally altered the existing phrase in the drafting, 'The State shall provide free primary education ... to read 'The State shall provide for free primary education.' The final draft became Art 42.4 of the Constitution.[151]

[9.030] With some notable and erudite exceptions,[152] the courts have generally held that the constitutional obligation on the state in regard to educational provision is an indirect obligation, ie to fund others (usually the churches) to provide education.[153] This minimalist interpretation of the state's role in educational provision, which has recently been upheld by the High Court, has permitted the state not only to evade full responsibility for the maintenance and repair of recognised schools, but also to avoid vicarious liability for the sexual abuse of children in national schools (day schools) who, as adults, were seeking to vindicate their rights.[154]

150. See a copy of O'Neill's letter in **Appendix 10.**

151. This change, among others, was made in the redraft made by De Valera on 7 April 1937, para 5, which later became Article 42.4; *De Valera Papers,* File 110, p 27, Archives of University College, Dublin.

152. In particular *McEneaney v Minister for Education* [1941] IR 430 (SC): *Maunsell v Minister for Education* [1940] IR 213 (HC) and *Fox v Higgins* (1912) ILTR 222.

153. *Crowley v Ireland* [1980] IR 102; *Conway v INTO* [1991] 2 IR 305; *Sheehan v INTO* [1997] 2 IR 327; *Hurley v INTO* [1991] 2 IR 328.

154. *O' Keefe v Minister for Education and Science* [2006] IEHC 13; *O'Callaghan v McDonnell, The Minister for Education and Science* [2006] IEHC 299; *TM v JH, JM and the Minister for Education* [2006] IECH 26; *Delahunty v South Eastern Health Board and St Joseph's Industrial School, Kilkenny* [2000] 4 IR 361 (the plaintiff in the last case was sexually abused by a housemaster while visiting a friend who was resident in an industrial school in Kilkenny).

Constitutional Guarantees

[9.031] Unlike the position in, *inter alia*, Spain and Germany, church-state relations in Ireland are not governed by concordats or agreements with the Holy See.[155] Neither has the Irish state any formal role in regard to higher ecclesiastical appointments.[156] Article 41 (the Family) and Art 42 (Education) of the Constitution are original and unusual provisions[157] inspired by Roman Catholic orthodoxy, especially the well-known encyclicals of modern popes.[158] The main source of law on church-state relations is Art 44 of the Constitution. Article 44.1 provides that the homage of public worship is due to Almighty God in terms which do not confine the benefits of that acknowledgment to members of the Christian faith. Freedom of conscience and the free profession and practice of religion are guaranteed to every Irish citizen, subject to public order and morality.[159] In Art 44.2.2°, the state guarantees not to endow any religion. Neither may the state impose any disabilities or make any discrimination on the ground of religious profession, belief or status.[160] Article 44.2.4° prohibits any discrimination between the management of different religious denominations in legislation providing state aid for schools,[161] nor may such legislation affect prejudicially the right of any child to attend any publicly funded school without attending religious instruction at that school. Every religious denomination has the right to manage its own affairs, together with the right to own, acquire and administer property and maintain institutions for

155. See further Whyte, *Church and State in Modern Ireland, 1923–70* (Gill & Macmillan, 1971) p 15: 'No concordat between the Irish State and the Catholic Church has ever been negotiated, nor, so far as is known, has one ever been suggested.' The 1st edition of this book was called *Church and State in Modern Ireland 1923–1970* and the 2nd edition is called *Church and State in Modern Ireland 1923–1979* (Gill and Macmillan, 1980).

156. Whyte, *Church and State in Modern Ireland, 1923–70* (Gill & Macmillan, 1971), and Casey, 'State and Church in Ireland', in Robbers (ed), *State and Church in the European Union* (Nomos, 2005) p 191.

157. The late Prof John Kelly, *Fundamental Rights in the Irish Law and Constitution* (2nd edn, Oceana Publications, 1968) p 57. See, however, *dictum* of Gavan Duffy J in *Re: Tilston, Infant* [1951] IR 1.

158. In particular two of Pope Pius X1, *Divini Illius Magistri* (1929) and *Casti Conubii* (1930). See further Glendenning, *Education and the Law*, Ch 3.

159. Article 44.2.

160. Article 44.2.3°; *Molloy v Minister for Education* [1975] IR 88.

161. The Education Act 1998, s 12.

religious or charitable purposes (eg schools).[162] Article 44.6 provides that the property of every religious denomination or any educational institution shall not be diverted except for necessary works of public utility and on payment of compensation. The extent to which the above provisions of the Irish Constitution are in line with the requirements of international law relating to freedom of religion and faith in a democratic society is quite striking, but whether they have been fully incorporated into educational practice is quite another matter.

School Ownership: National Schools

[9.032] Although the state has contributed substantially to the building of all schools, most primary schools and approximately 57 per cent of second-level schools are not state-owned but are vested in trustees of the various churches or religious orders. A number of the practices in the Stanley plan were operating until recently, particularly those relating to funding. Generally, a clergyman, on behalf of a bishop, made the application to the Department of Education and Science to establish a school.[163] Traditionally, the church provided the proposed school site free of charge together with 15 per cent of the capital costs[164] and 15 per cent of renovation costs. On completion, however, the church owned the school building. Since January 1999 onwards, the traditional model, outlined above, may still be used to establish mainstream schools subject to an agreement made with the Minister concerning the operation of the school.[165] On completion, however, the option is available for the establishment of new schools under which the patron (the person who at the commencement of Part 11 of the Education Act 1998 is recognised by the Minister as patron)[166] is to provide 5 per cent of the capital cost,[167] together with 10 per cent of renovation costs[168] but the state will then own the building which will be leased to the patron.

Under the pre-1999 model of establishing schools, the absence of any clear written legal agreements between church and state has led to some

162. Article 44.5.

163. See Rules for National Schools, 1965.

164. Rules for National Schools, 1965.

165. Presumably the agreement in the *Deed of Variation.*

166. Education Act 1998, s 8(1)(a) and (2); see further powers of the patron in the 1998 Act, eg ss 14(1), (4), 15(2)(b), 16, 17.

167. Which is 'capped' at €63,487.

168. Which is 'capped' at €31,743.

difficulties when schools are sold and the proceeds come to be distributed between church and state. Following the sale of the Christian Brothers school in Youghal, County Cork, there was a church-state dispute concerning the division of the proceeds of sale which reached the courts in 2004, but this dispute was settled prior to being heard by the Supreme Court.[169] This is a sphere which needs church-state negotiation and agreement if further unseemly disputes, and possible litigation, are to be avoided in the future when the proceeds of school sales are to be divided between the state and the churches.

The Constitution and Recognised Religions

[9.033] When the Constitution of 1937 was adopted, Art 44.1.2° recognised the special position of 'the Holy Catholic Apostolic and Roman Church' as the guardian of the faith professed by the great majority of Irish citizens, while Art 44.1.3° expressly recognised a plurality of religious denominations existing in Ireland at that time.[170] In *Re May, Minors*[171] Davitt J indicated that, for the purposes of that case, he was treating the Witnesses of Jehovah as a recognised religion. It is not the case that any religious sect or so-called 'new religion' whatsoever will be able to claim the protection of Art 44, however, since some practices, for example polygamy or human sacrifice, are such an outrage to public order and morality that no state should tolerate them.[172] In *Quinn's Supermarket v AG*,[173] which considered the legality of a ministerial order regulating hours of trading[174] which strove to accommodate Jewish observance of the Sabbath, the Supreme Court held that Art 44.1.3° was an express recognition of the separate co-existence of the religious denominations, named and unnamed, and that it did not prefer one denomination to the other, nor did it confer any privilege or impose any disability or diminution of status on any religious denomination, nor did it

169. See 'Bishop and State in moves to resolve row over school sale', (2004) *Irish Times,* 18 November. The proceeds of the sale realised €600,000.

170. Including the Church of Ireland, the Presbyterian Church in Ireland, the Methodist Church in Ireland, the Religious Society of Friends in Ireland and the Jewish Congregations.

171. *Re May, Minors* [1959] IR 334; 92 ILTR 1.

172. Mr Justice Barrington, writing extra-judicially in 81 *Irish Monthly* 381.

173. *Quinn's Supermarket v AG* [1972] IR 1 per Walsh J.

174. Made pursuant to the Shops (Hours of Trading) Act 1938, s 25.

permit the state to do so. Rather, the court held that the primary purpose of the constitutional guarantee against discrimination is to ensure the freedom of practice of religion.[175] Arts 44.1.2° and 44.1.3° conferred no special legal or constitutional rights on any church,[176] they led to difficulties leading up to the protracted peace negotiations with Northern Ireland and were finally repealed following a referendum in 1972.[177] Under the Constitution, the state is obliged to respect and honour religion but is prohibited from endowing any religion or from imposing any disabilities or making any discrimination on the ground of religious profession, belief or status.[178] Any legislative measures or administrative arrangements incompatible with the above principles, therefore, would be unconstitutional. However, Art 44 are undoubtedly supportive of religion, the Supreme Court has held that the primary purpose of the guarantee against discrimination in Art 44.2.3° is to ensure the freedom to practice religion.[179] Thus, where the free practice of religion and its profession necessitate an exemption from the provisions of a statute which is generally applicable, such exemption may lawfully be given.[180]

[9.034] While Arts 42 and 44 confer recognition on the right of the religious bodies and denominational school authorities to promote their ethos or characteristic spirit, that right must also respect the constitutional rights of those who profess a different religion, or who have no religious belief.[181] Article 44.2 guarantees freedom of conscience and the free practice of religion, subject to public order and morality, which given the state's guarantee in Art 44.2.3° not to impose any disabilities or make any discrimination 'on the ground of religious profession, belief or status',

175. Quinn's Supermarket v AG [1972] IR 1, citing Walsh J at pp 24–5.

176. *Re Tilston, Infants* [1951] IR 1; Kelly, *Fundamental Rights in the Irish Law and Constitution* (2nd edn, Oceana Publications, 1968) p 247.

177. The Fifth Amendment of the Constitution Act 1972.

178. *Mulloy v Minister for Education* [1975] IR 88; *Campaign to Separate Church and State v Minister for Education* [1998] 3 IR 321 at 355.

179. *Quinn's Supermarket v AG* [1972] IR 1; *Mulloy v Minister for Education* [1975] IR 88.

180. *Quinn's Supermarket v AG* [1972] IR 1; *Mulloy v Minister for Education* [1975] IR 88.

181. Article 44.2.3°: *Mulloy v Minister for Education* [1975] IR 88; *Quinn's Supermarket v AG* [1972] IR 1.

applies equally to persons of all religions and none. In *Molloy v Minister for Education*,[182] the Supreme Court held that the term 'status' in Art 44.2.3° related to the position or rank of a person in terms of religion in respect to others, either of the same religion, or of another religion or of no religion.

ENDOWMENT OF RELIGION

[9.035] In the 1960s, new second-level school types were established by agreed trust deeds following protracted church-state negotiations. These schools included comprehensive schools, community schools, and community colleges, the latter being public sector schools established under the VEC Acts 1930–1970. Publicly funded chaplains were introduced into the comprehensive and community schools (Catholic and Church of Ireland schools) in the early 1970s. This was not a novel concept since publicly funded chaplains were introduced into French *lycées* by Napoleon, but following the commencement of the Law of 1905 that funding was withdrawn.[183]

[9.036] In *Campaign to Separate Church and State v Minister for Education*[184] (the *Campaign* case), the constitutionality of the state's payment of salaries of community school chaplains was challenged by a secularist group alleging that such payment was in breach of the guarantee in Art 44.2.2° of the Constitution, which provides: 'The State guarantees not to endow any religion'.[185] In the Supreme Court, Barrington J stated that, in the light of Art 42, the Constitution contemplates children receiving religious education in schools recognised or established by the state but in

182. *Molloy v Minister for Education* [1975] IR 88.

183. Markham, 'The Revolution, Napoleon and Education', available online at http://napoleon-series.org/research/society/c_education.html.

184. *Campaign to Separate Church and State v Minister for Education* [1998] Vol 3, 11, 321–367, 357; [1996] 2 ILRM 241; [1998] 2 ILRM 81; 3 IR. 321, 356. See also *McGrath v Trustees of Maynooth College* [1979] ILRM 166.

185. The prohibition on the endowment of religion in Art 44.2.2° has been dealt with in the following cases: *McGrath and O'Ruairc v Trustees of Maynooth College* [1979] ILRM 166; *Re Article 26 and the Employment Equality Bill 1996* [1997] 2 IR 321 and *Campaign to Separate Church and State v Minister for Education* [1998] IR 357. For discussion of judicial interpretation of the constitutional prohibitions on religious endowment and religious discrimination, see further Hogan and Whyte, *J M Kelly: The Irish Constitution* (4th edn,Tottel Publishing, 2003) pp 2051–2068.

accordance with the wishes of parents and that it is in this context that one must read Art 44.2.4°,[186] which provides for the withdrawal of children from religious instruction if their parents make that request. Barrington J stated that:

> A child who attends a school run by a religious denomination different from his own may have a constitutional right not to attend religious instruction at that school but the Constitution cannot protect him from being influenced, to some degree, by the religious 'ethos' of the school. A religious denomination is not obliged to change the general atmosphere of its school merely to accommodate a child of a different religious persuasion who wishes to attend that school.[187]

The community and comprehensive schools, Barrington J pointed out, were an attempt to make post-primary education available to all children regardless of their means.

[9.037] Introducing a more dynamic note in the *Campaign* case, Barrington J stated that the Constitution distinguishes between 'religious education' and 'religious instruction', the former being the much wider term:

> In community schools it is no longer practicable to combine religious and academic education in the way that a religious order might have done in the past. Nevertheless parents have the same right to have religious education provided in the schools which their children attend. They are not obliged to settle merely for religious 'instruction'. The role of the chaplain is to help to provide this extra dimension to the religious education of the children. The evidence establishes that, besides looking after the pastoral needs of the children, the chaplain counsels them with advice about day to day problems.[188]

Accordingly, the judge concluded that the present system, whereby the salaries of chaplains in community schools are paid by the state, was simply a manifestation under modern conditions of recognised and approved principles in Arts 42 and 44 of the Constitution. Nonetheless, Barrington J entered two caveats, with which Keane J, as he was then, agreed:[189] that this judgment proceeded on the basis that the system of salaried chaplains be

186. *Campaign to Separate Church and State v Minister for Education* [1998] IR 357.

187. *Campaign to Separate Church and State v Minister for Education* [1998] IR 357, 357–8.

188. *Campaign to Separate Church and State v Minister for Education* [1998] IR 357, 358.

189. *Employment Equality Bill 1996* [1997] 2 IR 321, 367.

available to all community schools of whatever denomination on an equal basis in accordance with their needs; and that, while it was right and proper that a chaplain should advise and counsel any student who consulted him or her about problems, it would be unconstitutional for a chaplain to instruct a child in a religion other than the child's own without the knowledge and consent of the parents.

[9.038] Although the trust deeds of community and comprehensive schools expressly require their boards to ensure that there is religious instruction and religious worship (as distinct from religious education) for the pupils in these schools (with the exception of those whose parents make a written request to have their children withdrawn from religious instruction), the Supreme Court affirmed the role of 'religious education' in these schools as an option for parents who are not obliged to accept religious instruction.[190] In doing so, the court took account of the manifestation of religious freedom under modern conditions and adjusted its jurisprudence so as to reflect the changes in ecclesiastical law as the powers in second-level education moved from the churches to the state. and the growing secularity of life in modern Ireland.

[9.039] Approving the findings of the Supreme Court in *Employment Equality Bill 1996*, Barrington J held that the Constitution does not contemplate that the payment of moneys to a denominational school for educational purposes, is an 'endowment' of religion within the meaning of Art 44.2.2°. In addition, '... the Constitution contemplated that if a school was in receipt of public funds any child, no matter what his religion, would be entitled to attend it. But such a child was to have the right not to attend any course of religious instruction at the school.' Affirming the fact that each denominational school has its own ethos, Barrington J continued: 'Teachers of a particular religious persuasion do not convey their ideas merely through formal instruction but tend to organise the schools in such a way as best to promote the religious values which they themselves embrace.'[191]

[9.040] However, the court did not indicate the balance to be struck outside of formal religious instruction time between the ethos-related rights and the

190. Articles of Management, 2nd Schedule, para 11(i)–11(xi) in the Diocese of Dublin.

191. *Campaign to Separate Church and State v Minister for Education* [1998] IR 357, p 356 of the decision. On the issue of school 'ethos', see further *Employment Equality Bill 1996* [1997] 2 IR 321.

liberal rights in Art 44.2.4° in schools, nor did it impose any limitations on worship, preparation for the sacraments, or the saying of prayers during this time which might we seen as not respecting the freedom of religion principle for religious minorities. In view of the fact that the Integrated Curriculum of 1971,[192] which permitted religion to pervade the full school day was in operation at that time, the court had a singular opportunity to consider this curriculum and to weigh its merits in the denominational school setting against competing minority rights and other parental interests. Neither did the Court make any reference to the restrictions imposed by international human rights law on states to refrain from pursuing an aim of indoctrination when exercising functions which it assumes in relation to education and teaching that might be considered as not respecting parent's religious and philosophical convictions,[193] or to the obligation falling on the state to act in an objectively, critical and pluralist manner under international law.[194] Perhaps this was a lost opportunity for much needed clarification in these important spheres of life, which led to a lack of balance relating to religious freedoms in this decision.

[9.041] Keane J held that state payments to chaplains in community schools were constitutionally sanctioned having regard to the state's obligation in Art 42.4.[195] Thus, the Court qualified the non-endowment prohibition by reference to the state's obligation, acting through the education system, to assist parents with the religious and moral formation of their children[196] as required by Art 42.4.

[9.042] Hogan and Whyte state that, in addition to protecting the state funding of school chaplains, the reasoning in the *Campaign* case may also provide constitutional protection 'for the display of religious artefacts in publicly funded schools and for the public funding of a curriculum

192. Discussed at **para [9.047]** *et seq.*

193. Article 2 of Protocol 1 of the ECHR.

194. *Kjelsden, Busk Madsen and Pedersen v Denmark* (1976) 1 EHRR 711.

195. 'The State shall provide for free primary education and shall endeavour to supplement and give reasonable aid to private and corporate educational initiative and when the public good requires it, provide other educational facilities and institutions with due regard, however, for the rights of parents, especially in the matter of religious and moral formation.'

196. Hogan and Whyte, *J M Kelly: The Irish Constitution* (4th edn, Tottel Publishing, 2003) p 2054, para 7.8.59.

permeated by religious values, the "integrated curriculum".'[197] However, they consider that the reasoning in this case is not without its difficulties.[198] They observe both the High Court and the Supreme Court's reliance on the 'relatively weak obligation' in Art 42.4, 'to endeavour to supplement and give reasonable aid to private and corporate educational initiative' to qualify the more robust prohibition on state endowment of religion in Art 44.2.2°. Hogan and Whyte conclude that it would arguably do less violence to the text of the Constitution to reverse the priority of these two provisions: 'At best, one would have to accept that the constitutional text is indeterminate on this point and yet the Supreme Court decision does not offer any compelling reason for adopting its preferred interpretation over the alternative contended for by the plaintiffs.'

[9.043] McCrea argues that the historical approach employed by Barrington and Keane JJ in the *Campaign* case was neither helpful nor justified in contemporary times.[199] Moreover, neither judge addressed what would be expected to be the logical outcome to their rationale, ie that parents who are adherents of a minority religion must posses the same right as others to have provision made for religious instruction in their faith, as a constitutional right, and in the interests of equality and non-discrimination.[200] Cleary[201] contends that 'the excessive deference shown to institutions with a religious ethos' in the *Campaign* case and other cases,[202] 'has led to a weakening of the principle of religious equality and has undermined parental rights in relation to the education of children where parents are members of a religious minority or where they do not adhere to any religion.'

[9.044] Not only did the *Campaign* case validate the role of chaplains in community and comprehensive schools and their remuneration from public

197. Hogan and Whyte, *J M Kelly: The Irish Constitution*, para 7.8.69.

198. Hogan and Whyte, *J M Kelly: The Irish Constitution.*

199. McCrea, 'The Supreme Court and the School Chaplains Case', (1999) 2 *Trinity College Law Review* 19.

200. McCrea, 'The Supreme Court and the School Chaplains Case', (1999) 2 *Trinity College Law Review* 19.

201. Cleary, 'The Interaction Between Religious Freedoms and Non-Discrimination in Irish Jurisprudence', *University College Dublin Law Review,* Vol 7, pp 51–64 at 52.

202. *Quinn's Supermarket v AG* [1972] IR 1; *Employment Equality Bill 1996* [1997] 2 IR 321; *Murphy v IRTC* [1999] 1 IR 12.

funds,[203] it paved the way for the introduction of the state's programme of religious education in second-level schools, which is now part of the curriculum under the Education Act 1998, s 30. In summary, while the *Campaign* decision legitimised and clarified the ethos of denominational schools, it did not reconcile or harmonise the tensions which arise between the right of the denominational schools to protect their ethos and the rights of children of minority religions not to be indoctrinated in denominational schools. With the passage of the Education Act 1998 and the growth of a highly diverse society, these issues are likely to become more complex in the future.

THE RULES FOR NATIONAL SCHOOLS, 1965 (THE RULES)

[9.045] Between 1937 and 1998 no legislation was passed to provide state aid for schools,[204] or to give effect to the constitutional liberal protections in Art 44.2.4°. As a consequence, a legislative lacuna arose in educational matters, which led to the demise of the 'mixed education principle' introduced by Lord Stanley in 1831. A new approach is apparent in the Preface to the 1965 edition of the Rules, which amended Rule 68 (Religious Instruction) of the 1947 edition of the Rules by stating: 'In the pursuance of the provisions of these Articles [42 and 44.2.4] the State provides for free primary education for children in national schools and gives explicit recognition to the denominational character of these schools.' The Rules of 1965 retained the requirements to fix and timetable formal religious instruction,[205] to separate religious instruction from secular instruction,[206] and to display the timetable in a conspicuous place in the school.[207] Some six

---

203. 'The role of the chaplain is to help to provide this extra dimension to the religious education of the children. The evidence establishes that, besides looking after the pastoral needs of the children, the chaplain helps them with counsel and advice about their day to day problems. It therefore appears to me that the present system whereby the salaries of chaplains in community schools are paid by the State is merely a manifestation, under modern conditions, of principles which are recognised and approved by Articles 44 and 42 of the Constitution', at p 358 of the decision.

204. Other than the annual Appropriation Acts.

205. Rules for National Schools, 1965, rule 69(2)(a) and rule 69(5).

206. Rules for National Schools, 1965, rule 54(2)(a).

207. Rules for National Schools, 1965, rule 54(1).

years later, these important safeguards for the liberal rights were abandoned, however, when 'the integrated curriculum'[208] of 1971 was introduced. As will be seen, however, the current position appears to be that the liberal rules in the Rules for National Schools (1965) have been re-affirmed and incorporated in the Education Act 1998.

THE INTEGRATED CURRICULUM OF 1971

[9.046] It is important to note that, when the integrated curriculum (the 1971 curriculum), was introduced in 1971, each denomination provided education for its own faith almost exclusively in Irish schools. The 1971 curriculum conferred official recognition on the concept of integration in Irish education: 'That the separation of religious and secular subjects into differentiated subject compartments serves only to throw the whole educational function out of focus.'[209] This curriculum met the long-term demands of the Catholic Church for the full integration of religious instruction with secular education for the first time in the history of the state. Chapter IV (Religion) of the 1971 curriculum incorporates Rule 68 of the 1965 edition of the Rules:

> Of all the parts of a school curriculum Religious Instruction is by far the most important, as its subject matter, God's honour and service, includes the proper use of all man's faculties … Religious Instruction, is therefore, a fundamental part of the school course, and a religious spirit should inform and vivify the whole work of the school.[210]

[9.047] Writing in 1987, Clarke asserted that the integrated curriculum was incompatible with the ECHR[211] since children have a right to attend state-funded schools without being instructed in a denominational manner. In addition, he contended that the alleged widespread failure to implement the constitutional guaranteed right of withdrawal from religious instruction,

---

208. *Curraculum na Bunscoile,* Teachers' Handbook (Government Publications, 1971). See in particular Pt 1, pp 19 and 23.

209. *Curraculum na Bunscoile.*

210. *Curraculum na Bunscoile.* See Coolahan (ed), *Report on the National Education Convention. Ireland: The National Education Convention Secretariat* (Government Publications, 1994) p 71.

211. Clarke, 'Freedom of Thought and Educational Rights in the European Convention', (1987) *Irish Jurist,* 50–54, 51: See further Clarke, 'Freedom of Thought in Schools: A Comparative Study' in Simmonds and Hampton (eds), (1986) *International and Comparative Quarterly,* 35, 271–301.

together with the official recognition of the integration of religion in the curriculum, combined to privilege the majority religious denominations while ignoring the rights of the minority religions. Mawhinney points out[212] that, unlike timetabled religious instruction or worship, the implementation of 'the integrated curriculum' may of its very nature permit involuntary indoctrination to take place.[213] If the aim of 'the integrated curriculum' is indoctrination in any one religion, she asserts, then the state, by implicitly providing for it, is in breach of international human rights law since the state's duty of neutrality and impartiality is incompatible with any power on the state's part to access the legitimacy of religious beliefs.[214]

[9.048] Where several religions co-exist in a democratic society, the ECtHR has held that it may be necessary to place restrictions on certain freedoms so as to harmonise the interests of the various religious groups and ensure that everyone's belief is respected.[215] Thus, the state may restrict the freedom to manifest religion if the exercise of that freedom conflicts with the aim of protecting the rights and freedoms of others, public order and public safety.[216] Accordingly, when doctrinal religious instruction is given in schools, opt-out clauses are required to be provided for the children of parents who do not wish their children to attend such instruction, thus avoiding involuntary indoctrination.[217]

---

212. Mawhinney, 'The Opt-Out Clause: Imperfect Protection for the Rights to Freedom of Religion in Schools', (2006) *Education Law Journal* at p 380: 'A child cannot be opted out of unscheduled and potentially continuous religious teaching which is woven into the very fabric of daily education. Instead, the attention of international human rights bodies must switch to, and focus on, the nature and aim of the integrated curriculum being taught.' See also Mawhinney, 'Freedom of Religion in the Irish Primary School System', 27(3) *Legal Studies*, September 2007, pp 379–403. See also *Metropolitan Church of Bessarabia v Moldova*, Application no 45701/99, para 123, ECHR 2001–XII.

213. Clarke, 'Freedom of Thought and Educational Rights in the European Convention', (1987) *Irish Jurist*, 50–54, 51.

214. *Metropolitan Church of Bessarabia v Moldova*, Application no 45701/99, para 123, ECHR 2001–XII; *Hasam and Chaush v Bulgaria* [GC], Application no 30985/96, para 62, ECHR 2000–XI.

215. *Kokkinakis v Greece* (1993) 17 EHRR 397, p 18, para 33.

216. *Dahlab v Switzerland* Case 44774/98, 29 June 2004.

217. *Hartikainen v Finland* (Comm No 40/1078) UN Doc A/34/40, Decision of 9 April 1981; *Kjelsden, Busk Madsen and Pedersen v Denmark* (1976) 1 EHRR 711.

[9.049] Casey concedes that, at the very least, the arrangements made for an integrated curriculum in 1971 make it more difficult for students to avoid religious instruction of which their parents or guardians disapprove.[218] Article 44.2.4° specifically protects this right:

> Legislation providing State aid for schools shall not discriminate between schools under the management of different religious denominations, nor be such as to affect prejudicially the right of any child to attend a school receiving public money without attending religious instruction at that school.

In 1971 there was no substantive legislation[219] providing state aid for schools, but that changed with the coming into force of the Education Act 1998. Prior to the passing of the Education Act 1998, the Report of the Constitution Review Group 1996 (the 1996 Report) had stated, 'the present reality of the denominational character of the school system does not accord with Article 44.2.4 … either Article 44.2.4 should be changed or the school system must change to accommodate Article 44.2.4.'[220] Since, the 1996 Report did not recommend that Art 44.2.4° be changed, it implied that the school system be changed to comply with Art 44.2.4°. The 1996 Report advanced the following reasons for not changing Art 44.2.4°:

> if Article 44.2.4 did not provide these safeguards, the State might well be in breach of its international obligations, inasmuch as it might mean that a significant number of children of minority religions (or those with no religion) might be coerced by force of circumstances to attend a school which did not cater for their particular religious views or their conscientious objections. If this were to occur, it would also mean that the State would be in breach of its obligations under Article 42.3.1.[221]

Remarkably, there was scant public discussion regarding this significant finding. However, in 1997 the little publicised Deeds of Variation were agreed and introduced for all national schools.[222] The Deeds of Variation,

---

218. Casey, 'State and Church in Ireland', in Robbers (ed), *State and Church in the European Union* (Nomos, 2005) pp 18–208, p 198.

219. Other than the annual Appropriation Acts.

220. *Report of the Constitution Review Group, 1996* (Government Publications, 1996) pp 3754–5; 385–7.

221. *Report of the Constitution Review Group, 1996* (Government Publications, 1996) pp 3754–5; 385–7.

222. Hyland, 'Challenges for the Irish Education System for the next generation and beyond: the Issue of School Patronage', published in SEARCH, August 2006, p 2.

which were negotiated and agreed with the various school patrons, following discussion with 'the partners'[223] in education, aimed to protect the ethos of the denominational schools into the future as the system moved towards formality and the enactment of the Education Act 1998.

DEEDS OF VARIATION

[9.050] Effectively the Deeds of Variation (the Deeds) were, as the name implies, a 'variation' on the old leases or deeds of trust of national schools which had been established with the aid of a state grant (of generally between 80 per cent and 90 per cent of building costs) and was vested in trustees (generally diocesan trusts).[224] The original lease or deed of trust made no reference to the ethos or philosophy of the school but simply required that the building be used for national school purposes for a period of 99 years.[225] However, the Deeds of Variation vary the terms of the existing leases by revoking the existing Trust and by inserting a new Deed of Variation, supplemental to the existing lease, which lays down the ethos of the school patron and trustees and gives legal effect to this ethos. For example, the Deeds of Variation for Catholic primary schools under the patronage of the Roman Catholic Church declare:

> A new Trust that a National school in connection with the Minister adopting and reflecting in its management and in the education, whether moral, intellectual or social, offered and given by it in the School to the children thereat, a Roman Catholic ethos shall, during the term of the Lease and any renewal thereof, be maintained upon the Demised Premises and otherwise on the like Trusts as are declared in the Lease.[226]

---

223. The Minister for Education, the National Parent's Council (Primary) and the Irish National Teachers Organisation and the various patron bodies.

224. Hyland, 'Challenges for the Irish Education System for the next generation and beyond: the Issue of School Patronage', published in SEARCH, August 2006, p 3.

225. Hyland, 'Challenges for the Irish Education System for the next generation and beyond: the Issue of School Patronage', published in SEARCH, August 2006.

226. *Management Board Members' Handbook* (Catholic Primary School Managers' Association, Veritas, 2004) pp 10–14, para 6.

[9.051] The Deeds of Variation declare as part of the indenture that:

> ... The Present Trustees, for themselves, their successors and assigns, and with the Approbation of the Minister, as testified by his being a party hereto, hereby COVENANT with the Land Owners, their successors and assigns, that they, the present Trustees, their successors and assigns, shall take all reasonable steps, to ensure that any board of management which may from time to time, be appointed in accordance with the instrument of Management to manage the School (hereinafter called 'the board of management' and reference herein to a board of management shall be construed accordingly) shall firstly manage the school in accordance with the doctrines, practices and traditions of the Roman Catholic Church, and secondly, shall make and keep themselves familiar with the ethos of the Roman Catholic Church and the Roman Catholic Faith insofar as the same relates to education and schools and thirdly, shall manage and cause the School to be managed in a manner which will uphold and foster such ethos and fourthly, shall not do anything or permit anything to be done in relation to the School, or the management thereof, which would have or be likely to have a detrimental effect on the Roman Catholic ethos of the School.[227]

[9.052] The Report of the Constitution Review Group (pp 385–6) stated that it seems implicit in Art 44.2.4° of the Constitution that a school which receives public funding cannot insist on a policy such as admitting only co-religionists as pupils, and the practice of an integrated curriculum appeared to be at variance with this guarantee. Thus, prior to the enactment of the Education Act 1998, it was necessary to abandon the concept of the integrated curriculum and to re-affirm the liberal guarantees in the Rules for National School 1965, which have never been formally withdrawn. If implemented in practice, arguably these Rules would provide the mandatory safeguards for ensuring that the rights of children of minority religions or none are protected in denominational schools as required by the Constitution.[228]

Accordingly, the *Catholic Schools' Management Board's Handbook* (the Handbook) cites prominently the relevant Rules for National Schools, 1965:

(a) the separation of Religious Instruction from Secular Instruction by formal time-tabling;[229]

227. Management Board Members' Handbook, A (1) p 12.

228. Art 44.2.4 and *Mulloy v Minister for Education* [1975] IR 88.

229. Rules for National Schools (Government Publications, 1965), rule 54.2.

(b) the display of the said Time-Table in a conspicuous place in the school;[230]

(c) the Rule governing freedom to attend religious exercises;[231] and

(d) the obligation to withdraw pupils from any Religious Instruction of which his/her parents or guardians disapprove.

It would appear that the Rules for National Schools 1965 (as amended), and the Deeds of Variation, have been transposed by section 7(4)(a)(iv) of the Education Act 1998 which provides that the Minister, in carrying out his or her functions:

> shall have regard to ...
>
> (iv) the practices and traditions relating to the organisation of schools or groups of schools existing at the commencement of this Part and the right of the schools to manage their own affairs in accordance with this Act and any charters, deeds, articles of management or other instruments relating to their establishment or operation.

Whether this provision satisfies the international human rights requirements set down by the ECtHR in the *Metropolitan Church of Bessarabia* case[232] is another matter. In other words are they 'prescribed by law', foreseeable, precise, accessible to the people so that they can regulate their conduct accordingly and is the scope of their discretion sufficiently spelt out? In the opinion of this writer, these significant provisions need to be included in legislative measures so that they are accessable to the people whose children are affected by them.

A further interface arises with the Canon Law of the Catholic Church under which, by virtue of his office, the parish priest is to ensure that children are properly prepared for the sacraments by means of religious instruction and formation over an appropriate period of time.[233] This preparation is made through the agency of the Catholic school with the collaboration of the parents and family of the child.[234] The question then

230. Rules for National Schools, rule 54.1.

231. Rules for National Schools, rules 56.7 and 56.8.

232. *Metropolitan Church of Bessarabia v Moldova*, Application no 45701/99, para 123, ECHR 2001–XII; *Hasam and Chaush v Bulgaria* [GC], Application no 30985/96, para 62, ECHR 2000–XI

233. Code of Canon Law, Catechical Formation, No 777.2.

234. *Management Board Members' Handbook* (Catholic Primary School Managers' Association, Veritas, 2004) p 7.

arises as to whether this instruction and formation must necessarily be confined to the specified time for religious instruction on the school's time-table so as to protect the rights of pupils of minority religions or none. Another issue that is unclear is who is to monitor the implementation of the relevant Rules for National Schools in this regard?

[9.053] Because the Deeds of Variation brought about fundamental changes to a publicly-funded system of education, which enshrined a tradition of 126 years embodying safeguards for pupils of minority religions and none, one would expect that this measure would have been brought fully to the attention of the public prior to giving effect to such profound changes in legislation particularly at a time of growing secularity and diversity.

[9.054] The arrangement under the Deeds of Variation, under which the denominational schools accept the relevant Rules, as outlined above, are broadly in harmony with the principles laid down in *Kjelsden v Denmark* in which the ECHR stated with regard to Art 2 of Protocol 1 of the ECHR:

> It follows in the first place … that the setting and planning of the curriculum fall in principle within the competence of the Contracting States. This mainly involves questions of expediency on which it is not for the Court to rule and whose solution may legitimately vary according to the country and to the era. In particular, the second sentence of Article 2 of the Protocol does not prevent States from imparting through teaching or education information or knowledge of a directly or indirectly religious or philosophical kind. It does not even permit parents to object to the integration of such teaching or education in the school curriculum for otherwise all institutionalised teaching would run the risk of proving impracticable.[235]

Clearly, the ECHR permits a wide margin of appreciation to the state in this particular sphere. But there are limits to the state's discretion in that it may not enjoin a certain ethical or moral view of life and may not pursue an aim of indoctrination which might be considered as not respecting parents' religious and philosophical convictions.[236] The state must also ensure that information or knowledge conveyed in the curriculum is conveyed in an objective, critical and pluralist manner.[237]

One may conclude that the transposition of the Deeds of Variation and the re-affirmed Rules for National Schools, 1965 into the Education Act 1998

235. *Kjelsden, Busk Madsen and Pedersen v Denmark* (1976) 1 EHRR 711.

236. *Kjelsden, Busk Madsen and Pedersen v Denmark* (1976) 1 EHRR 711, p 712.

237. *Kjelsden, Busk Madsen and Pedersen v Denmark* (1976) 1 EHRR 711.

was effected with little publicity, and that because of the manner of their incorporation, many parents are currently unaware of the changes they have wrought. In the opinion of this author, it is important that these arrangements and those for the teaching of religious instruction and worship and religious education in national schools are included in secondary legislation pursuant to the Education Act 1998.

THE EDUCATION ACT 1998 AND RELIGION

[9.055] The Revised Curriculum for Primary Schools 1999 (the Curriculum) acknowledges the significance of the spiritual dimension of the person and the role of religious education, which 'enables the child to develop spiritual and moral values and to come to a knowledge of God.'[238] Furthermore, it recognises that 'The spiritual is a fundamental aspect of religious experience, and its religious and cultural expression is an inextricable part of Irish culture and history'[239] but it also emphasises the importance of tolerance towards the beliefs of others and aspires to develop that quality in children. However, the Curriculum recognises the freedom of religion principle, together with freedom of expression of religion. With regard to the school, it states:

> It is the responsibility of the school to provide a religious education that is consonant with its ethos and at the same time to be flexible in making alternative organisational arrangements for those who do not wish to avail of the particular religious education it offers. It is equally important that the beliefs and sensibilities of every child are respected.[240]

In the context of the Education Act 1998, the Department of Education and Science recognises the rights of the various church authorities to design curricula in religious education in primary schools, and to supervise their teaching and implementation. Accordingly, a religious education curriculum is not included in the curriculum documentation provided by the National Council for Curriculum and Assessment (NCCA).[241] However, the Education Act 1998 makes provision for the teaching of religious education and religious instruction.

---

238. Revised Curriculum for Primary Schools (Government Publications, 1999) p 58.
239. Revised Curriculum for Primary Schools.
240. Revised Curriculum for Primary Schools.
241. Revised Curriculum for Primary Schools.

[9.056] Under s 30 of the Education Act 1998, the Minister may prescribe the subjects to be offered, the syllabus of each secular subject, the amount of instruction time for each subject, including the time to be spent on religious instruction, but not the content thereof:[242] It is one of the functions of a recognised school to promote the moral, spiritual, social and personal development of students in consultation with their parents, having regard to the characteristic spirit of the school.[243] Thus, while the state may legitimately be concerned with moral education in such schools,[244] and may assist parents by providing for 'religious and moral formation', nonetheless, the spiritual dimension of a denominational school's function is essentially the responsibility of parents and the churches, acting on their behalf. Although s 30 of the 1998 Act provides for a period of religious instruction[245] in recognised denominational schools, the content and supervision of such instruction falls to the various religious authorities, although the instruction is given by the teachers, who are employees of the school boards, who in turn are remunerated by the state.

[9.057] Section 30(4) confers considerable discretion on a recognised school provided it discharges its obligation to teach the full state curriculum. Without prejudice to the generality of s 30(1), the Minister is required to have regard to the characteristic spirit of a school or class of school in exercising his/her functions under this section. Moreover, the Minister is required in s 30(2)(d) to ensure that the amount of instruction time to be allocated to curricular subjects as determined by him/her in each school day shall be such as to allow for 'such reasonable instruction time, as the board with the consent of the patron determines, for subjects relating to or arising from the characteristic spirit of the school ...'. In order to give effect to Art 44.2.4° of the Constitution, s 30(2)(e) of the 1998 Act provides[246] that the Minister: 'shall not require any student to attend instruction in any subject which is contrary to the conscience of the parent of the student or in

242. Section 30 (1) of the Act of 1998.

243. Section 9(d).

244. See Art 42.3.2° of the Constitution of Ireland and this is reflected in practice through the provision of religious education as a subject for Junior and Leaving Certificate. With regard to the human rights dimension, see further *Hartikainen v Finland* (Comm No 40/1078) UN Doc A/34/40, Decision of 9 April1981 and *Jimenez and Jimenez Merino v Spain*, Application no 51188/99.

245. Of 30 minutes duration daily; Rules for National Schools, rules 68 and 69.

246. 'Without prejudice to the generality of subsection (1) ...'.

the case of a student who has reached the age of 18 years, the student.' Section 30(4) provides: 'A school, may, subject to the requirement that the curriculum as determined by the Minister is taught in that school, provide courses of instruction in such other subjects as the board considers appropriate.'

[9.058] To date, there has been no judicial interpretation of these provisions and certain matters remain unclear. This was precisely the problem faced by the Minister in 2005, when it was alleged that a North Dublin Muslim primary school was spending too much time teaching the Koran,[247] giving rise to 'fears extremism could flourish.'[248] The school explained its practice of teaching religion for 45 minutes daily, rather than the allocated 30 minutes, which it claimed was 'within Ministerial guidelines' made under s 30 of the 1998 Act. Religion classes in the school included time for teaching Arabic, which was considered necessary by the patron in order to read the Koran. In addition, two classes weekly were devoted to the Koran, with a further three classes to moral education. From the perspective of s 30 of the 1998 Act, once the school could establish that the curriculum as determined by the Minister was taught, the board could provide courses of instruction in such other subjects as the patron considered appropriate.[249] Furthermore, with regard to the teaching of the Koran, since the Koran was revealed to Muhammad in Arabic, then arguably Arabic is a subject 'relating to or arising from the characteristic spirit of the school.'[250] If the school could show that the board, with the consent of the patron, had determined that Arabic be taught, that Arabic related to or arose out of the characteristic spirit of the school, and that the time spent on teaching Arabic amounted to 'reasonable instruction time' pursuant to s 30(2)(d),[251] then arguably this fell within the ambit of s 30 of the 1998 Act. One may conclude, therefore, that s 30 of the 1998 Act facilitates religious freedom in Ireland's recognised schools to a degree that is quite remarkable.

---

247. See (2005) *Irish Independent*, 10 October.

248. Murphy, 'Muslim school defends itself', (2005) *The Village*, 20 October.

249. Section 30(4).

250. Which indicates a dual test, either of which will suffice.

251. In addition, the school's position in regard to the teaching of the Koran would be strengthened by the fact that 'the integrated curriculum' appears to have been carried over into the 1998 Act thereby removing the strict boundaries that previously existed between secular education and spiritual instruction.

[9.059] If, however, any of the secular curricular subjects were not receiving the time allocated by the state curriculum, or if the students of the secular subjects were not achieving national standards in the state examinations, the Minister would be entitled to investigate such matters pursuant to the Education Act 1998, s 30. In addition, all schools are subject to the general law and the Constitution, which provides that fidelity to the nation and loyalty to the state are fundamental political duties of all citizens under Art 9.3. Indeed, the guarantee of freedom of conscience and the free profession and practice of religion in Art 44.2.1° of the Constitution is expressly made 'subject to public order and morality.'[252] Accordingly, if matters were being taught in any school which were contrary to the common good, or subversive of a democratic society,[253] then the state would not only have a right but a duty to intervene, since no recognised school is immune from the overall scrutiny of the state in regard to any subject taught on its premises.

Religious Education in Irish Schools

[9.060] In 1999, a new subject, religious education, was introduced under s 30 of the Act of 1998 and students may now opt to take this subject for the state examinations.[254] This broad comparative programme aims to provide students with a framework for encountering and engaging with a variety of religious traditions in Ireland and elsewhere. This provision by the state is in line with international human rights law provided this subject is taught in 'a neutral and objective way'[255] and with respect for the convictions of non-believers, and provided the state does not indoctrinate in any one religion.[256] By contrast with the position in Norway, Sweden, Finland, Greece and Turkey,[257] where the religious education/ethics programme is mandatory, the religious education programme in Ireland is a voluntary subject, which may be taken as a subject for the state examinations. In the case of Finland, for example, the UN Human Rights Committee have upheld the Finnish state's

252. Article 44.2.

253. See *Refah Partisi v Turkey* [2003] ECHR 87.

254. Junior Certificate Religious Education Syllabus and Leaving Certificate Religious Education Syllabus.

255. *Hartikainen v Finland* (Comm No 40/1078) UN Doc A/34/40, Decision of 9 April 1981.

256. *Kjelsden, Busk Madsen and Pedersen v Denmark* (1976) 1 EHRR 711.

257. **Para [4.002]**.

right to make a course of religious education compulsory for public schools since provision had been made for students to be withdrawn both from religious instruction or religious education if they were receiving comparable instruction outside of the school.[258] In *Hartikainen v Finland*,[259] the applicant, a teacher and General Secretary of the Union of Free Thinkers in Finland, challenged the teaching of religious education in public schools in Finland. He alleged that the content and teaching of a religious education class comprising the history of religions and ethics, which was compulsory for those students who had been exempted from the religious instruction programme (as is also the case in German public schools), was inherently religious in character and that the law requiring attendance at these classes[260] violated Art 18(4) of the ICCPR. That Article provides:

> States Parties to the present Convention undertake to have respect for the liberty of parents and, when applicable, legal guardians to ensure the religious and moral education of their children in conformity with their own convictions.[261]

[9.061] Finland admitted that difficulties had arisen with regard to the existing teaching plan to give effect to these provisions, which did, in part at least, appear to be religious in character. Nevertheless, the ICCPS found that the Finnish legislation concerning religious freedom and the School System Act were compatible with the ICCPR, indicating a considerable margin of appreciation for states in this sphere.

VOCATIONAL SCHOOLS IN IRELAND: PUBLIC SECTOR

[9.062] Vocational schools were established under the Vocational Education Act 1930, which devolved the control and management of vocational schools (trade schools as they were then)[262] to the local vocational education

258. Under para 6 of the School System Act, as amended.

259. *Hartikainen v Finland* (Comm No 40/1078) UN Doc A/34/40, Decision of 9 April 1981.

260. Paragraph 16(3) of the Comprehensive School Statute (No 443 of 26 June 1970), revised on 16 April 1982 (No 296) to correspond with the formulation of para 6 of the School System Act (No 467 of 26 July 1968).

261. The School System Act 1968, as amended, provides for one lesson weekly in ethics and history of religion.

262. Which had its roots in the previous two centuries: Byrne, 'Technical Education' in Hyland and Milne (eds) *Irish Educational Documents*, vol 1, pp 239 *et seq*.

committees (VECs), thus establishing a democratic, secular, non-denominational school system in state-owned schools.[263] The Act was confined to vocational and 'continuation education'[264] (education after the age of 14 years) and assurances were given by the state[265] to the Catholic bishops that general education would continue to be the preserve of the fee-paying denominational secondary schools.[266] Following church-state negotiations in 1942, however, the vocational schools introduced religious instruction to be given by priest-teachers in all VEC schools in the Dublin diocese (and later countrywide) and these teachers received state salaries in common with other teachers. Cooney observes the huge advantage which accrued to Catholic education interests as a result of this initiative, but he is critical of the undemocratic method of its achievement, since it circumvented the parliamentary process and was brought into effect without amendment to the Act of 1930.[267] Although there is no mention of religious instruction in the VEC Act, it was envisaged by the then Minister for Education (John Marcus O'Sullivan) that religious instruction would be provided by the VECs under 'our general powers of approval of courses…'.[268] During the late 1970s, when difficulties were encountered in recruiting priest-teachers, the teaching of religious instruction by lay teachers in vocational schools was facilitated by the state,[269] following

263. For a fascinating look at this development, see McCarthy, *The Distasteful Challenge*.

264. See 'Letter from the Minister for Education to Most Rev D Keane, Bishop of Limerick, dated 31 October, 1930', in Hyland and Milne (eds) *Irish Educational Documents,* Vol 2, pp 219–222; O'Buachalla, *Educational Policy in Twentieth Century Ireland*, p 64.

265. Through the then Minister for Education John Marcus O'Sullivan.

266. Hyland and Milne (eds) *Irish Educational Documents*, at p 220.

267. Cooney, *John Charles McQuaid: Ruler of Catholic Ireland*, p 146; see also Department of Education, Memorandum V.40 in this regard.

268. 'Letter from the Minister for Education to Most Rev D Keane, Bishop of Limerick, dated 31 October, 1930', published in Hyland and Milne (eds), *Irish Educational Documents,* vol 2, pp 221–222.

269. Department of Education, Circular Letter 7/79, 'Religious Instruction in Vocational Schools'; *O'Callaghan v Meath VEC*, (20 November 1990, unreported) HC, p 6. Mr Justice Costello, as he was then, when dealing with the appointment of a teacher of religion in a VEC school, stated 'If the VEC acted in breach of Circular 7/79 it would not follow that it acted *ultra vires*, as might well be the case if the procedures had been included in a statutory instrument.'

negotiation with the parties in education,[270] indicating the remarkably close relationship subsisting at that time between church and the state.[271]

[9.063] All VEC boards of management must now (through Department circulars) ensure that religious instruction and religious worship is provided in accordance with the rites, practice and teaching of the religious denomination to which the pupil belongs.[272] The board is also required to ensure there is a sufficient number of teachers in the school, appointed with the approval of the competent religious authority, to provide two hours of religious instruction per week in these schools.[273] There is constitutional authority for such provision in Art 42.4, provided parents require it.

With regard to the Education Act 1998, the Minister, in carrying out his or her functions under s 7(4)(iv) of the Act 1998, is required to have regard to ('shall have regard to'), among other matters:

> the practices and traditions relating to the organisation of schools or groups of schools existing at the commencement of this Part and the right of schools to manage their own affairs in accordance with this Act and any charters, deeds, articles of management or other such instruments relating to their establishment or operation.

Thus, the practices and traditions relating to the teaching of religious instruction and worship, grounded in Department of Education Circular Letters and its 'general power of approval of courses', are now recognised within the statutory context. Since parents of minority religions and none are unlikely to be fully aware of their rights in regard to their child's religious education, more detailed and transparent provision needs to made through secondary legislation, eg through statutory instruments or ministerial regulations. Otherwise, how are parents to exercise their significant rights in regard to religious freedom?

Community Colleges: Public Sector

[9.064] When the second-level community and comprehensive schools were established in the 1960s, the VECs pressed to retain their place as important education providers under the secular VEC Acts 1930–1962. Following

270. The VECs, the Teachers Union of Ireland and the state.

271. Whyte, Church and State in Modern Ireland, 1923–1979.

272. DES Circular 73/74, rule 11 B 9; see Farry, *Vocational Teachers and the Law* (1998), Blackhall, pp 34, 36–7

273. DES Circular 73/74, rule 10(e).

negotiation with the parties in education, community colleges were established by deeds of trust in which it was proposed to merge in one unit either a privately-owned (voluntary secondary) school with a school in the public sector (a VEC school), or to establish a new (Greenfield) community college. This plan necessitated the amendment of the VEC Acts 1930–1962, which was implemented by the VEC (Amendment) Act 1970 (the 1970 Act).[274] The 1970 Act permitted a VEC to establish and maintain in its area, in accordance with the VEC Acts 1930–1970, such courses of instruction, in the nature of continuation and technical education, as it considered necessary, subject to the consent of the Minister and to the agreed terms and conditions of the parties. Such courses, however, are restricted to those in the nature of 'continuation education' (defined in the Act of 1930 as 'education after the age of 14 years') and 'technical education'. Since the VEC Acts 1930–1962 were silent on religious instruction, it would have been more appropriate to amend those Acts in order to make provision for the teaching of religious instruction in these state-funded, public-sector colleges. However, no such amendment was made.

[9.065] Following a protracted period of negotiation with the parties in education, deeds of trust for community colleges were agreed and Model Agreements for Community Colleges or Memoranda formed part of these deeds: the wording and powers of which may vary somewhat from one college to another.[275] Under these agreements, boards of management are established, on which the religious authority has representation.[276] The religious authority also has a role in the selection and appointment of staff and a role in relation to the appointment, continuing suitability and discontinuance of teachers of religious instruction and worship.[277] Inspection of the teaching of religion is the responsibility of the catechetical inspectorate, in accordance with agreed procedures. Generally, the VEC is required to appoint a chaplain, nominated by the relevant religious authority,

274. Vocational Education (Amendment) Act 1970, which enabled a VEC, with ministerial consent, to jointly maintain a school, thereby facilitating the establishment of community colleges. See s 1 of the Act.

275. The author in this instance is using the Model Agreement for Community Colleges in County Cork VECs.

276. The main religious authority has three nominees and the minority church has one nominee out of a maximum of twelve members.

277. See, for example, *O'Callaghan v Meath VEC*, (20 November 1990, unreported) HC.

who is to be a full-time member of the staff. The chaplain receives the same state salary as a teacher. Suitable arrangements are to be made for members of other religions in consultation with the appropriate authorities.

[9.066] It will be recalled that the introduction of chaplains into community schools was affirmed as constitutional by the Supreme Court in *Campaign to Separate Church and State v Minister for Education*,[278] but this decision did not expressly encompass the appointment of publicly-funded chaplains in community colleges established under the VEC Acts 1930–2001. Nonetheless, chaplains were introduced into the community colleges through their model agreements, which may vary in wording and powers, as each VEC is independent. For example, the Model Agreement for Community Colleges, under the County Cork VEC,[279] states at para 13(x):

> The Committee will appoint a Chaplain nominated by the relevant religious authority who shall be employed outside the normal quota of the college. He shall be a full-time member of the staff and shall be paid a salary equivalent to that of a teacher in the school. Suitable arrangements will be made for members of other religions in consultation with the appropriate authorities.

There is constitutional authority for the state, when the public good requires it, to provide other educational facilities or institutions such as the community colleges.[280] The state must do so, however, with due regard for the rights of parents, especially in the matter of religious and moral formation.[281] Since Art 44.4 of the Constitution envisages that legislation would be employed for the provision of state aid for schools, arguably this provision should have been incorporated into the VEC Acts by amendment or included in secondary legislation. One way or another, in order to comply with international human rights freedom of religion principles, the rights of parents of minority religions or no religion must be prescribed by law and they must be accessible, foreseeable, precisely formulated and the scope of the discretion afforded to public authorities and denominational school authorities needs to be clearly specified.

---

278. *Campaign to Separate Church and State v Minister for Education* [1996] 2 ILRM 241; [1998] 2 ILRM 81; 3 IR 321, 356. See also *McGrath v Trustees of Maynooth College* [1979] ILRM 166.

279. In the dioceses of Cork and Ross.

280. Art 42.4 of the Constitution.

281. Art 42.4 of the Constitution.

EDUCATIONAL PROVISION: THE 'BLOCK GRANT' FOR PROTESTANT STUDENTS

[9.067] When free secondary education was being introduced in 1967, it became apparent that 75 per cent of Catholic students in secondary schools would benefit under the scheme, while only 7.5 per cent of Protestant students would benefit. This meant that the majority of the latter group, because of their size and geographical distribution, would have to attend Protestant boarding (residential) schools[282] if they were to receive an education in accordance with their parents' religious and philosophical convictions. Consequently, the then Minister for Education,[283] made special arrangements for the funding of the Protestant voluntary secondary schools, which is administered annually as 'the Block Grant' (the Grant). A *per capita* allocation, broadly equivalent to the capitation given to the other schools in the free scheme, is made for each day student attending a Protestant secondary school. A further allocation is made in respect of each residential student attending a Protestant voluntary secondary school or a Protestant comprehensive residential school. The total of these two allocations comprises the 'Block Grant', which is administered by the Secondary Education Committee of the Protestant school sector. Although the Grant is allocated in respect of families, it is paid to schools for administrative convenience and is used by them to offset fees payable by qualifying families on the basis of a means test.[284] While *prima facie* the Grant appears discriminatory, its underlying objectives indicate otherwise.[285] As Walsh J stated in *Quinn's Supermarket v AG*,[286] it would be completely contrary to the spirit and intendment of Art 44.2 to permit the guarantee against discrimination on the ground of religious profession or belief to be made the very means of restricting or preventing the free practice of religion. If the purpose of financial funding is to facilitate the protection of constitutionally-recognised rights or to aid in their exercise by right-holders, or to fulfil the state's obligations to respect them, then it cannot be

282. *Dáil Debates*, Vol 225, cols 1886/7, 30 November 1966; written submission of the TWG of the Secondary Education Committee.

283. The late Donough O'Malley TD.

284. *Dáil Debates*, Vol 225, cols 1886/7, 30 November 1966; written submission of the TWG of the Secondary Education Committee.

285. *McGrath v Trustees of Maynooth College* [1979] ILRM 166, SC, per Kenny J.

286. *Quinn's Supermarket v AG* [1972] IR 1.

constitutionally invalid to confer such aid.[287] Since the Grant is intended to aid the parents of Protestant students to exercise their right to free choice of school, so far as possible, in accordance with their religious or philosophical beliefs, this measure appears constitutional. If the Grant were denied to other denominations in similar circumstances, this would be unconstitutional because of the non-discrimination principle in Art 44.2.4° of the Constitution.

EMPLOYMENT EQUALITY

[9.068] By contrast with teachers in Germany, who are civil servants, the majority of teachers in Ireland are employees of denominational boards of management. However, teachers in Ireland are also classified as public servants paid by the state,[288] although they are not employed by the state, the exception being teachers in the vocational school sector[289] which educates approximately 26 per cent of second-level students. The duality of control in denominational schools, emanating from the church-state relationship, has led to some difficulties reconciling individual rights with the constitutionally-protected rights of the religious denomination.[290] When legislating for equality, therefore, the state had to respect the constitutional entitlements of the religious denominations by including certain exemptions in the legislation. When the Employment Equality Bill 1996 was referred by President Robinson to the Supreme Court to test its constitutionality, the Court rejected the challenge to the Bill based on the religion ground, holding that the legislative objective of the Bill was to authorise a form of positive discrimination so as to afford protection to the religious ethos of the various religious denominations, thus giving effect to Art 44 of the Constitution.[291] In allowing for such positive discrimination on the religion ground, the Court stated that the Oireachtas[292] had balanced the right of free profession

287. *Campaign to Separate Church and State v Minister for Education* [1996] 2 ILRM 241 HC and [1998] 2 ILRM 81.

288. *Maunsell v Minister for Education* [1940] 213 at 228.

289. Who are employees of the relevant VEC.

290. Whyte, 'Protecting Religious Ethos in Employment Law: a Clash of Cultures', (2005) 27 *DULJ* 169.

291. Employment Equality Bill 1996 [1997] 2 IR 321, p 321 at 325.

292. Parliament comprising two Houses, the Dáil and the Seanad.

and practice of religion, on the one hand, and the rights to equality before the law and the right to earn one's livelihood, on the other:

> The legislative objective behind both s 12 and s 37, sub-s 1 was to authorise a form of positive discrimination to afford protection to the religious ethos of various religious denominations, and in so doing, give effect to Article 44 of the Constitution. The provisions enacted represented a reasonable balancing by the Oireachtas between the conflicting principles.

The Court concluded that it is probably true to say that the respect for religion which the Constitution requires the state to show implies that each religious denomination should be respected when it says what its ethos is. The term 'ethos'[293] was not defined in the Bill but the court took notice of its definition in Chambers English Dictionary, as: 'the distinctive habitual character and disposition of an individual group.'[294] The final decision as to what is reasonably necessary to protect the ethos of a denominational school rests with the courts and, in arriving at a decision, the courts strive to balance and reconcile the various constitutional rights involved.[295] It is conceivable that the ECJ could require Ireland to narrow the exemptions provided for denominational schools, hospitals, state-funded adoption agencies and other charities in view of the fact that the provision made for religious institutions by Art 4(2) of EC Directive 2000/78/EC (the Framework Directive) establishing a general framework for equal treatment in employment and occupation, is considerably narrower in scope than that provided by s 37 of the 1998 Act, which became effective on 2 December 2003.[296]

[9.069] In what has proved to be a controversial and untimely move, the Equality Commissioner for the EU, Vladimir Spindla, sought a 'reasoned opinion' from the Irish government warning that certain exemptions for religious organisations from Equality Directives[297] under Irish law (discussed in **chapter 3**) were in conflict with EU law. Currently, institutions

293. The term 'ethos' is not used in the Education Act 1998, but rather 'the characteristic spirit of the school.' See further Norman, *Ethos and Education in Ireland.*

294. *Employment Equality Bill 1996* [1997] 2 IR 321, p 359 *per* Hamilton CJ.

295. *Employment Equality Bill 1996* [1997] 2 IR 321.

296. See Whyte, 'Protecting Religious Ethos in Employment Law: a Clash of Cultures', (2005) 27 *DULJ* 169; Walshe, 'State protection for church schools is at risk from the EU', (2008) *Irish Independent,* 5 April.

300 Council Directive 2000/43/EC (the Race Directive), which applies to education and to the churches, and Council Directive 2000/78/EC (contd .../)

of a religious character, including schools, are permitted when employing individuals to favour candidates who will uphold the religious ethos of the germane religion. Thus, for example, a school cannot be required to employ a person who openly ridicules the teaching of the relevant church. This exemption was negotiated some years ago and upheld by the Council of Ministers.[298] In February 2008, however, the Commission declared that the exemptions granted to these bodies were 'too broad' and it required the Irish government to align its legislation with the stricter Equality Directive or face a hearing at the ECJ. As Ireland approached its referendum on the Lisbon Treaty, it received a visit from President Manuel Barroso, who confirmed that the Commission would not be pursuing the case. However, the Commission's earlier intervention may have affirmed that unease on the part of the Irish people as to what would follow acceptance of the Lisbon Treaty. It is, of course, open to the Commission to revisit this issue at a future date, but it is now fully aware that any attempt to do so will be faced not just with the opposition of the Catholic Church, but possibly with the combined forces of all the main churches, which could prove divisive for the EU in the long term.

The Employment Equality Acts 1998–2004

[9.070] The Employment Equality Acts 1998–2004 prohibit discrimination on nine substantive grounds, one of which is religion, which includes the absence of religious belief. The Equality Act 2004 aims to implement three EU Directives: the Race Directive (2000/43/EC), the Framework Employment Directive (2000/78/EC) and the Revised Gender Equal Treatment Directive (2002/73/EC). These Directives require all member states to prohibit discrimination, harassment and victimisation on the grounds of gender, racial or social origin, religion or belief, disability, age or sexual orientation in regard to employment and occupational and vocational training.

---

297. (contd) (The Framework Directive) which establishes a general framework for equal treatment in employment and occupation in regard, *inter alia,* to the churches and in education and training.

298. Kelly, 'EU backs down in Church school row', (2008) *The Irish Catholic,* 24 April, p 1.

[9.071] Section 37 of the 1998 Act is of particular significance with regard to teacher employment in denominational schools. Section 37(1) of the Act provides:

> A religious, educational or medical institution which is under the direction or control of a body established for religious purposes or whose objectives include the provision of services in an environment which promotes certain religious values shall not be taken to discriminate against a person for the purposes of this Part or Part 11 if—
>
> (a) it gives more favourable treatment, on the religion ground, to an employee or a prospective employee over that person where it is reasonable to do so in order to maintain the religious ethos of the institution, or
>
> (b) it takes action which is reasonably necessary to prevent an employee or a prospective employee from undermining the religious ethos of the institution.

[9.072] Considerably narrower protection, however, is afforded religious interests in Art 4.2 of the Framework Directive, which establishes a general framework for equal treatment in employment and occupation and its object is the protection of minorities throughout the Union. It aims to protect the categories of individuals as set out in Art 13 of the EC Treaty[299] regarding access to employment. Consideration 23 of the Directive provides that 'in very limited circumstances' a difference of treatment may be justified where a characteristic relating to religion or belief, disability, age or sexual orientation constitutes a genuine and determining occupational requirement, provided that the objective is legitimate and the requirement is proportionate. The Framework Directive provides:

> Member States may maintain national legislation in force at the date of adoption of this Directive or provide for future legislation incorporating national practices existing at the date of adoption of this Directive pursuant to which, in the case of occupational activities within churches or other public or private organisations the ethos of which is based on religion or belief, a difference of treatment based on a person's religion or belief shall not constitute discrimination where, by reason of the nature of these activities or of the context in which they are carried out, a person's religion or belief constitute a genuine, legitimate and justified occupational requirement, having regard to the organisation's ethos. This difference of treatment shall be implemented taking account of Member States' constitutional provisions and

299. Inserted by Treaty of Amsterdam.

principles, as well as the general principles of Community law, and should not justify discrimination on another ground.

Provided that its provisions are otherwise complied with, this Directive shall thus not prejudice the right of the churches or other public or private organisations, the ethos of which is based on religion or belief, from acting in conformity with national constitutions and laws, from requiring individuals working for them to act in good faith and with loyalty to the organisation's ethos.

[9.073] An employer is to be afforded the Directive's protection if it can be established that, because of its occupational activities or the context in which they are exercised, the employee's religion or belief constitutes a genuine, legitimate and justified occupational requirement, having regard to the employer's ethos. Accordingly, Bolger argues: 'it will be necessary to show that a person's religion is a determining factor in her actual ability to discharge the duties of her job, rather than simply showing the employer's perception that such religion or belief is fitting in light of the organisation's ethos.'[300]

[9.074] Furthermore, the religious discrimination will only be lawful provided that it does not also constitute discrimination on any one of the other prohibited grounds.[301] Therefore, the dismissal of an unmarried pregnant female teacher could not now be justified under this provision since it would breach 'the family status' ground.[302] Neither would the dismissal of an openly homosexual teacher be lawful since it would breach 'the sexual orientation ground'.

Employment-Related Conflicts

[9.075] In the past, tensions arose between the individual rights of teachers and the rights of denominational schools to protect their ethos,[303] being two

300. Bolger, 'Discrimination on Grounds of Religion', in Costello and Barry (eds), *The New Equality Directives* (Irish Centre for European Law, 2003) p 384.

301. See further Whyte, 'Implications for Schools of Irish Equality Legislation' in Glendenning and Binchy (eds), *Litigation against Schools: Implications for School Management*, p 118 at 134; Beaumont, 'Christian Perspectives on the law: What makes them distinctive?' in O'Dair and Lennon, *Law and Religion* (OUP, 2001) p 538.

302. See the decision in an earlier case *Flynn v Power* [1985] IR 648; [1985] ILRM 336.

303. See O'Connell, A History of the INTO.

sets of competing legally established rights.[304] In *Memoir*,[305] the late John McGahern describes his dismissal from his position as a national teacher in Dublin in the mid-1960s. The school authorities[306] alleged the author had failed to live up to the ethos of his school by marrying a Finnish theatre director in a registry office in London and/or by publishing a novel (*The Dark*) in London in 1965, which was banned under the Irish Censorship of Publications Act 1929.[307] McGahern did not challenge his dismissal but departed quietly to London to pursue his burgeoning career as a writer. In *Memoir* he also refers to the many compatriot teachers he encountered during his sojourn in London who had 'run foul of a bishop or a priest, or had infringed some article of Catholic dogma and had no recourse but to disappear silently into Britain'.[308]

[9.076] One teacher who did not go silently, however, was the claimant in *Flynn v Power*[309] since the Unfair Dismissals Act 1977 (the 1977 Act) had by then provided some redress for employees who had been unfairly dismissed. The claimant, who had been residing with, and had become pregnant by, a married man in a provincial town, alleged unfair dismissal from her position as a consequence of matters 'wholly or mainly' arising from her pregnancy, contrary to the 1977 Act.[310] Prior to her pregnancy, however, the claimant had been requested by her employer, a religious order, to end the said relationship and it was alleged that some parents had complained about the claimant's lifestyle. The Employment Appeals Tribunal (EAT) held that the dismissal was not unfair.[311] Following an

---

304. *Fox v Higgins* (1912) 46 ILTR 222. For an interesting and erudite analysis of this matter, see Osborough, 'Education in the Irish Law and Constitution' (1978) 13 *Irish Jurist* (ns) 145 and Osborough, 'Irish Law and the Rights of National Teachers' (1979) *Irish Jurist*, 15, 36–60.

305. McGahern, *Memoir* (Faber and Faber, 2005), p 251 *et seq*.

306. The person who had authorised McGahern's dismissal was Archbishop John Charles McQuaid who was then patron of all the Catholic national schools in the Roman Catholic Dublin diocese.

307. Other banned authors were James Joyce, Samuel Beckett, Frank O'Connor and Brendan Behan.

308. McGahern, *Memoir* (Faber and Faber, 2005), p 252.

309. *Flynn v Power* [1985] ILRM 336.

310. Section 6(2)(f).

311. With its Chairperson, Mr Barry Hickson BL, dissenting.

unsuccessful appeal to the Circuit Court, the matter came before the High Court, where Costello J weighed the claimant's right to freedom from discrimination under the 1977 Act[312] against the constitutional rights of a voluntary secondary school to carry on its activities in the running of its school.[313] The judge held that the claimant was not dismissed for becoming pregnant but because her lifestyle did not accord with the ethos of the denominational secondary school and the norms of behaviour and ideals it was established to promote. Distinguishing a secular school from a religious school with long-established, well-recognised aims and objectives, Costello J referred to the Canadian Supreme Court case *Caldwell v Stuart*[314] which held that an employee's behaviour in sexual matters may justify dismissal if it is capable of damaging the employer's business. Finally, however, Costello J decided the case on the statutory grounds and ruled that the plaintiff was dismissed fairly. This decision was controversial, particularly in view of the fact that the plaintiff did not have an alternative option of employment as a teacher in a secular public school,[315] by contrast with Ms Caldwell in Canada. However, the Equality Acts 1998–2004 now prohibit discrimination, *inter alia*, on 'the family status ground" (that one has family status and the other has not).[316]

SCHOOL ADMISSION AND PARTICIPATION POLICIES

[9.077] Every recognised school is required to publish its 'Admissions and Participation Policies' in accordance with s 15(2)(d) of the Act of 1998. To date, there has been no judicial interpretation of this provision although there have been many referrals to the Equality Authority under the Equal

312. *Flynn v Power* [1985] ILRM 336.

313. Which is a right guaranteed by Art 44.5 of the Constitution.

314. *Caldwell v Stuart* (1985) 1 WWR 620. See further Glendenning, *Education and the Law*, at p 431.

315. The VEC schools are public sector schools, but although established in the secular VEC Acts, religious instruction is taught in them, so they could possibly argue that they too had an ethos to protect which had evolved through custom and practice from 1940 to date.

316. See further Whyte, 'Implications for Schools of Irish Equality Legislation', in Glendenning and Binchy, *Litigation against Schools: Implications for School Management*, p 118 at 134.

Status Acts 2000–2004, which prohibit discrimination on eight substantive grounds including the ground of religion.[317]

[9.078] Section 7 of the Equal Status Act 2000 (as amended):

(1) In this section 'educational establishment' means a pre-school service within the meaning of Part V11 of the Child Care Act, 1991, a primary or post-primary school, an institution providing adult, continuing or further education, or a university or any other third level institution, whether or not supported by public funds.

(2) An educational establishment shall not discriminate in relation to—

(a) the admission or the terms of admission of a person as a student to the establishment,

(b) the access of a student to any course, facility or benefit provided by the establishment,

(c) any other term or condition of participation in the establishment by a student, or

(d) the expulsion of a student from the establishment or any other sanction against the student.

(3) An educational establishment does not discriminate under subsection 2, *inter alia*, by reason only that—

...

(c) Where the establishment is a school providing primary or post primary education to students and the objective of the school is to provide education in an environment which promotes certain religious values, it admits persons of a particular religious denomination in preference to others or it refuses to admit as a student a person who is not of that denomination, and in the case of a refusal, it is proved that the refusal is essential to maintain the ethos of the school....

In the case of such a refusal under paragraph (c) the onus of proof falling on the school seems a stringent one. In order to discharge that onus, the school must prove that any such refusal (of a student) was 'essential to maintain the

317. See the Equality Authority, 'Equality in a Diverse Ireland', The Annual Report 2007, which shows there was a substantial number of case files relating to allegations of discrimination against public-sector government bodies including schools. The 'Traveller ground' was the second highest area of case files under the Equal Status Acts and these related mainly to educational establishments and accommodation provision. See further Whyte, 'Implications for Schools of Irish Equality Legislation' in Glendenning and Binchy, *Litigation against Schools: Implications for School Management*, p 134 *et seq*.

ethos of the school.' Given the heavy burden of proof falling on the school, the s 7(3)(c) exemption can scarcely be considered an absolute right. Since virtually all primary schools are denominational, together with approximately 57 per cent of second-level schools, if s 7(3)(c) an absolute right, it would violate the constitutional entitlement of parents of minority faiths, or no faith, (now a sizeable category)[318] to the constitutionally guaranteed free primary education and it would negate parental choice of schooling in certain circumstances.[319] An absolute right on the part of a denominational school with regard to admissions would discriminate on the religion ground to a degree that would deprive minority religions of access to education, which is constitutionally guaranteed at primary level. It will be recalled that in the *Campaign to Separate Church and State v the Minister for Education*,[320] the High Court ruled that the Constitution contemplated that if a school was in receipt of public funds, any child, no matter what his religion, would be entitled to attend it without being required to attend any course of religious instruction at the school.[321] In the light of that finding, which pre-dates the Equal Status Act 2000 (as amended), how would a court reconcile the rights in section 7(3)(c) with the constitutional guarantees?

[9.079] In the event of a legal challenge to s 7(3)(c) the courts would balance the child's right to education in the publicly funded school, together with the parental rights in Art 42[322] and Art 44[323] of the Constitution against the constitutional right of the religious denomination to manage its own affairs and to protect its characteristic spirit.[324] It would consider the full circumstances of the case: the diversity of modern Ireland; the virtual absence of non-denominational schools;[325] the lack of a permanent public sector at primary level and the limited provision of such schools at second level; the limited number of multidenominational schools in the area; the

318. A category now estimated to number 186,318 persons; see Central Statistics Office, 2006 Census, at www.csu.ie under category of Religion.

319. Articles 42.2 and 42.3.1°.

320. *Campaign to Separate Church and State v the Minister for Education* [1996] 2 ILRM 241; [1998] 2 ILRM 81.

321. *Campaign to Separate Church and State v the Minister for Education* [1996] 2 ILRM 241; [1998] 2 ILRM 81.

322. Articles 42.1, 42.2 , 42.3.1 and 42.4.

323. Art 44.2.1°, 44.2.3° and 44.2.4°.

324. Art 44.2.5°.

325. My understanding is that there is one such school in the country.

ethos of the school; and possibly the composition of the school enrolment from a faith perspective. Judicial notice would also be taken of germane international human rights[326] and, in particular, the obligation in Art 2 of Protocol 1 of the ECHR to respect the right of all parents to ensure that such education and teaching conforms with their own religious and philosophical convictions. A court would also consider EU anti-discrimination legislation and in particular the Equality Directives.[327] In an attempt to harmonise these competing rights, in the opinion of this writer, a court would be likely to impose quotas on a denominational school which would not unduly dilute the ethos of the school. If a legal challenge to s 7(3)(c) was lost in the national courts, it would most likely be appealed to the ECJ and/or in the ECtHR.

[9.080] In October 2006, the House of Lords voted down a second attempt to compel faith schools to take a quota of pupils from non-faith backgrounds. Lord Baker's amendment to permit local education authorities to force new faith schools to accept up to 25 per cent of non-faith pupils was rejected by 119 to 37 votes.[328] However, the position in England, in which an alternative public education sector exists to facilitate parental choice, must be distinguished from the position in Ireland, where no public sector exists at primary level and only a limited public sector exists at second level. Writing on the position prior to the passing of the Equal Status Acts 2000–2004, and the Education Act 1998, the Report of the Constitution Review Group (1996) stated:

> Accordingly, if a school under the control of a religious denomination accepts State funding, it must be prepared to accept that this aid is not given unconditionally. Requirements that the school must be prepared in principle to accept pupils from denominations other than its own and to have separate secular and religious instruction are not unreasonable or unfair.[329]

The Report concluded that there was no satisfactory answer to this potential conflict of rights.[330] In the light of the social realities of modern life in Ireland, however, quotas appear to be the only equitable way of dealing with

---

326. As set out in **chapter 4**.

327. Council Directive 2000/43/EC (The Race Directive) and Council Directive 2000/78/EC (The Framework Directive).

328. See online http://www.politics.co.uk.

329. *Report of the Constitution Review Group, 1996* (Government Publications, 1996) pp 386–7.

330. Report of the Constitution Review Group, 1996, p 186.

this intractable problem. It would, of course, be much less divisive for educational interests if such quotas were agreed by the denominational schools rather than having them conceivably imposed on them by the courts.

EMBRACING CHANGE

[9.081] There are some positive indications that the Catholic Church has begun to accept the notion of change and this is clear from its recent publication, *Primary Schools: a Policy for Provision into the Future*,[331] which recognised the need for a plurality of schools and educational providers to meet the needs of a diverse population. The fact that pilot enrolment policies for two Catholic schools are operating in the Dublin diocese, in which quotas of one-third of places have been assigned to non-Catholic students, is indicative of the church's willingness to revisit its Catholics-first admission's policy.[332] Qualitative research into parental choice is taking place and collaboration with other patron bodies is also occurring.[333] While critics may assert that the church has begun to adopt change now only because maintaining the *status quo* is impossible,[334] others see a church that is adapting to change and redefining its role into the future. The Church acknowledges, for example, that parents have a human right to access to non-denominational education[335] for their children, but arguably they also have that right pursuant to the Irish Constitution.[336] From a human rights perspective, in view of the fact that there are at least 186,318 persons who state they have no religion (up almost 35 per cent since the 2002 Census), there is a clear obligation on the state to respect the right of such parents to ensure such education and teaching in conformity with their own

331. Irish Bishop's Conference, Maynooth, 2007, available online at http://www.cpsma.ie/docs/vision0812pagedoc.pdf.

332. Kiernan, 'Embracing Change: The remodelling of Irish Catholic primary schools in the 21st century', in Littleton and Maher (eds), *Contemporary Catholicism: a Critical Appraisal* (Columba Press, 2008) p 43 at 56.

333. Kiernan, 'Embracing Change: The remodelling of Irish Catholic primary schools in the 21st century'.

334. Kiernan, 'Embracing Change: The remodelling of Irish Catholic primary schools in the 21st century'.

335. Kiernan, 'Embracing Change: The remodelling of Irish Catholic primary schools in the 21st century'.

336. Articles 42.1, 42.2, 42.3, 42.5, 44.2, and 44.2.3°.

religious and philosophical convictions[337] by establishing non-denominational schools if parents require them. Breaching a number of international human rights instruments, thereby bringing the state into disrepute.

Broadening Education Structures

[9.082] International human rights bodies have repeatedly stressed the need for Ireland to broaden its educational structures so as to equitably meet the needs of diversity and they have noted: the narrow base of existing provision; the conservative character of the upholding structures; the increasing demands of diversity; and the difficulties being experienced by foreign nationals in gaining access to denominational schools, despite their claims of being inclusive.[338] In 2006, the UN Committee on the Rights of the Child recommended that Ireland, which ratified the Convention on the Rights of the Child in 1992, should promote the establishment of non-denominational and multidenominational schools on human rights grounds, reaffirming an earlier recommendation made by the UN Committee on the Elimination of Racial Discrimination (CERD) in 2005:[339]

> **60. The Committee reiterates the concern raised by the Committee on the Elimination of Racial Discrimination (CERD/C/IRL/CO/2) that non-denominational or multi-denominational schools represent less than one per cent of the total number of primary education facilities.**
>
> **61. The Committee encourages the State party to take into consideration the recommendations made by the Committee on the Elimination of Racial Discrimination (CERD/C/IRL/2, para 18) which encourages the promotion of the establishment of non-denominational or multi-denominational schools and to amend the existing legislative framework to eliminate discrimination in school admissions.'** (bold in original text)

A further call for broadening the educational framework in Ireland has come from the Advisory Committee to the Council of Europe Framework

337. Article 2 of Protocol 1 of the ECHR.

338. Flynn, 'Bishops insist that Catholic schools are inclusive', (2008) *Irish Times*, 13 May.

339. United Nations Committee on Elimination of Racial Discrimination, 66th Session, 11 March 2005 at UN Office at Geneva. See also 'Schools must not be allowed favour Catholics, says UN', (2005) *Irish Independent*, 12 March, p 12; and further ETEN – The Electronic Newsletter from Educate Together, vol 6, No 4, 31 October 2006.

Convention for the Protection of National Minorities. In its second opinion on Ireland in 2006, the Council strongly recommended to the Irish state in its main recommendations to the Council of Ministers that it should widen school options in order to accommodate the growing diversity of Irish life. The Council stated at para 21: 'The growing diversity of Ireland is in many ways affecting the education system of Ireland, and in this context the authorities are encouraged to pursue their commitment to take into account the growing demand for non-denominational or multi-denominational schools.'

[9.083] In its third report on Ireland, the UN expressed concern, *inter alia*, that the majority of Ireland's primary schools are denominational and urged that alternative non-denominational primary education be provided.[340] As was indicated earlier, the state is currently piloting two new public sector 'community national schools', but it has now decided that these schools will be multifaith schools rather than non-denominational in character, it appears.[341] Parents need to be consulted widely on this very significant issue since the family/parents are the primary and natural educator of the children,[342] parents are constitutionally sovereign,[343] and they have a constitutional right[344] and a human right to non-denominational schools if they wish to have them established. In the opinion of this writer, it is insufficient to consult with school patrons and the key stakeholders in education in a matter of such pivotal significance for parents as happened in June 2008. Such a debate needs to be public, transparent, democratic and accountable and it needs to extent throughout the whole country.

[9.084] Recently, the Department of Education and Science has agreed to provide a grant for the Patron's costs of setting up a new school in the Educate Together (multidenominational) sector.[345] The lack of such funding was one of the two key restraints on Educate Together proceeding to apply to

340. See http://www.rightsmonitor.org.

341. Address from Mr Batt O'Keffe TD and Minister for Education and Science to the Conference on the Government Challenges for Future Primary School Needs, 27 June 2008, Kilmainham, available online at http://www.education.ie.

342. Article 42.1 of the Constitution.

343. Article 6(1).

344. Articles 42.1, 42.2, 42.3.1, 42.4, 44.2.1°, 44.2.3°.

345. The Electronic Newsletter from Educate Together, vol 7, no 5, 15 June 2007. I am grateful to Paul Rowe, CEO of Educate Together, for this information.

open a number of new schools in 2007, despite considerable parental demands, the other restraint being the lack of confirmed and credible building plans for permanent buildings for such schools.[346] With the removal of any further obstacles, the likelihood is that the Educate Together sector will increase considerably, but that the denominational national school model is likely to continue to be the choice of the majority of parents in the immediate future.

CHILD ABUSE IN SCHOOLS

[9.085] It is only in recent years that Irish society has become aware of the full extent of physical and sexual abuse of children in certain reformatory and industrial schools (residential schools)[347] and in some national schools (day schools) in the past.[348] Remarkably, the knowledge now in the public domain came mainly from the victims of child abuse in adulthood,[349] rather than from state or church authorities and, at the time of writing, these investigations are still ongoing. There is evidence, however, which indicates that both state and church bodies knew, or reasonably ought to have known,[350] that serious problems existed with child protection in Ireland for many decades.[351] In 1970, the Kennedy Report[352] recommended the closure

346. The Electronic Newsletter from Educate Together, vol 7, no 5, 15 June 2007.

347. Industrial schools were established under the Industrial Schools Act 1868 to cater for orphans and neglected, abandoned and homeless children: see further Raftery and O'Sullivan, *Suffer the Little Children: The Inside Story of Ireland's Industrial Schools* (Continuum Publishing, 2001).

348. Buckley, Skehill and O'Sullivan, *Child Protection in Ireland: A Case Study* (Oak Tree Press, 1997) pp 11–12.

349. In 1997 'Dear Daughter' was broadcast on RTÉ; in 1999 'States of Fear' by Mary Raftery and Eoin O'Sullivan was broadcast on RTÉ; in 1999 *Suffer the Little Children* was published by Mary Raftery and Eoin O'Sullivan.

350. The Ferns Report (Government Publications, 2005) pp 15–17 indicates that most Irish dioceses had obtained insurance policies to cover such risks between 1987 and 1990. See the Appendix of the report which includes a further five relevant complaints.

351. The Cussen Report (1934) had concerns over the large numbers of children in care, the inadequacy of their education, the absence of local support and the stigma attached to them

352. Written by the outstanding District Justice Eileen Kennedy who conducted the investigation.

of the industrial schools but that report was not acted upon. Furthermore, corporal punishment in schools was belatedly abolished by the Non-Fatal Offences against the Person Act 1997, although it had been prohibited by a Department of Education circular in 1982.[353] By way of response to the widespread reporting of child abuse in public institutions, the Commission to Enquire into Child Abuse was established pursuant to the Commission to Inquire into Child Abuse Act 2000 (the 2000 Act).

[9.086] The remit of the 2000 Act extended to the investigation of all types of abuse – physical, sexual, emotional – and neglect which took place in institutions, ie any place where a child was cared for other than by his or her own family, including orphanages, industrial schools, reformatory schools, hospitals, children's homes and day or boarding schools or in foster care. Some two years later, the Residential Institutions Redress Act 2002 provided for financial awards to assist in the recovery of certain persons who as children were resident in certain institutions in the state and who had received injuries consistent with child abuse while so resident. There has been considerable public concern that the division of resources agreed between church and state to meet the total bill paid out to child abuse victims in Ireland, which the Comptroller and Auditor General recently estimated to be approximately €1.35 billion, did not achieve an equitable balance for the taxpayer.[354]

[9.087] In order to facilitate those victims whose claims would otherwise be statute-barred, the Statute of Limitations (Amendment) Act 2000 made provision that certain persons would be considered to be under a disability for the purpose of bringing actions relating to sexual abuse committed

353. Department of Education, Circular Letters 9/82 and 7/88, which amended rule 130 of the Rules for National Schools, 1965.

354. Raftery, 'The €1.35 billion sting: how the religious orders outmanoeuvered the State', (2006) *The Village Magazine,* 9 February. The church-state agreement was made on 5 June 2002 between the Minister for Education (Mr Michael Woods TD) and the 18 religious orders who administered Ireland's child-care institutions. The said religious orders were effectively indemnified by the state in return for a transfer of property and money 'capped' at a value of €128 million towards the expenses of the redress scheme. The final bill ran to approximately €1.35 billion, it is estimated. At the time of writing the transfer of 64 properties from church to state is still awaited, John Drennan, 'Church still owes abuse payments: Negotiations bogged down over handover of €66m in property', (2008) *Sunday Independent*, 26 October, p 6

against them prior to their full age. Other relevant legislative measures were also enacted such as the Child Care Act 1991, the Protection of Persons Reporting Child Abuse Act 1998, the Child Trafficking and Pornography Act 1998, the Children Act 2000 and the Sex Offenders Act 2001. More recently, the Criminal Justice Act 2006 was passed and this Act included, *inter alia*, the offence of 'reckless endangerment of children'.[355] A person found guilty of an offence under the relevant section is liable on conviction on indictment to a fine, or to imprisonment for a term not exceeding ten years or both.

Vicarious Liability for Child Abuse in National Schools

[9.088] One unfortunate outcome of the state-aided system of education is that it led to legal complexity, not only in regard to the teacher's contract of employment,[356] but in regard to legal accountability for the abuse of children in publicly-funded institutions. In a series of recent High Court cases,[357] for example, those who suffered child abuse at the hands of teachers and clergy in national schools[358] failed later to establish vicarious liability against the state for the wrongs they had suffered. In *LOK*

355. Section 176(2) provides: 'A person having authority or control over a child or abuser, who intentionally or recklessly endangers a child by– (a) causing or permitting any child to be placed or left in a situation which creates a substantial risk to the child of being a victim of serious harm or sexual abuse, or (b) failing to take reasonable steps to protect a child from such a risk while knowing that the child is in such a situation, is guilty of an offence'.

356. Gibson J in *Fox v Higgins* (1912) 46 ILTR 222.

357. *LO'K v LH, the Minister for Education and Science and the AG* [2006] IECH 13; *TM v JH, JM and the Minister for Education and Science, Ireland and the AG* [2006] IEHC 261; *DO'C v AM McD, The Minister for Education and Science, Ireland and the AG* [2006] IEHC 299, and, in the context of an Industrial School, see *Delahunty v The South Eastern Health Board, St Joseph's Industrial School, Kilkenny and the Minister for Education & Science* [2003] 4 IR 361.

358. The Ferns Report states: 'As will be obvious from the allegations set out in this Report, some priests appear to have abused their position as Managers of national schools in order to access children. The powerlessness of children in such a situation was particularly acute and the Inquiry would urge all concerned to ensure that such situations as are described in this Report are prevented as far as possible', p 260, para 6.

v Minister for Education and Science,[359] the plaintiff sued the former lay principal teacher and the state for assaults perpetrated upon her when she was an eight-year old pupil in her national school in the 1970s. Applying 'the control test', which is at the heart of the vicarious liability doctrine,[360] the High Court held that the state did not exercise the control over teachers which is necessary to give rise to vicarious liability for their actions or omissions. Accordingly, the court held the state was not vicariously liable for the plaintiff's injuries since the selection and appointment of any person as a teacher or as principal was a prerogative of the manager (now the board of management). Awarding costs to the state, de Valera J indicated that, if the proceedings had been taken against the Catholic diocese of Cork and Ross, the action may have had a more favourable outcome.[361] This decision has been highly controversial and it has been alleged that it makes the 'subservient role of the state in education'[362] crystal clear. It should not be forgotten, however, that Art 42.2 of the Constitution provides a framework for the provision of education, *inter alia,* by the state: 'Parents shall be free to provide this education in their homes or in private schools or in schools recognised *or established by the State*.' (emphasis added) For whatever reason, parents have failed to exercise this constitutional entitlement at first level.[363] At the time of writing, the High Court has affirmed that the constitutional character of the education system remains state-aiding and that the constitutional obligation falling on the state merely requires it to 'provide for' education rather than provide it directly.[364]

The role of the state in Ireland seems somewhat 'out of step', so to speak, with the norm in the EU where the obligation to educate rests generally with

---

359. *LO'K v LH, the Minister for Education and Science and the AG* [2006] IECH 13.

360. McMahon and Binchy, *Law of Torts* (3rd edn, Tottel Publishing, 2000), at 43.02–43.03 and 43.08 and *Moynihan v Moynihan* [1975] IR 192.

361. Since the Catholic bishop was the patron of the school and he had appointed the board of management of the school.

362. In June 1998 the perpetrator had pleaded guilty at Cork Circuit Criminal Court to 21 charges of indecent assault from a sample of 380 counts relating to 21 girls and he was jailed for three years. See Carolan, 'State awarded costs in school abuse cases', (2006) *Irish Times*, 24 March. The costs in *LOK* were estimated at €500,000. See Doyle, 'Have a heart Minister', (2006) *Irish Times,* 30 March.

363. With the exception of the two 'community national schools' already mentioned.

364. *LO'K v LH, the Minister for Education and Science and the AG* [2006] IECH 13.

the state.[365] With regard to the role of the state in contemporary life, Glenn and De Groof state:

> In modern societies, the State typically has only a supportive role with respect to the arts, or the media, but it cannot avoid being the guarantor of the provision of schooling. Since the mid-19th century (and longer in some countries), the State in most Western democracies has been intimately involved with the educational system, but it has not been a simple matter to define precisely what the appropriate role of the State is in a sphere of life which so intimately involves the formation of values and ways of understanding the world.[366]

[9.089] These recent decisions have given rise to public concern that Ireland, a modern democratic state, with very substantial control of the education system, can evade responsibility for child abuse in national schools by reliance on the principle of vicarious liability. It is within the power of parents to alter that system by way of referendum,[367] if they so wish, so as to broaden the framework upholding education to include express direct state provision of education as well as indirect provision. Change in this significant sphere may also emerge incrementally through the establishment of permanent 'community national schools' or by way of judicial interpretation in the Supreme Court which can bring the law up to date with modern circumstances. The case of *L O'K v Minister for Education and Science*[368] has been appealed to the Supreme Court and its decision is awaited with interest.

[9.090] Why was child abuse permitted to happen and continue to exist in educational institutions in Ireland for many decades? It is generally accepted that a culture of secrecy and a fear of causing scandal informed many dimensions of Irish life,[369] including many state departments[370] in the past. Society was rigidly hierarchical and those who were uneducated knew their

365. Macbeth, 'The Child Between', *Studies* (Office for Official Publications, EC, 1984), p 11.

366. Glenn and de Groof, Finding the Right Balance: Freedom, Autonomy and Accountability in Education.

367. Art 47 of the Constitution.

368. *L O'K v LH, the Minister for Education and Science and the AG* [2006] IECH 13

369. The Ferns Report (2005) pp 255–6, para 7h; O'Toole, 'A Culture that refused to see evil', (2005) *Irish Times,* 1 November.

370. Sean O'Connor, a former Secretary of the Department of Education, refers to the long-standing practice of that Department 'never to reveal the nature of the action taken.' O'Connor, *A Troubled Sky,* p 27.

'rightful place' in that hierarchy. Authority in schools, both lay and clerical, was generally accorded a high degree of respect and even deference. Many feared the power of the church and the professions were virtually unassailable, recalling Shaw's aphorism: 'the professions were a conspiracy against the laity.'[371] Against this background, allegations of child abuse against those in authority were frequently met with incredulity, secrecy and indifference.

[9.091] Furthermore, parental autonomy, which was constitutionally protected, was upheld by the courts,[372] and children's rights were extremely slow in emerging.[373] Duncan, in the Report of the Constitutional Review Group (1996) states that 'historically it is fair to say that Art 42, with its emphasis on parental rights in matters of education, has indirectly consolidated the powers of the churches within the education system'.[374] Duncan traces the profound impact of this concept on many aspects of Irish life, including the interpretation of legislation and its drafting.[375] The Report of the Constitutional Review Group recommended that the Constitution be amended to include 'an express obligation to treat the best interests of the child as a paramount consideration in any actions relating to children.'[376] The 28th Amendment of the Constitution Bill 2007 proposes, *inter alia,* to insert, following a referendum, a new article into the Constitution: 'The State acknowledges and affirms the natural and imprescriptible rights of all children.' However, others assert that a constitutional referendum of children's rights should only be considered as a 'last resort', so to speak, which is unlikely to be necessary to establish a system of child protection. O'Malley is of the view that changes to the Constitution may have unintended consequences which would be difficult to remove or alter, while legislation can be flexible since it imposes 'strict' liability rather than

371. Shaw, The Doctor's Dilemma (1906).

372. *Article 26 and the School Attendance Bill 1942* [1943] IR 334; *Crowley v Ireland* [1980] IR 102.

373. Ferguson, 'Child Welfare, Child protection and the Child Care Act, 1991: key issues for Policy and Practice' in Ferguson and Kenny (eds), *On Behalf of the Child* (A & A Farmar, 1995).

374. Duncan, 'The Constitutional Protection of Parental Rights', *Report of the Constitutional Review Group, 1996*, p 612 at 618.

375. Duncan, 'The Constitutional Protection of Parental Rights', *Report of the Constitutional Review Group, 1996,* pp 612–3.

376. Duncan, 'The Constitutional Protection of Parental Rights', *Report of the Constitutional Review Group, 1996,* p 329.

'absolute' liability in the case of children in a younger age group (such as 13).[377]

In the opinion of this writer, there is much to be said for the flexibility of the legislative approach in child protection.

[9.092] With regard to legislation, the Children Act 1908, now substantially replaced by the Children Act 2001, was the main statute for safeguarding children at risk between 1908 and 1991. The Child Care Act 1991 is one of the most significant pieces of social legislation to reach the Irish statute book. Between 1908 and 1991, by permitting lacunae to arise in the 1908 Act and by failing to enact and implement further appropriate legislative measures, a fertile ground arose for the abuse of children both physically and sexually in certain publicly-funded church-state institutions. The Ferns Report (2005), which identified more then 100 allegations of child sexual abuse against certain clergy in the Roman Catholic Diocese of Ferns between 1962 and 2002,[378] points to the limited protection afforded by the 1908 Act for certain categories of children. While the 1908 Act empowered courts of summary jurisdiction to remove a child from a neglectful or abusive parent and place him or her in an alternative situation,[379] it made no provision for children who had been abused otherwise than by parental or

377. Genevieve Carbery, 'Vote on children's rights a "last resort"' (2008) *The Irish Times*, 6 November referring to Dr Tom O'Malley Barrister and Senior Law lecturer in National University of Ireland, Galway, in his advices to the Oireachtas Joint Committee on the Constitutional Amendment on Children. Thus, Dr O'Malley points out an accused person would be found guilty when it was established that they had sex with the child but they could raise a defence of due diligence to show that they had taken steps to establish the child's age but remained genuinely mistaken in that regard. He further suggested that for cases involving older children (such as between 13–17), there would be a defence of honest and reasonable mistake in which, for example, the jury could take into account the surrounding circumstances of the accused to establish the reasonableness of the mistake.

378. Ferns Report (Government Publications, 2005). This Report was chaired by Mr Justice Francis D Murphy and the other members were Dr Helen Buckley and Dr Laraine Joyce. The *Executive Summary* documents a further five relevant complaints in the Appendix. It should be noted, however, that the Ferns Inquiry did not express, and was not required to express, any view as to the truth or otherwise of any allegation.

379. The Elementary Education Act 1876, which made provision for a limited form of school attendance in cities and towns, meant that those children who failed to comply with its requirements were also within the remit of the 1908 Act.

carer neglect, leaving a critical gap in the legislation which was permitted to continue for almost a century. If there is one lesson to be learned from this disquieting chapter of Irish life, it is that vulnerable children generally require carefully considered statutory protections. Serious consideration also needs to be given to putting the official 'Children First National Guidelines for the Protection and Welfare of Children'[380] into statutory form, particularly in view of recent criticism of inconsistency of application of these guidelines.[381]

[9.093] As the late Professor Kelly frequently pointed out, the ultimate protection of human rights in a democracy lies with the people themselves and the most effective guarantee against the abuse of children is the vigilance of the sovereign people.[382] That vigilance was lacking. It was manifestly negligent to commit vulnerable children to the care of church or state, or to any person *in loco parentis*, without ensuring that statutory controls were in place for the protection of all children and that they were adequately monitored. It is easy, however, to apply contemporary standards to past circumstances and to point out pivotal deficits in both civil law and in Canon law. People appear to have trusted that Canon law[383] would ensure protection for all children in state-funded child-care institutions run by religious authorities. Some confusion appears to have arisen from the common perception of the legal status of Canon law and its interface with the civil law and as to which was superior.

Legal Status of Canon Law

[9.094] In *O'Keefe v Cardinal Cullen*,[384] discussed earlier, the House of Lords considered the relationship between the Canon law of the Roman

380. *Children First National Guidelines for the Protection and Welfare of Children* (Government Publications, 1999), with a Foreword by the Minister for State with Special Responsibility for Children, Frank Fahey TD.

381. O'Brien, 'Rules on child protection "implemented inconsistently"', (2008) *Irish Times,* 1 August; O' Brien, 'Child protection Services seen as hostile', (2008) *Irish Times,* 1 August.

382. Kelly, *Fundamental Rights in the Irish Law and Constitution*, pp 69 and 73.

383. Following the reform of the Second Vatican Council, Pope John Paul II promulgated the revised *Code of Canon Law* for the Latin Church in 1983. See online CatholicCanonLaw.com.

384. *O'Keefe v Cardinal Cullen* 2 QB 1873 CL 7 319.

Catholic Church and the civil law at a time when Ireland was under English dominion, and concluded that the law of the land was superior to the ecclesiastical law. In *O'Callaghan v O'Sullivan*,[385] O'Sullivan CJ stated the legal position in independent Ireland. The applicant had been removed from his position as parish priest by a Decree of Removal issued by the respondent bishop under the Canon law. It was admitted that the legal relationship of the parties was governed by the Laws, Ordinances and Canon Laws of the Roman Catholic Church, but the court was unambiguous regarding the status of Canon law:

> The Canon law of the Roman Catholic Church is foreign law, which must be proved as a fact and by the testimony of expert witnesses according to the well-settled rules as to proof of foreign law .... The corresponding position of members of the Church of Ireland after the disestablishment of the Church was defined in s 20 of the Irish Church Act, 1869.

[9.095] Vatican Council II stresses the ecclesiastical law principle that the temporal and the religious are two distinct competences with respective powers and faculties: 'The political community and the church are autonomous and independent of each other in their own fields' (*Gaudium et Spes*). The Ferns Report stated that the Irish legal system recognises Canon law as a scientific legal system and as a *corpus* of law, both substantive and adjective, whose rules order the conduct, regulate the social and domestic relations, and punish the disobedience of those who recognise that authority, and which gives judgments through its own tribunals. However, it went on to clarify its legal status:[386]

> Again like all other foreign laws, Canon law is without coercive power because the machinery of coercion is, in this State, kept in the exclusive control of the civil government and parliament for compelling obedience to such laws only as its parliament enacts.[387] No foreign law could exempt a person resident in this State from compliance with an obligation imposed by the Constitution or the laws enacted thereunder.[388]

While the Irish legal system recognises Canon Law as a scientific legal system, applying to those who accept its authority, having the status of foreign law, every person in the state is subject to the civil law and to the Constitution.

385. *O'Callaghan v O'Sullivan* [1925] 1 IR 90.

386. The Ferns Report (2005) p 37.

387. *O'Callaghan v O'Sullivan* [1925] 1 IR 90.

388. The Ferns Report (2005) p 38.

CONCLUSION

[9.096] Ireland has made remarkable strides towards implementing the democratic principles in its education system in latter decades but it still retains a number of covert practices and democratic deficits which derive largely from its deeply-embedded tradition of informality in education laid down between 1831–1998. Since the system of education is publicly-funded to a high degree, one would expect greater transparency in all areas of education but particularly in matters relating to the interface of education with religion.

Parents need to be fully informed of all aspects of school life but particularly of those elements of education which pertain to ideology and religion which are primarily within their constitutional remit. In particular, parents need to be made fully aware of the following:

(a) the character of the existing system of education;

(b) a denominational school's ethos rights and the protections afforded it by constitutional and statutory provisions and by the Deeds of Variation at primary level and the Deeds of Trust of Community and Comprehensive schools;

(c) the position of religion in the school and the rights of minority religions and none within the school;

(d) the variety of school types that may be established by parents under the constitutional provisions, including secular schools and how these may be established.

(e) the distinction between religious education (RE) and religious instruction (RI) and worship and the rights of parents in comprehensive and community schools to opt for RE for their children if they so wish.[389]

(f) the admissions and participation policy of the school.

The significance of full public debate prior to the establishment of new school types is pivotal since the family/parents are the primary educators and the people are constitutionally sovereign, but this right, of course, is not an absolute right, but must be balanced against the rights of others and within the context of available resources.

389. *Campaign to Separate Church and State v Minister for Education* [1998] vol 3, part 2, 321.

Now that the democratic principles are permeating Ireland's system of education, a broadly-based, transparent debate, not just with the key stakeholders in education, but with the general public, is necessary so as to chart the way forward for education within the structures of national and international human rights law. In particular, the issue of school admissions requires urgent clarification at first and second level. In addition, the Rules for National Schools (1965) need to be revised and updated.

The remarkable reluctance of the Irish people to debate matters of faith has been noted, but under their democratic mandate the people must take responsibility for their system of education particularly at this time when the religious orders, who have contributed so much to Irish education, are diminishing. It should not be forgotten that the ultimate protection of human rights in a democracy lies with the people and that the most effective guarantee against the abuse of children is the vigilance of the sovereign people.[390]

Significant changes in church-state relations pertaining to education are apparent in Ireland as the balance of power moves inexorably towards the state. Since the state now has much greater control of education, mainly as a result of a body of legislative measures, perhaps the time has come for it to bear greater responsibility for the provision of education, particularly at primary level. The constitutional obligation falling on the state in regard to the provision of free primary education remains an indirect obligation ('to provide for free primary education'). Perhaps the time is opportune for the people to re-visit this constitutional provision to consider whether it meets contemporary needs or whether it needs to be extended to include also direct provision of education by the state ('to provide free primary education').

[9.097] One advantage of Ireland's singular system of education is that it has avoided the excesses of the rigid imposition of a state ideology in education (Statism), particularly apparent in the French public schools. Another benefit accruing from Ireland's mainly denominational school system is that Muslims have integrated their children into existing denominational schools with, what appears to be, a greater degree of ease than in more secular systems of education, or they have established schools of their own school faith. Moreover, by contrast with some European countries, the Muslim community in Ireland has acquired significant representation rights with the other main churches and with the state, despite its members' disparate origins and ethnicity and relatively recent arrival in Ireland.

---

390. Kelly, *Fundamental Rights in the Irish Law and Constitution*, pp 69 and 73.

[9.098] It may be concluded that the existing system of education in Ireland, which has contributed so much over the centuries, needs to be expanded to enable it to fully meet the needs of contemporary society while respecting the principles of religious freedom for all persons and the philosophical convictions of those persons with no religion.

Chapter 10

RELIGION, EDUCATION AND THE LAW IN THE UNITED STATES

The place of religion in our society is an exalted one, achieved through a long tradition of reliance on the home, the church, and the inviolable citadel of the individual heart and mind. We have come to recognize through bitter experience that it is not within the power of government to invade that citadel ... (Abingdon v Schempp *374 US 203 (1963)* per Clark J).

INTRODUCTION

[10.001] One of the reasons the early colonists left Europe and sought freedom in the so-called 'New World' was to escape the bondage of laws which compelled them to support and attend established churches.[1] America's history echoes the history of the Quaker, the Puritan, the Catholic, the Baptist and the Jew and many others who fled their homelands in search of, *inter alia,* religious freedom. When some of the opponents of the established churches in Europe achieved sufficient control of colonial governments, they began to write their own prayers into law and enacted laws making their own religion the official religion of their respective colonies.[2] Thus, the practices of the old world were transplanted with considerable success into the soil of America but the outcome was far from conducive to societal peace.[3]

[10.002] In *Everson v Board of Education* Black J, when delivering the opinion of the US Supreme Court, referred to the 'turmoil, civil strife and persecutions generated in part by established sects determined to … maintain their absolute political and religious supremacy.'[4] Such

---

1. *Everson v Board of Education* (1947) 330 US 1.
2. *Engel et al v Vitale et al* (1962) 370 US 421, 423 *per* Black J.
3. See further Esbeck, 'Dissent and Disestablishment: The Church-State Settlement in the Early American Republic' (2004) *Brigham Young Univ L Rev* 1385 and further Stokes and Pfeiffer, *Church and State in the United States*, revised edition 1964.
4. *Everson v Board of Education* (1947) 330 US 1.

persecutions became so widespread that the freedom-loving colonials were shocked and indignant at their vehemence[5] and they resolved to seek a new approach to secure universal religious freedom. In seeking a new approach, the Founding Fathers were presented with an immense challenge, not least in striving to formulate a consensus among many states where close ties between religion and government had already been established during the colonial period. Thus, freedom of religion was a principle which emerged gradually over half a century as the ideology and language of secularism took hold in the US against a backdrop of considerable opposition.[6] As late as the Revolutionary wars, at least eight of the thirteen former colonies had established churches and there were established religions in at least four of the other five.[7] Finally, Thomas Jefferson and James Madison turned to the upholding ideology of the separationist policies of the Enlightenment writers of England and France as the key to a possible alternative approach.

SEPARATION OF CHURCH AND STATE

[10.003] The successful outcome of the Revolution against English political domination[8] was followed by intense debate and opposition to the practice of establishing religion by law; an opposition which was eventually

5. *Everson v Board of Education* (1947) 330 US 1.

6. See Boston, *Why the Religious Right is Wrong about Separation of Church and State* (Prometheus, 1993).

7. *Engel v Vitale* 370 US 421, 423. See further Russo's fascinating article, 'The Ten Commandments in American Public Schools: an Enduring *Controversy'* [2003] Education Law Journal, pp 90–99.

8 The *Three Charters of Freedom* in the United States are *The Declaration of Independence*, in Congress, 4 July 1776 (the unanimous Declaration of the thirteen United States of America); In the Declaration of Independence, the Founding Fathers laid down the foundation and the core principles on which the Constitution was to operate. *The Declaration of Independence* was ratified by all the states in the Union and has never been annulled: *the Constitution of the United States of America* (signed on 17 September 1787) to which 12 amendments were sought by the states to secure the immunities of individual citizens against the undue interference of the central government; the first three amendments were not ratified but nos 3–12 were ratified and these became the first 10 amendments: and *the Bill of Rights* (25 September 1789). I am grateful to the National Archives Experience for much of this information which is available on line at http://www.archives.gov/nae. (contd .../)

transformed into an effective political force in Virginia.[9] In 1785–86 Jefferson and Madison opposed the renewal of the tax levy for the support of the established church in Virginia and Madison published his famous *Memorial and Remonstrance* against this law.[10] Madison contended that a true religion did not need the support of law, that no person should be taxed to support a religious institution, that the best interests of society required that the minds of men be wholly free and that cruel persecutions were the inevitable result of government-established religions. In his letter to the committee of the Danbury Baptist Association in 1802, Jefferson, although not hostile to religion,[11] referred to his ideal of a clear separation between church and state:

> Believing with you that religion is a matter which lies solely between man and his God … I contemplate with sovereign reverence that act of the whole American people which declared that their legislature 'should make no law respecting an establishment of religion, or prohibiting the free exercise thereof', thus building a wall of separation between church and state.[12]

---

8. (contd) I also acknowledge the assistance of *The RJ & L Religious Liberty Archive, a Service of the Religious Institutions Group at Rothgerber Johnson & Lyons LLP*, online at file://G:\State Constitutions Religion Religious Liberty Archive Rothgerber Johnson, accessed by the author on 14 January 2008.

9. *Engel v Vitale* (1962) 370 US 421.

10. *Everson v Board of Education* (1947) 330 US 1.

11. Since he stated: 'We must reduce our volume to the simple evangelists, select, even from them, the very words only of Jesus …. There will be found remaining, the most sublime and benevolent code of morals which has ever been offered to man.' in Lipscomb and Bergh (eds), 16 *Writings of Thomas Jefferson* 281 (Thomas Jefferson Memorial Association of the United States, 1903).

12. Thomas Jefferson to the Danbury Baptist's Association, of 1 January 1802, Andrew (ed), *16 Writings of Thomas Jefferson 281* (1903). The concept of 'a wall or hedge of separation' between church and state is usually attributed to a Baptist theologian, Williams and his associates, see Millar, *Roger Williams: His Contribution to the American Tradition* (Atheneum, 1962): and further McBeth, *A Sourcebook for Baptist Heritage* (B&H Publishing Group, January 1990): and generally *Early Advocates for Separation: First American Advocate*, vol 3, no 1 (February 2002), accessible online at www.auok.org/early_advocates_for_separation.htm accessed by the author on the 17 January 2008.

Meanwhile Madison's *Memorial* received considerable support in Virginia, where the tax levy was postponed and it finally died in committee.[13]

[10.004] Two broadly distinct groups emerged: those who adhered to the separationist philosophy promoted by Jefferson's metaphorical 'wall of separation between church and state' (the separationists), and those who supported the view that church and state should not be rigidly separated but that there should exist some form of accommodation between them (the accommodationists).[14] In time, Jefferson brought forward his celebrated Virginia Bill for Religious Liberty (the Virginia Bill) which, when amended by Benjamin Franklin and John Adams, and altered stylistically and substantively by Congress, was enacted in 1785 as the Act for Establishing Religious Freedoms.[15] Similar, though less far-reaching, legislation was enacted in other states. Arguing on the basis of the natural rights of mankind, Jefferson posited the view that God had created the mind free and manifested his supreme will that free it should remain, making it altogether insusceptible of restraint. He contended that civil rights had no dependence on religious opinions and that the opinions of men were not under the jurisdiction of civil government; that truth was great and would prevail if left to herself, and that truth was the proper and sufficient antagonist to error.[16] Essentially, Jefferson believed that a person's religion was a matter for the private sphere, as he made clear in a letter written in 1814: 'our particular principles of religion are a subject of accountability to our god alone. I enquire after no man's and trouble none with mine; nor is it given to us in this life to know whether yours or mine, our friends or our foes, are exactly the right.'[17] Gradually a consensus was emerging that individual religious liberty could be best achieved under a government which was divested of all power to tax, support or otherwise assist any or all religions, or interfere with the beliefs of any religious individual or groups.[18] Following many

13. Thomas Jefferson to the Danbury Baptist's Association, of 1 January 1802, Andrew (ed), *16 Writings of Thomas Jefferson 281* (1903).

14. In *Lynch v Donnelly* (1984) 465 US 668 the Supreme Court accepted that absolute separation is not possible.

15. See further Foley (ed), Jefferson, *Writings* (The Library of America, 1984: The Jeffersonian Cyclopedia. 1900).

16. See the *Grolier Multimedia Encyclopedia*.

17. Thomas Jefferson to Miles King, 26 September 1814.

18. *Everson v Board of Education* (1947) 330 US 1 *per* Black J.

struggles and much opposition, the First Amendment to the US Constitution provided:

> Congress shall make no law respecting an establishment of religion or prohibiting the free exercise thereof; or abridging the freedom of speech, or of the press; or the right of the people peaceably to assemble, and to petition the Government for a redress of grievances.[19]

The first clause of the First Amendment – 'Congress shall make no law respecting an establishment of religion or prohibiting the free exercise thereof,' – has been at the centre of large amounts of litigation in the setting of public and private education. Under the second section of this clause, each person has the fundamental right to worship in accordance with his or her conscience-free from government intrusion.

[10.005] The First Amendment became a significant element of the United States Constitution in 1791 as part of the Bill of Rights.[20] While the US principle of church-state separation aims to prevent, as far as possible, the intrusion of the church and the state into the precincts of each other,[21] the principle itself is grounded in respect for the church and not in hostility,[22] since hostility would bring the courts into conflict with the national traditions of the US as embodied in the First Amendment guarantee of the free exercise of religion.[23] However, it has been alleged that three recent federal cases indicate a certain hostility to Christianity,[24] despite the

---

19. US Constitution, Amend 1. See further Esbeck, 'The Establishment Clause as a Structural Restraint on Governmental Power' (1998) 84 *Iowa L Rev.*
20. Russo, *Reutter's Law of Public Education* (6th edn, Foundation Press, 2006) 25 and generally ch 2 'Church-State Relations in Education.'
21. *Lynch v Donnelly* (1984) 465 US 668.
22. *Zorach v Clauson* (1952) 343 US 306 at pp 310–315: *Abingdon v Schempp* (1963) 374 US 203.
23. *McCollum v Board of Education* (1948) 333 US 203, 211–212: see also *Zorach v Clauson* (1952) 343 US 314, 343.
24. (1) *CH ex rel ZH v Oliva* (2000) (CH) 226 F 3d 198 (3d Cir), *cert denied sub nom.* The Third Circuit affirmed that school officials were not liable for preventing a student from reading a biblical story in a junior class in a public school, albeit on procedural grounds and in a Thanksgiving exercise from displaying a poster that he made giving thanks to Jesus: (2) In *Skoros v City of N York* (2007) 437 F3d (2d Cir 2006) cert denied, 127 S Ct 1245 the Second Circuit amazingly upheld as constitutional the decision of the Board of Education which permitted December 'holiday' displays containing a menorah celebrating Chanukah and the crescent and star commemorating Ramadan in public schools while excluding nativity scenes of Jesus on the grounds that the Christian displays were wholly religious. (contd .../)

principle laid down by *Lemon v Kurtzman*[25] that government activity should neither 'advance nor inhibit religion'. Referring to the later cases as examples of judicial hostility in the Second, Third and Ninth Circuits, Russo remarks:

> This hostility is all the more apparent in the light of the fact that the courts protect religious expression of faiths other than Christianity, belying a lack of even-handedness, often aided and abetted by school officials. While readily conceding that there are some cases where the courts did display even-handedness,[26] their systematic failure to adopt such a perspective consistently reflects judicial attitudes toward religion in public school.[27]

[10.006] Realistically speaking, however, the absolute separation of church and state is impossible and some relationship between government and religious organisations is inevitable.[28] For example, in *Lynch v Donnelly*,[29] the US Supreme Court observed that the government has long recognised, and even subsidised, holidays with religious significance.[30] Another striking example of accommodation is the fact that, in the same week that Congress approved the Establishment Clause as part of the Bill of Rights (1789) for submission to the states, Congress also passed legislation providing for publicly funded chaplains for the House and Senate, who would offer daily prayers in Congress.[31] There are countless other illustrations of the

24. (contd) (3) Even more surprising was the decision of the Ninth Circuit affirming the dismissal of a claim by parents who challenged a decision made by their children's School Board's policy to utilise Islamic-friendly curricular materials in *Eklund v Byron Union School District* (2006) 153 Fed Appx 648 (9th Cir 2005) cert denied, 127 S Ct 6.

25. *Lemon v Kurtzman* (1971) 403 US 602.

26. *Hansen v Ann Arbor Public Schools* (2003) 293 F Supp 2d 780 (ED Mich).

27. Russo, Judicial 'Hostility to all things Religious in Public Life' Or Healthy Separation of Religion and Public Education? (2008) Religion and Education, Vol 35, No 2 (Spring).

28. For a comprehensive assessment of ecclesiastical law in the US see Russo, *Reutter's The Law of Public Education* (6th edn, Foundation Press, 2006), chapter 2 'Church-State Relations in Education', 25–156.

29. *Lynch v Donnelly* (1984) 465 US 668, 673.

30. *Lynch v Donnelly* (1984) 465 US 668, 673 referring in particular to Thanksgiving and Christmas.

31. See further *Marsh v Chambers* (1983) 463 US 783.

government's sponsorship of and acknowledgment of religious heritage.[32] Many contemporary references also demonstrate respect for America's religious heritage. For instance, the national motto 'In God we Trust' was mandated by Congress and President for the US currency. Furthermore, the phrase 'One Nation under God' is part of the Pledge of Allegiance to the Flag, which thousands of public school students take every year (although much debate surrounds the nature of God in this context).[33] In *Aronow v United States,*[34] a Ninth Circuit court held that the phrase 'In God we Trust' has nothing to do with the establishment of religion,[35] but this matter has not been determined by the US Supreme Court. Again, however, there is much public debate on the meaning of 'God' in this particular context.[36] In *Lynch v Donnelly*[37] the Supreme Court considered the Jeffersonian 'wall of separation' to be a useful metaphor, but not an accurate description, of the practical aspects of the church-state relationship that exist in fact:

> The Constitution does not require complete separation of church and state; it affirmatively mandates accommodation, not merely tolerance of all religions and forbids hostility towards any. Anything else would require the 'callous indifference' that was never intended by the Establishment Clause.[38]

Because total separation is not possible, in every establishment case the courts must reconcile the inescapable tensions between the objective of preventing unnecessary intrusion of either the church on the state or the state on the church. As will be seen from the case law, there is no one particular test or criterion that can be applied by the courts, but a number of approaches or tests are evident.[39]

---

32. *Lynch v Donnelly* (1984) 465 US 668.
33. See for example Dershowitz, *America Declares Independence* (Wiley, 2003).
34. *Aronow v United States* (1970) 432 F 2d 242 (9th Cir).
35. See also *O'Hair v Murray* (1979) 588 F 2d 1144 (5th Cir), *cert denied sub nom O'Hair v Blumenthal* (1979) 442 US 930, 99 S Ct 2862, 61 L Ed 2d 298 (affirming the dismissal of a similar challenge).
36. See, for example Rinaldo, *Atheists, Agnostics and Deists in America* (DorPete Press, 2000): Novak, *God's Country: Taking the Declaration Seriously* (AEI Press, 2000): Kramnick and Moore, *The Godless Constitution: The Case against religious Correctness* (WW Norton & Co, 1991).
37. *Lynch v Donnelly* 465 US 668.
38. *Lynch v Donnelly* 465 US 668 at 672–673, the reference to '*callous indifference*' is from *Zorach v Clauson* (1952) 343 US 306, 314.
39. For a comprehensive discussion of these cases, see Russo, *Reutter's The Law of Public Education* (6th edn, Foundation Press, 2006), Ch 2 *et seq*.

EDUCATION IN THE CONSTITUTION

[10.007] Somewhat surprisingly, the US Constitution is silent on education but, nonetheless, it is a reserved power under the First Amendment. It casts no express obligation on states to provide schools and does not regulate state systems of education if the states see fit to maintain them, but states cannot, through school policy, invade rights secured to citizens by the Constitution.[40] However, the 10th Amendment, (ratified 15/12/1791), is relevant here in that it restricts federal state to those powers conferred on it in the Constitution: 'The powers not delegated to the United States by the Constitution, nor prohibited to it by the states, are reserved to the states respectively, or to the people.'[41] An abiding respect for the vital role of education in a free society is to be found in numerous opinions of the Supreme Court. As such, in a far-reaching phrase, the court in *San Antonio Independent School District v Rodriguez*, which challenged the Texan system of financing public education, indicated that no grounds exist for implying a right to education in the Constitution: 'education, of course is not among the rights afforded explicit protection under our Federal Constitution. Nor do we find any basis for saying that it is implicitly so protected.'[42] However, the court went on to state that education is essential to the effective exercise of the First Amendment freedoms and to the intelligent utilisation of the right to vote.[43]

[10.008] One of the citizen's secured rights is freedom from taxation to support a breach of the constitutional mandate that the authorities 'shall make no law respecting an establishment of religion, or prohibiting the free exercise thereof.'[44] As a result, the taxpayer is free from any obligation to fund religious schools in the US and moreover, the Supreme Court has been vigilant in ensuring that the American taxpayer, through his or her taxes, is

40. *Everson v Board of Education* (1947) 330 US, per Black J: see also *West Virginia Board of Education v Barnette* (1943) 319 US 624: *Newdow v US Congress* (2003) 292 F 3d 597 (9th Cir 2002); 203 WL 554742 (9th Cir); see also 166 Educ L Rep 85.

41. Available online at http://www.usconstitution.net/const.html accessed by this author on 29 August 2008.

42. *San Antonio Independent School District v Rodriguez* 411 US 1 (1973).

43. *San Antonio Independent School District v Rodriguez* 411 US 1 (1973).

44. *San Antonio Independent School District v Rodriguez* 411 US 1 (1973), Jackson J dissenting.

not required by law to promote or foster religious education or instruction in public schools. Two movements are constantly at work, in the name of education, seeking to bridge the division of religion and civil authority for which the Founding Fathers made provision in the First Amendment: the one, striving to introduce religious education and observance to the public schools; the other, striving to obtain public funds for the aid and support of various religious schools. Although both of these avenues were closed by the Constitution as the Supreme Court held in *Everson v Board of Education*,[45] they emerge regularly in the public forum and frequently come before the courts for resolution.

[10.009] As arbiter of these matters, the US Supreme Court has, for the most part, ensured that the metaphorical 'wall of separation' between church and state has been maintained in a relatively impregnable condition. Over the years, the court has been called upon to determine many issues arising from First Amendment rights relating to, for example:

(a) the right to preach in the streets;

(b) the parental right to establish private schools;

(c) the right of students to 'pure student expression';[46]

(d) 'school sponsored speech'[47] in public schools;

(e) 'government speech';[48]

(f) the right to open sessions of the legislature with a prayer; and

(g) the right to teach Darwinian evolution theory in the public schools.

A number of these cases are discussed later in this chapter.

---

45. *Constitution in Everson v Board of Education* 330 US 63 Black J delivering the opinion of the court.

46. The Supreme Court has evolved a different test for schools to that which is normally applied (the clear and present danger test): see *Tinker v Des Moines Independent Community School* (1969) 484 US 271. For a number of these cases see further Russo, *Reutter's The Law of Public Education* (6th edn, Foundation Press, 2006) p 867 *et seq*. Some of these cases are discussed below.

47. *Hazlewood School District v Kuhlmeier* (1988) 484 US 271.

48. *Wells v City of Denver* (2001) 257 F 3d 1132, 1144 (10th Cir).

THE FIRST AMENDMENT

[10.010] The Supreme Court has held that the first and most immediate purpose of the First Amendment is grounded in the belief that a union of government and religion tends to destroy government and to degrade religion.[49] That Amendment was framed, not merely to strike at the establishment of a single creed, sect or religion, but with the aim of uprooting all such relationships.[50] Clearly, the object of the First Amendment was much broader than merely separating church and state in this narrow sense;[51] it was to create a complete and permanent separation of the spheres of religious activity and civil authority by comprehensively prohibiting every form of public aid or support for religion.[52] The Amendment's actual wording and history combine with the constitutional *dicta* of the Supreme Court to unambiguously decide this very significant issue. It is therefore not simply an established church which is prohibited, but any law in respect of the establishment of religion.[53]

The Establishment Clause

[10.011] While the specific formulation of the Establishment Clause has been interpreted, expanded and refined over the decades, its essential meaning has not altered from the principles enunciated in *Everson v Board of Education.*[54] Although religion is mentioned only once in the First Amendment, it governs two prohibitions in like manner:[55] one narrow, to forbid an establishment and the other much broader, for securing 'the free exercise thereof.' The word 'thereof' draws down and engages the entire and exact content, from the first into the second guarantee, so that the states are as broadly restricted concerning the one guarantee as they are regarding the other.[56] The Establishment Clause itself also embodies two pivotal values,

49. See *dictum* of Black J in *Engel v Vitale* (1962) 370 US 421 at 431.

50. *Everson v Board of Education* (1947) 330 US 31.

51. *Watson v Jones* (1871) 80 US (13 Wall) 679 at 703.

52. *Watson v Jones* (1871) 80 US (13 Wall) 679 at 703.

53. *Watson v Jones* (1871) 80 US (13 Wall) 679 at 703.

54. *Everson v Board of Education* (1947) 330 US 31.

55. But it does not have two meanings.

56. *Everson v Board of Education* (1947) 330 US 31, 32.

voluntarism and pluralism, and it is precisely in the sphere of the public schools that the Supreme Court has indicated that these laws must be safeguarded most vigilantly because of their crucial role in American society.[57]

[10.012] In *McCollum v Board of Education*,[58] Frankfurter J[59] considered the role of the public schools which were designed to serve as perhaps 'the most powerful agency for promoting cohesion among a heterogeneous democratic people.' Thus, he stated, the public schools must be kept scrupulously free from entanglement in the strife of sects. In order to preserve the community from divisive conflicts, the government from irreconcilable pressures by religious groups and religions from censorship and coercion (however subtly exercised), the First Amendment requires the strict confinement of the state to secular instruction, leaving to the individual's church and home indoctrination in the faith of his choice.[60] The Founding Fathers in the US envisaged the public schools and public education as an agency for fostering unity and social cohesion, as the French Republic did following the Revolution although the means by which that objective was achieved differed considerably as **chapter 7** of this book illustrates.

[10.013] As the Supreme Court reiterated in *Lemon v Kurtzman*,[61] nothing it has stated can be construed to disparage the role of church-related elementary and secondary schools in national life and that their societal contribution has been, and is, enormous.[62] Burger CJ, when delivering the majority decision of the court, stated that every analysis, in this sphere, must begin with consideration of the cumulative criteria developed by the court over many years and that three tests may be identified from these sources:

> First the statute must have a secular legislative purpose; second, its principal or primary effect must be one that neither advances nor inhibits religion; finally,

57. *McLean v Arkansas Board of Education* (1982) 529 F Supp 1255 (ED Ark).
58. *McCollum v Board of Education* (1948) 333 US 203.
59. *McCollum v Board of Education* (1948) 333 US 203 at 216–217, Frankfurter J was joined in this decision by Jackson, Burton and Rutledge JJ.
60. *McCollum v Board of Education* (1948) 333 US 203, pp 216–217.
61. *Lemon v Kurtzman* 403 US 602.
62. *Lemon v Kurtzman* 403 US 602, see also Clark J's Comments on religion in *Abingdon v Schempp* (1963) 374 US 203 per Clark J at 239 above and those of Rutledge J (dissenting) in *Everson v Board of Education* (1947) 330 US 1, 58, 67.

the statute must not foster excessive governmental entanglement with religion.[63]

Further factors to be evaluated in the assessment of 'governmental entanglement' and the provision of state aid to religiously affiliated institutions, he stated, were the character and purposes of the institutions benefiting from the aid, the nature of the aid provided by the state and the resulting relationship between the government and the religious authority.[64] Applying the above criteria, the court found that the entire process of the subsidisation of parochial schools furthered a process of religious inculcation and that the 'continuing state surveillance' necessary to enforce the specific provisions of the laws would inevitably entangle the state in religious affairs. To ensure that teachers play a non-ideological role would require the state to become entangled with the church institutions. Moreover, the court considered that the teachers, whose salaries were partly paid by the state at that time, were agents who worked under the control of religious officials. It also noted the presence of an 'unhealthy divisive political potential' concerning legislation which appropriates support to religious schools. Accordingly, the court held unanimously that both statutes providing state aid to church-related elementary and secondary schools,[65] which were challenged by the appellant, fostered excessive governmental entanglement with religion and consequently they violated the Establishment Clause of the First Amendment.

The US Supreme Court clarified in *Lynch v Donnelly*,[66] approving *Lemon v Kurtzman*,[67] that the Establishment Clause, like the Due Process Clause, is not a precise, detailed provision in a legal code capable of ready application. Its purpose was to state an objective, not to write a statute and the line between permissible relationships and those barred by the Establishment Clause cannot be defined by a single stroke or phrase or test because it erects a blurred, indistinct and variable barrier depending on all the circumstances of a particular relationship. In each case the inquiry calls for line-drawing and no fixed, precise rule can be framed. Essentially, the Establishment Clause requires the government to remain neutral in religious matters and it may not take any action to advance, promote or inhibit

63. *Lemon v Kurtzman* 403 US 602, at 612–3.

64. *Lemon v Kurtzman* 403 US 602.

65. The Rhode Island Salary Supplement Act 1969 and the Pennsylvania Statute discussed in Russo, Reutter's *The Law of Public Education*, pp 91–98.

66. *Lynch v Donnelly* (1971) 403 US 602.

67. *Lemon v Kurtzman* (1973) 411 US 192.

religion. Clearly, the US Constitution did not create a nation or its religion and institutions, since these already existed. Rather, the Establishment Clause was framed with the object of protecting existing institutions and individuals under a republican form of government within the framework of the rule of law drawn up by the people, and for the people.[68] The Free Exercise Clause, on the other hand, is written in terms of what the government cannot do to the individual, not in terms of what the individual can exact from the government.[69]

[10.014] In a prayer-related case, *Santa Fe Independent School District v Doe*,[70] the Supreme Court applied the *Lemon* test, the endorsement test and the coercion test to strike down the policy of a school district board's policy of allowing student-led 'invocations' prior to high school games. The court held that 'the delivery of a pre-game prayer has the improper effect of coercing those present to participate in an act of religious worship.' Applying *Lemon,* the court found the prayer did not have a secular purpose. However, the court also used terminology redolent of the endorsement test (eg this policy was implemented with the intention of endorsing prayer). The court stated that the application of each of the three tests provided an independent ground for invalidating the statute at issue in *Santa Fe* and it proceeded to invalidate the school board's policy solely on the grounds of the coercion test.

RELIGIOUS INFLUENCES

Flag Salute

[10.015] The Pledge of Allegiance to the Flag reads: 'I pledge allegiance to the flag of the United States of America and to the Republic for which it

68. Feldman, *Divided by God* (Farrar, Straus and Giroux, 2005), 24.

69. *Sherbert v Verner* (1963) 374 US 398 in which a Seventh-day Adventist was discharged by her employer because she refused to work on Saturdays (her Sabbath). When she failed to get alternative employment she applied for and was refused unemployment compensation under South Carolina legislation. The Supreme Court upheld the principle laid down in *Everson v Board of Education* 330 US 1, 16 that no State may exclude the members of any faith or none from receiving the benefits of public welfare legislation and reversed and remanded the decision of the South Carolina Supreme Court.

70. *Santa Fe Independent School District v Doe* (2000) 530 US 290 at 310–316.

stands, one nation, under God, indivisible, with liberty and justice for all.' This is the normal method of honouring the nation in public schools and it is required by law, as part of the public schools' programme, in many states. In 1954, the words 'under God' were added to the pledge by Federal statute[71] following a campaign by a number of religious bodies.[72]

[10.016] There have been many controversial decisions relating to the constitutionality of the requirement to salute the American flag and repeat the Oath of Allegiance.[73] In 1939 the US Supreme Court summarily affirmed a decision that refused to prohibit a state statute that mandated the recital of the pledge by students.[74] In 1940 the court ruled that children of Jehovah's Witnesses were not exempted from participating in taking the pledge and that this requirement did not violate their religious freedoms.[75] A few years later, the court balancing the limits of state power against individual rights in another challenge taken by Jehovah's Witnesses, held that requiring children to salute the flag breached constitutional limits because it trespassed on the individual's sphere of intellect and spirit that is safeguarded by the First Amendment.[76] In 1966, the Supreme Court of New Jersey ordered the reinstatement of black Muslim students, who had been excluded from public school for refusing to pledge allegiance to the flag on the grounds that it violated their religious beliefs. The court noted that these students did not cause disruption but rather stood respectfully at attention while the pledge was being taken by the other students.[77]

[10.017] The California Education Code required that each day should begin in public schools in its jurisdiction with 'appropriate patriotic exercises'[78]

71. The Pledge was first codified by Congress in June 1942. An amendment to the Pledge was signed into law by President Eisenhower, Pledge of Allegiance to the Flag, 2003 but this amendment was later abolished and the Pledge is now contained in 4 USC, 4, 1998 (Title 4).

72. See Russo, '*The Pledge of Allegiance*, Patriotic Duty or Unconstitutional Establishment of Religion' citing Dolan, 2000 and Wagenseil, 2000, (2003) *School Finance*, July/August, 22–26. In this article Russo analyses the background, history and case law relating to the Pledge.

73. Many of these cases are discussed in Russo, *Reutter's The Law of Public Education* (6th edn, Foundation Press, 2006), 60–65.

74. See *Johnson v Town of Deerfield* (1939) 25 Fed Supp 918 (D Mass), affirmed, 306 US 621, 59 S Ct 791.

75. *Minersville v Gobitis* 310 US 586.

76. *West Virginia State Board of Education v Barnette* (1943) 319 US 624.

77. *Holden v Board of Education* (1966) 216 A 2d 387 (NJ).

and the recital of the pledge by willing pupils was one method of discharging that obligation.

One Californian public elementary school's policy stated: 'Each elementary school class [shall] recite the pledge of allegiance to the flag once a day.' However, in *Newdow v US Congress*[79] the non-custodial father of a pupil challenged the constitutionality of the school board's policy of permitting the recitation of the pledge in the public school since it included the words 'under God'. The applicant, a self-professed atheist, contended that although his daughter could opt to remain silent, she was harmed by hearing her state-employed teacher in her state-run school proclaim in a ritual that there is a God. He argued that the words 'under God' should be removed from the pledge since they were, he alleged, unconstitutional. A federal court dismissed the claim.[80] On appeal, the Ninth Circuit court of appeals[81] affirmed that the practice of teacher-led recitation of the pledge, together with the added words 'under God', violated the Establishment Clause[82] and was unconstitutional. The court held that the pledge, as currently codified, was an impermissible government endorsement of religion, which sent a message to 'unbelievers that they are outsiders and not full members of the political community and an accompanying message to adherents that they are insiders, favoured members of the political community.'[83] That was not the end of the matter, however. The reference to 'one nation under God' in the Pledge of Allegiance was adopted by resolution of the Senate and the House of Representatives and An Act to Reaffirm the Reference (2002) was passed incorporating that change. Congress admitted the significance that Americans, as a religious people, place a belief in God.[84] This matter remains controversial, however, and as

78. 52720 of 1989.

79. *Newdow v US Congress* (2003) 292 F 3d 597 (9th Cir 2002); 203 WL 554742 (9th Cir).

80. In an unpublished opinion, *Newdow 2,* 2003.

81. Which has jurisdiction over California, Arizona, Idaho, Hawaii, Montana, Nevada, Oregon and Washington.

82. *Newdow v US Congress* (2003) 292 F 3d 597 (9th Cir 2002); 203 WL 554742 (9th Cir).

83. *Newdow v US Congress* (2003) 292 F 3d 597 (9th Cir 2002); 203 WL 554742 (9th Cir) citing *Lynch v Donnelly* (1984) 465.

84. See also the statement 'We are a religious people whose institutions presuppose a Supreme Being', *Zorach v Clauson* 343 US 313 *per* Douglas J: see further Russo, *'The Pledge of Allegiance ....'*, p 23.

America, like Europe, becomes more increasingly diverse, that controversy is unlikely to diminish.

[10.018] In a case from Virginia, which was delayed on account of the *Newdow* case,[85] the Fourth Circuit rejected the argument of a father who claimed that the daily recitation of the pledge forced his children to worship a secular state. In affirming, the court was satisfied that the voluntary daily recitation of the pledge did not violate the Establishment Clause because it did not have a religious purpose or effect and did not create excessive government entanglement with religion, even though it was a religious statement, since it is mainly a patriotic expression.[86] The court also ruled that the non-attorney father of the minor students could not litigate their *pro se* claim.[87] However, approximately one month later, a federal trial court in California, relying on the case from the Ninth Circuit that the Supreme Court vacated as moot in *Newdow,*[88] granted the plaintiff's request to prevent students from reciting the phrase 'under God' in the pledge as being in violation of the Establishment Clause of the First Amendment.[89]

Judicial Expansion of Religious Freedoms

[10.019] When considering matters pertaining to religious freedoms and the church-state relationship, the courts have during the twentieth century mostly considered the Establishment Clause and the Free Exercise Clause of the First Amendment and Art VI, s 3 of the Religious Test Clause, which provides, *inter alia*, that no religious test shall ever be required for public office or public trust under the US Constitution. These are the sole provisions on religion in the Constitution and in matters relating to religious liberty and the relationship of state and church. However, they are seminal and have given rise to a significant corpus of judicial decisions. Prior to the 1940s, the Establishment and Free Exercise Clauses were not incorporated into the Fourteenth Amendment, so that they applied only to Congress at that time. *Cantwell v Connecticut*[90] incorporated the Free Exercise Clause

85. *Newdow v US Congress* (2003) 292 F 3d 597 (9th Cir 2002); 203 WL 554742 (9th Cir).
86. *Myers v Loudoun County Public Schools* (2005) 418 F 3d 395 (4th Cir).
87. *Myers v Loudoun County Public Schools* (2005) 418 F 3d 395 (4th Cir).
88. *Newdow v US Congress* (2003) 292 F 3d 597 (9th Cir 2002); 203 WL 554742 (9th Cir).
89. *Newdow v US Congress* (2003) 292 F 3d 597 (9th Cir 2002); 203 WL 554742 (9th Cir).
90. *Cantwell v Connecticut* (1940) 310 US 296.

and *Everson v Board of Education*[91] incorporated the Establishment Clause. In this manner, the Supreme Court extended the application of these clauses to the governments of all the states by virtue of the application of the Fourteenth Amendment. Consequently, with regard to the free exercise of religion and the establishment of religion, individuals now have the same rights against the federal and state governments and also against the legislature, and executive and judicial branches of government in the US.

[10.020] In *Lynch v Donnelly*[92] the court upheld as constitutional the inclusion of a nativity scene in an urban Christmas display in Pawtucket, Rhode Island, when it applied 'the endorsement test':

> The Establishment Clause prohibits government from making an adherence to religion relevant in any way to a person's standing in the political community. Government can run afoul of that prohibition in two principal ways. One is excessive entanglement with religious institutions which may interfere with the independence of the institutions, give the institutions access to government or governmental powers not fully shared by non-adherents of the religion, and foster the creation of political constituencies defined along religious lines. The second and more direct infringement is government endorsement of disapproval of religion. Endorsement sends a message to non-adherents that they are outsiders, not full members of the political community, and an accompanying message to adherents that they are insiders, favoured members of the political community.[93] Disapproval sends the opposite message.[94]Although *Lynch v Donnelly*[95] relates to a context other than schools, its endorsement test was applied to a number of later school related cases,[96] but it does not appear to have set aside the *Lemon* test or 'the coercion test'.

[10.021] Under 'the coercion test', 'school-sponsored' religious activity is analysed by the courts to determine the extent, if any, to which it has a

91. *Everson v Board of Education* (1947) 330 US 1.

92. *Everson v Board of Education* (1947) 330 US 1.

93. *Everson v Board of Education* (1947) 330 US 1, citing *Lynch v Donnelly* (1984) 465 US 668.

94. *Everson v Board of Education* (1947) 330 US 1, at 687–688 (omitting internal citations).

95. *Lynch v Donnelly* 403 US 603.

96. *Aguilar v Felton* (1985) 473 US 402 which held that New York's City's Title 1 Federally funded programmes of remedial education for disadvantaged children delivered, on a neutral basis, in religiously affiliated non-state schools was lawful as it did could not reasonably be viewed as endorsement of religion.

coercive effect on students.[97] The US Supreme Court has determined that unconstitutional coercion occurs when the government directs a formal religious exercise in such a way as to oblige the participation of objectors. In *Lee v Wiseman*[98] the Supreme Court declared that a school district's policy of inviting religious officials to give invocations and benedictions in the form of a non-sectarian, non-proselytising prayer at graduation ceremonies was an unconstitutional coercion in that it constituted 'a State-directed religious exercise.' By contrast, *Marsh v Chambers*[99] upheld the constitutionality of a prayer service at the opening of a state legislature, where adults were free to enter and exit, an atmosphere which cannot compare with the constraining potential of the one school event most important for the student to attend, that is a graduation ceremony.[100] In other words, the Court distinguished the context in which the prayer was recited, the ages of the participants and the fact that in the public school there was a more impressionable, captive, student audience which had to be protected.

Religious Guarantees in State Laws

[10.022] Following many decades of neglect, certain provisions of the individual states within the US are receiving greater judicial attention in recent years. These include the Acknowledgement of God Provisions, the Religion Provisions, the Education provisions and Finance/Property Tax provisions.[101] Some state guarantees and prohibitions are wider and more specific than those in the federal Constitution. All 50 states include express safeguards for religious liberty and all support the secular church-state separation principle, with some being absolute separationists.[102] Judicial interpretation of these state provisions have further clarified the relationship between church and state, or between governmental institutions and religious institutions, in the various states and these provisions have considerable potential for judicial interpretation in the future. A number of pivotal rights relating to religious freedoms have been established by the US

---

97. *Lee v Butler County Board of Education* (2002) 183 F Supp 2 d 1359. 869].

98. *Lee v Wiseman* (1992) 505 US 577.

99. *Marsh v Chambers* (1983) 463 US 783.

100. *Marsh v Chambers* (1983) 463 US 783, p 817.

101. See *The RJ & L Religious Liberty Archive*: http://www.churchstatelaw.com/. This is a very informative archive and I gratefully acknowledge internet access to it.

102. Doerr and Menendez, *Religious Liberty and State Constitutions* (Prmoetheus Books, 1993).

Supreme Court, some of which are germane to religion only, and others which are concerned with the interface of religion with education in public schools and a sample of these cases now follows.

The Right to Preach or Proselytise

[10.023] Some religions consider street preaching and door-to-door canvassing as an important vehicle for promoting their mission. The seminal issue of door-to-door canvassing and related First Amendment rights has come before the Supreme Court many times during the past half century.[103] Such canvassing, preaching or proselytising, in one form or another, has become a potent force in various religious movements over time and the courts have recognised that they are important vehicles for the dissemination of ideas. Consequently, this form of religious activity now occupies the same high status under the First Amendment as do worship in the churches and preaching from the pulpit,[104] as it has achieved the same entitlement to the guarantees of freedom of speech and freedom of the press.

[10.024] On the other hand, many cases also recognise and balance the interests of a town or village to some form of regulation of canvassing, preaching or proselytising. The right to preach in the streets was established in *Cantwell v Connecticut*.[105] The defendants in that case were Jehovah's Witnesses who had been proselytising on the street and door to door in a mainly Roman Catholic area. Two passers-by reacted angrily on overhearing their portable phonograph's anti-Catholic message, and the defendants were subsequently arrested for a breach of a local statute and for inciting a breach of the peace. The Supreme Court held that under the Constitutional guarantee in the First Amendment, freedom of conscience and of religious belief is absolute, although freedom to act in the exercise of religion is subject to regulation for the protection of society,[106] but that in achieving a permissible end, such regulation must not unduly infringe the protected

103. *Lovell v City of Griffin* (1938) 303 US 414; *Schneider v State (Township of Irvington)* (1939) 308 US 147; *Cantwell v Connecticut* (1940) 310 US 296; *Jamieson v Texas* (1943) 318 US 413; *Martin v City of Struthers* (1943) 319 US 141; *Murdock v Pennsylvania* (1943) 319 US 105 and *Hynes v Mayor and Council of Oradell* (1976) 425 US 610.

104. *Watchtower and Bible Tract Society of New York v Village of Stratton* (2002).

105. *Cantwell v State of Connecticut* 310 US 296, 60 S Ct, 900.

106 Compare with the guarantees in Art 9 of the ECHR in which the right to freedom of thought, conscience and belief is absolute but the right to manifest religion can be made subject to limitations in certain instances. (contd .../)

freedom.[107] The state statute in this instance, the Court continued, was a previous restraint upon the defendants' freedom of religion and a deprivation of liberty without due process of law being provided, and was in violation of the Fourteenth Amendment since it was applied to individuals engaged in distributing literature purporting to be religious and soliciting contributions to be used for that literature's publication.[108]

[10.025] While a state may by general and non-discriminatory legislation regulate the time, place and manner of soliciting upon its streets and of the conduct of meetings, and otherwise protect the peace, good order and comfort of the community, the statute in this instance was not such a regulation. If a certificate is issued, then soliciting is permitted without further restriction; if a certificate is denied, then soliciting is altogether prohibited.[109] In addition, the Court noted that the common law breach of the peace may arise not only by acts of violence, but also by acts and words likely to produce violence in others, and that no such violence or acts of inciting violence had occurred in this case.[110] Accordingly, the Court ruled that the defendant's conviction for the common law breach of the peace violated constitutional guarantees of religious liberty and freedom of speech in the First Amendment.

[10.026] Somewhat analogous rights have been considered by the Supreme Court in *Watchtower and Bible Tract Society of New York v Village of Stratton*[111] in what has been described as 'a ringing endorsement of speech and religious rights.'[112] In *Watchtower*, Stratton village had passed a statute banning door-to-door canvassing unless a permit had been granted by the

---

106. (contd) Where several religions so-exist in a democratic society in one and the same population, the ECHR has found that it may be necessary to place restrictions on this freedom so as to reconcile the interests of the various religious groups and ensure that everyone's beliefs is respected, *Kokkinakis v Greece* (1994) 17 EHRR 387.

107. *Cantwell v Connecticut* (1940) 310 US 296, pp 303–304.

108. *Cantwell v Connecticut* (1940) 310 US 296, p 304.

109. *Cantwell v Connecticut* (1940) 310 US 296, p 297.

110. *Cantwell v Connecticut* (1940) 310 US 296, p 308.

111. *Watchtower and Bible Tract Society of New York v Village of Stratton* (2002) 536 US 150.

112. Russo, *The Yearbook of Education Law 2003* (Education Law Association, 2003) p 268.

Mayor's office, and breach of this ordinance could result in criminal misdemeanour and loss of the right to canvass. In order to secure a permit, a wide range of personal information was required, some of which was intrusive, eg the purpose of the solicitation, the canvasser's whereabouts for the previous five years, and the specific addresses at which the proposed canvassing would take place. The Court considered 'the breath and unprecedented nature of the regulation', but concluded that this alone did not render the statute invalid. Central to the Court's decision to strike down the statute was that it was not tailored to the village's stated interest and so it did not pass the First Amendment's scrutiny. Consequently, the US Supreme Court remanded and reversed the appeal court's decision.[113]

PUBLIC EDUCATION

[10.027] In so far as public education is concerned, the US Supreme Court has for the past 40 years or so become identified with the secular separationist policy exemplified by Black J in *Everson v Board of Education*:

> The First Amendment has erected a wall between church and state. That wall must be kept high and impregnable. We could not approve the slightest breach.

In particular, the Court has been especially vigilant in monitoring compliance with the Establishment Clause in elementary and secondary public schools, since these institutions are in a position of trust to the majority of parents. As the Court observed in *Edwards v Aquillard*:

> Families entrust public schools with the education of their children, but condition their trust on the understanding that the classroom will not purposely be used to advance religious views that may conflict with the private beliefs of the student or his or her family. Students in such institutions are impressionable and their attendance is involuntary.[114]

It has been argued that in the culture war that has swept America, the Supreme Court has aligned itself with those who oppose religion and Christianity in particular, thereby excluding prayer and most religious activity from public schools. Among the critics has been Justice Scalia of that Court, who, albeit in a different context, stated in a dissenting opinion: 'It is clear from this that the Court has taken sides in the culture war

113. *Watchtower and Bible Tract Society of New York v Village of Stratton* 240 F 3d 553, reversed and remanded.

114. *Edwards v Aquillard* 482 US 583–584.

departing from its role of assuring, as neutral observer, that the democratic rules of engagement are observed.'[115]

[10.028] However, when interpreting the Establishment Clause of the First Amendment, the Supreme Court in *Everson* applied a broad interpretation.[116] In that case a New Jersey statute was challenged as a 'law respecting an establishment of religion' by a district taxpayer. The Act authorised, *inter alia,* the New Jersey Board of education to reimburse parents the money spent by them for the transportation of certain children to parochial schools, as part of a general programme of scheduled school buses. Part of the money expended by the Board was for the transport of Catholic children to Catholic parochial schools. The appellant alleged that the Board's practice of reimbursing bus fares to parents of Catholic students constituted a use of state power to support church schools contrary to the prohibition of the First Amendment, which the Fourteenth Amendment had made applicable to the states.[117] At issue was whether it was constitutional to tax the complainant to pay the cost of transporting pupils to church schools of one specified denomination (Roman Catholicism). The court analysed the ideology underpinning the US public school system of education.

[10.029] The American public school, if not a product of Protestantism, it found, was at least more consistent with Protestantism than with the Catholic culture and scheme of values, the system itself being a relatively recent development that dated from about 1840. The public schools are organised on the premise that secular education can be isolated from all religious teaching so that the school can inculcate all necessary temporal knowledge and also maintain 'a strict and lofty neutrality as to religion.' The assumption is that, after the individual has been instructed in worldly wisdom, he will be better fitted to choose his own religion, but whether such

115. *Lawrence v Texas* (2003) 539 US 558, 602–3 in which the court struck down a statute that criminalised the action of a same-sex couple to take part in a specified intimate sexual conduct as unconstitutional when applicable to adult males who participated in a consensual act of sodomy in the privacy of their home: see further Davison Hunter, *Culture Wars: the struggle to define America* (Basic Books, 1991).

116. *Everson v Board of Education* (1947) 330 US 1.

117. The decision in *Cantwell v Connecticut* (1940) incorporated the Free Exercise Clause and the decision in *Everson v Board of Education* (1947) incorporated the Establishment Clause and extended its application to the governments of all the states by virtue of the application of the Fourteenth Amendment.

a disjunction is possible – and if possible, whether it is wise – are questions which the court did not need to try to answer in *Everson.*[118] Black J clarified the constraints imposed on government by the Establishment Clause:

> The establishment of religion clause of the First Amendment means at least this: neither a state nor the Federal Government can set up a church. Neither can pass laws which aid one religion, aid all religions, or prefer one religion over another. Neither can force or influence a person to go or to remain away from church against his will or force him to profess a belief or disbelief in any religion. No person can be punished for entertaining or professing religious beliefs or disbeliefs, for church attendance or non-attendance. No tax in any amount, large or small, can be levied to support any religious activities or institutions, whatever they may be called or whatever form they may adopt to teach or practice religion. Neither a state nor the Federal Government can, openly or secretly, participate in the affairs of any religious organizations or groups and visa versa. In the words of Jefferson the clause against the establishment of religion by law was intended to erect 'a wall of separation between Church and State'.[119]

On the other hand, Black J balanced these prohibitions against the Free Exercise Clause of the First Amendment, which commands that New Jersey cannot hamper, as part of a general programme, its citizens in the free exercise of their own religion. Accordingly, the Court reasoned, the New Jersey law could not lawfully exempt the various faiths from receiving the benefits of its public welfare legislation which had a secular purpose. While the First Amendment mandates governmental neutrality between religion and religion, and between religion and non-religion, the Court held that the New Jersey law had not breached that neutrality in this case.[120] Accordingly, the Court upheld the power of a state to extend the benefits of the school bus transportation scheme to all children on a non-discriminatory basis without regard to their religious beliefs. Yet, the Court cautioned that it did not mean to intimate by its decision 'that a state could not provide transportation only to children attending public schools.' The Court appears to have left the discretion to the state since it pointed out that in *Board of Education of Central School District No 1 v Allen*[121] it had held that a state may, not that it must, adopt a programme for the purpose of furthering educational opportunities for the young under which secular text books are loaned free

---

118. *Everson v Board of Education* (1947) 330 US 1.
119. *Reynolds v United States* (1878) 98 US 145, 164.
120. Citing *Epperson v Arkansas* (1968) 393 US 97.
121. *Board of Education of Central School District No 1 v Allen* (1923) 392 US 236, 88 S Ct.

of charge to children attending parochial or private schools, a principle which was later affirmed in *Meek v Pittenger.*[122]

Evolution in Public Schools

[10.030] One issue which has confronted the courts with regularity since the mid-nineteenth century has been the teaching of the theory of evolution in public schools and, more particularly, the teaching of its competitor, the theory of creationism, which, as will be seen, has assumed a variety of names. The religious movement generally known as 'fundamentalism' came to the fore in America during the nineteenth century as an element of Evangelical Protestantism's response to social changes, new religions and Darwinism.[123] Religiously motivated groups pressed state legislatures to enact laws which prohibited public schools from teaching evolution. As part of that movement a heated debate arose concerning the teaching of evolution and biblical creationism in public schools and the wider ideological conflict between science and religion, which culminated in these issues being litigated in the US courts. Ever since the publication of Charles Darwin's *On the Origin of the Species* (1859) and *The Descent of Man* (1871), certain religions have assailed his theory of evolution[124] due to the perceived conflict between that theory and the biblical account of creation ('creationism') in the book of Genesis.[125] It was not, however, until 1925 that creationism and evolution faced their first major US courtroom battle (a criminal trial), the so-called 'Scopes Monkey Trial.' It was this bizarre case which brought the public controversy between religion and science in education into the US Supreme Court for the first time. More than eight decades later, the public debate continues unabated.[126] At issue in *Scopes* was the constitutionality of a Tennessee law[127] which provided:

> It shall be unlawful for any teacher in any of the Universities, normals and all other public schools of the State which are supported in whole or in part by the

---

122. *Meek v Pittenger* (1975).421 US 349.

123. Jones J in delivering the decision of the Supreme Court in *Kiltzmiller et al v Dover Area School Board et al* citing with approval *McLean v Arkansas Board of Education* (1982) 529 F Supp 1255 (ED Ark).

124. Darwin (1809–1882), *On the origin of the Species by Means of Natural Selection, or the Preservation of Favoured Races in the Struggle for Life* (1859).

125. Russo, 'Evolution v Creation Science in the US; Can the courts Divine a Solution?' (2002) 3 *Education Law Journal* 152 at 158.

126. Larson, *Summer of the Gods* (Basic Books, 1997). This book won the Pulitzer Prize for History.

127. The Butler Act 1925.

> public school funds of the State, to teach any theory that denies the story of divine creation of man as taught in the Bible and to teach instead that man has descended from a lower order of animals.[128]

This legislation prohibited the teaching of Darwin's theory of evolution in Tennessee's public schools and the teaching of any theory which denied the existence of creationism. A number of the citizens of Dayton, Tennessee challenged the constitutionality of the statute and they found a willing ally in the 24-year-old high school biology teacher, John Scopes. Scopes obligingly taught Darwinism, was duly prosecuted for violating the statute, and was found guilty by a jury, for which offence he was fined $100. On appeal from the Tennessee Supreme Court[129] which upheld the law's constitutionality, that decision was dismissed on a technicality, but the Court upheld the constitutionality of the Tennessee law prohibiting the teaching of human evolution in public school classrooms.

[10.031] The teaching of human evolution continued to be illegal in Tennessee until 1967 when a radical change was wrought in *Epperson v Arkansas*[130] by the Supreme Court, which struck down the Arkansas law's provision prohibiting the teaching of evolution in its public schools, that law being a product of an upsurge in fundamentalist religious fervour of the 1920s. While the state has the power to specify the public school curriculum, as it generally has in Europe, the Court found that the First Amendment does not permit it [the state] to require that teaching and learning must be tailored to the principles or prohibitions of any religious sect or dogma, since the First Amendment mandates government neutrality between religion and religion and between religion and non-religion.[131] Accordingly, neither a state nor the Federal government can pass laws which aid one religion, aid all religions, or prefer one religion over another.[132] The only reason for the enactment of the Arkansas law, the Court found, was that a particular religious group perceived a conflict between the evolution

---

128. *Scopes v State* (1924) 289 SW 363 (Tenn).

129. Larsen, *Summer for the Gods: The Scopes Trial and America's Continuing Debate over Science and Religion* (Basic Books, 1997).

130. *Epperson v Arkansas* (1968) 393 US 97.

131. *Epperson v Arkansas* (1968) 393 US 97 at pp 103–4.

132. *Epperson v Arkansas* (1968) 393 US 97, citing *Everson v Board of Education* (1947) 330 US 1, 15 with approval. In international law, the principles of State neutrality and objectivity are governed by the principles laid down in *Kjelsden, Busk Madsen and Pedersen v Denmark* (1976) 1 EHRR 711.

theory and the theory of creationism as documented in the Book of Genesis.[133]

The Challenge of Creationism

[10.032] Subsequently religious groups began to use scientific terminology to describe creationist theories. Words such as 'scientific creationism' and 'creation science' gained acceptance in the 1960s and, later on, the term 'Intelligent Design' (ID) found favour among the creationists. Supporters of ID contend that some features of the universe and nature are so exceedingly complex that they must have been designed by a higher intelligence. Opponents of ID argue that this is simply a disguise for 'creationism' which public schools were being encouraged to include in their science and biology classes on an equal treatment ('balanced treatment') footing with the theory of evolution. They perceived this as religion entering the public schools by stealth. However, this 'balanced treatment' fell foul of a federal court in *McLean v Arkansas Board of Education*[134] because it was held to cater for a religious doctrine, thus violating the Establishment Clause of the First Amendment. Again in *Edwards v Equalled*[135] the US Supreme Court struck down as unconstitutional a Lousiana law which required the 'balanced treatment' of evolution and creationism in its public schools, since it failed to pass all three parts of the *Lemon v Kurtzman*[136] test discussed previously. The evolution debate spread to the funding of pro-evolution school text books in *Willoughby v Stever*[137] when the National Science Foundation's director was sued for using public moneys for the funding of texts which allegedly promoted 'secular humanism' as the official religion of the US. However, that case was dismissed by the DC Circuit court of appeals on the grounds that the text disseminated scientific findings, not religion.

Evolution and Teacher Rights

[10.033] Some public school teachers may have conscientious objections to teaching evolution or creationism while others may perceive themselves as having a right to teach one or other. In *Webster v New Lennox School*

133. *Epperson v Arkansas* (1968) 393 US 97 pp 103, 107.

134. *McLean v Arkansas Board of Education* (1982) 529 F Supp 1255 (ED Ark).

135. *Edwards v Equalled* (1987) 482 US 578.

136. *Lemon v Kurtzman* (1971) 403 US 602.

137. *Willoughby v Stever* 504 F 2d 1975.

District,[138] a high school social science teacher sued his school board, alleging breach of his First and Fourteenth Amendment rights because he had been prohibited from teaching 'creation science' in his public school classroom. Applying *Edward v Aguillard*,[139] the Seventh Circuit court of appeals held that, in banning the teaching of 'creation science', the school district was simply discharging its obligation to ensure that the Establishment Clause was not violated, since it could not lawfully enact a curriculum that would bring religion into the public schools. The teacher remained free, however, to teach non-evolutionary theories and anything regarding the historical relationship of church and state, the court emphasised.[140] On the other hand, in *Peloza v Capistrano School District*[141] a teacher sued the school district, alleging a violation of the Free Exercise Clause since it required him to teach evolution theory. The Ninth Circuit court found that the school district's requirement did not violate its employee's Free Exercise Clause by mandating him to teach evolution.

[10.034] More recently, in Louisiana, a school board adopted a resolution which disclaimed the endorsement of evolution, following its failure to introduce creation science into its district curriculum, as a legitimate scientific alternative to evolution. Under both federal and state constitutions, parents brought a successful challenge to the school's disclaimer under the Establishment Clause of the First Amendment.[142] The court (the Fifth Circuit) affirmed that the school's disclaimer did not advance the articulated objective of encouraging informed freedom of belief or critical thought by students and that it advanced the purposes of disclaiming orthodoxy of belief and of reducing offence to the sensibilities of any student or parent.[143] Recently, a federal trial court in Georgia ruled that a school board's mandate to its officials requiring them to place stickers on biology text books, which stated that evolution was a theory, and not fact, and inviting students to approach material with critical views and with open minds and careful study,

138. *Webster v New Lennox School District* (1990) 122, 917 F 2d. 1004 (7th Cir).

139. *Edward v Aguillard* (1987) 482 US 578.

140. *Edward v Aguillard* (1987) 482 US 578.

141. *Peloza v Capistrano School District* 917 F 2d. 1004.

142. *Freiler v Tangipahoa Parish Board of Education* (2005) 185 F 3d 337[137 Educ. Law Rep. 581] (4th Cir).

143. *Freiler v Tangipahoa Parish Board of Education* (2005) 185 F 3d 337[137 Educ Law Rep 581] (4th Cir).

violated the Establishment Clause by impermissibly favouring religion.[144] On further review, however, the Eleventh Circuit vacated and remanded in favour of the school board on the grounds that it was essential to have further evidentiary enquiries and new findings of fact prior to proceeding.[145]

[10.035] In *Kitzmiller v Dover Area School District*[146] the teaching of evolution was once again before the Supreme Court and the boundaries between religion and science in public schools was again at issue. At the school board level a debate had arisen concerning whether ID theory should be: (a) part of the school curriculum; (b) part of an elective class in the school; or (c) part of a Sunday school class. The school's biology course for 15-year-old public school students was amended to include the ID theory and the school board decided that students participating in the ninth grade biology class would have a disclaimer read to them explaining that ID is an explanation of the origin of life which differs from Darwin's view and that students were encouraged to keep an open mind. The disclaimer read: 'Students will be made aware of gaps/problems in Darwin's theory and of other theories of evolution including, but not limited to, intelligent design. Note: Origins of Life not taught.'

[10.036] This arrangement was perceived by some parents as an attempt to introduce religion into public schools surreptitiously and eight families who disagreed with the policy challenged the board's decision. The Supreme Court, in its 139-page judgment delivered by Jones J on behalf of the Court, referred to the 'breathtaking inanity of the Board's decision' in adopting 'an imprudent and unconstitutional policy' for the school. While the Court did not question the *bona fides* and deeply held beliefs of the leading advocates of ID, nor did it controvert the view that ID should continued to be studied, debated and discussed, it ruled that it was unconstitutional to teach ID as an alternative to evolution in a public school science classroom. Not only did the school board's ID policy violate the Establishment Clause of the First Amendment of the US Constitution, the Court found, but it also violated

144. *Selman v Cobb County School District* (2005) 390 FSupp 2d 1286 [203 Educ L Rep 637] (n D Ga).

145. *Selman v Cobb County School District* (2006) 449 F 3d 1320 [210 Educ L Rep 52] (11th Cir).

146. *Kitzmiller v Dover Area School District* (2005) 400 F Supp. 2d 707 [205 Educ L Rep 250] (MD Pa). I am indebted to Professor Russo for drawing my attention to the last four cases all of which are discussed in *Reutter's The Law of Public Education* (6th edn, Foundation Press, 2006).

Art 1, para 3 of the (Pennsylvania) Constitution. The Court permanently enjoined the board from maintaining the ID policy and from requiring teachers to denigrate or disparage the scientific theory of evolution and from requiring teachers to refer to a religious, alternative theory known as ID.[147] The Court held that the school's policy amounted to an endorsement of religion and the violation of the Establishment Clause and that it also violated the *Lemon* test to the extent that the school policy had the primary effect of imposing a religious perspective into the biology course.[148] This precedent is likely to have a major impact on the content of science classes throughout the United States. It is unlikely, however, that the Supreme Court has heard the last of the evolution verus creation debate, which re-emerges from generation to generation as a testament to the immense mystery surrounding the origins of human persons. Another issue which confronts the courts from time to time is the wearing of religious garb in public schools.

Wearing Religious Garb in Public Schools

[10.037] Constitutional requirements applied by the courts in dress code cases generally fall under either the First Amendment or the Fourteenth Amendment in regard to due process.[149] Unlike the position in France, the judicial approach to the wearing of religious garb in US public schools is, generally speaking, one of accommodation. For the most part, the courts seem to be *ad idem* that educators must apply less restrictive alternatives to placing an express ban on those students who to wear religious garb to public schools.[150] In other words, schools are expected to explore alternatives when confronted with such problems and to choose the less restrictive alternatives to an outright ban. Such accommodation is in line with the underpinning ideology of the public schools elucidated by the court in a number of earlier cases. For example, it is well settled in American jurisprudence that neither teachers nor students leave their constitutional

147. *Reutter's The Law of Public Education* (6th edn, Foundation Press, 2006).

148. *Kitzmiller v Dover Area School District* (2005) 400 F Supp 2d 707 [205 Educ L Rep 250] (MD Pa).

149. For a comprehensive article on student dress codes see Kelso, 'Student Dress Codes', in 'SCHOOL LAW ISSUES', Kightlinger & Gray, Law Offices, presented at NBI School Law Issues in Indiana Seminar available at http://k-glaw.com: accessed on 24 June 2008.

150. Russo, *Reutter's The Law of Public Education* (6th edn, Foundation Press, 2006) p 65.

rights at the school gates.[151] Neither may state-operated schools be 'enclaves of totalitarianism'.[152] School officials do not have absolute authority over their students, who are persons under the Constitution, and are possessed of fundamental rights, which the state must respect, just as the student must also respect the state's rights.[153]

[10.038] For Sikhs the kirpan (a small ceremonial dagger) is a symbol of justice and it must be worn by orthodox Sikhs at all times. It will be recalled that the Canadian Supreme Court upheld the right of a 12-year-old Quebec student of the Sikh faith to wear his kirpan to school under strict conditions.[154] However, in the interests of safety, this dagger must be worn under the clothes and sewn into a wooden sheath. Thus, the Canadian Supreme Court pointed out, the argument relating to safety, could no longer reasonably succeed, since access to the kirpan is fully impeded by the cloth envelope sewn securely around the wooden sheath which is then sewn into the student's underclothing. In a unanimous decision, the Canadian Supreme Court held that the total prohibition of the kirpan by his school had infringed the Sikh student's guarantees of religious freedom under the Canadian Charter of Rights and Freedoms. Returning to the position in US public schools, in *Cheema v Thompson*[155] the Court held that school officials violated the rights of Sikh students by prohibiting them from wearing their ceremonial dagger beneath their clothes. The Court considered that the officials had exceeded their authority because they failed to show that a total ban on weapons was the least restrictive alternative available to them to promote campus safety.[156] By contrast, the wearing of a kirpan by a student in many European schools would be perceived as a risk to the safety of other students in the school.

[10.039] In the US, there is a considerable *corpus* of case law relating to the wearing of nuns' habits which may vary from state to state.[157] It seems clear, however, that if the state legislates specifically to ban nuns from teaching in

151. *Tinker v Des Moines Independent Community School* (1969) 484 US 271.

152. *Tinker v Des Moines Independent Community School* (1969) 484 US 271.

153. *Tinker v Des Moines Independent Community School* (1969) 484 US 271 and *Hines v Caston School Corp* 651 N E 2d 330 at 332.

154. *Multani v Commission Scolaire Marguerite-Bourgeoys* [2006] 1 SCR 256. Multani CBC News, 'Ban on Sikh kirpan overturned by Supreme Court', 2 March 2006 available at http://www.cbc.ca/news/background/kirpan/accessed on 5 October 2008.

155. *Cheema v Thompson* (1995) 67 F 3d 883 [104 Educ L Rep 57] (9th Cir).

156. *Cheema v Thompson* (1995) 67 F 3d 883 [104 Educ L Rep 57] (9th Cir).

their religious habits, the courts will affirm that decision.[158] In *Cooper v Eugene School District*,[159] a teacher who had adopted the Sikh faith, dressed entirely in white and donned a white turban, while teaching, contrary to Oregon's religious dress statute, which provided: 'No Teacher in any public school shall wear any religious dress while engaged in the performance of duties as Teacher.'[160] For breach of this provision, the teacher was suspended and had her teaching certificate revoked. The Supreme Court of Oregon held that the religious dress statute, when correctly interpreted, did not violate the state's guarantees of religious freedom or the federal First Amendment. The court stated that wearing religious clothing while teaching may leave a conscious or unconscious impression on students and their parents that the school endorses the particular religious commitment of the person.[161] However, the court also clarified that the religious dress statute did not prohibit teachers from wearing common decorations that a person might draw from a religious heritage, such as a necklace with a small cross or Star of David. Revocation of the teacher's teaching certificate did not arise from hostility to religious and political belief, the court concluded, and so it was not an excessive 'sanction' being no more than was necessary to achieve the First Amendment's purpose of maintaining religious freedom and neutrality in public schools.[162]

Religious Instruction in Public Schools

[10.040] In *McCollum v Board of Education*[163] the US Supreme Court decided that by permitting voluntary teachers of religion (Protestant, Catholic and Jewish) to come into public schools to teach religious instruction during the official school day, the school board had breached the Establishment Clause of the First Amendment. However, in *Zorach v Clauson*[164] the Court distinguished *McCollum* when it upheld in a 6:3

---

157. For a sample of these cases, see further Russo, *Reutter's The Law of Public Education* (6th edn, Foundation Press, 2006) p 65.

158. *Commonwealth v Herr* 78 A 68 (Pa 1910): also *O'Connor v Hendrick* (1906) 77 NE 612 (NY).

159. *Cooper v Eugene School District* No 4J 723 P 2d 298 [34 Ed L Rep 614].

160. (ORS 342.650).

161. *Cooper v Eugene School District* No 4J 723 P 2d 298 [34 Ed L Rep 614].

162. *Cooper v Eugene School District* No 4J 723 P 2d 298 [34 Ed L Rep 614].

163. *McCollum v Board of Education* (1948) 333 US 203.

164. *Zorach v Clauson* (1952) 343 US 306.

decision the constitutionality of New York state's education law policy, which permitted students to leave public schools so as to receive religious instruction off the public school premises. Since this latter programme of 'released time' did not coerce students to attend religion classes, the Court ruled that it did not violate the First Amendment, made applicable to states by the Fourteenth Amendment.[165]. By implementing this system, the state had neither prohibited the free exercise of religion nor made a law respecting the establishment of religion.[166] Writing for the majority, Douglas J stated that there was no constitutional requirement which made it necessary for government to be hostile to religion and to throw its weight against efforts to widen the effective scope of religious influence.[167]

Constitutionality of Prayers in US Public Schools

[10.041] The constitutionality of prayers in public schools depends on the circumstances: the nature of the prayer (eg officially required, sectarian, nondenominational etc); the context in which it is recited; who scrutinised the prayer; who endorsed or sanctioned the prayer; who recited the prayer; and whether the recital of the prayer was voluntary or mandated. The US Supreme Court has acknowledged that prayer in public schools raises particularly sensitive constitutional concerns,[168] however, and that 'prayer is a quintessential religious practice'[169] as the following cases illustrate.

[10.042] In *Engel v Vitale*,[170] the US Supreme Court considered the constitutionality of the mandatory recital of official school prayers in a New York state public school.[171] Acting in its official capacity under state law, the school district directed the principal to cause the following prayer to be recited aloud by each class in the presence of a teacher at the beginning of the school day: 'Almighty God, we acknowledge our dependence on Thee and we beg Thy blessings upon us, our parents, our teachers and our

165. Made applicable to states by the Fourteenth Amendment

166. See also *Grand Rapids v Ball* (1985) 473 US 373 in which a publicly- funded programme for students in religiously affiliated non-public schools was struck down by the Supreme Court as unconstitutional.

167. *Grand Rapids v Ball* (1985) 473 US 373, pp 310–315.

168. *Aquillard* (1987) 482 US 578, 583–584.

169. *Karen B v Treen* (1981) 653 F 2d 897, 901 (5th Circuit) affirmed 455 US 913 (1982).

170. *Engel v Vitale* (1962) 370 US 421.

171. Union Free School District No 9 (New York).

country.' A number of parents sued, alleging that this official mandatory requirement breached their children's freedom of religion, although they retained the freedom to refuse to take part in the non-denominational prayer. The parents of ten students challenged the recital of the prayer on the grounds that it violated the Establishment Clause in the First Amendment and the governments of 22 states signed on to an *amicus curiae* urging affirmation of the NewYork Constitutional court's appeal upholding the constitutionality of the state's decision.[172]

[10.043] In a decision grounded mainly in the rationale which emerged from the historical evolution of religion and its relationship with government in the US, the Supreme Court ruled in *Engle v Vitale*[173] that the daily prayer required by the New York state officials in its public schools violated the Establishment Clause of the First Amendment. Under that clause, as reinforced by the Fourteenth Amendment, the Court held that the state or federal government is without power to prescribe by law any particular form of prayer to be used as official prayer in discharging any programme of government-sponsored religious activity:

> State officials may not compose an official state prayer and require that it be recited in the public schools of the State at the beginning of each school day – even if the prayer is denominationally neutral and pupils who wish to do so may remain silent or be excused from the room while the prayer is being recited.[174]

One year later, the US Supreme Court expanded further on its decision in *Engel* when it considered *Abingdon School District v Schempp*,[175] which was a challenge to mandatory Bible-reading in Pennsylvania's public schools. In or about that time, another parent had also challenged the constitutionality of Bible-reading in a Baltimore public school as well as the recitation of the Lord's Prayer, and these two cases were consolidated and heard together by the US Supreme Court in *Abingdon*. The Court held that the recital of the Lord's Prayer in a public school, although mandated by officials, violated the Constitution since its purpose was to promote religion as did mandatory Bible-reading required by state officials.

172. However the following opposed the New York court's decision and submitted briefs: the American Ethical Union, the American Jewish Committee and the Synagogue Council of America.

173. *Engle v Vitale* 370 US 421.

174. *Engle v Vitale* 370 US 421.

175. *Abingdon School District v Schempp* (1963) 374 US 203.

Comparative Religious Education in Public Schools

[10.044] Another significant element of the *Abingdon* (1963) judgment is that it endorsed the teaching of comparative religious education in public schools as the Irish Supreme Court did in *Campaign to Separate Church and State v Minister for Education* (1998)[176] and the Constitutional Court in Germany (1998)[177] did more than three decades later. In *Abingdon* the US Supreme Court stated:

> It might well be said that that one's education is not complete without a study of comparative religion or the history of religion and its relationship to the advancement of civilization. Nothing we have said here indicates that such study of the Bible or religion, when presented objectively as part of a secular program of education, may not be effected consistently with the First Amendment.[178]

[10.045] At issue in *Wallace v Jafree*[179] was a constitutional challenge to an Alabama statute[180] which authorised a one-minute period for 'meditation or voluntary prayer' in its public schools. The District court found that the legislative measure was constitutional but the court of appeal reversed that decision. On appeal, the US Supreme Court applied the *Lemon* test principles, and the Court held the Alabama statute was unconstitutional since the record in *Wallace* showed that the purpose of the one-minute requirement was to endorse religion. In other words, it failed 'the endorsement test'.

[10.046] In *Lee v Wiseman*[181] the Supreme Court considered the constitutionality of the practice in the public schools of Providence, Rhode Island, whose school principals were permitted to invite clergy to offer invocation and benediction prayers as part of the official graduation ceremonies for middle and high school students. Petitioner Lee, the school principal, invited a Rabbi to offer such prayers, and he presented him with 'Guidelines for Civic Occasions' and advised him that the prayers should be

---

176. *Campaign to Separate Church and State v Minister for Education* [1996] 2 ILRM 241: [1998] 2 ILRM 81.

177. See Decision of 17 June 1998, *Deutsches Verwaltungsblatt* 1998, p 1344 ff and Decision of the 17 and 18 February 1999 (1 B v R 1840/98), NV WZ 1999, p 756.

178. 374 US 203 (1963).

179. *Wallace v Jafree* (1985) 472 US 38.

180. Statute no. (16–1–20.1).

181. *Lee v Wiseman* (1992) 505 US 577.

non-sectarian. The issue which eventually came before the Court[182] was whether this practice was consistent with the Establishment Clause of the First Amendment, which the Fourteenth Amendment made applicable to all the states. The court Found that the degree of school involvement in this case made it clear that the graduation prayers carried the imprint of the state and, accordingly, put children of school-going age, who objected to such prayers, in an untenable position. State officials had directed the performance of a formal religious exercise, the court noted. The principal's decision that prayers should be offered; his choice of the religious participant; and his verbal advice, through the pamphlet, that the prayer be non-sectarian meant that he (a state official) had directed and controlled the prayers' content.[183] The government may not establish an official or civic religion as a means of avoiding the establishment of a religion with more specific creeds, the court concluded.[184]

[10.047] At a minimum, a government may not coerce anyone to support or participate in religion or its exercise, or otherwise act in a manner which establishes a state religion or religious faith, or tends to do so.[185] The Court pointed out that the First Amendment protects speech and religion by quite distinctive mechanisms. Speech is safeguarded by ensuring its full expression, even when the government takes part. The mechanism for protecting freedom of worship and freedom of conscience in religious issues is quite the reverse. While the Free Exercise Clause includes a freedom of conscience element, which has similar parallels in the speech provisions of the First Amendment, the Establishment Clause specifically prohibits all forms of state intervention in religious matters with no precise parallel in the speech provisions. The Establishment Clause was inspired by the lesson, derived from historical experience, that in the hands of government what may commence as a tolerant expression of religious views may culminate in a policy of indoctrination and coercion. Prayer exercises in elementary and secondary schools carry a particular risk of indirect coercion, the Court stated.[186] A state-created orthodoxy puts at serious risk the freedom of belief

182. The District enjoined the petitioners from continuing the practice on the ground that it violated the Establishment Clause and the court of appeals affirmed that decision.

183. 505 US 577, pp 8–11.

184. 505 US 577, pp 7–8.

185. 505 US 577, citing with approval *Lynch v Donnelly* (1984) 465 US 668, 678.

186. 505 US 577, pp 11–15 citing with approval *Engel v Vitale* (1962) 370 US 421 and *Abington School District v Schempp* (1963) 374 US 203.

and conscience which are the sole assurance that religious faith is real, not imposed. The school district's supervision and control of a high school graduation ceremony placed subtle and indirect public and peer pressure on attending students to stand as a group or maintain respectful silence during the invocation and benediction.[187] Hence, the Court ruled that including clergy who offer prayers as part of an official public school graduation ceremony is prohibited by the Establishment Clause of the First Amendment.[188]

[10.048] In *Jones v Clear Creek Independent School*,[189] the Fifth Circuit held that a public school's policy of permitting a student-selected, student-given, non-proselytising, non-sectarian invocation and benediction at high school graduations did not violate the Establishment Clause of the First Amendment. Such invocations and benedictions could take the form of a non-denominational prayer and such 'generic prayers' to 'the Almighty' or 'to God' or to 'Our Heavenly Father or Mother' or the like, and such prayers would be permitted. The court warned, however, that the school should play no role whatever in selecting the students involved in such prayer, in scrutinising such prayers or in approving the contents of such prayers.

[10.049] It appears that in recent decades increasing numbers of Americans see a place for voluntary practice of religious beliefs and prayer in public schools; among them the former President Clinton, who has stated:

> Schools do more than train children's minds. They also help to nurture their souls by reinforcing the values they learn at home and in their communities. I believe that one of the best ways we can help out schools to do this is by supporting students' rights to voluntarily practice their religious beliefs, including prayer in schools .... For more than 200 years, the First Amendment has protected our religious freedom and allowed many faiths to flourish in our homes, in our work place and in our schools. Clearly understood and sensibly applied, it works.[190]

---

187. 505 US 577.

188. 505 US 577, pp 7–19.

189. *Jones v Clear Creek Independent School* (1992) 977 F 2d. 963 (5th Circuit). (Clear Creek 11) which was an appeal from the US District court for the Southern District of Texas.

190. 30 May 1998, Archived Information, Internet Research, US Department of Education, US Secretary of Education, Richard W Riley.

A Gallup Poll published in August 2001 found that 78 per cent of Americans were in favour of a constitutional amendment to permit voluntary prayer in public schools[191] and there have been a number of unsuccessful proposals to amend the US Constitution to permit this practice schools since then.[192]

Further Judicial Expansion of Separationism

[10.050] Further expansion of the court's separationist policy emerged in *Stone v Graham*[193] which arose out of challenged legislation in Kentucky[194] which mandated that each of the state's public schools should display on its walls a copy of the Ten Commandments purchased with private contributions.[195] A group of parents at the school objected and sued the state, alleging that this requirement violated the Establishment Clause. The Kentucky Supreme Court upheld the statute as constitutional, holding that the law had a secular purpose of fostering respect for the legal system, which is partly grounded in the Ten Commandments.[196] However, the US Supreme Court reversed that decision, being unimpressed by the inclusion of the following in the Kentucky statute: '[t]he secular application of the Ten Commandments is clearly seen in its adoption as the fundamental legal code of Western Civilization and the Common Law of the United States.' The Court ruled that such an avowed secular purpose was not sufficient to avoid conflict with the First Amendment. Clearly, the pre-eminent purpose of posting the Ten Commandments was religious and the Establishment Clause

---

191. More, 'Public Favors Voluntary Prayer for Public Schools' (2005) Gallup News Service, 26 August.

192. '*US Senator proposes Voluntary Prayer Amendment*', (2006) The Associated Press, 28 April. This report refers to Senator Byrd's introduction of a proposed constitutional amendment to permit, but not to require voluntary prayer in public schools and in extracurricular events, which would require to be approved by Congress and the legislatures of 75 per cent of the 50 states within seven years of the congressional vote. It also refers to similar proposals offered by Senator Byrd in 1962, 1979, 1982, 1993 see www.christianpost.com/article/20060428/21952_US_senator-proposes_voluntary_prayer-amendment accessed by the author on 28 January 2008.

193. *Stone v Graham* (1980) 449 US 39.

194. Kentucky Revised Statute no 158.178

195. See further Russo, 'Religious Neutrality in Public Schools and Elsewhere: An Assessment of the Supreme Court's Approach to Posting the Ten Commandments in Public Places in the US' (2006) 7 Education Law Journal 21.

196. 599 SW 2d 157.

requires the government to be neutral in relation to religious matters. Moreover, the posting served no constitutional educational function.[197] Determining the matter summarily,[198] the Court reiterated that any action which advances, promotes or inhibits religion is prohibited by the First Amendment. This was not a case in which the Ten Commandments were integrated into the school curriculum, where the Bible may constitutionally be employed in an appropriate study of history, civilization, ethics, comparative religion or the like. The Ten Commandments in the instant case served no such educational function. With no support beyond its own *ipse dixit,* the Court concluded that the relevant Kentucky statute was unconstitutional since it had no secular legislative purpose.[199]

[10.051] New guidelines were formulated by the Court in *Stone.* In determining whether a state law violates the First Amendment, a court has to decide: firstly, whether the law was enacted to promote a secular purpose or a religious purpose; secondly, whether the primary effect of such law inhibits or promotes religion; and thirdly, whether such law creates excessive entanglement of government and religion. Applying the first part of this test, the Supreme Court held that the Kentucky law was passed by the legislature to promote religion and was, therefore, unconstitutional since it violated the Establishment Clause.

[10.052] As with the evolution debate, public discourse surrounding the posting of the Ten Commandments in public schools continues unabated. However, since the *Stone* decision in 1980,[200] courts have largely prohibited the posting of the Ten Commandments in public schools. In the Sixth Circuit case *Baker v Adams County/Ohio Valley School,*[201] for example, the court affirmed an injunction against a public school board in Ohio which had displayed stone monuments upon which the Ten Commandments had been inscribed on the basis that the plaintiffs had standing to file suit and that the board has failed to establish a secular purpose for the display.[202] In another

197. See *Abingdon School District v Schempp* (1963) 374 US 203.

198. Hearing no oral evidence and supplying only a brief written opinion, 449 US 39, 101.

199. 449 US 41.

200. *Stone v Graham* (1980) 449 US 39.

201. *Baker v Adams County/Ohio Valley School* (2004) 86 Fed App 104 [184 Educ L Rep 745] 6th Cir, see Russo, *Reutter's The Law of Public Education* (6th edn, Foundation Press, 2006) pp 68–9.

202. Cited in Russo, *Reutter's The Law of Public Education* (6th edn, Foundation Press, 2006) pp 68–9.

case, the Sixth Circuit refused to accept the legality of changes made to displays in a Kentucky county courthouse and public schools which comprised a number of documents, including a quotation from the Bible on the grounds that it had the effect of advancing religion and, therefore, violated the Establishment Clause in the First Amendment.[203]

Display of Other Religious Symbols in Public Schools

[10.053] When deciding cases relating to other types of displays, there has been much less consistency in court decisions. In 2002, the Tenth Circuit court of appeal ruled in *Fleming v Jefferson County School District*[204] that the Columbine High School, in which a shooting led to the deaths of 15 persons in 1999, could lawfully prohibit the display on its public school walls of ceramic tiles bearing religious symbols or messages. These tiles were intended as part of a school memorial to students who lost their lives in the shooting. The school district invited parents to make tiles as part of the school's restoration programme and, observing the obvious church-state restrictions, it clarified from the outset that the tiles should not carry a religious theme. However, certain parents disregarded the school's prohibition and they created tiles bearing, *inter alia*, a Star of David, crosses, angels, graffiti and a skull dripping with blood. When the school refused to erect these tiles, a number of parents sued the school district alleging breach of their free speech claim under the First Amendment. The District court held in favour of the parents on free speech grounds but that decision was reversed by the Tenth US Circuit court of appeals holding that the school district had the right to censor a 'school sponsored' activity as defined in *Hazlewood School District v Kuhlmeier*.[205]

---

203. *American Civil Liberties Union v McCreary County, Kentucky* (2003) 354 F 3d 438 [184 Educ L Rep. 67] (6th Cir). This case is also cited in Russo, *Reutter's The Law of Public Education* (6th edn, Foundation Press, 2006) p 69.

204. *Fleming v Jefferson County School District* (DC No 99-D 1932) decided on 27 June 2002, 10th Circuit court of Appeal.

205. *Hazlewood School District v Kuhlmeier* 484 US at 271.

In *Fleming v Jefferson County School District*,[206] the US Supreme Court distinguished between the three main categories of speech in public schools, which are:

1. matters of 'pure student expression', for example, when students lawfully wore black armbands to manifest their objections[207] to the Vietnam war;[208]

2. the category of 'school sponsored speech', ie student speech which the school affirmatively promotes, as opposed to speech that it merely tolerates;[209] and,

3. the category of 'government speech', eg when a principal speaks at school assembly, as an agent of the government, and may choose what to say and what not to say.[210]

[10.054] When a principal teacher in Wisconsin refused permission to the school Bible club to display a mural containing a cross, some high school students challenged his decision and that of the school board in *Gernetzke v Kenosha School Board*[211] alleging that their First Amendment rights were breached. The Seventh Circuit court affirmed a grant of summary judgment in favour of the school board and held that the principal was striving to maintain order and discipline and was inured from liability by the Equal Access Act and that the school board did not violate First Amendment rights.[212] In another case, however, school officials were ordered by a court to remove a portrait of Jesus which hung in the school hall and had been painted by a school graduate on the grounds that it violated the Establishment Clause.[213] A more recent case reviewed a school board's decision to exclude the plaintiffs' bricks from the walkway in the front part

206. *Fleming v Jefferson County School District* (2002) (DC No 99-D 1932) decided on 27 June 2002, 10th Circuit court of Appeal.

207. Or perhaps their parents' conscientious objections.

208. Which are protected by the First Amendment, see *Tinker v Des Moines Independent Community School* (1969) 484 US 271.

209. *Hazlewood School District v Kuhlmeier* (1988) 484 US 271.

210. *Wells v City of Denver* (2001) 257 F 3d 1132, 1144 (10th Cir).

211. *Gernetzke v Kenosha Unified School District No 1* (2001) 274 F 3d 464 [160 Ed Law Reports 25] (7th Circuit); 525 US 1017 (2002).

212. *Gernetzke v Kenosha Unified School District No 1* (2001) 274 F 3d 464 [160 Ed Law Reports 25] (7th Circuit); 525 US 1017 (2002).

213. *Washegesic v Bloomingdale Public Schools* (1994) 33 F 3d 679 (6th Cir).

of the school because the writing on them contained Christian messages and/or made reference to Jesus. The court held that the school's action had violated the plaintiffs' right to free speech by taking part in viewpoint discrimination, but that the Establishment Clause had not been violated.[214] In 2004, an Arizona court refused the parents' application for summary judgment in a case against a school board for violations of their First and Fourteenth Amendment rights, because the board had required them to remove the word 'God' from their proposed inscriptions for erection on the internal school walls of a public school. The parents had proposed the following inscription 'God bless Quinn We love you Mom and Dad' and a similar inscription for their daughter.[215]

EXPRESSIVE ASSOCIATION

Value-Instilling Organisations

[10.055] In *Boy Scouts of America v Dale,*[216] the US Supreme Court held that bodies which instil values in young persons, such as the publicly-funded[217] Boy Scouts of America (BSA),[218] have a right of expressive association deriving from the First Amendment's Freedom of Speech Clause. This clause permits them to enlist and engage the services of like-minded persons even when doing so would otherwise violate a civil rights Act such as Title VII of the Civil Rights Act 1961 as amended. While this case is not a religion case or a school case, it has implications both for churches and for religiously-affiliated schools by virtue of the fact that they are all 'value instilling organisations' and it also illuminates expressive association and free speech rights. The BSA has a policy that prohibits, *inter alia,* 'known or avowed' homosexuals from membership in its scouting programme, since it considers it essential to instil into its members the values in the Scout Oath.

214. *Anderson v Mexico Academy and Cent School* (2003) 56 Fed Appx 549 (2d Cir).

215. *Seidman v Paradise Valley Unified School District No 69* (2004) 327 F Supp 2d 1089 [191 Educ L rep. 175] (d Ariz): see also *Kiesinger v Mexico Academy & Central School* (2003) 56 Fed Appx 549 [173 Educ L Rep 709] (2nd Cir).

216. *Boy Scouts of America v Dale* (2000) 530 US 640, 160 NJ 562, 734A 2d 1196, reversed and remanded.

217. In 2005 Congress passed a Resolution that the Dept. of Defence support the Boy Scouts of America: See further the Scouts Act 2005.

218. Which is the largest youth organisation in America.

This case arose out of New Jersey's anti-discrimination (or public accommodations) legislation,[219] which prohibited the BSA, a not-for-profit private organisation, from discriminating against the respondent by refusing to accept him as an assistant scoutmaster on the grounds of his sexual orientation. The respondent, James Dale, was a former Eagle Scout, whose membership was revoked when the BSA became aware that he was an avowed homosexual and gay rights activist. The BSA argued that homosexual conduct was inconsistent with the values it was striving to inculcate in youth, with its oath and law, and they invoked the Free Speech Clause and their freedom to associate without government intervention, although they are publicly funded.[220]

[10.056] When the matter came before the US Supreme Court, the Court held that in order to come within the scope of 'expressive association' and to be entitled to the protection of the First Amendment, a group must engage in some form of expression, public or private. The BSA is a private, non-profit organisation, with its aims set out in its mission statement: 'to serve others by helping to instil values in young people and in other ways to prepare them to make ethical choices over their lifetime in achieving their full potential …. The values we strive to instil are based on those found in the Scout Oath and law.'[221] Having considered their mission statement, the Court found that the BSA were not a place of 'public accommodation', as the New Jersey Supreme Court had found,[222] but rather a private organisation indisputably engaged in expressive activity.[223] Implicit in the right to engage in activities protected by the First Amendment, the Court stated, is a corresponding right to associate with others in pursuit of a wide variety of political, social, economic, educational, religious and cultural ends. Moreover, this freedom

---

219. New Jersey's Law against Discrimination (NJSA) 10 prohibits discrimination on the grounds, *inter alia,* of homosexuality.

220. New Jersey's Superior Courts Chancery Division granted summary judgment to the BSA holding that the First Amendment's Freedom of Expressive Association prevented the government from forcing them to accept Dale as an adult leader. New Jersey's Superior Court's Appellate Division affirmed the dismissal of Dale's common law claim, but otherwise reversed and remanded the further proceedings, 308 NJ Super. 516, 70A 2d, 270 (1988).

221. *Boy Scouts of America v Dale* (2000) 530 US 640, 160 NJ 562, 734A 2d 1196, reversed and remanded.

222. 734 A 2d 1196.

223. Approving *Roberts v US Jaycees* (1984) 468 US 609, 622.

to associate presupposes a freedom not to associate, which could not be unconstitutionally burdened by the government.

[10.057] The Court ruled that the New Jersey anti-discrimination law which required the BSA to admit an openly homosexual man as an assistant scoutmaster violated the First Amendment which protects expressive association rights. The Court clarified that the BSA was an expressive association, and not a place of public accommodation, and that the forced inclusion of Dale, as an assistant scoutmaster, would significantly affect the BSA's expressive association rights in the First Amendment, which were grounded in its oath and law. Since the Court re-affirmed that civil powers alone had been conferred on the civil authorities and they had no power to prescribe any religious exercise or to assume authority to prescribe any religious exercise. Accordingly, any such intervention by the government would be unconstitutional. The Court emphasised, however, that this was not an absolute right, but that it could be overridden by regulations adopted to serve compelling state interests, unrelated to the suppression of ideas, that could not be achieved through less restrictive means of associational freedoms.[224] In this highly controversial 5:4 decision, the Court grounded its decision on the bedrock constitutional tenet of a group's right to associate without state interference.[225] It considered that the forced inclusion of an unwanted person in a group infringes the group's freedom of expressive association if the presence of that person affects, in a significant manner, the group's ability to advocate public or private perspectives.[226]

[10.058] By analogy with the BSA, religious schools have the right to associate without state interference in the pursuit of education and religion, and their objectives, values and norms are generally specified in their foundational and ethos-related documents. Such schools frequently require their ministers, teachers, other staff and volunteers to adhere to and manifest in their behaviour the express beliefs and norms of the organisation itself. Hence, this case is of immense significance for religious organisations and church bodies. As discussed below, there are also a number of important exemptions for religiously affiliated schools under employment law.

224. Citing *Roberts v US Jaycees* (1984) 622 at 623.

225. *Roberts v US Jaycees* (1984) 622 at 623.

226. *Roberts v US Jaycees* (1984) 622 at 623, approving *New York State Club Assn, Inc v City of New York* (1988) 487 US 1.

The Doctrine of Church Autonomy

[10.059] In *Watson v Jones*[227] the US Supreme Court stated: 'The structure of our government has, for the preservation of liberty, rescued the temporal institutions from religious interference. On the other hand, it has secured religious liberty from the invasions of the civil authority.' While there is some disagreement as to whether the Doctrine of Church Autonomy, previously known as 'the abstension doctrine', has its source in the Establishment Clause, the Free Exercise Clause or both,[228] the better argued position is that it derives from the Establishment Clause. Esbeck states that the purpose of the Free Exercise Clause is to safeguard individual rights relating to religious belief or practice, while the task of the Establishment Clause is to act as a structural restraint on governmental power.[229] This, he observes, is remarkable in human history when the authority governing coercive power actually limits itself.[230] Accordingly, he argues, the Establishment Clause presupposes a constitutional model consisting of two spheres – government and religion: 'The subject matters that the Clause sets apart from the sphere of civil government – and thereby leaves to the sphere of religion – are those topics 'respecting an establishment of religion', eg ecclesiastical governance, the resolution of doctrine, the composing of prayers, and the teaching of religion.'[231]

[10.060] Professor Esbeck's reasoning is in line with Jefferson's writings in which he views the government of the US as being 'interdicted by the Constitution' from meddling with religious institutions, their dogma,

227. *Watson v Jones* 80 US (13 Wall) 677, 679, 730 (1871) (court of Appeals of South Carolina).

228. See, for example, Stackhouse, 'Religion, Rights and the Constitution', An Unsettled Arena: Religion and the Bill of Rights, White. and Zimmerman (eds), 1990: Esbeck, 'Religion and the First Amendment: some causes of recent confusion' (US Supreme Court). Esbeck, 'Dissent and Disestablishment: The Church-State Settlement in the Early American republic [2004] Brighton Young University Review.

229. Esbeck, The Establishment Clause as a Structural Restraint on Governmental Power (1998) 84 Iowa L Rev 1.

230. Esbeck, The Establishment Clause as a Structural Restraint on Governmental Power (1998) 84 Iowa L Rev 1, p 10, n. 34 citing Stackhouse.

231. Esbeck, The Establishment Clause as a Structural Restraint on Governmental Power (1998) 84 Iowa L Rev 1, pp 97, 101.

discipline and exercise and the objects properly pertaining to them.[232] In addition, Jefferson clearly indicates, every religious society retains the right to determine for itself the objects proper for them, the times for its religious exercise according to their own particular tenets and, he states: 'this right can never be safer than in their own hands, where the Constitution has deposited it.'[233] President Jefferson's views on this issue are also clear from his reply (dated 21 March 1804) to a letter from the Superior of the Sisters of St Ursula of New Orleans (Sr Therese de Xavier). Sr Xavier expressed her concerns in that letter, following the sale and transfer of New Orleans by the French Republic to the US in 1803,[234] regarding the impact this event could have on the property rights and religious freedoms of the Ursuline Order of nuns.[235] In his personal reply, dated 15 May 1804, Jefferson assures the nuns that the guarantees of religious liberty enshrined in the Constitution are a sure guarantee that the Order's property 'will be preserved to you sacred and inviolate, and that your institution will be permitted to govern itself according to its own voluntary rules, without interference from the civil authority.'[236] Somewhat similar guarantees are conferred on the religious denominations in the Irish Constitution.[237]

---

232. Peterson (ed), Thomas Jefferson, Letter to Rev Samuel Miller (1808) from *Thomas Jefferson: Writings, 1186–87* (1984), republished in *R & J Religious Liberty Archive* at www.churchstatelaw.com accessed on the 23 January 2008 by the author, Source, *Thomas Jefferson: Writings 1186–1187* (Merrill D Peterson, ed, 1984).

233. Peterson (ed), Thomas Jefferson, Letter to Rev Samuel Miller (1808) from *Thomas Jefferson: Writings, 1186–87* (1984), republished in *R & J Religious Liberty Archive* at www.churchstatelaw.com accessed on the 23 January 2008 by the author, Source, *Thomas Jefferson: Writings 1186–1187* (Merrill D Peterson, ed, 1984).

234. The Treaty of Cession between the USA and the French Republic, 30 April 1803 under which New Orleans was sold and transferred to the US.

235. Which is available at Archive, *R & J Religious Liberty Archive* at www.churchandstate.com which was accessed on the 23 January 2008. Source, Peterson (ed), *Thomas Jefferson: Writings 1186–1187* (Merrill, 1984).

236. Acopy of President Jefferson's letter is contained in the *R & L Religious Liberty Archive* and I am most grateful to the Archive for drawing my attention to this fascinating document at www.churchstatelaw.com.

237. In Arts 44.2.5° and 44.2.6°.

[10.061] With regard to the Doctrine of Church Autonomy, the landmark precedent is undoubtedly *Watson v Jones*[238] in which the Supreme Court was called upon to consider a dispute which arose among the elders of a Presbyterian Church. This celebrated case brought the court face to face with the pivotal issues which determine the character of the relationship between church and state in the US: the nature and extent of jurisdiction vested in US law in voluntary associations and their ecclesiastical courts; the degree to which these associations are independent of control of the civil authorities; and whether the church in regard to its civil interests is organised under the authority of the law or above it.[239] In *Watson,*[240] the Supreme Court cited with approval the following statement from *Harmon v Dreher*:[241]

> It belongs not to the civil power to enter into or review the proceedings of a spiritual court. The structure of our government has, for the preservation of liberty, rescued the temporal institutions from religious interference. On the other hand, it has secured religious liberty from the invasions of the civil authority.[242]

[10.062] The Court turned for guidance to Scottish law, the great field for litigation of this nature and the home of the Presbyterian religion. Having fully analysed the relevant Scottish precedents and *AG v Pearson,*[243] in particular, the court rejected the proposition laid down by Lord Eldon (Lord Eldon's Rule), the so-called 'departure from doctrine' test, in *Pearson* and sustained by his peers:

> that it is the duty of the court in such cases to inquire and decide for itself, not only what was the nature and power of such judicatories, but what is the true standard of faith in the church organization and which of the contending parties before the court holds to this standard ....[244]

---

238. *Watson v Jones* (1871) 80 US 679.

239. *Watson v Jones* (1871) 80 US 679.

240. *Watson v Jones* (1871) 80 US 679, 731.

241. *Harmon v Dreher* 2 Speers Equity Reports 87, 120 (SCCt Appeal), 1843.

242. *Watson v Jones* 80 US 679, 731.

243. *AG v Pearson* 3 Merivale, 353 and *Craigdallie v Aikman* (1813) 2 Bligh, 529; 1 Dow 1. See these cases on the Free Church of Scotland in Shaw's reports of Cases in court of sessions.

244. *AG v Pearson* 3 Merivale, 353 and *Craigdallie v Aikman* (1813) 2 Bligh, 529; 1 Dow 1. See these cases on the Free Church of Scotland in Shaw's reports of Cases in Court of Sessions.

In particular, the Court observed that the dissenting church in England was not a free church in that there did not exist that full, entire and practical freedom for all forms of belief and practice which lies at the foundation of the political principles in the US. In other words, when it came to a consideration of religious freedoms, the Supreme Court identified at the source of the English and US systems, fundamentally distinctive political principles and jurisprudential norms. Accordingly, the Court ruled in a singular passage, that the doctrines of the English Chancery Courts did not apply in US courts, since much broader principles of freedom of religion apply:

> In this country the full and free right to entertain any religious belief, to practice any religious principle, and to teach any religious doctrine which does not violate the laws of morality and property, and which does not infringe personal rights, is conceded to all. The law knows no heresy, and is committed to the support of no dogma, the establishment of no sect. The right to organize voluntary religious associations to assist in the expression and dissemination of any religious doctrine, and to create tribunals for the decision of disputed questions of faith within the association is and for the ecclesiastical government of all who unite themselves to such a body do so with implied consent to such government, and are bound to submit to it.

Furthermore, the Court was of the view that it would lead to the total subversion of such religious bodies, if any person aggrieved by one of their decisions could appeal to the secular courts, and have that decision reversed.[245] The Court concluded that those ecclesiastical decisions should be binding in all cases of ecclesiastical cognisance, subject only to such appeals as the organisation itself makes provision.

Application of *Watson*

[10.063] As the Court predicted, the influence of *Watson v Jones*[246] was wide-ranging. Numerous cases followed which applied the *Watson* principles, thus securing for religious organisations independence from secular control, freedom from state and federal interference, freedom relating to faith, dogma and discipline of the clergy, and freedom to select the clergy, where no improper methods of choice were proven to exist.[247] In *Kedroff v St*

245. See the case of *O'Keefe v Cardinal Cullen* 2 QB 1873 CL 7 319 discussed above at **para [5.012]**.

246. *Watson v Jones* (1871) 80 US (13 Wall) 679, 731.

247. *Kedroff v St. Nicholas Cathedral* 344 US at 116 citing *Watson v Jones* 80 US 679, 731,

Nicholas Cathedral,[248] the Supreme Court pointed out that the US government by the 'law of its being' allows no statute, state or national law that prohibits the free exercise of religion. However, there are occasions, the Court continued, when civil courts must draw lines between the responsibilities between church and state for the disposition or use of property. Even in those cases, however, when the property right follows as an incident from decisions of the church, the church rule controls the matter. Under the Constitution, these matters necessarily follow so that there may be free exercise of religion.[249] In view of the fact that the courts had held that the First Amendment deprived the civil courts of subject matter jurisdiction,[250] courts across the US have refused to adjudicate claims of clergy malpractice,[251] matters relating to church governance and clerical discipline,[252] spiritual doctrines and church-minister disputes,[253] since this would involve the sate in church matters in a way which is wholly prohibited by the First Amendment[254] and it would also lead to excessive church-state entanglement. Does the doctrine of Church autonomy extend to employment relationships?

---

248. *Kedroff v St Nicholas Cathedral* 44 US 94.

249. *Kedroff v St Nicholas Cathedral* 44 US 94.

250. *Hiles v Episcopal Diocese of Massachusetts* (2002) 773 NE 2d 929, 935 (Mass).

251. *Nelly v Grace Community Church of the Valley* (1988) 763 P 2d 948 (Cal) which laid down the principle that religious counsellors need not abide by the same legal standards that apply to other professionals see further Weitz, *Clergy Malpractice in America: Nally v Grace Community Church of the Valley* (Univ of Kansas, 2001): *Baumgartner v First Church of Christ, Scientist* (1986) 490 NE 2d 1319 (111 App) in which the court held that the question of a practitioner of the Church who had deviated from the Church's standard of care, was not a justiciable controversy.

252. *Williams v Episcopal Diocese of Massachusetts* (2002) 766 NE 2d 820, 825 (Mass): *Olson v Luther Memorial Church* (1996) WL 70102 (Minn): *Germain v Pullman Baptist Church* (1999) 980 P 2d 809 (Wash App).

253. *Minker v Baltimore v Conf. of United Methodist Church* (1990) 894 F 2d 1354, 1355, unless a church discriminates for reasons other than religion in which case the court does not foreclose Title VII suits, for example see *Petruska v Gannon Univ* (2005) US Ct of Appeal for Third Circuit, 83 F 3d 455 (DC), argued 20 October 2005.

254. *Bryan v Watchtower Bible and Tract Society* (1999) 738 A 2d 839, 848 (Me).

NON-PUBLIC SCHOOLS

[10.064] The rise of the public schools prepared the way for the development of the parochial schools of American Catholics. An independent Catholic parochial school system emerged in nineteenth-century America under the Baltimore Council which held its third plenary council at Baltimore in 1884. Public schools, it appears, were not only more receptive to the tenets of the Protestant religion, but some were even anti-Catholic.[255] *Pierce v Society of Sisters*[256] has been described as 'the *Magna Carta*' of the private school[257] because it upheld the constitutionality of private and parochial schools. Furthermore, in *Pierce* it was established by the Supreme Court that the state by its laws cannot mandate a parent to send a child to a public school. The other side of that coin, so to speak, is that there can be no denying the right of church schools to establish and maintain their private schools or the right of parents to choose these schools for their children's education provided they meet the state's curricular requirements. The Compulsory Education Act 1922 of Oregon sought to compel parents, guardians or other persons having control of a child between 8 and 16 years to send such children to public schools in the district in which they resided. However, the court ruled in *Pierce* that this would be an unreasonable interference with the liberty of parents to direct the upbringing of the children and that it would violate the Fourteenth Amendment:[258] 'The fundamental theory of liberty upon which all governments of this union rest excludes any general power of the State to standardise its children by forcing them to accept instruction from public teachers only.' Thus, the court recognised the right of parents, in discharging their duty under state compulsory education laws, to send their children to a religious school rather than a public school, provided the school met the state's reasonable minimum curricular requirements. Accepting the right of parental choice between public and private schools, it follows that the state could not, without manifesting hostility rather than the 'wholesome neutrality' mandated by the First

---

255. See Alilunas, 'The Image of Public Schools in Roman Catholic History Textbooks' (1963) History of Education Quarterly, vol 3, no 3 (September), 159–165: and further *US History Encyclopedia*, available online at http://www.answers.com/topic/private-school.

256. *Pierce v Society of Sisters* (1925) 268 US 510. The Plaintiffs in this case were 2 Oregon Corporations which owned and conducted schools in the state.

257. *US History Encyclopedia.*

258. *US History Encyclopedia,* p 529.

Amendment, prevent a parent from choosing a sectarian-sponsored private school for no reason other than its substantial religious nature.

Public Aid for Non-Public Schools

[10.065] Jackson J's dissenting opinion in *Everson* casts light on the distinctive character of Catholic schools, frequently referred to as 'parochial schools'. He emphasised that these schools are parochial only in name, and that they represent in fact a worldwide system of schools manifesting an age-old policy of the Roman Catholic Church established under the rubric 'Catholic Schools' in the Canon Law of the Church.[259] By contrast with public schools, he continued, parochial schools, in addition to secular education, give their students regular religious instruction conforming to the religious tenets and modes of worship of the Catholic faith and their superintendents, in this case Catholic priests:

> I should be surprised if any Catholic would deny that the parochial school is a vital, if not the most vital, part of the Roman Catholic Church. If put to the choice, that venerable institution, I should expect, would forego its whole service for mature persons before it would give up education of the young, and it would be a wise choice. Its growth and cohesion, discipline and loyalty, spring from its schools. Catholic education is the rock on which the whole structure rests, and to render tax aid to its Church school is indistinguishable to me from rendering the same aid to the Church itself.[260]

When it came to the public funding of parochial schools, it was inevitable that difficulties would arise.

[10.066] The Supreme Court reiterated in *Pierce* that a parent's right to choose a religious private school may not be equated with a right to insist that the state is mandated to fund his child's non-public education wholly or partly in order that he may obtain a religious education. Black J, in *Everson v Board of Education*,[261] sagely pointed out that with public funding comes public control: 'But we cannot have it both ways .... If the state may aid these religious schools, it may therefore regulate them. Many groups have sought aid from tax funds only to find that it carried political controls with it.' Applying the principles enunciated in the First Amendment of the US

259. *Everson v Board of Education* (1947) 330 US 1, Jackson J citing Canon Laws 1215, 1216, 1217, 1224 and 1373.

260. *Everson v Board of Education* (1947) 330 US 1.

261. *Everson v Board of Education* (1947) 330 US 1, 58, 67.

Constitution, the court made it clear that the state contributes no money to the private schools nor does it support them.

[10.067] The New Jersey statute which authorised its local school districts to formulate rules and make contracts for the purpose of transporting children to and from school. Part of the public funding which enabled this scheme was for the transportation of certain children in the community to Catholic parochial schools. The fact that a child, or his parent on his behalf, voluntarily chooses to forgo the exercise of the right to educational benefits provided in the public school system does not deprive him of anything by state action.[262] While the effect of this is to place an enormous financial burden on the various churches in the US, it confers on them much greater autonomy in the running of their own affairs than that which has been achieved in many of the co-operative systems of Europe. Rutledge J's remarks in *Everson* indicate a certain non-ideological sympathy for those parents who choose religious or private education for their children, because in effect they pay twice over:

> No one conscious of religious values can be unsympathetic toward the burden which our constitutional separation puts on parents who desire religious instruction mixed with secular for their children. They pay taxes for other children's education, at the same time the added cost of instruction for their own. Nor can one happily see benefits denied to children which others receive, because in conscience they or their parents for them desire a different kind of training others do not demand.[263]

[10.068] It does not follow, however, that the result of the voluntary choice of parent-plaintiffs is to impose an economic burden for educational provision on them such as to violate the Fourteenth Amendment, since this onus is equally shared by other taxpayers, eg childless couples, bachelors, corporations etc.[264] The scheme, as applied, the Court found did no more than provide a general programme to help parents get their children, regardless of their religion, safely and expeditiously to and from accredited schools.[265] The state contributed no money to the parochial schools nor did it support them. While the First Amendment had erected a wall between

262. *Everson v Board of Education* (1947) 330 US 1, 58, 67.

263. *Everson v Board of Education* (1947) 330 US 1, 58, 67.

264. *Everson v Board of Education* (1947) 330 US 1, 58, 67, *per* Routledge J; See also *Braunfeld v Brown* (1961) 366 US 599.

265. *Everson v Board of Education* (1947) 330 US 1, 58, 67, Black J.

church and state, which must be kept high and impregnable, the state of New Jersey has not breached it in this instance, the Court ruled.

The Provision of Secular Textbooks to Non-Public Schools

[10.069] In *Cochran v Louisiana State Board of Education*[266] the US Supreme Court held that using the money derived from public taxation to supply school books free for children in private as well as in public schools did not violate the Fourteenth Amendment. The books furnished for private schools are not granted to the schools themselves, but only to or for the use of the children, and are the same as those furnished for public schools and are not religious or sectarian in character. This was the result of an appeal from a decree of the Supreme Court of Louisiana affirming the refusal of a trial court to issue an injunction to restrain the state Board of Education from expending tax funds for the purchase of free school books to private as well as to public schools.

[10.070] New York's education law requires local public school authorities to lend text books free of charge to all students in grades seven to 12, including those in private schools. Appellant school boards challenged this provision and sought a declaration alleging that the statutory requirement violated the state and federal Constitutions since it was in breach of the First and Fourteenth Amendments. The US Supreme Court[267] held that the statute did not violate the Establishment or the Free Exercise Clause of the First Amendment since the express purpose of the statute was the furtherance of educational opportunities for the young, and the law merely makes available to all children the benefits of a general programme to lend school books free of charge, and the financial benefit accrues to parents and children, not to schools.[268]

[10.071] However, seven years later, in *Meek v Pittinger*[269] Supreme Court struck down a Pennsylvania a statute that permitted public school personnel to make provision for auxiliary services on-site in religiously affiliated parochial schools as being in breach of the Establishment Clause of the First Amendment. The auxiliary services included counselling, testing, psychological services, speech and hearing therapy, and related services for

---

266. *Cochran v Louisiana State Board of Education* (1930) 281 US 370.

267. Citing *Everson v Board of Education* (1947) 330 US 1 Pp 392 US 243–4.

268. *Board of Education v Allen* (1968) 392 US 236.

269. *Meek v Pittinger* (1975) 421 US 349.

exceptional, remedial or educationally disadvantaged students and 'such other secular, neutral non-ideological services as are beneficial to non-public school children' and are provided for those in public schools. The Court ruled that, since 75 per cent of Pennsylvania's non-public schools comply with the compulsory school attendance law, the massive state aid that the religiously affiliated schools received as a result of the loans was neither indirect nor incidental, and although it was ostensibly limited to secular instructional material and equipment, the inescapable result was the direct and substantial advancement of religious activity.[270] Moreover, the loans for 'auxiliary services' were provided at predominantly church-related schools, the Court stated, and this would involve the state in excessive entanglement in seeking to be assured that the public school teachers who provided the services did not advance the religious mission of the church-related schools in which they serve.[271] However, the textbook loans, provided under Part II of the statute, which were limited to textbooks for use in the public schools, were constitutional, since they 'merely [made] available to all children the benefits of a general program to lend school books free of charge,' and the 'financial benefit accrued to parents and children, and not to schools', the Court concluded.[272]

Employment of Staff in Religious Schools

[10.072] The employment of teachers is of particular importance for religious schools, since, as in other countries, such teachers are required to promote religious values and to support the ethos of the school. Because religious schools strive to retain their individual character and identity, which is necessary for their survival, and to promote their mission, the legal system has recognised the need to allow employers the right to confer certain employment preferences, in specific circumstances, on members of their own religion. The most significant federal statute concerning employees in religious schools, the preponderance of which are Catholic, is Title VII of the Civil Rights Act 1964, as amended (Title VII hereafter).[273] This legislation, which is applicable whether an employer receives federal funding or not, prohibits employers from discriminating against individuals when employing, dismissing or classifying employees on the grounds of

270. *Meek v Pittinger* (1975) 421 US 349, 362–366.

271. *Meek v Pittinger* (1975) 421 US 349, p 367–372. Cf. *Lemon v Kurtzman* 403 US 602 and 618.

272. Citing *Board of Education v Allen* (1968) 392 US 236.

273. 42 United States Code (USC) 2000.

race, colour, religion, sex or national origin.[274] However, there are significant exemptions for religious employers, including religious schools, since it allows them to establish *bona fide* occupational qualifications, which include religion, and permits them to restrict employment in pivotal spheres to members of their own faith or religion.

Exemptions for Religious Employers under Title VII

[10.073] Title VII does not apply to institutions with 15 employees or less, since they are generally considered to constitute part of a parish's larger organisational structures. An exemption also applies to those situations where: 'religion, sex or national origin is a *bona fide* occupational qualification reasonably necessary to the operations of the particular business or enterprise.'[275] However, in a number of cases the courts have declined to grant summary judgment in favour of Christian schools that had dismissed an unmarried female teacher who had become pregnant, holding that, if the dismissal had arisen from the teacher's adultery, the Title VII exemption would apply, but that dismissal for pregnancy alone would constitute prohibited sex discrimination.[276] For example, in *Cline v Catholic Diocese of Toledo*[277] the court considered the failure to renew the contract of a teacher in a Catholic elementary school in Ohio, who had premarital sexual relations and gave birth to a baby six months after her marriage. Refusing to uphold a grant of summary judgment in favour of the diocese, the court returned the case to the trial court for review, despite the restrictive wording in her contract, which stated: 'by word and example you will reflect the values of the Catholic Church'.[278] By way of contrast, in *Boyd v Harding Academy of Memphis*[279] a single, pregnant teacher was dismissed by her religiously affiliated school, which required all teachers to be Christian. The teacher subsequently sued the school on the grounds that her dismissal constituted discrimination on the grounds of sex in violation of Title VII of the Civil Rights Act 1964, as amended. By way of redress for the alleged gender discrimination, the complainant sought reinstatement with

---

274. 42 United States Code (USC) 2000, s 2000e–2(a).

275. 42 United States Code (USC) 2000, s 2000e–1.

276. See *Vigars v Vally Christian Centre of Dublin* (1992) Cal 805 F Supp, 802 (ND Cal): *Ganzy v Allen Christian School* (1998) 995 F Supp; 340 (EDNY).

277. *Cline v Catholic Diocese of Toledo* (2000) 206 F 3d 651 (6th Cir).

278. *Cline v Catholic Diocese of Toledo* (2000) 206 F 3d 651 (6th Cir), at 656.

279. *Boyd v Harding Academy of Memphis* CA 6, No. 95–5945, 7/9/96).

retroactive seniority rights, sick leave, vacation pay and all the other benefits she would have received if her employment hadn't been terminated. The Academy stated that it lawfully dismissed the teacher because of her violation of the New Testament's prohibition of premarital sex. The complainant stated that she was not informed that her employment would be terminated if she engaged in sex outside marriage, but the faculty book she had received stated: 'Christian character, as well as professional ability, is the basis for hiring teachers at Harding Academy. Each teacher at Harding is expected in all actions to be a Christian example for the students.' Evidence was given that married women employees did not have their employment terminated for pregnancy and had returned to work at Harding Academy after their maternity leave. Nonetheless, the US District court ruled in favour of Harding Academy. The US court of appeals for the Sixth Circuit ruled that there was no violation of Title VII of the Civil Rights Act of 1964 when Harding Academy terminated Andrea Boyd's position. This case is reminiscent of some older cases in other jurisdictions, such as *Caldwell v Stewart*[280] in Canada and *Flynn v Power*[281] in Ireland, which is discussed in **chapter 9**. It is worth noting, however, that in Canada, Ms Caldwell had an alternative employment option, since a full public education sector was available to her, but that Ms Flynn did not have this option since only a limited public sector was available to her in Ireland in which religious instruction formed part of the curriculum.[282]

[10.074] In the US, another exemption exists for religiously affiliated schools under Title VII of the US Civil Rights Act, which provides that the law will not apply to: 'a religious corporation, association, educational institution, or society with respect to the employment of individuals of a particular religion to perform work connected with the carrying on by such corporation, association, educational institution, or society of its activities.'[283] This exemption is frequently referred to as 'the ministerial exemption'. Under this exemption, the burden of proof falls on the employer to establish that the exemption applies. Thus, even though a person is not an ordained member of the clergy, so long as the religious organisation can prove that the employee's teaching, or other duties, are closely bound up with promoting the institution's spiritual and pastoral mission, then such

280. *Caldwell v Stuart* (1985) 1 WWR 620.

281. *Flynn v Power* [1985] IR 648; [1985] ILRM 336.

282. See further **chapter 9.**

283. 42 USC 2000 (e)–1(a).

teaching or other duties are likely to be considered ministerial in character. The ministerial exemption provides important safeguards for the churches when employing teachers in religious schools and it can impact significantly on employment and tenure in such schools and in religiously affiliated institutions of higher learning.[284] Russo points to the decision of the federal appellate court for the District of Columbia, which overruled the Catholic University's refusal of tenure to a religious sister who taught in the Department of Canon Law, thus agreeing that the teaching of Canon Law was caught by the ministerial exemption. However, it refused to consider the nun's related complaint that she had suffered gender-related discrimination under Title IX.[285] Some authors are critical of the considerable powers vested in the religious employers under Title VII and they question their constitutionality.[286]

[10.075] A further exemption for religious affiliated schools under Title VII applies provided the schools are 'in whole or in substantial part, owned, supported, controlled, or managed by a particular religion or by a particular religious corporation, association or society, or if the curriculum of such school, college, university, or other educational institution or institution of learning is directed towards the propagation of a particular religion.'[287] In *Hall v Baptist Memorial Health Care Corporation*[288] the court upheld the college's motion for summary judgment, thus permitting the dismissal of a

284. See, for example, *Curran v Catholic University of America* (1989) No 1562–87 (Sup Ct, DC February 28), in which the court held that a faculty member of the university did not have the right to continue to teach a theology course where he was found ineligible to do so because of his public departure from church teachings on sexual ethics and related matters. For a discussion of this case see Russo, 'Academic Freedom and Theology at the Catholic University of America: An Oxymoron?' (1997) Education Law Reporter, Vol 55 No 1, 1–6.

285. *Equal Employment Opportunity Commission (EEOC) v Catholic University of America* (1996) 83 F 3d 455 (DC Cir): for discussion on this case see Russo, 'The Camel's Nose in the Tent: Judicial Intervention in Tenure Disputes at Catholic Universities' (1997) Education Law Reporter, Vol 117, No 3, 813–831.

286. For example, see Corbin, 'Above the Law? The Constitutionality of the Ministerial Exemption from Antidiscrimination Law' *Fordham Law Rev*, vol 75, p 1965 2007 available at http://ssrn.com?abstract=981235: This is the Social Science Research Network website.

287. 42 USC 2000(e)(2).

288. *Hall v Baptist Memorial Health Care Corporation* (1998) 27 F Supp 1029 (WD).

person who was employed by a church with a large homosexual congregation, a case which is somewhat reminiscent of *Boy Scouts of America v Dale*,[289] albeit in a non-religious context.

Questions a Religious Employer May Ask Prospective Employees

[10.076] If a school is exempt under Title VII's religious discrimination provisions, it can pose questions to a prospective employee relating to his or her religious background, beliefs and religious practices and it may also determine employment decisions grounded in replies to such questions without violating any of Title VII's requirements. The 'religious organisation' exemptions, however, apply solely to those institutions and bodies whose 'purpose and character are primarily religious'. Although no single factor can determine this fact, significant factors include whether the organisation's articles of incorporation specify a religious purpose, whether its day-to-day operations are of a religious character and whether the organisation operates for profit or not. Such a determination must be grounded on significant religious and secular characteristics. It should be noted also that the exemptions for religious organisations are restricted to those discriminations based on the religion ground, since such bodies are not permitted to discriminate on any of the other protected spheres, eg race, colour, sex or national origin.[290]

What the Plaintiff must Prove under Title VII

[10.077] A plaintiff in a Title VII case must:

(a) be a member of a protected class;

(b) have made application for the post for which they are qualified;

(c) have been rejected under circumstances which give rise to an inference of unlawful discrimination; and

(d) having been rejected, show that the post remained unfilled and that the employer continued to seek other candidates for the same post with similar qualifications.[291]

289. *Boy Scouts of America v Dale* 530 US 640 (2000), 160 NJ 562, 734A 2d 1196, reversed and remanded.

290. Title VII, 42 United States Code (USC), s 2000e–2(a).

291. See further (under Title VII) Russo, *Reutters The Law of Public Education* (7th edn, Foundation Press) forthcoming.

When an employer succeeds in raising a genuine question of fact in relation to its non-discriminatory reasons for its actions, the burden of proof returns to the employee, who bears the ultimate burden of proof to establish that the employer acted with discriminatory intent or that the reasons presented were pretexts for discrimination.

Remedies under Title VII

[10.078] A plaintiff who succeeds may receive pay of up to two years or may be reinstated to a position and may be entitled to attorney's fees.[292] An aggrieved employee is also entitled to a jury trial and to recover monetary damages.[293] Such remedies are not, of course, unique to the US as most modern democracies have equality and non-discrimination legislation and there are entitlements under the common law for damages in certain circumstances.

CONCLUSION

[10.079] Unlike the European countries considered in this book, in the US two entirely separate spheres of life are envisaged, the civil and the religious. In practice, however, the separation of church and state is an imperfect one and there are some areas of inevitable intersection in the wider life and in school life, which is a microcosm of the wider society. Despite the establishment of a network of public schools as a highly effective agency for unity and social cohesion, religion frequently invades the citadel of public education, manifesting its presence in a variety of guises. The on-going public debate over the place of prayer and religiously-affiliated matters in the public schools shows how deeply divided the American public is in this regard and many are demanding greater accommodation in daily practice. The US Supreme Court has been the vigilant arbiter of this separation seeking to prohibit public schools and other governmental institutions from interfering with the individual's constitutional right to religious freedom, while ensuring that the state does not support religion or religious schools or churches from public taxes. However, the court's main emphasis over the years has been on the Establishment Clause and perhaps a greater jurisprudential balance needs to be achieved between the Free Exercise Clause and the Establishment Clause. Calls have been made for the court to adopt a more accommodationary approach for school officials and to

---

292. 42 USC, s 2003–5(g).

293. 42 USC, s 2000e.

promote a climate in the public schools where diversity of beliefs and opinions can flourish, at least to some degree. Moreover, demands are increasingly being made that a place should be found in the public schools for voluntary prayer.

[10.080] Issues such as the parental right to private schools and the place of religion in public schools raise very significant questions of how a modern democracy should balance the rights to freedom of religion and the guarantees in the First Amendment in practice. Although most children attend the public schools, parents have the constitutional right to choose private schools or religious schools for their children's education. This right, however, comes at a huge cost to parents because they must contribute both to the funding of the public schools and to the private school they have chosen for their children's education, since the latter are not publicly funded. It is difficult to escape the conclusion that in America such parents pay twice for the right to choose private education in accordance with their preference or religious convictions, a position which contrasts sharply with the arrangements made in France for the public funding of private schools under the provisions of the Debré law which are discussed in **[7.003]** above. On the other hand, because the state is precluded by the Establishment Clause from aiding the private schools, these schools are accorded a higher degree of autonomy than that achieved by publicly funded denominational (confessional) schools in the EU, an autonomy which is further reflected in the exemptions afforded religiously affiliated schools under the Civil Rights Act 1961 as amended.

[10.081] The US's more tolerant approach has been described as 'passive secularism', since the state reaches some level of accommodation with the churches, which contrasts with the more 'assertive secularism' of France in life generally speaking.[294] In the US, there is reasonable accommodation of the manifestation of religion in public life exemplified by the wearing of religious attire in schools provided it is not overly conspicuous. Other remarkable features of the US system are the toleration of preaching and proselytising in the streets, subject to certain constraints, and the doctrine of church autonomy, which as the name implies, leaves considerable autonomy to the various churches in church-related matters, a position which contrasts with certain elements in the member states of the EU where the EU Equality

294. Kuru, 'Passive and Assertive Secularism: Historical Conditions, Ideological Struggles, and State Policies toward Religion', *World Politics,* Vol 59, No 4, July 2007, pp 568–594.

Directives[295] have conflicted with the rights of the churches in England in regard to their publicly-funded adoptions agencies; in Germany in regard to same sex marriage; and in Ireland in regard to the full implementation of the Equality Directives.

[10.082] By contrast, a more assertive species of secularity, '*La Laïcité*' keeps watch over the secular character of public education in France. This ideological and doctrinal principle, distilled over the centuries in the crucible of church-state struggles, embodies certain elements of anti-clericism, deriving from France's fraught history, which has carried over into contemporary times, elements which are not generally apparent in the US system although some hostility to Christianity in recent case law is apparent. France's compromise with the churches under the *Debré* law, however, would be unthinkable in the US since it would violate the Establishment Clause of the First Amendment.

[10.083] Among the countries examined in this book, the author concludes that, despite the high prices exacted, the churches and private denominational schools in the US have achieved a greater degree of autonomy in their affairs than that achieved by any of the EU member states considered.

295. See **chapter 3** in general.

Chapter 11

CONCLUSIONS

> *Democracy is like a rising tide; it only recoils to come back with greater force, and soon one sees that ... it is always gaining ground. The immediate future of European society is completely democratic: this can in no way be doubted.*[1]

A. GENERAL CONCLUSIONS

[11.001] The provision of education is regarded as one of the principal functions of the modern democratic state. Education itself is closely linked to the transference of norms and values to future generations. Religious education in particular plays a significant role in developing value systems.[2] Something of a custody battle for the soul of the student, so to speak, has arisen between church and state in some countries as to whether the values taught in schools are to be those of state or church. Much depends on the civil ecclesiastical law structures (church-state structures) upholding the education system, which varies from country to country, and on the individual parent's choice of school. In France's public schools, for example, the ideological values will be those of the state, while in Ireland's mainly denominational system those values are more likely to be those of the church.

Conflict concerning religion, always tangible in US public schools, has become a common feature of education worldwide and a number of these disputes have reached the courts. These conflicts may relate to dress codes or the wearing of religious symbols in schools such as Islamic headscarves, Jewish kippas, Sikh turbans or kirpans, Hindu nose studs, Christian crucifixes or religious garb. Conflicts may also relate to the content of moral or citizenship state-promoted programmes which conflict with parents' religious or philosophical convictions. For example, the controversy surrounding the socialist government's radical reforms of education in Spain, which includes a new programme of morals in public schools, has recently brought thousands of parents on to the streets in protest against

---

1. de Tocqueville, *Journeys to England and Ireland,* trans by Lawrence, Mayer (ed), (Faber and Faber, 1957) p 67.

2. Ofsted, *The Annual Report of Her Majesty's Chief Inspector of Schools 2004/ 05*, Religious Education in Secondary Schools, London, Ofsted, 2005.

alleged state indoctrination of children. As was noted in **chapter 6**, the German Constitutional Court settled a controversy surrounding the introduction by the state of programmes of morality in public schools.[3] Meanwhile, controversy in France in recent years has centered on the decision of a Muslim girl to persist in wearing her Islamic headscarf in her public school, which was generally perceived there as an impermissible intrusion of religion and ethnicity into secular education, requiring a statutory ban on all 'conspicuous religious symbols'. In the context of Ireland's publicly-funded, mainly denominational school system, however, the main concern with the wearing of the Islamic headscarf seems to be that its colour should match the school uniform. The proposed increase in the number of faith schools was at the centre of a lively debate in England during the Blair administration while the statutory requirement on schools to arrange a collective act of worship '*wholly* or mainly of a broadly Christian character'[4] in England its diverse multi-religious schools in the state sector, has been an ongoing source of controversy.

[11.002] Clearly the right to equality and non-discrimination relating to freedom of religion is a right recognised across the developed world but, as society becomes more religiously diverse and secularism increases, the tensions between this right and the rights of others manifests itself more frequently in public schools. The various approaches to the interface of religion with education derive from the supporting ecclesiastic law structures (church-state) in the member states as reflected in their national laws, constitutions and other arrangements. In EU member states generally, the churches' right to self-determination is not limited to ecclesiastical activities, so the concept of religious freedom may also extend to publicly-funded institutions founded on religious objectives such as hospitals, schools and adoption agencies. This is certainly the case in Germany, Spain, Ireland and England, where the main churches have considerable autonomy, in certain social spheres. Robbers observes a degree of convergence in this regard across the Community:

> Despite all the differences between the systems there does, however, seem to be a measure of convergence. In some countries the earlier anticlerical attitudes faded as the centuries passed and their legal consequences are being gradually reduced. Religious communities are given space for action and allowed greater freedom. Religion is acknowledged as an important element of social life; and, further, the conditions for meeting religious needs are created

3. See **para [6.034]** *et seq.*

4. SSFA 1998, ss. 69 and 70; EA 2002, ss 100 and 101.

> by the State. .... Finally it is generally acknowledged that, given a comprehensive support by the State of social activities, the religious communities may not be excluded from such support and so discriminated against.[5]

Whether the EU will accommodate the broad remit of the churches in the social spheres in the member states is a matter of concern for the churches now experiencing firsthand the restrictive impact of the EU's equality and non-discrimination legislation. Nonetheless, the Union depends on the churches for social solidarity and social cohesion in the member states while the churches depend on the Union for reasonable accommodation within the compass of its laws and structures. As the Union enters the social policy sphere, the churches are likely to challenge harmonisation and integration processes, unless they are accorded reasonable accommodation within the EU.

Pluralism v Secularism

[11.003] The provision of education in most European countries reflects the pluralist outlook and a Church right to self-determination, in a stricter sense, is also generally recognised.[6] While it is axiomatic in a democracy that no religion is above the rule of law, the vast majority of member states have provided systems of education within which the churches have been accommodated within their laws, constitutions and other arrangements. In Europe, it is generally accepted that freedom of religion and freedom of education principles embrace the concept that systems of education should be sufficiently broadly-structured and inclusive to meet the needs of all religions and none, for as one author puts it: 'Grace is not so poor a thing that it cannot present itself in any number of ways.'[7] Most national constitutions enshrine the principles of equality and non-discrimination between the churches in their constitutions although the extent to which these are reflected in practice varies considerably in the countries considered

Whether the EU adopts and applies the principle of pluralism or the principle of secularism as its jurisprudence evolves will be of pivotal significance. If the EU follows the consensus currently emerging from the member states, it will adopt the pluralist principle, but since the member states are gravitating towards secularism, this is likely to be reflected

5. Robbers (ed), *State and Church in the European Union* (Nomos, 2005) p 580.

6. Robbers (ed), *State and Church in the European Union* (Nomos, 2005) p 580.

7. Robinson, *Gilead* (Virago Press, 2004).

ultimately in EU law since, as Art 6 of the Declaration on the Rights of Man and the Citizen 1780 reminds us, 'Law is the expression of the general will.'

[11.004] The UN's Special *Rapporteur* on the right to education has emphasised that diversity 'is the cornerstone of education' which manifests itself in intercultural community life and in respect for differences.[8] This implies that by engaging positively with plurality in a manner which fosters tolerance, human rights and equality principles, education can serve important social objectives which are necessary to lead a dignified life.[9] Moreover, the European Court of Human Rights (ECtHR) has held that pluralism is a fundamental principle of a democratic society and in *Sahin v Turkey*[10] it held that 'pluralism, tolerance and broadmindedness are hallmarks of a 'democratic society'". The court considered that, although individual interests must on occasion be subordinated to those of a group, democracy does not simply mean that the views of a majority must always prevail: a balance must be achieved which ensures the fair and proper treatment of people from minorities and avoids any abuse of a dominant position.[11]

[11.005] However, the ECtHR has also applied the principle of secularism, which is inimical to religion and the churches, in a number of cases. In *Refah Partisi v Turkey*, for example, the court found that 'secularism was one of the indispensable conditions of democracy.'[12] Secularism carries with it the notion that government and society must be protected from religious overreaching in order to preserve the secular character of government and the public.[13] In public schools, the application of the secularist principle

---

8. United Nations Committee on Human Rights, 61st session, Economic, Social and Cultural Rights, *The Right to Education.* Report submitted by the Special Rapporteur on the Right to Education, Mr Vernor, Munoz Vilalos, E/CN4/2005/50, 17 December 2004, para 70.

9. United Nations Committee on Human Rights, 61st session, Economic, Social and Cultural Rights, *The Right to Education.* Report submitted by the Special Rapporteur on the Right to Education, Mr Vernor, Munoz Vilalos, E/CN4/2005/50, 17 December 2004, para 70.

10. *Sahin v Turkey* (2005) 41 EHRR 8, para 108: see also *Young, James and Webster v UK* (1982) 4 EHRR 38, para 62.

11. *Sahin v Turkey* (2005) 41 EHRR 8, p1ara 108.

12. *Refah Partisi v Turkey* [2003] ECHR 87*; Jimenez and Jimenez Merino v Spain* Application No 51188/99 EHRR.

13. Kuru, 'Muslims and the Secular State in France', online at http://europe.byu.edu/islam/pdfs/Kuru-paper.pdf, p 27, accessed on 5 October 2008.

excludes all religion from the school curriculum and from the school ethos, as in France and the USA, while the principle of pluralism accommodates all religions, and none, within the public sphere. It is notable that neither the ICCPR or the ECHR make any provision for secularism as a ground on which the manifestation of religious belief may be curtailed. Neither instrument posits the view that religious freedom, *inter alia,* is linked to the protection of secular government when secular means protected from the influence of religion.[14] There are clear conflicts between the principle of pluralism, emerging from the majority consensus of the member states, and the principle of secularism which need to be reconciled by the ECJ in conjunction with the ECtHR as the EU moves towards closer unity.

Moral and Civic Education

[11.006] As the power of the churches in education lessens, the state's advance into the moral and civic subjects of school curricula is apparent in all five European countries considered in this book. As some of the cases illustrate, this sphere, in which the state asserts its powers over the moral education of children, has brought national policies and legislative measures into conflict with minority wishes, where the new policies are perceived by some parents as posing a threat to religious freedoms and established cultural and religious values or as attempted assimilation or 'indoctrination' by the state[15] There is huge potential for conflict in this sphere between the rights of individual parents, frequently reflected in religious and cultural values, and the collective interests of the majority, echoed in state policies and legislative measures. In striving to balance such rights, the upholding premise in the ECtHR appears to be that the accommodation of individual parental rights could threaten the right of the state in a democratic society to direct the education system and manage resources for the common good when seeking to deliver national objectives. One would expect, however, that the application of the principle of plurality, which accommodates all religions, and none within the public sphere, would enable the Court to reasonably accommodate such parental convictions within public schools, since this has already been achieved in many member states.

14. Kuru, 'Muslims and the Secular State in France', online at http://europe.byu.edu/islam/pdfs/Kuru-paper.pdf, p 35, accessed on 5 October 2008.

15. Ahdar and Leigh, *Religious Freedom in the Liberal State,* p 261.

The Identity of the Union

[11.007] The EU respects the principles of freedom of religion and freedom of education and it gives a number of assurances and guarantees to the churches in that regard: it also recognises the rights of other parties not to be unlawfully subjected to discrimination in accordance with its relevant Directives. The right to self-determination of the churches finds its genesis in the freedom of religion principle which has been acknowledged by the ECJ in *Prais v Council.*[16] Art 6.2 TEU respects Art 9 of the European Convention which, in turn, protects the freedom of thought, conscience and religion, individually and collectively. Churches and religious communities have a right of complaint before the ECtHR if they have a claim to being injured in their rights under Art 9 or otherwise[17] of the ECHR.[18] With regard to EU law, the principle of subsidiarity acts as a constraint on Community action in the member states. Although the EU, as yet, enjoys no significant jurisdiction in the social policy sphere of the member states, the equality and non-discrimination Directives,[19] which penetrate the national laws, represent a significant advance in the Union's social policy. These Directives comprise part of the basic rights of the European citizen and they have immense potential for the future.

B. CONCLUSIONS RELATING TO SPECIFIC COUNTRIES

(i) EU Countries (England, France, Germany, Ireland and Spain)

[11.008] In the above-mentioned countries, with the exception of France and Germany, one religion became identified with the cause of nationalism, history and culture. In Spain and Ireland the Catholic Church became *primus inter pares* while the Church of England remains the Established Church in England, all other churches being mere voluntary associations. Despite guarantees of parity and non-discrimination in its Basic Law,

16. *Prais v Council* C–130/75 [1976] ECR 1589.

17. Arts 8, 9, 10, 11 and 14 as well as Article 2 of Protocoll of the European Convention on Human Rights may also be of assistance depending on the context.

18. Robbers (ed), *State and Church in the European Union* (Nomos, 2005) p 583.

19. Directive 2000/78/EC (the Race Directive) and Directive 2000/78/EC (the Framework Directive.

Germany accords a special legal status to its two main churches, (Catholicism and Lutheranism), together with the Jewish Church, since they are classified as public law corporations, entitling them to fiscal and other advantages above and beyond their sister churches. Furthermore, the German state collects the Church Tax (*Kirchensteuer*) for the two main churches and disburses most of it to the churches which provide many social services including hospitals, schools and retirement homes. Somewhat similar taxes are to be found, *inter alia*,[20] in Spain[21] and in Italy.[22] Spain also makes significant distinctions between its treatment of the Catholic Church and other churches through state-funding arrangements and through its recognition of concordats with the Holy See: the concordata have the status of international treaties in Spanish law. Despite the principle of non-recognition of the churches in France, religious bodies fall under complex and specific rules which are discussed in some detail in **chapter 7**.[23] In Ireland there is no distinction between the status of the various churches nor is there any requirement to register as a church. While there is remarkable freedom for religious interests in the Constitution, there is no express protection for those who profess no religious faith. Although the courts have implied that right, it has been cogently argued that it is a weak right and an aspect of religious freedom which has been inadequately protected constitutionally and by the Irish courts.[24] Furthermore, parents in Ireland have been dilatory in exercising the full range of entitlements afforded them in the Constitution in regard to the provision of a variety of school types.[25]Accordingly, certain constraints on the exercise of religious freedom and freedom of education have arisen, mainly from the narrow base of educational provision; the absence of a full public education sector; the centrality of existing educational provision; and the absence of secular education.

---

20. In Austria and in some parts of Switzerland while Greece directly funds the Orthodox Church.

21. See **para [8.010]** *et seq*.

22. Ferrari, 'State and Church in Italy', Robbers (ed), *State and Church in the European Community*, p 209 at pp 221–4.

23. **Para [7.011]** *et seq*.

24. Cleary, 'The Interaction Between Religious Freedoms and Non-Discrimination in Irish Constiutional Jurisprudence', *University College Dublin Law Review*, Vol 7, 2007, p 51.

25. Art 42.2 of the Constitution of Ireland.

[11.009] Among the countries considered, the two most polarised approaches are those of France and Ireland. France generally finds no place for religion in its public schools during the course of the official school day, while Ireland finds it difficult to conceive of publicly-funded education without religion.[26] Indeed, it may not be without some ideological relevance that France and Ireland were two of the three countries instrumental in delaying the progress of integration in the EU. If afforded the same opportunity as France, the Netherlands and Ireland, however, other countries may have made the same decisions. Whether the polarised approaches of France and Ireland can be harmoniously accommodated in the EU will depend on the flexibility afforded by EU legislation, the ECJ and the ECt HR in the future.

[11.010] Ireland is not alone in its general perception that religion is an important pillar of the educational edifice which is worth retaining. While the presence of religiously–affiliated schools within the state education system in England, giving parents the choice of a denominational education, might be viewed as obviating the need for religion to play a part in the remainder of the state system, that is not the case.[27] Even the secular community schools in England[28] are required to provide a daily act of collective worship.[29] Germany and Spain also make provision for religion in their public schools as may be seen in **chapters 6** and **8** on this book. This study has found that, in the five European countries in this book, despite evidence of increasing secularisation, religion matters, not just as an element of social life but as an issue of growing political significance. Further research in this sphere is needed as Europe moves towards closer unity.

[11.011] In denominational systems of education, it is generally accepted that the relevant church has control of religious instruction (instruction in

26. But it provides generously for private schools most of which are Catholic, see further **chapter** 7, note also the Wednesday exemption for the possibility of receiving religious instruction or religious education and the exception made for the Alsace-Moselle region.

27. Harris, *Education, Law and Diversity,* p 430.

28. Harris, *Education, Law and Diversity,* p 430: he indicates that the community schools comprise 13,000 schools out of the 21,000 state schools but excluding special schools.

29. SSFA 1998, ss 69 and 70; EA 2002, ss 80 and 101.

the faith of the relevant denomination),[30] while in the public school sector the state had the right to determine programmes of morality, ethics or citizenship. When new school types are established by the state,[31] the national courts in Germany[32] and Ireland[33] have upheld the right of the state to teach a programme of morality in these schools as an option for parents, who may elect that programme, or who may choose religious instruction if available. Although the German state may make its Ethics programme compulsory for all students in the public schools who choose not to attend religious instruction,[34] the Irish state may not mandate its secular comparative religious education programme in any publicly-funded schools. This distinction arises from the wide-ranging control the German Constitution has over 'the entire curriculum' in the Basic Law, which contrasts with the restricted remit of the Irish state in Art 42 of the Constitution of Ireland, which leaves the spiritual dimension of education with the family/parents, who have generally exercised that right through their churches. In giving effect to the constitutional provisions, however, the Education Act 1998 makes broad provision for the ethos of the school, and for reasonable instruction for subjects relating to that ethos, but it does not require any student to attend instruction in any subject to which is contrary to the conscience of the parent or the adult student. While such constitutional principles have ensured that the imposition of a state ideology in publicly-funded education in Ireland was avoided, some of the disadvantages accruing from indirect state provision of education are discussed in **chapter 9**. Ultimately, it is for the people of Ireland to decide whether such restrictions on the state permit it to adequately meet the diverse needs of its democratic society at a time of immense change as the laws across the EU move towards greater harmonisation.

---

30. In Germany this is done in co-operation with the State, while in England the local contribution is accommodated as is discussed in **chapter 5**.

31. For example, community and comprehensive schools in Ireland and Christian Communal Schools in Germany.

32. See **para [6.034]**.

33. See **para [9.036]**, *Campaign to Separate Church and State v Minister for Education* [1996] 2 ILRM 24; [1998] 2 ILRM 81.

34. Provided a complete equality is maintained between the Ethics programme and the Ethics programme and in the assessments thereof.

Advance of Secularism

[11.012] With regard to the EU countries considered in this book, there is clear evidence of the advance of secularism both in society and in schools. Voas and Crockett found that 'in Britain institutional religion now has a half-life of one generation.'[35] While observing the strong presence of Catholicism in Spain, Iban considers that this should be seen 'in the context of an increasingly secular society which considers that standards of conduct should not be determined by any official religion.'[36] In modern Germany, Avensarius describes 'a creeping process of secularization and pluralization that has taken hold of all strata of society', which is mirrored by the fact that: 'religious values and traditions have lost to a great extent their vital influence in school.'[37] Harris found that, notwithstanding the inclusion of religious education within the statutory basic curriculum in England, religious education has tended to become marginalised within the education system.[38] The process of secularisation has been slower in Ireland than in the other countries examined, but it is nonetheless tangible. Recent Census figures (2006) indicate that the process of secularisation has advanced in Ireland, but it is still very far from a secular society as **chapter 9** illustrates.

[11.013] France's concept of controlling the place of religion in society, encapsulated in the concept of *laïcité*, was forged over centuries of fraught relationships with the Catholic Church in particular, and while it is not formally hostile to that church, it is assertive of the rights of the individual to a degree that is unusual in Europe. But *laïcité,* by its very nature, lacks the saving grace of tolerance of religion and of the new religions in particular. *Laïcité* has now assumed the function of a state ideology, or an alternative belief system: it is a secular faith (*foi laïque*) inspired by the centrality of the *laic* principle.[39] But, even France has been unable to consign religion entirely to the private sphere in that, while banning religion from the curriculum of the public schools, in response to public demands and out of a

35. Voas and Crockett, 'Religion in Britain: Neither believing nor Belonging', (2005) 39 *Sociology* 11, 2005, 21.

36. Iban, 'State and Church in Spain', Robbers (ed), *State and Church in the European Union*, p 140 (2005).

37. Aversarius, *Religious Education in Public Schools* (2006).

38. Harris, *Education, Law and Diversity,* p 431 (2007).

39. Chevalier, *Histoire de la Franc-Maconnerie Francaise, 2. Law Maconnerie: Missionaire du liberalisme,* (180–1877), Paris, Fayard, 1974, 550.

sense of justice, the French state decided to fund generously the predominantly Catholic private school sector albeit on strict legislative conditions. It was the principle of freedom of education which enabled France to justify this remarkable compromise which appears to have worked well.

[11.014] With the exception of France, the other EU countries covered in this book (England, Germany, Spain, and Ireland) tend to perceive religion as a societal benefit generally speaking. Accordingly, religion usually forms part of the state-provided education system, although, as we have seen, its impact has been eroded by the advance of secularism in society generally. Thus, although the Constitutions of Germany, Spain and Ireland specifically provide for religious instruction in schools, parents are frequently opting out of religious education for a 'new' secular subject variously termed 'Religious Education', Ethics, Citizenship, etc. The antecedents of these 'new' programmes are to be found in the Ferry Laws of the 1880s France when secular elementary schools were established. As the influence of the churches in public education lessens in Europe, many member states are concerned to ensure that their citizens have some moral values and accordingly a 'new' form of civic religion is now discernible in publicly-funded schools which has received the backing of the ECHR.[40] Thus, the process of secularisation is occurring at two levels – within the member states considered, and arising from EU law and international human rights law.

[11.015] However, there are new factors to be considered including the fact that there is now an estimated 15–20 million Muslims in Europe who are unlikely to succumb to secularism. This adds a very significant dimension to the law relating to religious freedom and freedom of education in the EU which needs to be equitably accommodated. The fact that the Islamic community has no central authority to negotiate as a 'partner' with the state in each country had led to considerable difficulties for this particular faith in accessing their rights to freedom of religion. Paradoxically, Ireland's so called 'sectarian system' provides the greatest degree of religious freedom for, *inter alia*, the Muslim community among the EU countries considered. Germany and England are exploring a number of new avenues for addressing the problems encountered by the Muslim community while Spain permits religious instruction in the Islamic faith in its public schools.

40. *Jiminez & Jiminez Marino v Spain*, Application No 51188/99, Reports of Judgments and Decisions 2000–VI.

The case of Muslim integration in education in Europe calls for an urgent official response, for the pooling of expertise, for dialogue and for further research.

(ii) The USA

[11.016] The concept of separation of church and state embodied in the First Amendment to the US Constitution is quite distinctive to that prevailing in any of the EU countries considered since it envisages total separation, in so far as that is possible, between government and religion in all 50 states. In practice, however, this separation [of church and state] is an imperfect one. Despite the establishment of a network of secular public schools, which operate as a highly effective agency for unity and social cohesion, religion frequently invades the citadel of public education, manifesting its presence in a variety of guises as the short review of cases in **chapter 10** illustrates. The on-going public debate over the place of prayer and religiously affiliated issues in the public schools shows how deeply divided the American public is in this regard. The fact that two separate spheres of activity exist in American life, one pertaining to civil authority, the other relating to religion, and that the First Amendment of the US Constitution mandates their separation, confers on the American churches much greater autonomy than that experienced by the churches in any EU country. Such autonomy comes at a high price, however, since the churches must be self-financing in all matters including education, and since the government is strictly prohibited by the First Amendment from funding any religious activity. For more than 200 years the US Supreme Court has been the arbiter of the extent of the division or separation that must exist in practice between church and state and it has been particularly vigilant in ensuring that the state does not trespass on the jurisdiction of the churches, or that the tax-payer is nor called upon to fund any religious activity. Nowhere has the US Supreme Court been more vigilant to guard against the violation of First Amendment rights of students and their parents than in the public schools as the case law in **chapter 10** illustrates.

[11.017] On the other hand, the court has also ensured, through the application of the constitutional doctrine of 'the autonomy of the churches,' that the churches have retained a remarkable independence over their own affairs. In *Watson v Jones* (1871) the Supreme Court's interpretation of the separation of church and state principle radiates a freedom that vests in religious organisations an independence from secular control in matters of church governance such as church dogma and doctrine, ecclesiastical governance, prayers, the teaching of religion and clerical discipline. This freedom is particularly notable in employment matters, in that the churches in the US are free from interference by way of state laws, regulations or otherwise relating to equality or non-discrimination. Accordingly, the sensitive areas of mutual church-state interest that are the cause of tensions in certain European countries simply do not arise in the US since it belongs not to the civil powers to enter into or review the affairs of a church/religion unless the law has been infringed.

[11.018] Although most children attend the public schools, parents have the constitutional right to choose private schools or religious schools for their children's education. But this right comes at a huge cost to parents because they must contribute both to the funding of the public schools and to the private school chosen since the latter are not publicly-funded. This situation contrasts sharply with the arrangements made by France for private schools under the provisions of the Debré law which are discussed earlier.[41] In the US because the state is precluded by the Establishment Clause from aiding the private schools, these schools are accorded a higher degree of autonomy than that achieved by publicly funded denominational (confessional) schools in the EU, an autonomy which is further reflected in the exemptions afforded religiously affiliated schools under the Civil Rights Act 1961 as amended.

[11.019] Other remarkable features of the US system are the toleration of preaching and proselytising in the streets, subject to certain constraints, and the doctrine of church autonomy, arising out of the separation of church and state as it exists. Kuru describes the US's more tolerant approach as 'passive secularism', since it reaches some level of accommodation with the churches, which contrasts with the more 'assertive secularism' of France[42] and with that of Turkey. Generally speaking, there is reasonable accommodation of the manifestation of religion in public life exemplified by the wearing of religious attire in schools provided it is not overly conspicuous. Possibly, the most impressive element in the US system is its overarching tolerance of such a wide variety of religions and the absence of any religion together with the scope of the freedom of religion principle as it applies across the 50 states.

---

41. See **paras [7.033]** and **[7.038]**.

42. Kuru, 'Passive and Assertive Secularism: Historical Conditions, Ideological Struggles, and State Policies toward Religion', *World Politics,* Vol 59, No 4, July 2007, pp 568–594.

Appendix 1A

DECLARATION OF INDEPENDENCE: TRANSCRIPTION 1776[1]

The unanimous Declaration of the thirteen united States of America,

When in the Course of human events, it becomes necessary for one people to dissolve the political bands which have connected them with another, and to assume among the powers of the earth, the separate and equal station to which the Laws of Nature and of Nature's God entitle them, a decent respect to the opinions of mankind requires that they should declare the causes which impel them to the separation.

We hold these truths to be self-evident, that all men are created equal, that they are endowed by their Creator with certain unalienable Rights, that among these are Life, Liberty and the pursuit of Happiness.—That to secure these rights, Governments are instituted among Men, deriving their just powers from the consent of the governed, —That whenever any Form of Government becomes destructive of these ends, it is the Right of the People to alter or to abolish it, and to institute new Government, laying its foundation on such principles and organizing its powers in such form, as to them shall seem most likely to effect their Safety and Happiness. Prudence, indeed, will dictate that Governments long established should not be changed for light and transient causes; and accordingly all experience hath shewn, that mankind are more disposed to suffer, while evils are sufferable, than to right themselves by abolishing the forms to which they are accustomed. But when a long train of abuses and usurpations, pursuing invariably the same Object evinces a design to reduce them under absolute Despotism, it is their right, it is their duty, to throw off such Government, and to provide new Guards for their future security.—Such has been the patient sufferance of these Colonies; and such is now the necessity which constrains them to alter their former Systems of Government. The history of the present King of Great Britain is a history of repeated injuries and usurpations, all having in direct object the establishment of an absolute Tyranny over these States. To prove this, let Facts be submitted to a candid world.

1. http://www.archives.gov/exhibits/charters/declaration.html.

He has refused his Assent to Laws, the most wholesome and necessary for the public good.

He has forbidden his Governors to pass Laws of immediate and pressing importance, unless suspended in their operation till his Assent should be obtained; and when so suspended, he has utterly neglected to attend to them.

He has refused to pass other Laws for the accommodation of large districts of people, unless those people would relinquish the right of Representation in the Legislature, a right inestimable to them and formidable to tyrants only.

He has called together legislative bodies at places unusual, uncomfortable, and distant from the depository of their public Records, for the sole purpose of fatiguing them into compliance with his measures.

He has dissolved Representative Houses repeatedly, for opposing with manly firmness his invasions on the rights of the people.

He has refused for a long time, after such dissolutions, to cause others to be elected; whereby the Legislative powers, incapable of Annihilation, have returned to the People at large for their exercise; the State remaining in the mean time exposed to all the dangers of invasion from without, and convulsions within.

He has endeavoured to prevent the population of these States; for that purpose obstructing the Laws for Naturalization of Foreigners; refusing to pass others to encourage their migrations hither, and raising the conditions of new Appropriations of Lands.

He has obstructed the Administration of Justice, by refusing his Assent to Laws for establishing Judiciary powers.

He has made Judges dependent on his Will alone, for the tenure of their offices, and the amount and payment of their salaries.

He has erected a multitude of New Offices, and sent hither swarms of Officers to harrass our people, and eat out their substance.

He has kept among us, in times of peace, Standing Armies without the Consent of our legislatures.

He has affected to render the Military independent of and superior to the Civil power.

He has combined with others to subject us to a jurisdiction foreign to our constitution, and unacknowledged by our laws; giving his Assent to their Acts of pretended Legislation:

For Quartering large bodies of armed troops among us:

For protecting them, by a mock Trial, from punishment for any Murders which they should commit on the Inhabitants of these States:

For cutting off our Trade with all parts of the world:

For imposing Taxes on us without our Consent:

For depriving us in many cases, of the benefits of Trial by Jury:

For transporting us beyond Seas to be tried for pretended offences

For abolishing the free System of English Laws in a neighbouring Province, establishing therein an Arbitrary government, and enlarging its Boundaries so as to render it at once an example and fit instrument for introducing the same absolute rule into these Colonies:

For taking away our Charters, abolishing our most valuable Laws, and altering fundamentally the Forms of our Governments:

For suspending our own Legislatures, and declaring themselves invested with power to legislate for us in all cases whatsoever.

He has abdicated Government here, by declaring us out of his Protection and waging War against us.

He has plundered our seas, ravaged our Coasts, burnt our towns, and destroyed the lives of our people.

He is at this time transporting large Armies of foreign Mercenaries to compleat the works of death, desolation and tyranny, already begun with circumstances of Cruelty & perfidy scarcely paralleled in the most barbarous ages, and totally unworthy the Head of a civilized nation.

He has constrained our fellow Citizens taken Captive on the high Seas to bear Arms against their Country, to become the executioners of their friends and Brethren, or to fall themselves by their Hands.

He has excited domestic insurrections amongst us, and has endeavoured to bring on the inhabitants of our frontiers, the

> merciless Indian Savages, whose known rule of warfare, is an undistinguished destruction of all ages, sexes and conditions.

In every stage of these Oppressions We have Petitioned for Redress in the most humble terms: Our repeated Petitions have been answered only by repeated injury. A Prince whose character is thus marked by every act which may define a Tyrant, is unfit to be the ruler of a free people.

Nor have We been wanting in attentions to our Brittish brethren. We have warned them from time to time of attempts by their legislature to extend an unwarrantable jurisdiction over us. We have reminded them of the circumstances of our emigration and settlement here. We have appealed to their native justice and magnanimity, and we have conjured them by the ties of our common kindred to disavow these usurpations, which, would inevitably interrupt our connections and correspondence. They too have been deaf to the voice of justice and of consanguinity. We must, therefore, acquiesce in the necessity, which denounces our Separation, and hold them, as we hold the rest of mankind, Enemies in War, in Peace Friends.

We, therefore, the Representatives of the united States of America, in General Congress, Assembled, appealing to the Supreme Judge of the world for the rectitude of our intentions, do, in the Name, and by Authority of the good People of these Colonies, solemnly publish and declare, That these United Colonies are, and of Right ought to be Free and Independent States; that they are Absolved from all Allegiance to the British Crown, and that all political connection between them and the State of Great Britain, is and ought to be totally dissolved; and that as Free and Independent States, they have full Power to levy War, conclude Peace, contract Alliances, establish Commerce, and to do all other Acts and Things which Independent States may of right do. And for the support of this Declaration, with a firm reliance on the protection of divine Providence, we mutually pledge to each other our Lives, our Fortunes and our sacred Honor.

Appendix 1B

Bill of Rights: Transcription 1789[2]

The Preamble to The Bill of Rights

Congress of the United States begun and held at the City of New-York, on Wednesday the fourth of March, one thousand seven hundred and eighty nine.

THE Conventions of a number of the States, having at the time of their adopting the Constitution, expressed a desire, in order to prevent misconstruction or abuse of its powers, that further declaratory and restrictive clauses should be added: And as extending the ground of public confidence in the Government, will best ensure the beneficent ends of its institution.

RESOLVED by the Senate and House of Representatives of the United States of America, in Congress assembled, two thirds of both Houses concurring, that the following Articles be proposed to the Legislatures of the several States, as amendments to the Constitution of the United States, all, or any of which Articles, when ratified by three fourths of the said Legislatures, to be valid to all intents and purposes, as part of the said Constitution; viz.

ARTICLES in addition to, and Amendment of the Constitution of the United States of America, proposed by Congress, and ratified by the Legislatures of the several States, pursuant to the fifth Article of the original Constitution.

Note: The following text is a transcription of the first ten amendments to the Constitution in their original form. These amendments were ratified December 15, 1791, and form what is known as the 'Bill of Rights.'

Amendment I

Congress shall make no law respecting an establishment of religion, or prohibiting the free exercise thereof; or abridging the freedom of speech, or of the press; or the right of the people peaceably to assemble, and to petition the Government for a redress of grievances.

2. http://www.archives.gov/exhibits/charters/bill_of_rights_transcript.html.

Amendment II

A well regulated Militia, being necessary to the security of a free State, the right of the people to keep and bear Arms, shall not be infringed.

Amendment III

No Soldier shall, in time of peace be quartered in any house, without the consent of the Owner, nor in time of war, but in a manner to be prescribed by law.

Amendment IV

The right of the people to be secure in their persons, houses, papers, and effects, against unreasonable searches and seizures, shall not be violated, and no Warrants shall issue, but upon probable cause, supported by Oath or affirmation, and particularly describing the place to be searched, and the persons or things to be seized.

Amendment V

No person shall be held to answer for a capital, or otherwise infamous crime, unless on a presentment or indictment of a Grand Jury, except in cases arising in the land or naval forces, or in the Militia, when in actual service in time of War or public danger; nor shall any person be subject for the same offence to be twice put in jeopardy of life or limb; nor shall be compelled in any criminal case to be a witness against himself, nor be deprived of life, liberty, or property, without due process of law; nor shall private property be taken for public use, without just compensation.

Amendment VI

In all criminal prosecutions, the accused shall enjoy the right to a speedy and public trial, by an impartial jury of the State and district wherein the crime shall have been committed, which district shall have been previously ascertained by law, and to be informed of the nature and cause of the accusation; to be confronted with the witnesses against him; to have compulsory process for obtaining witnesses in his favor, and to have the Assistance of Counsel for his defence.

Amendment VII

In Suits at common law, where the value in controversy shall exceed twenty dollars, the right of trial by jury shall be preserved, and no fact tried by a jury, shall be otherwise re-examined in any Court of the United States, than according to the rules of the common law.

Amendment VIII

Excessive bail shall not be required, nor excessive fines imposed, nor cruel and unusual punishments inflicted.

Amendment IX

The enumeration in the Constitution, of certain rights, shall not be construed to deny or disparage others retained by the people.

Amendment X

The powers not delegated to the United States by the Constitution, nor prohibited by it to the States, are reserved to the States respectively, or to the people.

Appendix 2

DECLARATION OF THE RIGHTS OF MAN AND OF THE CITIZEN (LA DÉCLARATION DES DROITS DE L'HOMME ET DU CITOYEN) 1789[3]

Approved by the National Assembly of France, August 26, 1789

The representatives of the French people, organized as a National Assembly, believing that the ignorance, neglect, or contempt of the rights of man are the sole cause of public calamities and of the corruption of governments, have determined to set forth in a solemn declaration the natural, unalienable, and sacred rights of man, in order that this declaration, being constantly before all the members of the Social body, shall remind them continually of their rights and duties; in order that the acts of the legislative power, as well as those of the executive power, may be compared at any moment with the objects and purposes of all political institutions and may thus be more respected, and, lastly, in order that the grievances of the citizens, based hereafter upon simple and incontestable principles, shall tend to the maintenance of the constitution and redound to the happiness of all. Therefore the National Assembly recognizes and proclaims, in the presence and under the auspices of the Supreme Being, the following rights of man and of the citizen:

Articles:

1. Men are born and remain free and equal in rights. Social distinctions may be founded only upon the general good.

2. The aim of all political association is the preservation of the natural and imprescriptible rights of man. These rights are liberty, property, security, and resistance to oppression.

3. The principle of all sovereignty resides essentially in the nation. No body nor individual may exercise any authority which does not proceed directly from the nation.

4. Liberty consists in the freedom to do everything which injures no one else; hence the exercise of the natural rights of each man has no limits

3. http://www.constitution.org/fr/fr_drm.htm.

except those which assure to the other members of the society the enjoyment of the same rights. These limits can only be determined by law.

5. Law can only prohibit such actions as are hurtful to society. Nothing may be prevented which is not forbidden by law, and no one may be forced to do anything not provided for by law.

6. Law is the expression of the general will. Every citizen has a right to participate personally, or through his representative, in its foundation. It must be the same for all, whether it protects or punishes. All citizens, being equal in the eyes of the law, are equally eligible to all dignities and to all public positions and occupations, according to their abilities, and without distinction except that of their virtues and talents.

7. No person shall be accused, arrested, or imprisoned except in the cases and according to the forms prescribed by law. Any one soliciting, transmitting, executing, or causing to be executed, any arbitrary order, shall be punished. But any citizen summoned or arrested in virtue of the law shall submit without delay, as resistance constitutes an offense.

8. The law shall provide for such punishments only as are strictly and obviously necessary, and no one shall suffer punishment except it be legally inflicted in virtue of a law passed and promulgated before the commission of the offense.

9. As all persons are held innocent until they shall have been declared guilty, if arrest shall be deemed indispensable, all harshness not essential to the securing of the prisoner's person shall be severely repressed by law.

10. No one shall be disquieted on account of his opinions, including his religious views, provided their manifestation does not disturb the public order established by law.

11. The free communication of ideas and opinions is one of the most precious of the rights of man. Every citizen may, accordingly, speak, write, and print with freedom, but shall be responsible for such abuses of this freedom as shall be defined by law.

12. The security of the rights of man and of the citizen requires public military forces. These forces are, therefore, established for the good of all and not for the personal advantage of those to whom they shall be intrusted.

13. A common contribution is essential for the maintenance of the public forces and for the cost of administration. This should be equitably distributed among all the citizens in proportion to their means.

14. All the citizens have a right to decide, either personally or by their representatives, as to the necessity of the public contribution; to grant this freely; to know to what uses it is put; and to fix the proportion, the mode of assessment and of collection and the duration of the taxes.

15. Society has the right to require of every public agent an account of his administration.

16. A society in which the observance of the law is not assured, nor the separation of powers defined, has no constitution at all.

17. Since property is an inviolable and sacred right, no one shall be deprived thereof except where public necessity, legally determined, shall clearly demand it, and then only on condition that the owner shall have been previously and equitably indemnified.

Appendix 3

UNIVERSAL DECLARATION OF HUMAN RIGHTS[4]

Adopted and proclaimed by General Assembly resolution 217A (III) of 10 December 1948

Article 18

Everyone has the right to freedom of thought, conscience and religion; this right includes freedom to change his religion or belief, and freedom, either alone or in community with others and in public or private, to manifest his religion or belief in teaching, practice, worship and observance.

Article 26

1. Everyone has the right to education. Education shall be free, at least in the elementary and fundamental stages. Elementary education shall be compulsory. Technical and professional education shall be made generally available and higher education shall be equally accessible to all on the basis of merit.

2. Education shall be directed to the full development of the human personality and to the strengthening of respect for human rights and fundamental freedoms. It shall promote understanding, tolerance and friendship among all nations, racial or religious groups, and shall further the activities of the United Nations for the maintenance of peace.

3. Parents have a prior right to choose the kind of education that shall be given to their children.

---

4. file:///F:/2008_Religion,%20Education%20and%20the%20Law/UN%20Human%20Rights/UDHR_20021124/eng_print.htm.

Appendix 4

EUROPEAN CONVENTION ON HUMAN RIGHTS[5]

ROME 4 November 1950

Article 9

1. Everyone has the right to freedom of thought, conscience and religion; this right includes freedom to change his religion or belief, and freedom, either alone or in community with others and in public or private, to manifest his religion or belief, in worship, teaching, practice and observance.

2. Freedom to manifest one's religion or beliefs shall be subject only to such limitations as are prescribed by law and are necessary in a democratic society in the interests of public safety, for the protection of public order, health or morals, or the protection of the rights and freedoms of others.

Article 10

1. Everyone has the right to freedom of expression. this right shall include freedom to hold opinions and to receive and impart information and ideas without interference by public authority and regardless of frontiers. This article shall not prevent States from requiring the licensing of broadcasting, television or cinema enterprises.

2. The exercise of these freedoms, since it carries with it duties and responsibilities, may be subject to such formalities, conditions, restrictions or penalties as are prescribed by law and are necessary in a democratic society, in the interests of national security, territorial integrity or public safety, for the prevention of disorder or crime, for the protection of health or morals, for the protection of the reputation or the rights of others, for preventing the disclosure of information received in confidence, or for maintaining the authority and impartiality of the judiciary.

Article 11

1. Everyone has the right to freedom of peaceful assembly and to freedom of association with others, including the right to form and to join trade unions for the protection of his interests.

---

5. http://www.unesco.org/most/rr4echr.htm.

2. No restrictions shall be placed on the exercise of these rights other than such as are prescribed by law and are necessary in a democratic society in the interests of national security or public safety, for the prevention of disorder or crime, for the protection of health or morals or for the protection of the rights and freedoms of others. this article shall not prevent the imposition of lawful restrictions on the exercise of these rights by members of the armed forces, of the police or of the administration of the State.

Article 13

Everyone whose rights and freedoms as set forth in this Convention are violated shall have an effective remedy before a national authority notwithstanding that the violation has been committed by persons acting in an official capacity.

Article 14

The enjoyment of the rights and freedoms set forth in this Convention shall be secured without discrimination on any ground such as sex, race, colour, language, religion, political or other opinion, national or social origin, association with a national minority, property, birth or other status.

Protocol

Article 2

No person shall be denied the right to education. In the exercise of any functions which it assumes in relation to education and to teaching, the State shall respect the right of parents to ensure such education and teaching in conformity with their own religions and philosophical convictions.

Appendix 5

CONVENTION AGAINST DISCRIMINATION IN EDUCATION[6]

Adopted by the General Conference of the United Nations Educational, Scientific and Cultural Organization on 14 December 1960

The General Conference of the United Nations Educational, Scientific and Cultural Organization, meeting in Paris from 14 November to 15 December 1960, at its eleventh session,

Recalling that the Universal Declaration of Human Rights asserts the principle of non-discrimination and proclaims that every person has the right to education,

Considering that discrimination in education is a violation of rights enunciated in that Declaration,

Considering that, under the terms of its Constitution, the United Nations Educational, Scientific and Cultural Organization has the purpose of instituting collaboration among the nations with a view to furthering for all universal respect for human rights and equality of educational opportunity,

Recognizing that, consequently, the United Nations Educational, Scientific and Cultural Organization, while respecting the diversity of national educational systems, has the duty not only to proscribe any form of discrimination in education but also to promote equality of opportunity and treatment for all in education,

Having before it proposals concerning the different aspects of discrimination in education, constituting item 17.1.4 of the agenda of the session,

Having decided at its tenth session that this question should be made the subject of an international convention as well as of recommendations to Member States,

Adopts this Convention on the fourteenth day of December 1960.

---

6. http://www.unhchr.ch/html/menu3/b/d_c_educ.htm.

Article 1

1. For the purpose of this Convention, the term 'discrimination' includes any distinction, exclusion, limitation or preference which, being based on race, colour, sex, language, religion, political or other opinion, national or social origin, economic condition or birth, has the purpose or effect of nullifying or impairing equality of treatment in education and in particular:

(a) Of depriving any person or group of persons of access to education of any type or at any level;

(b) Of limiting any person or group of persons to education of an inferior standard;

(c) Subject to the provisions of article 2 of this Convention, of establishing or maintaining separate educational systems or institutions for persons or groups of persons; or

(d) Of inflicting on any person or group of persons conditions which are incompatible with the dignity of man.

2. For the purposes of this Convention, the term 'education' refers to all types and levels of education, and includes access to education, the standard and quality of education, and the conditions under which it is given.

Article 2

When permitted in a State, the following situations shall not be deemed to constitute discrimination, within the meaning of article 1 of this Convention:

(a) The establishment or maintenance of separate educational systems or institutions for pupils of the two sexes, if these systems or institutions offer equivalent access to education, provide a teaching staff with qualifications of the same standard as well as school premises and equipment of the same quality, and afford the opportunity to take the same or equivalent courses of study;

(b) The establishment or maintenance, for religious or linguistic reasons, of separate educational systems or institutions offering an education which is in keeping with the wishes of the pupil's parents or legal guardians, if participation in such systems or attendance at such institutions is optional and if the education provided conforms to such standards as may be laid down or approved by the competent authorities, in particular for education of the same level;

(c) The establishment or maintenance of private educational institutions, if the object of the institutions is not to secure the exclusion of any group but to provide educational facilities in addition to those provided by the public authorities, if the institutions are conducted in accordance with that object, and if the education provided conforms with such standards as may be laid down or approved by the competent authorities, in particular for education of the same level.

Article 3

In order to eliminate and prevent discrimination within the meaning of this Convention, the States Parties thereto undertake:

(a) To abrogate any statutory provisions and any administrative instructions and to discontinue any administrative practices which involve discrimination in education;

(b) To ensure, by legislation where necessary, that there is no discrimination in the admission of pupils to educational institutions;

(c) Not to allow any differences of treatment by the public authorities between nationals, except on the basis of merit or need, in the matter of school fees and the grant of scholarships or other forms of assistance to pupils and necessary permits and facilities for the pursuit of studies in foreign countries;

(d) Not to allow, in any form of assistance granted by the public authorities to educational institutions, any restrictions or preference based solely on the ground that pupils belong to a particular group;

(e) To give foreign nationals resident within their territory the same access to education as that given to their own nationals.

Article 4

The States Parties to this Convention undertake furthermore to formulate, develop and apply a national policy which, by methods appropriate to the circumstances and to national usage, will tend to promote equality of opportunity and of treatment in the matter of education and in particular:

(a) To make primary education free and compulsory; make secondary education in its different forms generally available and accessible to all; make higher education equally accessible to all on the basis of individual capacity; assure compliance by all with the obligation to attend school prescribed by law;

(b) To ensure that the standards of education are equivalent in all public education institutions of the same level, and that the conditions relating to the quality of education provided are also equivalent;

(c) To encourage and intensify by appropriate methods the education of persons who have not received any primary education or who have not completed the entire primary education course and the continuation of their education on the basis of individual capacity;

(d) To provide training for the teaching profession without discrimination.

Article 5

1. The States Parties to this Convention agree that:

(a) Education shall be directed to the full development of the human personality an d to the strengthening of respect for human rights and fundamental freedoms; it shall promote understanding, tolerance and friendship among all nations, racial or religious groups, and shall further the activities of the United Nations for the maintenance of peace;

(b) It is essential to respect the liberty of parents and, where applicable, of legal guardians, firstly to choose for their children institutions other than those maintained by the public authorities but conforming to such minimum educational standards as may be laid down or approved by the competent authorities and, secondly, to ensure in a manner consistent with the procedures followed in the State for the application of its legislation, the religious and moral education of the children in conformity with their own convictions; and no person or group of persons should be compelled to receive religious instruction inconsistent with his or their conviction;

(c) It is essential to recognize the right of members of national minorities to carry on their own educational activities, including the maintenance of schools and, depending on the educational policy of each State, the use or the teaching of their own language, provided however:

(i) That this right is not exercised in a manner which prevents the members of these minorities from understanding the culture and language of the community as a whole and from participating in its - activities, or which prejudices national sovereignty;

(ii) That the standard of education is not lower than the general standard laid down or approved by the competent authorities; and

(iii) That attendance at such schools is optional.

2. The States Parties to this Convention undertake to take all necessary measures to ensure the application of the principles enunciated in paragraph 1 of this article.

Article 6

In the application of this Convention, the States Parties to it undertake to pay the greatest attention to any recommendations hereafter adopted by the General Conference of the United Nations Educational, Scientific and Cultural Organization defining the measures to be taken against the different forms of discrimination in education and for the purpose of ensuring equality of opportunity and treatment in education.

Article 7

The States Parties to this Convention shall in their periodic reports submitted to the General Conference of the United Nations Educational, Scientific and Cultural Organization on dates and in a manner to be determined by it, give information on the legislative and administrative provisions which they have adopted and other action which they have taken for the application of this Convention, including that taken for the formulation and the development of the national policy defined in article 4 as well as the results achieved and the obstacles encountered in the application of that policy.

Article 8

Any dispute which may arise between any two or more States Parties to this Convention concerning the interpretation or application of this Convention which is not settled by negotiations shall at the request of the parties to the dispute be referred, failing other means of settling the dispute, to the International Court of Justice for decision.

Article 9

Reservations to this Convention shall not be permitted.

Article 10

This Convention shall not have the effect of diminishing the rights which individuals or groups may enjoy by virtue of agreements concluded between two or more States, where such rights are not contrary to the letter or spirit of this Convention.

Article 11

This Convention is drawn up in English, French, Russian and Spanish, the four texts being equally authoritative.

Article 12

1. This Convention shall be subject to ratification or acceptance by States Members of the United Nations Educational, Scientific and Cultural Organization in accordance with their respective constitutional procedures.

2. The instruments of ratification or acceptance shall be deposited with the Director-General of the United Nations Educational, Scientific and Cultural Organization.

Article 13

1. This Convention shall be open to accession by all States not Members of the United Nations Educational, Scientific and Cultural Organization which are invited to do so by the Executive Board of the Organization.

2. Accession shall be effected by the deposit of an instrument of accession with the Director-General of the United Nations Educational, Scientific and Cultural Organization.

Article 14

This Convention shall enter into force three months after the date of the deposit of the third instrument of ratification, acceptance or accession, but only with respect to those States which have deposited their respective instruments on or before that date. It shall enter into force with respect to any other State three months after the deposit of its instrument of ratification, acceptance or accession.

Article 15

The States Parties to this Convention recognize that the Convention is applicable not only to their metropolitan territory but also to all non-self-governing, trust, colonial and other territories for the international relations of which they are responsible; they undertake to consult, if necessary, the governments or other competent authorities of these territories on or before ratification, acceptance or accession with a view to securing the application of the Convention to those territories, and to notify the Director-General of the United Nations Educational, Scientific and Cultural Organization of the territories to which it is accordingly applied, the notification to take effect three months after the date of its receipt.

Article 16

1. Each State Party to this Convention may denounce the Convention on its own behalf or on behalf of any territory for whose international relations it is responsible.

2. The denunciation shall be notified by an instrument in writing, deposited with the Director-General of the United Nations Educational, Scientific and Cultural Organization.

3. The denunciation shall take effect twelve months after the receipt of the instrument of denunciation.

Article 17

The Director-General of the United Nations Educational, Scientific and Cultural Organization shall inform the States Members of the Organization, the States not members of the Organization which are referred to in article 13, as well as the United Nations, of the deposit of all the instruments of ratification, acceptance and accession provided for in articles 12 and 13, and of notifications and denunciations provided for in articles 15 and 16 respectively.

Article 18

1. This Convention may be revised by the General Conference of the United Nations Educational, Scientific and Cultural Organization. Any such revision shall, however, bind only the States which shall become Parties to the revising convention.

2. If the General Conference should adopt a new convention revising this Convention in whole or in part, then, unless the new convention otherwise provides, this Convention shall cease to be open to ratification, acceptance or accession as from the date on which the new revising convention enters into force.

Article 19

In conformity with Article 102 of the Charter of the United Nations, this Convention shall be registered with the Secretariat of the United Nations at the request of the Director-General of the United Nations Educational, Scientific and Cultural Organization.

DONE in Paris, this fifteenth day of December 1960, in two authentic copies bearing the signatures of the President of the eleventh session of the General Conference and of the Director-General of the United Nations Educational, Scientific and Cultural Organization, which shall be deposited in the archives of the United Nations Educational, Scientific and Cultural Organization, and certified true copies of which shall be delivered to all the States referred to in articles 12 and 13 as well as to the United Nations.

The foregoing is the authentic text of the Convention duly adopted by the General Conference of the United Nations Educational, Scientific and Cultural Organization during its eleventh session, which was held in Paris and declared closed the fifteenth day of December 1960.

IN FAITH WHEREOF we have appended our signatures this fifteenth day of December 1960.

Appendix 6

INTERNATIONAL COVENANT ON CIVIL AND POLITICAL RIGHTS[7]

Adopted and opened for signature, ratification and accession by General Assembly resolution 2200A (XXI) of 16 December 1966

entry into force 23 March 1976, in accordance with Article 49

Article 18

1. Everyone shall have the right to freedom of thought, conscience and religion. This right shall include freedom to have or to adopt a religion or belief of his choice, and freedom, either individually or in community with others and in public or private, to manifest his religion or belief in worship, observance, practice and teaching.

2. No one shall be subject to coercion which would impair his freedom to have or to adopt a religion or belief of his choice.

3. Freedom to manifest one's religion or beliefs may be subject only to such limitations as are prescribed by law and are necessary to protect public safety, order, health, or morals or the fundamental rights and freedoms of others.

4. The States Parties to the present Covenant undertake to have respect for the liberty of parents and, when applicable, legal guardians to ensure the religious and moral education of their children in conformity with their own convictions.

7. http://www.unhchr.ch/html/menu3/b/a_ccpr.htm.

Appendix 7

INTERNATIONAL COVENANT ON ECONOMIC, SOCIAL AND CULTURAL RIGHTS[8]

Adopted and opened for signature, ratification and accession by General Assembly resolution 2200A (XXI) of 16 December 1966

entry into force 3 January 1976, in accordance with article 27

Article 10

The States Parties to the present Covenant recognize that:

1. The widest possible protection and assistance should be accorded to the family, which is the natural and fundamental group unit of society, particularly for its establishment and while it is responsible for the care and education of dependent children. Marriage must be entered into with the free consent of the intending spouses.

2. Special protection should be accorded to mothers during a reasonable period before and after childbirth. During such period working mothers should be accorded paid leave or leave with adequate social security benefits.

3. Special measures of protection and assistance should be taken on behalf of all children and young persons without any discrimination for reasons of parentage or other conditions. Children and young persons should be protected from economic and social exploitation. Their employment in work harmful to their morals or health or dangerous to life or likely to hamper their normal development should be punishable by law. States should also set age limits below which the paid employment of child labour should be prohibited and punishable by law.

Article 13

1. The States Parties to the present Covenant recognize the right of everyone to education. They agree that education shall be directed to the full development of the human personality and the sense of its dignity, and shall strengthen the respect for human rights and fundamental freedoms. They

8. http://www.unhchr.ch/html/menu3/b/a_cescr.htm.

further agree that education shall enable all persons to participate effectively in a free society, promote understanding, tolerance and friendship among all nations and all racial, ethnic or religious groups, and further the activities of the United Nations for the maintenance of peace.

2. The States Parties to the present Covenant recognize that, with a view to achieving the full realization of this right:

(a) Primary education shall be compulsory and available free to all;

(b) Secondary education in its different forms, including technical and vocational secondary education, shall be made generally available and accessible to all by every appropriate means, and in particular by the progressive introduction of free education;

(c) Higher education shall be made equally accessible to all, on the basis of capacity, by every appropriate means, and in particular by the progressive introduction of free education;

(d) Fundamental education shall be encouraged or intensified as far as possible for those persons who have not received or completed the whole period of their primary education;

(e) The development of a system of schools at all levels shall be actively pursued, an adequate fellowship system shall be established, and the material conditions of teaching staff shall be continuously improved.

3. The States Parties to the present Covenant undertake to have respect for the liberty of parents and, when applicable, legal guardians to choose for their children schools, other than those established by the public authorities, which conform to such minimum educational standards as may be laid down or approved by the State and to ensure the religious and moral education of their children in conformity with their own convictions.

4. No part of this article shall be construed so as to interfere with the liberty of individuals and bodies to establish and direct educational institutions, subject always to the observance of the principles set forth in paragraph I of this article and to the requirement that the education given in such institutions shall conform to such minimum standards as may be laid down by the State.

Appendix 8

DECLARATION ON THE ELIMINATION OF ALL FORMS OF INTOLERANCE AND OF DISCRIMINATION BASED ON RELIGION OR BELIEF[9]

The General Assembly,

Considering that one of the basic principles of the Charter of the United Nations is that of the dignity and equality inherent in all human beings, and that all Member States have pledged themselves to take joint and separate action in co-operation with the Organization to promote and encourage universal respect for and observance of human rights and fundamental freedoms for all, without distinction as to race, sex, language or religion,

Considering that the Universal Declaration of Human Rights and the International Covenants on Human Rights proclaim the principles of nondiscrimination and equality before the law and the right to freedom of thought, conscience, religion and belief,

Considering that the disregard and infringement of human rights and fundamental freedoms, in particular of the right to freedom of thought, conscience, religion or whatever belief, have brought, directly or indirectly, wars and great suffering to mankind, especially where they serve as a means of foreign interference in the internal affairs of other States and amount to kindling hatred between peoples and nations,

Considering that religion or belief, for anyone who professes either, is one of the fundamental elements in his conception of life and that freedom of religion or belief should be fully respected and guaranteed,

Considering that it is essential to promote understanding, tolerance and respect in matters relating to freedom of religion and belief and to ensure that the use of religion or belief for ends inconsistent with the Charter of the United Nations, other relevant instruments of the United Nations and the purposes and principles of the present Declaration is inadmissible,

Convinced that freedom of religion and belief should also contribute to the attainment of the goals of world peace, social justice and friendship among

9. http://www.unhchr.ch/html/menu3/b/d_intole.htm.

peoples and to the elimination of ideologies or practices of colonialism and racial discrimination,

Noting with satisfaction the adoption of several, and the coming into force of some, conventions, under the aegis of the United Nations and of the specialized agencies, for the elimination of various forms of discrimination,

Concerned by manifestations of intolerance and by the existence of discrimination in matters of religion or belief still in evidence in some areas of the world,

Resolved to adopt all necessary measures for the speedy elimination of such intolerance in all its forms and manifestations and to prevent and combat discrimination on the ground of religion or belief,

Proclaims this Declaration on the Elimination of All Forms of Intolerance and of Discrimination Based on Religion or Belief:

Article 1

1. Everyone shall have the right to freedom of thought, conscience and religion. This right shall include freedom to have a religion or whatever belief of his choice, and freedom, either individually or in community with others and in public or private, to manifest his religion or belief in worship, observance, practice and teaching.

2. No one shall be subject to coercion which would impair his freedom to have a religion or belief of his choice.

3. Freedom to manifest one's religion or belief may be subject only to such limitations as are prescribed by law and are necessary to protect public safety, order, health or morals or the fundamental rights and freedoms of others.

Article 2

1. No one shall be subject to discrimination by any State, institution, group of persons, or person on the grounds of religion or other belief.

2. For the purposes of the present Declaration, the expression 'intolerance and discrimination based on religion or belief' means any distinction, exclusion, restriction or preference based on religion or belief and having as its purpose or as its effect nullification or impairment of the recognition, enjoyment or exercise of human rights and fundamental freedoms on an equal basis.

Article 3

Discrimination between human being on the grounds of religion or belief constitutes an affront to human dignity and a disavowal of the principles of the Charter of the United Nations, and shall be condemned as a violation of the human rights and fundamental freedoms proclaimed in the Universal Declaration of Human Rights and enunciated in detail in the International Covenants on Human Rights, and as an obstacle to friendly and peaceful relations between nations.

Article 4

1. All States shall take effective measures to prevent and eliminate discrimination on the grounds of religion or belief in the recognition, exercise and enjoyment of human rights and fundamental freedoms in all fields of civil, economic, political, social and cultural life.

2. All States shall make all efforts to enact or rescind legislation where necessary to prohibit any such discrimination, and to take all appropriate measures to combat intolerance on the grounds of religion or other beliefs in this matter.

Article 5

1. The parents or, as the case may be, the legal guardians of the child have the right to organize the life within the family in accordance with their religion or belief and bearing in mind the moral education in which they believe the child should be brought up.

2. Every child shall enjoy the right to have access to education in the matter of religion or belief in accordance with the wishes of his parents or, as the case may be, legal guardians, and shall not be compelled to receive teaching on religion or belief against the wishes of his parents or legal guardians, the best interests of the child being the guiding principle.

3. The child shall be protected from any form of discrimination on the ground of religion or belief. He shall be brought up in a spirit of understanding, tolerance, friendship among peoples, peace and universal brotherhood, respect for freedom of religion or belief of others, and in full consciousness that his energy and talents should be devoted to the service of his fellow men.

4. In the case of a child who is not under the care either of his parents or of legal guardians, due account shall be taken of their expressed wishes or of any other proof of their wishes in the matter of religion or belief, the best interests of the child being the guiding principle.

5. Practices of a religion or belief in which a child is brought up must not be injurious to his physical or mental health or to his full development, taking into account article 1, paragraph 3, of the present Declaration.

Article 6

In accordance with article I of the present Declaration, and subject to the provisions of article 1, paragraph 3, the right to freedom of thought, conscience, religion or belief shall include, inter alia, the following freedoms:

(a) To worship or assemble in connection with a religion or belief, and to establish and maintain places for these purposes;

(b) To establish and maintain appropriate charitable or humanitarian institutions;

(c) To make, acquire and use to an adequate extent the necessary articles and materials related to the rites or customs of a religion or belief;

(d) To write, issue and disseminate relevant publications in these areas;

(e) To teach a religion or belief in places suitable for these purposes;

(f) To solicit and receive voluntary financial and other contributions from individuals and institutions;

(g) To train, appoint, elect or designate by succession appropriate leaders called for by the requirements and standards of any religion or belief;

(h) To observe days of rest and to celebrate holidays and ceremonies in accordance with the precepts of one's religion or belief;

(i) To establish and maintain communications with individuals and communities in matters of religion and belief at the national and international levels.

Article 7

The rights and freedoms set forth in the present Declaration shall be accorded in national legislation in such a manner that everyone shall be able to avail himself of such rights and freedoms in practice.

Article 8

Nothing in the present Declaration shall be construed as restricting or derogating from any right defined in the Universal Declaration of Human Rights and the International Covenants on Human Rights.

Appendix 9

CHARTER OF FUNDAMENTAL RIGHTS OF THE EUROPEAN UNION

(2000/C 3 64/01)

SOLEMN PROCLAMATION

Done at Nice on the seventh day of December in the year two thousand.

For the European Parliament

PREAMBLE

The peoples of Europe, in creating an ever closer union among them, are resolved to share a peaceful future based on common values.

Conscious of its spiritual and moral heritage, the Union is founded on the indivisible, universal values of human dignity, freedom, equality and solidarity; it is based on the principles of democracy and the rule of law. It places the individual at the heart of its activities, by establishing the citizenship of the Union and by creating an area of freedom, security and justice.

The Union contributes to the preservation and to the development of these common values while respecting the diversity of the cultures and traditions of the peoples of Europe as well as the national identities of the Member States and the organisation of their public authorities at national, regional and local levels; it seeks to promote balanced and sustainable development and ensures free movement of persons, goods, services and capital, and the freedom of establishment.

To this end, it is necessary to strengthen the protection of fundamental rights in the light of changes in society, social progress and scientific and technological developments by making those rights more visible in a Charter.

This Charter reaffirms, with due regard for the powers and tasks of the Community and the Union and the principle of subsidiarity, the rights as they result, in particular, from the constitutional traditions and international obligations common to the Member States, the Treaty on European Union, the Community Treaties, the European Convention for the Protection of Human Rights and Fundamental Freedoms, the Social Charters adopted by the Community and by the Council of Europe and the case-law of the Court of Justice of the European Communities and of the European Court of Human Rights.

Enjoyment of these rights entails responsibilities and duties with regard to other persons, to the human community and to future generations.

The Union therefore recognises the rights, freedoms and principles set out hereafter.

CHAPTER I: Dignity

Article 1: Human dignity

Human dignity is inviolable. It must be respected and protected.

Article 2: Right to life

1. Everyone has the right to life.

2. No one shall be condemned to the death penalty, or executed.

Article 3: Right to the integrity of the person

1. Everyone has the right to respect for his or her physical and mental integrity.

2. In the fields of medicine and biology, the following must be respected in particular:

- the free and informed consent of the person concerned, according to the procedures laid down by law,
- the prohibition of eugenic practices, in particular those aiming at the selection of persons,
- the prohibition on making the human body and its parts as such a source of financial gain,
- the prohibition of the reproductive cloning of human beings.

Article 4: Prohibition of torture and inhuman or degrading treatment or punishment

No one shall be subjected to torture or to inhuman or degrading treatment or punishment.

Article 5: Prohibition of slavery and forced labour

1. No one shall be held in slavery or servitude.

2. No one shall be required to perform forced or compulsory labour.

3. Trafficking in human beings is prohibited.

CHAPTER II: Freedoms

Article 6: Right to liberty and security

Everyone has the right to liberty and security of person.

Article 7: Respect for private and family life

Everyone has the right to respect for his or her private and family life, home and communications.

Article 8: Protection of personal data

1. Everyone has the right to the protection of personal data concerning him or her.

2. Such data must be processed fairly for specified purposes and on the basis of the consent of the person concerned or some other legitimate basis laid down by law. Everyone has the right of access to data which has been collected concerning him or her, and the right to have it rectified.

3. Compliance with these rules shall be subject to control by an independent authority.

Article 9: Right to marry and right to found a family

The right to marry and the right to found a family shall be guaranteed in accordance with the national laws governing the exercise of these rights.

Article 10: Freedom of thought, conscience and religion

1. Everyone has the right to freedom of thought, conscience and religion. This right includes freedom to change religion or belief and freedom, either alone or in community with others and in public or in private, to manifest religion or belief, in worship, teaching, practice and observance.

2. The right to conscientious objection is recognised, in accordance with the national laws governing the exercise of this right.

Article 11: Freedom of expression and information

1. Everyone has the right to freedom of expression. This right shall include freedom to hold opinions and to receive and impart information and ideas without interference by public authority and regardless of frontiers.

2. The freedom and pluralism of the media shall be respected.

Article 12: Freedom of assembly and of association

1. Everyone has the right to freedom of peaceful assembly and to freedom of association at all levels, in particular in political, trade union and civic matters, which implies the right of everyone to form and to join trade unions for the protection of his or her interests.

2. Political parties at Union level contribute to expressing the political will of the citizens of the Union.

Article 13: Freedom of the arts and sciences

The arts and scientific research shall be free of constraint. Academic freedom shall be respected.

Article 14: Right to education

1. Everyone has the right to education and to have access to vocational and continuing training.

2. This right includes the possibility to receive free compulsory education.

3. The freedom to found educational establishments with due respect for democratic principles and the right of parents to ensure the education and teaching of their children in conformity with their religious, philosophical and pedagogical convictions shall be respected, in accordance with the national laws governing the exercise of such freedom and right.

Article 15: Freedom to choose an occupation and right to engage in work

1. Everyone has the right to engage in work and to pursue a freely chosen or accepted occupation.

2. Every citizen of the Union has the freedom to seek employment, to work, to exercise the right of establishment and to provide services in any Member State.

3. Nationals of third countries who are authorised to work in the territories of the Member States are entitled to working conditions equivalent to those of citizens of the Union.

Article 16: Freedom to conduct a business

The freedom to conduct a business in accordance with Community law and national laws and practices is recognised.

Article 17: Right to property

1. Everyone has the right to own, use, dispose of and bequeath his or her lawfully acquired possessions. No one may be deprived of his or her possessions, except in the public interest and in the cases and under the conditions provided for by law, subject to fair compensation being paid in good time for their loss. The use of property may be regulated by law in so far as is necessary for the general interest.

2. Intellectual property shall be protected.

Article 18: Right to asylum

The right to asylum shall be guaranteed with due respect for the rules of the Geneva Convention of 28 July 1951 and the Protocol of 31 January 1967 relating to the status of refugees and in accordance with the Treaty establishing the European Community.

Article 19: Protection in the event of removal, expulsion or extradition

1. Collective expulsions are prohibited.

2. No one may be removed, expelled or extradited to a State where there is a serious risk that he or she would be subjected to the death penalty, torture or other inhuman or degrading treatment or punishment.

CHAPTER III: Equality

Article 20: Equality before the law

Everyone is equal before the law.

Article 21: Non-discrimination

1. Any discrimination based on any ground such as sex, race, colour, ethnic or social origin, genetic features, language, religion or belief, political or any other opinion, membership of a national minority, property, birth, disability, age or sexual orientation shall be prohibited.

2. Within the scope of application of the Treaty establishing the European Community and of the Treaty on European Union, and without prejudice to the special provisions of those Treaties, any discrimination on grounds of nationality shall be prohibited.

Article 22: Cultural, religious and linguistic diversity

The Union shall respect cultural, religious and linguistic diversity.

Article 23: Equality between men and women

Equality between men and women must be ensured in all areas, including employment, work and pay.

The principle of equality shall not prevent the maintenance or adoption of measures providing for specific advantages in favour of the under-represented sex.

Article 24: The rights of the child

1. Children shall have the right to such protection and care as is necessary for their well-being. They may express their views freely. Such views shall be taken into consideration on matters which concern them in accordance with their age and maturity.

2. In all actions relating to children, whether taken by public authorities or private institutions, the child's best interests must be a primary consideration.

3. Every child shall have the right to maintain on a regular basis a personal relationship and direct contact with both his or her parents, unless that is contrary to his or her interests.

Article 25: The rights of the elderly

The Union recognises and respects the rights of the elderly to lead a life of dignity and independence and to participate in social and cultural life.

Article 26: Integration of persons with disabilities

The Union recognises and respects the right of persons with disabilities to benefit from measures designed to ensure their independence, social and occupational integration and participation in the life of the community.

CHAPTER IV: Solidarity

Article 27: Workers' right to information and consultation within the undertaking

Workers or their representatives must, at the appropriate levels, be guaranteed information and consultation in good time in the cases and under the conditions provided for by Community law and national laws and practices.

Article 28: Right of collective bargaining and action

Workers and employers, or their respective organisations, have, in accordance with Community law and national laws and practices, the right to negotiate and conclude collective agreements at the appropriate levels and, in cases of conflicts of interest, to take collective action to defend their interests, including strike action.

Article 29: Right of access to placement services

Everyone has the right of access to a free placement service.

Article 30: Protection in the event of unjustified dismissal

Every worker has the right to protection against unjustified dismissal, in accordance with Community law and national laws and practices.

Article 31: Fair and just working conditions

1. Every worker has the right to working conditions which respect his or her health, safety and dignity.

2. Every worker has the right to limitation of maximum working hours, to daily and weekly rest periods and to an annual period of paid leave.

Article 32: Prohibition of child labour and protection of young people at work

The employment of children is prohibited. The minimum age of admission to employment may not be lower than the minimum school-leaving age, without prejudice to such rules as may be more favourable to young people and except for limited derogations.

Young people admitted to work must have working conditions appropriate to their age and be protected against economic exploitation and any work likely to harm their safety, health or physical, mental, moral or social development or to interfere with their education.

Article 33: Family and professional life

1. The family shall enjoy legal, economic and social protection.

2. To reconcile family and professional life, everyone shall have the right to protection from dismissal for a reason connected with maternity and the right to paid maternity leave and to parental leave following the birth or adoption of a child.

Article 34: Social security and social assistance

1. The Union recognises and respects the entitlement to social security benefits and social services providing protection in cases such as maternity, illness, industrial accidents, dependency or old age, and in the case of loss of employment, in accordance with the rules laid down by Community law and national laws and practices.

2. Everyone residing and moving legally within the European Union is entitled to social security benefits and social advantages in accordance with Community law and national laws and practices.

3. In order to combat social exclusion and poverty, the Union recognises and respects the right to social and housing assistance so as to ensure a decent existence for all those who lack sufficient resources, in accordance with the rules laid down by Community law and national laws and practices.

Article 35: Health care

Everyone has the right of access to preventive health care and the right to benefit from medical treatment under the conditions established by national laws and practices. A high level of human health protection shall be ensured in the definition and implementation of all Union policies and activities.

Article 36: Access to services of general economic interest

The Union recognises and respects access to services of general economic interest as provided for in national laws and practices, in accordance with the Treaty establishing the European Community, in order to promote the social and territorial cohesion of the Union.

Article 37: Environmental protection

A high level of environmental protection and the improvement of the quality of the environment must be integrated into the policies of the Union and ensured in accordance with the principle of sustainable development.

Article 38: Consumer protection

Union policies shall ensure a high level of consumer protection.

CHAPTER V: Citizens' Rights

Article 39: Right to vote and to stand as a candidate at elections : to the European Parliament

1. Every citizen of the Union has the right to vote and to stand as a candidate at elections to the European Parliament in the Member State in which he or she resides, under the same conditions as nationals of that State.

2. Members of the European Parliament shall be elected by direct universal suffrage in a free and secret ballot.

Article 40: Right to vote and to stand as a candidate at municipal elections

Every citizen of the Union has the right to vote and to stand as a candidate at municipal elections in the Member State in which he or she resides under the same conditions as nationals of that State.

Article 41: Right to good administration

1. Every person has the right to have his or her affairs handled impartially, fairly and within a reasonable time by the institutions and bodies of the Union.

2. This right includes:

- the right of every person to be heard, before any individual measure which would affect him or her adversely is taken;
- the right of every person to have access to his or her file, while respecting the legitimate interests of confidentiality and of professional and business secrecy;
- the obligation of the administration to give reasons for its decisions.

3. Every person has the right to have the Community make good any damage caused by its insti-tutions or by its servants in the performance of their duties, in accordance with the general principles common to the laws of the Member States.

4. Every person may write to the institutions of the Union in one of the languages of the Treaties and must have an answer in the same language.

Article 42: Right of access to documents

Any citizen of the Union, and any natural or legal person residing or having its registered office in a Member State, has a right of access to European Parliament, Council and Commission documents.

Article 43: Ombudsman

Any citizen of the Union and any natural or legal person residing or having its registered office in a Member State has the right to refer to the Ombudsman of the Union cases of maladministration in the activities of the Community institutions or bodies, with the exception of the Court of Justice and the Court of First Instance acting in their judicial role.

Article 44: Right to petition

Any citizen of the Union and any natural or legal person residing or having its registered office in a Member State has the right to petition the European Parliament.

Article 45: Freedom of movement and of residence

1. Every citizen of the Union has the right to move and reside freely within the territory of the Member States.

2. Freedom of movement and residence may be granted, in accordance with the Treaty establishing the European Community, to nationals of third countries legally resident in the territory of a Member State.

Article 46

Diplomatic and consular protection

Every citizen of the Union shall, in the territory of a third country in which the Member State of which he or she is a national is not represented, be entitled to protection by the diplomatic or consular authorities of any Member State, on the same conditions as the nationals of that Member State.

CHAPTER VI: Justice

Article 47: Right to an effective remedy and to a fair trial

Everyone whose rights and freedoms guaranteed by the law of the Union are violated has the right to an effective remedy before a tribunal in compliance with the conditions laid down in this Article.

Everyone is entitled to a fair and public hearing within a reasonable time by an independent and impartial tribunal previously established by law. Everyone shall have the possibility of being advised, defended and represented.

Legal aid shall be made available to those who lack sufficient resources in so far as such aid is necessary to ensure effective access to justice.

Article 48: Presumption of innocence and right of defence

1. Everyone who has been charged shall be presumed innocent until proved guilty according to law.

2. Respect for the rights of the defence of anyone who has been charged shall be guaranteed.

Article 49: Principles of legality and proportionality of criminal offences and penalties

1. No one shall be held guilty of any criminal offence on account of any act or omission which did not constitute a criminal offence under national law or international law at the time when it was committed. Nor shall a heavier penalty be imposed than that which was applicable at the time the criminal offence was committed. If, subsequent to the commission of a criminal offence, the law provides for a lighter penalty, that penalty shall be applicable.

2. This Article shall not prejudice the trial and punishment of any person for any act or omission which, at the time when it was committed, was criminal according to the general principles recognised by the community of nations.

3. The severity of penalties must not be disproportionate to the criminal offence.

Article 50: Right not to be tried or punished twice in criminal proceedings : for the same criminal offence

No one shall be liable to be tried or punished again in criminal proceedings for an offence for which he or she has already been finally acquitted or convicted within the Union in accordance with the law.

CHAPTER VII: General Provisions

Article 51: Scope

1. The provisions of this Charter are addressed to the institutions and bodies of the Union with due regard for the principle of subsidiarity and to the Member States only when they are implementing Union law. They shall therefore respect the rights, observe the principles and promote the application thereof in accordance with their respective powers.

2. This Charter does not establish any new power or task for the Community or the Union, or modify powers and tasks defined by the Treaties.

Article 52: Scope of guaranteed rights

1. Any limitation on the exercise of the rights and freedoms recognised by this Charter must be provided for by law and respect the essence of those rights and freedoms. Subject to the principle of proportionality, limitations may be made only if they are necessary and genuinely meet objectives of general interest recognised by the Union or the need to protect the rights and freedoms of others.

2. Rights recognised by this Charter which are based on the Community Treaties or the Treaty on European Union shall be exercised under the conditions and within the limits defined by those Treaties.

3. In so far as this Charter contains rights which correspond to rights guaranteed by the Convention for the Protection of Human Rights and Fundamental Freedoms, the meaning and scope of those rights shall be the same as those laid down by the said Convention. This provision shall not prevent Union law providing more extensive protection.

Article 53: Level of protection

Nothing in this Charter shall be interpreted as restricting or adversely affecting human rights and fundamental freedoms as recognised, in their respective fields of application, by Union law and international law and by international agreements to which the Union, the Community or all the Member States are party, including the European Convention for the Protection of Human Rights and Fundamental Freedoms, and by the Member States' constitutions.

Article 54: Prohibition of abuse of rights

Nothing in this Charter shall be interpreted as implying any right to engage in any activity or to perform any act aimed at the destruction of any of the rights and freedoms recognised in this Charter or at their limitation to a greater extent than is provided for herein.

Appendix 10

LETTERS OF NOTE

THE STANLEY LETTER

Copy of a Letter from the Chief Secretary for Ireland, to His Grace the Duke of Leinster, on the Formation of a Board of Commissioners for Education in Ireland; this, the so called 'Stanley Letter' became the basis of the system of primary education in Ireland; two versions of this letter exist, see Report of the Powis Commission 1831/2, Vol XXIX, p 757, reprinted 1837 Vol IX p 585.

Irish Office, London, October, 1831.

My Lord – His Majesty's Government having come to the determination of empowering the Lord Lieutenant to constitute a Board for the Superintendence of a System of National Education in Ireland, and Parliament having so far sanctioned the arrangement as to appropriate a sum of money in the present year as an experiment of the probable success of the proposed system, I am directed by His Excellency to acquaint your Grace that it is his intention, with your consent, to constitute you the President of the new Board: And I have it further in command, to lay before your Grace the motives of the Government in constituting the Board, the powers which it is intended to confer upon it, and the objects which it is expected that it will bear in view, and carry into effect.

The Commissioners, in 1812, recommended the appointment of a Board of this description to superintend a system of education, from which should be banished even the suspicion of proselytism, and which, admitting children of all religious persuasions, should not interfere with the peculiar tenets of any. The Government of the day imagined that they had found a superintending body, acting upon a system such as was recommended, and intrusted the distribution of the National grants to the care of the Kildare street Society. His Majesty's present Government are of opinion that no private society deriving a part, however small, of their annual income from private sources, and only made the channel of the munificence of the Legislature, without being subject to any direct responsibility, could adequately and satisfactorily accomplish the end proposed; and while they do full justice to the liberal views with which that society was originally instituted, they cannot but be sensible that one of its leading principles was calculated to defeat its avowed objects, as experience has subsequently proved that it has. The determination to enforce, in all their schools, the reading of the Holy Scriptures without note or comment, was undoubtedly taken with the purest motives; with the wish at once to connect religious with moral and literary education, and, at the same time, not to run the risk of wounding the peculiar feelings of any sect by catechetical instruction, or comments which might tend to subjects of polemical controversy. But it seems to have been overlooked that the principles of the Roman Catholic Church (to which, in any system intended for general diffusion throughout Ireland, the bulk of the pupils must necessarily belong) were totally at variance with this principle; and that the indiscriminate reading of the Holy Scriptures without note or comment, by children, must be peculiarly obnoxious to a Church which denies, even to adults, the right of unaided private interpretation of the sacred volume with respect to articles of religious belief.

Shortly after its institution, although the society prospered and extended its operations under the fostering care of the Legislature, the vital defect began to be noticed, and the Roman Catholic system to which they were on principle opposed, and which they feared might lead in its results to proselytism, even though no such object were contemplated by its promoters. When this opposition arose, founded on such grounds, it soon became manifest that the system could not become one of National Education.

The Commissioners of Education, in 1824–5, sensible of the defects of the system, and of the ground, as well as the strength of the objection taken, recommended the appointment of two teachers in every school, one Protestant and the other Roman Catholic, to superintend separately the religious education of the children; and they hoped to have been able to agree upon a selection from the Scriptures, which might have been generally acquiesced in by both persuasions. But it was soon found that these schemes were impracticable; and, in 1828, a Committee of the House of Commons, to which were referred the various Reports of the Commissioners of Education, recommended a system to be adopted which should afford, if possible, a combined literary and a separate religious education, and should be capable of being so far adapted to the views of the religious persuasions which prevail in Ireland, as to render it, in truth, a system of National Education for the poorer classes of the community.

For the success of the undertaking much must depend upon the character of the individuals who compose the Board; and upon the security thereby afforded to the country, that while the interests of religion are not overlooked, the most scrupulous care should be taken not to interfere with the peculiar tenets of any description of Christian pupils.

To attain the first object, it appears essential that the Board should be composed of men of high personal character, including individuals of exalted station in the Church, to attain the latter that it should consist of persons professing different religious opinions. It is the intention of the Government that the Board should exercise a complete control over the various schools which may be erected under its auspices, or which, having been already established, may hereafter place themselves under its management, and submit to its regulations. Subject to these, applications for aid will be admissible from Christians of all denominations; but as one of the main objects must be to unite in one system children of different creeds, and as much must depend upon the co-operation of the resident clergy, the Board will probably look with peculiar favour upon applications proceeding either from –

> 1st The Protestant and Roman Catholic clergy of the parish; or
>
> 2nd One of the clergymen, and a certain number of parishioners professing the opposite creed; or
>
> 3rd Parishioners of both denominations.

Where the application proceeds exclusively from Protestants, or exclusively from Roman Catholics, it will be proper for the Board to make inquiry as to the circumstances which lead to the absence of any names of the persuasion which does not appear. The Board will note all applications for aid, whether granted or refused, with the grounds of the decision, and annually submit to, Parliament a Report of their proceedings.

They will invariably require, as a condition not to be departed from, that local funds shall be raised upon which any aid from the public will be dependent.

They will refuse all applications in which the following objects are not locally provided for:

> 1st A fund sufficient for the annual repairs of the school-house and furniture. 2nd A permanent salary for the master, not less than pounds.
>
> 3rd A sum sufficient to purchase books and school requisites at half-price.
>
> 4th Where aid is sought from the Commissioners for building a school-house, it is required that at least one-third of the estimated

expense be subscribed, a site for building, to be approved of by the Commissioners, be granted for the purpose, and that the school-house, when finished, be vested in trustees, to be also approved of by them.

They will require that the schools be kept open for a certain number of hours, on four or five days of the week, at the discretion of the commissioners, for moral and literary education only, and at the remaining one or two days in the week be set apart for living, separately, such religious education to the children as may approved of by the clergy of their respective persuasions.

They will also permit and encourage the clergy to give religious instruction to the children of their respective persuasions, either before or after the ordinary school hours, on the other days of the week.

They will exercise the most entire control over all books to be used in the schools, whether in the combined moral and literary, or separate religious instruction; none to be employed in the first except under the sanction of the Board, nor in the latter, but with the approbation of those members of the Board who are of the same religious persuasion with those for whose use they are intended. Although it is not designed to exclude from the list of books for the combined instruction, such portions of Sacred history or of religious or moral teaching as may he approved of by the Board, it is to he understood that this is by no means intended to convey a perfect and sufficient religious education, or to supersede the necessity of separate religious instruction on the day set apart for that purpose.

They will require that a register shall be kept in the schools, in which shall be entered the attendance or non-attendance of each child on Divine Worship on Sundays.

They will, at various times, either by themselves or by their Inspectors, visit and examine into the state of each school, and report their observations to the Board. They will allow to the individuals or bodies applying for aid, the appointment of their own teacher, subject to the following restrictions and regulations:

1st He (or she) shall be liable to be fined, suspended, or removed altogether, by the authority of the Commissioners, who shall, however, record their reasons.

2nd He shall have received previous instruction in a model school in Dublin, to be sanctioned by the Board.

NB It is not intended that this regulation should apply to prevent the admission of masters or mistresses of schools already established, who may be approved of by the Commissioners

3rd He shall have received testimonials of good conduct, and of general fitness for the situation, from the Board.

The Board will be intrusted with the absolute control over the funds which may be annually voted by Parliament, which they shall apply to the following purposes:

> 1st Granting aid for the erection of schools, subject to the conditions hereinbefore specified.
>
> 2nd paying Inspectors for visiting and reporting upon schools.
>
> 3rd Gratuities to teachers of schools conducted under the rules laid down, not exceeding pounds each.
>
> 4th Establishing and maintaining a model school in Dublin, and training teachers for country schools.
>
> 5th Editing and printing such books of moral and literary education as may be approved of for the use of the schools, and supplying them and school necessaries, at not lower than half-price.
>
> 6th Defraying all necessary contingent expenses of the Board.

I have thus stated the objects which His Majesty's Government have in view, and the principal regulations by which they think those objects may be most effectually promoted: and I am directed by the Lord Lieutenant to express His Excellency's earnest wish that the one and the other may be found such as to procure for the Board the sanction of your Grace's name, and the benefit of your Grace's attendance.

A full power will of course be given to the Board to make such regulations upon matters of detail, not inconsistent with the spirit of these instructions, as they may judge best qualified to carry into effect the intentions of the Government and of the legislature. Parliament has already placed at his Excellency's disposal a sum which may be available even in the course of the present year; and as soon as the Board can be formed, it will be highly desirable that no time should be lost, with a view to the estimates of the ensuing year, in enabling such schools, already established, as are willing to subscribe to the conditions imposed, to put in their claims for protection and assistance; and in receiving applications from parties desirous to avail themselves of the munificence of the Legislature in founding new schools under your regulations.

I have the honour to be, &c.

(Signed) E C Stanley.

THE O'NEILL LETTER

Extract from a letter from Seosamh O'Neill, Secretary of the Department of Education, dated the 2nd July 1934. This letter is contained in the De Valera Papers, File No 1074 and also in the State Papers' Office File s 2979.[10]

RE ARTICLE 10

Article 10 has never bee fully invoked, and we have not so far obtained a legal interpretation of it, or of the obligation which it imposes.

The present position is that elementary education is free except in a few of the Model schools, and in these schools the practice of charging fees is being gradually terminated and in a few years it will have disappeared.

Apart however from the obligation that elementary education should be free, there are other claims which might possibly be made under the Article in question. These include

> Whether a small number of children, say two, three or four, living on an island, or at a long distance from a National School: could successfully claim the right to be transported daily to a National School; or to have a school established for their own use;
>
> Whether the Article could be construed to put an obligation on the State not only to pay the teachers but also to build, equip and maintain schools and provide free books and requisites for the schoolchildren.

In my opinion the present position is that the principle underlying the Article is fundamental and should be preserved if possible, but in the absence of a clear definition of the State's obligation under the Article, it would be undesirable to put it in such a position as to make it more difficult to deal by legislation with any problem which might arise thereunder.

10. This letter is reprinted by the kind permission of the Franciscan Fathers.

INDEX

[all references are to paragraph number]